# ECONOMETRIC APPLICATIONS

# ECONOMETRIC APPLICATIONS

## EMPIRICS OF SIMULTANEOUS EQUATIONS, TIME SERIES, QUALITATIVE RESPONSE AND PANEL DATA MODELS

T. Lakshmanasamy

KALPAZ

First Published, 2020

*Published by*

Kalpaz Publications
C-30, Satyawati Nagar,
Delhi – 110052
Ph.: 011-47034999, 9811692060
www.kalpazpublications.com
E-mail: kalpaz@hotmail.com

*Printed at:* G. Print Process, Delhi

**Cataloging in Publication Data—DK**
Courtesy: D.K. Agencies (P) Ltd. <docinfo@dkagencies.com>

**Lakshmanasamy, T., author.**
Econometric application / Dr. T. Lakshmanasamy.
pages cm
ISBN 9789353240530

1. Econometrics. 2. Equations, Simultaneous. I. Title.

LCC HB139.L35 2019 | DDC 330.15195 23

# Contents

## Section - IV
## Panel Data Econometrics

# Preface

Understanding the nuances of empirical analysis of economic data in relation with economic theory and econometric applications to derive meaningful inferences from the econometric estimates is an art that comes only with sustained practice and deep understanding of the issues involved both in theory and in data. Any amount of theoretical knowledge in economic theory and econometric methods is incomplete unless one learns how to translate them into applied and analytical methods of empirical analysis. However sophisticated an economic theory is, it needs support from empirical estimation to derive sound policy implications. An aptitude to empirical work is therefore a very essential quality of applied econometric analysis. It has often been the case in empirical works that many methodological challenges are posed by the data itself and the hitherto existing techniques are inappropriate or inefficient. In many instances the challenges of data analysis have led to many interesting novel econometric techniques and improved methods to solve those issues. Applied econometric analysis requires specialised skills to identify the issues and appropriate methods to solve them.

In this broad sense, the papers in this volume are unique and interesting. This volume comprises papers on applied econometric analysis originally carried out by the students as a project work for the masters degree programme in econometrics. Since the project work is taken so earnestly by the students, the hardwork put by them should not go unnoticed. It is only appropriate to make their work known to the outside world. Hence, this modest attempt is undertaken to put together the applied econometric works of students as a book. Every research work in this book follows serious empirical analysis with equally important strong methodological foundations. The research issues are discussed in detail and appropriate econometric methodologies are carefully identified on various issues and methods. All the econometric works in this volume use relevant data and empirical methods to substantiate the research issues and offer insightful solutions.

The aim of bringing together these works is to motivate young researchers to better appreciate the empirical approach, estimation methodology and apply appropriate econometric techniques on relevant data in order to derive meaningful inferences from empirical estimates. It is heartening to note that many of the so called empirical studies in India do not follow sound methodological approaches even for the issues that warrant quite a strong systematic analysis of data. Even the available and much tested simple methodological frameworks have largely been ignored and it is quite common to find research works that simply add or duplicate the existing works. In this regard, the present volume may serve as a basis for identifying methodological approaches for undertaking rigorous empirical analysis. With the increasing availability of nationwide large scale data sets and user friendly softwares along with the readily accessible upto date literature and computer programming made possible by the developments in information technology, there is no handicap for the modern day researchers to venture into explorations of new frontiers of knowledge. It is hoped that this book will serve as a stimulant to the young researchers to explore new vistas in research and empirics.

It is always a pleasant duty to acknowledge the contributions of wellwishers in the academic career of a teacher and researcher. First and foremost, I thank all my students whose research works comprise this volume for their research insights and analytical skills. Without their involvement, it would not have been possible for me to learn the different econometric methods and their applications in the diverse fields of applied econometrics. Also many academicians have contributed to my academic pursuits over the years in many ways. I am ever thankful to my teachers, colleagues and students who are the sources of inspiration, involvement, understanding and improvement in my academic learnings. They constantly motivate and infuse my research interests in various fields of economics and econometrics and sharpen my understanding of the subjects that form the basis of this present volume. It is a pleasure to recall the academic interactions I had with my research guide Prof. A.M. Nalla Gounden without whose thoughtful academic insights and critical inputs, I would not have become a researcher in applied econometrics. I also acknowledge the academic interactions with my colleagues Prof. U. Sankar, Prof. S.S. Sivakumar, Dr. K. Shanthi, Dr. G. Mythili, Dr. D. Sathiyavan, Dr. P. Mahendra Varman and Dr. R. Mariappan and their encouragement and cooperation throughout my association with the Department of Econometrics in the University of Madras.

Life is not complete if one fails to duly recognise the numerous sacrifices of people who shape one's life, most importantly one's academic career. I wish to place on record the constant encouragement, extraordinary support and untiring cooperation always pleasantly extended by my family in my academic pursuits. I acknowledge the evergreen wishes of my father Thiru. Thangamuthu Gounder, innocent faith of my mother Thirumathi. Muthayammal, honoured wishes of my brother Mr. T. Ramasamy, and innumerable sacrifices of my sisters Mrs. Kannammal, Mrs. Parvathy, Mrs. Rajathi, wife Dr. K. Parimala and my son Mr. L. Ashwanth.

**T. Lakshmanasamy**

# List of Tables

# List of Figures

# Section - I

# Simultaneous Equations Econometrics

# 1

# The Effect of Parental Education on Child Education: 2SLS-IV Estimation of Intergenerational Education Mobility

**Abstract**

*Analyses of intergenerational relations focus on the extent to which economic and social status of children are influenced from that of their parents. Intergenerational effects may reflect mere selection, parents with higher ability having higher ability children, or causal effect, parental social and economic characteristics affect child outcomes. Persistence of intergenerational relations shows transmission, whereas intergenerational mobility relates to the progress occurring from one generation to the next generation. Among various aspects of intergenerational social and economic relations, income, occupation and education mobility are the basic intergenerational effects that determine the progress of a society. This paper estimates the intergenerational education mobility in India using the IHDS-II (2011-2012) data. To overcome the endogeneity issue, parental education correlated with ability, this paper uses an instrumental variables approach. The instrument used is the New Scheme of Elementary Education (NSEE) introduced in 1953 which made schooling compulsory. The 2SLS-IV estimates show a high degree of intergenerational persistence in education. The Indian society seems to be less mobile educationally, and especially, mother-child educational relations reflect intergenerational educational transmission.*

**Keywords:** *Intergenerational education mobility, endogeneity, 2SLS-IV estimation, parent-child pairs, educational transmission*

## 1.1 Introduction

In every society, every generation moves ahead of its predecessors, only to be overtaken by its subsequent generations, almost in every respect of life, importantly in social and economic spheres. This intergenerational mobility of individuals as well as society is not only a much desirable attribute but also is a measure of quality of life improvements, equality of opportunity, progress, development and freedom. Although such social and economic mobility concerns differ in their meaning and nature between developed and developing countries, and between different strata within society, every change is taken to be a positive progress. Also, country, education, income and social mobility form the cornerstone for the provision of opportunity for development as well as change. The extent to which economic status is transmitted from one generation to the next has long been the interest of social scientists. Economists' interest in intergenerational relationship between generations is in its effects on individual mobility, equality of opportunity, economic progress, and income distribution. Persistence of intergenerational transmission in economic status is an important mechanism in retarding intergenerational mobility that also perpetuates inequality of opportunities in a society. Such persistence of intergenerational effects may differ across groups of people in a society typically by race, community, gender and religion, implying differential access to opportunities for different groups.

It is well known that the aim of free public education in most of the societies is to increase the equality in opportunity. The education system has always been considered as the most effective and equalising process for individuals to improve one's economic and social status. It is a widespread knowledge that there is a strong correlation between education and increasing one's economic mobility. Despite the increasing availability to education for all, family background plays a huge role in determining economic success of generations. If the relationship between children's and parent's education is too strong, there is a lack of opportunity for those who are with less educational background.

Education is a very important aspect of every human life. In almost all countries worldwide, school level education is generally compulsory and free provided by the public sector. Even in the private sector, it is almost free or heavily subsidised. In India, education is recognised as a fundamental right by the Constitution of India. It provided to every child in the age of 6 to 14 and has been made compulsory and free in government schools. By the Right to Education Act, 25 percent of seats in private schools are reserved for weaker sections of the society. The ratio of public school and private school is 7:5. In India, a person aged 7 years and above who can both read and write with understanding in any language has been taken as literate. The adult literacy rate has shown an upward trend for females as well as males. As per the 2011 Census of India, it has increased from 61 percent to 69.3 percent during the period 2001-2011. As per the NSS 71$^{st}$ round findings, adult literacy rate stands 70.5 percent for the year 2014 (Education Statistics at a Glance, 2016). This indicator is generally considered as the stock of human capital of an economy.

It is widely known that more educated parents have more educated children. More educated parents have more resources – via higher returns to higher education – to provide a better environment for their children to do well in school. The parent's education level has greater impact than their income level on the probability of young people pursuing and completing graduation. Better educated parents also provide their children with better environment that is more conducive to the child's cognitive development from birth, and become apparent in various ways, including higher grades. Educated parents have higher educational aspirations for their children and are more likely to transmit them to children.

Most studies on intergenerational mobility focus on developed countries. Income and occupational mobility are the common topics of analysis, whereas education mobility has also been receiving serious attention in developed countries in recent years. The studies on intergenerational mobility are rather scanty in developing countries, limited by lack of data availability. India is particularly a relevant laboratory for the study of intergenerational mobility because of its diversity, variations, caste religion and culture. In India, society is deeply stratified by caste which has historically been associated with poor outcomes and very low mobility (Borkotoky et al., 2015). Further, the rigid caste structure is coupled with unity in diversity. In recent decades, India also experiences rapid economic transformation and one of the fastest growing economies in the world. However, how far these contrasting features of India contribute to social and economic mobility of its diverse populations is not yet known clearly making India an intriguing case study. Mobility analysis by social group shows that scheduled castes (SC) and scheduled tribes (ST) – historically socially deprived communities – have done much better than others in attaining intergenerational educational mobility (Azam and Bhatt, 2015). Of the SC/ST children who were born to parents with no formal education, the proportion of those who cleared secondary school rose from 8 percent to 20 percent between the two generations. In other words, SC/ST children from less educated families witnessed 12 percentage point rise in their upward mobility. The corresponding increase in mobility for non-SC/ST children has been only 4 percentage point.

Intergenerational relations is a term that describes the relationship between two or more generations in a society. The term was coined as a social movement within or between social classes and occupations, the change occurring from one generation to the next generation. Intergenerational relations describes a wide range of patterns of interaction among individuals in different generations of a family: for example, between those in older generations, such as parents and grandparents, aunt, uncle, and those in younger generations, such as children and grandchildren, nieces and nephews. Intergenerational mobility is when the background, resources, income, occupation, education, ethnicity, culture, place of residence, etc. of one generation determines the social and economic status of future generation. The term is also frequently used to describe behaviours involving older and younger people in society at a large, even if they are unrelated to one another. Such intergenerational relations comprise two mutually exclusive components: the intergenerational relations may simply transmit or deviate. The former is generally described as intergenerational transmission and the latter is called as intergenerational mobility. For example, genetic characteristics simply transmit from one generation to another. But, income or education of one generation moves upward or higher income or education of the next generation. That is, intergenerational mobility brings positive changes between the generations.

Intergenerational education mobility analysis focuses on the causal relationship between the education of parents and their children. It concentrates on how children's education correlates with the education of their parents. There is not much empirical evidence available, especially in developing countries, that too in India. It is only recently that empirical studies in developed countries have begun to focus on disentangling the intergenerational relations in education, either mobility or transmission, i.e. differentiating causal relationship from mere selection in which better educated parents having better educated children. The few available empirical studies on intergenerational effects of education that are around produce conflicting findings. There is dearth of empirical evidence on the exact role of parental education in the educational attainment of children.

Therefore, this paper tries to disentangle the intergenerational links between in educational outcomes using educational attainment of parents and their children. Specifically, this paper tests the mobility or transmission aspects of intergenerational educational relationship in India, focusing on the relationship between parent's education and child education. use the nationwide Indian Human Development Survey (IHDS-II 2011-2012), and the Instrumental Variable-Two Stage Least Squares (2SLS-IV) method, the paper examines the impact of parental education on child education to assess the nature of intergenerational relations in education in the state of Tamil Nadu in India.

## 1.2 A Brief Review of Recent Studies

Literature on intergenerational economic mobility in developed countries mostly focuses on intergenerational correlation between father-son incomes (Solon, 1999; Black and Devereux, 2011). The early intergenerational relations research concentrated on estimating the intergenerational regression and correlation coefficients, and later refining the estimation methods. Hertz et al. (2008) review the trends in intergenerational transmission of education for a sample of 42 countries. They document large regional differences in educational persistence, with Latin America displaying the highest intergenerational correlations, and the Nordic countries the lowest. The correlation coefficient is about 0.60 in South America; about 0.40 in Western Europe, 0.46 in the US, and 0.20 in Nordic countries. They estimate the global average correlation between parent's and child's schooling to be around 0.420 for the fifty years under review. Interestingly, they also find a 30 point reduction in the estimated mean regression coefficient over the 60 years, from 0.80 in 1920 to 0.50 in 1980.

Some studies focus on intergenerational mobility in education. Results from the US and UK suggest intergenerational education elasticity between 0.20 and 0.45 (Dearden et al., 1997; Mulligan, 1999; Corak, 2013). Most studies find that parental education has at least a small impact on children's schooling. In order to deal with endogeneity of the parental education, another group of studies use instrumental variable estimates. The instrumental variable approach provides exogenous variations and permits causal effects of parental education across generations without affecting parental innate abilities or their endowments. This way enables the estimation of the causal effect of increase in parental education on children's education. Oreopoulos et al. (2006) consider IV estimation with historical changes in compulsory schooling legislation in the US as instrument for parental educational attainment and find that an increase in the schooling of either parent reduces the probability that a child repeats a grade and that 15-16 years old will drop out of school.

Black et al. (2005) using a Norwegian education system reform as IV for parental education, estimate the casual link between parent's and children's education in Norway. The census data from Norway Statistics provides little evidence of a causal relationship between father's education and children's education, despite significant and large OLS relationships. There is a small but significant causal relationship between mother's education and her son's education but no causal relationship between mother's and daughter's education. Thus, studies find conflicting statistical intergenerational educational relations when IV estimation is employed.

The issue of intergenerational mobility in India has recently started to receive attention in India (Jalan and Murgai, 2007; Maitra and Sharma, 2009; Majumdar, 2010; Hnatkovska et al., 2013; Azam and Bhatt, 2015; Borkotoky et al., 2015; Kishan, 2018). The issues analysed ranges over mobility in income, occupation, education, and mobility differentials across social groups. Jalan and Murgai (2008) investigate the educational mobility of the age group 15-19, using 1992-93 and 1998-99 National Family Health Survey (NFHS) data. They found that educational mobility for age group 15-19 has increased significantly between 1992-1993 and 1999-2000, and that education gaps between backward and forward castes are not that large once other attributes are controlled for. However, in the NFHS data, parental outcomes are not directly known for child-parent pairs living in the same household. As a result, they only focus on children aged 15-19 years who are more likely to be living with their parents.

Sinha (2018) examine the differential effect of economic development in India on the educational and occupational attainment of caste groups over the period 1983 and 2009-10. Using the six rounds of NSS data, the educational and occupational outcomes of coresident father-son pairs of social groups of SC/ST and non-SC/ST are compared. The results show that the intergenerational educational mobility gap is closing. Though the gap is converging at the no education level of father, large absolute gap exists at higher level of father education.

Some studies use the India Human Development Survey data that directly identifies the children-parent pairs residing in the same household. Maitra and Sharma (2009) use the India Human Development Survey 2004-2005 (IHDS-I) to explore the effect of parental education (both father and mother) on years of schooling of children among the parent-child pairs residing in the same household. They find that the average intergenerational correlation in educational attainment in India is 0.52, significantly higher than the global average of 0.42, reported by Hertz et al. (2008). Hnatkovska et al. (2013) use five rounds of NSS surveys (1983, 1987–1988, 1993–1994, 1999–2000, and 2004–2005), and aggregate occupations in three groups (white collar, blue collar and agriculture) to study occupation mobility in India. Based on occupation switches (sons' occupation being different than fathers' occupation, they find that the overall probability of an occupation switch by next generation relative to the household head has steadily increased from 32 percent in 1983 to 41 percent in 2004–2005. For non-SC/STs the switch probability increased from 33 percent to 42 percent, while for SC/STs it has gone from 30 to 39 percent. They conclude that the difference in intergenerational occupational mobility between SC/STs and non-SC/STs has not changed over this period. Majumdar (2010) also use NSS data to study trends in educational and occupational mobility gaps over time among social groups.

Borkotoky et al. (2015) use a district level household survey conducted in 2007-2008 to estimate the process of partner selection and differential fertility with the intergenerational transmission of education. The educational attainment of children was estimated by fitting the estimated marriage probabilities and children ever born in the intergenerational transmission model. To estimate this intergenerational transmission model they use logit, probit and ordered probit used for their analysis. The paper considers both direct and indirect pathways that might influence education attainment of women, their age at marriage, age at first birth and choice of marriage partner in estimating distribution of children's education. The study concludes that the intergenerational transmission model of education is appropriate in the India. Women who are having higher education will marry late, marry well educated and employed men, and have fewer children. Their findings suggest that children are getting higher education than their parents, and better educated mothers do not show partiality in providing higher education among the children.

In short, studies find that the global average correlation between parental and child schooling is around 0.42, the intergenerational elasticity ranges between 0.20 in US and 0.45 in UK, and the average intergenerational correlation in educational attainment in India is about 0.52. Studies also find significant relationship between parent's and child education when the IV estimation is employed. Some studies find that children are getting higher education than their parents suggesting intergenerational transmission. The present study is unaware any study that examine the impact of parental education on child education in Tamil Nadu.

## 1.3 Data and Methodology

The IHDS-II (2011-12) survey is a nationally representative multi-level household survey, a collaborative project by National Council of Applied Economic Research (NCAER) and the University of Maryland. It consists of 42152 households in 1420 villages and 971 urban neighbourhoods across India. The 2011-12 data is mostly re-interviews of 83 percent households that were interviewed for IHDS-I in 2004-05. There are two distinct advantages of using the IHDS data for the analysis of intergenerational education mobility, over the larger and commonly used household surveys for India such as National Sample Survey (NSS) and National Family Health Survey (NFHS). First, the IHDS contains additional questions which are not asked in the NSS or NFHS. These questions allow the identification of parental education for the adult population (in the age group 15-24), including parent-child pairs who do not co-reside. The "ID of father" column in the household roster helps linking individuals to their fathers in the IHDS data set. Second, although the primary goal of the IHDS was the collection of data on income and education of each household, questions on educational history were asked about all household members. These questions allow the calculation of the number of years of schooling for every individual in the sample. An added advantage is that the IHDS contains data on actual years of schooling rather than levels of schooling completed which is generally reported in the NSS data. This avoids the discontinuities in schooling distribution as a result of the attribution of years of schooling from the categorical variable containing level of schooling completed. Moreover, the IHDS collects direct information on household consumption expenditures or household income. Besides, the IHDS also includes the standard data on household characteristics (caste, religion and demographics), characteristics of the household's dwelling, ownership of various assets, information on health, employment, education, social status, employment, marriage, fertility, wage etc., and even panchayat composition. For this study, the IHDS-II data pertaining to Tamil Nadu state of India has been used. The sample size is 678 households.

Figure 1.1 shows the mean years of education of children by parental age. The figure 1.1 shows that older parents have children with more education. Figures 1.2 and 1.3 compares the educational attainment of children with that of mother's and father's educational attainment. Illiterate parents have higher proportion of children with secondary education as well as higher education. The proportion of children with high school and above is higher for parents with secondary level education. In fact, percentage of children with high school education and above is higher for fathers with high school education than that of mothers.

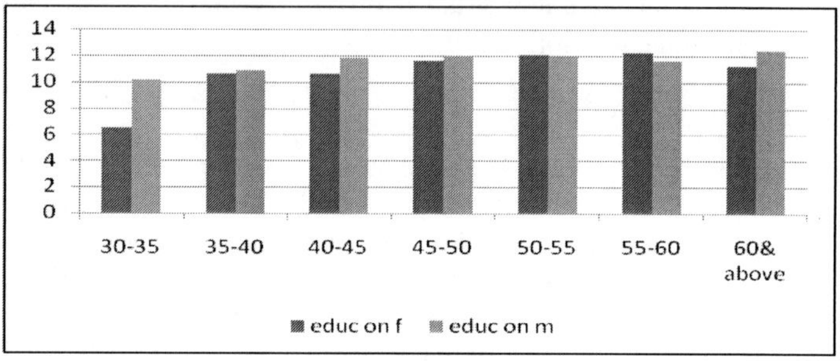


***Figure 1.1 Mean Years of Child Education by Parental Age***

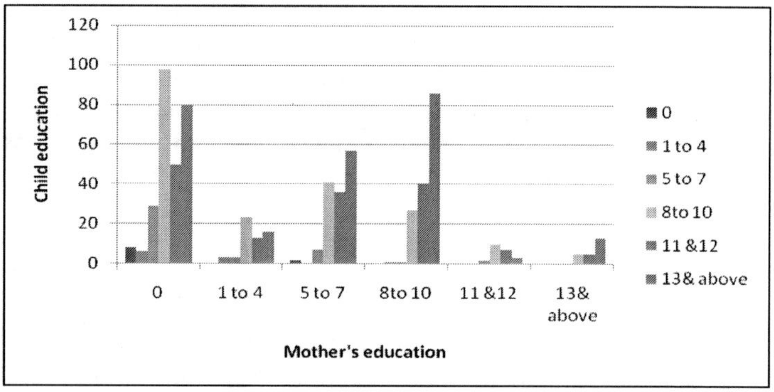


***Figure 1.2 Child Education by Mother's Education***

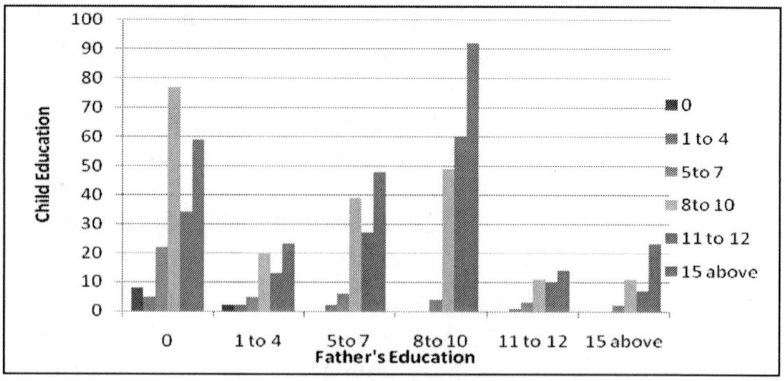


***Figure 1.3 Child Education by Father's Education***

## Instrumental Variable Estimation Methodology

The high intergenerational link between parental education and child schooling may simply a correlation or there may be a causal effect. Even if there is causation, there may also be the problem of endogeneity. Higher educated parents may choose to give higher education for their children. Therefore, child schooling is influenced by parental ability, and hence father's education and mother's education are endogenous variable. To identify the causal effects of parent's education on child's education, it is useful to have variation in parent's education that is exogenous to parental ability and other factors. Therefore, an instrumental variables (IV) approach is used in this paper to overcome the problem posed by endogeneity. The choice of instrumental variable is the New Scheme of Elementary Education (NSEE) introduced in 1953 which made schooling compulsory. Parental education is highly influenced by this scheme while child schooling is not correlated with this. Therefore, parental education is instrumented by the NSEE.

Consider a structural equation,

$$y_1 = \beta_0 y_2 + \beta_2 z_1 + u_1 \tag{1.1}$$

where the $y$ variables are endogenous; the $z$ variable is exogenous. With endogeneity, the OLS point estimates will be biased and inconsistent, since the error term will be correlated with $y_2$. Therefore, $y_2$ need to be replaced with an instrumental variable ($z_2$) such that the IV is correlated with $y_2$, but not correlated with the error term, $u_1$. Rewriting the endogenous explanatory variable in terms of the exogenous variable, including the instrument, $z_{2,}$

$$y_2 = \pi_0 + \pi_1 z_1 + \pi_2 z_2 + v_1 \tag{1.2}$$

The key identification condition is that $\pi_2 \neq 0$; that is, after partialing out $z_1$, $y_2$ and $z_2$ are still meaningfully correlated. Under the assumption that cov ($z_2$, $v_1$) = 0, the instrumental variable estimator of equation (1.1) is derived by writing down the normal equations for the least squares and solving them for the point estimates.

## Two Stage Least Squares Estimation Method

Consider the structural model with two exogenous variables, $z_2$ and $z_{3,}$ excluded from equation (1.1), and, under the assumption of exclusion restrictions, are uncorrelated with the error term $u_1$. If $z_2$ and $z_3$ are both correlated with $y_2$, then each variable could be used as an IV. However, there will be two IV estimators, and neither of these would, in general, be efficient. As a way out, any linear combination of the exogenous variable can be a valid IV, since each of $z_{1,} z_2$ and $z_3$ is uncorrelated with $u_1$. The best linear combination IV is the one that is most highly correlated with $y_2$. This is given by the reduced form equation for $y_2$. Therefore,

$$y_2 = \pi_0 + \pi_1 z_1 + \pi_2 z_2 + \pi_3 z_3 + v_2 \tag{1.3}$$

where $E(v_2) = 0$, cov $(z_1, v_2) = 0$, cov $(z_2, v_2) = 0$, cov $(z_3, v_2) = 0$.

Then, the best IV for $y_2$ is the linear combination of the z's, which can be written as $y_2^*$ given by,

$$y_2^* = \pi_0 + \pi_1 z_1 + \pi_2 z_2 + \pi_3 z_3 \tag{1.4}$$

For this IV not to be perfectly correlated with $z_1$ need at least one of $\pi_2$ or $\pi_3$ to be different from zero, which is a key identification assumption, once all *z's* are assumed to be exogenous. The structural equation is not identified if $\pi_2 \neq 0$ and $\pi_3 \neq 0$, which can tested with an F-statistic. The variable $y_2$ into two components: the first component is $y_2^*$, the part of $y_2$ that is uncorrelated with the error term $u_1$; the second component is $v_2$, which is possibly correlated with the error term with $u_1$, thus making $y_2$ possibly endogenous.

Given data on the $z$'s, $y_2^*$ can be computed for each observation, provided the population parameters π 's are known. As the population parameters are not known in practice, the reduced form equation may be estimated by OLS. Using the sample, $y_2$ is regressed on $z_1, z_2$ and $z_3$ to yield the fitted values,

$$\hat{y}_2 = \hat{\pi}_0 + \hat{\pi}_1 z_1 + \hat{\pi}_2 z_2 + \hat{\pi}_3 z_3 \tag{1.5}$$

The estimated $\hat{y}_2$ can then be used as an IV for $y_2$,

$$\begin{aligned} &\textstyle\sum_{i=1}^{n}(y_{i1} - \hat{\beta}_0 - \hat{\beta}_1 y_{i2} - \hat{\beta}_2 z_{i1}) = 0 \\ &\textstyle\sum_{i=1}^{n}[z_{i1}(y_{i1} - \hat{\beta}_0 - \hat{\beta}_1 y_{i2} - \hat{\beta}_2 z_{i1})] = 0 \\ &\textstyle\sum_{i=1}^{n}\{z_{i2}(y_{i2} - \hat{\beta}_0 - \hat{\beta}_1 y_{i2} - \hat{\beta}_2 z_{i1})\} = 0 \end{aligned} \tag{1.6}$$

The three equations for estimating $\beta_0, \beta_1$ and $\beta_2$ are the first two equations with the third replaced by,

$$\textstyle\sum_{i=1}^{n}[\hat{y}_{i2}(y_{i2} - \hat{\beta}_0 - \hat{\beta}_1 y_{i2} - \hat{\beta}_2 z_{i1})] = 0 \tag{1.7}$$

Solving the three equations in three unknowns gives the IV estimators.

## 1.4 Empirical Analysis

The estimating empirical specifications are,

$$Ed_C = \beta_0 + \beta_1 Ed_P + \beta_2 \ln(HINC) + \beta_3 \ln(OINC) + \beta_4 SG + u_i \tag{1.8}$$

$$Ed_P = \alpha_0 + \alpha_1 NSEE_P + \alpha_2 \ln(HINC) + \alpha_3 \ln(OINC) + \alpha_4 SG + v_i \tag{1.9}$$

where $Ed_C$ is years of education of child, $Ed_P$ (p = father, mother) is years of education of parents, ln(HINC) is log of total household earned income, ln(OINC) is log of income of the household from other sources like interest income, rent etc., and SG is social group, i.e. community to which the household belongs. The instrumental variable NSEE equals 1 if the parent has gone through the New Scheme of Elementary Education, and 0 otherwise. That is, the variable NSEE essentially captures whether the parents went to school before or after 1953 when the scheme was introduced. The equations are estimated by the 2SLS-IV method so that equation (1.9) is the first stage and NSEE serves as an instrumental variable for parental education. Social categories is included as in India, caste is an important socioeconomic factor that plays a crucial role in determining education, occupation, and earnings. The coefficients $\beta_1$ and $\beta_2$ which relate the education level of the child with that of parents and their income are the measures of intergenerational mobility. A higher value for the coefficients implies that parental education has stronger effects on the schooling of their children, and therefore less mobility i.e. there is intergenerational transmission. The extent to which these coefficients are less than unity describe how fast differences in education tend to systematically lessen across generations.

**Table 1.1: Percentage Distribution of Education Before and After NSEE**

| *Education level* | *Father* | | *Mother* | |
|---|---|---|---|---|
| | *Before NSEE* | *After NSEE* | *Before NSEE* | *After NSEE* |
| 0 | 33.83 | 21.85 | 43.24 | 41.65 |
| 1 – 4 | 12.03 | 8.51 | 2.70 | 8.26 |
| 5 – 7 | 14.28 | 18.70 | 18.92 | 22.81 |
| 8 – 10 | 23.30 | 31.85 | 16.22 | 21.82 |
| 11 – 12 | 10.52 | 4.63 | 2.70 | 3.14 |
| 13 – 15 | 5.26 | 3.89 | 8.11 | 2.31 |
| > 16 | 1.50 | 2.78 | 5.41 | 0.83 |

The Table 1.1 presents the proportion of individuals whose distribution of education prior to NSEE introduction in 1953 and after the scheme. It can be observed that while the proportion of fathers who were illiterates before the introduction of NSEE in 1953 has declined drastically, there has been only moderate improvement in the case of mothers. However, proportion mothers with primary and secondary education has increased substantially. Further, the proportion of both fathers and mothers in post secondary education has declined, perhaps due to the location and distance to higher education institutions.

The summary statistics of the variables in empirical analysis are presented in Table 1.2. It can be noted that the mean years of education of the child is higher than the education of parents. From the correlation matrix presented in Table 1.3, it is also to be noted that mother's education has more statistically significant correlation than father's education. Similarly, other income of mother has significant positive correlation with child education, whereas father's other income has no statistically significant correlation with the schooling of the child. Household income also has a positive correlation with years of education of the child. Social group of the household has a negative relation with the educational attainment of children belonging to the backward and deprived community.

**Table 1.2: Descriptive Statistics of Variables in the Analysis of Intergenerational Education Mobility**

| *Variable* | *Child* | *Father* | *Mother* |
|---|---|---|---|
| Age | 22.68 (6.12) | 51.78 (7.81) | 45.13 (7.43) |
| Education | 11.88 (3.56) | 5.70 (4.73) | 4.43 (4.39) |
| ln (HINC) | - | 11.77 (0.80) | - |
| ln (OINC) | - | 9.44 (3.82) | 11.45 (1.39) |
| No of obs. | | 678 | |

**Note:** Standard deviations in parentheses.

**Table 1.3: Correlation Matrix of Variables in Intergenerational Education Mobility**

| *Variable* | $Edu_c$ | *SG* | $Ed_f$ | *ln(HINC)* | $ln(OINC_f)$ | $Ed_m$ | $ln(OINC_m)$ |
|---|---|---|---|---|---|---|---|
| $Edu_c$ | 1.00 | - | - | - | - | - | - |
| SG | -0.10 (0.12) | 1.00 | - | - | - | - | |
| $Ed_f$ | 0.23** (0.00) | -0.01 (0.84) | 1.00 | - | - | - | - |
| ln(HINC) | 0.11*** (0.09) | 0.02 (0.75) | 0.30** (0.00) | 1.00 | - | - | - |
| $ln(OINC_f)$ | 0.04 (0.52) | 0.05 (0.39) | -0.15** (0.02) | 0.156** (0.01) | 1.00 | - | - |
| $Ed_m$ | 0.25** (0.00) | -0.003 (0.95) | 0.62* (0.00) | 0.347* (0.00) | -0.11** (0.07) | 1.00 | - |
| $ln(OINC_m)$ | 0.12** (0.05) | 0.10 (0.12) | 0.05 (0.41) | 0.44** (0.00) | 0.08 (0.19) | 0.15** (0.01) | 1.00 |

**Note:** Absolute t-values in parentheses. ** Significant at 5 percent level *** Significant at 10 percent level.

**Table 1.4: OLS Estimates of Intergenerational Education Mobility Dependent variable: Years of education of child**

| *Variable* | *Spec.1* | *Spec.2* | *Spec.3* | *Spec.4* | *Spec.5* |
|---|---|---|---|---|---|
| $Ed_f$ | 0.172** (0.00) | - | 0.121** (0.00) | 0.081** (0.01) | 0.098** (0.00) |
| $Ed_m$ | - | 0.200** (0.00) | 0.191** (0.00) | 0.129** (0.00) | 0.130** (0.00) |
| ln(HINC) | - | - | - | 0.234 (0.15) | 0.071 (0.72) |
| $ln(OINC_f)$ | - | - | - | - | 0.056*** (0.093) |
| $ln(OINC_m)$ | - | - | - | - | 0.213** (0.042) |
| SG (SC/ST) | - | - | - | -0.529** (0.035) | -0.56** (0.024) |

*(Contd...)*

| Constant | 10.57** (0.00) | 10.64** (0.00) | 9.48** (0.00) | 7.97** (0.00) | 8.99** (0.00) |
|---|---|---|---|---|---|
| R-square | 0.209 | 0.226 | 0.433 | 0.383 | 0.459 |
| F-statistics | 30.12 | 35.36 | 50.38 | 46.63 | 55.30 |

**Note:** Absolute t-values in parentheses. ** Significant at 5 percent level *** Significant at 10 percent level.

The Table 1.4 presents the OLS estimates of intergenerational education mobility. The years of education of parents, $Ed_f$, and $Ed_m$, has a positive and statistically significant effect on the years of education of child. Though the effect of household income on child schooling is positive, it is not statistically significant. However, non-earned income of parents is significantly and positively related to educational of child. Note that the effect of both mother education and non-labour income on child education is higher than those of father. Clearly, women's education has a strong influence on children, not only on child education but also on health and behaviour, as has been documented in numerous studies. It is also to be observed that the social group (SC/ST) has s significant negative effect on the education of children belonging to the deprived communities.

As has been pointed out earlier, in order to overcome the endogeneity issue of OLS estimation, the intergenerational education mobility model has been estimated by 2SLS-IV method instrumenting parental education with the New Elementary School Education Scheme of 1953. In the 2SLS-IV estimation, the first stage equation (1.9) is first estimated for father education and mother education separately by regressing on all other exogenous variables and the excluded instrument to obtain predicted values. In the second stage estimation, child education (equation 1.8) is regressed on the predicted values from the first stage. The Table 1.5 presents the 2SLS results, where the instrument NSEE is the indicator variable whether father and mother attended school before or after 1953. The 2SLS results show that only mother's education and community are statistically significant, while father's education and incomes have no significant effect on child education. While mother's education has a strong positive effect on years of education of child, the negative effect of SC/ST community on child schooling is even stronger in 2SLS-IV estimates. Thus, the 2SLS-IV estimates show that there is no intergenerational mobility, but there may be some intergenerational transmission of mother's education.

**Table 1.5: OLS and IV Estimates of Intergenerational Education Mobility Dependent variable: Years of education of child**

| *Variable* | *OLS* | *2SLS-IV* |
|---|---|---|
| $NSEE_f$ | -0.415 (0.66) | 0.047 (0.99) |
| $NSEE_m$ | 0.437** (0.00) | 0.604** (0.00) |
| ln(HINC) | 0.515 (0.64) | 0.879 (0.78) |
| ln($OINC_f$) | 0.074 (0.97) | 0.749 (0.77) |

*(Contd...)*

| | | |
|---|---|---|
| ln($OINC_m$) | 0.054 (0.86) | 0.438 (0.75) |
| SG (SC/ST) | -0.578** (0.00) | -0.828*** (0.08) |
| Constant | 5.71** (0.00) | 6.38** (0.00) |
| R-square | 0.228 | 0.357 |
| Wald-Chi 2(6) | 51.32 | 14.37 |

**Note:** Absolute t-values in parentheses. ** Significant at 5 percent level
*** Significant at 10 percent level.

The Table 1.6 presents the OLS and IV results of intergenerational mobility among the pairs of parent-child households. It can be clearly observed that mother's education is more influencing than the fathers in both parent-son and parent-daughter pairs. Further, only mother's education is positive and statistically significant in the IV estimates, whereas father's education is insignificant in parent-child educational relationship. This result is similar to Black et al. (2005) who observe that the IV estimates, compared to OLS estimates, of mother's education has significant influence on children's education than the father's education.

**Table 1.6: Relationship between Parental and Child Education**

| *Variable* | *OLS estimates* | *IV estimates* |
|---|---|---|
| Mother-all | 0.191** (0.00) | 0.600** (0.05) |
| Mother-son | 0.213** (0.00) | 0.638*** (0.08) |
| Mother-daughter | 0.173** (0.00) | 0.611*** (0.08) |
| Father-all | 0.121** (0.00) | 0.3942 (0.66) |
| Father-son | 0.184** (0.00) | -0.382 (0.80) |
| Father-daughter | 0.124** (0.00) | -0.345 (0.68) |

**Note:** p-values in parentheses. ** Significant at 5 percent level
*** Significant at 10 percent level.

## 1.5 Conclusion

Education is a primary determinant of long term economic success and a key mechanism of social mobility, capable of lifting disadvantaged children and improving their chances for success. Also, people who are well educated are likely to have children who are also well educated. The converse holds for people who have low education. The parent-child educational outcomes may simply reflect intergenerational transmission or there may be intergenerational mobility. Thus, there is a strong intergenerational association between parental education and education of their children. This intergenerational mobility is a measure of the change in social status which occurs from parent's to the children's generation. Intergenerational mobility studies concentrate on how children's income or education correlates with the income, occupation or education of their parents. This paper analyses the intergenerational educational relations in India between parental education and educational attainments of their children using the Indian Human Development Survey 2011-12 (IHDS-II) data pertaining to the 678 households in the state of Tamil Nadu.

As there may be endogeneity problem in econometric estimation of intergenerational education mobility in that parental ability may be correlated with parental education, this paper employs an instrumental variable two stage least squares (2SLS-IV) method for estimation. The instrument chosen is the New Scheme of Elementary Education Scheme implemented in Tamil Nadu in 1953, making primary education compulsory. The NSEE scheme provides for variation in parental education that is exogenous to parental ability, and hence NSEE is IV for parental education.

Initial OLS estimation results show that there is some significant positive impact of parent's education on child's education, suggesting intergenerational mobility. Also, mother's education has strong influence than father's education on the educational outcomes of children. The 2SLS-IV estimates show that mother's education positively and statistically significantly influences child schooling. The results are reinforced by the IV estimates of the parent-child pairs of both sons and daughters. Thus, both OLS and 2SLS-IV estimates exhibit the strong relevance of mother's education relative to father's education on their child education. Overall, there is intergenerational educational relationship in India, which is positively influenced by female education. With strong intergenerational educational persistence, the Indian society seems to be less mobile intergenerationally, and there is significant intergenerational transmission of education.

# 2

# The Relationship between Income and Nutrition: Non-parametric LOWESS and Parametric TSLS-IV Estimation of Calorie Intake from Cereals Consumption

**Abstract**

*The unprecedented economic growth and the increasing incomes of households have not been accompanied with a corresponding reduction in poverty and hunger and malnutrition in many poor economies. The inadequate calorie intake is further hampered by rising food prices in developing economies. This paper analyses the relationship between income and calorie intake from cereals, as cereals is core of Indian food system, and the effect of food prices on calorie shares of cereals among the poor and non-poor households in Tamil Nadu. In the empirical analysis, parametric TSLS-IV and non-parametric LOWESS methods has been applied to the 68th round (July 2011-June 2012) of NSSO data of rural and urban Tamil Nadu. Both methods of estimation show a significant positive relationship between per capita calorie share of cereals in total calorie intake and monthly per capita expenditure. Rising prices of cereals and other food items reduce the calorie consumption from cereals. There is not much difference in cereals consumption between poor and non-poor in Tamil Nadu.*

**Key words:** *Income, nutrition, cereals, calorie intake, LOWESS, TSLS-IV estimation*

## 2.1 Introduction

The economic growth of India has been unprecedented since economic reforms of 1990s and now India is one of the fastest growing economies in the world. However, despite this spectacular growth of the economy, the problems of poverty, undernourishment, malnutrition, underweight birth and child stunting continue to plague the population. Inadequate nutrition is perhaps the most important problem faced by the poor people in the world today. Despite the efforts to improve nutrient availability in household consumption, a large proportion of poor households in developing countries still have inadequate access to sufficient food. Further, malnutrition is a great and widespread problem in the developing world. The decline in calorie intake, especially from cereals across expenditure classes during a period of accelerated economic growth is puzzling. The World Bank articulates this view forcefully: "There is now a wide measure of agreement on several broad propositions. Malnutrition is largely a reflection of poverty: people do not have income for food. Given the slow income growth that is likely for the poorest people in the foreseeable future, large numbers will remain malnourished for decades to come. The most efficient long-term policies are those that raise the income of the poor" (World Bank, 1981, p. 59). Thus, such malnutrition will disappear only with the improvements in income that accompany the development process.

The nutritious food consumption or calorie intake has been found to have a strong linkage with both human health and productivity. The human body needs dietary calorie energy to maintain normal body metabolic function and engage in activity related to good health and hygiene. In addition, calorie intake is the main determinant of under nutrition and malnutrition among the people. It is needed for growth and assimilation of micronutrients among children. Inadequate supply of calorie lowers productivity, hinders learning and increases the risk of diseases. Although per capita daily calorie intake in developing countries has increased substantially, the number of under nourished people is still around 923 million and the increase in food prices triggers hunger worldwide (FAO, 2008).

The importance of calorie intake for health and development, coupled with the concern about undernourishment in developing countries, has led to increasing number of studies on the determinants of calorie intake. More prominent in the empirical studies is the relationship between income and calorie intake (Abdulai and Aubert, 2004). There has been an intense debate on the exact nature of the relationship between income and calorie intake (Gibson and Rozelle, 2002). From the debates there emerged two types of empirical literatures. The first group is of the opinion that the level of per capita calorie intake has a strong positive but non-linear relationship with income, and that increases in income will lead to substantial increase in calorie intake (Subramanian and Deaton, 1996). On the contrary, the second group suggests that the linkage between income and calorie intake is weak and therefore, increases in income will not result in substantial improvement in calorie intake (Behrman and Deolalikar, 1987; Bouis and Haddad, 1992).

The main objective of this paper is to understand the nature of relationship between income and calorie intake in India. This paper analyses the impact of monthly per capita expenditure and food prices on calorie shares of cereals, the cheapest and largest source of calories in India, among the poor and non-poor households in rural and urban Tamil Nadu. In the empirical analysis, the

68th round (July 2011-June 2012) of NSSO data pertaining to Tamil Nadu has been used. The estimates are obtained by applying the parametric IV/2SLS and the non-parametric LOWESS (Locally Weighted Scatter Plot Smoothing) methods. The variables used in this paper are calorie share of cereals, per capita monthly expenditure, prices of food items such as cereals, pulses, sugar, oil, fruits and vegetables and demographic variables such as household size, age of the household head, gender of the household head and proportion of adult males in the household.

## 2.2 A Brief Review of Recent Studies

Pitt and Rosenzwieg (1985) analyse the changes in nutrient consumption and health of individual family members for changes in the price of particular food faced by a household. They use the National Socio-Economic Survey of Indonesia (April-June 1978 sub-round) data that provides information for a national probability sample of farm household on itemised weekly household consumption expenditures and on the incidence and severity of illness in the seven day period preceding the survey. They assess the conditions under which inferences can be drawn about the health status of individual family members from information on commonly available household aggregate consumption data. They find that the incidence of illness significantly reduces for an increase in calorie consumption.

Variyam, Baylock and Smallwood (1996) estimate the relationship between the fiber-specific nutrition information level of US household meal planners and their dietary fiber intake. They use the 1989 and 1990 Continuing Survey of Food Intake of Individuals (CSFII) and the Diet and Health Knowledge Survey (DHKS) for US and apply Probit latent variable method. They incorporate information variables as endogenous and separate the indirect effects of various exogenous variables on intake (acting through information variables) from the direct effects of exogenous variables on intake. They find that the diet has a marginally significant negative direct effect, implying that those on a special diet tend to have slightly lower fiber intake than those not on a diet. However, those on a diet tend to possess a higher level of disease awareness as well as a better attitude toward consuming fiber-rich food.

Ohri-Vachaspati, Rogers, Kennedy and Goldberg (1998) study the calorie-income relationship using data from the 1986 (January and November) Dominican Republic household survey of over 1400 households applying two stage least squares method with an aim to improve the diets of the poor. The approach is to compare the calorie-expenditure elasticity derived from two sources of information on household calorie consumption: food prepared for consumption (PFC) and food purchased including home produced (PIHP). The change in consumption with changing income level has been measured in terms of calorie-income elasticity. The dependent variable has been the log of average calories computed from up to seven days of recall on PFC or PIHP divided by number of adult equivalents in the household. From the estimated results, they infer that the calorie expenditure elasticity estimates vary due to a difference in the type of calorie variable used and purchase data provide less reliable estimates.

Skouas (2003) use the Indonesian 1996 and 1999 SUSENAS survey data to study whether the relationship between income changes and caloric availability has changed and if so how the relationship between income changes and caloric availability has changed, using nonparametric as well as regression methods. Empirically, they examine two important relationships: the relationship between income and total calories, and the relationship between income and calories from cereals and other foods (excluding cereals and root crops). The estimated empirical results show that the income elasticity of the demand for total calories has been slightly higher in1999 (the crisis year with dramatically different relative prices) compared to its level in1996. In addition, the calorie-income elasticity for cereals as a group increases while the calorie-income elasticity for other food items decreases, consistent with the presence of a binding subsistence constraint.

Abdulai and Aubert (2004), employing both nonparametric and parametric methods, examine the impact of household expenditure on household demand for calories in Tanzania. They find a strong significant positive relationship between household expenditure and calorie demand and a negative and significant relationship between food prices and calorie demand. These results support the conventional wisdom that income growth can alleviate inadequate calorie intake and that effectively targeted food subsidies for very poor households may play a role in improving their calorie intake.

Orewa and Iyanbe (2010) attempt to identify the socio-economic and household characteristics that have major impact on the level of food calorie intake of rural and low-income urban households in Nigeria using a primary cross sectional survey of 90 households applying the OLS multiple regression method. The study concludes that household size, age, educational level, sex, and salary earnings have positive impact on the daily per capita calorie intake while dependency ratio and non-engagement in farming negatively affected it.

Ngwenya (2008), using the 2002 Vietnamese living standardised survey data and applying instrumental variable method, investigate how widowhood influences food consumption choices and calorie intake in Vietnam. The focus has been on food poverty (calorie power) in widowhood instead of total expenditure poverty (general poverty). The IV estimates of the logarithm of per capita calorie intake shows that widows and widowers are more calorie vulnerable than non-widowed households. The calorie intake in widowed households responds slowly to improvements in income, compared to the sensitivity observed in non-widowed households.

Ayinde, Akerele and Dipeolu (2010) examine the calorie intake status in Nigeria, using data on 346 household members in 60 households applying multiple regression analysis. The study shows that calorie intake of male household members has been significantly higher than that of their female counterparts across all age groups. The main socioeconomic factors that affect calorie intake of household members are household monthly income and farm size, among others factors. The study recommends that school meal subsidies, rural family nutrition enlightenment programmes and policies that would help improve household income, among others.

Babatunde, Adejobi and Fakayode (2010) investigate the relationship between income and calorie intake in rural areas of Nigeria, using a primary data collected in 2006 from 220 farm households across 40 villages in Kwara state of Nigeria. The use nonparametric kernel density estimation as well as parametric instrumental variable method. Estimating the effect of total income per capita in Naira on per capita daily calorie intake, the paper suggests that the study area is generally calorie-deficient and more attention is needed to bring calorie consumption to the recommended level of 2500 kilo calories per capita per day.

In India, Behrman and Deolalikar (1987) investigate the calorie-income relationship among the relatively poor population of rural south India. They estimate direct as well as indirect calorie-income elasticity. Direct elasticity estimation is the conversion of food group quantities into aggregate calories before estimation and indirect elasticity estimation is when food group's expenditure elasticities are calculated and a weighted average is computed. They calculate calorie-income elasticities for the same households from two different methods viz. calorie intake as a function of predicted total expenditure (from a two hourly recall of 120 foods) and food group expenditure as a function of predicted total expenditure in a non-system framework (for only 6 aggregate food groups). The estimated results show that the direct nutrient elasticities are not significantly different from zero whereas indirect nutrient elasticities are close to one.

Sinha (2005) focus on investing the nutrition demand pattern for rural households in India, using the nonparametric approach of quantile regression that characterise the entire distribution of calorie consumption. The estimated effect of income on per capita calorie consumption in rural India suggests that while providing food subsidy, the nature of food subsidies is also important. A subsidy on certain commodities might actually reduce the nutritional level of the households. A subsidy on a less nutritious food might not be effective in improving the nutrition of the undernourished households whereas it might provide over nutrition for the over-nourished households.

Kaicker and Gaiha (2013) study the relationship between calorie share of cereals and monthly per capita expenditure, using a panel data of 1993 and 2004 NSSO Consumer Expenditure Survey data. It is argued that food prices induce substitutions between different sources of calories. They estimate the effect on the proportion of calories obtained from cereals of per capita monthly expenditure, vector of food prices, household size, and proportion of adult males in the household, and a vector of state and caste dummy variables. The estimated results show significant food price elasticities. While the food price elasticities vary between food commodities across different subsamples and over time, they are substantially lower than expenditure elasticities, implying that expenditure has a much larger influence on calorie shares.

## 2.3 Data and Methodology

In the empirical analysis of the household calorie intake from cereals, this paper uses the nationwide 68th round (July 2011-June 2012) NSSO consumer expenditure survey data pertaining to Tamil Nadu. The 68th round NSSO survey is the ninth quinquennial consumer expenditure survey of India. The NSSO provides estimates of household monthly per capita expenditure (MPCE) and the distribution of households and persons over the MPCE range separately for the rural and urban sectors of the country, for states and union territories, and for different socio-economic groups. The sample size for this study has been 6646 households, 3319 rural and 3327 urban households, covering all 31 districts of Tamil Nadu. The data has been collected using the schedule type II of NSSO questionnaire, using 'last 7 days' for general food items and 'last 365 days' for the infrequently purchased categories. The food items contain 142 items of food including cereals, pulses, salt and sugar items, milk products, fruits, vegetables, oil, egg, meat, etc. Among these 142 items, this paper considers cereals for empirical analysis.

In the empirical analysis, the dependent variable is the proportion of calorie intake from cereals per capita per day. The calorie intake of an item is derived from the quantities reported as consumed by the sample households. The nutrient content of each item per unit of quantity is based on the source Nutritive Values of Indian Foods (Gopalan, Rama Sastry and Balasubramanian, 2012). Per capita proportion of calorie from cereals is calculated from calorie intake from cereals divided by total calorie intake and household size. The independent variables include income, price of various food items and demographic variables. As the income data is not available, the monthly per capita expenditure has been used as a proxy for income. As is widely understood, the MPCE is commonly used for comparison of average living standards between countries, between regions, and between social and occupational groups. The NSSO calculates MPCE as,

$$\text{MPCE} = \frac{\text{Household monthly consumption expenditure}}{\text{Household size}}$$

The natural logarithm of MPCE and its square are used along with other explanatory variables.

Fluctuations in food prices are also key factor for calorie consumption of the households. The NSSO data does not provide prices of the food items directly, but the total value of these food items is provided. Therefore, using the data on total value and total quantity of consumption of various food items, prices of cereals, pulses, salt and sugar, oils fruits and vegetables are computed in terms of rupees per unit (kg/litre) as,

$$\text{Price} = \frac{\text{Total value of consumption}}{\text{Total quantity of consumption}}$$

The other independent variables used are defined and described in the descriptive statistics table. It is to be noted that the household size, the number of persons living together and taking food from a common kitchen, is used as an instrumental variable for MPCE.

Empirically, parametric and non-parametric approaches are used to estimate the determinants of calorie share of cereals. The relationship between calories and MPCE is generally characterised by non-linearities because the least well-nourished persons are likely to make the largest nutritional responses as their budget shifts (Ravallion, 1990). In other words, the poor may have much to gain from an increase in calorie intake while the rich have little to gain. Thus, it is important to identify the full range of nutritional responses, rather than aggregating them into a single point estimate. To better understand the relationship between calorie and MPCE, nonparametric regression may be an appropriate tool because it makes no assumptions about functional form and allows the data to 'speak for themselves' (Delgado and Robinson, 1992). The non-parametric approach provides useful tools for non-linear modeling and helpful diagnostics. When there is sufficient data, it can also reveal features of the data that are invisible under parametric techniques. However, generally the nonparametric approach is restricted to bivariate relationship only (Gibson and Rozelle, 2002). Ideally, it would be better to examine the effect of income on calorie intake after controlling for household and demographic characteristics. Therefore, this paper supplements the non-parametric estimates with parametric estimations.

## Locally Weighted Scatter Plot Smoothing Method

A special non-parametric regression method, the Locally Weighted Scatter Plot Smoothing (LOWESS) approach, combines multiple regression models in a *k*-nearest neighbour based meta model. The LOWESS method, by looking at the data, uses locally weighted linear regression to smooth data. The smoothing process is considered as local because, like the moving average method, each smoothed value is determined by neighbouring data points defined within the span. The process is weighted because a regression weight function is defined for the data points contained within the span. The locus of each smoothed value given by weighted linear least squares regression over the span is known as LOWESS curve. The local regression smoothing process follows the following steps for each data point,

1. Compute the regression weights for each data point in the span. The weights are given by the tricube function.

$$w_i = \left(1 - \left|\frac{x - x_i}{d(x)}\right|^3\right)^3 \tag{2.1}$$

   where $x$ is the predictor value associated with the response value to be smoothed, $x_i$ are the nearest neighbours of $x$ as defined by the span, and *d(x)* is the distance along the abscissa from $x$ to the most distant predictor value within the span. The weights have the characteristics that (i) the data point to be smoothed has the largest weight and the most influence on the fit, and (ii) the data points outside the span have zero weight and no influence on the fit.

2. A weighted linear least-squares regression is performed. For LOWESS, the regression uses a first degree polynomial.
3. The smoothed value is given by the weighted regression at the predictor value of interest.

If the smooth calculation involves the same number of neighbouring data points on either side of the smoothed data point, the weight function is symmetric. However, if the number of neighbouring points is not symmetric about the smoothed data point, then the weight function is not symmetric. It is to be noted that unlike the moving average smoothing process, the span never changes. For example, when the data points are smoothed with the smallest predictor value, the shape of the weight function is truncated by one-half, the left-most data point in the span has the largest weight, and all the neighbouring points are to the right of the smoothed value. In this paper, the LOWESS smoothing of proportion of calories from cereals with logarithm of monthly per capita expenditure is adopted, without specifying any functional form, with a bandwidth of 0.8 in order to fit the data closely.

The non-parametric LOWESS analysis of this paper is supplemented with parametric analysis. As the proportion of calorie share of cereals and monthly per capita expenditure are endogenous, the parametric approach used is the simultaneous equation model. When a structural equation is over identified, the Two Stage Least Squares (TSLS) method is used. Under the circumstances that the structural equation is over identified, each equation in a simultaneous equation model is instrumented with all exogenous variables. Hence, the two stage least squares method is also called as Instrumental Variables (IV) method. The IV method is used when the dependent variable's error terms are correlated with the independent variables. The TSLS-IV method performs the OLS estimation at two stages.

Consider the structural model,

$$y_1 = \beta_0 + \beta_1 y_2 + \beta_2 z_1 + u_1 \tag{2.2}$$

where the variables $y_2$, and $z_1$, are the explanatory variables and $u_1$ is the error term. This is a structural equation as the interest is in the estimation of $\beta_j$, the casual relationship. But, the dependent variable $y_1$ is endogenous as it is correlated with $u_1$. Assuming $z_1$ is exogenous, $E(u_1)=0$ and $z_1$ is uncorrelated with $u_1$, the OLS estimates of equation (2.2) is biased and inconsistent. Hence, the variable $y_2$ need to be instrumented with an exogenous variable that does not appear in equation (2.2), say $z_2$. The key assumptions are that $z_1$ and $z_2$ are uncorrelated with $u_1$. Thus, for IV estimation,

$$E(u_1) = 0,\ \ Cov(z_1, u_1) = 0,\ \ Cov(z_2, u_1) = 0 \tag{2.3}$$

Given the zero mean assumption, the latter two assumptions are equivalent to $E(z_1 u_1) = E(z_1 u_1) = 0$. Then, the method of moments approach suggests obtaining estimators $\beta_0$, $\beta_1$ and $\beta_2$ by solving the sample counterparts of equation (2.3),

$$\begin{aligned} &\textstyle\sum_{i=1}^{N}(y_{i1} - \beta_0 + \beta_1 y_{i1} + \beta_2 z_{i1}) = 0 \\ &\textstyle\sum_{i=1}^{N} z_{i1}(y_{i1} - \beta_0 + \beta_1 y_{i2} + \beta_2 z_{i1}) = 0 \\ &\textstyle\sum_{i=1}^{N} z_{i2}(y_{i1} - \beta_0 + \beta_1 y_{i2} + \beta_2 z_{i1}) = 0 \end{aligned} \tag{2.4}$$

This is a set of three linear equations in the three unknowns $\beta_0$, $\beta_{01}$ and $\beta_0$, and it is easily solved given the data on $y_1$, $y_2$, $z_1$ and $z_2$.

With more than one exogenous variables $z_2$ and $z_3$ excluded from (not appear in equation (2.2) and are both correlated with $y_2$, each of these variables could be used as an instrumental variable. There are two IV estimators and neither of these would in general be efficient. Since each of $z_1$, $z_2$ and $z_3$ is uncorrelated with $u_1$, any linear combination is also uncorrelated with u1, and therefore any linear combination of the exogenous variables is a valid instrumental variable. The best IV is the linear combination of $z_1$, $z_2$ and $z_3$ that is most highly correlated with $y_2$, given by the reduced form equation for $y_2$, given by,

$$y_2 = \pi_0 + \pi_1 z_1 + \pi_2 z_2 + \pi_3 z_3 + v_2 \tag{2.5}$$

where, $$E(v_2) = 0,\ \ Cov(z_1, v_2) = 0,\ \ Cov(z_2, v_2) = 0\ Cov(z_3, v_2) = 0 \tag{2.6}$$

For this IV not to be perfectly correlated with $z_1$, at least one of $\pi_2$ or $\pi_3$ to be different from zero,

$$\pi_2 \neq 0 \text{ or } \pi_3 \neq 0 \tag{2.7}$$

which can be tested using the F-statistic. This is the key identification assumption, when all $z_j$ are exogenous.

A useful way is to estimate the structural equation in (2.2) is to break $y_2$ into two components, the first is a part of $y_2$ that is uncorrelated with the error term, $u_1$, and the second component is a part of $y_2$ possibly correlated with $u_1$, which is why $y_2$ is possibly endogenous. Given data on the $z_j$, for each observation $y_{2i}$ is computed, by regressing $y_2$ on $z_j$.

$$\hat{y}_2 = \hat{\pi}_0 + \hat{\pi}_1 z_1 + \hat{\pi}_2 z_2 + \hat{\pi}_3 z_3 \tag{2.8}$$

At this stage, it is important to verify the joint significant of $z_2$ and $z_3$ for IV estimation. Thus, $y_2$ is thus an instrument of $y_2$. The three equations for estimating $\beta_0$, $\beta_1$ and $\beta_2$ are the first two equations of (2.4), with the third replaced by,

$$\sum_{i=1}^{N} \hat{y}_{2i}\left(y_{1i} - \hat{\beta}_0 - \hat{\beta}_1 y_{2i} - \hat{\beta}_2 z_{1i}\right) = 0 \tag{2.9}$$

Thus, the three equations given as,

$$\begin{aligned} &\sum_{i=1}^{N}(y_{i1} - \beta_0 + \beta_1 y_{i1} + \beta_2 z_{i1}) = 0 \\ &\sum_{i=1}^{N} z_{i1}(y_{i1} - \beta_0 + \beta_1 y_{i2} + \beta_2 z_{i1}) = 0 \\ &\sum_{i=1}^{N} \hat{y}_{2i}\left(y_{1i} - \hat{\beta}_0 - \hat{\beta}_1 y_{2i} - \hat{\beta}_2 z_{1i}\right) = 0 \end{aligned} \tag{2.10}$$

solves for the three unknown parameters giving the IV estimators.

In general, at least as many excluded exogenous variables as there are included endogenous explanatory variables in the structural equation are needed for IV estimation. With multiple instruments, the IV estimator is also called the two stage least squares (TSLS) estimator. Using the algebra of OLS, when $y_2$ is used as an IV for $y_2$, the IV estimates $\beta_0$, $\beta_1$ and $\beta_2$ are identical to the OLS estimates from the regression of $y_1$ on $y_2$ and $z_1$. In other words, the TSLS estimator is obtained in two stages. The first stage is to run the regression in equation (2.8), where the fitted value $y_2$ is obtained. The second stage is the OLS regression of $y_1$ on $y_2$ and $z_1$. The TSLS estimates can differ substantially from the OLS estimates because $y_2$ is used in place of $y_2$.

## 2.4 Empirical Analysis

Without specifying any functional form, the LOWESS (Locally Weighted Scatter Plot Smoothing) smoothing with a default bandwidth of 0.8 is fitted with the data. The dependent variable is the share of calories from cereals and the explanatory variables are income of the household per capita, as approximated by the log of monthly per capita expenditure (MPCE). The Figure 2.1 presents the LOWESS results for rural Tamil Nadu for the 68th round NSSO data for the year 2011-12. The LOWESS plots strongly suggest a positive linear relationship between the proportion of calorie intake from cereals and monthly per capita expenditure. The calorie share threshold occurs at 0.20 and the corresponding MPCE is Rs.19.28. About 40 percent of individuals are expected to be below the calorie threshold and MPCE, 23 percent of individuals are consuming above the calorie threshold and spend above Rs. 19.28, 18 percent of individuals consume above the calorie threshold and MPCE and 19 percent of individuals consume less than 0.20 Kcal and spend above Rs. 19.28.

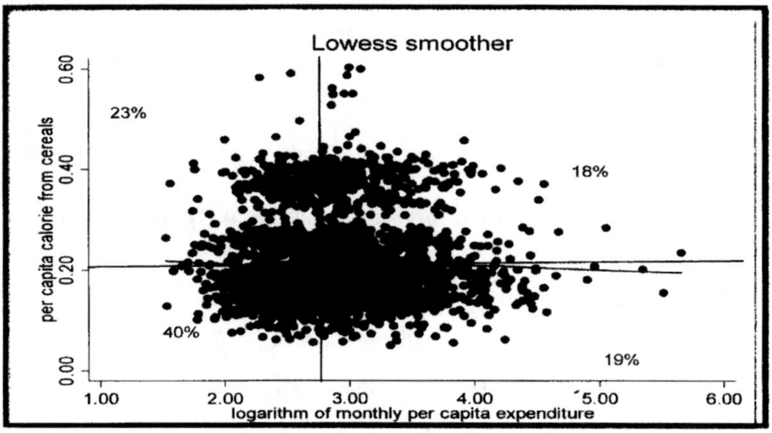


***Figure 2.1: Distribution of Calories Intake from Cereals by MPCE in Rural Tamil Nadu.***

The Figure 2.2 presents the LOWESS results for urban Tamil Nadu for the 68th round NSSO data for the year 2011-12. The results for urban Tamil Nadu also show a strong and positive relationship between calorie share from cereals and monthly per capita expenditure. The calorie share again threshold occurs at 0.20 and the corresponding MPCE is Rs. 23.47. Around 37 percent of individuals are below the calorie threshold and MPCE, 22 percent of individuals consume above the calorie threshold and spend above Rs. 23.47, 21 percent of individuals consume above calorie threshold and MPCE, and 20 percent of individuals consume less than 0.20 Kcal and spend more than Rs. 23.47. In Tamil Nadu, urban people spend about four rupees more than rural people to consume 0.20 shares of calories from cereals.

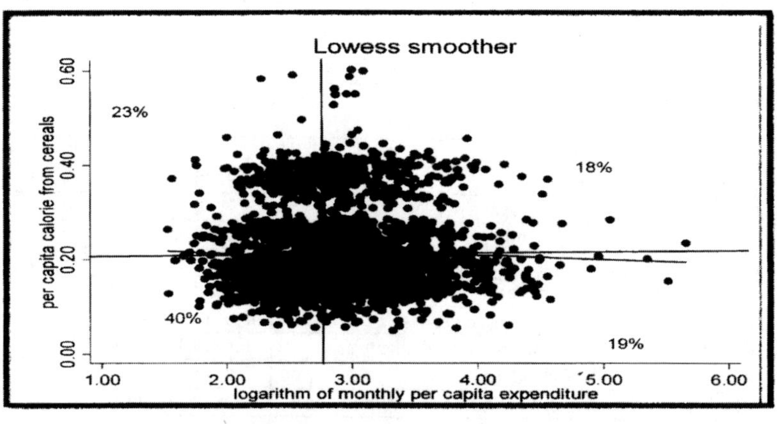


***Figure 2.2: Distribution of Calories Intake from Cereals by MPCE in Urban Tamil Nadu.***

In the parametric analysis, the share of calories from cereals is estimated as a function of monthly per capita expenditure, prices of food items and demographic variables. As the MPCE is expected to correlate with random disturbance term in the calorie share equation, the MPCE is treated as endogenous variable. The endogenous variable MPCE is instrumented by household size and proportion of adult males as they are expected to influence strongly the MPCE, which in turn, determines the share of calorie intake from cereals. The structural equation for calorie share from cereals consumption and monthly per capita expenditure are specified as,

$$CI_i = \beta_0 + \beta_1 \ln(MPCE) + \beta_2 \, ln(MPCE)^2 + \beta_3 \ln(PC) + \beta_4 \ln(PP)$$

$$+\beta_5 \ln(PS) + \beta_6 \ln(PO) + \beta_7 \ln(PF) + \beta_8 \ln(PV) + \beta_9 HHAage$$

$$+\beta_{10} HHMale + \beta_{11} ST + \beta_{12} BC + \beta_{13} GC + \sum \gamma_j \, District_j + u_i \quad (2.11)$$

$$\ln(MPCE) = \delta_0 + \delta_1 HHSize + \delta_2 HHAdults + v_1 \quad (2.12)$$

where $CI_i$ is the proportion of calorie intake share from cereals consumption. The Table 2.1 presents the descriptive statistics of all the variables used in the empirical analysis. The mean value of natural logarithm of proportion of per capita calorie intake from cereals is 0.24 Kcal and its standard deviation is 0.14 in rural Tamil Nadu, and urban has mean value of 0.23 and its standard deviation is 1.13. The mean of the natural logarithm of MPCE is 2.90 in rural Tamil Nadu and urban Tamil Nadu has average lnMPCE of 3.12. The log of prices ranges from 0.48 to 4.18. The mean household size is 3.8 and the proportion of adults is 20 percent.

**Table 2.1: Descriptive Statistics of Variables in the Calorie Intake Analysis of Rural and Urban Tamil Nadu.**

| *Variable* | *Description* | *Rural Tamil Nadu* | *Urban Tamil Nadu* |
|---|---|---|---|
| CI | Calorie intake share from cereals in total calorie intake (Kcal/person/day) | 0.24 (0.14) | 0.23 (1.13) |
| ln(MPCE) | Log of monthly per capita expenditure (Rs.) | 2.90 (0.50) | 3.12 (0.58) |
| $\ln(MPCE)^2$ | Log of monthly per capita expenditure square (Rs.) | 8.69 (3.09) | 10.07 (3.81) |
| ln(PC) | Log of price of cereals | 2.76 (0.39) | 2.92 (0.42) |
| ln(PP) | Log of price of pulses | 3.91 (0.22) | 3.96 (0.23) |
| ln(PS) | Log of price of sugar | 2.72 (0.29) | 2.80 (0.31) |
| ln(PO) | Log of price of oil | 4.14 (0.46) | 4.17 (0.46) |
| ln(PF) | Log of price of fruits | 0.48 (1.21) | 0.72 (1.26) |
| ln(PV) | Log of price of vegetables | 2.35 (0.33) | 2.45 (0.32) |
| HHHAge | Age of household head (years) | 48.01 (12.89) | 48.10 (12.69) |
| HHHMale | If male household head=1, 0 otherwise | 0.85 (0.35) | 0.85 (0.32) |
| HHSize | No. of household members | 3.87 (1.63) | 3.71 (1.52) |
| HHAdults | Proportion of adult males | 0.28 (0.23) | 0.22 (0.24) |

*(Contd...)*

| | | | |
|---|---|---|---|
| SC | If schedule caste community=1, 0 otherwise | 0.20 (0.40) | 0.13 (0.34) |
| ST | If schedule tribe community=1, 0 otherwise | 0.01 (0.12) | 0.01 (0.08) |
| BC | If backward class community=1, 0 otherwise | 0.76 (0.42) | 0.80 (0.39) |
| GC | If general community=1, 0 otherwise | 0.01 (0.13) | 0.04 (0.21) |
| N | Number of sample observations | 3079 | 3019 |

**Table 2.2: OLS and TSLS Estimates of Calorie Intake from Cereals in Tamil Nadu**
**Dependent variable: CI (calorie share from cereals in total calorie intake)**

| ***Variable*** | ***Rural Tamil Nadu*** | | ***Urban Tamil Nadu*** | |
|---|---|---|---|---|
| | ***OLS*** | ***TSLS*** | ***OLS*** | ***TSLS*** |
| ln(MPCE) | 0.195* (6.03) | 7.029* (10.16) | 0.174* (6.39) | 6.260* (9.57) |
| $\ln(MPCE)^2$ | -0.016* (3.05) | -1.083* (10.02) | -0.013* (3.22) | -0.910* (9.43) |
| ln(PC) | -0.064* (9.22) | -0.186* (6.26) | -0.057* (7.61) | -0.193* (7.31) |
| ln(PP) | -0.044* (3.86) | -0.027 (0.59) | -0.015 (1.31) | -0.084*** (1.71) |
| ln(PS) | -0.073* (8.92) | -0.189* (5.55) | -0.044* (5.54) | -0.035 (1.07) |
| ln(PO) | -0.018* (3.49) | -0.072* (3.49) | 0.001 (0.22) | -0.141* (5.14) |
| ln(PF) | -0.018* (9.54) | -0.033* (4.49) | -0.024* (12.72) | -0.043* (3.32) |
| ln(PV) | -0.057* (8.22) | -0.160* (5.51) | -0.079* (10.88) | -0.175* (5.45) |
| HHHAge | 0.002* (7.63) | 0.002* (2.59) | 0.0008* (5.18) | 0.002* (3.26) |
| HHHMale | -0.131* (21.91) | -0.114* (4.84) | -0.129* (21.38) | -0.153* (6.01) |
| ST | 0.031*** (1.81) | 0.127*** (1.87) | -0.011 (0.44) | -0.044 (0.42) |
| BC | 0.010** (1.98) | -0.049** (2.29) | -0.003 (0.50) | -0.142* (4.74) |
| GC | 0.009 (0.61) | -0.026 (0.43) | 0.003 (0.32) | -0.038 (0.80) |
| Constant | 0.607* (9.42) | -9.033* (9.11) | 0.444* (7.28) | -7.797* (8.58) |
| District dummies | yes | yes | yes | yes |
| $R^2$/Wald $Chi^2$ | 0.35 | 209.06 | 0.32 | 166.92 |

**Note:** Absolute t-values (OLS) and z-values (TSLS) in parentheses. * Significant at 1 percent level ** Significant at 5 percent level *** Significant at 10 percent level.

The OLS and TSLS-IV estimates of the per capita share of calorie intake from cereals in total calorie intake for rural and urban Tamil Nadu in 2011-12 are presented in Table 2.2. In both rural and urban Tamil Nadu, the estimated TSLS coefficients of MPCE is positive and its square is negative and both are statistically significant at 1 percent level. The estimated results indicate that a 1 percent increase in household MPCE increases the calorie share from cereals by 29.3 percent in rural and by 27.1 percent in urban households of Tamil Nadu. An increase in the price of cereals significantly reduces its calorie intake by 1.08 percent in rural and 0.91 percent in urban Tamil Nadu. Similarly, the calorie intake significantly decreases in Tamil Nadu with increases in prices of other food items. The calorie share of cereals in food consumption is influenced not just by expenditure and food prices but also by demographic characteristics. The variable age of the household head influences the calorie share positively and its effect is statistically significant at 1 percent level while the effect of male household head on calorie intake is significantly negative. The coefficients of schedule tribe and backward community are significantly positive and negative respectively in rural households of Tamil Nadu compared to scheduled caste households. In urban Tamil Nadu only the BC dummy is statistically significant and its coefficient is also negative. Among the district dummies, the estimated coefficients are generally positive in relatively developed districts and negative for most of the backward districts of Tamil Nadu. Thus, the calorie share is sensitive to household income/expenditure, food prices and household demographic characteristics. Hence, the finding of this paper does not support the notion that cereal consumption will not increase with higher standard of living.

The results of Durbin and Wu-Hausman tests for endogeneity and Sargan and Basmann tests for identification restrictions for rural and urban samples are presented in Table 2.3. The endogeneity test has been performed to determine whether endogenous repressors in the model are in fact exogenous. The difference between the Durbin and Wu-Hausman tests of endogeneity is that the former uses estimates of the error variance based on the model assumption that the variables being tested are exogenous, while the latter uses estimates of the error variance based on the model assumption that the variables being tested are endogenous. Both tests are highly significant for both rural and urban Tamil Nadu, so both reject the null of exogeneity. Therefore, the MPCE has to be treated as endogenous, and the chosen instruments are not weak because minimum Eigen value statistics of 52.9 for rural and 48.48 for urban exceed the critical value of the F statistic.

The Sargan and Basmann tests for over-identifying restrictions tests two different things simultaneously: whether the instruments are uncorrelated with the error term, and whether the equation is miss-specified in that one or more of the excluded exogenous variables should in fact be included in the structural equation. In both the tests, the null hypothesis is rejected at 10 percent level of Chi-square significance for rural and 5 percent level for urban Tamil Nadu. Thus, the two instrumental variables, household size and proportion of adult males in the household, are valid and the structural model is specified correctly.

**Table 2.3: Endogeneity and Identification Restrictions Tests**

| *Hypothesis* | *Test* | *Rural Tamil Nadu* | | *Urban Tamil Nadu* | |
|---|---|---|---|---|---|
| | | *Estimate* | *p-value* | *Estimate* | *p-value* |
| Endogeneity | Durbin $chi^2$ | 1581.44 | 0.000 | 1588.81 | 0.000 |
| | Wu-Hausman F | 3204.00 | 0.000 | 3304.96 | 0.000 |
| Identification | Sargan $chi^2$ | 2.958 | 0.085 | 3.873 | 0.049 |
| | Basmann $chi^2$ | 2.919 | 0.088 | 3.821 | 0.051 |

A calorie intake of 2400 Kcal per day is considered as adequate for a typical adult engaged in physically strenuous work of certain duration in rural India. If an individual consumes per capita calorie intake per day less than 2400 Kcal per day, he is considered as poor or in poverty, and consumption of more than 2400 Kcal per day is considered to be above poverty or non-poor. Therefore, the paper also performs empirical analysis for poor and non-poor samples or order to identify the differential effects of the determinants of calorie intake from cereals in poor and non-poor households in Tamil Nadu. The Table 2.4 presents the descriptive statistics for poor and non-poor households in rural and urban Tamil Nadu. The mean of calorie intake from cereals is 0.23, 0.28, 0.22 and 0.26 respectively for poor and non-poor in rural and urban Tamil Nadu.

**Table 2.4: Descriptive Statistics of Variables in the Calorie Intake Analysis for Poor and Non-Poor Households in Rural and Urban Tamil Nadu**

| *Variable* | *Rural Tamil Nadu* | | *Urban Tamil Nadu* | |
|---|---|---|---|---|
| | *Poor* | *Non-poor* | *Poor* | *Non-poor* |
| CI | 0.23 (031) | 0.28 (0.17) | 0.22 (0.12) | 0.26 (0.16) |
| ln(MPCE) | 2.82 (0.45) | 3.36 (0.53) | 3.01 (0.55) | 3.51 (0.52) |
| $\ln(MPCE)^2$ | 8.20 (2.67) | 11.61 (3.80) | 9.37 (3.48) | 12.62 (3.92) |
| ln(PC) | 2.74 (0.39) | 2.84 (0.40) | 2.89 (0.41) | 3.02 (0.38) |
| ln(PP) | 3.90 (0.21) | 3.96 (0.21) | 3.94 (0.23) | 4.02 (0.20) |
| ln(PS) | 2.71 (0.29) | 2.77 (0.30) | 2.79 (0.30) | 2.86 (0.32) |
| ln(PO) | 4.12 (0.46) | 4.22 (0.41) | 4.14 (0.47) | 4.27 (0.39) |
| ln(PF) | 0.33 (1.14) | 1.37 (1.24) | 0.51 (1.18) | 1.47 (1.25) |
| ln(PV) | 2.35 (0.33) | 2.38 (034) | 2.44 (0.31) | 2.49 (0.32) |
| HHHAge | 47.59 (12.94) | 49.23 (12.53) | 17.48 (13.19) | 49.08 (11.97) |
| HHHMale | 0.86 (0.33) | 0.78 (0.41) | 0.86 (0.34) | 0.83 (0.37) |
| SC | 0.21 (0.40) | 0.15 (0.36) | 0.14 (0.35) | 0.10 (0.30) |
| ST | 0.01 (0.12) | 0.01 (0.09) | 0.08 (0.08) | 0.01 (0.06) |
| BC | 0.75 (0.43) | 0.81 (0.38) | 0.79 (0.40) | 0.84 (0.36) |
| GC | 0.02 (0.14) | 0.01 (0.12) | 0.04 (0.20) | 0.05 (0.22) |
| N | 2641 | 438 | 2372 | 647 |

**Note:** Standard deviations in parentheses.

**Table 2.5: TSLS Estimates of Calorie Intake from Cereals of Poor and Non-Poor in Tamil Nadu**

| *Variable* | *Rural Tamil Nadu* | | *Urban Tamil Nadu* | |
|---|---|---|---|---|
| | *Poor* | *Non-poor* | *Poor* | *Non-poor* |
| ln(MPCE) | 8.523* (8.88) | 10.504* (3.16) | 8.594* (6.92) | 11.028* (2.86) |
| $\ln(MPCE)^2$ | -1.392* (8.80) | -1.413* (3.13) | -1.312* (6.86) | -1.426* (2.85) |
| ln(PC) | -0.111* (3.68) | -0.463* (2.92) | -0.033* (5.53) | -0.383** (2.51) |
| ln(PP) | -0.027 (0.56) | -0.102 (0.58) | -0.089 (1.34) | -0.192 (1.01) |
| ln(PS) | -0.187* (5.04) | -0.355** (2.35) | -0.041 (0.89) | -0.272** (2.09) |
| ln(PO) | -0.060* (2.74) | -0.272* (2.40) | -0.153** (4.03) | -0.353** (2.36) |
| ln(PF) | -0.031 (1.58) | -0.047*** (1.80) | -0.028** (2.47) | -0.051*** (1.93) |
| ln(PV) | -0.167* (5.16) | -0.184*** (1.71) | -0.203* (4.43) | -0.170*** (1.70) |
| HHHAge | 0.002* (2.74) | -0.0003 (0.12) | 0.003* (3.18) | -0.0005 (0.20) |
| HHHMale | -0.134* (5.07) | 0.035 (0.39) | -0.154* (4.31) | -0.180** (2.24) |

*(Contd...)*

| ST | 0.144** (1.98) | -0.288 (0.87) | -0.061 (0.44) | -0.245 (0.57) |
|---|---|---|---|---|
| BC | -0.012 (0.86) | -0.114 (1.24) | -0.156* (3.76) | -0.066 (0.66) |
| GC | -0.003 (0.04) | 0.102 (0.41) | 0.077 (1.16) | 0.105 (0.65) |
| Constant | -11.033* (8.17) | -15.030* (2.92) | -10.92* (6.45) | -15.857* (2.71) |
| District dummies | yes | yes | yes | yes |
| Wald $Chi^2$ | 155.99 | 27.17 | 78.94 | 24.53 |

**Note:** z-values in parentheses. * Significant at 1 percent level ** Significant at 5 percent level *** Significant at 10 percent level.

The estimated two-stage least square regression results are presented in Table 2.5 for poor and non-poor in rural and urban Tamil Nadu. In both the poor and non-poor rural households, the household expenditure and its square have significant positive and negative effects respectively on calorie intake from cereals. The results indicate that a 1 percent increase in MPCE results in a 38.72 and 37.5 percent increase in calorie intake from cereal consumption in poor and non-poor rural households in Tamil Nadu. The poor rural schedule tribe households consume relatively higher calorie share than schedule caste households. The prices of cereals, sugar, oil and vegetables have significant negative effect on calorie consumption from cereals indicating higher prices of food products lead to lower household calorie consumption from cereals. In rural Tamil Nadu, relative to poor households, for non-poor households calorie consumption from cereals is less for an increase in food prices, probably due to shift towards junk food in non-poor households. Again, both poor and non-poor households in the relatively developed districts consume more calories than their counter parts backward districts of Tamil Nadu.

The TSLS results for urban Tamil Nadu are somewhat different from the rural estimates in some respects. Among the urban households, though the expenditure elasticities are significantly positive and negative respectively for MPCE and its square and its square, the effects are higher relative to rural households of Tamil Nadu. A 1 percent increase in MPCE results in 39.04 percent increase in calorie intake from cereal consumption in poor urban households and a much higher 42.38 increase in calorie intake from cereal consumption in non-poor urban households. The backward class poor households have lower calorie share relative to scheduled caste households. The price effects and regional effects are the same as that of rural Tamil Nadu.

The endogeneity tests for poor and non-poor in rural and urban Tamil Nadu, presented in Table 2.6, are highly significant and reject the null of exogeneity and allow lnMPCE as endogenous. The instruments are also not weak as the minimum Eigen value statistics exceed the critical value of F statistic. The tests of over-identifying restrictions reject the null hypothesis suggesting that the two instrument variables are valid and the structural model is specified correctly.

**Table 2.6: Endogeneity and Identification Restrictions Tests for Poor and Non-Poor Households in Rural and Urban Tamil Nadu**

| *Hypothesis* | *Test* | *Rural Tamil Nadu* | | *Urban Tamil Nadu* | |
|---|---|---|---|---|---|
| | | *Poor* | *Non-poor* | *Poor* | *Non-poor* |
| Endogeneity | Durbin $chi^2$ | 1333.59 (0.00) | 225.46 (0.00) | 1340.26 (0.00) | 300.06 (0.00) |
| | Wu-Hausman F | 2649.02 (0.00) | 417.94 (0.00) | 3022.83 (0.00) | 520.68 (0.00) |
| Identification | Sargan $chi^2$ | 5.004 (0.03) | 0.010 (0.92) | 1.004 (0.32) | 1.115 (0.29) |
| | Basmann $chi^2$ | 4.930 (0.03) | 0.009 (0.93) | 0.986 (0.32) | 1.039 (0.31) |

## 2.5 Conclusion

Around the world, economic growth is supposed to improve not only standards and quality of life, but also to eliminate poverty, hunger, hygiene, disease, ill-health, and child mortality. For these to be achieved, there has to be proper availability and access to nutrition for the poor and undernourished. The nutritious food consumption or calorie intake has strong linkages with not only human health but also determines the efficiency and productivity and even the learning and achievement of children. Despite all-round development of economies, and all-out efforts to improve nutrient availability inadequate nutrition is perhaps the most important problem faced by the poor people and poor economies around the world today. The decline in calorie intake, especially from cereals across expenditure classes during a period of accelerated economic growth is puzzling. The relationship between income and nutrition or calorie intake has been at the core of an intense debate. The empirical literature has produced controversial findings. Some evidences suggest that the level of per capita calorie intake has a strong positive but non-linear relationship with income, and that increases in income will lead to substantial increase in calorie intake. On the contrary, some results suggest that the linkage between income and calorie intake is weak and therefore, increases in income will not result in substantial improvement in calorie intake. Further, rising food prices and household composition have been shown to have significant effects on the calorie intake.

Therefore, this paper tries to understand the nature of relationship between income and calorie intake in India. As the cereal consumption forms the core of Indian food system, this paper analyses the effect of income (monthly per capita expenditure) and food prices on calorie shares of cereals, the cheapest and largest source of calories in India, among the poor and non-poor households in Tamil Nadu. In the empirical analysis, the 68th round (July 2011-June 2012) of NSSO data pertaining to rural and urban Tamil Nadu has been used and methods of parametric TSLS-IV and non-parametric LOWESS (Locally Weighted Scatter Plot Smoothing) are used. The non-parametric LOWESS estimation on the relationship between per capita calorie share of cereals in total calorie intake and monthly per capita expenditure reveal a positive and non-linear relationship. In Tamil Nadu, urban people spend about four rupees more than rural people to consume 0.20 shares of calories from cereals. The results of the parametric analyses also indicate a positive and strongly significant relationship between per capita calorie share of cereals and monthly per capita expenditure. Increases in the price of cereals, pulses, oil, fruits and vegetables lead to decline in the calorie consumption from cereals in both rural and urban Tamil Nadu. Analysis of poor and non-poor calorie intake from cereals shows that there is not much difference between poor and non-poor in cereal consumption in urban Tamil Nadu, indicating not much difference in life style between poor and non-poor in urban Tamil Nadu.

The empirical results of this paper suggest that the shifting pattern calorie intake by non-poor with growing income from cereals to more expensive non-cereal food products need to be taken into designing food subsidy programmes. A subsidy on a less nutritious food might not be effective in improving the nutrition of the under-nourished households whereas it might provide over-nutrition for the over-nourished households. Further, lowering food prices may play a critical role in improving calorie intake of poor households, for which effective targeted food subsidies could be used to improve the nutritional needs of very poor households. Further, lowering food prices may play a critical role in improving calorie intake of poor households, for which effective targeted food subsidies could be used to improve the nutritional status of vulnerable poor households.

# 3

# Gender Bias in Education Expenditure: 3SLS Estimation of Budget Share of Household Expenditure on Education of Children

**Abstract**

*In the Indian patriarchal society, the resource allocation within household is not equal between the sexes and there exists a significant gender bias in favour of males and against females. Such bias is also exhibited even in education of children, and the expenditure on education among the boys and girls are unequal. This paper analyses the issue of gender bias and the influence of bargaining power in the budget share of education expenditure in the household expenditure using the 68th round (2011-2012) of NSSO data pertaining to Bihar and Kerala following the collective household model approach and applying the three stage least square estimation method. The 3SLS estimates show significant gender gap in the budget share of education expenditure of households in rural and urban Bihar and Kerala and there is not much difference in the gender allocation patterns in households in these two states. Though the urban households allocate more of resources on education, the gender disparities are more both in urban Bihar and Kerala compared to rural areas. The budget share of education expenditure of households increases more with an increase in the proportion of boys than girls in the household. The male bargaining power has some effect within the household on the budget share of household education expenditure in urban households, but not in rural households, of Bihar and Kerala.*

**Key words:** *Gender, bargaining, education expenditure, budget share, 3SLS estimation*

## 3.1 Introduction

In the post-independence 1951 Census of India, the literacy rates of females and males were only 9 percent and 27 percent respectively. The slow progress of education sector continued in that in the 1991 Census the corresponding rates were 39.3 percent and 64.1 percent. With economic reforms of 1991, there has been increased public attention on the benefits of schooling and government policies have been revitalized to improve the supply side and incentivise households to enrol children in schools. Consequently, dramatic changes in enrolment have occurred. Also, significant efforts have been made to promote female schooling which is important for reducing the gender differential in literacy rates. The Sarva Shiksha Abhiyan (SSA, Education for All) education programme, implemented in 2002, has specific provisions to boost female participation through changes in the education system as well as societal attitudes. As a result, the proportion of out of school children fell from 66 percent in 2005 to 3.5 percent in 2010 for children between the ages of 6 and 14 in rural India. Further, in recognition of education as a national priority, government investment in education has increased considerably. Many state governments have increased their elementary education budget over the years. However, there remains an acute shortfall in terms of infrastructure and quality in government schools which necessitates further action by the government to improve education system in India.

India's rapid economic growth since l980 has also been accompanied by increasing inequality in many outcomes, raising concerns that may be due to growing inequality in opportunities. Inequality in opportunities is manifested across different groups like caste, community, gender or class and the poor, women, and weaker sections of population have unequal chances of acquiring assets, unequal return to assets or other basic services. In recent years, the growing inequality creep the educational outcomes and even the household allocation of resources for boys and girls. While the mean years of schooling have grown noticeably across successive generations, for both men and women, in both rural and urban areas, gender gaps in education has increased. The most significant gains have been among urban females; in rural areas, mean years of schooling grew at comparable rates for both men and women. In a study of 41 countries, a World Bank (2001) report finds that "in most countries the ratio of boys to girls enrolled in secondary school is 40 percent for poorest countries and 20 percent for rich countries". The gap remains large and gender inequality increases over the year in developing and underdeveloped countries. According to 2001 Census of India, "the gender gap in literacy ranges from 24.6 percent in rural India and 13.4 percent in urban India. In northern part of India, literacy rates vary from 27.7 from rural and Bihar 17.5 percent in urban Bihar, whereas in Uttar Pradesh figures are 30.3 in rural areas and 16.1 for the urban areas. In the southern states of India like Kerala the literacy gap between the rural and urban areas is much less compared to other states of India, standing at 6.7 percent for the rural areas and 5.2 percent for the urban areas".

The issue of gender bias against girls within the household is particularly important in the Indian context as there exists widespread social sanction for son preference and the skewed property rights. But it is difficult to observe the inner working of household due to lack of data. The best way to gauge the extent of gender bias against girls within households is to look at the issue by using external observable outcomes like education expenditure on children by the household. A general approach is to understand how household expenditure on any particular good like education changes with respect to gender composition of household. It tests the significance of gender differential between marginal impact of boy and girl child on the expenditure share of education in budget share of household. This can be stated that if one replaces girl child on the particular age group with a boy in that same age group, then the extent to which expenditure share of education changes. This gives a measure of gender bias in the household expenditure allocation of an education item.

The main objectives of this paper are to examine the nature and existence of gender bias in household allocation of resources to education on children and to analyse the effects of the bargaining power of the household decision-maker on the budget share of educational expenditure. This paper follows the theoretical approach of the collective household model of Browning and Chiappori (1998) and applies the three stage least square (3SLS) estimation method on the 68th round NSSO (2011-2012) data pertaining to Kerala and Bihar. The empirical methodology that is adopted for testing gender bias is based on the difference between the expenditure share of education in the household budget associated with an addition of a boy and a girl child in the household. If the differential is statistically significant, then gender bias is said to exist, with the sign of the differential indicating the direction of the bias. Stated differently, if one replaces a girl in a certain age group with a boy in that same age group, holding everything else constant, then the extent to which the expenditure share of education changes gives a measure of gender bias in the household allocation of the education expenditure.

To understand the effects of the bargaining power of the household decision-maker on the budget share of household educational expenditure, a two-step approach is followed. Assuming that each member of the household cares about the welfare of the other member, following Bourguignon and Chiappori (1992) and Bourguignon, Browning, Chiappori and Lechene (1993), the efficient household behaviour in resource allocation is characterized by an income sharing rule as follows. In the first stage the household acts as if the members pool and allocate income to each member according to some household sharing rule, which depends on the welfare weight of each individual. The years of schooling of the household head is used as a proxy for welfare weight of household head as it directly affects the earnings or income. In the second stage, each individual maximises his/her sub-utility subject to the income allocated. The estimation methodology followed is the extended approach of Basu (2006), examining whether the earnings of the household head is a true measure of the bargaining power of the head within the household and whether household head has an effect on expenditure patterns or budget share of education in the household expenditure.

## 3.2 A Brief Review of Recent Studies

A concern for the high gender inequality in India and the importance of female education has evolved many studies that investigate the effects of gender inequality in the allocation of resources towards education. There are several studies that estimate gender bias and household member (specifically household head) bargaining power over allocation of resources or budget share for education expenditure. Studies by Bardhan (1974) and Das Gupta (1987) clearly show evidence of discrimination against females in India, although the explanations put forward by the two authors are quite different. Further, the empirical evidence on the intra-household allocations also demonstrates the substantially low level of resources directed towards female child education. However, the problem of detecting discrimination at the household level comes from two kinds of limitations: a lack of data on consumption at the individual level and the fact that the lower allocations of one good to the girls relative to the boys may be offset by higher allocations of other goods.

Deaton (1989) proposes a novel technique, an outlay equivalent/adult good approach, for detecting gender bias at the household level. Using data from Thailand and Cote d' Ivoire, Deaton fails to find any evidence of a significant level of gender bias in Cote d' Ivoire and find evidence for some gender discrimination in Thailand. Subramanian and Deaton (1991) test gender gap in the intra-household consumption patterns in Maharashtra using the outlay equivalent/adult good approach. The study finds a pro-male preference for educational and medical expenditures in the urban areas while expenditures on basic food stuffs are either gender neutral or pro-female. In rural households, discrimination against the girls has been found in the young age groups. The study, however, did not find any evidence of major gaps in the allocation of resources within the household. Following the same methodology, Haddad and Reardon (1993) test gender discrimination in Burkina Faso, disaggregating by agro-economical zones (rural versus urban) and income strata. The study finds that there is no significant gap in the intra-household allocations towards male and female children in Burkina Faso.

Subramanian (1995) applies the outlay equivalent technique for adult goods and educational and medical expenditures for rural areas of five Indian states – Andhra Pradesh, Maharashtra, Punjab, Rajasthan and Tamil Nadu. He fails to find any evidence of gender discrimination in the northern states, although Andhra Pradesh and Maharashtra show some evidence of gender discrimination in the 5-9 age group. Andhra Pradesh and Rajasthan also depict evidence of gender discrimination in the 10-14 age group for educational expenditure whereas Rajasthan (0-4 age group) and Punjab (0-4, 5-9 and 10-14 age groups) show evidence of discrimination in medical expenditures.

Lancaster, Maitia and Ray (2008) use two sets of data, the Standard Living Survey for Uttar Pradesh and Bihar and the 50th round of NSSO data (1993-94) for Bihar, Maharashtra and Kerala, to understand the nature of gender bias in rural and urban India applying 3SLS method. Analysing the budget shares of expenditure on food, cloth, tobacco, education, energy, transport, medical, alcohol and other expenditure, they also estimate how the effects of male bargaining power on budget shares of each item. The estimated results show that in general household size has a statistically significant negative effect on education expenditure patterns. In the standard living survey data, they find, holding household size constant, a unit increase in the number of boys aged 6-9 in the household increases the budget share of education by 4.5 percentage points while a unit increase in the number of girls aged 6-9 in the household increases the budget share of education by 2.1 percentage points. And a unit increase in the number of boys aged 10-16 in the household increases the budget share of education by 9.2 percentage points whereas a unit increase in the number of girls aged 10-16 in the household increases the budget share of education by 0.7 percentage points. There is therefore a significant gender bias in household educational expenditure in both age groups and the bias is in favour of boys, and the boys-girls difference estimate is positive and statistically significant in both age categories. In the national sample survey data, they find statistically significant gender bias in resources allocation, the budget of education runs in favour of the boys and against girl in the age group 11-16. Further, the male bargaining power and household income have statistical significant positive impact on the household budget share of education.

Aslam and Kingdon (2008), using the fourth round of the Pakistan Integrated Household Survey (PIHS) 2001-2002 and applying a Hurdle model, investigate whether the intra-household allocation of educational expenditure in Pakistan favour males over females. They identify two potential channels of gender bias: bias in the decision whether to enrol/keep both sons and daughters in school, and bias in the decision of education expenditure conditional on keeping both sons and daughters in school. The Hurdle model is a two-tier model as the hurdle or first tier is the decision of whether to enrol or not and the second tier is the decision on how much to spend conditional on spending a positive amount. The key variable in the analysis is the share of educational expenditure in total household expenditure and it is regressed on the log of per capita expenditure and its square, log of household size, and the age-gender composition variables. In the junior and secondary school ages, the estimates show a significant male bias in both the enrolment decision as well as the decision on education spending. However, in the primary school age-group, there is only enrolment bias. They also find that education budget share increases significantly more when an extra boy aged 5-9 is added to the household than when an extra girl of that age is added. This suggests very significant bias against females in education expenditure in the 5-9 age range. There is very significant pro-male bias in the 10-14 and 15-19 age groups as well. Much of this bias manifests itself in rural areas. They conclude that girls receive lower educational expenditure allocations than boys within households.

Husain (2011) studies gender gap in enrolment, educational attainment and educational expenditure in India using the 64th round of NSSO data (2009). The study also uses district level data from the 2001 Census and data from district information on education (2005-06). They apply OLS, probit and double hurdle models to estimates the gender bias in terms of educational resources allocation. The empirical estimates of household educational expenditure show that at individual level the coefficient of male dummy is positive and statistically significant and households spend more on boys.

## 3.3 Data and Methodology

In order to empirically analyse whether there is gender bias in India in educational expenditure and how the bargaining power effects on budget share of education, this paper uses the 68th round of NSSO data (2011-12) using three stage least square method for both rural and urban areas of Kerala and Bihar. Kerala and Bihar are the two contrasting states in India in terms of literacy rate; Kerala has the highest literacy rate and Bihar is one of the lowest literacy rates in India. The data on household consumption expenditure in the 68th round of NSSO data consists of 59,695 rural and 41,967 urban households. The use of the NSSO data also allows examining whether there are rural-urban disparities in the principal results. An analysis of the NSSO data helps to answer the question: whether gender bias is prevailing in selected parts of India or is it specific to certain regions alone?

Theoretically, this paper follows the collective household model of Browning and Chiappori (1998) and Bourguignon, Browning, Chiappori and Lechene (1993). The assumptions of the collective household model are that the household members have separate utility functions and the household resources are shared according to the bargaining power of the members and such resource allocations within the household are Pareto efficient. The household objective function can be written as a weighted sum of utilities of household members. Consider a household with two members, male *(m)* and female *(f)* and assume that the household utility function depends upon the consumption of commodities *(x)* and leisure *(l)* of each member separately. The household utility function can be written as,

$$Max[\theta u_m(x_m, x_f, l_m, l_f) + (1-\theta)u_f(x_m, x_f, l_m, l_f)] \qquad (3.1)$$

subject to income constraint,

$$\sum_{i=m,f} px_i \leq \sum_{i=m,f} w_i(T_i - l_i) + I \quad (3.2)$$

The $u_i$ represents the utility of member *i* (*i=m, f*), $x_i$ represents a vector of private consumption goods of individual *i*, *w*; $T_i$, $l_i$, and $w_i$ represent the time endowment, leisure and wage rate of individual *i*, I represents total household unearned income, *p* represents a vector of prices of goods *x*, where the prices and wages are assumed to be exogenous, and θ ($\theta \in 0,\ 1$) which denotes thewelfare weight of member i depends on the bargaining power of individual *i* within the household. The separate utility function of household members shows that the utility function of each member in consumption and leisure. The household allocates resources to each individual according to a sharing rule and then each individual maximises his/her sub-utility subject to the income allocated to him/her.

The household member m then solves the following utility maximisation problem,

$$Max\ u_m\ (x_m) \text{ subject to } px_m = \theta S \quad (3.3)$$

And individual *f* solves the following utility maximisation problem,

$$Max\ u_f\ (x_f) \text{ subject to } px_f = (1- \theta)\text{S} \quad (3.4)$$

where *S* denotes total household income. The equations (3.3) and (3.4) can be solved to obtain the individual member's demand equations for good *x* in budget share form i.e. as the share of that member's allotted expenditure,

$$b_m^x = \alpha_m^x + \beta_m^x[\theta S] + \varepsilon_m^x \quad (3.5)$$

$$b_f^x = \alpha_f^x + \beta_f^x[(1-\theta)S] + \varepsilon_f^x \quad (3.6)$$

where $\varepsilon_m^x$ ande $\varepsilon^x_f$ are stochastic error terms. However, the demands for individual goods $b^x_m$ and $b^x_f$ are not typically observable as surveys do not collect data on gender speci?cexpenditure on specific commodities. Hence, studies assume that the household level budget share of good *x*, ($b^x$), is the θ weighted average of the budget share of that good of the spouses (*m, f*),

$$b^x = [\theta b_m^x + (1-\theta)b_f^x] \quad (3.7)$$

Substituting for $b^x_m$ and $b^x_f$ obtained from equations (3.5) and (3.6) in equation (3.7) and including standard demographic variables (household size and composition variables) as additional explanatory variables, the estimating equation can be written as,

$$b^x = \alpha_0^x + \alpha_1^x\theta + \beta_m^x\theta^2 S + \beta_f^x(1-\theta)^2 S + \lambda^x\, ln(n) + \sum_{i=m.f}\sum_{k=1}^{K}\phi_{ik}^x\left(\frac{n_{ik}}{n}\right) + \varepsilon^x \quad (3.8)$$

where *x = 1,...X,* denotes the goods, *n* denotes the size of household and *nik* denotes the number of individuals in the household in the gender *i* and age category *k*.

If the household size and expenditures are sufficient to explain the demand, then the coefficients $\phi$ will all be zero. However, in general, household composition will matter and the coefficients $\phi_{ik}$ measure the effect of changing household composition (in proportion terms) on budget shares. A test of the statistical significance of the estimated difference $(\phi^x_{mk} - \phi^x_{fk})$ constitutes a test of gender bias in the age group $k$ in the expenditure allocation of good $x$. In other words, the null hypothesis, $(\phi^x_{mk} = \phi^x_{fk})$ maintains that there is no gender bias in case of age group $k$ and good $x$. This paper considers the age groups 6-10 years and 11-16 years for empirical analysis because, in India, children in the age group 6-10 are enrolled in primary school (grade 1-grade 5) and children in the age group 11-16 are enrolled in middle and high schools. If it is the case that the coefficients for boys and girls are different, then, everything else constant, expenditure on a particular commodity depends on the gender composition of children.

A significant feature of this approach is that the male welfare weight, θ, which is a determinant of budget shares (in equation 3.8) is jointly estimated with household expenditure and the budget shares, $b^x$. The welfare weight θ is measured by the household head's (male) share of education as a proxy of males hare of income, showing the male income earner's bargaining power within the household, so that (1–θ) is the bargaining strength of female income earner. As the bargaining strength θ could be correlated with the unobserved determinants of budget shares, θ is potentially endogenous in budget share equation. The monthly per capita household expenditure is used as a proxy for household income. However, household expenditure is also likely to be correlated with unobserved determinants of the household budget shares and hence this potential endogeneity could result in inconsistent estimates. To consider the potential endogeneity of male bargaining power and monthly per capita household expenditure, the male bargaining power and monthly per capita household expenditure and education budget share are jointly estimated as a set of simultaneous equations using 3SLS model. The three estimating equations are specified as,

$$\theta = g(z_1) + v_1 \tag{3.9}$$

$$Exp = h(z_2) + v_2 \tag{3.10}$$

$$b^x = \psi(\theta, Exp, z_3) + v_3 \tag{3.11}$$

where EXP is per capita household expenditure, $z_1$, $z_2$ and $z_3$ are the vectors of exogenous determinants in the three equations and the other variables are as defined above.

The budget share of education is calculated as a ratio of household education expenditure to total household expenditure. The 3SLS estimation of the budget share equation estimates the gender bias in education expenditure and the effect of bargaining power of the household head on the budget share of education. The bargaining power of the household head is measured by the ratio [Edum/(Edum+Eduf)] where Edum is the years of education of the most educated male member of the household and Eduf is the years of education of the most educated female member of the household. The square of this relative educational attainment of the most educated male member of the household allows for the possibility of non-linearity in the effect of the male bargaining power on the budget share of educational expenditure in total household expenditure.

## Three Stage Least Squares Estimation Method

The three stages least squares estimation method considers the general linear model containing G jointly endogenous variables and *k* predetermined variables. There are *i* equations that can be written as,

$$y_i = \beta_i x_i + \gamma_i z_i + u_i \tag{3.12}$$

where $y_i$ is an $nx_i$ vector of sample observations on the dependent variable in the ith equation, $x$ is an nxgi matrix of observations on the other endogenous variables in the equation, $z$ is an nxk matrix of predetermined variable in the equation. The β and γ are the vectors of structural parameters and $u$ is a vector of disturbance terms. Rewriting equation (3.12) as,

$$y_i = \omega_i z_i + u_i \tag{3.13}$$

where $z_i = [x_i, z_i]$ and $\omega_i = \binom{\beta}{\gamma}$, the model specification is,

$$\begin{bmatrix} y_1 \\ y_2 \\ \cdot \\ \cdot \\ y_G \end{bmatrix} = \begin{bmatrix} Z_1 & 0 & \cdot & \cdot & 0 \\ 0 & Z_2 & \cdot & \cdot & 0 \\ \vdots & \vdots & \vdots & \vdots & \cdot \\ 0 & 0 & \cdot & \cdot & Z_G \end{bmatrix} \begin{bmatrix} \omega_1 \\ \omega_2 \\ \cdot \\ \cdot \\ \omega_G \end{bmatrix} + \begin{bmatrix} u_1 \\ u_2 \\ \cdot \\ \cdot \\ u \end{bmatrix} \tag{3.14}$$

where $u$ has a zero mean and variance-covariance matrix **Σ⊗I** are possible correlations between the disturbances. Applying GLS on the whole system yields,

$$\hat{\omega}_{GLS} = [z^T(I \otimes x)\Sigma^{-1} \otimes (x'x^{-1})][(I \otimes x')z]^{-1}[z^T(I \otimes x)\Sigma^{-1} \otimes (x'x^{-1})] [(I \otimes x^T)y] \tag{3.15}$$

Simplifying,

$$\hat{\omega}_{GLS} = [z^T(\Sigma^{-1} \otimes I)z]^{-1}[z^T(\Sigma^{-1} \otimes I)y] \tag{3.16}$$

However, an estimate of S for ith equation is needed. Estimating by 2SLS, the residuals are obtained so that $u_i = y_i - \omega_i z_i$ and the estimate of ε is given by = $\Sigma = |\hat{\sigma}_{ij}|$ where,

$$\hat{\sigma}_{ij} = \frac{(y_i - \hat{\delta}_i z_i)'(y_j - \hat{\delta}_j z_j)}{\sqrt{T - g_i - k_i}\sqrt{T - g_j - k_j}} \tag{3.17}$$

Hence, the 3SLS estimator is estimated as,

$$\widehat{\omega}_{3SLS} = [\hat{\boldsymbol{z}}'(\boldsymbol{\Sigma}^{-1} \otimes \boldsymbol{I})\hat{\boldsymbol{z}}]^{-1}\hat{\boldsymbol{z}}'(\boldsymbol{\Sigma}^{-1} \otimes \mathbf{I})\boldsymbol{y} \tag{3.18}$$

## 3.4 Empirical Analysis

The Table 3.1 presents the descriptive statistics of the main variables. In general, the average household income, measured by monthly per capita consumption expenditure, is higher in urban areas compared to rural areas, both in Kerala and Bihar. Generally, in India, there is discrimination against girls over boys in terms resources allocation. The average years of education of most educated male in the household is greater over females and in rural Bihar the average year of most educated male in household is twice greater than the year of schooling of most female educated, whereas in both rural and urban Kerala the year of schooling of most educated male and female in the household are approximately same. Households in urban areas allocate more resources to education in the total budget of household. The household size is higher in rural areas of India.

**Table 3.1: Descriptive Statistics of Variables in the Budget Share of Household Education Expenditure Analysis**

| *Variable* | *Urban Bihar* | *Rural Bihar* | *Urban Kerala* | *Rural Kerala* | *Urban India* | *Rural India* |
|---|---|---|---|---|---|---|
| Per capita monthly expenditure (proxy for income) (Rs.) | 1600.79<br>(1314.68) | 698.16<br>(434.57) | 2846.46<br>(2822.96) | 3381.28<br>(1449.69) | 2612.47<br>(4388.63) | 1656.05<br>(4026.19) |
| Education of most educated male in the household (yrs) | 8.54<br>(5.98) | 6.11<br>(5.52) | 7.57<br>(5.64) | 6.10<br>(5.10) | 8.76<br>(5.88) | 5.75<br>(5.44) |
| Education of most educated female in the household (yrs) | 3.49<br>(4.92) | 2.04<br>(3.80) | 5.23<br>(4.94) | 4.90<br>(4.76) | 5.23<br>(5.75) | 2.71<br>(4.33) |
| Household size | 5.05<br>(2.65) | 5.31<br>(2.35) | 4.49<br>(2.42) | 4.36<br>(2.02) | 4.17<br>(2.20) | 4.78<br>(2.25) |
| Budget share of education expenditure (Rs.) | 0.075<br>(0.089) | 0.037<br>(0.049) | 0.092<br>(0.224) | 0.061<br>(0.102) | 0.086<br>(0.137) | 0.266<br>(0.254) |
| Sample | 1720 | 3312 | 3382 | 5318 | 41967 | 59695 |

**Note:** Standard deviations in parentheses.

The Table 3.2 presents the description and measurement of variables used in the empirical analysis of the determinants of the budget share of education expenditure in total household expenditure.

The 3SLS estimating equations are specified as,

$$b^x = \delta_0 + \beta_1\theta + \beta_2(EXP) + \beta_3(HHSize) + \beta_k \textstyle\sum_{k=1}^{K} \phi_{ik}^x \left(\frac{n_{ik}}{n}\right) + \xi_1 \tag{3.19}$$

$$\theta = \delta_1 + \beta_4(Maleedu) + \beta_5(Maleedu)^2 + \beta_6(HHSize) + \beta_7(SocialGroup) + \beta_8(Religion) + \xi_2 \tag{3.20}$$

$$Exp = \delta_2 + \beta_9(HHHage) + \beta_{10}(HHHmaritalstatus) + \beta_{11}(HHType) + \beta_{12}(HHHedulevel) + \beta_{12}(HHLandholding) + \xi_3 \quad (3.21)$$

The estimated 3SLS results of the budget share of the household education expenditure are presented in Table 3.3 for rural and urban Bihar and in Table 3.4 for rural and urban Kerala.

**Table 3.2: Description and Measurement of Variables in the Budget Share of Household Education Expenditure Analysis**

| *Variable* | *Description* | *Measurement* |
|---|---|---|
| Budget share of education expenditure | Education expenditure as a share in total household expenditure | Education expenditure/Total household expenditure |
| Male bargaining power | Bargaining strength of male household head | Years of education of the most educated male member of the household/(Years of education of the most educated male member of the household + Years of education of the most educated female member of the household) |
| Male education share | Education of the most educated male member of the household | Years of education |
| Female education share | Education of the most educated female member of the household | Years of education |
| Household income | Proxied by household expenditure | Monthly per capita household expenditure |
| Size of household | All members of the household | Number of members in the household |
| Age of household head | Age of the head of the household | Age in years |
| Marital status | Marital status of the household head | If married=1, 0 otherwise |
| Head education1 | Education level of the household head | If no formal schooling=1, 0 otherwise |
| Head education2 | Education level of the household head | If upto higher secondary schooling=1, 0 otherwise |
| Head education3 | Education level of the household head | If graduate=1, 0 otherwise |
| Land | Land possessed by the household | Land in acres |

The 3SLS estimates for rural Bihar presented in Table 3.3 shows that an increase in the proportion of boys in the age group 11-16 significantly increases the budget share of education by 2.17 percentage points while an increase in the number of girls aged 11-16 increases the budget share of education by 0.7 percentage points only. In urban Bihar, the coefficient estimates show that an increase in proportion of boys in the age group 11-16 increases household budget share of education by 1.4 percentage points while an increase in the number of girls aged 11-16 increases the budget share of education by 1 percentage point. Thus, the results imply that there is a significant gender bias in household educational expenditure and in both 6-10 and 11-16 age groups the bias runs in favour of boys, though statistically significant only for the age category 11-16. The male household bargaining power has a statistically significant positive effect on budget share of education in urban Bihar, but statistically insignificant in rural Bihar. In urban Bihar, a unit increase in household head male bargaining power increases the budget share of education increase by a sizable 16.8 percent.

**Table 3.3: 3SLS Estimates of Gender Bias in the Budget Share of Household Education Expenditure in Bihar**

| *Dependent variable* | *Independent variable* | *Rural Bihar* | | *Urban Bihar* | |
|---|---|---|---|---|---|
| | | *Coefficient* | *z-value* | *Coefficient* | *z-value* |
| Household budget share of education expenditure | Male bargaining power | 0.00323 (0.0057) | 0.56 | 0.168* (0.020) | 8.27 |
| | Per capita monthly household expenditure | 0.00003* (0.00001) | 5.90 | -0.00007* (0.00001) | 5.85 |
| | Household size | -0.0105 (0.0037) | 0.27 | -0.733* (0.012) | 6.12 |
| | Male child-0-5 years | 0.00023 (0.0014) | 0.16 | -0.00019 (0.0049) | 0.04 |
| | Male child 11-16 years | 0.0217* (0.0013) | 4.74 | 0.01396* (0.004) | 3.37 |
| | Female child-0-5 years | -0.00029 (0.0016) | 0.18 | 0.0011 (0.0051) | 0.21 |
| | Female child 11-16 years | 0.0070* (0.0017) | 4.25 | 0.0108** (0.0046) | 2.34 |
| | R-square | 0.15 | | 0.22 | |
| | Chi-square | 14.35 | | 94.75 | |
| Male bargaining power | Male education share | 1.843* (0.098) | 18.68 | 2.696* (0.250) | 10.75 |
| | Male education share square | -1.497* (0.075) | 19.76 | -2.183* (0.181) | 12.03 |
| | SC/ST household | -0.086* (0.0158) | 5.45 | -0.067* (0.081) | 2.89 |
| | Hindu household | 0.067* (0.0173) | 3.91 | 0.120* (0.0287) | 4.21 |
| | Household size | -0.186* (0.015) | 11.72 | -0.224* (0.020) | 11.18 |
| | R-square | 0.18 | | 0.22 | |
| | Chi-square | 5.54 | | 13.41 | |

(*Contd...*)

| | | | | | |
|---|---|---|---|---|---|
| Per capita household expenditure | Age of household head | 5.91* (1.093) | 5.24 | 2.56 (3.550) | 0.72 |
| | Married household head | -7.601* (1.554) | 4.94 | -4.184** (1.824) | 2.29 |
| | Nuclear household | 11.827* (3.144) | 3.43 | 9.423 (8.239) | 1.17 |
| | Head secondary school educated | 8.683* (2.172) | 3.75 | 6.849* (1.206) | 5.62 |
| | Head graduate and above | 7.557* (2.880) | 4.14 | 11.936* (1.459) | 8.20 |
| | Land owned | 0.0551* (0.0084) | 6.55 | -0.0084 (0.061) | 0.14 |
| | R-square | 0.16 | | 0.14 | |
| | Chi-square | 4.35 | | 25.73 | |

**Note:** Standard errors in parentheses. * Significant at 1 percent level.

In the estimates of male bargaining power in Bihar, the positive sign and statistical significance of the of the coefficients of education share of the most educated male in the household and the statistically significant negative sign of its square term show that the male bargaining power increases with education which could make males to allocate more budget to educating children, but the male bargaining power declines beyond a certain level of education. Education increases male bargaining power by 18 percent in rural Bihar and 27 percent in urban Bihar. The results also show that males belonging to Hindu households have higher bargaining power compared to other religious households. The SC/ST community status of households reduces male bargaining power by 8.6 percent in rural Bihar and 6.7 percent in urban Bihar compared to other social groups. Similarly, an increase in household size decreases male bargaining power in both rural and urban Bihar, by about 2 percent.

In the per capita household expenditure estimation of Bihar, the dummy variables of education of household head are positive and statistically significant. Similarly, higher age of the household head increases per capita household expenditure. While land owned increases per capita household expenditure in rural Bihar, marriage reduces household expenditure in both rural and urban Bihar.

**Table 3.4: 3SLS Estimates of Gender Bias in the Budget Share of Household Education Expenditure in Kerala**

| *Dependent variable* | *Independent variable* | *Rural Bihar* | | *Urban Bihar* | |
|---|---|---|---|---|---|
| | | *Coefficient* | *z-value* | *Coefficient* | *z-value* |
| | Male bargaining power | -0.011 (0.017) | 0.63 | 0.0537** (0.0211) | 2.55 |

*(Contd...)*

| | | | | | |
|---|---|---|---|---|---|
| Household budget share of education expenditure | Per capita monthly household expenditure | 7.83* (1.95) | 4.03 | 1.09 (6.80) | 0.02 |
| | Household size | 0.0163*** (0.009) | 1.74 | 0.014 (0.014) | 1.08 |
| | Male child-0-5 years | -0.0056 (0.0048) | 1.16 | 0.0032 (0.0066) | 0.49 |
| | Male child 11-16 years | 0.0094** (0.0043) | 2.19 | 0.0122** (0.0061) | 1.99 |
| | Female child-0-5 years | -0.0070 (0.0049) | 1.42 | 00.0128*** (0.0071) | 1.81 |
| | Female child 11-16 years | 0.0072 (0.0045) | 0.24 | 0.0107*** (0.0061) | 1.75 |
| | R-square | 0.14 | | 0.28 | |
| | Chi-square | 36.08 | | 27.33 | |
| Male bargaining power | Male education share | 1.57* (0.119) | 13.16 | 2.240* (0.218) | 10.23 |
| | Male education share square | -1.269* (0.100) | 12.68 | --1.773* (0.174) | 10.16 |
| | SC/ST household | -0.130* (0.015) | 8.68 | -0.114* (0.0260) | 4.50 |
| | Hindu household | 0.048* (0.0112) | 4.30 | 0.020 (0.180) | 0.25 |
| | Household size | -0.0018* (0.0112) | 13.23 | -0.241* (0.020) | 11.80 |
| | R-square | 0.12 | | 0.13 | |
| | Chi-square | 3.29 | | 3.84 | |
| Per capita household expenditure | Age of household head | -0.743 (0.0122) | 0.46 | 9.66 (6.32) | 1.06 |
| | Married household head | -7.441 (11.501) | 0.28 | -2.520* (0.578) | 4.17 |
| | Nuclear household | 15.943** (6.123) | 2.29 | 2.632 (1.985) | 1.29 |
| | Head secondary school educated | 19.211* (9.201) | 1.28 | 10.194* (2.781) | 3.04 |
| | Head graduate and above | 5.104* (2.012) | 2.76 | 21.717* (3.291) | 7.38 |
| | Land owned | 0.350** (0.156) | 2.01 | 0.161** (0.083) | 1.91 |
| | R-square | 0.20 | | 0.23 | |
| | Chi-square | 5.41 | | 21.47 | |

**Note:** Standard errors in parentheses. * Significant at 1 percent level ** Significant at 5 percent level *** Significant at 10 percent level.

In the 3SLS estimation of budget share of household education expenditure in Kerala presented in Table 3.4, the household monthly household expenditure, household size and presence of male child in the age group 11-16 have statistically significant positive effect on the budget share of education expenditure, while the male bargaining power has significant negative effect. Also, the presence of school going female children influences the budget share of education, and the male bargaining power turns out to be significantly positive in urban Kerala. In rural Kerala, a unit increase in proportion of boys in the age group 11-16 increases budget share of education by 0.94 percentage points while a unit increase in the number of girls aged 11-16 increases the budget share of education by 0.072 percentage points. In urban Kerala, a unit increase in the proportion of boys in the age group 11-16 increases budget share of education by 1.22 percentage points while a unit increase in the number of girls aged 11-16 increases the budget share of education by 1.07 percentage points. Thus, the results imply that there exists significant gender bias in the household educational expenditure in favour of boys. In urban Kerala, with a unit increase in household head male bargaining power the budget share of education increase by 5.37 percent.

In the estimates of male bargaining power in Kerala, the coefficients of the education share of the most educated male in the household and its square are respectively positive and negative, and both the coefficients are statistically significant. The bargaining power in the household increases with their education possibly giving rise to more resource allocation to children education. However, as the square term shows the male bargaining power declines beyond a certain level of education. The results also show that males in Hindu households have more bargaining power and the males in SC/ST households have less bargaining power by 4.8 percent in rural and 2 percent in urban Kerala compared to other social groups. In the per capita household expenditure estimates, the coefficients of nuclear household, education, and land possessed are positive statistically significant in both rural and urban Kerala. In urban Kerala, the marital status of household head has a significant negative effect on income.

## 3.5 Conclusion

The educational investments both by the governments and households have increasing tremendously in recent years as showing by the growing enrolments and schooling expenditure. However, the household expenditure on education among the boys and girls are not the same. There has been gender bias and generally males are favoured than girls in the household allocation of resources. The scenario is the same either in most advanced and literate states like Kerala and in the most backward and illiterate states like Bihar. The gender bias in household expenditure against girl child in India has been the subject of analysis in many scholarly studies and the gender gap refuses to die even in the face of globalisation, women education, property and legal rights, and labour force participation. A partial explanation is in the patriarchal system if Indian society and a part of such gender differentials could be the result of the control of family resources by males in the household. This basic structure of the household coupled with higher male education attainment and labour force attachment increases the male bargaining power in the differential allocation of resources towards educational expenditure on boys and girls within the household.

This paper analyses the issue of gender bias in education expenditure within the household. The main objectives of this paper are the two vexed questions central to the household resource allocations pattern: does the allocation of household educational resources favour boys over girls and does the relative bargaining power of the decision-maker in household influence the budget share of household education expenditure. In order to understand such gender bias in education in a diverse country like India, this paper considers two contrasting scenarios, Bihar and Kerala and rural and urban areas. The data used is from the 68th round (2011-2012) of NSSO data pertaining to Bihar and Kerala. This paper follows the theoretical approach of the collective household model and applies the three stage least square (3SLS) estimation method, as the decision variables are endogenous, on the share of education expenditure in the household budget associated with an addition of a boy and a girl child in the household.

The 3SLS estimation results of this paper show significant gender gap in the budget share of education expenditure of households in rural and urban Bihar and Kerala. Even with notable differentials between the developed state of Kerala and backward state of Bihar, there is not much difference in the gender allocation results in households in these two states. The urban households allocate more of resources on education as compared to rural areas. The gender disparities are more strongly prevalent in urban Bihar and Kerala whereas in rural areas it is much less. An increase in the proportion of boys in the household increases the budget share of education expenditure in the household relative the increase in the same due to an increase in the proportion of girls in the household. The male bargaining power within the household on the budget share of household education expenditure has some effect in urban households of Bihar and Kerala but no effect in rural households.

# Section - II

# Time Series Econometrics

# 4

# The Effect of Volatility on Future Volatility: GARCH and EGARCH Estimation of Stock Prices and Stock Price Volatility Forecasts


## Abstract

*In any stock market, the stock prices are generally volatile and fluctuate over time. While stock prices either increase or decrease gradually in short periods, the fluctuations are wide and sometimes persistent in long periods. This paper analyses the effects of such long period and short period stock price volatility on stock prices and using error variance i.e. the volatility in residuals forecasts the future volatility in stock prices. Using the data on the stock prices of TATA Steel Limited for 1237 days, between 1st January 2013 and 29th December 2017, the effects of short period and long period stock price fluctuations on stock prices and on stock price volatility are predicted. First, ARIMA model has been applied to forecast the stock prices, and to the resultant residuals, GARCH and EGARCH models have been applied to predict the future stock price volatility. The EGARCH fitting shows that the long period fluctuations have significant effect on the future stock price volatility relative to the GARCH fitting. The forecast of the EGARCH model has been compared with the actual stock price volatility for 69 days, for January 1-April 13, 2018. The econometric forecasts show that the long period stock price volatility is more reliant than the short period volatility in forecasting future stock price volatility as well as the stock prices.*



**Key words:** *Stock price volatility, forecasting, error variance, volatility clustering, asymmetry, leverage effect, GARCH models*

## 4.1 Introduction

A stock or capital market is a network of transactions of shares or securities of companies or firms and a place where buyers and sellers make crucial decisions on stock trading at certain stock prices. A stock market also acts as the basement of major investment decisions. Participants in the stock market include individuals, brokers, agencies, non-bank financial institutions like insurance companies, chit fund companies and many more. The prices of shares generally fluctuate both during the time of transactions and over time also. Fluctuations in stock prices include both positive and negative changes. The stock price of any product is affected by a host of factors such as inflation, demand for that good in the market, government policies, changes in budget, the worth of the organisation or company that manufactures that particular good, etc. Generally stock prices fluctuate on the basis of the performance of the company whose shares are traded in the stock market. There are systematic and unsystematic risks in a stock market that also influence stock prices. Calendar effects like January effect, Friday the 13th effect, first half of the month effect are some of the factors that influence the investors to buy or sell stocks at a particular time. The stock price variation or volatility in the stock market is measured by the degree of variation of a trading price series over time, the standard deviation of returns on stocks.

In India, there are two major stock exchanges: National Stock Exchange of India (NSE) and Bombay Stock Exchange (BSE). The NSE is the first demutualised electronic exchange stock market in the country that provides a fully automated screen-based electronic stock trading system that offers easy online trading facility to the investors. As on March, 2017, NSE is the world's tenth largest stock exchange. The performance of stocks in an exchange is measured by some indices, the NIFTY 50 is the index of the NSE. The NIFTY 50 covers major sectors of the Indian economy, including financial services, information technology, automobiles, energy, metal, engineering, etc., and offers investment managers a vibrant exposure to the Indian market. The NIFTY 50 stock index is used extensively by investors in India and around the world as a barometer of the Indian capital markets. The other stock exchange in India, the Bombay Stock Exchange (BSE) is the oldest financial market in the country. The BSE's index, BSE 30 or Sensex, is a premier stock index in India. The index is constructed on the market capitalisation of highly liquid stocks of 30 largest companies. In India, the corporate sector, whose shares are traded in the stock exchanges, accounts for only 12 to 14 percent of its GDP. Of all the companies in India's corporate sector, only 7800 companies are listed in NSE, out of which about 4000 companies only trade on both the NSE and BSE. Hence, the contribution of stock trading at NSE and BSE to India's GDP is only 4 percent, unlike the US where nearly 70 percent of its GDP is derived from larger corporate companies.

Over the course of stock trading in a day, the stock prices are bound to fluctuate in between the open price and the close price of the day due to various reasons. It is also possible that the stock price of a day is the result of stock price that it experienced a day or a month ago. If such is the case then today's price may have an effect on the price that comes into effect on tomorrow or later. Thus, there may be lagged effects of own price in the current stock price. It is also possible that current stock price volatility is a reflection of past fluctuations. Therefore, the past stock prices and its volatility may be crucial to forecast future prices and their volatilities. Econometrically, based on previous prices, the future price of a stock can be forecasted and also its volatility can be forecasted. Among the many econometric models of forecasting, autoregressive integrated moving average (ARIMA) and generalised autoregressive conditional heteroscedasticity (GARCH) models are commonly used to forecast the future stock prices and their volatilities. While the ARCH and ARIMA models are based on the assumption of constant common variance, the GARCH model takes into account the time-varying conditional variance of the stock prices. In the conditional variance, autoregressive term includes the past variances and moving average term is the square of residual from the autoregression of present variance on the past variance.

This paper analyses the impact of long term and short term stock price volatility on the future stock price as well as on the variance of the forecasted stock price. Specifically, this paper forecasts the future prices using datasets for long and short time periods and forecasts the variance from the long term and short term stock price fluctuations. The analysis is carried out on the daily stock prices of important manufacturing company, the TATA Steel Limited, a listed company in the NSE that manufactures metal steels. The Tata Steel Limited is an Indian multinational steel manufacturing company, a subsidiary of the Tata Group. It is also one of the top steel producing companies globally with annual crude steel deliveries of 27.5 million tons in 2017, and the second largest steel company in India in terms of domestic production with an annual capacity of 13 million tons after Steel Authority of India Limited, a public sector undertaking in India. Metal manufacturing sector is one of the growing sectors in India. It contributes to almost 2.5 percent of India's GDP. The daily data on the stock prices of TATA Steel for five years from January 1, 2013 to April 13, 2018. 2013 to 2017 from the National Stock Exchange of India has been used. The paper follows the Box-Jenkins methodology for forecasting. The ARIMA model residuals are used in GARCH and EGARCH models to understand the effect of error variance on the forecast of the future volatility in stock prices.

## 4.2 A Brief Review of Recent Studies

In many stock market applications, the autoregressive integrated moving average (ARIMA) model is the most widely used Box-Jenkins model for forecasting, since it can handle non-stationary data. While ARIMA model can be used to forecast only the future values, ARIMA-GARCH model is used to forecast the future values along with the fluctuations of their variances also over time.

Maity and Chatterjee (2012) applying ARIM of order (1,2,2) for the period 1959 to 2011 to forecast the GDP for India for the following ten years from 2012 to 2021. The forecasted GDP shows an increasing trend and its rate of growth rates shows a decreasing trend. In the maximum likelihood estimates, the coefficient of AR terms is negative and less than 1 and the coefficients of MA are more than 1. Statistical validity of the model is checked by modified Ljung-Box statistics. The estimates show a parsimonious model with only one AR coefficient and one MA coefficient statistically significant, which is very effective to forecast GDP and its growth rates in India.

Guha and Bandyopadhyay (2016) forecast the gold price using a non-stationary data of gold prices from November 2003 to January 2014 by ARIMA method. A comparison of various fit statistics like root mean squared error, mean absolute error, mean absolute percentage error of models of different orders, the ARIMA (1,1,1) provides the most accurate forecasts for the data. The forecasts showed an increasing trend in gold prices.

Ashik and Kannan (2017) apply the ARIMA model on 2015 NSE Nifty 50 closing price to forecast the future stock prices. Among all the tentative ARIMA models, the ARIMA (0,1,1) model provides the most accurate forecasts, with lowest BIC value and small mean absolute percentage error. The closing stock price of Nifty 50 shows a trend with slow decreasing fluctuations for future trading days.

It is common that not all time series errors satisfy the assumption of common variance. The errors also fluctuate, showing volatility in variance. Sometimes, the variance is time-varying and conditional. Engle (1982) developed autoregressive conditional heteroscedasticity (ARCH) class of models to describe a series with time-varying conditional variance. These models are generalised by Bollerslev (1986) as GARCH models. The GARCH models are capture volatility clustering or the periods of fluctuations and predict volatility of the future prices. In the GARCH model, variances of residuals of the forecasted values using AR or MA or ARMA or ARIMA are used to forecast their future variances. When there is leverage effect, i.e. an asymmetry in volatility induced by big positive and negative returns on stocks, the GJR-GARCH or TGARCH is used for forecasting the variance (Glosten, Jagannathan and Runkle, 1993). The TGARCH model captures the effects of positive news hitting on the financial market with the market being in a calm period and the negative news hitting on the financial market with the market entering into a fluctuating period with high volatility.

Ahmad et al. (2015) use a hybrid of linear ARIMA and GJR-GARCH in modeling and forecasting Malaysian gold price and compared it with the forecasting performance of ARIMA model. The gold prices are forecasted using the best fit ARIMA model whose order is (2,1,2). Then, the residuals of the forecasted values are subjected to TGARCH analysis. GJR-GARCH model of order (1,1) has been applied after checking the residuals for ARCH effects using the ARCH-LM test. Based on the lowest AIC values, the ARIMA (2,1,2)-GJR GARCH (1,1) hybrid model performs better than the ARIMA in forecasting gold price. In terms of forecasting, the mean absolute percentage error of both in-sample and out-sample using ARIMA-GJR are lower than that using ARIMA only.

Yaziz et al. (2013) use ARIMA-GARCH hybrid model to forecast the gold price in Malaysia. A total of 40 daily gold price data series in USD/grams is used from November 26, 2005 to January 18, 2006 of 5-day-per-week frequencies. The ARIMA (1,1,1) has been fitted to the 35 observations, and the remaining 5 observations are used to check the accuracies of the forecasts. To the residuals of these forecasts, GARCH has been fitted to forecast the variance of the prices. The result show that ARIMA (1,1,1)-GARCH (0,2) is the most significant model and provide optimum results with low values of mean absolute error and mean square error.

Epaphra (2017) use GARCH and EGARCH models to study the volatility of exchange rates in Tanzanian. For the data on Tanzanian Shilling per USD exchange rate from January 4, 2009 to July 27, 2015, GARCH (1, 1) model has been used to model the variance and EGARCH (1,1) has been used to capture any possible asymmetry and leverage effects. The negativity of the coefficient of asymmetric volatility signifies that positive shocks create less volatility than the negative shocks. The results show that GARCH (1,1) model provides good fit on the basis of low root mean square error.

## 4.3 Data and Methodology

This study uses daily data on the stock prices of TATA Steel Limited, listed in the National Stock Exchange of India. The time period considered is five years, from January 1, 2013 to April 13, 2018. The daily data on stock prices from January 1, 2016 to December 29, 2017, consisting of 495 observations is used for short run variance forecasting, and for long run variance forecasting, data from January 1, 2013 to December 29, 2017, a total of 1237 observations is used. The forecast accuracies are validated with the data for 69 days, from January 1, 2018 to April 13, 2018. The daily stock price data of TATA Steel is collected from the NSE website that contains information on open, close, high, low, previous close, last stock prices, volume weighted average price (VWAP), total traded quantity, turnover, number of trades, total deliverable quantity, percentage of deliverable quantity to traded quantity, etc.

### Empirical Methodology

The volume weighted average price (VWAP) has been taken for fitting the ARIMA model, since unlike open, close and last prices, VWAP takes into account all the prices that existed throughout the day and the total trades that have taken place for different prices.

$$VWAP = \frac{\sum Stock\ price\ \times Number\ of\ Stocks\ Bought\ at\ that\ Price\ that\ Day}{Total\ Number\ of\ Stocks\ Traded\ for\ that\ Day} \quad (4.1)$$

Empirically, the ARIMA model is used to forecast future prices and on the residuals of the forecasts the GARCH is applied. First, to check for stationarity, the data are plotted at level and Augmented Dickey-Fuller (ADF) test is performed on the levels data. The series are then differenced and the ADF test is conducted on the differenced data yet again. After differencing, the series achieves stationarity. Based on the Autocorrelation Function (ACF) and the Partial Autocorrelation Function (PACF) plots of the differenced series tentative orders of the autoregressive and moving average terms are taken just to get a point to begin from. The best model is taken on the basis of significance of coefficients and lowest AIC values. The variables in the resultant estimating equation will be in differenced forms. Hence, the difference is eliminated from the equation by using basic sum-difference arithmetic and then forecasting is carried out. The residuals of these forecasts are tested for serial correlation and ARCH effects using Breusch-Godfrey LM and ARCH LM tests respectively. Once the existence of ARCH and GARCH effects is confirmed, the GARCH model is applied thereby obtaining forecasts of the varying conditional variance i.e. volatility. After checking for the significance of the coefficients, EGARCH model is applied to the residuals of the forecasts generated from the data set taken for long time period.

## Stationarity Test

A random or stochastic process is stationary if its mean and variance are constant over time and the value of the covariance between the two time periods depends only on the distance or gap or lag between the two time periods and not the actual time at which the covariance is computed. That is, a random variable ordered over time has,

Mean: $E(y_t) = \mu$ (4.2)

Variance: $var\ (y_t) = E\ (y_t - \mu)^2 = \sigma^2$ (4.3)

Covariance: $\rho_k = E[(y_t - \mu)(y_{t+k} - \mu)]$ (4.4)

where $k$ is the number of lags considered.

The Augmented Dickey Fuller test is used to test the presence of unit root in case the errors are correlated. This test is conducted by augmenting the equations of a random walk, random walk with drift, and random walk with drift around a stochastic trend, by adding the lagged values of the time series,

$Y_t$ is a random walk: $\Delta y_t = \Delta y_{t-1} + u_t$ (4.5)

$Y_t$ is a random walk with drift: $\Delta y_t = \beta_1 + \Delta y_{t-1} + u_t$ (4.6)

$Y_t$ is a random walk with drift around a stochastic trend:

$$\Delta y_t = \beta_1 + \beta_2 t + \Delta y_{t-1} + u_t \tag{4.7}$$

The ADF test consists of estimating the following regression,

$$\Delta y_t = \beta_0 + \beta_t + \Delta y_{t-1} + \Sigma\beta_i \Delta Y_{t-k} + u_t\ k = 1, 2 \ldots T \tag{4.8}$$

where $u_t$ is a pure white noise error term and Δ is the first difference. The number of lagged difference terms to include is often determined empirically using Akaike Information Criteria (AIC), Schwarz Information Criteria (SIC), etc. The idea is to include enough terms so that the error term is serially uncorrelated. In ADF, the test is whether $\Delta = 0$ i.e. if $\rho = 1$ for the presence of unit root in the time series.

## Box-Jenkins Methodology

A time series data ordinarily does not reveal itself whether it follows a purely autoregressive (AR) process, and if so, the value of *p*, or a purely moving average (MA) process, and if so, the value of *q*, or an autoregressive moving average (ARMA) process, and if so, the values of *p* and *q*, or an autoregressive integrated moving average (ARIMA) process, and if so, the values of *p, d,* and q. The Box-Jenkins (B-J) methodology addresses these issues. The B-J method consists of four steps: (i) identification, (ii) estimation, (iii) diagnostic checking, and (iv) forecasting. The identification of ARIMA model involves determining the order (*p, d, q*) of the model to be fitted, where *p* is order of autoregressive process, *d* is order of integration, and *q* is order of moving average process.

First, the order of integration *d* is identified by unit root test on series before and after differencing. If there is no unit root in the undifferenced series i.e. the series is stationary at level, then the order of integration is zero. In the presence of unit root in the undifferenced series and in the absence of unit root in the differenced series, the order of integration is one. The differencing process continues until the unit root is eliminated from the series. The level of differencing at which unit root is eliminated and the series is stationarised is the order of integration *d*. After the time series is stationarised by differencing, the next step in fitting an ARIMA model is to determine whether AR or MA terms are needed to correct any autocorrelation that remains in the differenced series. The autocorrelation function (ACF) and partial autocorrelation (PACF) plots of the differenced series can tentatively identify the numbers of AR and/or MA terms needed. The ACF plot is a bar chart of the coefficients of correlation between a time series and lags of itself. The PACF plot is a plot of the partial correlation coefficients between the series and its own lags. In the case of time series, the partial correlation propagates to higher order lags, and is therefore the difference between the actual correlation at lags and the expected correlation due to the propagation of correlation at previous lags. If the PACF of the differenced series displays a sharp cut-off and/or the lag-1 autocorrelation is positive i.e. if the series appears slightly under differenced, then an AR term may be added to the model. The lag at which the PACF cuts off is the indicated number of AR terms, AR(*p*). If the ACF of the differenced series displays a sharp cut-off and/or the lag-1 autocorrelation is negative i.e. if the series appears slightly over differenced, then an MA term may be added to the model. The lag at which the ACF cuts off is the indicated number of MA terms, MA(*q*).

After the order (*p, d, q*) of the model has been identified, the ARIMA model is estimated by ordinary least squares regression of the integrated series of order *d* on *p* auto regressive terms and *q* moving average terms obtained from the identification step. In the ARIMA model of stock prices, the current price is expressed in terms of sum of past prices $Y_{t-p}$'s and sum of moving average terms or past error terms *ut-q*'s. Each $u_{t-q}$ is obtained by regressing $Y_{t-p}$ on $Y_{t-p-1}$ ($p = 0, 1, 2\ldots n$). There may exist many other models that better fit the data, as the order of the autoregressive and moving average terms is determined solely on the basis of correlogram and partial correlogram. The best fit model among different orders of the AR and MA terms is generally chosen on the basis of significance of coefficients and certain criteria like log likelihood, Akaike Information Criteria (AIC), Bayesian Information Criteria (BIC) or Schwarz-Bayesian Information Criteria (SBIC). These criteria are given by,

$$AIC = \{n(1 + log2\pi) + nlog\sigma^2 + 2m\} \tag{4.9}$$

$$BIC = -2\log(L) + klog(n) \tag{4.10}$$

$$SBIC = log\sigma^2 + [\{\text{mlog(n)}\}/\text{n}] \tag{4.11}$$

where *n* is sample size and *k* is number of parameters to be estimated.

After choosing the best fit ARIMA model, the next step is to check if there is more information available i.e. to check if there are any more significant autocorrelations and partial autocorrelations at any lags present. In essence, diagnostic checking is to confirm that the residuals are white noise. In correlogram and partial correlogram analysis, the Ljung-Box *q*-statistic or Box-Pierce *q*-statistic is used to test the joint hypothesis that all the autocorrelations upto certain lags are simultaneously equal to zero. The *q*-statistic is defined as,

$$\text{Box-Pierce q-statistic: } Q = n\sum_{k=1}^{m}\hat{\rho}_k \tag{4.12}$$

$$\text{Ljung-Box q-statistic: } Q = n(n+2)\sum_{p=1}^{h}(n-k)^{-1}\hat{\rho}_p^2 \tag{4.13}$$

where n is sample size and *m* is lag length.

The best fit ARIMA model obtained through the foregoing identification, estimation and diagnostic checking steps can now be used for forecasting the future stock prices. The estimating equation consists of $Y_{t-p}$ autoregressive and $u_{t-q}$ moving average terms that are taken based on the order. Thus, the ARIMA model is a self-determining model as there are only current and past values of the data series that depends on the own autoregression of the variable and the moving average of the errors, and no exogenous variables are there in the model.

## Arima Model

Generally, the autoregressive model AR($p$) is defined as,

$$y_t = a + \gamma_1 y_{t-1} + \gamma_2 y_{t-2} + \cdots + \gamma_p y_{t-p} + u_t \quad (4.14)$$

where $y_t$ is a finite linear sum of its past values, ut is the random shock or white noise term identically and independently distributed, $u_t \sim NIID(0,\sigma^2)$,, γi ($i$=1,….., $p$) are the parameters of the model, and $y_t$ is assumed to be stationary. The moving average model MA(q) is defined as,

$$y_t = u_t - \lambda_1 u_{t-1} - \lambda_2 u_{t-2} - \cdots - \lambda_q u_{t-q} \quad (4.15)$$

where $y_t$ is linearly dependent upon the weighted sum of the current and past values of the random shock series, and the $\lambda_i$ ($j$ = 1, ……, $q$) are the moving average parameters. When the series is non-stationary at level, the series $y_t$ is reduced to stationarity by differencing,

$$\Delta y_t = y_t - y_{t-1} \quad (4.16)$$

Therefore, the AR model (4.14) for the differenced series can be written as,

$$\Delta y_t - \gamma_1 \Delta y_{t-1} - \cdots - \gamma_p \Delta y_{t-p} = u_t \quad (4.17)$$

Combining the AR and MA models, and taking the appropriate degree of differencing (integrated), the ARIMA (p,d,q) model can be written as,

$$y_t = a + \gamma_1 y_{t-1} + \gamma_2 y_{t-2} + \cdots + \gamma_p y_{t-p} + u_t - \lambda_1 u_{t-1} - \lambda_2 u_{t-2} - \cdots - \lambda_q u_{t-q} \quad (4.18)$$

or $$\Delta y_t - \gamma_1 \Delta y_{t-1} - \cdots - \gamma_p \Delta y_{t-p} = u_t - \lambda_1 u_{t-1} - \lambda_2 u_{t-2} - \cdots - \lambda_q u_{t-q} \quad (4.19)$$

Using the backward shift operator B, the ARIMA model can be is expressed more compactly as,

$$y_{t-1} - y_{t-2} = By_t - B^2 y_t \quad (4.20)$$

$$\Rightarrow y_{t-1} = B(1-B)y_t;\ \Delta y_{t-2} = B^2(1-B)y_t;\ (1-B)y_t = y_t - y_{t-1}$$

where $B^d\ y_t = Y_{t-d}$. Therefore, assuming the degree of differencing is $d$, the general ARIMA ($p$, $d$, $q$) model can be expressed as,

$$(1 - \gamma_1 B - \gamma_2 B^2 - \gamma_3 B^3 - \cdots - \gamma_p B^p)(1-B)y_t = (1 - \lambda_1 B - \lambda_2 B^2 - \cdots - \lambda_q B^q)u_t \quad (4.21)$$

Then, the OLS method can be applied to the ARIMA model. The differenced series are regressed on the auto-regressive and moving average terms. Fitting the model to the data, errors bound to arise showing the deviation of the fitted values from the actual. The estimated residuals can be written as,

$$\hat{u}_t = y_t - \hat{y}_t \quad (4.22)$$

Then, the GARCH model is applied to estimate of the error variance i.e. volatility in residuals. The ARCH-LM test is applied to test the common variance of errors.

## GARCH Model

When the time series errors exhibit time-varying errors, then the OLS method can not be applied. For the series with time-varying conditional variance Engle's (1982) autoregressive conditional heteroscedasticity (ARCH) class of models can be applied. The Bollerslev's (1986) generalised autoregressive conditional heteroscedasticity (GARCH) model captures the volatility clustering or the periods of fluctuations, and predicts volatilities in the future. In the GARCH model, past variances and past variance forecasts are used to forecast future variances. The standard GARCH model is symmetric in response to past volatility and variance. The basic structure of symmetric and normal GARCH (*p, q*) model as given by Brooks (2008) can be written as,

$$y_t = \gamma_0 + \gamma_1 y_{t-1} + \cdots + \gamma_q y_{t-q} + u_t \tag{4.23}$$

where the error term $u_t$, conditional on information of period *t*-1, is distributed as,

$$u_t \sim [N(0, (\gamma_0 + \gamma_1 u_{t-1}^2 + \lambda\sigma_{t-1}^2)] \tag{4.24}$$

Thus, the variance of the error ut follows the ARCH (1) process. This error variance not only depends on the squared error in the previous period but also on its conditional variance in the previous period. As the variance is not directly observed, Engle suggests that GARCH model conditional variance as,

$$u_t = v_t\sigma_t^2 \tag{4.25}$$

where $v_t \sim N(0,1)$ and,

$$\sigma_t^2 = \delta + (\gamma_1 u_{t-1}^2 + \gamma_2 u_{t-2}^2 + \cdots) + (\lambda_1\sigma_{t-1}^2 + \lambda_2\sigma_{t-2}^2 + \cdots) \tag{4.26}$$

$$\sigma_t^2 = \delta + \sum \gamma_i \varepsilon_{t-q}^2 + \sum \lambda_j \sigma_{t-p}^2 \tag{4.27}$$

where $\delta = \gamma_0(1-\lambda_1)$. The GARCH term is $\sigma^2$, the conditional variance, where the last period forecast variance is of order *p*, the ARCH term is $\varepsilon^2$, which is the information about volatility from the previous period measured as the lag of squared residual from the mean equation and of order *q*.

## Egarch Model

The GARCH model is restrictive in that it assumes non-negative constraints on the parameters $\alpha_i$ and $\beta_j$ and symmetry in residuals. Nelson and Cao (1992) propose an Exponential Conditional Heteroscedasticity (EGARCH) model that takes into account the leverage effect i.e. asymmetry in the residuals induced by big positive and negative changes. The EGARCH model can be specified as,

$$log\sigma_t^2 = \omega + \sum_{k=1}^{q} \beta_k g(z_{t-k}) + \sum_{k=1}^{p} \alpha_k \, log\sigma_{t-k}^2 \quad (4.28)$$

$$(z_t) = az_t + b[|z_t| - E|z_t|] \quad (4.29)$$

$$z_t = \frac{\varepsilon_t}{\sqrt{\sigma_t^2}} \quad (4.30)$$

$$E|z_t| = \sqrt{\frac{2}{\pi}} \text{ if } z_t \sim N(0,1) \quad (4.31)$$

Substituting equations (4.30) and (4.31) in equation (4.29) gives,

$$g(z_t) = a\frac{\varepsilon_t}{\sqrt{\sigma_t^2}} + b\left[\frac{|\varepsilon_t|}{\sqrt{\sigma_t^2}} - \sqrt{\frac{2}{\pi}}\right] \quad (4.32)$$

Substituting one period lagged form of equation (4.32) in equation (4.28) gives,

$$log\,\sigma_t^2 = \omega + \lambda ln\sigma_{t-1}^2 + \theta\frac{\varepsilon_{t-1}}{\sqrt{\sigma_{t-1}^2}} + \gamma\left[\frac{|\varepsilon_{t-1}|}{\sqrt{\sigma_{t-1}^2}} - \sqrt{\frac{2}{\pi}}\right] \quad (4.33)$$

where $\sigma_t^2 = \gamma_0 + \gamma_1\varepsilon_{t-1}^2 + \lambda_1\sigma_{t-1}^2 + \theta\varepsilon_{t-1}^2 I_{t-1}$, $I$ being the information asymmetry. As the $\sigma_t^2$ is modeled in this specific way, a significant advantage of EGARCH models is that even if the parameters are negative, the $\sigma_t^2$ will be positive.

The logarithmic value of conditional variance is taken since the sign restrictions that are present in GARCH are not considered in EGARCH. Equation (4.18) is an EGARCH model of the first order. $\sigma_t^2$ is the conditional variance, it is an asymmetric function of lagged disturbances $u_{t-k}$. An advantage of the EGARCH model is that even if the parameters are negative, $\sigma_t^2$ is always positive. The term λ measures the persistence of conditional volatility, irrespective of anything that is happening in the market. If λ is relatively large, then the volatility takes a long time to decay in the market. The θ parameter measures the asymmetry or the leverage effect. If θ=0, the model is symmetric; θ<0 implies positive shocks generate less volatility than negative shocks, and θ>0 implies good news generate more volatility than bad news. The γ measures the symmetric effect or the GARCH effect of the model.

## 4.4 Empirical Analysis

As shown in Figures 4.1 and 4.2, the stock prices of TATA Steel Limited in NSE have experienced fluctuations during the time period from January 1, 2013 to the end of December 29, 2017. The Figure 4.1 presents the plot VWAP data at levels. While the stock prices show ups and downs during long period from 2013 to 2017, the stock prices from 2016 to 2017 show steady increase. Hence, there is no mean reversal phenomenon in the plot. Since VWAP comprises all the prices that exist throughout the day including open and close prices, the plot of VWAP resembles with that of open and close prices.

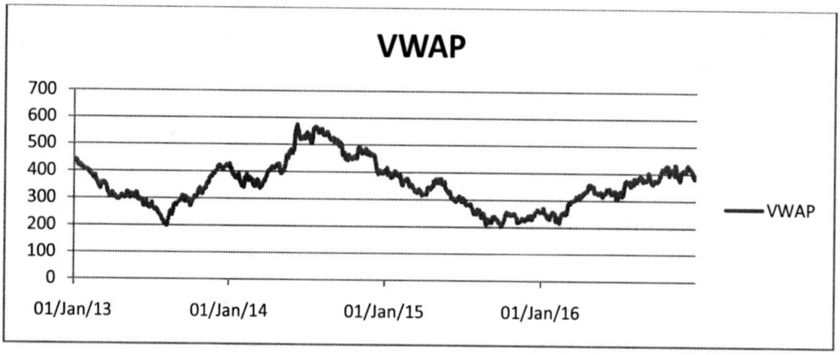


*Figure 4.1: Plot of TATA Steel Stock Prices at Levels*

The stationarity of the series is checked by plotting VWAP data at the first difference. The plot of the differenced data in Figure 4.2 shows the phenomenon of mean reversal i.e. the graphs are frequently cutting the mean line. Thus, the data has become stationary after differencing it once.

Table 4.1 presents the descriptive statistics of the VWAP both for long and short data sets. The average stock price is Rs. 397 during the long period and Rs. 455 during the short period. The standard deviations and variances for both periods show considerable fluctuations in the stock prices.

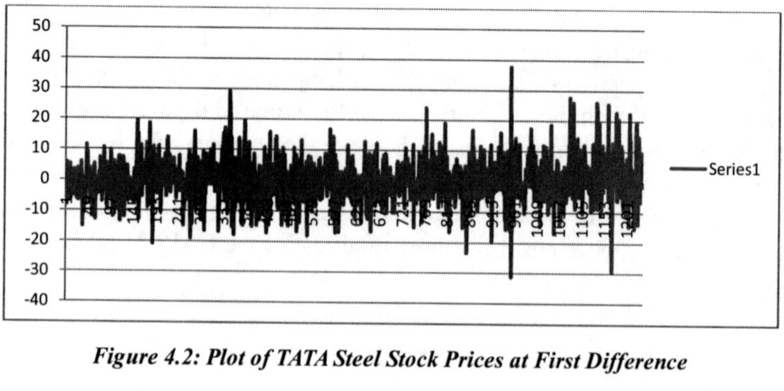


*Figure 4.2: Plot of TATA Steel Stock Prices at First Difference*

**Table 4.1: Descriptive Statistics of TATA Steel Stock Prices**

| *Period* | *Mean* | *Median* | *Mode* | *Standard deviation* | *Sample variance* |
|---|---|---|---|---|---|
| January 1, 2013 to December 29, 2017 | 397.09 | 377.67 | 377.74 | 122.15 | 14920.61 |
| January 1, 2016 to December 29, 2017 | 454.57 | 427.63 | 375.08 | 138.74 | 19249.69 |

Towards the fitting of ARIMA model for the data, identification of the orders (*p, d, q*) of autoregressive, integration or differencing and moving average terms are to be determined performing the standard tests on the data series. The Augmented Dickey Fuller test for stationarity is performed both at the levels and on the first difference. The ADF test results presented in Table 4.2 show that the series is non-stationarity at levels as the *p*-value is greater than 0.05. Hence, the series at levels has a unit root, which is also revealed by the time series plot of the differenced series. The series has become stationary at first difference, as the *t*-statistics is greater than the *p*-value. Thus, the data series is integrated of order 1 i.e. I(1).

**Table 4.2: ADF Stationarity Test on TATA Steel Stock Prices**

| *At level* | | *At first difference* | |
|---|---|---|---|
| t-statistic | Probability | t-statistic | Probability |
| -2.053651 | 0.2639 | -35.21691 | 0.0000 |

The orders of the autoregressive and moving average terms are determined by checking the partial autocorrelation function and autocorrelation function of the data series. The Figures 4.3 and 4.4 present the ACF and PACF correlograms of the short period and ling period autocorrelation of the differenced series. The plots reveal a significant autocorrelation at the first lag in both PACF and ACF.

Therefore, based on the correlogram and unit root test, the (*p, d, q*) order of the model has to be (1, 1, 1) due to the presence of autocorrelation at the first lag itself. However, correlogram is only indicative about the orders and do not identify the appropriate order for the ARIMA model. Therefore, the Akaike Information Criteria has to be applied for the identification of the most appropriate order to be chosen for model fitting. The model with the lowest AIC value will be taken as the best fit model. The Table 4.3 presents the AIC and SIC values for both short period and long period series for various orders. Based on the significance and the lowest AIC, the orders (1, 1, 2) and (3, 1, 3) are identified as the best fit models for short run and long run data respectively.

The Table 4.4 presents the OLS regression estimates of the best fit ARIMA model for first differenced series on the autoregressive and moving average terms.

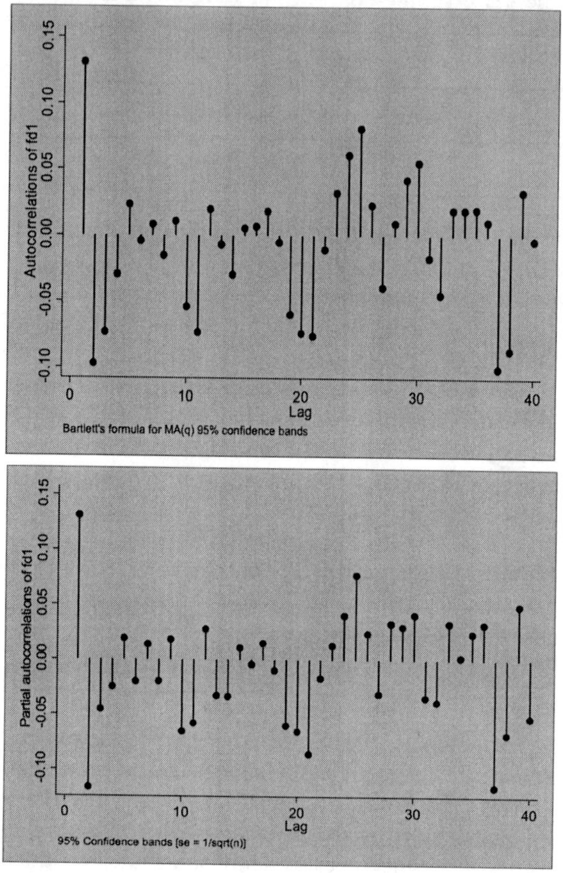


***Figure 4.3: Short Period Autocorrelations of First Differenced Series***

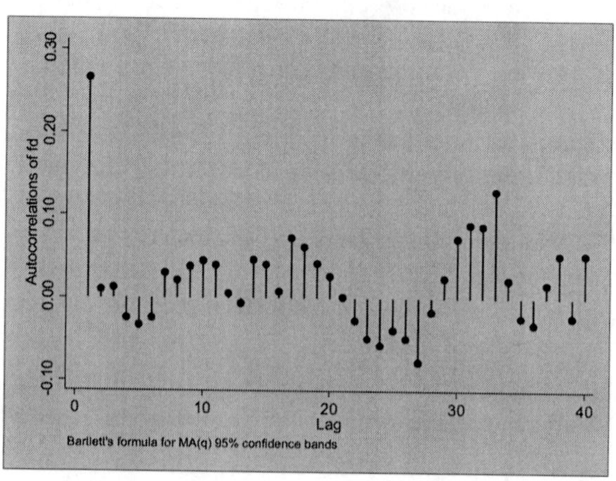

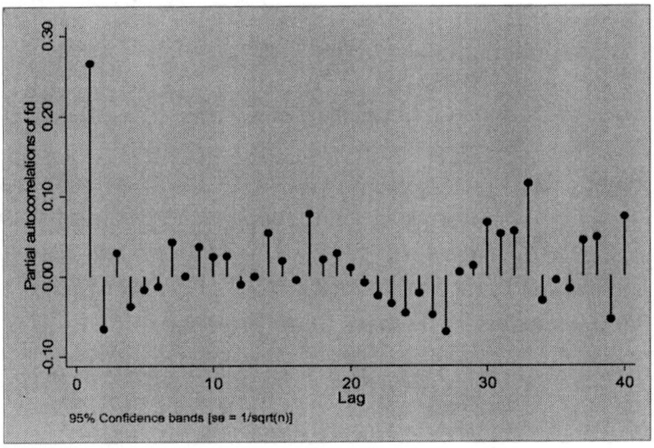


***Figure 4.4: Long Period Autocorrelations of First Differenced Series***

**Table 4.3: AIC for Orders (p, d, q)**

| *Order (p,d,q)* | *Short period* | | *Long period* | |
|---|---|---|---|---|
| | *AIC* | *SIC* | *AIC* | *SIC* |
| (1,1,1) | 6.9628 | 6.9883 | 6.7672 | 6.7796 |
| (1,1,2) | 6.9571 | 6.9911 | 6.7684 | 6.7849 |
| (1,1,3) | 6.9631 | 7.0055 | 6.7699 | 6.7907 |
| (2,1,1) | 6.9587 | 6.9927 | 6.7683 | 6.7848 |
| (2,1,2) | 6.9627 | 7.0051 | 6.7684 | 6.7891 |
| (2,1,3) | 6.9667 | 7.0176 | 6.7700 | 6.7949 |
| (3,1,1) | - | - | 6.7685 | 6.7892 |
| (3,1,2) | - | - | 6.7698 | 6.7946 |
| (3,1,3) | - | - | 6.7629 | 6.7920 |

**Table 4.4: OLS Estimates of the Best Fit ARIMA Model**

| *Data period* | *Parameter* | *Coefficient* | *Standard error* | *t-statistic* | *p-value* |
|---|---|---|---|---|---|
| Short run | AR(1) | 0.877* | 0.0721 | 12.1642 | 0.000 |
| | MA(1) | -0.733* | 0.0814 | -9.0044 | 0.000 |
| | MA(2) | -0.187* | 0.0451 | -4.1503 | 0.000 |
| | Constant | 1.016* | 0.2362 | 4.3023 | 0.000 |
| Long run | AR(1) | -1.715* | 0.1127 | -15.222 | 0.000 |
| | AR(2) | -1.302* | 0.1658 | -7.8511 | 0.000 |
| | AR(3) | -0.220** | 0.1093 | -2.0143 | 0.044 |
| | MA(1) | 1.948* | 0.1037 | 18.7918 | 0.000 |
| | MA(2) | 1.668* | 0.1539 | 10.835 | 0.000 |
| | MA(3) | 0.454* | 0.1025 | 4.4261 | 0.000 |
| | Constant | 0.247 | 0.2418 | 1.0203 | 0.308 |

**Note:** * Significant at 1 percent level ** Significant at 5 percent level.

Thus, the short period model is,

$$\Delta y_t = 1.016 + 0.877\Delta y_{t-1} + u_t - 0.733u_{t-1} - 0.187u_{t-2} \tag{4.34}$$

The long period model would be,

$$\Delta y_t = 0.247 - 1.715\Delta y_{t-1} - 1.302\,\Delta y_{t-2} - 0.220\Delta y_{t-3} + u_t + 1.948u_{t-1} + 1.668u_{t-2} + 0.454u_{t-3} \quad (4.35)$$

Since the regression is on the differenced series, the resultant forecasted prices would be in differenced forms as well. Hence, using ordinary sum-difference arithmetic, the difference term from the equations are eliminated to get estimated equations in terms of actual values of prices which can be used to forecast the stock prices in the base form. From equation (4.34),

$$y_t - y_{t-1} = 1.016 + 0.877(y_{t-1} - y_{t-2}) + u_t - 0.733u_{t-1} - 0.187u_{t-2}$$

$$\Rightarrow y_t = 1.016 + 0.123y_{t-1} + 0.877y_{t-2} + u_t - 0.733u_{t-1} - 0.187u_{t-2} \quad (4.36)$$

From equation (4.35),

$$y_t - y_{t-1} = 0.247 - 1.715(y_{t-1} - y_{t-2}) - 1.302(y_{t-2} - y_{t-3}) - 0.220(y_{t-3} - y_{t-4}) + u_t + 1.948u_{t-1} + 1.668u_{t-2} + 0.454u_{t-3}$$

$$y_t = 0.247 - 0.715y_{t-1} - 0.414y_{t-2} - 1.082y_{t-3} - 0.220y_{t-4} + u_t + 1.948u_{t-1} + 1.668u_{t-2} + 0.454u_{t-3} \quad (4.37)$$

Therefore, based on short data and long data, equations (4.36) and (4.37) respectively are used to forecast the stock prices of TATA Steel.

Before forecasting the stock prices, following the Box-Jenkins methodology, the residuals of the best fit models are tested if they are white noise terms. The Figures 4.5 and 4.6 show the correlograms of residuals

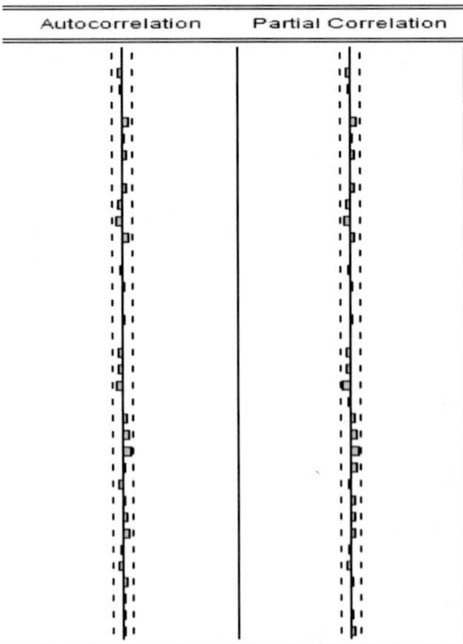

| | AC | PAC | Q-Stat | Prob |
|---|---|---|---|---|
| 1 | -0.007 | -0.007 | 0.0232 | |
| 2 | -0.038 | -0.038 | 0.7607 | |
| 3 | -0.021 | -0.021 | 0.9754 | |
| 4 | 0.004 | 0.003 | 0.9846 | 0.321 |
| 5 | 0.053 | 0.052 | 2.4195 | 0.298 |
| 6 | 0.010 | 0.011 | 2.4681 | 0.481 |
| 7 | 0.034 | 0.038 | 3.0393 | 0.551 |
| 8 | -0.004 | -0.001 | 3.0476 | 0.693 |
| 9 | 0.038 | 0.040 | 3.7602 | 0.709 |
| 10 | -0.029 | -0.031 | 4.1956 | 0.757 |
| 11 | -0.056 | -0.055 | 5.7965 | 0.670 |
| 12 | 0.043 | 0.038 | 6.7356 | 0.665 |
| 13 | 0.002 | -0.003 | 6.7388 | 0.750 |
| 14 | -0.020 | -0.024 | 6.9424 | 0.804 |
| 15 | 0.016 | 0.021 | 7.0819 | 0.852 |
| 16 | 0.005 | 0.007 | 7.0955 | 0.897 |
| 17 | 0.020 | 0.020 | 7.3069 | 0.922 |
| 18 | 0.004 | 0.007 | 7.3136 | 0.948 |
| 19 | -0.045 | -0.043 | 8.3651 | 0.937 |
| 20 | -0.047 | -0.045 | 9.5106 | 0.923 |
| 21 | -0.058 | -0.069 | 11.260 | 0.883 |
| 22 | 0.002 | -0.009 | 11.263 | 0.915 |
| 23 | 0.029 | 0.028 | 11.703 | 0.926 |
| 24 | 0.047 | 0.046 | 12.874 | 0.913 |
| 25 | 0.071 | 0.082 | 15.516 | 0.839 |
| 26 | 0.024 | 0.046 | 15.805 | 0.863 |
| 27 | -0.037 | -0.024 | 16.508 | 0.869 |
| 28 | 0.017 | 0.027 | 16.657 | 0.894 |
| 29 | 0.035 | 0.027 | 17.320 | 0.899 |
| 30 | 0.053 | 0.038 | 18.797 | 0.877 |
| 31 | -0.015 | -0.024 | 18.910 | 0.901 |
| 32 | -0.041 | -0.048 | 19.804 | 0.899 |
| 33 | 0.025 | 0.022 | 20.137 | 0.913 |
| 34 | 0.012 | 0.007 | 20.214 | 0.931 |
| 35 | 0.011 | 0.010 | 20.281 | 0.946 |
| 36 | 0.022 | 0.040 | 20.540 | 0.955 |

*Figure 4.5: Correlogram of Residuals of Short Period Data*

generated by the short period and long period models respectively. As can be seen from the correlograms, no significant spikes can be noticed in both ACF and PACF, implying that the residual of the identified ARIMA models are white noise, and no further information is available. Hence, there is no need to consider AR ($p$) and MA ($q$) any further.

Using the identified models for forecasting, ARIMA models have been fitted for long period with 1237 observations and short period with 495 observations, and TATA Steel stock prices have been predicted for the next 70 working days of the National Stock Exchange of India. The plots of these static forecasts are compared with the plot of actual for the period January 1, 2018 to April 18, 2018 for checking the forecasting accuracy. The Figures 4.7 and 4.8 present the plots of actual and forecasted stock prices of TATA Steel for short period and long period respectively. Remarkably, the forecasted values closely follow the actual stock prices in both cases. The validity of the fit of the models is also signified by low root mean squared error and mean absolute percentage error, presented in Table 4.5.

| Autocorrelation | Partial Correlation | | AC | PAC | Q-Stat | Prob |
|---|---|---|---|---|---|---|
| | | 1 | 0.001 | 0.001 | 0.0013 | |
| | | 2 | -0.000 | -0.000 | 0.0013 | |
| | | 3 | -0.013 | -0.013 | 0.2166 | |
| | | 4 | -0.023 | -0.023 | 0.8764 | |
| | | 5 | 0.002 | 0.002 | 0.8821 | |
| | | 6 | -0.001 | -0.001 | 0.8828 | |
| | | 7 | 0.010 | 0.009 | 0.9992 | 0.317 |
| | | 8 | 0.014 | 0.014 | 1.2562 | 0.534 |
| | | 9 | 0.029 | 0.029 | 2.3190 | 0.509 |
| | | 10 | -0.010 | -0.010 | 2.4540 | 0.653 |
| | | 11 | 0.008 | 0.009 | 2.5372 | 0.771 |
| | | 12 | 0.004 | 0.006 | 2.5593 | 0.862 |
| | | 13 | 0.003 | 0.004 | 2.5678 | 0.922 |
| | | 14 | 0.015 | 0.015 | 2.8556 | 0.943 |
| | | 15 | 0.013 | 0.014 | 3.0725 | 0.961 |
| | | 16 | 0.018 | 0.018 | 3.4959 | 0.967 |
| | | 17 | 0.036 | 0.036 | 5.1562 | 0.923 |
| | | 18 | 0.022 | 0.023 | 5.7706 | 0.927 |
| | | 19 | 0.004 | 0.005 | 5.7890 | 0.953 |
| | | 20 | -0.023 | -0.022 | 6.4273 | 0.955 |
| | | 21 | -0.012 | -0.010 | 6.5992 | 0.968 |
| | | 22 | -0.012 | -0.012 | 6.7765 | 0.977 |
| | | 23 | -0.008 | -0.010 | 6.8596 | 0.985 |
| | | 24 | 0.017 | 0.014 | 7.2398 | 0.988 |
| | | 25 | 0.009 | 0.006 | 7.3488 | 0.992 |
| | | 26 | 0.009 | 0.006 | 7.4507 | 0.995 |
| | | 27 | -0.049 | -0.050 | 10.488 | 0.972 |
| | | 28 | -0.004 | -0.003 | 10.507 | 0.981 |
| | | 29 | 0.038 | 0.040 | 12.380 | 0.964 |
| | | 30 | 0.047 | 0.046 | 15.155 | 0.916 |
| | | 31 | 0.034 | 0.032 | 16.647 | 0.894 |
| | | 32 | 0.015 | 0.014 | 16.924 | 0.911 |
| | | 33 | 0.067 | 0.068 | 22.583 | 0.707 |
| | | 34 | 0.022 | 0.025 | 23.186 | 0.724 |

***Figure 4.6: Correlogram of Residuals of Long Period Data***

the residuals of the ARIMA forecasts of the short period to forecast the variances. Therefore, GARCH (1,1) has been fitted to the forecasts of the resultant residuals of ARIMA forecasting. The estimated GARCH model is

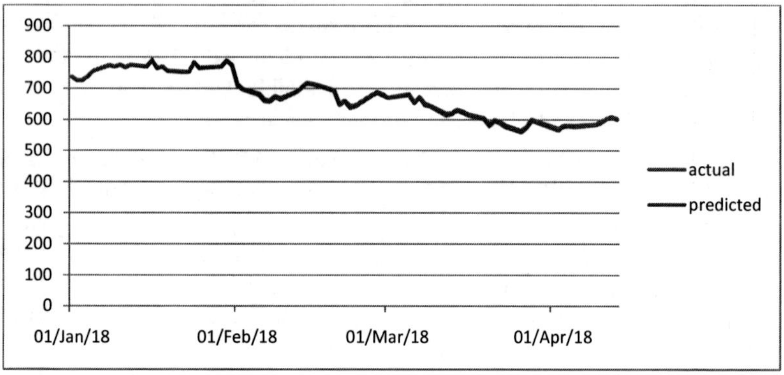


***Figure 4.7: Plot of Short Period Actual and Forecasted TATA Steel Stock Prices***

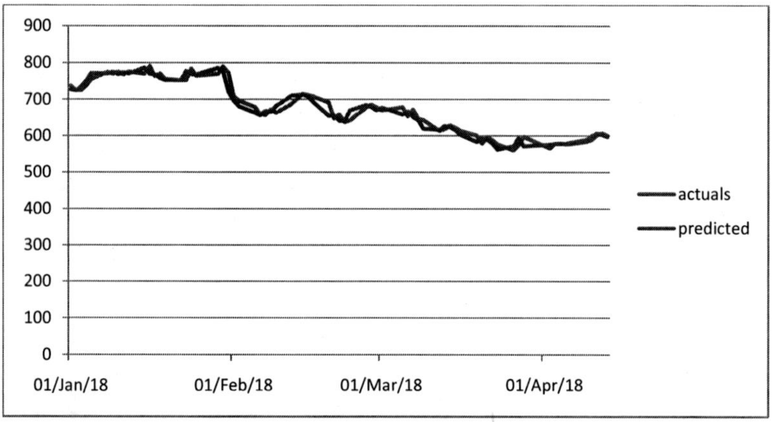


***Figure 4.8: Plot of Long Period Actual and Forecasted TATA Steel Stock Prices***

**Table 4.5: Forecasting Performance of the Model**

| *Period* | *p* | *d* | *q* | *RMSE* | *MAPE* |
|---|---|---|---|---|---|
| Short period data | 1 | 1 | 2 | 14.824 | 1.729 |
| Long period data | 3 | 1 | 3 | 14.341 | 1.665 |

The Figure 4.9 plots the conditional variance of stock prices from January 1, 2013 to December 29, 2017, and the Figures 4.10 and 4.11 plot the volatility clustering for short period and long period respectively.

The ARIMA residuals are tested for ARCH effects by the ARCH-LM test and the results are presented in Table 4.6. Since the ARCH-LM test probabilities are less than the level of significance, the null hypothesis that there are no ARCH-GARCH effects is rejected. Hence, GARCH model can be fitted to

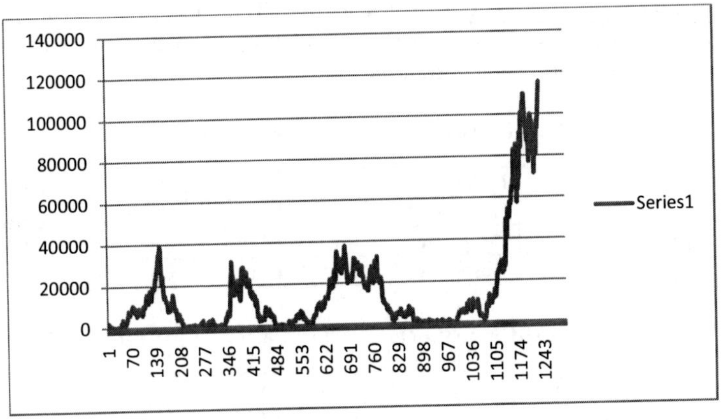


***Figure 4.9: Plot of Conditional Variance of Stock Price Series 2013 to 2017.***

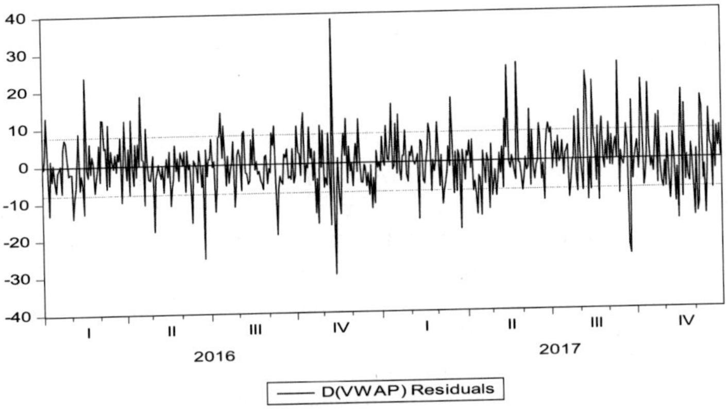


***Figure 4.10: Plot of Volatility Clustering in ARIMA Residual for Short Period.***

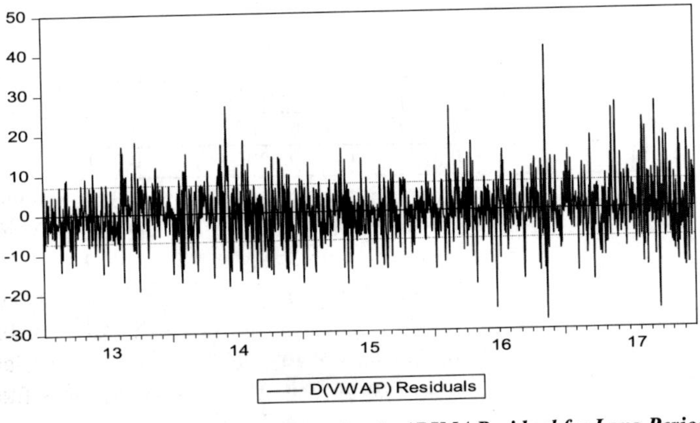


***Figure 4.11: Plot of Volatility Clustering in ARIMA Residual for Long Period.***

presented in Table 4.7. The estimates of GARCH model provide the effects of both past variances of the forecasted residuals and squares of residuals of those variances on current variances.

**Table 4.6: Heteroscedasticity Test for ARIMA Residuals**

| | | | | |
|---|---|---|---|---|
| Short period data | F-statistic | 4.094 | Prob. F(1, 492) | 0.0436 |
| | Observed $R^2$ | 4.076 | Prob. Chi square (1) | 0.0435 |
| Long period data | F-statistic | 14.155 | Prob. F(1, 1230) | 0.0002 |
| | Observed $R^2$ | 14.017 | Prob. Chi square (1) | 0.0002 |

**Table 4.7: GARCH Estimates of Short Period ARIMA Residuals**

| *Variable* | *Coefficient* | *Standard error* | *p-value* |
|---|---|---|---|
| Constant | 108.7559 | 238.8774 | 0.6489 |
| Residual $(-1)^2$ | -0.1036 | 0.223803 | 0.6436 |
| GARCH (-1) | 0.5856 | 1.063476 | 0.5819 |

Thus, the estimation variance forecasting GARCH equation can be written as,

$$\sigma_t^2 = 108.7559 - 0.1036\varepsilon_{t-1}^2 + 0.5856\sigma_{t-1}^2 \tag{4.38}$$

Since the forecast of variances by GARCH fitting on short time data produces highly insignificant results, the stock price variance is neither effected by its past value nor by the residuals of the variance. As none of the residuals has any effect on the forecast of variances, the short period effect is not observed on the stock price volatility. Therefore, the variances are forecasted again with long period data for 5 years and this time fitting EGARCH model for the time series. The estimated EGARCH results presented in Table 4.8 show that three out of four coefficients are highly significant.

**Table 4.8: GARCH Estimates of Long Period ARIMA Residuals**

| *Parameter* | *coefficient* | *standard error* | *p-value* |
|---|---|---|---|
| α | 1.4448 | 0.0097 | 0.000 |
| λ | -0.6194 | 0.0176 | 0.000 |
| θ | -0.1258 | 0.0463 | 0.006 |
| γ | 0.8237 | 0.0006 | 0.000 |

Therefore, the estimated variance forecasting EGARCH equation can be written as,

$$\log \sigma_t^2 = 1.444 - 0.619 ln\sigma_{t-1}^2 - 0.126\frac{\varepsilon_{t-1}}{\sqrt{\sigma_{t-1}^2}} + 0.824\left[\frac{|\varepsilon_{t-1}|}{\sqrt{\sigma_{t-1}^2}} - \sqrt{\frac{2}{\pi}}\right] \tag{4.39}$$

The estimated coefficient λ, which measures the persistence of conditional volatility, is the least in terms of magnitude out of all the parameters and is highly significant. Hence, it takes a very short time for the volatility to decrease in the market. Since θ, the asymmetry parameter, is significantly negative, there is leverage effect implying that negative shocks generate more volatility than the positive shocks. The coefficient γ, measuring the GARCH effect, is positive and statistically significant, there is GARCH effect i.e. the present variance is effected by its past values. The plot of the EGARCH variance is shown in Figure 4.12.

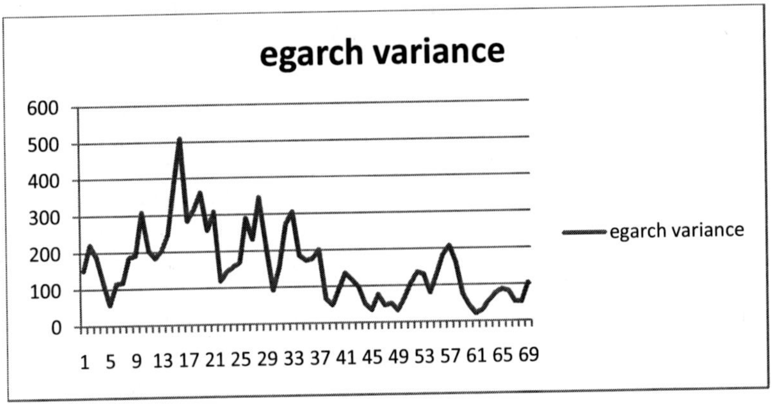


***Figure 4.12: Plot of EGARCH Model Variance for Long Period***

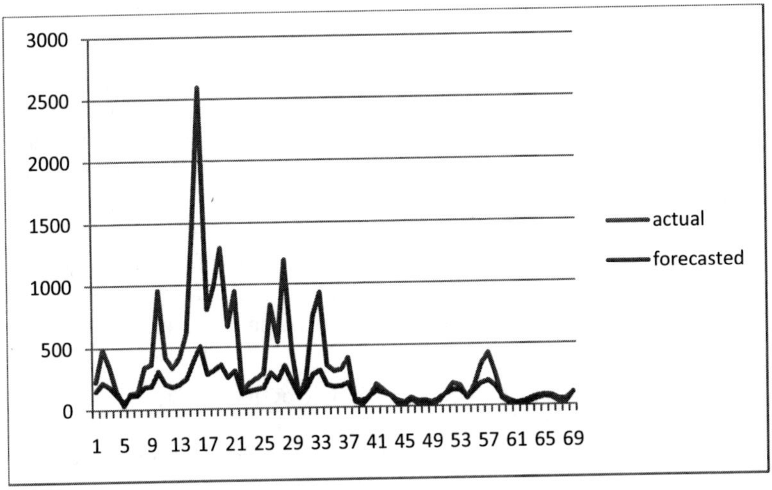


***Figure 4.13: Performance of Actual vs Forecasted Variance Model of Stock Prices***

The Figure 4.13 presents the plot of actual forecasted variance by fitting EGARCH model on stock prices of TATA Steel Limited for the first four months of 2018 (69 days), January1, 2018 to April 18 i.e. from 1238th day to 1307th day. The graph shows remarkably close fit of the EGARCH model to the actual, especially showing the high volatility in the first half of the period slowly decays in the second half of the time period considered as the EGARCH model explains. It is to be noted that the actual variance is calculated by taking standard deviations of the actual stock prices for the 69 days and then squaring them to variances, whereas the forecasted variance is generated as a result of the heteroscedasticity model with error variance that includes certain factors like leverage effects, asymmetry, etc. Therefore, in Figure 4.12 the plot of calculated actual variance shows slightly higher volatility than the plot of the forecasted variance.

It can be observed that the stock prices are highly volatile in the month of January 2018. This volatility is caused by negative shocks as shown by the $\theta$ coefficient. It is meaningful to relate the high volatility of stock prices in the month of January to the phenomenon of 'January effect' in the stock market (Thaler, 1987). This happens as investors buy more stocks during the month of December owing to the fall in stock prices that happen during the end of a year and sell them during the last week of January of the next year when stock prices rebounds. Also, generally the total trade volume of stock in December is relatively high in the month of January, leading to relatively more volatility in January. The volatility in stock prices that is present during the month of January will not last long as it will decay in the following days, as the coefficient of $\lambda$ parameter reveals. The forecasting performance of the EGARCH model is evaluated by the root mean square which is 14.373 for the fitted EGARCH model.

While fitting the ARIMA model for short period data, the price on the present working day is dependent on prices in the preceding periods along with the errors made in two preceding periods, and for long period data, the price on the present working day is dependent on longer preceding periods and the errors made in those periods. The parameters in the fitted ARIMA model to short data are all significant, hence the plot for the forecasted values almost overlapped the actual stock prices. In the case of long period data, all the parameters other than the intercept and the third autoregressive term are highly significant, thus the plot for the forecasted series closely follow the plot of the actual series of stock prices.

However, the residual plots of both time period models show volatility clustering as a result of which GARCH model has been used to study the variances in the prices in the short data. As the coefficients of fitted GARCH model are highly insignificant, the ARCH and GARCH terms are quite ineffective in studying the fluctuations in the conditional variance. As the GARCH model is symmetric, EGARCH model has been estimated to study the variance fluctuations for a relatively long period data to capture any possible asymmetry in the stock prices. The parameters that signify symmetry, persistence of volatility and leverage effect are significant implying that the volatility in the stock prices will die out within a very short span of time. The plot of forecasted variance shows that the volatility in the stock prices of TATA Steel that is observed in the month of January 2018 does not extend to February. Hence, the volatility in the stock prices of TATA Steel is not quite persistent. Thus, the forecasted stock price variance on the basis of long period price series is more reliant than the one forecasted on short period price series.

## 4.5 Conclusion

Generally, the performance of the stock market is identified with the health of the economy. An increasing trend in stock market indices implies the growth of the economy and a decreasing trend indicates poor performance. In any stock market, the stock prices are generally volatile and fluctuate over time which is measured by various indices. This paper analyses the effects of long period and short period stock price variations on stock prices and using the volatility in residuals i.e. error variance, the future volatility in stock prices are forecasted. Empirically, based on the stock prices of TATA Steel Limited in the NSE for 1237 days, between 1st January 2013 and 29th December 2017, the short period and long period stock prices are used to predict the future stock price and future volatility. First, ARIMA model has been fitted to forecast the stock prices, and to the resultant residuals, GARCH and EGARCH models have been applied to examine the effects of short period and long period price fluctuations on the forecasts of future price variations respectively. The EGARCH fitting shows that the long period fluctuations have significant effect on the future stock price volatility relative to the GARCH fitting. The predictability of the EGARCH model has been compared with the actual stock price variations for 69 days, for January-April 2018. The econometric forecasts show that the long period stock price volatility is more reliant than the short period volatility in forecasting future stock price volatility as well as the stock prices.

# 5

# The Effect of FDI on Economic Growth and Domestic Investment: Vector Autoregression Estimation


## Abstract

*There is evidence that foreign direct investment promotes growth in developing economies. At the same time, economic development also attracts FDI. Further, FDI inflows may also induce investment by national investors. In order to analyse the effect of FDI inflows on economic growth and domestic investment in developing countries, this paper has applied the vector autoregressive model for five Asian countries - India, Malaysia, Pakistan, Sri Lanka and Thailand - for the period 1980-2008. In the VAR framework, the relationship between GDP, FDI, exports, infrastructure and population growth are estimated endogenously by taking two period lags of each of these variables. The estimated VAR results show that there is a positive impact of FDI on growth in these economies, except Pakistan, and the infrastructure facility is an important factor for attracting FDI. The impact of FDI inflows on domestic investment in India is significantly positive, a more than two fold increase in investment by the national investors.*



**Key words:** *FDI inflows, economic growth, domestic investment, causality, VAR estimation*


## 5.1 Introduction

The most striking aspect of globalisation process has been the exponential growth of FDI inflows and the spread of multinational enterprises (MNEs) activity in most developing countries. Increasing demand for global brands and opening of the economy provides a significant platform for multinational enterprises (MNEs) to exert vital influence on the economic activities of most developing countries. Growing collaboration by international companies with domestic business houses and enlarging direct business activities by subsidiaries in local markets envisage FDI flows. New information technology system and decline in global communication costs have made management of foreign investments far easier than in the past. In the sea change, trade and investment policies and the global regulatory environment including trade policy and tariff liberalisation, easing of restriction on foreign investments and acquisitions in many nations and the deregulation and privatisation of many industries have been the main significant catalyst for FDIs expanded growth. Global changes in technology, growing liberalisation of the national regulatory frameworks governing investment in enterprises and changes in capital market have changed the size, scope and methods of FDI. Many countries that favour FDI provide investment incentives by offering specifically design incentives and channels to attract MNEs to locate their production facilities in their territories. Governments in both developed as well as developing countries alike attract MNEs with various incentive packages to access their resources viz. capital, technology, skilled labour and market access among others to expedite the process of their development. Tax incentives are prominent and found to have a greater effect on the FDI inflows and affiliate outputs than the extent of their localisation. Such mechanisms have been found to be favourably associated with MNE operations in the country.

With global market integration and mobility of capital and labour, foreign direct investment (FDI) has become an integral part of global as well as in domestic business and economic activities. For a host country which receives the FDI flows, FDI provides a strong impetus to economic growth. FDI can generate direct and indirect effect on the host economies. Direct gains from FDI are obtained when it raises financial capital, technological know-how, managerial techniques and productivity in the host country and the foreign investor does not wholly appropriate this increase. Direct gains accrue to the labour in the form of lower prices and to the government in the form of tax revenues. In a sense, the extent of direct contribution of FDI to the growth of host economies depends on their efficiency relative to the domestic firms. In addition, FDI may exert indirect effects in the host economies. The indirect effects largely relate to the external effects or spillovers (Blomstrom and Persson, 1983). FDI also play a major role in the promotion of entrepreneurship and internalisation of businesses. Thus, the FDI flows not only provide the much need capital investments, but also provide the firm with new markets, marketing channels, low cost production facilities, access to new technology, processing, products, organisational technology and management skills.

It is against this background that FDI has been viewed by some as a panacea for declining domestic investment and higher costs of borrowing abroad. FDI appears attractive because it involves risk sharing relationship with investors from the home country. Such risk sharing does not exist in the formal contractual arrangements for foreign loans. FDI appears particularly attractive when existing stocks are low. Low stocks of foreign owned capital imply low flows of repatriated profits. Over time, however, success in attracting

FDI will increase this counter flow which could exceed the alternative flow of interest payments in the longer run. However, not everything about FDI is positive for the host countries (Ram and Zhang, 2002). Sometimes the economies of the host countries may suffer rather than prosper because of FDI. It is often said that FDI is the Trojan Horse the MNEs bring to the low income countries. In the race for seeking more and more FDI inflows however the countries have overlooked the fact that all the flows of FDI do not benefit their host countries similarly. In fact, some FDI inflows may actually bring pretty little, if at all.

Further, with the growing role of WTO in international business regulations, multilateral agreements in investments aim for security of foreign investments with virtually unfettered rights to invest in all sectors of the host country and to obtain for them the same treatment as domestic investors. The host country has to agree with the multilateral agencies to open the market, deregulate the industries, remove protective regulations, and most importantly to abide by the international standards and regulations. In some developing countries the MNEs might adversely affect the development of domestic firms and otherwise be a source of economic exploitation. The MNEs may put a pressure on domestic business as local firms have to compete with the MNEs and in the course of time domestic firms may face the risk of elimination. Some specific drawbacks that the LDCs may suffer as a result of the entry by MNE are: (i) MNCs may repatriate more funds than they bring in to their home countries, (ii) MNCs may transfer inferior technologies to the host countries, (iii) MNCs may monopolise some markets in the host countries by destroying domestic competition through price cutting, (iv) MNCs may focus only on the domestic markets of the host country and may not contribute to the exports from the host country, (v) MNCs may exert undue influence on the political and regulatory system of the host countries so as to benefit the foreign investors, and (vi) MNCs may have a negative impact on the cultural and social norms of the host countries by imposing alien standards.

Since 1997 East Asian financial crisis, the relationship between FDI, exports and economic growth has gained importance and attention among policy-makers and researchers. The long term benefits of FDI and the impacts of FDI flows on growth and income distribution are not clearly established. Without an understanding with certainty how FDI is attracted to the country and its effects in short term and long term, the task is more difficult when it is not clear about the mechanisms through which FDI will bring about changes in the economy. In order to explore the nexus between the FDI inflow and economic growth, it is necessary to evaluate the relationship along with other economic factors like exports, imports, trade policy and infrastructure development and in general economic forces operating in the domestic markets. Further, it is also important to understand the direction of causation: is it the FDI inflows that cause economic growth or the other way. Another important question is: whether FDI crowds out or increase domestic private investment.

Therefore, the main objectives of this paper are to examine the relationship between FDI inflows and economic growth, and analyse the relationship between FDI inflows and domestic private investment. The impact of FDI inflows on growth is estimated by Vector Autoregressive (VAR) method for five Asian economies for the period 1980 to 2008. The impact of FDI inflows on domestic investment is estimated for the period I991-2008 for India by OLS.

## 5.2 A Brief Review of Recent Studies

From the theoretical point of view, FDI inflows are expected to accelerate economic growth of the host country. Fry (1993) examines the question of whether FDI inflows affect national savings both directly and indirectly in the presence of incentive-disincentive packages and other economic distortions by analysing the rate of economic growth in l6 Pacific Basin developing countries with a control group of 11 other developing countries. The estimated reduced form current account equations show that FDI has a significant negative impact on national savings in all the l6 countries. For the control group, this negative effect is similar in magnitude to FDI's negative effect on domestic investment implying a zero effect on the current account. Fry concludes that the FDI has a negative effect on economic growth in the control group countries but a positive effect on growth in the Pacific Basin countries.

Borensztein, Gregorio and Lee (1998) test the effect of FDI on technology diffusion and economic growth in a cross country analysis of 69 developing countries for the period 1970-1989. The seemingly unrelated least squares (SURE) estimates show that there exists a positive effect on economic growth of FDI inflows and also FDI exerts a positive effect on domestic investment.

Agrawal et al. (2000) also finds a strong positive impact of FDI inflows on GDP growth rate in five South Asian countries - India, Pakistan, Bangladesh, Sri Lanka and Nepal - during late eighties and early nineties, supporting the view that FDI is more likely to be beneficial in more open economies. Further, increase in the FDI inflows in South Asia is also associated with a 4-5 percent increase in nationally owned investment suggesting a complementarity and linkage effects between foreign and domestic investments.

Banga (2008) examines the relationship between FDI inflows and infrastructure using aggregate FDI inflows in 15 developing South, East and South East Asian countries for the period 1980-81 to 1999-2000.The study finds that availability of electricity is indeed an important factor in FDI flows. The paper also emphasises the role of labour costs, labour productivity and educational attainment in attracting FDI into Asian countries. The panel random effects estimates show that fiscal incentives have insignificant impact on aggregate FDI, but removal of restrictions or lower tariffs attract aggregate FDI and attract FDI notably from developing countries. Further, bilateral investment treaties with developed countries have significant impact on aggregate FDI inflows.

Lumbila (2005) estimates the effects of FDI inflows on economic growth in 47 African countries over the period 1980-2000. The weighted seemingly unrelated least squares results show that FDI inflows exert a positive impact on growth in Africa. The FDI inflows not only bring fresh capital to African countries but also allow these economies to take advantage from technology and managerial practices. A ten percent increase in the inflows of FDI impacts the host economy to grow by 0.34 percent. The impact of FDI inflows on growth in host country is further enhanced by trained human capital, attractive investment climate stemming from a developed infrastructure from a lower country risk and stable macro environment. The results are also supportive of a small crowding-in-effect i.e. one dollar increase in the net inflow of FDI is associated with an increase in domestic investment in the host economy of about 0.048 dollars.

An IMF (2005) study analyses the significant determinants of FDI inflows in India. Estimating a reduced form equation of fixed effects model, the study significantly finds that the most important factors influencing FDI into India are not FDI-specific policies but rather the broader economic policies including corporate taxes, trade openness and other business climate issues like regulatory quality and burden. Also, some institutional factors and the quality of infrastructure are the significant determinants of India's FDI inflows.

Reddy and Mohanty (2007) examines the interrelations among the variables FDI, GDP, exports and imports of four countries - China, India, Malaysia and Singapore - using panel data methods. They estimate that one dollar of FDI inflow adds to about 3.27 dollars to the GDP for each country suggesting that FDI promotes economic growth. Further, an autoregressive forecast of the FDI inflows to these countries shows that China has been able to attract $15 billion more in FDI than India because of the combined effects of its policies.

Miankhel, Thangavelu and Kalirajan (2009) adopt a time-series framework of a vector autoregressive model to examine the relationship between growths in export, FDI and GDP among the emerging economies a multivariate causality study. The paper further examines whether the established causality between FDI and growth is effective in the short run or in the long run. In the analysis, export growth precedes GDP growth and then GDP growth precedes FDI growth implying that it is exports that drives FDI through channeling effect of GDP. The results show that in South Asian countries, the export-growth hypothesis holds both in the short and long runs. However, it is the GDP growth in the long run that attracts FDI in India, and on the other hand, GDP leads to exports growth in Pakistan. In Thailand, there exists a bidirectional relationship between GDP and FDI under a block exogeneity test. There is no specific relationship either in the short run or in the long run in the case of Malaysia. In the case of Mexico, exports precede FDI in the short and long runs while in Chile, it is FDI which is driving other economic variables in the short and long runs.

Empirically, while the studies have used a slightly different sets of independent variables in addition to FDI, the dependent variable in almost all studies, is either the logarithm of the growth in per capita GDP or the logarithm of the GDP growth rate itself. Also, the independent variable representing FDI is scaled as the ratio of FDI inflows to the GDP of the country or the ratio of FDI inflows to the gross capital formation of the country. The studies are generally based on the conventional neoclassical production function approach adding foreign capital as an additional variable and the estimation techniques are SURE, VAR and autoregressive methods.

Overall, the time series and panel studies show that FDI inflows promotes economic growth, but the extent to which a country is benefited by FDI depends on its trade policies, labour force skills, business climate, domestic investment, infrastructure, and other factors.

## 5.3 Data and Methodology

This paper analyses the impact of FDI inflows on economic growth of five Asian countries - India, Malaysia, Pakistan, Sri Lanka and Thailand - for the period 1980 to 2008, and the effect of FDI inflows on domestic investment in India for the period 1991-2008. Malaysia and Thailand from East Asia have been included as these countries have been successful in attracting FDI, being among the top ten FDI recipient countries. India, Pakistan and Sri Lanka from South Asia have been considered as they have sizably liberalised their economy. The data for the study on GDP, FDI, exports and control variables have been collected from the UNCTAD Handbook of Statistics 2009, IMF International Financial Statistics 2009 and the World Bank World Development Indicators 2009. All variables are defined in real values by deflating them to 2000 prices using GDP deflators and are expressed in US$ for comparison. The time series data on domestic investment have been collected from the RBI Handbook of Statistics on the Indian Economy 2009.

The growth of output is measured as the current per capita GDP. Net FDI inflow measure is defined as the net inflow of investment to acquire a lasting management interest (10 percent or more of voting stock) in an enterprise operating in an economy other than that of the investor. The net FDI inflow is the sum of equity capital, reinvestment of earnings, other long term capital and short term capital as shown in the balance of payments. The level of infrastructure development in an economy is measured by the telephone mainlines, which are telephone lines connecting a customer's equipment to the public switched telephone network. The size of population represents the demand side of the economy. The Table 5.1 presents the descriptive statistics of the variables used in the empirical analysis of this paper. The Table 5.1 shows that Thailand and Malaysia have received the largest FDI inflows and the FDI inflow into them is also substantial compared to Pakistan. Malaysia is better positioned in terms of infrastructure.

**Table 5.1: Descriptive Statistics of the Variables in VAR Analysis**

| *Variable* | *India* | *Malaysia* | *Pakistan* | *Sri Lanka* | *Thailand* |
|---|---|---|---|---|---|
| GDP per capita(US$) | 445.80<br>(204.14) | 3637.78<br>(1651.94) | 561.36<br>(151.34) | 742.97<br>(426.26) | 1874.27<br>(928.52) |
| Net FDI inflows(US$) | 18950.97<br>(31223.87) | 27782.43<br>(21445.26) | 6004.35<br>(7138.87) | 1388.11<br>(1012.45) | 25253.39<br>(28738.41) |
| Exports(US$) | 40965.46<br>(43400.49) | 67296.17<br>(54601.49) | 8072.00<br>(4939.07) | 3526.81<br>(2219.41) | 51454.13<br>(45532.45) |
| Telephone mainlines (per 100 persons) | 1.77<br>(1.48) | 12.71<br>(6.09) | 1.54<br>(0.98) | 1.54<br>(0.98) | 3.80<br>(2.04) |
| Population growth rate (annual percent) | 1.82<br>(0.30) | 2.40<br>(0.38) | 2.49 (0.18) | 1.07<br>(0.32) | 1.29<br>(0.52) |

*Source:* UNCTAD Handbook of Statistics, 2009.

**Note:** Standard deviations in parentheses.

The Figure 5.1 plots the scatter matrix and the Table 5.2 presents the correlation matrix of the variables for India, where all variables are expressed in logarithms. From the Figure 5.1 and Table 5.2 it is observed that the variables, GDP, FDI, exports and infrastructure are highly, positively and significantly related to each other, while population growth rate is negatively related with other variables. Further, the same results are obtained from the scatter matrix and correlation matrix of the variables in other four countries.

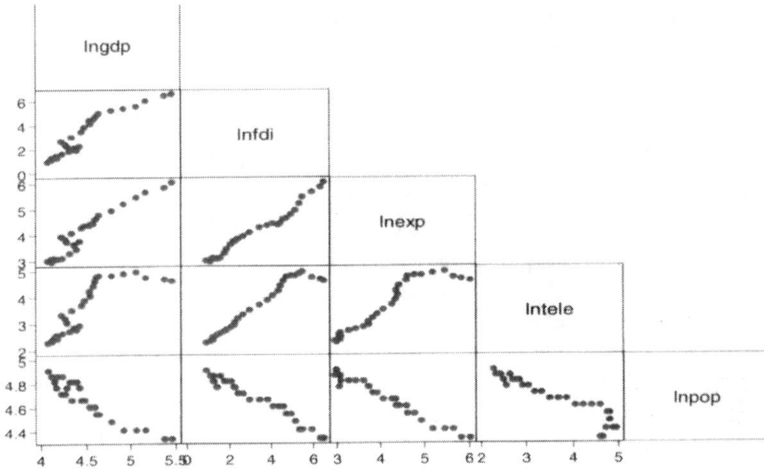


***Figure 5.1: Scatter Matrix of VAR Variables for India***

## Vector Auto-Regressive (VAR) Method

The VAR analysis of causal relationship between the economic variables requires the initial testing for the presence of unit root and cointegration. Granger (1988) states that long run equilibrium exists when two or more non-stationary time series [integrated of order 1 or I (l)] are integrated of order I(0). With the presence of unit root, stationarity is achieved by trend stationarity. Then by applying the VAR approach of Johansen and Juselius (1990), test for cointegration can be performed, and if cointegration is present, Granger Causality test with an error correction term can be applied. If there is no cointegration, the VAR model can be used for estimation.

**Table 5.2: Correlation Matrix of VAR Variables for India**

| *Variable* | *GDP* | *FDI* | *Exports* | *Infrastructure* |
|---|---|---|---|---|
| FDI | 0.931* | - | - | - |
| Exports | 0.956* | 0.933* | - | - |
| Infrastructure | 0.830* | 0.970* | 0.933* | - |
| Population growth rate | -0.941* | -0.980* | -0.983* | -0.938* |

**Note:** Significant at 1 percent level.

## Unit Root Test

The common test of stationarity (or non-stationarity) is the unit root test. A stochastic process is stationary if its mean and variance are constant over time i.e. they are time invariant and the value of the covariance between the two time periods depend only on the distance or gap or lag between the two time periods and not the actual time at which the covariance is computed. A non-stationary time series will have a time varying mean or a time varying variance or both. The unit root test consists of testing for significance the term ρ in the equation,

$$y_t = \rho y_{t-1} + u_t \tag{5.1}$$

where $u_t$ is the white noise or purely random error term. The error term $u_t$ is white noise if the stochastic process has zero mean, constant variance and is serially uncorrelated. If $|\rho|<l$, then $y_t$, is stationary i.e. $y$ is having short memory influence of $y_{t-1}$ and tends to zero as $t$ increases, finite variance (time independent) and autocorrelation function decays fast. $y_t$ is non-stationary if $|\rho|=l$ i.e. $y_t$ has infinite memory influence of $y_{t-1}$ which persists as $t$ increases, with unbounded variance, grows with $t$ and autocorrelation function persists. If |?|>l, $y_t$ is non-stationary and explosive. Under the null hypothesis (i.e. ρ=l), the $t$-value of the estimated coefficient of $y_{t-1}$ does not follow the $t$-distribution even in large samples i.e. it does not have an asymptotic normal distribution. Dickey and Fuller (1979) have shown that under the null hypothesis that ρ=l, the estimated $t$-value of the coefficient of $y_{t-1}$ follows the τ (tau) statistic. When ρ=l is rejected i.e. time series is stationary, $t$-test can be used.

A random walk process may have no drift, or it may have drift or it may have both deterministic and stochastic trends. To allow various possibilities Dickey-Fuller test is estimated in three different forms, that is under three different null hypotheses,

$y_t$ is a random walk: $\Delta y_t = \delta y_{t-1} + u_t$ (5.2)

$y_t$ is a random walk with drift: $\Delta y_t = \beta_0 + \beta_1 t + \delta y_{t-1} + u_t$ (5.3)

$y_t$ is a random walk with drift around a stochastic trend:

$\Delta y_t = \beta_0 + \beta_1 t + \delta y_{t-1} + u_t$ (5.4)

where $\delta = (\rho - 1)$ and $\Delta$ is the first difference operator. In each case, the null hypothesis is that $\delta = 0$ i.e. there is unit root and the time series is non-stationary. The alternative hypothesis is that the $\delta < 0$ i.e. the time series is stationary with 0 mean or with a non-zero mean or around a deterministic trend respectively. Under the assumption that the error term ut is uncorrelated, the Dickey and Fuller test is applied to the time series. When the error term ut is correlated, the Augmented Dickey-Fuller (ADF) test is used. The ADF test consists of estimating the regression,

$$\Delta y_t = \beta_0 + \beta_1 t + \delta y_{t-1} + \sum \alpha_i \Delta y_{t-i} + \varepsilon_t \quad (5.5)$$

where $\varepsilon_t$ is a pure white noise error term. The number of lagged difference terms to be included is determined empirically. Thangavelu and Rajaguru (2004) show that the ADF test corrects for higher order serial correlations by adding differenced terms of the lagged variables on the right side of the equation. If the ADF test shows the presence of unit root, the series is transformed to a difference stationary process or trend stationarity.

In this paper, all variables in the VAR model are tested for stationarity by applying the ADF test for both the level and trend stationarity and the results are presented in Table 5.3.

**Table 5.3: ADF Unit Root Test for Stationarity of VAR Variables**

| *Variable* | | *India* | *Malaysia* | *Pakistan* | *Sri Lanka* | *Thailand* |
|---|---|---|---|---|---|---|
| GDP | Level | 2.61 | 0.39 | 0.64 | 2.05 | -0.45 |
| | Trend | 11.21* | 14.23* | 8.79* | 29.75* | 11.32* |
| FDI | Level | 2.17 | -0.39 | 0.69 | -0.87 | -0.78 |
| | Trend | 34.14* | 17.65* | 19.42* | 24.71* | 33.65* |
| Exports | Level | 3.06** | 0.31 | 0.04 | -0.06 | -0.06 |
| | Trend | - | 29.26* | 24.98* | 25.88* | 25.50* |
| Infrastructure | Level | -1.09 | -6.01* | -1.47 | -4.64* | 1.08 |
| | Trend | 21.70* | - | 25.59* | - | 4.34* |
| Population growth rate | Level | 0.22 | 1.52 | -1.53 | -1.98 | -0.50 |
| | Trend | -21.77* | -7.43* | -13.43* | -4.45* | -8.37* |

**Note:*** Significant at 1 percent level ** Significant at 5 percent level.

The ADF test results show that FDI and GDP of all the five countries are stationary after transformation and significant at 1 percent level. For India, exports is stationary at level and significant at 5 percent level, while it is significant at 1 percent level in trend in all other four countries. Infrastructure also exhibits stationarity at level for Malaysia and Sri Lanka and other countries it is trend.

## Cointegration Test

The cointegration analysis captures the dynamic relationship among the variables. The multivariate cointegration test based on Johansen and Juselius (1990) is used to determine the long run relationship. Two variables are cointegrated if they have a long term or equilibrium relationship between them, and such cointegrated series leads to spurious regression situation. The test procedure for cointegration is: Determine whether $y_t$, and $x_t$ are I(1) which is equivalent to determining whether or not they contain unit roots, and if they are both I(1), then estimate the parameters of the cointegrating regression $y_t = \beta_0 + \beta_1 x_{t-1} + u_t$ and test whether the estimated residual ut is I(0) or not using ADF test statistic. If the null hypothesis of unit root ut is rejected, then it may be inferred that there exists cointegration between $y_t$ and $x_t$ denoted as CI(l,1) [cointegrated of order 1,1].

## Error Correction Model

When the variables are cointegrated, there is a long run relationship between the variables, while there may be disequilibrium in the short run, and the error term may not be treated as the equilibrium error. In fact, this error term can be used to tie the short run behaviour to its long run value. The Engle and Granger (1987) error correction mechanism (ECM) corrects for disequilibrium. The notion of error correction is that a part of the disequilibrium from one period is corrected with the next period, and therefore cointegrated series can be represented by the error correction model. In essence, under the restriction that the variables are CI (1,1), showing that an error correction is needed, for any set of I(1) variables, error correction and cointegration are equivalent. The error correction model (ECM) is a more comprehensive test of causality because, in addition to the standard causality between the cointegrated variables, the ECM captures yet another causal linkage between the two variables - the impact of long run equilibrium on the short run dynamics.

Thus, the cointegration explains the extent of deviation from the long run equilibrium relationship by non-stationary series. If the series of variables are not cointegrated i.e. no long run equilibrium, usual VAR model can be applied. When the variables are cointegrated, an error correction term in VAR framework, vector error correction mechanism (VECM) is to be included to study the dynamic relationship among the cointegrated variables. In the empirical analysis of this paper, GDP and FDI are not cointegrated for India, Malaysia, Pakistan and Thailand except Sri Lanka. For Sri Lanka, since the variables are cointegrated, a proper VAR framework to study the dynamic relationship among them must include an error correction term and for the other countries since there is no cointegration among the variables, we can estimate it by the usual VAR model.

### Vector Autoregressive Regression Model

In the vector autoregressive modeling (VAR) several endogenous variables are considered together with each endogenous variable is explained by its lagged and the lagged values fall other endogenous variables in the model. That is, a vector of variables is explained by the own lagged or past values of the dependent variables themselves. Hence, there is autoregression of the variables together. A vector autoregressive process of order p [VAR(p)] for a system of M variables $y_t = (y_{1t}, y_{2t}, \ldots, y_{mt})$ may be defined as,

$$y_t = v + \Lambda_1 y_{t-1} + \cdots + \Lambda_p y_{t-p} + u_t \tag{5.6}$$

In this system of M equations $v = (v_1, \ldots, V_m)'$ is an M-dimensional vector, the $\Lambda_i$ are (MxM) coefficient matrix and $u_t = (u_{1t}, \ldots, u_{mt})'$ is the stochastic error terms called impulses or innovations or shocks. The $u$'s are white noise with mean zero, $E[u_t] = 0$, and non-singular covariance matrix, $\Sigma v = E[u_t, u_t']$ for all $t$, and $u_t$ and $u_s$ are uncorrelated for $t \neq s$. In estimating the model by VAR, the maximum lag length $k$ is usually decided by lowest values of the Akaike or Schwarz information criteria defined by,

$$AIC(n) = \ln det(\Sigma_n) + 2M^2 n / N \tag{5.7}$$

$$SIC(n) = \ln det(\Sigma_n) + M^2 n \ln N / N \tag{5.8}$$

where $M$ is the number of variables in the system, $N$ is sample size, and $\Sigma n$ is an estimate of the residual covariance matrix $\Sigma_v$ obtained with a VAR($n$) model. The elements of $\Sigma_n$ are computed as,

$$\sigma_{ij} = [(y_i - x\beta_i)'(y_j - x\beta_j)]N \tag{5.9}$$

that is, the sum of squares or cross-products divided by the sample size.

In the empirical estimation, the VAR model for the dependent variables (GDP, FDI, exports, infrastructure, population) are specified as a function of $k$ lag values of all the variables,

$$y_t = \beta_0 + \sum \beta_i y_{t-i} + \sum \gamma_i x_{t-i} + \varepsilon_{1t} \tag{5.10}$$

$$x_t = \beta_0 + \sum \theta_i y_{t-i} + \sum \gamma_i x_{t-i} + \varepsilon_{2t} \tag{5.11}$$

## 5.4 Empirical Analysis

### Effects of FDI on Economic Growth

The estimated VAR results are not the same for all the countries as each country is at a different level of development and has been followed different policies to attain their goal of development. The VAR estimates presented in Table 5.4 shows that, in all the countries the one period lagged GDP is positively and significantly associated with the current level of GDP. A unit increase in the previous year GDP increases the current year GDP by 0.47, 2.13, 0.77, 1.30 and 0.64 units in India, Malaysia, Pakistan, Sri Lanka and Thailand respectively. However, the effect of two period lagged GDP is not the same on GDP in these countries. It has no significant impact on the current GDP in most countries, except Malaysia where it has a significant negative effect on GDP. There is a positive relationship between previous year's FDI in all countries. A unit increase in the previous year FDI increases the current year GDP by 0.28 units for India, 0.44 units for Malaysia, 0.40 units for Thailand and 0.13 units for Sri Lanka, In the case of India, Pakistan, and Thailand, there is a significant negative relationship between the two period lag of FDI and the current GDP. The previous exports of India, Malaysia, Sri Lanka and Thailand have a positive relationship with the current year GDP. A unit increase in the exports will lead to 0.198, 0.89, 0.15 and 0.413 unit increase in GDP of these countries. The lagged effects of infrastructure and population growth are mixed in these countries. For India is that the lagged effects of infrastructure and population growth rate on current GDP are negative. Two noteworthy results are that, in the case of Pakistan, almost all the lagged effects are statistically insignificant, and in the case of Sri Lanka, the variables are cointegrated.

**Table 5.4: VAR Estimates of GDP**
**Dependent variable: ln GDP**

| *Variable* | *India* | | *Malaysia* | | *Pakistan* | | *Sri Lanka* | | *Thailand* | |
|---|---|---|---|---|---|---|---|---|---|---|
| | *Lag1* | *Lag2* | *Lag1* | *Lag2* | *Lag1* | *Lag2* | *Lag1* | *Lag2* | *Lag1* | *Lag2* |
| GDP | 0.47*<br>(0.15) | 0.23<br>(0.16) | 2.13*<br>(0.46) | -2.58*<br>(0.99) | 0.77*<br>(0.20) | -0.12<br>(0.22) | 1.30*<br>(0.26) | 0.23<br>(0.25) | 0.64*<br>(0.15) | -0.26<br>(0.17) |
| FDI | 0.28*<br>(0.08) | -0.21**<br>(0.11) | 0.44**<br>* (0.26) | 0.34<br>(0.49) | 0.03<br>(0.08) | -0.20*<br>(0.070 | 0.13**<br>(0.14) | -0.02<br>(0.26) | 0.40*<br>(0.06) | -0.34*<br>(0.06) |
| Exports | 0.19***<br>(0.11) | -0.48*<br>(0.13) | 0.03<br>(0.34) | 0.89***<br>(0.54) | 0.02<br>(0.13) | 0.01<br>(0.16) | 0.15**<br>(0.13) | -0.10<br>(0.12) | 0.41*<br>(0.13) | 0.05<br>(0.15) |
| Infrastructure | -0.51*<br>(0.12) | 0.48*<br>(0.11) | 2.06*<br>(0.69) | -2.22*<br>(0.74) | 0.05<br>(0.18) | 0.11<br>(0.18) | -0.24***<br>(0.12) | 0.23***<br>(0.11) | 0.88*<br>(0.19) | -1.09*<br>(0.21) |
| Population growth rate | -0.53***<br>(0.25) | -0.97*<br>(0.22) | -0.44<br>(0.79) | 0.07<br>(0.66) | -0.65<br>(0.49) | 0.10<br>(0.47) | -0.04<br>(0.04) | 0.03<br>(0.04) | -0.09<br>(0.12) | 0.13<br>(0.09) |
| ECM | - | - | - | - | - | - | 0.30<br>(0.32) | 0.12<br>(0.14) | - | - |
| AIC | -14.91 | | -15.11 | | -11.93 | | -48.93 | | -4.17 | |
| SIC | -12.26 | | -12.47 | | -9.29 | | -44.55 | | -1.53 | |
| R-square | 0.97 | | 0.96 | | 0.95 | | 0.97 | | 0.98 | |
| N | 27 | | 27 | | 27 | | 26 | | 27 | |

**Note:** Standard errors in parentheses. Lag1 and Lag2 are lags of 1 and 2 periods.

* Significant at 1 percent level ** Significant at 5 percent level *** Significant at 10 percent level.

**Table 5.5: VAR Estimates of FDI**
**Dependent variable: ln (FDI)**

| *Variable* | *India* | | *Malaysia* | | *Pakistan* | | *Sri Lanka* | | *Thailand* | |
|---|---|---|---|---|---|---|---|---|---|---|
| | *Lag1* | *Lag2* | *Lag1* | *Lag2* | *Lag1* | *Lag2* | *Lag1* | *Lag2* | *Lag1* | *Lag2* |
| GDP | 0.51* (0.31) | -0.41 (0.31) | -0.49 (0.42) | 2.61* (0.91) | 0.85* * (0.40) | 0.17 (0.42) | 0.59** * (0.34) | 0.53 (0.33) | -1.54* (0.41) | 0.87** * (0.47) |
| FDI | 1.05* (0.15) | -0.67* (0.20) | 0.31 (0.24) | -1.56* (0.45) | 0.91* (0.16) | -0.44* (0.14) | -0.01 (0.18) | 0.78* * (0.34) | 0.62* (0.17) | 0.03 (0.18) |
| Exports | 0.06 (0.21) | 0.47** * (0.25) | 0.61* * (0.30) | -0.32 (0.52) | -0.80* (0.25) | 0.20 (0.32) | 0.09 (0.15) | 0.005 (0.15) | 1.73* (0.36) | -0.65 (0.410 |
| Infrastru-cture | 0.55** (0.26) | -0.05 (0.21) | 1.57* (0.630 | -0.47 (0.68) | 1.46* (0.36) | - 0.75* * (0.35) | 0.08 (0.15) | 0.28* * (0.14) | 0.18 (0.55) | -0.49 (0.61) |
| Populati-on growth rate | 0.41 (0.47) | -1.17* (o.43) | -0.63 (0.73) | -1.31* (0.60) | -3.37* (0.96) | -0.12 (0.92) | 0.13** (0.06) | -0.04 (0.05) | 0.17 (0.34) | -0.04 (0.27) |
| ECM | - | - | - | - | - | - | 1.48* (0.42) | 0.33* ** (0.19) | - | - |
| AIC | -14.91 | | -15.11 | | -11.93 | | -48.03 | | -4.17 | |
| SIC | -12.26 | | -12.47 | | -9.29 | | -44.55 | | -1.53 | |
| R-square | 0.97 | | 0.96 | | 0.97 | | 0.98 | | 0.97 | |
| N | 27 | | 27 | | 27 | | 26 | | 27 | |

**Note:** Standard errors in parentheses. Lag1 and Lag2 are lags of 1 and 2 periods.
* Significant at 1 percent level ** Significant at 5 percent level *** Significant at 10 percent level.

As the VAR estimates presented in Table 5.5 shows there is a significant and positive effect of the previous year GDP on the current year FDI in India and Sri Lanka, while in Malaysia, Pakistan and Thailand, the relationship between one period lagged GDP and FDI inflows is negative. A unit increase in the GDP of the previous year leads to an increase in the current year FDI by 0.51, -0.49, 0.85, 0.59 and -1.54 units for India, Malaysia, Pakistan, Sri Lanka and Thailand respectively. For the countries India, Pakistan and Thailand, a unit increase in the previous year's FDI will significantly increase the current year FDI by 1.05, 0.91 and 0.62 units. For India, Malaysia and Pakistan, there is a significant negative relationship between the second period lag of FDI and current year FDI by -0.67, -1.56 and -0.44 units. Similarly, the other variable lagged effects are interpreted. The VAR estimates for exports, infrastructure and population growth have similar results but are not presented here.

## FDI and Domestic Investment

This section empirically estimates the impact of FDI on domestic investment by national investors of India using time series data for the period

1991-2008 by OLS method. The Table 5.6 presents the description of explanatory variables along with summary values used in the analysis of the effect of FDI on domestic investment. The FDI can promote domestic investment through the backward and linkage effects with the domestic industries. Further, the foreign borrowing can be used as a source of funds for investment. The relative effectiveness of foreign borrowing and FDI inflows in promoting investment has to be analysed. An improvement in terms of trade can increase investment by increasing real income, making capital goods cheaper relative to the domestic goods. An increase in real exchange rate would increase the price of imported capital and intermediate goods and result in a contraction of investment. The real lending rate is critical for domestic borrowings and a decrease in it will promote investment. The gross fixed domestic investment includes the foreign direct investment. Therefore, the nationally owned gross fixed investment is defined as gross fixed domestic investment minus the net FDI inflows. In the empirical analysis, the dependent variable is defined as the ratio of nationally owned gross fixed investment to GDP.

**Table 5.6: Descriptive Statistics of the Variables in FDI and Domestic Investment**

| *Variable* | *Description* | *Mean* | *Std. dev.* |
|---|---|---|---|
| $INV_{ni}$ | Nationally owned gross fixed investment – net FDI inflows | 581448.2 | 461980.9 |
| FDI | FDI inflows as a share of GDP (FDI/GDP) | 25438.61 | 36937.21 |
| FB | Total foreign borrowing as share of GDP (FB/GDP) | 13.99 | 2.42 |
| TOT | Terms of trade (unit price of exports/unit price of imports) | 139.0 | 25.9 |
| RER | Real exchange rate (nominal prime-lending rate of the banks - average of current and next year's inflation rates) | 39.21 | 7.79 |
| RLR | Real lending rate (domestic interest rate) | 13.66 | 2.42 |

*Source:* RBI: Handbook of Statistics on the Indian Economy 2009.

The estimating equation is specified as,

$$\text{In}(INV_{ni})_t = \beta_0 + \beta_1 \text{InFDI}_t + \beta_2 \text{InFB}_t + \beta_3 \text{InTOT}_t + \beta_4 \text{inRER}_t + \beta_5 \text{inRLR}_t + u_t \quad (5.12)$$

Theoretically, the coefficient of FDI/GDP should be zero if FDI has no impact on investment by national sources. If FDI is associated with a decline in domestic investors, it should be negative while if FDI inflows are associated with an increase in investment by local investors, it should be positive. The estimated OLS results are presented in Table 5.7.

**Table 5.7: OLS Estimates of the Effect of FDI on Domestic Investment Dependent variable: ln ($INV_{ni}$)**

| *Variable* | *Coefficient* |
|---|---|
| lnFDI | 2.63* (3.50) |
| lnFB | 0.35 (0.21) |
| lnTOT | 0.010* (0.001) |
| lnRER | -0.007* (0.002) |
| lnRLR | -0.01 (0.01) |
| R-square | 0.80 |
| F-value | 9.33 |
| N | 18 |

**Note:** Standard errors in parentheses.
* Significant at 1 percent level.

It is seen that most of the variables have the expected sign. The crucial variable, the ratio of net FDI inflows to GDP, has a strong positive effect on the investment by national investors and is statistically significant. The elasticity of domestic investment with respect to FDI increases is 2.63 implying investment by national investors more than doubles when there are significant FDI inflows. The impact on domestic investment of total foreign borrowings (FB) and terms of trade (TOT) are positive effect. The effect of real lending rate (RLR) on national investment is negative by 0.01 units. Similarly, an increase in the real exchange rate (RER) has a significant negative effect on investment by national investors.

## 5.5 Conclusion

The experience of the East Asian financial crisis that resulted in the volatility of the short term capital flows has forced economies to shift their policies towards attracting foreign direct investments. However, the FDI inflows have not been the same, and it differs depending on the national incentives and opportunities. There is overwhelming evidence that the FDI inflows promote growth in developing economies. At the same time, economic development also attracts FDI. Further, FDI inflows may also induce investment by national investors. In order to analyse the effect of FDI inflows on economic growth and domestic investment in developing countries, this paper has adopted a time-series analysis of a vector autoregressive model for five Asian countries - India, Malaysia, Pakistan, Sri Lanka and Thailand - for the period 1980-2008. In the VAR framework, it is possible to examine whether it is FDI that promotes GDP or GDP that promotes FDI. In the VAR framework of this paper, the relationship between GDP, FDI, exports, infrastructure and population growth are estimated endogenously by taking two period lags of each of these variables.

The estimated VAR results are not the same for all the countries since each country is at a different level of development and has followed different policies to attain the present level of development. The results point out that for India, Malaysia, Sri Lanka and Thailand there is a positive impact of FDI on growth whereas Pakistan does not show any relation at all. Exports and infrastructure too have a positive impact on the GDP for all the countries except Pakistan. Further, from the analysis it is observed that the infrastructure facility is an important factor for attracting FDI. The impact of FDI inflows on domestic investment, this paper applied OLS estimation to a time-series data on India for the period 1991-2008. The estimated results suggest that an increase in FDI inflows in India is associated with a more than two fold increase in investment by the national investors.

The estimated empirical results provide some support for more liberal policies towards FDI. Identifying the FDI impacts and its mechanism can help governments to develop effective policy to promote greater investment activities in the domestic economy. However, it should be remembered that FDI is not beneficial under all conditions. Just like high import tariffs, excessive concessions to attract FDI could harm domestic investors as they may not be able to compete with MNCs and even eliminate national investors. Therefore, developing countries need to negotiate hard to ensure that they do not give unreasonable concessions under the multilateral investment agreement under the WTO negotiations, especially unlimited access to domestic markets, at least not without getting adequate concessions in return from developed countries. Instead, the developing countries should focus on developing their own human capital, skilled and trained labour, and develop infrastructure networks that will encourage domestic investment by national investors.

# 6

# The Twin Deficit Hypothesis: Structural Vector Autoregression Estimation of the Relationship between Fiscal Deficit and Current Account Deficit


## Abstract

*This paper tests the validity of the twin deficit hypothesis, the causal relationship between fiscal deficit (FD) and current account balance (CAB), in India for the period 1994-2016 by estimating a structural model that includes interest rate and exchange rate as interlinking variable. The SVAR estimates show a negative effect implying that a positive shock given to FD worsens the CAB. The current account deficit, while not directly determined by fiscal deficit, is significantly influenced by RIR and REER. The IRF indicates that a positive shock to FD leads to an increase in the domestic interest rate which appreciates the real exchange rate of the domestic currency making the exports costlier and imports cheaper and thereby widening the current account deficit. The SVAR, IRF and Granger causality analyses show that fiscal deficit affects the current account balance in India through the interlinking variables RIR and REER for the time period 1994 (quarter-I) to 2016 (quarter-IV). This result validates the relevance of twin deficit hypothesis in the Indian economy and is consistent with the Keynesian proposition in Indian economy during the period 1994-2016.*



**Key words:** *Fiscal deficit, current account balance, interest rare, exchange rate, SVAR estimation*


## 6.1 Introduction

Most of the developing countries have fiscal or deficit as well as current account deficits. Fiscal deficit refers to the budget deficit wherein tax revenues are less than the government expenditure. The current account deficit refers to the trade deficit where imports exceed exports. The simultaneous occurrence of the two deficits are has been referred as twin deficit hypothesis and the causal relationship between the two deficits has been controversial. Many studies have attempted to test the validity of both the views on current account and fiscal deficit in different origins and contexts using different methodologies. Some studies find that higher fiscal deficit leads to higher current account deficit while other studies find the opposite and observe no significant relationship between the two. Thus, the empirical evidences on the causality and validity of the twin deficit hypothesis have been inconclusive.

Most Asian countries experience the twin deficits. But, in Saudi Arabia and Kuwait there is reverse causality from current account balance to the fiscal deficit (Alkswani, 2000; Merza, Alawin and Bashayreh, 2012). This is because both the countries are oil-based economy and the current account balance is more sensitive to the fluctuations in oil prices than to the changes in fiscal balance. However, in Turkey the validity of the twin deficit hypothesis is different. The differential validity of twin deficit hypothesis in the western Asia is attributed to the difference in the income levels in these countries. While Kuwait and Saudi Arabia belong to the high-income economy, Turkey is a middle-income country. The former countries are highly oil-based economies which yield them higher income (making the current account more sensitive to the income) than in the latter country and hence, creating an income gap between these countries which leads to varying results of the twin deficit hypothesis. In African countries like Egypt, South Africa and Ghana, there is a twin divergence between the fiscal balance and the current account balance implying that a fiscal deficit would lead to improvement of the current account deficit. However, among most of the African countries, twin deficit hypothesis is found to be valid only in Nigeria (Onafowora and Owoye, 2006). The validity of twin deficit hypothesis in 10 European countries shows on one hand absence of any relationship between fiscal deficit and current account for Austria, Finland, Germany, Greece, Netherlands and Portugal and on the other hand valid twin deficit hypothesis for France, Ireland, and Spain (Deltoro, 2015). Thus, the validity of the twin deficit hypothesis for different countries depends on the economic conditions of the country.

India is one of the many countries with both current account deficit and fiscal deficit. India has been experiencing the twin deficits since 1980s. The average fiscal deficit of the central government has remained at 5.8 percent during 1980-2010. It is argued that the main reason behind the financial crisis of 1991 has been the inability to finance the high current account deficit via capital inflows leading to BOP crisis. In fact, the financial crisis in mid 1980s has led to BOP crisis in the next decade. In the first half of the 1980s, the fiscal deficit has been around 6 to 7.5 percent and it has increased to 9 percent in the next half. The fiscal deficit is driven more by the revenue deficit. By 1990s, the fiscal deficit and current account deficit have risen at 9.4 percent and 3.5 percent respectively. With an aim to control the fiscal deficit, the fiscal responsibility and budget management act (FRBM) was introduced in

2003. The FRBM Act warrants a medium term target for balancing current revenues and expenditures and restricts the overall limits to the fiscal deficit at 3 percent of GDP to be achieved by a phased deficit reduction roadmap by 2008. However, with the implementation of massive social security schemes under national rural employment guarantee programme (MGNREGA) and the sixth pay commission, and without any reduction in subsidies, the high government expenditures improved the domestic demand of the economy and a contraction of Indian exports.

During the financial crisis in 1991, the current account deficit of India has been above 3 percent. The structural reforms undertaken subsequently have reduced the current account deficit and in fact there has been a trade surplus between 2001-02 and 2003-04. However, from 2004-05 onwards, the current account experienced deficit in high magnitude and the trade deficit has increased to 4.2 percent in 2011-12. Thus, with the recovery of the economy, the current account deficit also started to widen (Mitra and Khan, 2014). The biggest contributors to the trade deficit of India are the oil and gold imports, followed by factor income paid to abroad and government grants made to the foreigners. The current account deficit is about 0.7 percent of India's GDP in 2016-17 (IMF, BOP Statistics Yearbook).

The Figure 6.1 shows the trends in fiscal deficit (FD) and current account balance (CAB) of the Indian economy as percentage of real GDP from 1994-95 to 2016-17. It can be observed that both FD and CAB are fluctuating over the years. India has been experiencing fiscal deficit in all the years except in the second and third quarter of 2007-08. This is due to the rise in tax revenues from excise and custom duties of the central government. Though the fiscal deficit was high in 1980s and in the early 1990s, it had dropped down in the later years especially in the post FRBM act period. The FD is seen to be fluctuating between 0-4 percent which is due to the government's effort to reduce the deficit by 0.5 percent and bring it down to 3 percent as per the FRBM act. The components of CAB include imports, exports, net transfers and net factor income. The current account balance is negative for most of the years indicating that there has been current account deficit. The negative balance in the current account from 1994 to 2001 can be attributed to the rising imports and falling exports caused by currency appreciation. Between 2002-03 and 2004-05, there has been a surplus in the current account balance due to high surplus from transfers and net income (GOI, Economic Survey, 2005). However, the current account experienced deficit of more than 4 percent in 2011 due to sharp rise in oil prices and fall in growth of the economy. With continuous growth in gold and electronic imports and fall in pharma exports, the deficit in CAB further expanded to around 8 percent till 2014. Though the deficit in CAB reduced to around 2 percent by 2016, it is seen that there is persistent deficit in CAB since 2009-10.

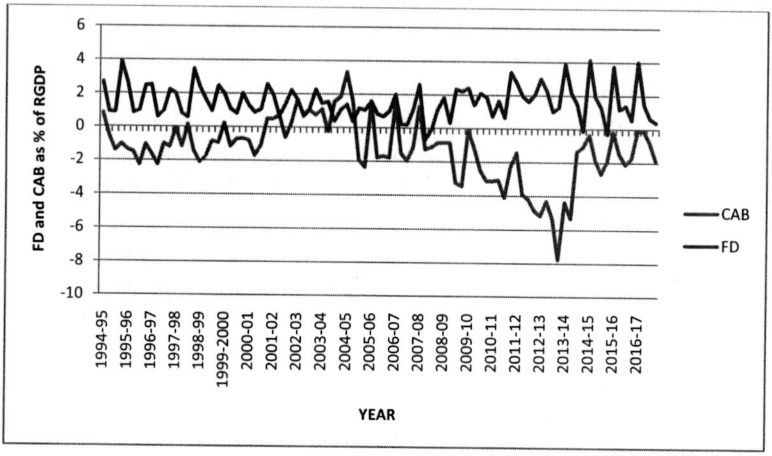


***Figure 6.1: Trends in Fiscal Deficit and Current Account Balance in India 1994-2017***

From Figure 6.1, it can also be observed that when the fiscal deficit is on a rise, the current account balance is running into a deficit indicating the possibility of a causal relationship between FD and CAB. And both FD and CAB have been fluctuating over the years. However, there is no similarity in the trends of FD and CAB in India. Therefore, it is necessary to examine the nature of relationship between fiscal deficit and current account deficit and verify if fiscal deficit fuels the deficit in the external account of India. The previous attempts to test the validity of twin deficit hypothesis in India considered only these two variables, the fiscal deficit and current account balance, and ignored other relevant variables like interest rate and exchange rate which could act as interlinking variables between FD and CAB.

Therefore, the main objective of this paper is to analyse the nature of relationship between fiscal deficit and current account balance in India including the interlinking variables interest rate and exchange rate. The causal relationship between FD and CAB is examined for the time period beginning from quarter I of 1994 to quarter IV of 2016 applying the Structural Vector Autoregressive (SVAR) model for the time series data obtained from the Handbook of Statistics on Indian Economy of the RBI and the International Financial Statistics of the IMF.

## 6.2 A Brief Review of Recent Studies

The theoretical background of twin deficit hypothesis that explores the relationship between current account balance and fiscal deficit are derived from the Keynesian proposition and the Ricardian equivalence hypothesis. The Keynesian proposition argues for the existence of a positive relationship between fiscal deficit and current account deficit and proposes that fiscal deficit leads to a current account deficit. In the Mundell-Fleming framework, in an open economy, the government's expansionary fiscal policy leads to fiscal deficit which induces the domestic rate of interest to rise above the global rate of interest causing capital inflows into the domestic economy. Hence, the exchange rate gets appreciated leading to trade deficit and current account deficit. Therefore, the Keynesian proposition states that a fiscal surplus by contraction of government expenditure will improve the current account balance.

In contrast to the Keynesian approach, the Ricardian equivalence hypothesis denies any relationship between the fiscal deficit and the current account deficit instead it proposes the 'twin divergence hypothesis'. Using the rational expectations framework, it argues that rational individuals know that the reduction in taxes, which leads to fiscal deficit, is temporary and hence they will increase their savings anticipating higher taxes in the future. The impact of such changes in fiscal deficit is adjusted in the national savings and therefore the fiscal deficit has no effect on the current account deficit.

The relationship between these two variables can be put in the national income accounting identity as given by,

$$Y = C + I + G + (X - M) \tag{6.1}$$

where $Y$ is national income, $C$ is private consumption expenditure, $I$ is investment, $G$ is government expenditure on final goods and services, $X$ is exports of goods and services, and $M$ is imports of goods and services. Also the individual dispose of income ($Y$) is either consumption ($C$), saving ($S$), or taxes ($T$). Therefore,

$$Y = C + S + T \tag{6.2}$$

Combining equations (6.1) and (6.2) yields,

$$C + S + T = C + I + G + (X - M) \tag{6.3}$$

$$(X - M) = (S - I) + (T - G) \tag{6.4}$$

The equation (6.4) is the basis for the relationship between fiscal deficit and current account balance which states that the current account balance equals the sum of excess of private savings over investment and fiscal deficit. If the difference between private savings and investment is assumed to be stable over time, as the Keynesian proposition holds, the fluctuations in the public sector balance which is FD will be fully translated to current account (CAB) and vice versa. Therefore, the twin deficit hypothesis will hold. In the second case, the Ricardian equivalence hypothesis states that the change in fiscal deficit is fully offset by the change in savings.

There is an extensive theoretical and empirical literature that has examined the relationship between current account deficits and fiscal deficit and among other macroeconomic variables. An early paper by Bernheim (1988) investigates the relationship between fiscal deficits and trade deficits for the

US and several of its major trading partners (Canada, UK, West Germany, Mexico and Japan) for the period 1960-1984. The growth of real GDP is also included to control for the effects of business cycle. The results show that the fiscal deficit does significantly affect the trade deficit, suggesting the validity of twin deficit hypothesis for the US. The twin deficit relationship also holds true for all the other nations in the study except for Japan.

Kim and Roubini (2008) examine the impact of fiscal policy on current account and real exchange rate of US for the period 1973-2004 by considering a variable system containing budget deficit, current account deficit and real exchange rate employing Vector Autoregressive (VAR) method that allows dynamic interactions among the variables. The empirical results suggest twin divergence rather than twin deficits in the US data as the fiscal accounts worsen the current account improves and vice versa. Further, an expansionary fiscal policy shock (or a fiscal deficit shock) improves the current account and depreciates the real exchange rate. The private saving rises and the investment falls contributing to the current account improvement while the nominal exchange rate depreciation is mainly responsible for the real exchange rate appreciation. They explain the twin divergence of fiscal deficit and current account balance by the prevalence of output shocks and cyclical fluctuations of output. Normandin (1999) gauge the twin deficit hypothesis for the Canadian and US economies for the period 1950 to 1992 by examining the responses of the external deficit to changes in the fiscal deficit. The empirical results show that the responses are positively affected by the degree of persistence of the fiscal deficit, as well as by the birth rate, and the great persistence of the fiscal deficits yields numerically large and statistically positive responses.

Merza, Alawin and Bashayreh (2012) examine the twin deficit hypothesis for Kuwait for the period 1993-2010 using quarterly data and applying time series tests and the VAR estimation method. The causality analysis shows that there is unidirectional causality that runs from current account balance to fiscal balance in the short run. However, in the long run, there is a significant negative relationship between the two deficits. Thus, the twin deficits hypothesis rejected in the case of Kuwait. A similar study by Onafowora and Owoye (2006) observe a statistically significant short run and long run bidirectional relationship among the two deficits in Nigeria during the period 1970-2008. However, Mukhtar, Zakaria and Ahmed (2007) and Saeed and Khan (2012), investigate twin deficit hypothesis in Pakistan using Granger-causality tests, claim the presence of twin deficits in Pakistan.

Lau and Baharumshah (2006) analyse the twin deficits hypothesis of SEACEN countries, including India, using panel VAR framework covering the period 1957-1993. The results support the presence of unidirectional reverse causality from current account deficit to fiscal deficit with inflation, interest rate and exchange rate playing the role of interlinking variables.

Basu and Datta (2005) investigate the nature of the statistical relationship between fiscal and trade deficits in India both in levels as well as in percentage terms using quarterly data for the period 1985-2003. From the empirical results, there seems no long run relation exists between the two deficits either at their levels or at percentages and thus, no evidence in favour of twin deficit phenomenon in India. The study by Mitra and Khan (2014) on the twin deficits hypothesis in India for the period 1994-95 to 2013-14 show that the lagged values of CAB jointly predict the present value of FB statistically significantly and vice versa, Therefore, they conclude that there exists a bi-directional causality among the variables and the causality is positive. The impulse response function results further supported the prevalence of bidirectional causality between current account balance and fiscal balance and the causality is positive supporting the twin deficit hypothesis in India. Suresh and Gautam (2015) consider the endogenously determined structural breaks in both unit root and cointegration tests to test the relevance of twin deficit hypothesis in India for the period 1973-1974 to 2013-2014. While there is no evidence of a cointegrating relationship i.e. no long term relationship between fiscal deficit and current account deficit, the Granger causality test indicates the presence of a bi-directional causality between the FD and CAB. Therefore, they conclude that the twin deficit hypothesis is invalid in India.

As this brief review of empirical studies on the validity of the twin deficit hypothesis in various economic shows the twin deficit hypothesis turned out to be inconclusive for different countries and for different estimation techniques. Especially, the evidence in India is mixed and warrants further examination with improved estimation methods. Hence, this paper attempts to analyse the relevance of the twin deficit hypothesis on the relationship fiscal deficit and current account deficit in India with interlinking variables interest rate and exchange rate, applying the structural vector autoregressive (SVAR) estimation method for the period first quarter of 1994 to fourth quarter of 2016.

## 6.3 Data and Methodology

In the empirical analysis on the relationship between budget deficit and trade deficit in India, this paper uses quarterly data for the time period from 1994-I to 2016-IV. The variables considered are fiscal deficit (FD), current account balance (CAB), real effective exchange rate (REER) and real interest rate (RIR). Fiscal deficit is measured as the excess of government expenditure over revenue receipts and non-debt capital receipts. Current account balance is a measure of trade balance, the sum of exports and imports of goods and services, net factor income and net transfers that have taken place in a year. The real effective exchange rate is the weighted average of Indian currency in relation to an index of currencies of 36 countries. The real interest rate is the lending interest rate. The FD and CAB are expressed as a percentage of real gross domestic product (RGDP) where the RGDP is adjusted for cyclical fluctuations using Hodrick-Prescott filter and REER and RIR is obtained after adjusting for inflation using wholesale price index (WPI). Data for FD, CAB and REER have been obtained from the Reserve Bank of India Handbook of Statistics on Indian Economy and that of RIR have been obtained from the IMF International Financial Statistics. For the period quarter-I of 1994 to quarter-IV of 2016, there are 92 observations on FD, CAB, REER and RIR.

Before examining the relevance of the twin deficit hypothesis in India, the data is subjected to various time series diagnostics. The first test is the stationatity test and the Augmented Dickey-Fuller (ADF) test has been applied to the regression equation,

$$\Delta Y_t = \beta_1 + \beta_2 t + \delta Y_{t-1} + \sum_{i=1}^{m} \alpha_i \Delta Y_{t-i} + \varepsilon_t \qquad (6.5)$$

where $Y_t$ is a variable at time $t$, $\varepsilon_t$ is the disturbance term that is generated from a white noise process. The ADF test is to test for the null hypothesis that the series has a unit root ($\delta = 0$) meaning that the series is non-stationary against the alternative hypothesis of the series being stationary. If a unit root (non-stationarity) exists, then $\delta$ would not be statistically different from zero. If the p-value of the coefficient of $Y_{t-1}$ is less than 0.05 at 5 percent level of significance, the null hypothesis is rejected indicating that the series is stationary.

If two time series data are non-stationary, there is a possibility that the two variables may be cointegrated. In other words, the two variables may have a long term or equilibrium relationship between them and there may exist a linear combination of the two variables such that the error term is stationary. The existence of cointegration between the variables is tested on the null hypothesis H0: no cointegration ($r$=0) against H1: presence of cointegration ($r$>0) by the eigen value and trace statistics defined as,

$$\text{Trace statistic: Trace} = -T \sum log\,(1 - \lambda_t^l) \;\; t=r+1,\ldots, p \qquad (6.6)$$

$$\text{Maximum eigen value statistic: } \lambda_{max}\,(r, r+1) = -T log(1 - \lambda_{t+1}^l) \qquad (6.7)$$

where $\lambda^1_{r+1},\ldots,\lambda^1_p$ are ($p$-$r$) number of estimated eigen values. When the absolute value of the computed trace statistic and the computed eigen value statistic are greater than their respective critical values, then the null hypothesis is rejected and there may exist at least one cointegrating relation between the variables. Then, the cointegration test is to test the hypothesis, H0: presence of one cointegrating relation ($r$=1) against H1: presence of more than one cointegrating relation among the variables ($r$>1). Based on the value of the computed trace statistic and the eigen value, null hypothesis is either accepted or rejected.

The existence of corelationship between variables does not necessarily imply causation or the direction of influence. The Granger-causality test allows determining the short-run or forecasting direction of the relations between the variables. In the two variable relations model, the Granger causality test postulate that *y* and *z* are affected by their own lags and the lags of the other variable,

$$y_t = \sum_{i=1}^{n} \alpha_i \, z_{t-i} + \sum_{i=1}^{n} \beta_j \, y_{t-j} + u_{1t} \tag{6.8}$$

$$z_t = \sum_{i=1}^{n} \gamma_i \, z_{t-i} + \sum_{j=1}^{n} \delta_j \, y_{t-j} + u_{2t} \tag{6.9}$$

There are two null hypotheses in case of a two variable system, H0: one variable does not granger cause the other against the alternative hypothesis (Ha): the variable granger causes the other. The coefficients $\alpha_i$, $\beta_j$, $\gamma_i$ and $\delta_j$ are jointly tested for their significance in order to determine the direction of causality.

## Structural Vector Auto-Regressive (SVAR) Method

The Vector Auto-regression (VAR) model is used to estimate the relationship between a group of variables where there is no a priori distinction of variables as endogenous and exogenous variables. Instead, the VAR model treats all variables on an equal footing and symmetrically by including lags of each of the dependent variable in the model. The information criteria like Akaike Information Criterion (AIC) or Schwarz Information Criterion (SIC) are used to choose the appropriate lag length for the VAR model. A two variable SVAR is given by,

$$y_t = b_{10} - b_{12} z_t + \gamma_{11} y_{t-1} + \gamma_{12} z_{t-1} + \varepsilon_{yt} \tag{6.10}$$

$$z_t = b_{20} - b_{21} y_t + \gamma_{21} y_{t-1} + \gamma_{22} z_{t-1} + \varepsilon_{zt} \tag{6.11}$$

where $y_t$ and $z_t$ are the current endogenous variables and $y_{t-1}$ and $z_{t-1}$ are the lags of $y_t$ and $z_t$ respectively and are predetermined. Assuming that $y_t$ and $z_t$ are stationary, $\varepsilon_{yt}$ and $\varepsilon_{zt}$ are white noise disturbances and are uncorrelated, equations (6.10) and (6.11) represent first-order SVAR with lag length of one. Both $y_t$ and $z_t$ affect each other and the coefficients are: $-b_{12}$ is the contemporaneous effect of a unit change of $z_t$ on $y_t$ and $y_{11}$ and $y_{12}$ are the effect of a unit change in $y_{t-1}$ and $z_{t-1}$ respectively on $y_t$. Similarly, $-b_{21}$ is the contemporaneous effect of a unit change of $y_t$ on $z_t$ and $y_{21}$ and $Y_{22}$ are the effect of a unit change in $y_{t-1}$ and $z_{t-1}$ respectively on $z_t$.

The matrix form of the S VAR equations can be written as,

$$\begin{bmatrix} 1 & b_{12} \\ b_{21} & 1 \end{bmatrix} \begin{bmatrix} y_t \\ z_t \end{bmatrix} = \begin{bmatrix} b_{10} \\ b_{20} \end{bmatrix} + \begin{bmatrix} \gamma_{11} & \gamma_{12} \\ \gamma_{21} & \gamma_{22} \end{bmatrix} \begin{bmatrix} y_{t-1} \\ z_{t-1} \end{bmatrix} + \begin{bmatrix} \varepsilon_{yt} \\ \varepsilon_{zt} \end{bmatrix} \tag{6.12}$$

Or $Bx_t = z_0 + z_1 x_{t-1} + \varepsilon_t$ (6.13)

where B = $\begin{bmatrix} 1 & b_{12} \\ b_{21} & 1 \end{bmatrix}$, $x_t = \begin{bmatrix} y_t \\ z_t \end{bmatrix}$, $z_0 = \begin{bmatrix} b_{10} \\ b_{20} \end{bmatrix}$, $z_1 = \begin{bmatrix} \gamma_{11} & \gamma_{12} \\ \gamma_{21} & \gamma_{22} \end{bmatrix}$, $x_{t-1} = \begin{bmatrix} y_{t-1} \\ z_{t-1} \end{bmatrix}$, $\varepsilon_t = \begin{bmatrix} \varepsilon_{yt} \\ \varepsilon_{zt} \end{bmatrix}$ (6.14)

Pre-multiplying equation (6.13) by $B^{-1}$,

$$B^{-1}Bx_t = B^{-1}z_0 + B^{-1}z_1x_{t-1} + B^{-1}\varepsilon_t \tag{6.15}$$

$$x_t = A_0 + A_1x_{t-1} + e_t \tag{6.16}$$

where $$A_0 = B^{-1}z_0,\ A_1 = B^{-1}z_1,\ e_t = B^{-1}\varepsilon_t \tag{6.17}$$

and $a_{i0}$ is element $i$ of the vector $A_0$, $a_{ij}$ is element in row $i$ and column $j$ of matrix $A_1$ and $e_{it}$ is the element $i$ of the vector $e_t$. The equations in standard SVAR form are,

$$y_t = a_{10} + a_{11}y_{t-1} + a_{12}z_{t-1} + e_{1t} \tag{6.18}$$

$$z_t = a_{20} + a_{21}y_{t-1} + a_{22}z_{t-1} + e_{2t} \tag{6.19}$$

The resulting SVAR model in matrix notation, with $p$ lag is,

$$y_t = \alpha_0 + \phi_1 y_{t-1} + \dots + \phi_p y_{t-p} + v_t \tag{6.20}$$

where $y_t$ and its lagged values are vectors of endogenous variables $v_t$ is a vector of non-auto-correlated disturbances, and $\phi$s are matrices of coefficients to be estimated.

The SVAR associated Impulse Response Function (IRF) defines the response of the dependent variable in the VAR model to shocks in the error terms, that is, the IRF detects the impact of a one-time shock in one of the innovations (the impulse) on current and future values of the endogenous variables (the responses). The general form for the IRF is,

$$y_t = \alpha + \varepsilon_t + \theta_1\varepsilon_{t-1} + \theta_2\varepsilon_{t-2} + \dots + \theta_i\varepsilon_{t-i} \tag{6.21}$$

where $y_t$ is a vector of the dependent variables, $\alpha$ is a vector of the constants, $\varepsilon_i$ is a vector of innovations for all variables that have been included in the SVAR model, and $\theta_i$ is a vector of parameters that measure the reaction of the dependent variable to innovations in all variables included in the SVAR model.

## 6.4 Empirical Analysis

The descriptive statistics of the variables used in the empirical relationship between fiscal deficit and current account balance along with their measures are presented in Table 6.1. The average fiscal deficit is 1.55 percent of RGDP and the mean current account balance is -1.29 percent of RGDP, indicating a deficit in CAB on an average. While the average REER is 90.001, the mean of RIR is 9.11 percent. The standard deviation of the variables shows the spread of the values, fiscal deficit has the lowest standard deviation of 0.99 and real effective exchange rate has the highest standard deviation of 6.72.

In the first step of econometric analysis, the variables are tested for the presence of unit root at levels as well as at first difference using the Augmented Dickey-Fuller (ADF) unit root test. The null hypothesis states the presence of

**Table 6.1: Descriptive Statistics of Variables used in the Twin Deficit Hypothesis Analysis**

| *Variable* | *Description* | *Mean* |
|---|---|---|
| FD | Fiscal deficit (percent of RGDP) | 1.5589 (0.997) |
| CAB | Current account balance (percent of RGDP) | -1.2931 (1.838) |
| REER | Real effective exchange rate | 90.001 (6.721) |
| RIR | Real interest rate | 9.1139 (2.778) |

**Note:** Standard deviations in parentheses.

unit root that is, the series is non-stationary against the alternative hypothesis that the series is stationary. From Table 6.2 which shows ADF unit root test, it can be observed that FD, RIR, REER and CAB are non-stationary at levels as their probability values exceed 0.05 leading to the acceptance of the null hypothesis that the series are non-stationary. However, they become stationary after taking the first difference and therefore are integrated of order 1, that is, the variables are I(1).

**Table 6.2: Augmented Dickey Fuller (ADF) Unit Root Test**

| *Variable* | *Description* | *At levels* | | *At first difference* | |
|---|---|---|---|---|---|
| | | *t-statistics* | *p-value* | *t-statistics* | *p-value* |
| FD | Fiscal deficit | -2.3978 | 0.1453 | -21.678 | 0.0001* |
| RIR | Real interest rate | -4.1758 | 0.2875 | -9.459 | 0.0000* |
| REER | Real effective exchange rate | -1.9038 | 0.3293 | -9.719 | 0.0000* |
| CAB | Current account balance | -2.5613 | 0.3744 | -10.751 | 0.0000* |

**Note:** *Rejection of null hypothesis of presence of unit root at 5 percent level of significance.

The Cointegration test is used to test the presence of a long term relationship between variables which are integrated of order 1. The null hypothesis is that there is no cointegration against the alternative hypothesis of cointegration between the variables. The result of the Johansen cointegration test presented in Table 6.3 shows that the p-values are high at 5 percent level of significance and the 0.05 critical values are greater than both the trace statistic and eigen value statistic indicating that there are no cointegrating equations between FD, RIR, REER and CAB. Therefore, the vector

**Table 6.3: Johansen Cointegration Test**

| *Hypothesised no. of Cointegrating equations* | *Trace statistic* | *0.05 critical value* | *Proba-bility* | *Maximum eigen statistic* | *0.05 critical value* | *proba-bility* |
|---|---|---|---|---|---|---|
| None | 38.90 | 40.17 | 0.06 | 29.18 | 34.162 | 0.08 |
| At most 1 | 9.72 | 24.27 | 0.87 | 4.976 | 17.80 | 0.96 |
| At most 2 | 4.75 | 12.32 | 0.60 | 4.588 | 11.22 | 0.54 |
| At most 3 | 0.16 | 4.13 | 0.74 | 0.158 | 4.13 | 0.74 |

autoregression can be applied to examine the relationship among the variables in the model.

The Table 6.4 presents the optimal lag length in the VAR model selected using VAR lag order selection criteria. The optimal lag length is 4 as indicated by LR, FPE, AIC and HQIC criteria. This suggests that each variable is lagged by 4 periods and the equation for each endogenous variable is regressed on 4 lags of itself and other endogenous variables in the system.

**Table 6.4: Lag Length Selection for VAR Estimation**

| *Lag* | *Log L* | *LR* | *FPE* | *AIC* | *SIC* | *HQIC* |
|---|---|---|---|---|---|---|
| 0 | -766.7995 | NA | 1097.583 | 18.3523 | 18.4681 | 18.3989 |
| 1 | -646.3550 | 226.5503 | 91.3456 | 15.8656 | 16.4443 | 16.0982 |
| 2 | -607.5589 | 69.2787 | 53.2301 | 15.3228 | 16.3646* | 15.7416 |
| 3 | -594.4610 | 22.1417 | 57.4232 | 15.3919 | 16.8967 | 15.9968 |
| 4 | -554.9175 | 63.0813* | 33.1991* | 14.8313* | 16.7991 | 15.6224* |
| 5 | -545.8359 | 13.6222 | 39.9603 | 14.9960 | 17.4269 | 15.9732 |
| 6 | -528.7335 | 24.0248 | 40.1502 | 14.9698 | 17.8636 | 16.1331 |
| 7 | -509.2533 | 25.5098 | 38.6207 | 14.8869 | 18.2438 | 16.2364 |
| 8 | -491.2327 | 21.8821 | 39.0913 | 14.8388 | 18.6587 | 16.3744 |

**Note:** * Lag order selected by the criterion. LR: sequential modified LR test statistic, FPE: Final prediction error, AIC: Akaike information criterion, SC: Schwarz information criterion, HQIC: Hannan-Quinn information criterion.

The structural VAR (SVAR) model accounting for the four variables along with their four lags are,

$$FD_t = c_{10} - b_{12}RIR_t - b_{13}REER_t - b_{14}CAB_t + \beta_{11}FD_{t-1} + \beta_{12}RIR_{t-1} + \beta_{13}REER_{t-1} + \beta_{14}CAB_{t-1} + \gamma_{11}FD_{t-2} + \gamma_{12}RIR_{t-2} + \gamma_{13}REER_{t-2} + \gamma_{14}CAB_{t-2} + \alpha_{11}FD_{t-3} + \alpha_{12}RIR_{t-3} + \alpha_{13}REER_{t-3} + \alpha_{14}CAB_{t-3} + \delta_{11}FD_{t-4} + \delta_{12}RIR_{t-4} + \delta_{13}REER_{t-4} + \delta_{14}CAB_{t-4} + \varepsilon_{FD_t}$$

$$RIR_t = c_{20} - b_{21}FD_t - b_{23}REER_t - b_{24}CAB_t + \beta_{21}FD_{t-1} + \beta_{22}RIR_{t-1} + \beta_{23}REER_{t-1} + \beta_{24}CAB_{t-1} + \gamma_{21}FD_{t-2} + \gamma_{22}RIR_{t-2} + \gamma_{23}REER_{t-2} + \gamma_{24}CAB_{t-2} + \alpha_{21}FD_{t-3} + \alpha_{22}RIR_{t-3} + \alpha_{23}REER_{t-3} + \alpha_{24}CAB_{t-3} + \delta_{21}FD_{t-4} + \delta_{22}RIR_{t-4} + \delta_{23}REER_{t-4} + \delta_{24}CAB_{t-4} + \varepsilon_{RIR_t}$$

$$REER_t = c_{30} - b_{31}FD_t - b_{32}RIR_t - b_{34}CAB_t + \beta_{31}FD_{t-1} + \beta_{32}RIR_{t-1} + \beta_{33}REER_{t-1} + \beta_{34}CAB_{t-1} + \gamma_{31}FD_{t-2} + \gamma_{32}RIR_{t-2} + \gamma_{33}REER_{t-2} + \gamma_{34}CAB_{t-2} + \alpha_{31}FD_{t-3} + \alpha_{32}RIR_{t-3} + \alpha_{33}REER_{t-3} + \alpha_{34}CAB_{t-3} + \delta_{31}FD_{t-4} + \delta_{32}RIR_{t-4} + \delta_{33}REER_{t-4} + \delta_{34}CAB_{t-4} + \varepsilon_{REER_t}$$

$$CAB_t = c_{40} - b_{41}FD_t - b_{42}RIR_t - b_{43}REER_t + \beta_{41}FD_{t-1} + \beta_{42}RIR_{t-1} + \beta_{43}REER_{t-1} + \beta_{44}CAB_{t-1} + \gamma_{41}FD_{t-2} + \gamma_{42}RIR_{t-2} + \gamma_{43}REER_{t-2} + \gamma_{44}CAB_{t-2} + \alpha_{41}FD_{t-3} + \alpha_{42}RIR_{t-3} + \alpha_{43}REER_{t-3} + \alpha_{44}CAB_{t-3} + \delta_{41}FD_{t-4} + \delta_{42}RIR_{t-4} + \delta_{43}REER_{t-4} + \delta_{44}CAB_{t-4} + \varepsilon_{CAB_t}$$

In matrix form,

$$\begin{bmatrix} 1 & b_{12} & b_{13} & b_{14} \\ b_{21} & 1 & b_{23} & b_{24} \\ b_{31} & b_{32} & 1 & b_{34} \\ b_{41} & b_{42} & b_{43} & 1 \end{bmatrix} \begin{bmatrix} FD_t \\ RIR_t \\ REER_t \\ CAB_t \end{bmatrix} = \begin{bmatrix} c_{10} \\ c_{20} \\ c_{30} \\ c_{40} \end{bmatrix} + \begin{bmatrix} \beta_{11} & \beta_{12} & \beta_{13} & \beta_{14} \\ \beta_{21} & \beta_{22} & \beta_{23} & \beta_{24} \\ \beta_{31} & \beta_{32} & \beta_{33} & \beta_{34} \\ \beta_{41} & \beta_{42} & \beta_{43} & \beta_{44} \end{bmatrix} \begin{bmatrix} FD_{t-1} \\ RIR_{t-1} \\ REER_{t-1} \\ CAB_{t-1} \end{bmatrix} +$$

$$\begin{bmatrix} \gamma_{11} & \gamma_{12} & \gamma_{13} & \gamma_{14} \\ \gamma_{21} & \gamma_{22} & \gamma_{23} & \gamma_{24} \\ \gamma_{31} & \gamma_{32} & \gamma_{33} & \gamma_{34} \\ \gamma_{41} & \gamma_{42} & \gamma_{43} & \gamma_{44} \end{bmatrix} \begin{bmatrix} FD_{t-2} \\ RIR_{t-2} \\ REER_{t-2} \\ CAB_{t-2} \end{bmatrix} + \begin{bmatrix} \alpha_{11} & \alpha_{12} & \alpha_{13} & \alpha_{14} \\ \alpha_{21} & \alpha_{22} & \alpha_{23} & \alpha_{24} \\ \alpha_{31} & \alpha_{32} & \alpha_{33} & \alpha_{34} \\ \alpha_{41} & \alpha_{42} & \alpha_{43} & \alpha_{44} \end{bmatrix} \begin{bmatrix} FD_{t-3} \\ RIR_{t-3} \\ REER_{t-3} \\ CAB_{t-3} \end{bmatrix} +$$

$$\begin{bmatrix} \delta_{11} & \delta_{12} & \delta_{13} & \delta_{14} \\ \delta_{21} & \delta_{22} & \delta_{23} & \delta_{24} \\ \delta_{31} & \delta_{32} & \delta_{33} & \delta_{34} \\ \delta_{41} & \delta_{42} & \delta_{43} & \delta_{44} \end{bmatrix} \begin{bmatrix} FD_{t-4} \\ RIR_{t-4} \\ REER_{t-4} \\ CAB_{t-4} \end{bmatrix} + \begin{bmatrix} \varepsilon_{FD_t} \\ \varepsilon_{RIR_t} \\ \varepsilon_{REER_t} \\ \varepsilon_{CAB_t} \end{bmatrix}$$

where the ordering of the variables is: fiscal deficit, real interest rate, real effective exchange rate and current account balance. That is,

$$BX_t = z_0 + z_1X_{t-1} + z_2X_{t-2} + z_3X_{t-3} + z_4X_{t-4} + \varepsilon_t \tag{6.22}$$

where,

$$B = \begin{bmatrix} 1 & b_{12} & b_{13} & b_{14} \\ b_{21} & 1 & b_{23} & b_{24} \\ b_{31} & b_{32} & 1 & b_{34} \\ b_{41} & b_{42} & b_{43} & 1 \end{bmatrix} \quad X_t = \begin{bmatrix} FD_t \\ RIR_t \\ REER_t \\ CAB_t \end{bmatrix} \quad z_0 = \begin{bmatrix} c_{10} \\ c_{20} \\ c_{30} \\ c_{40} \end{bmatrix} \quad z_1 = \begin{bmatrix} \beta_{11} & \beta_{12} & \beta_{13} & \beta_{14} \\ \beta_{21} & \beta_{22} & \beta_{23} & \beta_{24} \\ \beta_{31} & \beta_{32} & \beta_{33} & \beta_{34} \\ \beta_{41} & \beta_{42} & \beta_{43} & \beta_{44} \end{bmatrix}$$

$$z_2 = \begin{bmatrix} \gamma_{11} & \gamma_{12} & \gamma_{13} & \gamma_{14} \\ \gamma_{21} & \gamma_{22} & \gamma_{23} & \gamma_{24} \\ \gamma_{31} & \gamma_{32} & \gamma_{33} & \gamma_{34} \\ \gamma_{41} & \gamma_{42} & \gamma_{43} & \gamma_{44} \end{bmatrix} \quad z_3 = \begin{bmatrix} \alpha_{11} & \alpha_{12} & \alpha_{13} & \alpha_{14} \\ \alpha_{21} & \alpha_{22} & \alpha_{23} & \alpha_{24} \\ \alpha_{31} & \alpha_{32} & \alpha_{33} & \alpha_{34} \\ \alpha_{41} & \alpha_{42} & \alpha_{43} & \alpha_{44} \end{bmatrix}$$

$$z_4 = \begin{bmatrix} \delta_{11} & \delta_{12} & \delta_{13} & \delta_{14} \\ \delta_{21} & \delta_{22} & \delta_{23} & \delta_{24} \\ \delta_{31} & \delta_{32} & \delta_{33} & \delta_{34} \\ \delta_{41} & \delta_{42} & \delta_{43} & \delta_{44} \end{bmatrix} \quad \varepsilon_t = \begin{bmatrix} \varepsilon_{FD_t} \\ \varepsilon_{RIR_t} \\ \varepsilon_{REER_t} \\ \varepsilon_{CAB_t} \end{bmatrix}$$

The VAR in standard form is given by,

$$X_t = A_0 + A_1X_{t-1} + A_2X_{t-2} + A_3X_{t-3} + A_4X_{t-4} + e_t \tag{6.23}$$

where,

$$A_0 = B^{-1}z_0,\ A_1 = B^{-1}z_1,\ A_2 = B^{-1}z_2,\ A_3 = B^{-1}z_3,\ A_4 = B^{-1}z_4, e_t = B^{-1}\varepsilon_t \tag{6.24}$$

The standard form of the equations of VAR which are to be estimated in this paper are,

$$\begin{aligned} FD_t = c_{10} &+ \omega_{11}FD_{t-1} + \omega_{12}RIR_{t-1} + \omega_{13}REER_{t-1} + \omega_{14}CAB_{t-1} + \varphi_{11}FD_{t-2} \\ &+ \varphi_{12}RIR_{t-2} + \varphi_{13}REER_{t-2} + \varphi_{14}CAB_{t-2} + \theta_{11}FD_{t-3} + \theta_{12}RIR_{t-3} \\ &+ \theta_{13}REER_{t-3} + \theta_{14}CAB_{t-3} + \rho_{11}FD_{t-4} + \rho_{12}RIR_{t-4} + \rho_{13}REER_{t-4} \\ &+ \rho_{14}CAB_{t-4} + e_{1t} \end{aligned}$$

$$RIR_t = c_{20} + \omega_{21}FD_{t-1} + \omega_{22}RIR_{t-1} + \omega_{23}REER_{t-1} + \omega_{24}CAB_{t-1} + \varphi_{21}FD_{t-2} + \varphi_{22}RIR_{t-2} + \varphi_{23}REER_{t-2} + \varphi_{24}CAB_{t-2} + \theta_{21}FD_{t-3} + \theta_{22}RIR_{t-3} + \theta_{23}REER_{t-3} + \theta_{24}CAB_{t-3} + \rho_{21}FD_{t-4} + \rho_{22}RIR_{t-4} + \rho_{23}REER_{t-4} + \rho_{24}CAB_{t-4} + e_{2t}$$

$$REER_t = c_{30} + \omega_{31}FD_{t-1} + \omega_{32}RIR_{t-1} + \omega_{33}REER_{t-1} + \omega_{34}CAB_{t-1} + \varphi_{31}FD_{t-2} + \varphi_{32}RIR_{t-2} + \varphi_{33}REER_{t-2} + \varphi_{34}CAB_{t-2} + \theta_{31}FD_{t-3} + \theta_{32}RIR_{t-3} + \theta_{33}REER_{t-3} + \theta_{34}CAB_{t-3} + \rho_{31}FD_{t-4} + \rho_{32}RIR_{t-4} + \rho_{33}REER_{t-4} + \rho_{34}CAB_{t-4} + e_{3t}$$

$$CAB_t = c_{40} + \omega_{41}FD_{t-1} + \omega_{42}RIR_{t-1} + \omega_{43}REER_{t-1} + \omega_{44}CAB_{t-1} + \varphi_{41}FD_{t-2} + \varphi_{42}RIR_{t-2} + \varphi_{43}REER_{t-2} + \varphi_{44}CAB_{t-2} + \theta_{41}FD_{t-3} + \theta_{42}RIR_{t-3} + \theta_{43}REER_{t-3} + \theta_{44}CAB_{t-3} + \rho_{41}FD_{t-4} + \rho_{42}RIR_{t-4} + \rho_{43}REER_{t-4} + \rho_{44}CAB_{t-4} + e_{4t}$$

In these equations, ω's are the coefficients of the variables lagged by one year, φ's are the coefficients of the variables lagged by two years, θ's are the coefficients of the variables lagged by three years and ρ's are the coefficients of the variables lagged by four years. The VAR estimates of the coefficients of the equations are presented in Table 6.5.

**Table 6.5: VAR Estimates of the Parameters of FD, RIR, REER and CAB**

| *Parameter* | *FD* | *RIR* | *REER* | *CAB* |
|---|---|---|---|---|
| $\omega_{j1}$ | -0.1701***<br>(1.84) | -0.0586<br>(0.22) | 0.8662***<br>(1.87) | -0.3743**<br>(1.98) |
| $\varphi_{j1}$ | -0.2681*<br>(2.88) | 0.0007<br>(0.00) | 0.7459<br>(1.61) | -0.3387***<br>(1.78) |
| $\theta_{j1}$ | -0.1952**<br>(2.33) | -0.1543<br>(0.63) | -0.0595<br>(0.14) | -0.1513<br>(0.88) |
| $\rho_{j1}$ | 0.5312*<br>(6.43) | 0.1008<br>(0.42) | 1.1229*<br>(2.73) | 0.0307<br>(0.18) |
| $\omega_{j2}$ | -0.0683<br>(1.52) | 0.434*<br>(3.30) | 0.2811<br>(1.25) | 0.0014<br>(0.02) |
| $\varphi_{j2}$ | 0.0498<br>(1.05) | 0.2848**<br>(2.05) | -0.3348<br>1.41) | -0.1185<br>(1.22) |
| $\theta_{j2}$ | 0.0831***<br>(1.78) | 0.0592<br>(0.43) | -0.3214<br>(1.38) | -0.0039<br>(0.04) |
| $\rho_{j2}$ | 0.0277<br>(0.67) | 0.0560<br>(0.46) | -0.0649<br>(0.31) | 0.2361*<br>(2.77) |
| $\omega_{j3}$ | 0.0141<br>(0.57) | -0.2774*<br>(3.79) | 0.7917*<br>(6.37) | 0.0070<br>(0.14) |

*(Contd...)*

| | | | | |
|---|---|---|---|---|
| $\varphi_{j3}$ | -0.0132 (0.36) | 0.3209* (2.98) | 0.2454 (1.34) | -0.0231 (0.31) |
| $\theta_{j3}$ | -0.0376 (0.97) | -0.0211 (0.18) | -0.1694 (0.87) | -0.0047 (0.06) |
| $\rho_{j3}$ | 0.0734* (2.60) | -0.0385 (0.47) | -0.1104 (0.78) | 0.0285 (0.49) |
| $\omega_{j4}$ | -0.1303** (2.43) | -0.0445 (0.28) | 0.1545 (0.58) | 0.5330* (4.85) |
| $\varphi_{j4}$ | -0.0386 (0.61) | 0.1165 (0.62) | 0.2047 (0.67) | 0.0108 (0.08) |
| $\theta_{j4}$ | -0.0356 (0.57) | -0.1639 (0.87) | -0.0842 (0.26) | -0.1117 (0.85) |
| $\rho_{j4}$ | 0.0551 (1.00) | -0.0072 (0.04) | -0.2163 (0.79) | 0.2517** (2.24) |
| $c_{j0}$ | -2.6191*** (1.94) | 2.9340 (0.74) | 21.7918* (3.23) | -0.8564 (0.31) |
| R-square | 0.8709 | 0.8503 | 0.9345 | 0.9220 |
| Adjusted R-square | 0.7967 | 0.7715 | 0.8972 | 0.8368 |
| S.E. of regression | 0.6195 | 1.8138 | 3.0893 | 1.2683 |
| Sum squared residual | 27.2551 | 233.5922 | 677.6511 | 114.2260 |
| Log likelihood | -73.2944 | - 167.8212 | -214.6836 | -136.3437 |
| F-statistic | 9.0479 | 8.2529 | 22.3761 | 7.3022 |
| Prob. (F-statistic) | 0.0000 | 0.0000 | 0.0000 | 0.0000 |
| Mean of dependent variable | 1.5347 | 8.9860 | 89.9105 | -1.3280 |
| Std.dev. of dependent variable | 0.9757 | 2.7710 | 6.8604 | 1.8637 |
| AIC | 2.0521 | 4.2004 | 5.2655 | 3.4850 |
| SIC | 2.5307 | 4.6790 | 5.7441 | 3.9636 |
| HQIC | 2.2449 | 4.3932 | 5.4583 | 3.6778 |
| Durbin-Watson statistic | 1.9323 | 2.0402 | 2.0536 | 2.0154 |

**Note:** Absolute t-values in parentheses. j denotes variables FD, RIR, REER and CAB. Time lags are denoted as 1,2,3,4, and constant is denoted as cj0. * Significant at 1 percent level. ** Significant at 5 percent level. *** Significant at 10 percent level.

The results of the VAR estimates show that fiscal deficit is significantly influenced by its own lags. The first and third lags of real interest rate and the fourth lag of real effective exchange rate have significant impact on FD at 5 percent level of significance. However, only the first lag of CAB is affecting FD and the other lags do not have any significant effect on FD. The first and third lag of FD is significantly affecting RIR at 5 percent level of significance. The first two lags of RIR, CAB and REER have a statistically significant impact on RIR and CAB does not have any significant impact on RIR at

5 percent level of significance. While only the first and fourth lags of FD significantly affect the real effective exchange rate, the first 3 lags of RIR have a significant impact on REER. Except for the third lag, all the other lags of REER are affecting REER significantly and CAB has no impact on REER. While RIR has no impact on CAB at 5 percent level of significance, the first two lags of FD and the first, second and fourth lags of REER are significantly impacting CAB. Also, CAB is significantly affected by its own lags of first, second and fourth years.

Though the coefficients of the variables in the VAR model are estimated, it is important for the sequences of the variables to be stationary which holds true only if the stability condition of VAR is satisfied. Also, it is important to examine the stability of the model as it will indicate if the impact of the shocks in one variable on the other will die out or explode over the period. The stability condition of VAR requires that the characteristic roots of the polynomial lie outside the unit circle. From Figure 6.2 it is observed that the inverse roots of the AR characteristic polynomial lie inside the unit circle. Hence, the VAR model is stable and the sequences of FD, RIR, REER and CAB have a finite and time-invariant mean and variance.

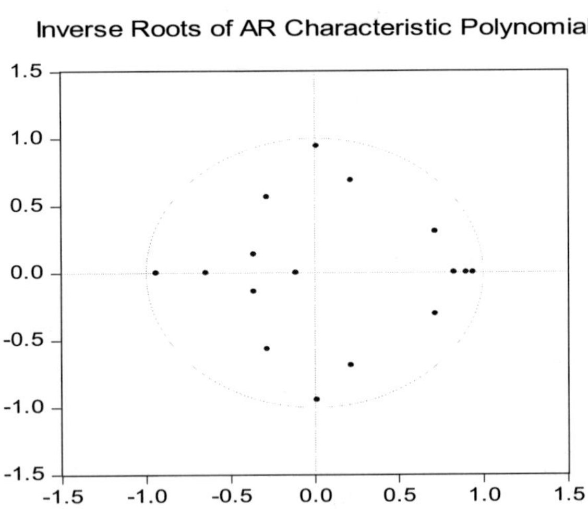


***Figure 6.2: Stability of VAR Model***

Further, the residuals obtained by estimating the equations in a VAR model are required to be tested for autocorrelation and heteroscedasticity as these may affect the efficiency of the estimated coefficients. The coefficients are efficient if the residuals are homoscedastic and serially uncorrelated. The variances of the residuals are tested for heteroscedasticity using White's heteroscedasticity under VAR residual heteroscedasticity test. The null hypothesis is that there is no heteroscedasticity against the alternative hypothesis of heteroscedasticity of the residuals. The residual test is presented in Table 6.6. The estimated results show that the residuals are homoscedastic. The null hypothesis of no heteroscedasticity is accepted at 5 percent level of significance as the p-value is 0.2 which is higher than 0.05. Also, the individual probabilities are greater than 0.05 leading to the acceptance of the null hypothesis and thereby supporting the homoscedasticity of the residuals. The residuals obtained from VAR are tested for serial correlation. The Table 6.7 presents the results of VAR residual serial correlation LM test. At all the four lags, the p-values exceed 0.05 at 5 percent significance level leading to the acceptance of the null hypothesis that the residuals are serially uncorrelated. Thus, the residuals are serially uncorrelated and homoscedastic and therefore the estimates of the VAR model are efficient. Therefore, the estimates of the Structural VAR (SVAR) coefficients can be obtained by placing appropriate restrictions.

**Table 6.6: VAR Residual Heteroscedasticity Test**

| *Chi-square* | | *df* | | *Probability* | |
|---|---|---|---|---|---|
| *439.7370* | | *320* | | *0.2000* | |
| ***Residual*** | ***R-square*** | ***F(32,55)*** | ***Probability*** | ***Chi-sq(32)*** | ***Probability*** |
| res1*res1 | 0.3595 | 0.9648 | 0.5339 | 31.6396 | 0.4847 |
| res2*res2 | 0.6314 | 2.9445 | 0.2002 | 55.5656 | 0.2060 |
| res3*res3 | 0.4361 | 1.3295 | 0.1740 | 38.3826 | 0.2026 |
| res4*res4 | 0.5678 | 2.2584 | 0.2039 | 49.9709 | 0.1224 |
| res2*res1 | 0.5341 | 1.9708 | 0.1133 | 47.0069 | 0.1423 |
| res3*res1 | 0.4298 | 1.2956 | 0.1963 | 37.8238 | 0.2206 |
| res3*res2 | 0.6772 | 3.6061 | 0.3000 | 59.5959 | 0.1022 |
| res4*res1 | 0.5043 | 1.7486 | 0.2338 | 44.3788 | 0.1715 |
| res4*res2 | 0.6117 | 2.7082 | 0.1006 | 53.8345 | 0.2092 |
| res4*res3 | 0.4190 | 1.2396 | 0.2380 | 36.8745 | 0.2536 |

**Note:** * Significant at 5 percent level.

**Table 6.7: VAR Residual Serial Correlation LM Test**

| *Lags* | *LM-statistics* | *Probability* |
|---|---|---|
| 1 | 12.47449 | 0.7107 |
| 2 | 22.84126 | 0.1180 |
| 3 | 14.60267 | 0.5539 |
| 4 | 11.66858 | 0.7665 |

**Note:** * Significant at 5 percent level.

The estimated coefficients of the VAR method report only the effects of the lags of other endogenous variables in the system for each of the endogenous variable. However, the current period effects of one variable on the other endogenous variables are not obtained in the VAR model. This necessitates the estimation of SVAR coefficients as they estimate current period impact also. The coefficients of the structural VAR model can be estimated by placing restrictions based on the theory of twin deficit hypothesis. The matrix of structural coefficients is given by,

$$B=\begin{bmatrix} 1 & b_{12} & b_{13} & b_{14} \\ b_{21} & 1 & b_{23} & b_{24} \\ b_{31} & b_{32} & 1 & b_{34} \\ b_{41} & b_{42} & b_{43} & 1 \end{bmatrix} \tag{6.25}$$

In the matrix B, the $b_{ij}$ is an element where *i* indicate the response variable and *j* includes the other endogenous variables in the system. The ordering of the variables is: fiscal deficit, real interest rate, real effective exchange rate and current account balance.

According to the twin deficit hypothesis, a deficit in fiscal balance leads to a deficit in the current account balance. According to the Mundell-Fleming model, this impact takes place through the RIR and REER. An increase in FD increases the domestic interest rate which leads to appreciation of REER. This further leads to a deficit in the CAB. Therefore, these can be imposed as restrictions and the restricted matrix B is given as,

$$B=\begin{bmatrix} 1 & 0 & 0 & 0 \\ b_{21} & 1 & 0 & 0 \\ b_{31} & b_{32} & 1 & 0 \\ b_{41} & b_{42} & b_{43} & 1 \end{bmatrix} \tag{6.26}$$

With these restrictions, the estimated SVAR coefficients of the matrix B are presented in Table 6.8.

**Table 6.8: SVAR Estimates of the Twin Deficit Hypothesis**

| *Parameter* | *Coefficient* | *Std. error* | *z-statistics* | *Probability* |
|---|---|---|---|---|
| $b_{21}$ | 0.9818 | 0.10660 | 9.2108 | 0.0000* |
| $b_{31}$ | -0.3958 | 0.14939 | -2.6499 | 0.0080* |
| $b_{32}$ | 0.71603 | 0.10660 | -6.7170 | 0.0000* |
| $b_{41}$ | -0.10004 | 0.15524 | -0.6444 | 0.0193* |
| $b_{42}$ | 0.06459 | 0.13111 | 0.4926 | 0.0223* |
| $b_{43}$ | -0.8674 | 0.10660 | -0.0813 | 0.0351* |

**Note:** * Significant at 5 percent level.

All the SVAR coefficients are significant at 5 percent level of significance. On average, the RIR increases by 9.8 percent for one percent increase in the fiscal deficit ($b_{21}$). The rise in RIR by one percent leads to 7.1 percent appreciation in the real exchange rate (indicated by $b_{32}$). While fiscal deficit directly affects CAB such that, a percentage change in FD leads to 1 percent rise in the current account deficit ($b_{41}$), the REER appreciation (due to rise in RIR caused by an increase in FD) by a unit increases the current account deficit by 8.6 percent ($b_{43}$).

The VAR results are augmented by the impulse response function (IRF) and the forecast error variance decomposition (FEVD). The IRF shows the persistence of the impact of a unit shock in one variable on the other variables in the system and FEVD shows the variation in the errors of a variable due to its own shocks and the shocks to other variables. The IRFs generates the effects of shocks to the e's on the entire time paths of the variables contained in the VAR system. In Figure 6.3, the IRFs are shown for a period of 8 quarters.

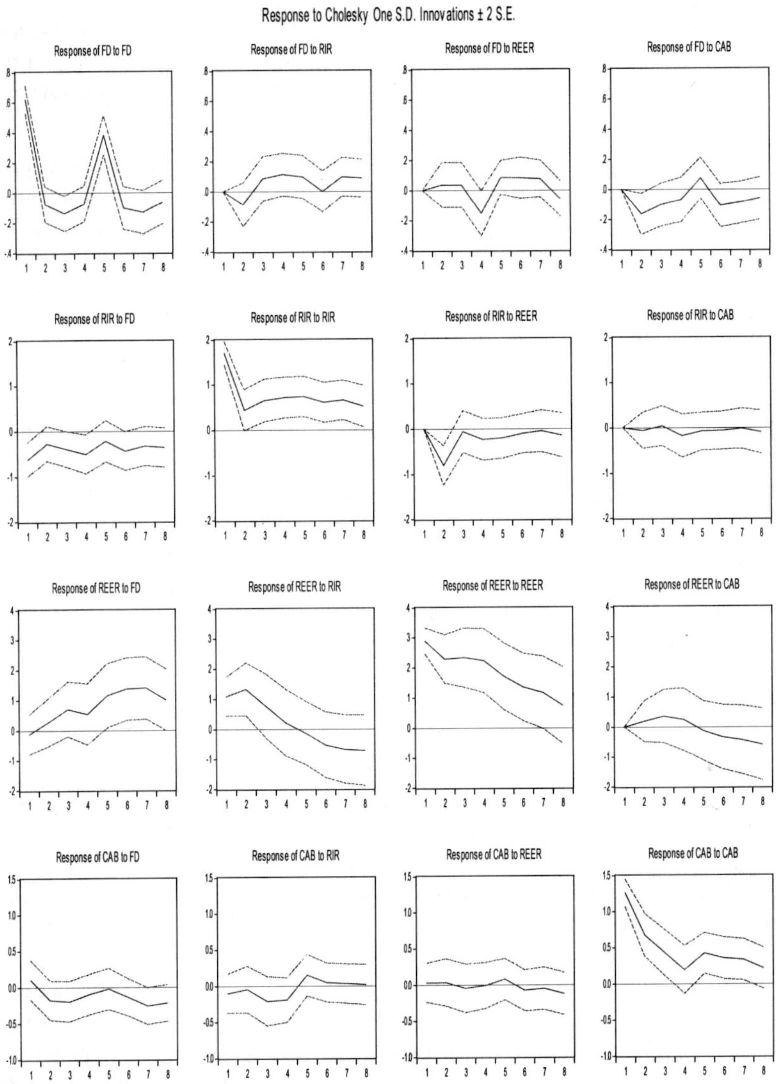


***Figure 6.3: Impulse Response Functions***

In Figure 6.3, the diagonal graphs show the response of a variable to its own shock by one standard deviation. The off diagonal graphs show the response of a variable to shock in other variables in the system by one standard deviation. The shortfalls in collections of indirect taxes due to sluggish growth in industrial production and imports are captured by the shocks to FD. A shock to fiscal deficit leads to a decline in fiscal deficit till the second quarter. However, it increases from the third quarter to the fifth quarter and starts declining thereafter. While both RIR and CAB decline initially and then become stable in response to their own shocks, a shock to REER leads to continuous decline in itself till the 8th quarter. RIR follows a cyclical pattern in response to shocks in FD and does not respond to shocks in current account balance. Also, REER is on an increasing trend over the 8 quarters to shocks in FD and is decreasing to shocks in RIR. However, when there are shocks in real effective exchange rate, current account balance is on the zero line till the 5th quarter indicating that there is no response. It increases slightly and then starts falling from the sixth quarter and becomes negative over time.

The Table 6.9 presents the variance decomposition of fiscal deficit over 10 quarters. In the first quarter, 100 percent of the variation in FD is due to its own shocks. Over the period that is in the 5th quarter, the variation in FD due to its own shocks reduces to 83.2 percent and 7 percent variation is explained by shocks to CAB. In the tenth quarter, around 9 percent of fluctuations in FD is caused by shocks to CAB and 14 percent variations is caused by shocks to RIR and REER each contributing to around 7 percent fluctuation in FD. About 88 percent of variation in RIR is due to its own shocks and the remaining 12 percent is divided between FD and CAB in the first quarter. However, in the tenth quarter, REER causes 8.5 percent fluctuations in RIR and variations in RIR due to shocks in FD, itself and CAB are 14 percent, 72 percent and 5 percent respectively. Around 82 percent and 17 percent of the fluctuations in REER is due to its own shocks and shocks in RIR respectively and FD and CAB do not lead to any significant variation in the first quarter. By tenth quarter, variation in REER due to shocks in FD and CAB has increased to 12 percent and 1.5 percent respectively. The fluctuation in REER caused by its own shocks has declined to 64 percent over the quarters. Almost 100 percent of the variation in CAB is due to its own shocks in the first quarter. This has fallen to 87 percent in the 10th quarter. The contribution of shocks to RIR and REER to fluctuations in CAB has risen from zero percent in the first quarter to 3.6 percent and 1.05 percent respectively in the tenth quarter and shocks in FD causes 8 percent fluctuations in CAB in the same period.

The Table 6.10 presents the results of Granger causality test at lag length 4. The null hypothesis under the test is that the variable under consideration does not Granger cause the other variable against the alternative hypothesis that the variable Granger cause the other variable. The FD Granger causes all the other variables RIR, REER and CAB. The null hypothesis that FD does

**Table 6.9: Variance Decomposition of FD, RIR, REER and CAB**

| *Variable* | *Period* | *Std. error* | *FD* | *RIR* | *REER* | *CAB* |
|---|---|---|---|---|---|---|
| FD | 1 | 0.6227 | 100.000 | 0.0000 | 0.0000 | 0.0000 |
| | 2 | 0.6536 | 92.2224 | 1.9848 | 0.1687 | 5.6236 |
| | 3 | 0.6830 | 88.8220 | 3.3227 | 0.2785 | 7.5766 |
| | 4 | 0.7150 | 82.1644 | 5.0738 | 4.6026 | 8.1589 |
| | 5 | 0.8198 | 83.1557 | 5.2072 | 4.6395 | 6.9974 |
| | 6 | 0.8357 | 81.6871 | 5.0109 | 5.1667 | 8.1350 |
| | 7 | 0.8602 | 79.5823 | 6.1689 | 5.4297 | 8.8189 |
| | 8 | 0.8721 | 78.0423 | 6.9346 | 5.5528 | 9.4701 |
| | 9 | 0.9357 | 78.1198 | 7.2084 | 6.0237 | 8.6479 |
| | 10 | 0.9415 | 77.4515 | 7.1264 | 6.3525 | 9.0695 |
| RIR | 1 | 2.9528 | 11.3956 | 88.062 | 0.0000 | 0.5419 |
| | 2 | 3.8514 | 11.1910 | 76.4192 | 11.5922 | 0.7968 |
| | 3 | 4.4488 | 13.3140 | 75.4010 | 10.5505 | 0.7343 |
| | 4 | 4.7750 | 15.5907 | 73.2240 | 9.2715 | 1.9137 |
| | 5 | 4.9384 | 14.6048 | 74.3641 | 8.4951 | 2.5358 |
| | 6 | 5.0471 | 15.3466 | 73.1345 | 8.3060 | 3.2127 |
| | 7 | 5.1218 | 14.8603 | 73.4098 | 8.3248 | 3.4049 |
| | 8 | 5.1394 | 14.7733 | 73.0725 | 8.1443 | 4.0097 |
| | 9 | 5.1592 | 14.5193 | 72.7702 | 8.4691 | 4.2413 |
| | 10 | 5.1709 | 14.3411 | 72.2590 | 8.4874 | 4.9123 |
| REER | 1 | 1.2766 | 0.4196 | 17.0986 | 82.4569 | 0.0247 |
| | 2 | 1.4581 | 0.7069 | 27.6507 | 71.3961 | 0.2460 |
| | 3 | 1.5508 | 2.5194 | 27.1576 | 69.3481 | 0.9747 |
| | 4 | 1.5787 | 2.7511 | 25.0967 | 70.7284 | 1.4235 |
| | 5 | 1.6474 | 5.8296 | 23.7998 | 68.8713 | 1.4991 |
| | 6 | 1.6980 | 9.1591 | 22.8203 | 66.5727 | 1.4477 |
| | 7 | 1.7541 | 11.5071 | 22.3010 | 64.7857 | 1.4058 |
| | 8 | 1.7862 | 11.7631 | 22.2591 | 64.4996 | 1.4777 |
| | 9 | 1.8061 | 12.1132 | 22.1000 | 64.2852 | 1.5013 |
| | 10 | 1.8218 | 12.2462 | 22.0003 | 64.2075 | 1.5459 |
| CAB | 1 | 1.8114 | 0.6152 | 0.0000 | 0.0000 | 99.3842 |
| | 2 | 1.9875 | 2.0065 | 0.0159 | 0.0020 | 97.9751 |
| | 3 | 2.1043 | 3.4474 | 1.2098 | 0.1760 | 95.1667 |
| | 4 | 2.2571 | 3.7886 | 2.3658 | 0.1880 | 93.6574 |
| | 5 | 2.3585 | 3.5091 | 3.5638 | 0.2560 | 92.6709 |
| | 6 | 2.4445 | 4.0398 | 3.5856 | 0.5597 | 91.8145 |
| | 7 | 2.5208 | 6.2406 | 3.4742 | 0.6148 | 89.6702 |
| | 8 | 2.5646 | 7.6754 | 3.3752 | 0.9745 | 87.9747 |
| | 9 | 2.5953 | 7.5365 | 3.5885 | 1.0352 | 87.8396 |
| | 10 | 2.6148 | 7.9946 | 3.6354 | 1.0585 | 87.3113 |

not Granger cause RIR, REER and CAB are rejected as the p-values are less than 0.05 at 5 percent level of significance. The real interest rate (RIR) also causes REER and CAB through its impact on capital inflows. Also, the null hypothesis that REER does not granger cause CAB is rejected at 5 percent level. This result is obvious as the change in exchange rate affects the imports and exports which is one of the principal component of CAB. However, the CAB does not Granger cause any of the variables in the system as the p-values indicate. Therefore, from the SVAR, IRF and Granger causality analyses, it can be inferred that the fiscal deficit affects the current account balance in India through the interlinking variables RIR and REER for the time period 1994 (quarter-I) to 2016 (quarter-IV) validating the relevance of twin deficit hypothesis in the Indian economy.

**Table 6.10: Pairwise Granger Causality Test of Twin Hypothesis**

| *Null hypothesis* | *F-Statistics* | *Probability* |
|---|---|---|
| REER does not Granger cause FD | 1.35427 | 0.2575 |
| FD does not Granger cause REER | 2.42824 | 0.0447 |
| RIR does not Granger cause FD | 1.47310 | 0.2184 |
| FD does not Granger cause RIR | 1.01460 | 0.0451 |
| CAB does not Granger cause FD | 0.47526 | 0.7538 |
| FD does not Granger cause CAB | 4.24717 | 0.0037 |
| RIR does not Granger cause REER | 1.29642 | 0.0188 |
| REER does not Granger cause RIR | 4.92751 | 0.1014 |
| CAB does not Granger cause REER | 2.55451 | 0.1454 |
| REER does not Granger cause CAB | 1.71920 | 0.0442 |
| CAB does not Granger cause RIR | 3.24180 | 0.2163 |
| RIR does not Granger cause CAB | 1.94639 | 0.0111 |
| Sample: 1994Q1 2016Q4 | Lags 4 | No. of obs.: 88 |

## 6.5 Conclusion

The causal relationship between fiscal deficit (FD) and current account balance (CAB) has been referred as twin deficit hypothesis and both the theoretical explanations and the empirical evidences have been controversial. This paper examines the relevance of twin deficit hypothesis in India for the period 1994-2016 by including the interlinking variable interest rate (RIR) and exchange rate (REER). Treating these variables as endogenous, the Structural Vector Autoregressive (SVAR) model has been estimated. The empirical results of this paper lend support to the existence of a causal relationship between budget deficit and trade deficit in India during 1994-2016. The SVAR coefficients show a negative impact implying that a positive shock given to FD worsens the CAB. The current account deficit, while not directly determined by fiscal deficit, is significantly influenced by RIR and REER. The IRF indicates that a positive shock to FD leads to an increase in the domestic interest rate. This appreciates the real exchange rate of the domestic currency which makes the exports costlier and imports cheaper and thereby widening the current account deficit.

The expansionary fiscal policy of the Indian government leads to a rise in government expenditure inducing the fiscal balance to run in deficit. This rise in government expenditure leads to increase in RIR inducing the exchange rate of the economy (rupees) to appreciate. With appreciation of the rupee, the import of foreign goods and services rises such that the trade balance runs into deficit. This trade deficit leads to current account deficit in the Indian economy. Hence, there is unidirectional causality from fiscal deficit to current account deficit. Therefore, policy changes by the internal sector of the economy affects the external sector in India. Thus, the results of this paper are consistent with the Keynesian proposition and validate the twin deficit hypothesis in Indian economy during the period 1994-2016.

# Section - III
# Limited Dependent Variables Econometrics

# 7

# The Effects of Birth Spacing and Maternal Education on Child Mortality: Probit and Logit Estimation of Child Survival in India

## Abstract

*Within the household, mother's decision on the number of children, birth spacing and investments in child health are crucial for survival and growth of children. Maternal education is an important factor that affects the female age at marriage, age at first birth, spacing between child births and child healthcare practices, and ultimately determines the risk of child death in a household. If the mother is educated the health of child improves and the risk of child death is reduced. This paper estimates the effects of mother's education and birth spacing on child mortality using the NFHS-3 data for 2005-06 pertaining to the state of Rajasthan, and applying the probit and logit models. The results of the econometric estimation of this study shows that birth spacing and maternal education have high statistically significant negative effect on both male and female child mortality. As spacing between births and mother's education increases, the probability of child death in a household decreases. The estimated results show that the effects of mother's education and birth spacing are more negatively pronounced on the risk of male child death than the death of a female child. The study also shows that the risk of death of the female child is high than male child when there are more number of children in the family. Improving maternal education and increasing spacing between births will reduce not only the number of children born to a woman but also the chance of child dying before the age of 5.*

**Key words:** *child mortality, birth spacing, female education, probit and logit estimation*

## 7.1 Introduction

Child mortality, especially in rural areas, continues to be a major challenge despite rapid progress in health care. Nearly two million children below the age of 5 die every year in India. Further, India accounts for one-fifth of newborn deaths, those dying within a month of birth and also India accounts for one-third of the undernourished children. According to World Bank, India's child mortality rate, with 65.5 per 1000 live births in 2009, is worse than that of many less developed countries like Bangladesh and Sri Lanka whose mortality rates are only 61 and 21 per 1000 live births. The average rate of reduction in child mortality in India is only 2.9. The high child mortality rate in less developed countries like India is primarily due to the poor socio-economic conditions with lack of mother's education, poor family, limited parental resources, lack of public services in rural areas like safe drinking water, sanitation, etc. Moreover, in developing countries, poor families have more number of children in order to raise the future income. When the income is limited, and there are many children in family, parents are not able to provide enough resources necessary to nourish the children and then children become victims of many diseases which lead to child mortality (Makepeace and Pal, 2008). Hence, children in low income countries face much higher risk of mortality compared to developed countries. In India the main cause for death of a child is diarrhea due to lack of safe drinking water. According to NFHS-3, 2005-06 data, in India only 64 percent of children living in rural areas are treated for diarrhea. When child suffers from health problems and if immediate treatments are not given, it naturally leads death of child. This problem is faced by illiterate parents who are unable to diagnosis the illness of their child and thus lack in providing the treatment to the child. Therefore, parental education, especially mother's education, plays a vital role in reducing child mortality. The low level of maternal education predisposes children to higher death risk (Arulampalam and Bhalotra, 2008).

Since the seminal work by John Caldwell who examined the role of maternal education on child mortality in Nigeria and outlined potential pathways through which mother's level of schooling could affect the child health (Caldwell, 1979), a great deal of research has focused on substantiating the independent and causal relationship between maternal schooling and child health. Mother's education plays vital role in reducing the child mortality. The mother monitors the health of her children, diagnoses illness, treats and follows up for complications, and in many developing countries, the mother is often the only source of this care. In addition, her daily decisions with respect to nutrition, hygiene and exposure to environmental hazards area major determinant of the health of her children. If mother is literate she can take care of herself during pregnancy which brings better health outcome of her offspring. According to the Census of India 2011, population growth slowed down and the number of literates has grown, especially among women. India's literacy rate has gone up to 74 percent nationwide for people aged 7 and older from 65 percent in 2001. For males it has risen to 82 percent from 75 percent and for females it has risen to 65 percent from 54 percent. Percentage growth in literacy during 2001-2011 is 38.8 percent, for males it is 32 percent and for females it is 49 percent; Kerala is at highest rate with 94 percent and lowest is Bihar and Rajasthan with 64 percent and 67 percent respectively.

The 2011 Census also shows a disturbing fact that the sex ratio for children below 6 years has dropped between 2001 and 2011. While the overall sex ratio has shown improvement, from 933 women per 1000 men to 940, child sex ratio (0-6 yrs) has worsened from 927 to 914 girls for every 1000 boys. The total number of children in 0-6 age group is 159 million, 5 million less since 2001. Haryana is at the lowest 830 per 1000 boys, while Mizoram, Meghalaya and Arunachal Pradesh have the highest child sex ratio. The gender imbalance continues despite a ban on SDT (sex determination test) based on ultrasound scans and sex selection abortion. In many parts of India there is very strong male preference in the family, expecting the future income to be raised. In order to have at least one male child in the family, women have to give birth many children till the male child is born, importantly with very short birth intervals. When birth spacing between the siblings is too close, it affects the health of not only the mother, but also the health of both the older and younger siblings (Makepeace and Pal, 2008). With limited resources, parents are strained to allocate limited resources among many children at the same time. If there is enough spacing between the births the older may not require so much attention as the younger and parents can pay their attention in bringing up the younger one. Moreover, most educated mothers prefer to have fewer, one or two, children and spacing between births, that ultimately leading to lower child mortality.

There has been a long tradition in social sciences investigating the relationship between fertility and mortality in low income countries. There has also been a long literature in demography that suggests that longer birth spacing (and therefore lower fertility) is associated with lower child mortality. Spacing between births also impacts the health of the child. The explanation for this inverse relationship between birth spacing and child mortality include, among others, less maternal depletion and more resources and parental care per child. Therefore, the spacing child birth has important consequences not only for the child health but also for older and younger siblings (Rosenzweig, 1986). With low birth intervals and hence poor health, the risk of child mortality is high.

Hence, this paper aims to analyse the effects of birth spacing, maternal education and number of children on child mortality in a household. Mother's education is the single most important intervening factor from the point of view of health of children and decision-making in the household that influences both birth spacing and number of children. Empirically, the paper estimates the probability of a child death in a household using the NFHS-3 for 2005-06 for the state of Rajasthan consisting of 2023 samples, and applying the probit and logit models.

## 7.2 A Brief Review of Recent Studies

Many empirical studies have found a positive cross-sectional association between maternal education and child health and a negative relationship between birth spacing and child mortality in diverse settings and in the same settings at different points in time. Further, examination of the role increasing women's education plays in reducing infant or child mortality has produced more nuanced results (Fuchs, Pamuk and Lutz, 2010). Though the strength of the relationship between mother's education and child health seems to be gradually reduced, when other factors such as family income or other material resources, family size or structure, reproductive behaviour indicators (age at first birth and birth intervals), piped water, sanitation improvements, communication with spouse, female status, health information and knowledge and health services utilisation are introduced into the model, but not eliminated (Heaton et al., 2005). In fact, the observed results show that maternal education working through a variety of causal pathways, such as increasing economic resources, knowledge, and empowerment and through more proximate mechanisms, such as change in reproductive behavior and health services utilisation, that improve the health of children and reduce child mortality. Further, to the extent that increased mother's schooling delays childbearing into adulthood, the greater risk of infant mortality as a consequence of maternal physical immaturity is reduced. In addition, since low maternal education is associated with a larger number of children ever born and childbearing continuing late into the reproductive years, increased maternal education reduces the risks associated with late childbearing and short birth interval (Hobcraft, 1993).

Examining the relative contribution of a number of factors to the decline in infant mortality in Malaysia between 1946 and 1975, Da Vanzo and Hadicht (1986), using the Malayasian Family Life Survey, finds that increases in maternal education level explained nearly half of the reduction in infant mortality rate over the period. They also observe that, contrary to their expectation, the relationship between maternal education and infant mortality has been stronger during 1961-1975 than during 1946-1960.

Pena et al. (1999) examining both fertility and infant mortality trends in Leon, Nicaragua between 1964 and 1993 conclude that while the observed dramatic increase in female education instituted by the revolutionary government in 1979 was a major contributor to the overall drop in the fertility during the 1980s, the decline in infant mortality was primarily the result of the concomitant expansion of primary health services that mainly benefited uneducated mothers.

In India, examining the mother education-child health relationship at a more specific level, Jalan and Ravallion (2003) finds that maternal education compensated for poverty in rural India by providing knowledge related to both water safety and treatment of diarrhea, especially the piped water source located within the house of mothers with no education.

However, Cleland and van Ginneken (1988) combining data from 16 WFS surveys in developing countries and adjusting for the reproductive variables, finds no reduction in the effect of 4-6 years of maternal schooling on post-neonatal mortality, and only minimal reduction for women with 7+ years of education. Similarly, analysing the DHS survey data, Bicego and Boerma (1993) finds that inclusion of 'family formation' variables (maternal age, birth order and birth interval) has either no effect or acted to increase the risk ratio of the lowest to highest maternal education group for both neo-natal deaths and deaths at ages 1-23 months.

It has also long been hypothesised that increasing education of women in developing countries improves child health by providing familiarity with more modem behaviour, including personal behaviour related directly or indirectly to health and use of 'modem' health services - as opposed to traditional sources of medical care. There is some evidence that more educated women make greater use of antenatal care during pregnancy in both more developed and less developed countries (Wong et al., 1987; Bicego and Boerma, 1993; Pebley et al., 1996; Raghupathy, 1996; Govindasamy and Ramesh, 1997). In developing countries, higher maternal education has been shown to be a significant predictor not only of earlier and more frequent antenatal visits, but also to a shift from traditional to modem care providers in both urban and rural settings (Wong et al., 1987).

For India, Arulampalam and Bhalotra (2008) investigate whether the actual event of death of a child results in a higher risk of death for the next child in the family. This scarring effect, a positive correlation of sibling death risk, given the natural sequencing of siblings in time, is related to the maternal education. Family with low level of maternal education predisposes their children to higher death risk. In almost all the states of India, the scarring effect is large except Punjab (the richest state) and Kerala (the state that is most advanced in socio-economic terms) in which the evidence of scarring was weak. Thus, with educated mother in the family, the survival chances of child are higher as she can avoid the risk that caused child death not to happen to other children.

The death of a child in a family shortens the time to the next birth. This process may be set off in either of two ways. One possibility, which is referred to as the fecundity hypothesis, is that the death of an infant results in the mother ceasing to breastfeed, and thereby, being able to conceive sooner than otherwise (Bongaarts and Potter, 1983). An alternative is the replacement hypothesis, according to which the death of a child leads parents to (intentionally) conceive sooner in a desire to replace their loss (Preston, 1978; Rosenzweig and Schultz, 1983). Whatever may be the mechanism for reduced birth interval, reduced birth intervals cause high risk of child death, because it takes time for an under-nourished mother to recover physiologically from a birth, and to replenish her stock of the nutrients essential to support the next pregnancy. There is plenty of evidence in the demographic and medical literature that short preceding birth intervals result in higher death risk (Cleland and Sathar, 1984; Stephansson et al., 2003), especially amongst poor women (Rawlings et al., 1995). Many studies have suggested that a minimum interval of about 24 months is needed (Pebley and Da Vanzo, 1993), but in India, almost 40 percent of birth intervals are shorter than 24 months.

Makepeace and Pal (2006) emphasise birth spacing between children so that the family can make the optimum use of the limited resources before each child is born. If there is limited spacing between the children, the older child may not receive as much attention as required by the younger sibling, otherwise it is constraint for parents to allocate the limited resources to both the children at same time. This indirectly affects the health of the child as parents are not able to pay attention to all the children simultaneously. Similarly, too long gap between siblings can again have adverse effect on the health of the child. According to psychology literature, the older child may resent the attention paid to the younger sibling as the child has had more time alone with parents. Further, if the spacing is short, an older sibling may not be independent when the younger sibling is born and both children would require the close attention of their parents, which in turn may cause a strain on parents, adversely affecting health of both the current and the elder child.

Thus, this brief review shows that birth order and birth spacing are crucial for child survival and maternal education is strongly associated with reduction in child mortality. Even in poor families, maternal education has great impact on the health of the child, as mother is the decision-maker at home. Educated mother takes right decision regarding the health of the child and prefer small and nuclear family. Mothers who are educated make the optimum use of health services provided, and their reproductive behaviour is also towards less desired children, spacing between births, concentration on nutrients to improve health of children.

## 7.3 Data and Methodology

This paper uses the nationwide National Family Health Survey 2005-06 (NFHS-3) data in the empirical analysis. The NFHS-3 is the third in a series of national surveys; earlier NFHS surveys were carried out in 1992-93 (NFHS-1) and 1998-99 (NFHS-2). The NFHS is a household survey which will provide indicators of population, health, and nutrition by background characteristics at the national and state levels. The NFHS-3 survey included more than 2,30,000 women aged 15-49 and men aged 15-54 throughout India. This paper uses the NFHS-3 data for the state of Rajasthan including rural and urban areas to study the impact of birth spacing, number of children, and maternal education on child mortality. The sample for Rajasthan is 2023 households. The survey contains rich data on health, education, standard of living, family size, contraceptive use, birth spacing and other aspects of household collected through 1164 questions.

The characteristics of the NFHS-3 samples are discussed below. The Figure 7.1 shows the education level of both men and women of age 15-49 in India for the year 2005-06. Among men only 18 percent of population has no education, whereas 41 percent of women are uneducated. While 35 percent of men have completed education of 10 years and above, among women only 14 percent of women have 8-9 years of completed education, and 22 percent of women have attained 10 years and above education.

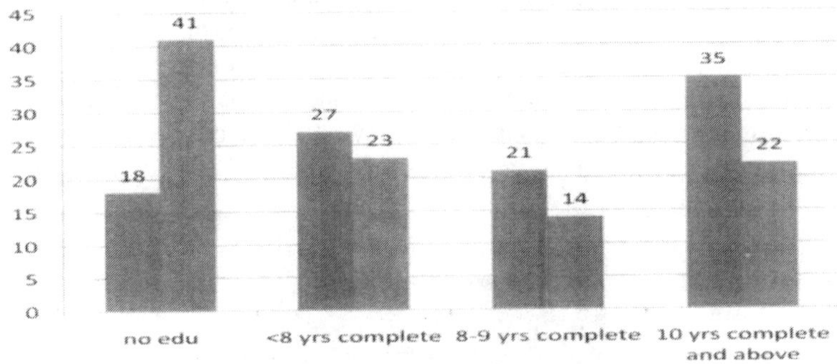


***Figure 7.1: Distribution of NFHS Samples by Education (percent)***

The Figure 7.2 shows health indicators for male and female children. For both sexes, child mortality is high; female child mortality is 79 per 1000 live births and for male it is 70 per 1000 live births. Infant mortality is almost the

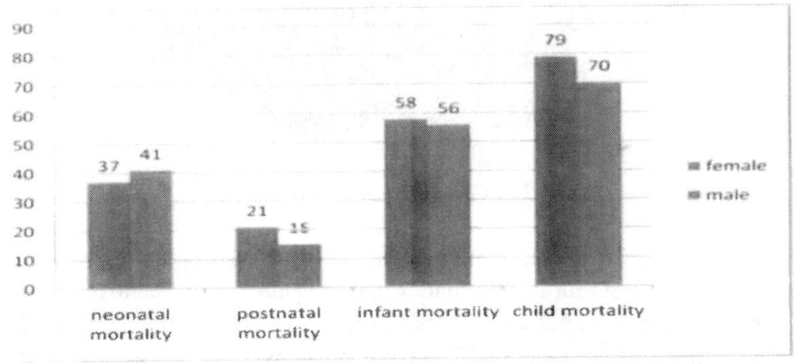


***Figure 7.2: Child Mortality Rates by Sex (percent)***

same, 56 and 58, for both male and female children. Neonatal mortality is high for male children compared to female children, 41 per 1000 live births for males and 37 per 1000 live births for females. However, postnatal mortality is high for female children with 21 per 1000 live births compared to male children with 15 per 1000 live births.

Length of birth intervals also has impact on the health of child. Birth intervals are strongly associated with child mortality. Children born too close to a previous birth are at increased risk of health problems and of dying at an early age. The Figure 7.3 shows the statistics of birth intervals in India for the year 2005-06 from NFHS-3. Nearly 34 percent of births occur within 24-35 months after the previous child is born. Only 10 percent births take place with gap if 60 months and above from the previous born. With birth intervals of 36-47 months 19 percent of births occur. With 48-59 months of birth intervals only 9 percent of births occur. Eleven percent of births occur within 7-17 months after the previous child is born. Thus, about 61percent of non-first births occur less than 36 months after the preceding birth. The Figure 7.4 shows the nutritional status of children in the states of India for the year 2005-06. On the average, India has 43 percent of underweight children, below the age 5. Among the states, Sikkim has the lowest, 20 percent of underweight children, whereas Madhya Pradesh has the highest, 60 percent of children who are underweight.

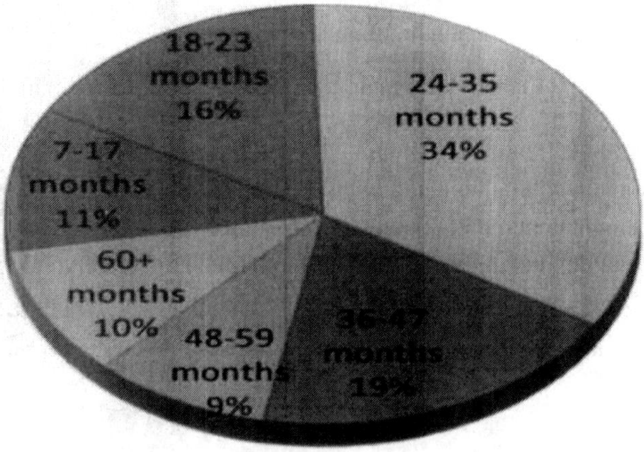


*Figure 7.3: Child Birth Intervals (percent)*

The Figure 7.5 presents the percentage of population among men and women in India both rural and urban who are regularly exposed to media like TV, radio and newspaper for the year 2005-06. In urban India, compared to the 93 percent of men, about 87 percent of women are exposed to media. In rural areas, 73 percent of men are exposed to media, but only 54 percent rural women are exposed to media. The media exposure facilitates household awareness of health and hygiene practices not only for women but also for children, as well as exposure to modern contraceptive methods that also facilitates birth spacing. As can be observed from the Figure 7.6, the contraceptive use has increased through the successive periods of NFHS-I, NFHS-II, NFHS-III both in rural and urban areas. Overall, the contraceptive use increased from 41 percent to 56 percent between 1992-93 and 2005-06. The Figure 7.7 presents the trends in fertility rate during this period clearly showing a decreasing trend.

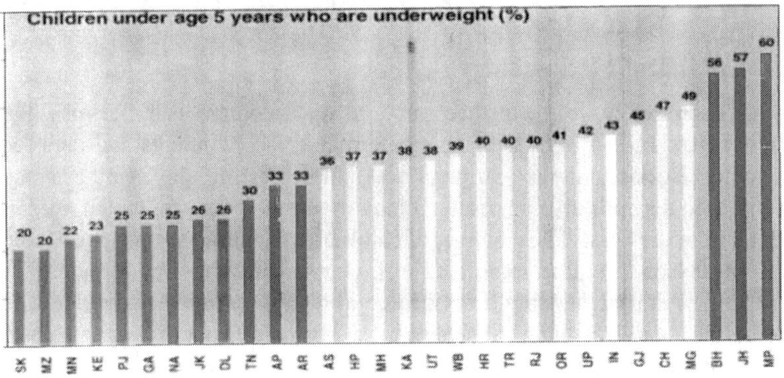


*Figure 7.4: Child Nutritional Status (percent)*

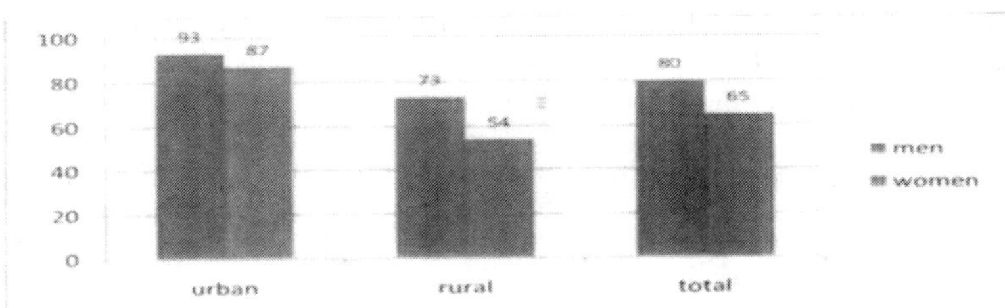


*Figure 7.5: Media Exposure of Population in India (percent)*

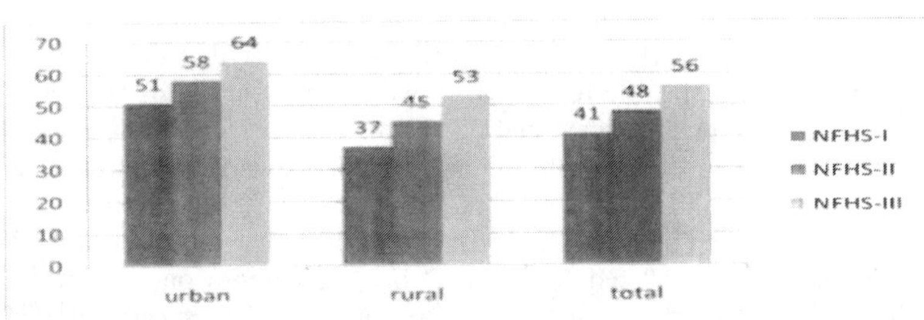


*Figure 7.6: Contraceptive Use in India (percent)*

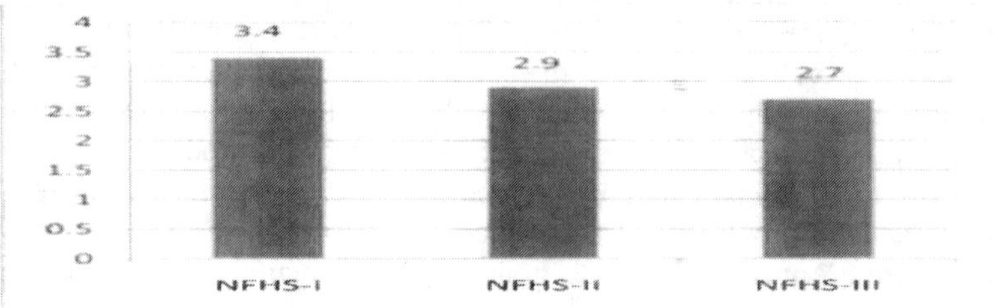


*Figure 7.7: Trends in Fertility in India*

## 7.4 Empirical Methodology

Theoretically, following the standard microeconomic framework, the family maximises the total income of the household, parents and children together. Besides, market earnings non-labour income, the income of the household depends also on health, which in turn, depends on the number of children in the family. The number of children is supposed to raise household income by contributing more earnings. But, raising more children means reduced birth spacing and diminished child quality in terms of child health. When the family's resources are constrained, resource distribution among many children reduces the health of the children and thereby the future earnings capacity of children. This trade-off between quantity and quality (measured by health) is central to the neoclassical approach to household behaviour (Becker, 1965; 1981; Becker and Tomes, 1976), essentially a static model, later extended by Rosenzweig (1986) as a sequential model incorporating birth spacing and sibling effects on child health.

### Health Production Function

A key feature of the household production function approach is the health production function, defined as,

$$H_{ij} = \alpha_1 A_{ij} + \alpha_2 (A_{i,j} - A_{i-1,j}) + \alpha_3 (A_{i+1,j} - A_{i,j}) + \alpha_4 Z_{ij} + \lambda_j + u_{ij} \quad (7.1)$$

where $H_{ij}$ the quality of child $i$ born to the family $j$ is assumed to depend on its birth order $i$, the age of mother at the time of birth of this child $A_i$, the intervals between its birth and prior and subsequent births, measured by the age of the mother, and child specific resources $Z_{ij}$, with $\alpha_1$ measuring the impact of mother's age, $\alpha_2$ prior spacing and $\alpha_3$ posterior spacing, $\alpha_4$ child specific resources, $\lambda_j$ an unobserved quality component common to all children in the family, and $\varepsilon_{ij}$ a child specific random error. The prior birth spacing is not observed for the first born child and posterior birth spacing for last born child. For the first child $\alpha_2 = 0$ and for last child $\alpha_3 = 0$. Therefore, only for middle order children the birth spacing effects are considered. The specification of equation (7.1) describes the household health production technology, displaying a jointness of spacing decision - an increase in the parental age at birth of child *i*, affects its older and younger siblings post and prior birth intervals. This interdependence implies that, even in the absence of differences in child specific endowments ($u_{ij} = 0$), it is unlikely that parents could simultaneously equalise child specific resource across children and equalise quality outcomes because of the sequential nature of childbearing. Thus, child specific investment in health will be correlated with birth order and spacing as well as children's endowments. It is also to be noted here that the effects of siblings on child health are not the same if parents are characterised by male preference because of higher expected earnings (Rosenzweig and Schultz, 1982) or son preference prejudice. Therefore, empirical estimation of health production function is separate for male and female children to allow for the possibility that the treatment of a child by the parents may depend on its gender.

## Child Mortality Function

The household chooses the number and age composition (birth interval) of its children to maximise the income produced by family members. This is possible only if the child is surviving. The surviving chances of the child depend on the spacing of births. Therefore, the primary cause of child death is hypothesised to be the prior and posterior birth spacing of children. Again, only for middle order children the birth spacing effects on child mortality are considered as the prior birth spacing is not observed for the first born child and posterior birth spacing for last born child. The mortality equation given below describes the probability that a child dies within 5 years of birth. For the *ith* child born to the *jth* mother, the propensity to die is given by,

$$D_{ij} = \beta_1 Z_{ij} + \beta_2 X_j + \beta_3 PREV_{ij} + \beta_4 NEXT_{ij} + \lambda_j + \varepsilon_{ij} \qquad (7.2)$$

where $D_{ij}$ =1 if the child *i* has died in family *j*, PREV and NEXT are the prior and posterior birth spacing variables showing the gap between the current and previous/next child birth, *Z* and *X* are vectors of child-specific and household-specific covariates, $\lambda_j$ an unobserved quality component common to all children in the family, and $\varepsilon_{ij}$ is error term.

## Birth Spacing Function

Parents can devote more time to rearing a child if prior or post birth spacing is longer which improves the child health outcomes, and hence the probability of child death decreases.

## Posterior Birth Spacing

The log hazard rate of spacing from the time of birth of child *i*, born to the jth women till the arrival of the next sibling (NEXT) is a function of calendar time (T(t)) and household ($X2_j$) and individual child-specific ($Z2_j$) characteristics and a family specific heterogeneity component $v_j$ common to all children in the $j^{th}$ family,

$$Ln(BS_{ij}^{NEXT}) = \gamma_0 + \gamma_1 T(t) + +\gamma_2 Z_{nj}(t) + \gamma_3 X_{nj}(t) + \lambda_j + \upsilon_{nj} \quad (7.3)$$

## Prior Birth Spacing

In the same way, previous sibling (PREV) is specified as,

$$Ln(BS_{ij}^{PREV}) = \delta_0 + \delta_1 T(t) + +\delta_2 Z_{pj}(t) + \delta_3 X_{pj}(t) + \lambda_j + \xi_{pj} \quad (7.4)$$

The probability of a child death is a latent variable, as the outcome is known only after the death of the child. Let the latent variable is specified as,

$$y_i^* = a_0 + a_1 x_i \quad (7.5)$$

where the occurrence of a child death depends on an unobserved index function $y_i$* that is determined by a set of variables $x$ in such a way that the larger the value of the index, the greater the probability of a child death occurring.

Then, $y = 1$, if the child dies, and $y = 0$, if the child survives. There is critical or threshold level of the index $y_i$* such that if y exceeds $y_i$*, the event will occur otherwise it will not. That is,

$$\begin{aligned} y &= 1 \quad if y_i^* \geq 0 \\ &= 0 \quad if y_i^* < 0 \end{aligned} \quad (7.6)$$

Then, given the assumption of normality, the probability of a child death can be computed from the standardised normal CDF as,

$$D_i = P(y = 1|x) = P(y_i \geq y_i^*) = P(y_i \geq a_0 + a_1 x_i) = \phi(a_0 + a_1 x_i) \quad (7.7)$$

where, $P(y=1|x)$ is the conditional probability that an event occurs given the values of the explanatory variables. If $Y \sim N(\mu, \sigma^2)$, its CDF and PDF are given respectively by,

$$\Phi(y) = \int_{-\infty}^{y_0} \frac{1}{\sqrt{2\sigma^2 \pi}} e^{-(y-\mu)^2/2\sigma^2} \quad (7.8)$$

$$\phi(y) = \frac{1}{\sqrt{2\pi}} e^{-(y-\mu)^2/2\sigma^2} \quad (7.9)$$

If $y$ follows logistic distribution, the logit model can be applied. Then, the probability of death of a child is given by,

$$P_i = \frac{1}{1+e^{-z_i}} = \frac{e^z}{1+e^z} \quad (7.10)$$

Then, $(1-P_i)$ is the probability of child surviving, given by,

$$(1 - P_i) = \frac{1}{1+e^{-z_i}} \quad (7.11)$$

where $z = a_0 + a_1 x_i$. Then, the odds ratio can be written as,

$$\frac{P_i}{1-P_i} = \frac{1+e^{z_i}}{1+e^{-z_i}} = e^{z_i} \quad (7.12)$$

Taking natural log of equation (7.12), the log of the odds ratio L is not only linear in X's, but also linear in parameters,

$$L_i = ln\left(\frac{P_i}{1-P_i}\right) = z_i = a_0 + a_1 x_i \qquad (7.13)$$

Thus, the odds ratio is estimated by the maximum likelihood estimation of the logit equation to find the effect of independent variables on child death.

## 7.5 Empirical Analysis

In this paper, child death is the dependent variable which depends on a set of household characteristics. The descriptive statistics of the variables used in the empirical analysis are presented in Table 7.1. In the sample of 2023 households, there are 1079 male and 944 female children. During 2005-06, sample households reported 6 percent of male child died and 9 percent female child died. The mother's age at first birth is 19 years. On average, previous birth spacing is 33 months and posterior birth spacing is 26 months. About 4 percent of mothers had delivery problems associated with child birth. Among the sample households, nearly two thirds of mothers (68 percent) have no education, only 12 percent of mothers have primary level, 15 percent have attained secondary level and 4 percent of mothers have higher level education. Only 33 percent households have television in the house, which is used as a proxy for awareness of modern contraception. Since the NFHS data does not provide the data on income, agriculture land owned and pucca house (build with bricks)are used as indicators of income of the household. In the sample, 65 percent of households own land and 41 percent of population live in pucca house. About 74 percent of households live in rural areas. In rural areas, the public services like drinking water, sanitation, and other health inputs are poor and hence the probability of child death in high. Majority of child birth are single birth and only one percent of child births are twin birth. Nearly 40 percent of households have more than three children. Number of children in the family affects the health of child as children will be undernourished and becomes the victim of diseases and hence child death by limiting the share of each child in the household resource allocation.

**Table 7.1: Descriptive Statistics of Variables in the Child Survival Analysis**

| *Variable* | *Description* | *Male child* | *Female child* |
|---|---|---|---|
| Child death | Child death = 1, 0 otherwise | 0.06 (0.24) | 0.09 (0.28) |
| Mother education | Mother is educated = 1, 0 otherwise | 0.31 (0.90) | 0.30 (0.88) |
| Television | Household has television = 1, 0 otherwise | 0.33 (2.00) | 0.31 (2.02) |
| No. children | More than 3children in the household =1, 0 otherwise | 0.39 (0.49) | 0.40 (0.49) |
| Age at first birth | Age of mother at first child birth (years) | 19.11 (3.07) | 19.00 (2.98) |
| Delivery problem | Mother had delivery problem = 1, 0 otherwise | 0.04 (0.21) | 0.03 (0.19) |
| Twins | Child is twin = 1, 0 otherwise | 0.01 (0.17) | 0.006 (0.16) |

*(Contd...)*

| Prior spacing | Preceding birth interval (months) | 33.3 (16.70) | 32.76 (15.35) |
|---|---|---|---|
| Posterior spacing | Succeeding birth interval (months) | 26.3 (9.63) | 25.79 (9.33) |
| Land | Household owns land = 1, 0 otherwise | 0.65 (0.47) | 0.66 (0.47) |
| Rural | Household lives in rural area = 1, 0 otherwise | 0.74 (0.43) | 0.75 (0.43) |
| Pucca house | Household lives in pucca house = 1, 0 otherwise | 0.41 (1.62) | 0.41 (1.64) |
| Religion | Household is Muslim = 1, 0 otherwise | 0.12 (0.53) | 0.11 (0.44) |
| N | No. of observations | 1079 | 944 |

**Note:** Standard deviations in parentheses.

The impact of spacing on child is also estimated by introducing three variables as dummy separately for prior and posterior birth spacing between 12 months and more than 60 months in the estimating equation. As noted earlier, the prior birth spacing is not observed for the first born child and posterior birth spacing for last born child. Therefore, only for middle order children the birth spacing effects on child mortality are considered in the empirical analysis.

| PREV2 = 1 | Previous child birth spaced between 12- 24 months |
|---|---|
| PREV3 = 1 | Previous child birth spaced between 25- 60 months |
| PREV4 = 1 | Previous child birth spaced more than 60 months |
| POST2 = 1 | Posterior child birth spaced between 12- 24 months |
| POST3 = 1 | Posterior child birth spaced between 25- 60 months |
| POST4 = 1 | Posterior child birth spaced more than 60 months |

The probit estimates of child death, separately for male and female child are presented in Table 7.2. Mother's education has negative effect on both male and female child death and the coefficient is significant for female child death. The estimated coefficients imply that an increase in mother's education reduces the probability of female child death by 0.72 and male child death 0.22. It is inferred that mother's education plays a vital role in child survival as better educated mothers provide better child care, health and nutrition, and have better awareness of healthy practices. More importantly, birth spacing effects are significantly negative on child death, implying the longer the gap between births more the chances of survival of the child. Prior and posterior spacing reduces the probability of death of child by 0.55 and 0.02. Similarly, an increase in age at firth birth also reduces child death in a household, the negative effect on the probability of male child death is more pronounced than on the probability of female child dying. The awareness variable, presence of television in the house, reduces child death. The income variable, land, has a negative effect on child death, whereas pucca house has a positive effect, but both are statistically insignificant. Religion also has no significant effect on child death in a family. Overall, the effects of almost all the variable on child death are higher for male child than for female child. Therefore, there seems to be some evidence for sex preference and the evidence is against the female child.

**Table 7.2: Probit Estimates of Child Death**
**Dependent variable: Death of a child =1, 0 otherwise**

| *Variable* | *Male child* | | *Female child* | |
|---|---|---|---|---|
| | *Coefficient* | *p-value* | *Coefficient* | *p-value* |
| Mother education | -0.226 (0.364) | 0.534 | -0.7187** (0.344) | 0.037 |
| Age at first birth | -0.535 (0.055) | 0.330 | -0.0118 (0.035) | 0.738 |
| Prior spacing | -0.290*** (0.016) | 0.070 | -0.0048 (0.008) | 0.537 |
| Posterior spacing | -0.549** (0.020) | 0.007 | -0.0206*** (0.011) | 0.082 |
| Television | -0.788 (0.384) | 0.837 | -0.0911*** (0.272) | 0.073 |
| No. of children | -0.26976 (0.287) | 0.925 | 0.5663** (0.183) | 0.002 |
| Land | -0.805 (0.308) | 0.794 | -0.2721 (0.208) | 0.192 |
| Rural | -0.404 (0.362) | 0.264 | -0.2471 (0.305) | 0.418 |
| Pucca house | 0.460 (0.350) | 0.188 | 0.1838 (0.226) | 0.419 |
| Religion | - | - | 0.1473 (0.318) | 0.643 |
| Log likelihood | -47.2832 | | -105.7462 | |

**Note:** Standard deviations in parentheses ** Significant at 5 percent level
*** Significant at 10 percent level.

The Table 7.3 presents the effects of birth spacing on child mortality. Both prior and posterior birth intervals decrease the probability of child death in a household. However, only the posterior birth spacing variables are statistically significant. As prior birth spacing increases from 24 to 60 months, the probability of a female child dying decreases from 0.16 to 0.37. More months of posterior spacing of child birth decreases the probability of both male and female child death more strongly. The effect of mother's education has significant negative effect on female child mortality and an insignificant negative effect on male child mortality. An increase in a year of female education reduces the probability of female child death by 0.41, and male child by 0.22. An increase in age at firth birth of the mother also decreases the probability of child death. Further, the presence of television, land ownership, rural residence and pucca housing decrease the probability of child death in a household. However, problems faced at the time of delivery increases the probability of death of the male child, as shown by the statistically significant positive coefficient of 0.83, relative to the female child. Thus, higher spacing of births and better education and age at first birth of females reduce the risk of child dying below 5 years.

**Table 7.3: Probit Estimates of Prior and Posterior Birth Spacing on Child Mortality Dependent variable: Death of a child =1, 0 otherwise**

| *Variable* | *Male child* | | *Female child* | |
|---|---|---|---|---|
| | *Coefficient* | *p-value* | *Coefficient* | *p-value* |
| Mother education | -0.224 | 0.169 | -0.409** | 0.018 |
| Age at first birth | -0.027 | 0.226 | -0.038 | 0.101 |
| Television | -0.273 | 0.113 | -0.070 | 0.680 |
| Previous 12-24 months | -0.162 | 0.674 | 0.165 | 0.649 |

*(Contd...)*

| | | | | |
|---|---|---|---|---|
| Previous 25-60 months | -0.240 | 0.529 | -0.250 | 0.485 |
| Previous 60 months above | -0.100 | 0.794 | -0.371 | 0.320 |
| Posterior 12-24 months | -0.683** | 0.039 | -0.910** | 0.010 |
| Posterior 25-60 months | -1.443 | 0.000 | -0.846** | 0.015 |
| Posterior 60 months above | -1.432* | 0.000 | -1.336* | 0.000 |
| Delivery problem | 0.829* | 0.000 | -0.173 | 0.708 |
| Twins | 0.262 | 0.621 | 0.500 | 0.275 |
| Religion | -0.086 | 0.678 | -0.070 | 0.718 |
| Land | -0.112 | 0.410 | 0.100 | 0.461 |
| Rural | -0.225 | 0.188 | -0.060 | 0.731 |
| Pucca house | - | - | -0.122 | 0.389 |
| Log likelihood | -216.4905 | | -254.0660 | |

**Note:** ** Significant at 5 percent level *** Significant at 10 percent level.

The estimated odds ratio of child death presented in Table 7.4 shows that the effect of urban residence, mother's education, wealth position, television, and religion are reducing the likelihood of child death. The values of odds ratio less than one have the effect of reducing the risk of child dying before the age of 5. If mother is educated at degree level, the probability of child death reduces by 0.76. At no education or lower levels of mother's education, the probability of child death increases by 0.01 and 0.94. Similarly, rich income households have less 0.76 probability of child death compared to poor and middle income families. Urban residence and ownership of television also reduces the likelihood of child death by 0.69 and 0.67. House type has no statistical effect on child mortality.

**Table 7.4: Logistic Estimates of Child Mortality**
**Dependent variable = Death of a child**

| *Variable* | | *Odds ratio* | *p-value* |
|---|---|---|---|
| Urban | | 0.6944 | 0.129 |
| Television | | 0.6712 | 0.108 |
| Religion | | 0.7688 | 0.349 |
| Mother education | Illiterate | 1.9441** | 0.033 |
| | Primary | 1.0125 | 0.975 |
| | Higher | 0.7642 | 0.683 |
| Wealth | Poor | 1.0644 | 0.815 |
| | Middle-class | 1.1083 | 0.706 |
| | Rich | 0.9424 | 0.842 |
| House type | Kachha | 1.3290 | 0.433 |
| | Semi-pucca | 1.4926 | 0.260 |
| | Pucca | 1.4893 | 0.274 |

**Note:** ** Significant at 5 percent level.

## 7.5 Conclusion

Child mortality depends on many socio-economic factors like mother's education and age, age at first birth, spacing between child birth, family income, wealth, residence, awareness, etc. Among them, mother's education and birth spacing are vital for child survival. If the mother is educated the health of child improves and the risk of child death is reduced. The increase in the age of the mother increases the age at child birth that can also reduce the chances of child mortality. To bear a child physically she has to be matured. Early childbearing can lead to many delivery problems which affects the survival outcome of the child. The family planning and health awareness of mothers acquired through television, provides parents the knowledge of modem contraceptive methods, hygiene, healthy practices in child rearing and benefits of birth spacing, all of which lower both the fertility and child mortality of the family.

This paper has estimated the effects of mother's education and birth spacing on child mortality using the NFHS-3 data for 2005-06 pertaining to the state of Rajasthan, applying the probit and logit models. The main finding from this study is that birth spacing has high statistically significant negative effect on both male and female child mortality. As birth spacing increases, the chances of child survival improves. Similarly, mother's education has also the effect of reducing child death. In the context of family, these results imply that parents are able to devote more time and resources for better childcare. More number of children in the family also has impact on the death of the child. The study shows that the risk of death of the female child is high than male child when there are more number of children in the family. The estimated results further show that the effects of mother's education and birth spacing are more negatively pronounced for the risk of male child death than the death of a female child. Thus, improving maternal education and increasing spacing between births will reduce not only number of children born to a woman but also the chance of child dying before the age of five.

# 8

# Subjective Well-being, Money and the Easterlin Paradox: An Ordered Probit Estimation of Life Satisfaction

**Abstract**

*The original question posed by Easterlin in 1974, does economic growth improve the human lot, still rages the literature on economic of happiness. Easterlin's explanation for the lack of association between rising aggregate income and average happiness in terms of relative income and social comparison is examined in this paper using the five waves of world value survey during 1990-2006 for eight states in India. The ordered probit estimates show that the relative income effect is significantly positive and the absolute income has no significant effect on the happiness level of individuals. The OLS estimate of rank position on life satisfaction is positive. These results imply that individuals in India are concerned more with relative status than with their own income, and hence, average happiness does not increase with aggregate or per capita state income. Pursuing economic growth with the aim to increase income of all proportionately may not raise the happiness of all individuals.*

**Key words:** *Happiness, absolute and relative income, rank position, WVS, ordered probit*

## 8.1 Introduction

Happiness of humans is the utmost concern for both the individual and the society. World Happiness Report 2018 of the United Nations ranks India in 133rd position, a drop of 11 places from 2017 ranking of 122nd rank. Happiness, as defined by the Cambridge Advanced Learner's Dictionary, is generally understood as a state of mind or feeling characterised by contentment, love, satisfaction, pleasure, or joy of life. As happiness is a state of feeling that encompasses all aspects of human life, a wide variety of biological, psychological, social, religious, and philosophical approaches have striven to define happiness and identify its sources. Economics measures human well-being in terms of utility, progress, welfare, quality of life, well-being, or standard of living, mostly relating well-being to consumption, income, GDP, growth in GDP, economic growth, per capita income, or some other indicators like, maximum utility, reduction in poverty, decrease in inequality, indicators of health, or indicators of environment standards. Economics reduces happiness to yet another aspect of human behaviour that is related with material goods and services in that command over physical resources, simply money, buys human happiness. But, psychologists frequently measure happiness by subjective well-being by self-reported levels of subjective life satisfaction. Positive psychology researchers use theoretical models that include describing happiness as consisting of positive emotions and positive activities, or that describe some kinds of happiness: pleasure, engagement, and meaning. While economists are concerned with objective measures of well-being, psychologists rely on self-reported subjective evaluations of life satisfaction. Research has identified a number of attributes that correlate with happiness: personal relationships, social interaction, extraversion, marital status, employment, health, democratic freedom, optimism, endorphins released through physical exercise and eating chocolate, religious involvement, income and proximity to other happy people. Frey and Stutzer (2002) argue that "happiness is a 'subjectivist' measure of individual welfare and is much broader than the way individual utility is normally defined... while happiness is not derived from actual behaviour, it is systematically and closed connected with generally accepted manifestations of well-being". Therefore, happiness, subjective well-being and life satisfaction are commonly and interchangeably used to refer the same thing, the general human well-being.

A fundamental assumption of standard economic analysis is that people's well-being increases with consumption. Consumption is the most important argument in the utility function used by economists in order to capture the extent to which consumption translates into the well-being of an individual. It is primarily due to this assumption that GDP is so often taken as the yardstick of well-being and progress. More systematic evidence on the limitations of using GDP as a yardstick for well-being come from more direct indicators of quality of life (Easterlin and Angelescu, 2010). Given the myriad issues surrounded the economics measures of such as welfare that try to quantify happiness, the recent trend to use direct measures of happiness, such as survey tools asking people to self-evaluate how happy they are, challenge traditional income indicators like GDP. Some of these indicators are objective (increases in nutrition or life expectancy increase quality of life, while increases in crime rates or congestion decrease it), others subjective (self-reported status of well-being by people in surveys of happiness, life satisfaction, or prevalence of positive moods). As the objective function of a government is increasing people's well-being, it is argued that government policies should focus, once basic needs are met, on increasing Gross National Happiness (GNH), not on simply economic growth or GDP. In fact, Gross National Happiness is a concept introduced by the King of Bhutan as an alternative to GDP.

The general conclusion on the income-well-being relationship is that while cross-country data shows a correlation between GDP per capita and objective indicators of quality of life (for example, richer countries tend to have higher life expectancy), time series data provides very little support for GDP per capita causation of improvements in the objective indicators (for example, in a large number of countries the turning point towards sustained economic growth anteceded by many decades of sustained improvements in life expectancy). A comprehensive and systematic cross-country and time-series study by Easterly (1999) on the relationship between GDP growth and improvements in objective indicators of well-being finds that there is only robust indication that GDP growth was the prime cause for the improvement in three out of possible 81 indicators (calorie intake, protein intake, and telephones). In addition, the evidence shows that growth comes along accompanied with objective indicators of some bad or negative factors that lowers quality of life, such as higher levels of pollution and, beyond a certain income threshold, dietary habits increase obesity. Thus, income growth also brings with it the consumptions that tend to lower well-being.

As well-being is multidimensional, conceptualising well-being in a more holistic way goes beyond the GDP stance. One adjustment to GDP is to allow purchasing power parity among countries, and another, further adjustment to GDP to include differences in income distribution, for example, by providing weighted shares of growth by population groups, as income per capita as a national average does not provide the real income picture of the different population subgroups or regions. Yet another approach is to construct objective measures to complement GDP that include social and environmental information beyond the economic realm. Since the 1970s many non-economic indicators have been developed to complement GDP, like HDI, that encompass education, health and nutrition, environment and empowerment and participation to complement GDP. Another approach is to adjust GDP by monetising different aspects that are not counted in the GDP measurement, like social and environmental factors (McGillivray, 2007). The problem with these adjustments is that it is difficult to quantify and monetise some of these additional factors. Even more complex adjustment is, for example, to take into account social and environmental factors such as the value of leisure or the damage of pollution (Nordhaus and Tobin, 1973). Beyond adjusting GDP, like the Physical Quality of Life Index (PQLI) UNDP's Human Development Index (HDI),World Bank's Genuine Savings, Happy Planet Index, Happy Life Years (Veenhoven, 1984; 2004), etc. try to construct composite measures that would capture the multidimensional aspect of well-being.

Beyond income measure, economic freedom, democracy, federalism and political participation are also found to correlate strongly with happiness

(Frey and Stutzer, 2001). A more active role for citizens enables better monitoring of government and politics by citizens, which leads to greater satisfaction with government output. Also, the ability for citizens to get involved in and have control over the political process increases well-being. According to Glaeser et al. (2014), though humans constantly strive to make them happy, the choices that that they make tend decrease their happiness, because they have also other important aims that clash with the aim of happiness and choices are made under certain constraints. Ultimately all the economic and social policy should be diverted toward what matters most, the people's well-being.

Thus, well-being is one of the more elusive concepts of economic research and hence an understanding of the relationship between economic growth and happiness is warranted. While objective measurement of happiness presents challenges, subjective measures like self-reported life satisfaction levels, the tools developed by surveys like the World Value Survey and Gallup world poll are frequently used by researchers to quantify happiness. Using such a subjective measure of well-being, this paper analyses the relationship between life satisfaction and income in India. Using a panel of World Value Database for the period 1990-2006 for eight states of India, and applying pane econometric methods, this paper analyses the effect of per capita state income on the average level of happiness in the states of India. The eight states are Andhra Pradesh, Gujarat, Karnataka, Kerala, Maharashtra, Rajasthan, Tamil Nadu and West Bengal. For which the WVS data are available. The specific objectives of the paper are to identify and estimate the effects of absolute income and relative income on the level of happiness i.e. to explain how much a person's happiness depends on his/her income in absolute term and in relation to the income of others. The paper also tests if the rank position of an individual in the income order is significant in explaining the satisfaction level and to estimate the level of its effect. Further, the paper also attempts to estimate how large is the effect of income on happiness compared to the effects of non-pecuniary factors such as personal relationships, employment, health, etc.

## 8.2 A Brief Review of Recent Studies

In the early 1960s, Hadley Cantril, a social psychologist, conducted an intensive survey in 14 countries worldwide, to know what people want out of life – what they would need for their life to be completely satisfied (Cantril, 1965). A startling finding of the survey is that the answer was strikingly similar and apparent, despite vast disparities in every respect of the life– material circumstances, especially levels of living was the most often said in every country. In the same vein, Warner Wilson (1967) concluded that a happy person is a "young, healthy, well-educated, extroverted, optimistic, worry-free, religious, married person with high self-esteem, job morale, modest aspirations, of either sex and of a wide range of intelligence" (Wilson, 1967, p. 294, as quoted in Diener, Suh, Lucas and Smith, 1999, p. 276). The most significant result of the Cantril study, for the economist, is that despite vast differences in income levels, the average level of happiness seems to be close to each other. The Cantril's findings are depicted in Figure 8.1. It can be observed that for more developed countries like Germany and for less developed countries like Nigeria, the average happiness level is almost the same, in spite of their vast differences in per capita income. Also, across countries the mean happiness level hovers around 4 to 6 in 7 point Ladder scale.

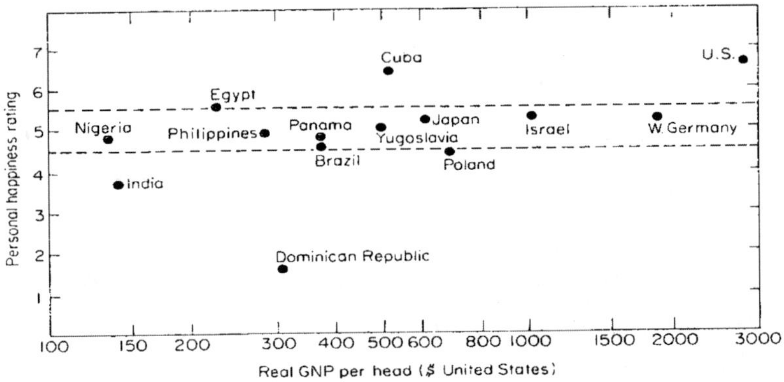


*Source:* Cantril (1965).

***Figure 8.1: Cantril's (1965) Happiness and GDP per head in 14 Countries in 1960***

Starting with the seminal work of Easterlin (1974), the research in economics on the relationship between income and happiness produced mixed and controversial results. Easterlin (1974) posed the questions: does economic growth improve the human lot? Does higher income make people happier? Will raising incomes of all increase the happiness of all? Analysing the US data on income and happiness, Easterlin concluded that there is a lack of growth in aggregate happiness in the US despite a massive rise in GDP per capita. Though a rise in absolute income at individual level seems to raise happiness, at the aggregate level, rise in average income has no effect on average happiness. In spite of the many fold increase in per capita income in the US between 1972 and 2002, the level of average happiness remained the same. This is the famous Easterlin Paradox, which has become a key concept as well as major controversy in the economics of happiness literature (Easterlin, 2003; 2017; Easterlin and Sawangfa, 2010; Easterlin et al., 2010; Hagerty and Veenhoven, 2003). Easterlin explains the lack of association between average income and GDP growth in terms of income adaptation and social comparison. That is, when the income of all people rises, their relative position remains unchanged, and given their relative income levels, people care little or not at all about their absolute income levels and care only about their relative incomes. The Figure 8.2 presents the income-happiness relationship for the US as reported by Easterlin.

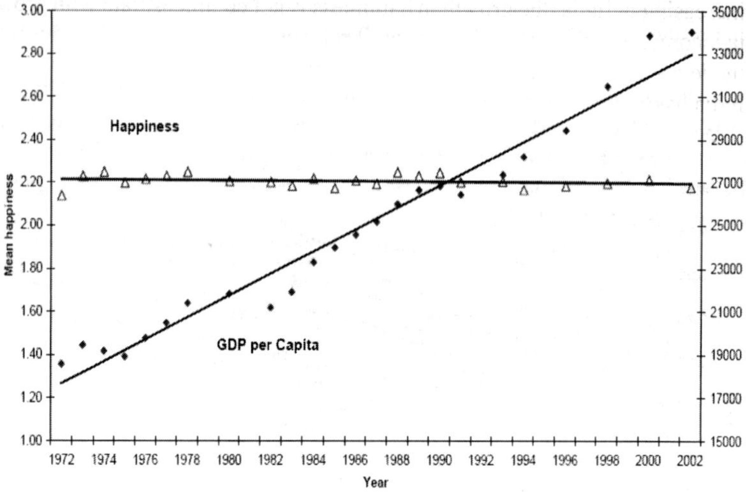


*Source:* Easterlin and Angelescu (2010).

***Figure 8.2: Easterlin Paradox: Happiness and Real GDP per capita in US, 1972-2002***

The Easterlin Paradox is a key concept in happiness economics. In subsequent cross country analysis also Easterlin fails to find a strong association between income and happiness across countries, though within the country, there is a positive happiness-income relationship (Easterlin, 1995). The stylised finding of the literature on Easterlin paradox are: at a point in time both among and within nations, happiness varies directly with income, but over time, happiness does not increase when a country's income increases; no long run relationship between income and happiness; and economic growth in nations does not buy greater happiness for the average citizen over time. Subsequent studies that challenged the Easterlin hypothesis find some evidence of a positive relationship between average income and happiness (Layard, 2005; Stevenson and Wolfers, 2008; 2010; Deaton, 2008; Clark, Frijters and Shields, 2008; Sacks and Stevenson, 2012). The stylised findings of this literature are: the nil relationship between economic growth and happiness does not actually imply the absence of a relationship between the two; there exists a statistically significant positive long run relationship, at least the relationship does not become zero; and the time series income-happiness relationship is generally weaker in the developed countries, but generally stronger in the developing countries.

The Figure 8.3 presents the subjective well-being-income relationship worldwide. The Figure 8.3 reveals two distinct facts: in Latin American countries, though poorer relative to OECD countries, have almost comparable levels of subjective well-being, and the ex-communist or transition economies subjective well-being is lesser than even that of some developing countries. The Figure 8.4 presents the trends in happiness in India. Though happiness is increasing in India, the growth in happiness is not commensurate with growth in income, especially after the economic reforms of 1991. As Figure 8.5 reveals the level of happiness in India is low, compared with other countries, though India has been experiencing one of the highest rates of growth of the economy.

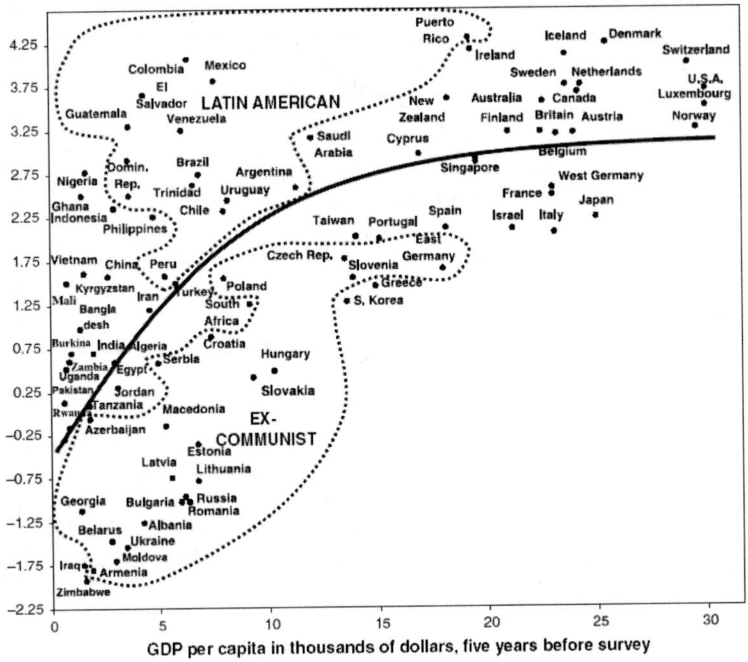


***Figure 8.3: Relationship between Income and Subjective Well-being 1995-2007***

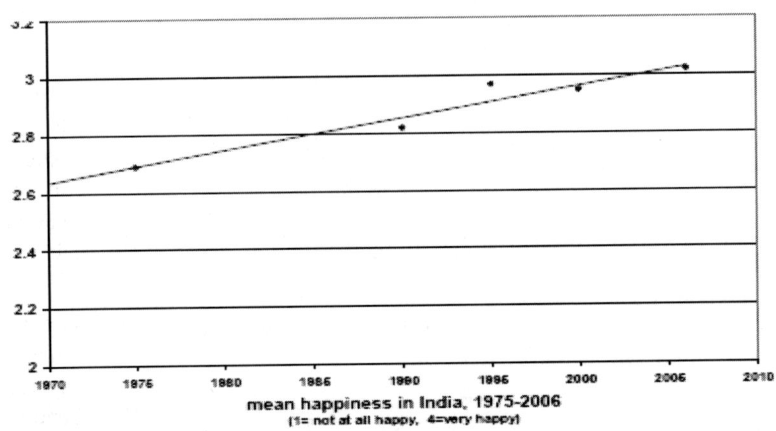


*Source:* Inglehart, Foa, Peterson, Welzel (2008).

***Figure 8.4: Happiness Trend in India 1975-2006***

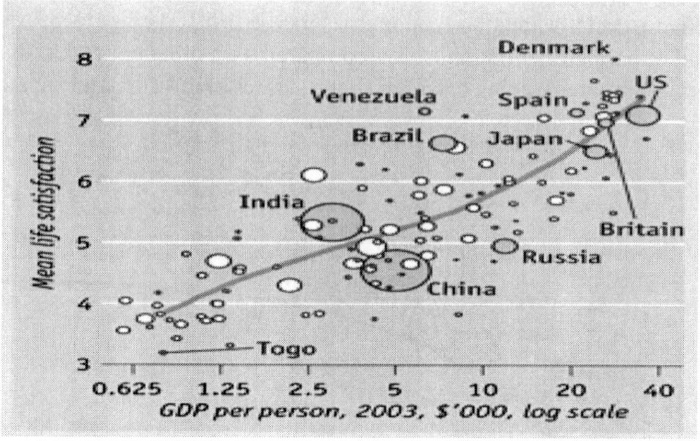


*Source:* Deaton (2008).

***Figure 8.5: Life Satisfaction in India Compared to Other Countries, 2003.***

In contrast to these absolute income and relative income models, some researchers have used rank-based model which suggest that people gain utility/satisfaction from occupying a higher ranked position within an income distribution rather than from either absolute income or their position relative to a reference income (Smith, Diener and Wedell, 1989; Hagerty, 2000; Brown, Gardner, Oswald and Qian, 2008; Clark, Kristensen and Westergard-Nielsen, 2009; Clark, Masclet and Villeval, 2010). The ranked position of an income will be highly correlated with the position of that income relative to a mean, so reference-income account may be consistent with a rank-income account. According to the rank-income hypothesis, there is no simple causal relationship between money and happiness: an increase in income need not increase ranked position and hence need not increase happiness. Clark et al. (2009), in a study of 9,000 small neighbourhoods, finds that satisfaction with economic conditions increased with ranked position within a neighbourhood. Brown et al. (2008) observes, in a study of 16,000 British workers, wage satisfaction depended on the ordinal rank of an individual's wage within a workplace. Boyce et al. (2010) tests the rank income hypothesis using the 1997-2004 British household panel survey with 86,679 observations, and observes that relative rank income positively predicts the life satisfaction, and subsumes the effect of absolute income in Britain. Further, they show that satisfaction is gained for better-than comparison and lost for worse than comparison. Other studies have considered rank in the broader context of range-frequency theory (Hagerty, 2000; Smith, Diener and Wedell, 1989).

Though some cross-country studies include India also in their analysis, most studies are either are psychological or simple correlational analyses. The causal impact of income on happiness in India is never fully analysed. Lakshmanasamy (2010) is the first attempt to examine Easterlin paradox in

India. For a primary survey data, the ordered probit estimation of the relationship between income and happiness in India shows a significant positive effect of both absolute income and relative income on happiness. However, the relative income effect vanishes when interactions between absolute income and relative income are allowed. Thus, as the Easterlin paradox holds, proportionate shift in the relative position does not change the happiness level. Another study by Majumdar and Gupta (2015) examine several correlates of happiness such as unemployment, poverty, literacy rate, life expectancy, inflation rate, crime rate and political stability at the aggregate level. They find that employed are more satisfied than unemployed, married people are more happier than divorced, separated and widowed etc. Further, it is shown that the Easterlin Paradox does not hold for India as happiness is found to be more sensitive to absolute than to relative income. Focusing on consumption rather than income, Linssen (2009) examine happiness among Indian rural poor, using a 2008 primary data from Orissa consisting of 697 individuals within 375 households. Applying linear multilevel regressions, the study finds insignificant effects of absolute and relative consumption on subjective well-being, but a significant negative effect of status intensive goods consumption on subjective well-being.

Borooah (2006) conducts an econometric investigation into what makes people happy in Ireland by examining the relation between standards of living and levels of happiness. The results show that money does not buy happiness and money may not even fully be convertible in terms of satisfaction of having money. The satisfaction of one's standard of living depends on comparison with standard of living of others, a relative income effect. Further, the study importantly reveals the significance of social capital, the area we live in, the people we have as our neighbours are very important in lifting happiness levels. On the other hand, Litchfield, Reilly and Veneziani (2012) studying life satisfaction in Albania using heteroscedastic ordered probit model find that a measure of absolute household welfare is important for life satisfaction, but there is no role for a relative measure.

Yushkina (2010) study the determinants of life satisfaction and its changes in modern Russia. The effects of living space, perceived economic rank, other subjective attitudes and perceptions on well-being are analysed for a panel data applying the ordered logit model. The factors subjective attitudes that describe an individual's perceived power rank, respect rank and economic value in society are shown to have consistently positive significant effects on happiness.

Hajdu and Hajdu (2014) evaluate different econometric methodologies in explaining the association between subjective well-being and income. The OLS regression is compared with quantile regression and the ordered probit model with generalised ordered probit model. It results show that income has a positive impact on satisfaction under OLS regression and this association is not so strong at the upper end of the conditional distribution of life satisfaction and stronger at the lower end. The ordered probit model predicts a moderate positive income effect: higher income decreases the probability of dissatisfaction and increases the probability of satisfaction. Contrary to this result, the generalised ordered probit model shows a more negative effect of income on the probability of lower levels of satisfaction, but income does not affect the probability of the highest satisfaction.

The literature on happiness has grown a lot since Easterlin's (1974) seminal findings. Several surveys and reviews on happiness research have indicated a number of correlates of happiness, World data base of happiness lists hundreds of correlates of happiness identified by research. Many of such findings remain controversial. Central to all such study of happiness and well-being is the role of income. Different schools of thoughts have evolved and empirical studies struggle to identify the relevant concept of income - absolute income, relative income and rank income, and establish the exact relationship between happiness and income. Taking all evidences together from all sides on whether income and happiness are directly or inversely related to happiness, it is somewhat clear that all these studies show that the concern in economics of improving the human welfare through greater material wealth is exaggerated, at least in economically developed countries.

## 8.3 Data and Methodology

This paper uses the World Value Survey (WVS) data pertaining to India for empirical analysis. The World Value the success of Survey the European Values Study (EVS) has led to the emergence of the World Value Survey in 1981, when the methods were extended to 14 countries outside Europe. The 1981 WVS covered 22 countries worldwide. Since then the WVS is being conducted in over 70 countries, till 2006 five waves of WVS have been conducted. India was included in WVS since 1990, the second wave of WVS. The years of survey for India are 1990, 1995, 2001 and 2006.The WVS is being conducted in eight states in India viz. Andhra Pradesh, Gujarat, Karnataka, Kerala, Maharashtra, Rajasthan, Tamil Nadu and West Bengal. The four waves of the WVS in 1990, 1995, 2001 and 2006 consisting of 2807 observations. The WVS methodology is face-to-face interviews with a detailed questionnaire consisting of about 250 questions with some 400 to 800 measurable variables. The WVS data provides information on personal values and attitudes towards a wide range of social issues such as life satisfaction, religion, family, work and democracy.

This paper uses the self-reported answers to some of the questions as empirical variables. The WVS provides two ways of assessing the happiness/satisfaction levels of individuals. For both measures, the respondents are asked to give a qualitative assessment on their happiness on a Likert scale. To measure the feeling of happiness, the question in WVS is "Taking all things together, would you say you are: 1 - Very happy, 2- Rather happy, 3 - Not very happy and 4 - Not at all happy". The measure of individual's life satisfaction is the responses to item al70 of WVS in which it is asked "all things considered, how satisfied are you with your life as a whole these days?". The respondents are asked to give integer rating from 1 (least satisfied) to 10 (most satisfied).This paper takes the latter, life satisfaction, as the measure of happiness, as it has ten categories than happiness that has only four categories, in the ordered probit analysis. The measures of absolute income and relative income are both derived from item X047cs titled Income (country specific). In this item, each respondent is presented with 10 income brackets. In second and third waves income is expressed as rupees per annum and in fourth and fifth waves income is expressed as rupees per month. The reported monthly income is converted into annual income for the last two waves, and the midpoint of each individual's income bracket is considered as approximation of absolute income. Relative income is the ratio of an individual's absolute income with the mean income level of the states. The other variables considered for analysis are age, health, marital status, gender, employment, and number of children.

For health, the WVS asks "all in all, how would you describe your state of health these days?". Respondents are asked to choose among five categories: very good, good, fair, poor and very poor. The coding that is done as 1,2,3,4 and 5 in the WVS codebook have been reversed as 5,4,3,2 and 1 respectively so that it is consistent with the coding of other ordinal variable used in this paper, higher values correspond to better health states. For religion, the WVS asks "how important is God in your life?", and respondents are asked to answer on an integer scale from 1 (not at all important) to 10 (very important). For the income of the states, the Net State Domestic Product per capita (NSDP) data is taken from the RBI's Handbook of Statistics on Indian Economy.

In the empirical analysis, since individual's self-rating of their overall happiness is measured by an ordered categorical variable, the estimation is based on ordered probit model. Ordered response data are mutually exclusive qualitative categories that have a natural ordering, but they do not have natural numerical values. Ordered probit is a generalisation of the probit analysis, used for ordinal multinomial dependent variable in which the probabilities of each outcome conditional on the independent variables are modeled using the cumulative normal distribution. The assumption underlying the ordered probit model is that, although the respondents to the WVS report their happiness levels on the prescribed 1 through 10 integer scale, happiness can be measured by an unobserved (or latent) variable that can take on any real value. Therefore, the ordered probit model is based on the underlying model with single index function and constant thresholds.

Let $y$ be an ordered response of happiness, and happiness is rated on a scale from 1 to 10, with $y$=10 representing the highest rating i.e. most satisfied, and $y$=1 the lowest rating i.e. least satisfied. The fact that 10 is a better rating than 9 conveys useful information, even though the happiness rating itself only has ordinal meaning. Therefore, *y* is an ordered response taking on the values {1,2,…..,10} for some known integer J. Then, the ordered probit model for *y* (conditional on explanatory variables) can be derived from a latent variable model. Assume that a latent variable *Y** is determined by,

$$y^* = \beta x + u|x \sim N(0, \sigma^2) \tag{8.1}$$

As *y** is unobserved, the observed *y* can be expressed as,

$$\begin{aligned} y &= 1 \quad if y^* \leq c_1 \\ y &= 2 \quad if c_1 \leq y^* \leq c_2 \\ &\cdots\cdots\cdots\cdots\cdots \\ y &= 9 \quad if c_8 \leq y^* \leq c_9 \\ y &= 10 \quad if y^* > c_9 \end{aligned} \tag{8.2}$$

The *c*'s are the unknown threshold levels (cut points) to be estimated along with the probabilities. Given the assumption that the error term *u* is distributed normally, the conditional distribution of *y* given x is derived as the response probability for each *y*,

$$\begin{aligned} P(y = 1/x) &= P(y^* = c_1/x) = P(\beta x + u \leq c_1/x) = \Phi(c_1 - \beta x) \\ P(y = 2/x) &= P(c_1 \leq y^* \leq c_2/x) = \Phi(c_2 - \beta x) - \Phi(c_1 - \beta x) \\ &\cdots\cdots\cdots\cdots\cdots \\ P(y = 9/x) &= P(c_8 \leq y^* \leq c_9/x) = \Phi(c_9 - \beta x) - \Phi(c_8 - \beta x) \\ P(y = 10/x) &= P(y^* \geq c_9/x) = 1 - \Phi(c_9 - \beta x) \end{aligned} \tag{8.3}$$

In probability, these sums to unity, and hence when J = 1, the binary probit model is given by,

$$P(y = 1/x) = 1 - P(y = 0/x) = 1 - \Phi(\alpha_1 - \beta x) = \Phi(\beta x - \alpha_1) \tag{8.4}$$

where $\alpha_1$ is the intercept inside Φ. Therefore, *x* does not contain an explicit intercept in this formulation of the ordered probit model. The predicted probabilities can be expressed as,

$$P(y = j/x) = \Phi(\alpha_j - \beta x) - \Phi(\alpha_{j-1} - \beta x) \tag{8.5}$$

where *j* represents the (ten) happiness levels. The parameters α and β can be estimated by the maximum likelihood method. The log-likelihood function of the ordered probit model is specified as,

$$\begin{aligned} L(\alpha, \beta) = 1(y = 0)\log[(\Phi(\alpha_1 - \beta x)] + 1(y = 1)\log[(\Phi(\alpha_2 - \beta x)] \\ +1(y = 2)\log[(\Phi(\alpha_2 - \beta x)] + \ldots\ldots\ldots +1(y = 10)\log[(\Phi(\alpha_{10} - \beta x)] \end{aligned} \tag{8.6}$$

That is,

$$lnL = \sum_{i=1}^{n}\sum_{j=1}^{J} I(y_j = j)log[\Phi(\alpha_j - \beta x) - \Phi(\alpha_{j-1} - \beta x)] \quad (8.7)$$

where $I$ is a binary indicator function that equals 1 if $y_i = j$, and 0 otherwise. Since the latent happiness measure is assumed to be a linear function of a set of explanatory variables, the estimating panel ordered probit model can be written as,

$$y_{it} = x_{itk}\beta_k + u_{it} \quad (8.8)$$

where $y_{it}$ denotes the happiness of the i[th] individual at time t. Specifying the estimating equation with respect to income, the happiness function can be expressed as,

$$y_{it} = \beta_1 \, ln(absy_{it}) + \beta_2 \, ln(rely_{it}) + x_{itk}\beta_k + u_{it} \quad (8.9)$$

where ln(absy) is the individual absolute income and ln(rely) is the relative income, and $X_{itk}$ is a vector of other exogenous variables, and $\beta_k$ is a conformable vector of coefficients.

The paper also tests the rank income happiness model, according to which individuals compare their rank position with others within the income distribution. The number of people who have income 'worse than' that of the individual (i-1) is compared with the total number of people within the individual's reference group i.e. the state (*n* - 1). The ratio gives the individual a rank (Ri) normalised between 0 and 1,

$$R_i^s = (i-1)/(n^s - 1) \quad (8.10)$$

For the rank income analysis, the 2006 (fifth wave) WVS data of all the eight states are used.

## 8.4 Empirical Analysis

This paper starts by examining the relationship between individual's reported happiness in the eight states of India and the state income per capita (NSDP). The Table 8.1 presents the distribution of samples across states over the four waves of WVS during 1990-2006 in India.

**Table 8.1: Distribution of WVS Samples across States in India**

| *State* | *1990* | *1995* | *2000* | *2006* | *Total* |
|---|---|---|---|---|---|
| Andhra Pradesh | 134 | 136 | 25 | 143 | 438 |
| Gujarat | 92 | 73 | 6 | 97 | 268 |
| Karnataka | 93 | 64 | 3 | 102 | 262 |
| Kerala | 70 | 67 | 13 | 56 | 206 |
| Maharashtra | 169 | 135 | 15 | 196 | 515 |
| Rajasthan | 94 | 58 | 12 | 112 | 276 |
| Tamil Nadu | 143 | 51 | 33 | 161 | 388 |
| West Bengal | 140 | 155 | 4 | 155 | 454 |
| Total | 935 | 739 | 111 | 1022 | 2807 |

The Table 8.2 and Figure 8.6 present distribution of happiness in the eight states. It is observed that, out of 2807 sample, 703 people have indicated their happiness level as 5 i.e. neither most satisfied nor least satisfied, 1596 people have indicated their happiness level above 5 and the rest have satisfaction level below 5. Thus, on average, majority people in the states of India during 1990-2006 are satisfied with their life, reporting between 5 and 7 happiness level. But, there also exists differential in happiness between the states. In Gujarat, more than 20 percent are most happy or satisfied with their life, whereas in West Bengal only 5 percent are most happy. Relatively, more people in Andhra Pradesh and Gujarat, states with higher NSDP and per capita income, are lest satisfied, whereas in Rajasthan, a less income state, only few people are less satisfied and majority of people in West Bengal are at level 5. While most states have more or less the same percentage of people who are most satisfied, Kerala, the highly literate state, has the least number of most satisfied people.

**Table 8.2: Distribution of Happiness across States in India**

| *Happiness level* | *Andhra Pradesh* | *Gujarat* | *Karnataka* | *Kerala* | *Maharashtra* | *Rajasthan* | *Tamil Nadu* | *West Bengal* | *Total* |
|---|---|---|---|---|---|---|---|---|---|
| 1 | 22 | 13 | 7 | 2 | 11 | 7 | 3 | 65 | 130 |
| 2 | 2 | 0 | 4 | 2 | 10 | 0 | 2 | 7 | 27 |
| 3 | 36 | 17 | 45 | 12 | 36 | 12 | 18 | 77 | 253 |
| 4 | 13 | 3 | 24 | 4 | 18 | 3 | 16 | 16 | 97 |
| 5 | 103 | 40 | 80 | 41 | 148 | 67 | 75 | 149 | 703 |
| 6 | 25 | 21 | 20 | 57 | 18 | 21 | 19 | 36 | 217 |
| 7 | 91 | 44 | 21 | 40 | 96 | 68 | 103 | 33 | 496 |
| 8 | 44 | 36 | 13 | 6 | 62 | 40 | 52 | 26 | 279 |
| 9 | 44 | 26 | 9 | 9 | 51 | 12 | 31 | 19 | 201 |
| 10 | 58 | 68 | 39 | 33 | 65 | 46 | 69 | 26 | 404 |
| Total | 438 | 268 | 262 | 206 | 515 | 276 | 388 | 454 | 2807 |

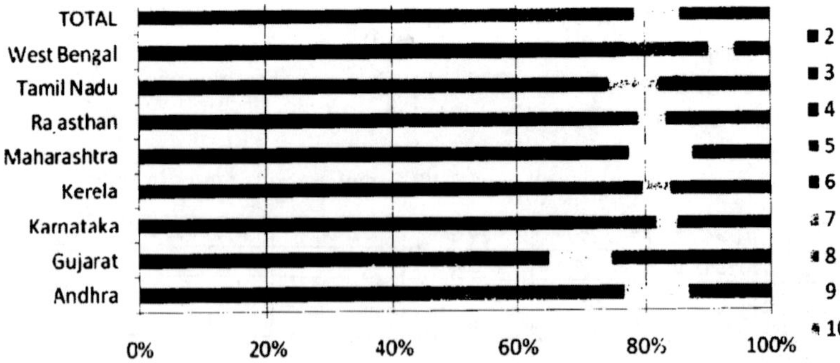


***Figure 8.6: Distribution of Happiness across States in India***

The Table 8.3 presents the average level of happiness and average income in the eight states. The mean happiness is highest in Gujarat, whereas the lowest average happiness is reported in West Bengal. The least per capita income state, Rajasthan, has mean happiness higher than Andhra Pradesh and West Bengal, the higher income states. Thus, there are variations in mean happiness across states in India with similar income per capita.

**Table 8.3: Average Happiness and NSDP per capita across States in India**

| *State* | *Mean happiness* | *NSDP pc* | *ln NSDP pc* |
|---|---|---|---|
| Andhra Pradesh | 5.56(1.890) | 26226 | 10.17 |
| Gujarat | 7.27 (2.7138) | 32991 | 10.40 |
| Karnataka | 6.19(2.8623) | 29185 | 10.28 |
| Kerala | 6.29 (2.2215) | 32450 | 10.39 |
| Maharashtra | 6.28 (2.2906) | 36048 | 10.49 |
| Rajasthan | 6.08 (2.3942) | 17997 | 9.80 |
| Tamil Nadu | 6.58 (2.1784) | 31663 | 10.36 |
| West Bengal | 4.57(1.6496) | 24533 | 10.11 |

**Note:** Standard deviations in parentheses.

The Figure 8.7 presents the scatter plot of the relationship between mean happiness and NSDP per capita of the eight states. The plot suggests that there is a positive relationship between happiness and income.

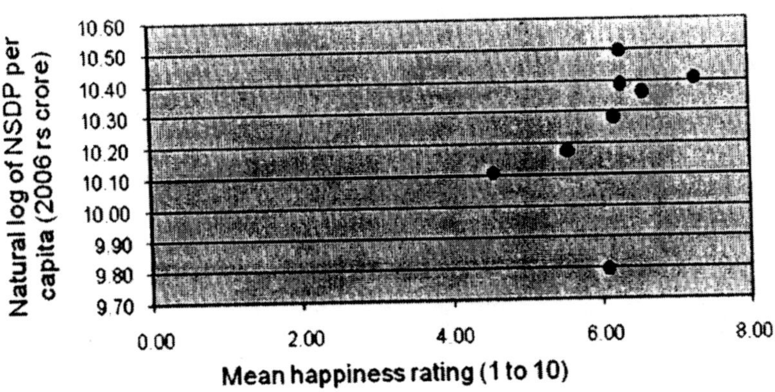


*Figure 8.7: Scatter Plot of Average Happiness on NSDP per capita*

In the empirical analysis of the ordered probit model, the happiness level is the dependent variable. The explanatory variables are defined as given in Table 8.4. Two income measures absolute income and relative income are considered as explanatory variables with other control variables. The Figure 8.8 presents the histograms of relative income and absolute income. The density plots show that both incomes are highly skewed towards the left.

The estimated coefficients of ordered probit model are presented in Table 8.5. The relative income effect is significantly positive showing that an

**Table 8.4: Description of Variables in the Ordered Probit Analysis of Happiness**

| *Variable* | | *Description* |
|---|---|---|
| Happiness | Life satisfaction rating 1 (least satisfied) to 10 (most satisfied) (item al70) | |
| Income | ln(absy) | Log of absolute income (itemX047cs) |
| | ln(rely) | Log of relative income, the ratio of individual income to the average income of the state |
| Marital status | Partner | Marital partner present = 1, 0 otherwise (itemX007) |
| | Split widow | Separated/widowed = 1, 0 otherwise (itemX007) |
| Sex | Female | Female = 1, 0 otherwise (itemX001) |
| Age | Age in years (itemX003) | |
| Children | kid1 | One child = 1, 0 otherwise (itemX011) |
| | kid2plus | More than two children = 1, 0 otherwise (itemX011) |
| Occupation | Retired | Retired = 1, 0 otherwise (itemX028) |
| | Unemployed | Unemployed = 1, 0 otherwise (itemX028) |
| | Housewife | Housewife = 1, 0 otherwise (itemX028) |
| | Student | Student = 1, 0 otherwise (itemX028) |
| Health | Health status 1 (least healthy) to 5 (most healthy) (itema009) | |
| Religion | Religion 1 (least important) to 10 (most important)(itemf063) | |
| No. of observations | | 2807 |

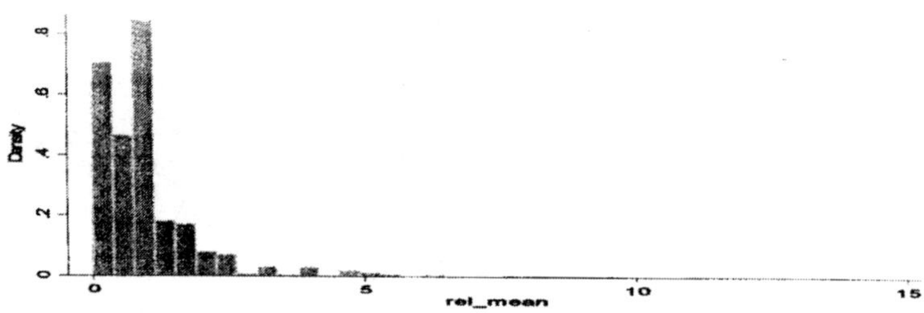


i. **Relative Income(rel_mean)**

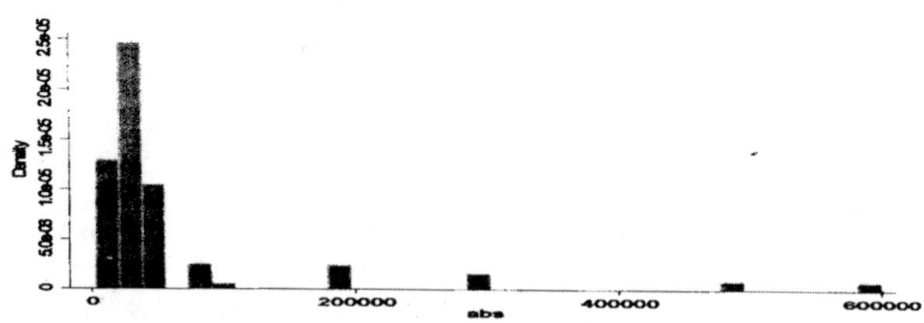


ii. **Absolute Income**

***Figure 8.8: Histograms of Relative and Absolute Incomes***

increase in relative income of an individual will increase the probability of happiness by 0.17. An increase in individual income in relation to the state average income increases the probability of reporting higher satisfaction. The effect of absolute income on happiness is negative, but not statistically significant. Hence, people in India are more concerned with relative income than with their absolute income. This is also supported by the significantly high correlation (0.93) between ln(absy) and ln(rely). The coefficients of marital status show that, married people, living with partners as well as separated and widowed, are less happy than single people, but these results are statistically insignificant. Females are happier than males, and age reduces happiness. Children make people happy and having more than two children makes people more than doubly happy, and the latter is statistically significant. This shows the significance of the value attached to having children in India. The coefficients of all the occupation dummies are negative and statistically significant showing that working individuals, employed or working as part-time or self-employed, are happier than who are unemployed, retired or housewife. This finding is in line with many studies that find negative relationship between unhappiness and unemployment. More healthy people are happier than least healthy individuals and the estimated coefficient is positive and statistically significant. Similarly, religious people are happier than people who give less importance to religion.

**Table 8.5: Ordered Probit Estimates of Happiness in India**
**Dependent variable: Happiness level**

| Variable | | Coefficient | Standard error | p-value |
|---|---|---|---|---|
| Income | ln(absy) | -0.00505 | 0.034084 | 0.882 |
| | ln(rely) | 0.165896** | 0.033918 | 0.000 |
| Marital status | partner | -0.0808 | 0.062142 | 0.194 |
| | split widow | -0.094 | 0.11895 | 0.429 |
| Sex | Female | 0.003524 | 0.040337 | 0.930 |
| Age | | -0.00132 | 0.001669 | 0.429 |
| Children | kid1 | 0.131728 | 0.090249 | 0.144 |
| | kid2plus | 0.338928** | 0.071782 | 0.000 |
| Occupation | Retired | -1.4734** | 0.110778 | 0.000 |
| | unemployed | -0.15346* | 0.060232 | 0.011 |
| | housewife | -0.9633** | 0.056795 | 0.000 |
| | student | -0.5092** | 0.080332 | 0.000 |
| Health | | 0.472347** | 0.024757 | 0.000 |
| Religion | | 0.061001** | 0.007153 | 0.000 |
| Log likelihood function | | -5247.4343 | | |

**Note:** * Significant at 1 percent level. ** Significant at 5 percent level.

The Table 8.6 presents the effects of rank position within the reference group on happiness in India. The estimated coefficient shows that as the rank of a person within his reference group increases his happiness level also increases by 1.82 times, and such effect is statistically significant at 1 percent level. Thus, people do compare their status position with some reference group. Individuals will report higher satisfaction level to the extent that they perceive themselves as ranking higher in happiness relative to others.

**Table 8.6: OLS Estimate of the Effect of Income Rank on Happiness in India Dependent variable: Happiness level**

| *Variable* | *coefficient* | *t-value* | $R^2$ | *N* |
|---|---|---|---|---|
| Income rank (by reference group) | 1.8238 | 7.77* | 0.382 | 1022 |

**Note:** * Significant at 1 percent level.

## 8.5 Conclusion

Pursuing economic growth alone, though remains the key political goal, might not make people in a country happy. Increasing the income of all may not raise the happiness of all, even though wealth and happiness are correlated within a society at a given point of time. Based on WVS data for eight states and for the period 1990-2006, on the question of whether individual's self-reported happiness or satisfaction is influenced by their absolute income or by relative income, the estimated ordered probit results of this paper shows that relative income matters whereas absolute does not affect happiness level. Also, an improvement in rank position of an individual over the reference group will increase his/her happiness level. Thus, the findings of this paper are consistent with the Easterlin (1974) hypothesis that only relative income/ position matters for happiness than the absolute income.

The finding of this paper that people are not concerned much about their absolute income suggests that distribution-neutral increase in average income will not change the happiness level; when everybody's income is increased, on average, individual happiness will remain at the same level. The finding that people care much about their relative income/position suggests that if some people's income grows more slowly than others, the relative looser will end up feeling worse-off. Hence, in this sense any unequal increase in income will lead to unequal changes in happiness level on average. The policy implication of this study is that governments should focus on reducing income inequality rather than increasing the net income so that overall happiness level would increase.

# 9

# Gender and Remittances: Probit and Tobit Estimation of Decision to Remit and Remittances Behaviour of Migrants


## Abstract

*India is on the top of international remittance inflows with Kerala receiving substantial international remittances. Though female migration is also substantial, there is wide gender difference in the remittance behaviour of migrants. This paper analyses the determinants and their effects on migrant's remittance behaviour, the decision to remit and the amount of remittances from the gender perspective in Kerala using the 2008 Kerala Migration Survey. The decision to remit by migrants is estimated by LPM and probit methods, and conditional on decision to remit, the amount of remittances is estimated by Tobit model for both males and females separately. The empirical estimates of this paper show gender difference in decision to remit as well as in the amount of remittances. Female migrants have lower probability to remit, and the amount remitted is lower, than those of male migrants. The estimates of the amount of remittances show that married, rural, head of household and educated migrants remit more and female and young migrants send low remittances, whereas household size, number of migrants in a household and age of migrants increase the amount of remittances. The gender difference in Kerala migration is noticeable and female migrants, unless they are the head of the household, have lower probability to remit and their level of remittances is low compared to male migrants.*



**Key words:** *Kerala migration, gender, decision to remit, remittances, probit and tobit estimation*


## 9.1 Introduction

With increasing globalisation and the rapid growth of information technology resulting in global labour mobility, international migration has become a significant global phenomenon in recent years. Consequently, international migrant remittance inflows into the developing countries have experienced significant increase over the past decades. For many developing countries, such migrant remittances constitute one of the largest sources of foreign exchange earnings, even exceeding export revenues, FDI, aid, or private capital flows. International migrant remittances become, therefore, a relatively attractive source of foreign earnings for developing countries. The IMF, in balance of payments, mentions three components as constituting remittances - compensation of employees (part of income component of current account), worker remittances (part of current transfers in current account) and migrant transfers (part of capital account). Migrant remittances commonly refer to the monetary transactions that are initiated by individuals living or working outside their country of birth or origin and related to their migration. Worker remittances are current private transfers from migrant workers who are considered resident (living in the host country for a year or longer) of the host country to recipients in their country of origin.

The international remittance inflows in developing countries has significantly increased from US$31.2 billion in 1990 to US$160 billion in 2004. The World Bank has estimated that the global remittances totalled $443.4 billion in 2008, of which $338 billion went to developing countries (World Bank, 2010). The World Bank projects that global remittances will reach US$689 billion in 2018 of which the developing countries will receive about US$528. In 2009, remittance inflows in 11 countries were equal to more than 20 percent of their GDP, and in 22 countries, remittances accounted for more than 10 percent of GDP. India received US$52 billion as remittances in 2008, equivalent of 4.2 percent of its GDP, and accounts for close to 10 percent of

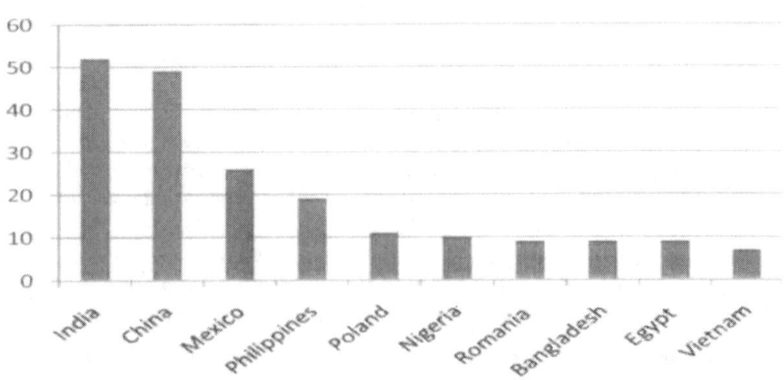


*Source:* World Bank (2010).

***Figure 9.1: Top 10 Recipient of Remittances, 2008 (US$ billions)***

global remittances. The Figure 9.1 shows the top 10 recipients of international remittances. Among them, India ranked number one with the largest recipient of remittances, followed by China with US$49 billion remittances and Mexico and Philippines. The pattern is the same in 2018 also with India retaining the top spot as the country receiving the largest amount of remittances followed by China, Mexico, Philippines and Egypt.

The Figure 9.2 shows the dominant position of Indian remittances, with the remittance inflow increasing approximately 20 fold during the period 1991-2008. In 1990-1991, for instance, the RBI reported that remittances from overseas Indians were a modest $2.1 billion. This has risen gradually over the years, and dramatically recently. Remittance inflows rose to $12.3 billion in 1996-1997 and jumped to $22 billion in 2003-2004. Between 2000-2001 and 2003-2004, remittances almost doubled. The Reserve Bank of India (RBI) reported that Indian migrants transferred $24.1 billion to India in 2005-2006. Despite the global financial crisis of 2007-08, there was sharp increase in remittance inflows to India in 2008 in absolute term. International remittance inflows to India actually increased from US$44 billion in 2008-09 to US$52 billion in 2009-10. In 2018, India received US$80 billion as remittances.

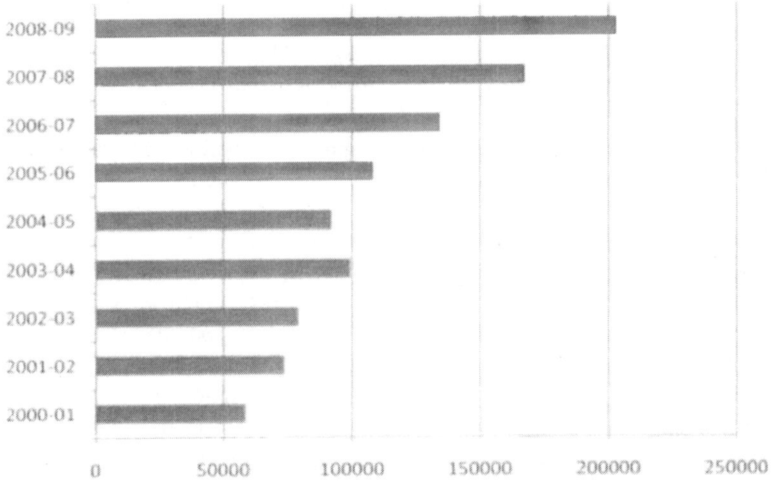


*Source:* RBI: Handbook of Statistics on Indian Economy (2009-10).

***Figure 9.2: Remittance Inflows to India (Rs. crores)***

Traditionally, the Gulf countries are the major source of international remittance inflows to India. In 1990-91, 40 percent of the remittances came from Gulf countries and 24 percent from North America. However, the change in patterns of emigration towards more skilled and technical manpower has led to a significant shift in the source regions of remittance inflows to India. As shown in Figure 9.3, recently North America has replaced the Gulf countries as the most important source for remittances. The RBI estimates that 44 percent of remittances originate in North America, 24 percent in the Gulf region and 13 percent in Europe.

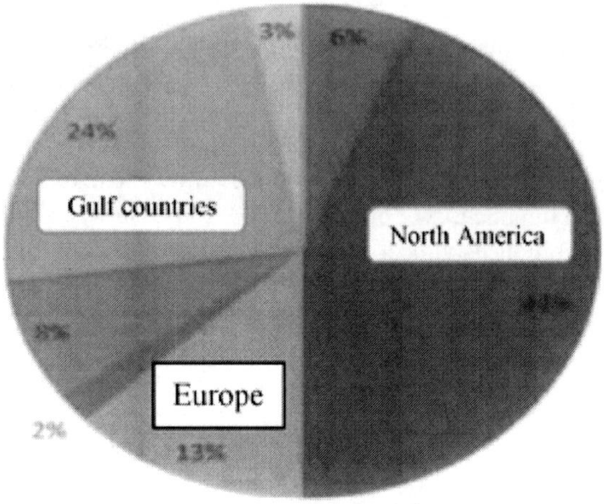


*Source:* RBI (2006): Invisibles in India's Balance of Payments.

***Figure 9.3: Source Regions of Remittance Inflows to India***

Remittances are among the most tangible links between migration and development, both at individual and state levels. While remittance inflows could positively influence economic growth and reduce poverty, the rapid increase in such inflows could also possibly generate adverse effects to the overall economy, notably retarding economic growth. Empirical evidence on the effect of worker remittances on economic growth and poverty reduction are mixed. While Taylor (1992) and Faini (2005) find a positive relationship between remittances and economic growth, Chami et al. (2003; 2008) and IMF (2005) find either negative or no impact on economic growth. Likewise, while Stahl (1982) find that remittances would not benefit the poor, Adams and Page (2005) find positive and significant impact of remittances on poverty reduction.

It is also argued that in a large economy like India, the impact of remittances on overall development is negligible, compared to some key economic and fiscal factors. However, the impact of remittances on incomes of households and non-economic factors, their relative importance of remittances can not be dismissed as insignificant. Especially, the effect of remittances is more pronounced in parts of the country that have experienced higher volumes of emigration and in regions where is not much scope for either industrialisation or IT sector development. In India, Kerala is one such region, which sends the highest proportion of emigrants to the Gulf countries and receives the highest amount of remittances. The contribution of remittances to Kerala economy is more significant compared to its contribution to the overall Indian economy.

While the share of remittances from all countries to Indian economy is about 4.2 percent of its GDP, the share of remittances is nearly 30 percent of the NSDP of Kerala. Kerala received about 20 percent of remittances which come to India. Including remittances, Kerala's per capita income is 60 percent higher than the national per capita income. Remittances to Kerala were 174 times the revenue receipts of the state, 7 times of the transfers to the state from the central government and 1.8 times the annual expenditure of the Kerala government. Remittances were sufficient to wipe out 60 percent of the Kerala state's debt. According to the Kerala migration survey, out of the 34 million population of Kerala, 2.2 million are emigrants (residents of Kerala who left for studies or work abroad), 1.2 million are return emigrants (those who worked or studied abroad and returned to Kerala) and 3.4 million are non-resident Keralites. Emigrants account for 7 percent of the total resident population. About 90 percent of the emigrants are in six countries in the Gulf region, the United Arab Emirates, Saudi Arabia, Oman, Qatar, Bahrain and Kuwait. With such size of emigrants, one out of five households in Kerala received remittances.

According to the Kerala migration survey 2003, there is an incredible increase in the flow of remittances to Kerala. As shown in Figure 9.4, remittances to Kerala have increased from 1156 crores in 1989-90 to

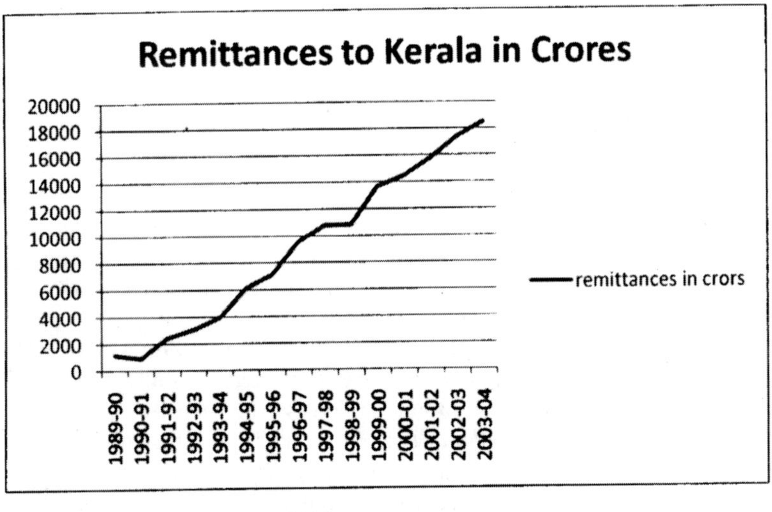


*Source:* Kerala Migration Survey (2003)

***Figure 9.4: Remittances to Kerala***

14438 crores in 2000. In 2002-03, it was 17362 crores which again increased to 18465 crores in 2003-04. Each emigrant, on an average, supports a minimum of four persons (the average household size in Kerala is 5 persons). In other words, 2.2 million emigrants provide livelihoods for 8.8 million persons left behind in Kerala - women, children and parents. It simply means that 32 percent of Kerala's population is either directly or indirectly benefited by the international migration alone. The proportion of households that used remittances for education is about 40 percent. About 50 percent of the cash remittances are used for subsistence, 25 percent on education, an item which accounted for 25 percent of the cash remittances, 8 percent for debt repayment, 4.6 percent for savings, 4.4 percent for constructing houses. Remittances also contributed to investments in businesses and accumulation of both movable and non-movable assets.

It is also important to understand the motivation for emigration and subsequent remitting behaviour. With regard to the motivation, the risk-sharing motive suggests that remittances are part of a risk management strategy (Stark, 1991; Stark and Lucas, 1988). The remittances provide benefits to the emigrant who intends to return home and the recipient household, providing security and the maintenance of a sufficient income in the event of external shocks. These may be the result of a loss of employment on the part of the remitter or drought in the case of a rural beneficiary. Remittances are thus a mutual benefit and are an enforceable contract between the remitter and the recipients. Therefore, risk sharing motive suggests that remittances are a contractual premium that is not affected by the number of migrants from the same family that are remitting or the poverty status of the receiving household. Any altruistic behaviour is seen as coincidental to personal self-interest. However, one of the main problems of this approach is that it assumes the migrant is a rational economic being, whereas some evidences suggest that family bonds of trust and not simply economic expediency play an important role in the decision to remit (Kannan and Hari, 2002; Yang, 2011; Budijanto et al., 2016).

There is another view that remittances fullfil an obligation to the household, based on affection and responsibility towards the family (Chimhowu, Piesse, and Pinder, 2005). The migrant is simply part of a spatially extended household that is reducing the risk of impoverishment by diversifying across a number of activities (Banerjee, 1984; de Haan, 1999; Agarwal and Horowitz, 2002). Thus, emigration is a one such diversification strategy, and hence, migration of a member of household is a collective family decision. With such a diversification motive, the migrant uses established networks for both potential employment opportunities and the transfer of funds and other resources. When motivated by altruism, remittances can vary depending on the number of household members that migrate and the poverty status of the receiving household. It has been observed that poorer households receive a greater proportion of their total income more than the non-poor ones. The third model is a combination of the two, where altruism and self-interest both are determinants of the decision to migrate and remit (Clarke and Drinkwater, 2001; Ballard, 2005). Migrants are motivated by self-interest, but this is usually within the context of existing kinship ties. Remittances that are part of productive investment tend to have an impact on long-term poverty reduction, resulting in less vulnerability at both household and community level. There may also be a reduction in inter-household inequality.

There are significant differences between men and women in several aspects of migration such as motivation, risks, norms and consequences. De La Cruz (1995) observes some gender dimensions that male migrants are more likely to follow self-interest whereas female migrants remit more out of altruism. From the remitter perspective, women comprise a small but growing percentage of migrants and are generally considered to be the more reliable remitters. Female migrants also have influence in the use of their remittances while they are away from home. Evidence of female preferences for expenditure on welfare enhancing consumption are noted, for example, the education of the younger siblings and health of parents. Conversely, male migrants tend to remit money to savings account for themselves or for investment on their behalf in land and hosing for the future. Female remitters are more likely to contribute to household consumption needs as a risk reduction strategy, out of altruism, whereas males invest in risk management, largely out of self-interest.

Thus, there is wide gender difference in the remittance behaviour of migrants. The motivation and decision to migrate, destination, type of job, ability, risks faced, norms followed, motive to send remittance, intended purpose of remitting, expectations from remittance receiving individual, and return migration aspects are all likely to be influenced by gender. Therefore, this paper analyses the determinants and their effects on migrant's remittance behaviour, the decision to remit and the amount of remittances from the gender perspective in Kerala using the 2008 Kerala Migration Survey. Empirically, the Probit model is used to estimate the decision to remit and Tobit model is used to estimate the level of remittances, conditional on decision to remit, for both males and females separately.

## 9.2 A Brief Review of Recent Studies

There have been a number of that determine the remittance behaviour, the decision to remit and the level of remittances. The major factor that affects the remittance behaviour is the gender difference. The other major factors affecting remittance behaviour are the earnings in the destination country, education, migrant's legal status, job, number of household members in the home country, etc.

According to Amuedo-Dorantes and Pozo (2006), remittances are the result of three main motives-asset accumulation, altruism, and insurance. They use data on Mexican immigrants who work in the US to test the insurance motive for sending remittances, relating host economy risk levels to remittance flows. They report that an increase in income risk associated with earnings and employment in the US significantly raises both the propensity and the proportion of labour earnings sent home for family provided insurance and for self-insurance. Income risk proxies (e.g. being an undocumented immigrant or not having social networks within the United States) are associated with a higher propensity to remit and with a higher level of remittances. Undocumented immigrants send a significantly higher fraction of their earnings to Mexico, as do migrants lacking social networks in their US based communities. In contrast, immigrants with longer work and residency histories in the US remit less. They also observe that Mexican immigrants who remit for family provided insurance tend to be male, younger, less educated wage and salaried workers employed in the agricultural sector, and with families back home and those who lack social networks in the US. In contrast, Mexican immigrants who are motivated by self-insure via remittances for asset accumulation are older migrants with US based social networks. They have used Tobit model to explain the likelihood of transferring money home and fraction of earnings remitted.

Agarwal and Horowitz (2002) using data from Guyana links the behavioural differences of migrants from multiple versus single migrant households to remittance motivation by estimating the Probit model for remittance behaviour of multiple and single migrants. Empirical results show that per-migrant remittances decline in the number of migrants, suggesting altruistic incentive to remit.

Adams (2008) using instrumental variable method study the effect of skill composition, identified with education level, on migrant behaviour. High skilled migrants remit less because they are more likely to bring family members and to remain in their newly adopted country and so they are less concerned with any eventual return to their home country. By contrast, low skilled migrants tend to remit more because their migration is more temporary in nature and they are more concerned with returning home.

Markova and Reilly (2007) study the remittance behaviour of Bulgarian immigrants in Spain using Tobit model. They observe that a Bulgarian migrant with legal status to remain and work in Spain remits less than someone without the status. Those without legal status retain stronger connections with their Bulgarian based family members given the greater degree of uncertainty that attaches to their status in Spain, a form of insurance against the risk of being repatriated. Legal status guarantees a greater degree of certainty for the migrant thus potentially reducing reliance on the Bulgarian household to act as an insurer for the last resort. Further findings of this study are males remit more than females, married individual remit more than those in other marital status categories, and remittances rise with the number of family members.

Funkhouser (1995) makes a comparative study on remittances behaviour in the regions of El Salvador and Nicaragua. The Probit model is used to estimate probability to remit separately for both regions and Tobit and OLS are used to estimate the determinants of level of remittances. They find that sex and age do not influence the probability or the level of remittances. Education is negatively correlated with the probability of remitting, and among those who remit, the educated are likely to remit more. The migrants who have their spouse left in their home country remit more.

Holst, Schafer, Scrooten (2011) examining the immigrants of Germany who are on the transnational network contract, using Tobit model, find that women remit less than men, contrary to the findings of earlier studies. However, females remit a higher share of their own labour income than men. A second interesting finding is that immigrant women with foreign citizenship remit less than men if they have remigration plans. They find that remittances increase with the age of a migrant, being married and planning to re-migrate. The household size in Germany has a negative impact on remittances. Structure of the existing social network in Germany and the network structure in the home country both play important roles in explaining remittances. With remittances, women's economic importance within the transnational network increases.

Semyonov and Gorodzeisky (2005), for Philippine migrants, find that men send more money than do women to households in Philippines. The gender gap in the amount of remittances is attributed to the gender gap in the earnings in overseas markets. Consequently, due to difference in amount of remittances, households with men employed overseas enjoy higher income than households with women overseas. Thus, earnings inequality between men and women in the global economy has significant consequence for income inequality among households within Philippines.

Orozco, Lowell, Schneider (2006) observe opposite results for the gender differences in remittance behaviour among the migrants of Latin America, the Caribbean, and West Africa, showing that women appear to remit lesser amounts than men. An interesting finding of this study is that women remit more than men to other than their spouse, especially to more distant family members including siblings and others, while men increase the amount of the remittances only when sending to their spouse, which shows that women indeed act more altruistically. Further, both men and women remit more the longer they have been sending remittances but women remit yet more than men over time.

Thus, empirical studies show that there are significant differences in the remittance behaviour among males and females. Generally, males remit more than females, chiefly as insurance or self-interest. When women remit more, it is generally altruistic concern. The main reason for this is the differences in earnings of individuals in host countries and the commitment to the family in the sending countries. In most of the studies, the Probit model is used to analyse the decision to remit and Tobit model is used to model the remittances function.

## 9.3 Data and Methodology

This paper uses the 2008 Kerala Migration Survey in the empirical analysis of migration and remittances behaviour. The Kerala Migration Survey has been conducted by the Centre for Development Studies in all the fourteen districts of Kerala. Over the past 12 years, five large scale migration surveys have been conducted covering 15,000 representative sample households which have both migrants including both emigrants and out-migrants and non-migrants, in order to monitor and assess the migration situation in terms of employment and remittances for policy formulation at the state level. The survey covers a wide range of topics including information on the migration process, socio-economic characteristics of the migrants, demographic and other characteristics of the household. The survey also includes details about sources for financing migration, expenses incurred for emigration, and utilisation of remittances.

This paper considers only the emigrants, migrants who moved from Kerala to other countries. Sample size used in this analysis contains 2742 emigrants, consisting of 2489 male emigrants and 253 female emigrants. The female sample is low compared to male emigrants as 2422 emigrants are unmarried, and most female emigrants are married women who migrate with husband. A majority of the emigrants are literate, 28 percent of female emigrants are graduates compared to only 9 percent of the male emigrants with degree.

The main dependent variables in the empirical analysis are the decision to remit and the amount of remittances, defined as the total value of the money/goods that the migrant sent to their relatives during the 12-month period immediately prior to the survey. To analyse the decision to remit, the linear probability and Probit models are used. The dependent variable is a binary or dichotomous variable indicating whether the emigrant remits or not. Linear probability model is estimated using OLS method and probit model by the maximum likelihood method. Remittances are observed only for those emigrants who choose to remit and the size of the remittance is normally above a minimum level, thus making the sample a censored sample. Therefore, for estimating amount of remittances, the Tobit model is used taking into account the censored nature of the dependent variable.

### Linear Probability Model

As the objective is to know the probability to remit or not, the LPM provides the probabilities by applying the OLS method to the estimating model given by,

$$y = \alpha_0 + \alpha_1 x_1 + \alpha_2 x_2 + \cdots + \alpha_k x_k + u \qquad (9.1)$$

where $x$'s are explanatory variables and $y = 1$ if the emigrant remits and 0 if not remitting. The LPM is a typical linear regression model except that the regressand is binary. However, the LPM assumes that the probability $P = E(y=1|x)$ increases linearly with $x$, that is, the marginal effect of $x$ remains constant throughout the distribution. There is also the possibility that the estimated probability of $y$, $\hat{y}$, lying outside the 0-1 range. These limitations of the LPM can be overcome by the Probit model.

## Probit Model

In the probit model, the remittance decision depends on an unobservable utility index $I_i$ that is determined by the explanatory variables, in such a way that the larger the value of index the greater the probability of the emigrant to remit. The index function is stated as,

$$I_i^* = \beta_0 + \beta_1 x_1 + \beta_2 x_2 + \cdots + \beta_k x_k + v_i \tag{9.2}$$

$$y = 1 \quad if\ I_i^* \geq 0 \tag{9.3}$$

$$= 0 \quad if\ I_i^* < 0$$

$y = 1$ if the emigrant remits and $y = 0$ if he doesn't remit. For each individual there is a critical or threshold level of the index $I_i^*$, such that if $I_i^*$ exceeds the threshold, remittances are observed and hence it is taken as the emigrant has decided to remit, and when $I_i^*$is less than the threshold, remittances are not observed and hence it is taken as the emigrant has decided not to remit. As the threshold is not directly observed but assumed to be normally distributed with constant mean and variance, it is possible not only to estimate the parameters of the index given in equation (9.2) but also to get some information about the unobservable index itself.

Given the assumption of normality, the probability that if $I_i^*$ is less than or equal to the critical value $I_i$ can be computed from the standardised normal CDF as,

$$P_i = P(y = 1/x) = P(I_i^* \geq I_i) = P(z_i \geq \alpha_0 + \alpha_1 x_i) = \Phi(\alpha_0 + \alpha_1 x_i) \tag{9.4}$$

where $P(y = 1/x)$ is the conditional probability that individual remits given the values of explanatory variables, $z$ is the standard normal variable with $z \sim N(0,\sigma^2)$, and $\Phi$ is the standard normal CDF. The CDF is given by,

$$\Phi(I_i) = \frac{1}{\sqrt{2\pi}} \int_{-\infty}^{I_i} e^{\left(-\frac{z^2}{2}\right)} dz = \frac{1}{\sqrt{2\pi}} \int_{-\infty}^{\alpha_0 + \alpha_1 x_i} e^{\left(-\frac{z^2}{2}\right)} dz \tag{9.5}$$

Since P represents the probability that emigrant remits, it is measured by the area of the standard normal curve from 0 to $I_i$ the threshold level. The probit model is estimated by the maximum likelihood method.

## Tobit Model

An extension of the Probit model is the Tobit model, which could be applied to estimate the amount of remittances from the censored sample. The Tobit model is defined as a latent variable model,

$$R_i^* = \gamma_0 + \gamma x_i + \varepsilon \quad \varepsilon|\mathrm{x} \sim \mathrm{N}(0, \sigma^2) \tag{9.6}$$

$$R_i = \max(0, R^*) \tag{9.7}$$

$$R_i = R_i^* if R_i^* > 0 \tag{9.8}$$

$$= 0 \; if R_i^* \leq 0$$

where $R_i^*$ is the unobservable individual propensity to remit. The equation (9.7) implies that the observed variable, amount remitted, $R$ equals $R^*$ when $R^* > 0$, but $R = 0$ when $R^* < 0$ as given in equation (9.8). Because $R^*$ is normally distributed, $R$ has a continuous distribution over strictly positive values. The remittances equation is a censored regression model because observations on at or below zero are censored. As the values fall at or below zero are censored, it is left censoring of the data, as not all individuals remit positive amounts in a given year. For the maximum likelihood estimation of censored sample, the likelihood function is expressed as,

$$L = \prod[1 - \Phi(\beta x/\sigma_\varepsilon)] \prod\left[\phi\left(\frac{R_i - \beta x}{\sigma_\varepsilon}\right)/\sigma_\varepsilon\right] \tag{9.9}$$

where $\Phi(.)$ and $\phi(.)$ are the cumulative distribution and probability density functions of the standard normal. The unconditional expectation of remittances is given by,

$$E(R_i/x, \beta, \sigma) = x\Phi(\beta x/\sigma_\varepsilon) + \sigma_\varepsilon\phi(\beta x/\sigma_\varepsilon) \tag{9.10}$$

It is also known that the censored Tobit model estimates are subject to bias and inconsistency in the presence of heteroscedasticity. The main form of heteroscedasticity is given by,

$$\sigma_\varepsilon = e^{\delta\,\omega_i} \tag{9.11}$$

where $\omega_i$ comprises a matrix of variables found to be the source for the residual dispersion and $\delta$ is a vector of unknown parameters. The likelihood function incorporating heteroscedasticity is given by,

$$L^H = \prod[1 - \Phi(\beta x/(\sigma_\varepsilon e^{\delta\,\omega_i})] \prod\left[\phi\left(\frac{R_i - \beta x}{\sigma_\varepsilon e^{\delta\,\omega_i}}\right)/\sigma_\varepsilon e^{\delta\,\omega_i}\right] \tag{9.12}$$

Then, the unconditional expectation of remittances can be expressed as,

$$E(R_i/x, \omega; \beta, \sigma) = x\Phi\left(\beta x/\sigma_\varepsilon e^{\delta\,\omega_i}\right) + \sigma_\varepsilon e^{\delta\,\omega_i}\phi(\beta x/\sigma_\varepsilon) \tag{9.13}$$

## 9.4 Empirical Analysis

In the empirical analysis of remittances behaviour, the Probit model is used to estimate the probability to remit and heteroscedastic Tobit model is used to estimate the remittances of emigrants, for both males and females. The Table 9.1 presents the description and descriptive statistics of the variables used in the empirical analysis. About 90 percent of male emigrants reported positive remittances, whereas only 79 percent of female migrants remitted. On average, over the relevant 12 months frame, men actually remitted slightly more than women. The mean remittances reported is Rs.76,600 per year. It also shows that most of the women are married compared to men when they migrate. While out of 10 percent of female emigrants, 83 percent of female migrants are married, about 80 percent male migrants are married. On average, three females are migrants in a household, 1.3 males are migrants, showing female migration is largely family migration. Majority of migrants, 76 percent, are from rural areas. The mean of the dummy variable for the household head shows that more men are household head compared to women. More number of males and females, on average 62 percent, are employed in the private sector. Majority of male migrants are in the age group of 35-55, while more number of female migrants are in the ages 25-35, implying most of them are migrating after marriage. On average, males are less educated than females. Most men, 20 percent have secondary school education, whereas degree holders are more, 25 percent, among the females compared to males. Males are migrating from the rural areas compared to females. Male migrants are from households with more members compared to females.

**Table 9.1: Descriptive Statistics of Variables in the Remittances Analysis**

| *Variable* | *Description* | *Males* | *Females* | *Total sample* |
|---|---|---|---|---|
| Remit | Individual remits = 1, 0 otherwise | 0.902 (0.30) | 0.791 (0.41) | 0.892 (0.31) |
| Remittance | Remittances (Rs./annum) | 76657.73 (75577.9) | 75939.98 (115926.3) | 76603.92 (79612.3) |
| HHsize | Number of household members in home country | 04.85 (2.61) | 3.55 (2.16) | 4.670 (2.60) |
| NOEmg | Number of emigrants in the household | 1.39 (0.89) | 3.10(2.12) | 1.557(1.25) |
| Female | Female = 1, 0 otherwise | - | - | 0.093 (0.29) |
| Married | Married = 1, 0 otherwise | 0.795 (0.41) | 0.830 (0.39) | 0.768 (0.46) |
| Job1 | Government sector worker = 1, 0 otherwise | 0.010 (0.10) | 0.111 (0.31) | 0.020 (0.14) |
| Job2 | Semi-government sector worker = 1, 0 otherwise | 0.009 (0.10) | 0.012 (0.11) | 0.012 (0.11) |
| Job3 | Private sector worker = 1, 0 otherwise | 0.61 (0.49) | 0.73 (0.46) | 0.625 (0.48) |
| Job4 | Self-employed = 1, 0 otherwise | 0.388 (0.19) | 0.20 (0.14) | 0.039 (0.20) |
| Job5 | Family work = 1, 0 otherwise | 0.002 (0.04) | 0.012 (0.10) | 0.003 (0.05) |
| Job6 | Non-agricultural sector labourer = 1, 0 otherwise | 0.327 (0.47) | 0.071 (0.23) | 0.295(0.46) |

*(Contd...)*

| | | | | |
|---|---|---|---|---|
| HHead | Head of the household = 1, 0 otherwise, | 0.250 (0.43) | 0.063 (0.24) | 0.212 (0.41) |
| Rural | Rural area = 1, 0 otherwise | 0.777 (0.42) | 0.670 (0.47) | 0.760(0.43) |
| Edu1 | Illiterate = 1, 0 otherwise | 0.003 (0.06) | 0.020 (0.14) | 0.005 (0.07) |
| Edu2 | Not completed primary = 1, 0 otherwise | 0.020 (0.14) | 0.00 (0.00) | 0.018 (0.13) |
| Edu3 | Primary education = 1, 0 otherwise | 0.066 (0.25) | 0.024 (0.15) | 0.059 (0.24) |
| Edu4 | Upper primary to secondary = 1, 0 otherwise | 0.474 (0.50) | 0.130 (0.38) | 0.435 (0.50) |
| Edu5 | Secondary passed = 1, 0 otherwise | 0.295 (0.46) | 0.245 (0.43) | 0.290 (0.45) |
| Edu6 | Degree holder = 1, 0 otherwise | 0.090 (0.29) | 0.249 (0.43) | 0.118 (0.32) |
| Age1 | Age < 25 years = 1, 0 otherwise | 0.062 (0.24) | 0.065 (0.25) | 0.079 (0.27) |
| Age2 | Age 25-35 years= 1, 0 otherwise | 0.395 (0.49) | 0.513 (0.50) | 0.415 (0.49) |
| Age3 | Age 36-55 years= 1, 0 otherwise | 0.497 (0.50) | 0.355 (0.48) | 0.464 (0.50) |
| N | No. of observations | 2489 | 253 | 2742 |

The Table 9.2 presents the OLS estimates of LPM and maximum likelihood estimates of the Probit model for remittances decision. In both the models, almost all coefficients are statistically significant at 5 percent level, except age and number of emigrants from a household. In estimated probabilities are higher in Probit model relative to the LPM, showing the limitations of the LPM discussed earlier. This is also reflected in the low R-square of the LPM relative to the log-likelihood of the probit model. In both LPM and probit estimates, the coefficient of the dummy variable female shows that remitting female migrants are lesser than that of male migrants. It may be because women migrate with their children. Expenses of education and other purposes for children leave them with little money to remit. The coefficient of the dummy variable married shows that married migrants have higher probability to remit than unmarried migrants. The coefficient of the household head is positive and the coefficient of the dummy variable rural is also positive, indicating rural migrants have higher probability to remit compared to urban migrants. An increase in one member of the household in the home country, increases the probability of remitting by the migrants. All the coefficients of education dummies are positive indicating that education increases the probability to remit. The coefficient of the dummy variable for lower age is negative showing that if a migrant age is below 25 years, the probability to remit decreases, whereas the probability of remitting by migrants aged above 25 years increases. The number of emigrants from a household decreases the probability to remit, but the coefficient is not statistically significant in any of the specifications.

In the probit estimates of remittance decision of males and females presented separately in Table 9.2, the coefficient of married dummy is positive 0.27 for males and negative 0.35 for females. This implies that married male migrants have 0.27 higher probability to remit and married females migrants have 0.35 lower probability of remitting than the unmarried male and female migrants. The coefficients of all job dummies are negative and statistically significant for both male and female samples. This is so because most migrants are employed in low paying private sector jobs or self-employed, and hence their earnings are low irrespective of occupation in the host country. Moreover, most of the female migrants who are working jobs migrate with their children, and hence they have to sustain their family in the destination country as well. The coefficients of education variables are positive for both males and females, but the probability is significant only in male estimates and none of the education dummies are significant in the female specification. Male education coefficients are also high, implying higher probability to remit with education beyond secondary level. The female migrants in the age group 26 and 35 have 0.93 higher probability to remit than other age groups. Number of emigrants in the household has no statistical effect on the probability of remitting either in male or in female equations.

**Table 9.2: LPM and Probit Estimates of Remittances Decision**

| *Variable* | *Pooled sample* | | *Males* | *Females* |
|---|---|---|---|---|
| | *LPM (OLS estimates)* | *ML Probit estimates* | *ML Probit estimates* | *ML Probit estimates* |
| Female | -0.067** (0.003) | -0.294** (0.01) | - | - |
| Married | 0.065** (0.00) | 0.235** (0.001) | 0.269** (0.00) | -0.349 (0.246) |
| HHead | 0.089** (0.00) | 0.985** (0.000) | 0.853** (0.00) | 0.775*** (0.07) |
| Rural | 0.027** (0.04) | 0.176** (0.023) | 0.190** (0.03) | 0.029 (0.89) |
| HHsize | 0.006** (0.006) | 0.043** (0.004) | 0.045** (0.00) | 0.008 (0.86) |
| Job1 | - | - | -0.679** (0.00) | -0.414** (0.00) |
| Job2 | - | - | -0.539** (0.00) | -0.436** (0.00) |
| Job3 | - | - | -0.856** (0.00) | -0.841** (0.00) |
| Job4 | - | - | -0.638** (0.00) | -0.236** (0.00) |
| Job6 | - | - | -0.770** (0.00) | -0.697** (0.00) |
| Edu1 | - | - | - | 0.236 (0.74) |
| Edu3 | 0.067** (0.045) | 0.293 (0.164) | - | - |
| Edu4 | 0.063** (0.009) | 0.247** (0.048) | 0.297** (0.03) | 0.060 (0.86) |
| Edu5 | 0.080** (0.001) | 0.329** (0.007) | 0.406** (0.00) | -0.001 (0.99) |
| Edu6 | 0.061** (0.021) | 0.250*** (0.062) | 0.331** (0.04) | 0.184 (0.47) |

*(Contd...)*

| | | | | |
|---|---|---|---|---|
| Age1 | -0.115** (0.003) | -0.282 (0.268) | -0.441 (0.13) | 0.046 (0.94) |
| Age2 | 0.018 (0.535) | 0.282 (0.222) | - | 0.931*** (0.09) |
| NOEmg | -0.005 (0.324) | -0.015 (0.578) | -0.019 (0.60) | 0.004 (0.94) |
| Constant | 0.693** (0.00) | 0.128 (0.846) | 0.523** (0.00) | 0.993** (0.00) |
| Log likelihood | $R^2 = 0.084$ | -823.757 | -689.513 | -116.817 |

**Note:** Standard errors in parentheses. ** Significant at 5 percent level.

The Table 9.3 presents the maximum likelihood as well as the heteroscedastic maximum likelihood Tobit estimates for the amount of remittances. Most of the variables have statistically significant coefficients in pooled sample and male sample. In the female sample, almost all variables are statistically insignificant, except household head and age group 26-35, showing that if only a female is head of a family she could remit. This is clear from the estimated coefficients that female heads remit more compared to male heads. Female head of the households remit Rs. 25,000-27,000 per annum, whereas male heads remit Rs. 9000 per annum. The positive sign of the coefficient of dummy variable for married shows that married migrants send more amount of money than the unmarried. Married males remit Rs. 2000-8000 more than unmarried males. The coefficient of married dummy is negative, but statistically insignificant. The coefficient of the household size shows that when there is an increase in the number of household members, the amount of remittances increases by Rs. 700 per annum. If the migrant is from a rural sector, the amount of remittances will increase by Rs. 3000 rupees. All the occupation variables in both male and female specifications are negative and statistically insignificant, except government job in the destination country. The coefficients of education dummies show that as education increases amount that remittances by male migrants also increases. The estimate of the number of emigrants in a household shows that when there is an increase in number of migrants, the amount remittances will decrease by Rs.1000-2000 per annum.

**Table 9.3: Tobit Estimates of Amount of Remittances**

| *Variable* | *Pooled sample* | | *Males* | | *Females* | |
|---|---|---|---|---|---|---|
| | *ML Tobit estimates* | *Heteroscedastic ML Tobit estimates* | *ML Tobit estimates* | *Heteroscedastic ML Tobit estimates* | *ML Tobit estimates* | *Heteroscedastic ML Tobit estimates* |
| Female | -0.075** (0.003) | -0.103** (0.00) | - | - | - | - |
| Married | 0.074** (0.000) | 0.014 (0.145) | 0 .087** (0.00) | 0.025** (0.003) | -0.128 (0.168) | -0.155 (0.736) |
| HHead | 0.098** (0.00) | 0.080** (0.00) | 0.085** (0.00) | 0.068** (0.00) | 0.275*** (0.052) | 0.256*** (0.08) |

*(Contd...)*

| | | | | | | |
|---|---|---|---|---|---|---|
| Rural | 0.030** (0.047) | 0.023* (0.098) | 0.031** (0.04) | 0.018 (0.15) | 0.005 (0.94) | 0.049 (0.52) |
| HHsize | 0.007** (0.006) | 0.007** (0.002) | 0.007** (0.009) | 0.007** (0.001) | 0.001 (0.91) | 0.001 (0.94) |
| Job1 | - | - | -0.260* (0.06) | -0.124 (0.31) | 0.008 (0.99) | 0.026 (0.96) |
| Job2 | - | - | -0.152 (0.29) | -0.072 (0.57) | -0.379 (0.46) | -0.272 (0.60) |
| Job3 | - | - | -0.101 (0.43) | -0.014 (0.90) | -0.201 (0.68) | -0.155 (0.75) |
| Job4 | - | - | -0.177 (0.18) | -0.018 (0.88) | -0.293 (0.58) | -0.408 (0.47) |
| Job6 | - | - | -0.088 (0.49) | -0.025 (0.82) | -0.061 (0.90) | -0.075 (0.88) |
| Edu1 | - | - | - | - | 0.094 (0.69) | -0.354 (0.35) |
| Edu3 | 0.076** (0.042) | 0.098** (0.004) | - | - | - | - |
| Edu4 | 0.072** (0.008) | 0.086** (0.001) | 0.078** (0.006) | 0.114** (0.00) | 0.034 (0.77) | 0.012 (0.92) |
| Edu5 | 0.090** (0.001) | 0.080** (0.002) | 0.100** (0.00) | 0.115** (0.00) | 0.004 (0.96) | -0.061 (0.56) |
| Edu6 | 0.070** (0.019) | 0.074** (0.009) | 0.081** (0.01) | 0.110** (0.00) | 0.073 (0.39) | 0.044 (0.63) |
| Age1 | -0.132** (0.003) | -0.100 (0.116) | -0.147** (0.001) | -0.014 (0.83) | 0.016 (0.94) | -0.172 (0.53) |
| Age2 | 0.020 (0.538) | 0.024 (0.37) | - | - | 0.369** (0.05) | 0.349* (0.07) |
| NOEmg | -0.006 (0.317) | -0.017** (0.001) | -0.006 (0.38) | -0.022** (0.00) | 0.0006 (0.97) | -0.005 (0.77) |
| Constant | 0.657 (0.317) | 0.602** (0.00) | 0.798** (0.00) | 0.836** (0.00) | 0.673** (0.00) | 0.714 (0.31) |
| Log likelihood | -1224.374 | -445.371 | -957.245 | -127.479 | -201.081 | -166.864 |

**Note:** Standard errors in parentheses. ** Significant at 5 percent level.

The coefficient of female dummy in the pooled sample is negative and statistically significant, indicating that females remit about 10 percent less amount of money than males. On average a female migrant remits Rs. 1000 less per annum than a male migrant. The coefficient of the dummy variable for age less than 25 years is negative and statistically significant which shows that if a person is less than age 25 the amount that he remits will be less by Rs.13000-14000 per annum. In the estimates without correcting for heteroscedasticity of female migrant sample, there is a significant positive effect of female age between 26-35 years wherein they remit Rs. 35000-37000 per annum more than the other age group female migrants. Thus, the estimates of the amount of remittances show that married, rural, educated and head of household migrants send more remittances, whereas female and young migrants send lower remittances. Also, household size, number of migrants in a household and higher age of migrants increases the remittances amount.

## 9.5 Conclusion

International remittances are a significant factor in economic development. India also receives substantial international remittances. Especially, Kerala has a large number of migrants working mostly in Gulf countries and the remittances of the emigrants are crucial for Kerala's economy. The Kerala migration survey shows that migration from Kerala and remittance inflows into Kerala are significant not only for the household, but also for the development of Kerala. In this context, it is important to understand the motives for migration and the subsequent remittance behaviour of the migrants. Studies also show that there is wide gender difference in the remittance behaviour of migrants. This paper analyses the determinants and their effects on migrant's remittance behaviour, the decision to remit and the amount of remittances from the gender perspective in Kerala using the 2008 Kerala Migration Survey. The decision to remit by migrants is estimated by LPM and Probit methods, and conditional on decision to remit the amount of remittances is estimated by Tobit model for both males and females separately.

The empirical results this paper shows gender difference in both decision to remit and the amount of remittances. Probit estimates of pooled data shows that females have lower probability to remit and Tobit results show that the amount remitted is less than those of male migrants. The plausible reason may be in the differences in earnings of males and females in the destination country. The other main factor that affects the probability to remit is being a head of the household. The migrant being the head of the household increases the probability to remit for both males and females. Similarly, married migrants have higher probability to remit as well as higher amount of remittances. While education of migrants increases the probability to remit, the occupation of migrants in the host country decreases the probability of remitting. Further, the migrant job has no impact on the amount of remittances. Overall, the estimates of the amount of remittances show that married, rural, head of household and educated migrants send more remittances, whereas female and young migrants send low remittances. Also, household size, number of migrants in a household and age of migrants increase the remittances amount. As female migrants constitute a small percentage of total migrants and most of them are family migrants with children, in the empirical estimation of female remittance behaviour most of the coefficients of the explanatory variables are rather statistically insignificant. Thus, gender differences in Kerala migration is noticeable and female migrants, unless they are the head of the household, have lower probability to remit and their level of remittances is low compared to male migrants.

# 10

# The Demand for Children: Poisson Regression Estimation of Household Fertility Decisions

**Abstract**

*With economic growth and the associated development in social and demographic changes of an economy contributing to declining fertility and mortality rates, population growth depends mainly on household fertility decisions. This paper analyses the determinants of household demand for children in India using the 2011-2012 India Human Development Survey II and applying the Poisson regression method. The estimates of Poisson regression show that wife's age and employment and household income have positive effects on the number of children while female education and household urban residence reduces the number of children a household has in India.*

**Key words:** *Household fertility decision, number of children, count data, Poisson regression*

## 10.1 Introduction

The historically unprecedented increase in economic and social development in the 20th century has been accompanied by considerable declines fertility and mortality rates thereby in reducing population growth rates across the world (Myrskyla et al., 2013). The negative association between human fertility and socio-economic development has been one of the most solidly established and generally accepted empirical regularities in the social sciences. In the early stages of economic development, in most countries women averaged six to seven births during their reproductive years, as development progresses this number falls to two or even fewer births per woman. A decline in fertility rate of a country does not necessarily a result in economic growth. This fertility decline can also happen due to poor healthcare conditions, increased infant mortality rate, improper sanitation facilities, poverty, unemployment and various other social factors. On the other hand, fertility decline can be mainly due to increased women's education and labour force participation which postpones age at marriage and pregnancy especially of first births. Another factor often cited as the reason for the sharp decline in western fertility in the 1960s and 1970s is the modern contraceptive pill. Fertility, however, began to decline in the late 1950s, long before the pill became widely available.

In India, fertility level has been declining gradually since 1971. The 2011 Census of India shows that there has been a decline in the total fertility rate, the average number of children born per woman during her entire span of reproductive period, from 5.2 to 4.5 during the period 1971-1981 and further decline from 3.6 to 2.4 during the period 1991 to 2011. As Figure 10.1 reveals, the average fertility rate of India in 2011 is 2.4. Bihar has the highest fertility rate of 3.5 and Tamil Nadu has the lowest fertility rate of 1.6. Uttar Pradesh, Rajasthan, Madhya Pradesh, Jharkhand and Chhattisgarh have fertility rates more than the average fertility of India. The variations in the fertility rates are due to various socio-economic factors. As age of the women is considered to be an important factor affecting fertility levels, the relationship between women's age and the number of children is expected to be negative. The Figure 10.2 shows that the general fertility rate in India, the number of live births per thousand women in the reproductive age, reaches peak in the age group 20-24 and declines after that irrespective of place of residence. Compared to rural women, the urban women's fertility is low. The rural age specific fertility curve has declined very steeply after attaining peak for age 20-24 whereas urban fertility curve has gradually declined up to the age 25-29 after attaining peak at the age group 20-24.

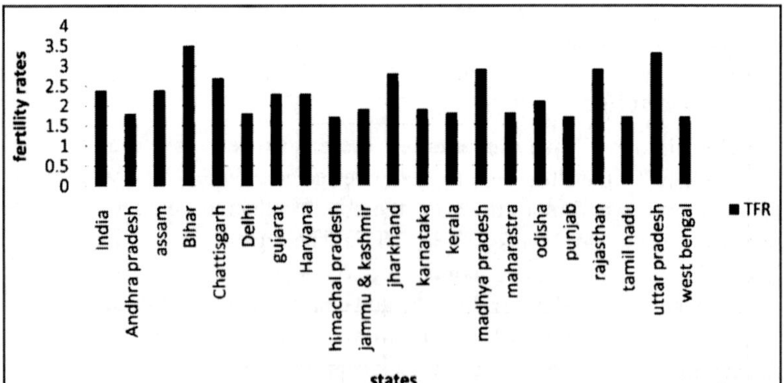


*Source:* Census of India, 2011.

***Figure 10.1: Total Fertility Rates in India and States, 2011***

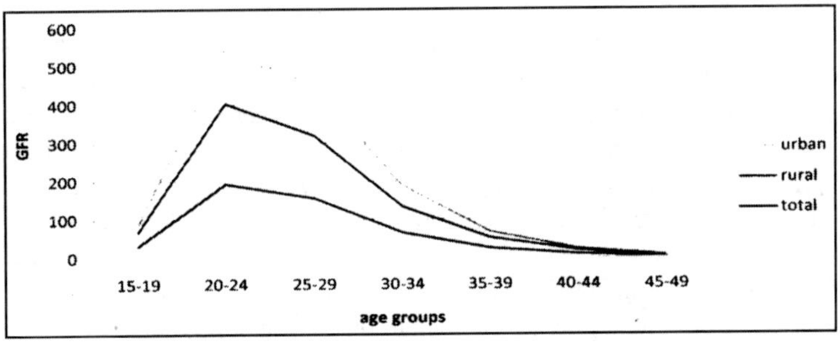


*Source:* Census of India, 2011.

***Figure 10.2: General Fertility Rates of Women in India by Age Group, 2011***

The literature on fertility has evidence that the educational attainment of women is directly related to her opportunity cost of time and inversely related to fertility. The inverse relationship is predicted to be stronger the higher the women's education level lower will be her preference. It is evident from Table 10.1 that there exists a negative relationship between the education level of women and their fertility rate. However, a different scenario is reported in Kerala. It is the only state where the general fertility rate increases as the women get better education.

**Table 10.1: Total Fertility Rates of Women by Education in India and States, 2011**

| *State* | *Illiterate* | *Below primary* | *Primary* | *Middle* | *Class X* | *Class XII* | *Graduate and above* |
|---|---|---|---|---|---|---|---|
| Andhra Pradesh | 1.8 | 1.9 | 2.1 | 2.1 | 1.8 | 1.1 | 1.6 |
| Assam | 3.2 | 2.2 | 3.0 | 2.4 | 1.7 | 1.2 | 1.4 |
| Bihar | 4.6 | 2.5 | 2.7 | 2.7 | 2.0 | 1.6 | 2.1 |
| Chhattisgarh | 2.8 | 2.7 | 3.1 | 2.7 | 2.1 | 1.9 | 1.9 |
| Delhi | 2.7 | 1.6 | 2.4 | 1.7 | 1.5 | 1.1 | 1.3 |
| Gujarat | 3.0 | 2.2 | 2.6 | 2.2 | 1.5 | 1.4 | 1.5 |
| Haryana | 2.9 | 2.1 | 2.6 | 2.3 | 1.9 | 1.8 | 2.0 |
| Himachal Pradesh | 3.7 | 1.7 | 1.6 | 1.4 | 1.9 | 1.8 | 1.9 |
| Jammu & Kashmir | 2.2 | 1.6 | 2.4 | 2.0 | 1.6 | 1.2 | 1.3 |
| Jharkhand | 1.6 | 2.3 | 2.6 | 2.2 | 1.9 | 1.7 | 1.6 |
| Karnataka | 2.2 | 1.9 | 2.4 | 2.1 | 1.7 | 1.5 | 1.5 |
| Kerala | 1.6 | 1.8 | 1.5 | 1.7 | 1.7 | 2.0 | 2.3 |
| Madhya Pradesh | 3.2 | 2.8 | 3.3 | 2.5 | 2.0 | 1.7 | 1.8 |
| Maharashtra | 1.6 | 1.8 | 1.9 | 2.3 | 1.7 | 1.5 | 1.4 |
| Odisha | 2.9 | 2.0 | 2.3 | 2.0 | 1.5 | 1.4 | 1.4 |
| Punjab | 2.0 | 1.7 | 1.8 | 1.7 | 1.7 | 1.4 | 1.7 |
| Rajasthan | 3.6 | 2.5 | 2.8 | 2.6 | 1.7 | 1.5 | 1.6 |
| Tamil Nadu | 1.0 | 1.7 | 1.8 | 1.9 | 1.8 | 1.6 | 1.9 |
| Uttar Pradesh | 4.0 | 2.9 | 3.4 | 2.9 | 2.6 | 2.0 | 2.1 |
| West Bengal | 1.8 | 1.7 | 2.0 | 1.5 | 1.4 | 1.2 | 1.3 |
| India | 3.2 | 2.9 | 2.5 | 2.2 | 1.8 | 1.6 | 1.7 |

*Source:* Census of India, 2011.

In his seminal work on household behaviour, Becker (1960) argues that household fertility decisions are just like household decisions on consumption and therefore children can be considered as consumer durable goods. Each family produces its own children and tries to achieve their desired number of children. Families with excess children consume less of other goods, especially goods that are close substitutes for quantity of children. As usual there is a positive relation between income of the household and the number of children and a negative relationship between price of children and number of children. The price of children is the amount spent on having and raising children as well as the opportunity cost of time of parents measured in terms of wage rates. Becker also takes into account the knowledge of contraceptive use by parents. Therefore, according to Becker income, knowledge of contraceptive use and cost of children are the significant fertility determinants.

Easterlin (1975) and Easterlin and Crimmins (1985) point out that family fertility decisions depend also on potential output of children and the costs of fertility regulation besides demand for the children. The demand for children is the number of surviving children parents would want if the fertility costs were low which is determined by the income, the price of children compared with other goods. The potential output is the number of children parents would want to produce if they did not deliberately limit their fertility depends on the natural fertility (biological and physiological factors) and the survival prospects of the child. Motivation for fertility regulation also has huge influence where if the family doesn't receive any incentive upon following the regulation or the costs of fertility control are high then they are likely to increase the output. On other hand, if the situation is an excess supply where the motivation of fertility control is high than the fertility costs, then the family is likely to produce less number of children. The growing literature on household fertility decisions also incorporates models of intrahousehold conflict and bargaining to bear on fertility choice, as the review by Doepke and Kindermann (2017) shows.

Therefore, deciding on the number of children a household would like to have is an important household decision as it influences the economic status of the family. It is therefore important to understand how the education and employment of women affect the fertility decisions of households and what happens to household preferences for children when the income of family increases? Further, it is also useful to know whether the place of residence of the household has an influence over the fertility decision and whether the social factors like religion have any impact on the household decisions on fertility. Hence, the main objective of this paper is to identify the factors influencing household fertility decisions in India. This paper uses the 2011-2012 India Human Development Survey II in the empirical analysis. Since the variable of interest in this paper, the number of children, is in the form of counts, the appropriate statistical tool to be used is the Poisson regression method.

## 10.2 A Brief Review of Recent Studies

Theoretically much work on household fertility decisions are stimulated by Becker (1960) who formulated the economic theory of household behaviour. The economics of population literature has advanced many theories of fertility, the prominent being the new home economics based on the micro economic theory of consumer behaviour (Becker, 1960). For most parents children are a source of pleasure, a psychic income or satisfaction and therefore children are treated as 'consumer durables'. Accordingly, in the household production function approach, children are viewed household production and the demand for children is influenced by the cost-benefit calculations, the chief cost being the value of time inputs of parents evaluated by the wage rates. Easterlin (1975) and Easterlin and Crimmins (1985) incorporate supply side considerations like biological birth function and costs of fertility regulations. Within the microeconomic tradition of fertility behaviour Rosenzweig (1977) and Rosenzweig and Evenson (1977) regard children as a form of 'capital' – a means of earning income, and Nugent (1985, Nugent et al. (1983), Cain (1983) and Chennichovsky (1982) view children as a source of 'security against risk and old age'. However, many non-economists object the reduction of children as commodities and favour fertility as outcome of biological factors that are 'proximate' determinants and the diverse socio-economic and cultural conditions (Blake, 1968). Moreover, neither the money income nor the old age security provided by children is fixed and reliable as they vary with the age and earnings of children, making children a vulnerable durable consumption and production good.

One of the problems faced by economists is the decline in fertility as income rises, implying that children are 'inferior' goods, in economics sense. However, children cannot be treated as inferior goods as they are demanded by all households irrespective of income status. Education, especially female education, is often seen as a significant factor in fertility decisions of couples. Most couples often cite that they need more births in order to achieve a given number of surviving children, and women's education plays a significant role in bringing about reductions in infant mortality. Moreover, an increase in female education increases the opportunity cost of women's time and thereby childcare costly. Hence, fertility decisions respond to education through the price of women's time and relative income within the household. Becker and Tomes (1976) develop such price of time model with a 'quantity-quality' trade-off, where potential parents can trade quantity for quality. Parents have a demand for quality as well as quantity of children, and then as income increases the demand for quality rises more rapidly than the demand for quantity. In economic sense, it is meant that an increase in income should increase both the quantity and quality of children, but the quantity elasticity is small compared to the quality elasticity.

In the related literature, the Easterlin (1975) model of relative income explains that individuals focus on their per capita disposable income and make the necessary adjustments to keep it on a par with material aspirations. In case of less developed economies, wages of younger workers progress more slowly than those of older workers due to labour market crowding. The earnings of the worker will be low compared to his material aspirations. So the young couples either postpone or forego marriage in order to maintain their level of per capita disposable income. Thus, both the models are based on the common assumption of an underlying positive relationship between income and fertility, and both attempt to put forward explanations for the negative relationship, which has often been observed in modem experience. It appears that the 'price of time' and 'relative income' models are relevant in developing countries as well as developed countries to explain the fertility transition.

Empirically, Wang and Famoye (1997) analyse the household fertility decisions using a US national level longitudinal data applying the generalized Poisson regression method of estimation. The effects of income of the household, employment status of wife and her educational level on the number of children in the household are significantly negative. The substitution effect due to higher price associated with high quality of child is larger than the income effect. The empirical results of this paper also support the neoclassical theory of the opportunity cost of raising children.

Pandey et al. (1998) analyse the fertility differentials due to socioeconomic and demographic factors for all India and also state wise using the 1992-93 National Family Health Survey data. The paper uses the method of parity progression ratios to explain the family building process and apply the multivariate analysis to fertility. The results show that when a woman has one son, her preference to have another child is lower than the woman who has no son. Also, rural women have high progression ratios than urban women, but this vanishes when controlled for education level. Urban women are likely to have fewer children as they have high educational status compared to rural women. One of the key findings of the paper is when woman is more exposed to electronic mass media, her progression ratio is much lower than those who do not have frequent access to electronic media.

## 10.3 Data and Methodology

This paper uses from the India Human Development Survey II (2011-2012) in the empirical analysis of household fertility decisions. The IHDS II sample is spread across 33 states and union territories covering urban as well as rural households. From the IHDS II survey, this paper considers households with married women aged between 18 to 40 years. The sample size for this study has been 27,275 households. As the fertility variable, number of children, is of discrete count data ranging from 0-18, this paper uses the Poisson regression model in the empirical estimation. The Poisson regression model restricts the variance of the data to be equal to the mean, conditional on explanatory variables.

## Poisson Regression Model

The Poisson regression assumes the response variable *y* is a count data in which the observations can take only the non-negative integer values {0, 1, 2, 3...} where these integers arise from counting and therefore follows a Poisson distribution. A Poisson regression model is similar to an ordinary linear regression with two exceptions. The Poisson regression model assumes that the errors follow a Poisson, not normal, distribution and rather than modeling *y* as a linear function of the regression coefficients, the logarithm of the expected value of *y* can be modeled as a linear combination of the unknown parameters.

Given a vector of independent variables *x*, the Poisson regression model is expressed as,

$$ln[E(y|x)] = \alpha + \beta'x = \theta'x \tag{10.1}$$

where *x* is a $(n+1)$ dimensional vector consisting of *n* independent variables combined with a vector of ones and θ is simply a concatenated to β. Thus, given a Poisson regression model θ and an input vector *x*, the predicted mean of the associated Poisson distribution is given by,

$$[E(y|x)] = e^{\theta' x} \tag{10.2}$$

If $y_i$ are independent observations with corresponding $x_i$ of the predictor variables, then θ can be estimated by the maximum likelihood estimation. Given a set of parameters θ and an input vector x, the mean of the predicted Poisson distribution is given by,

$$\lambda = [E(y|x)] = e^{\theta' x} \tag{10.3}$$

The probability mass function of Poisson distribution is given by,

$$p(y|x;\theta) = \frac{\lambda^y}{y!}e^{-\lambda} = \frac{e^{y\theta' x}e^{-e^{\theta' x}}}{y!} \tag{10.4}$$

If a data set consists of m vectors $x_i$ $(i=1,2,..., m)$ along with a set of *m* values $y_i$ $(i=1,2,..., m)$, then for a given set of parameters θ, the probability of attaining this particular set of data is given by,

$$p(y_1, y_2, ..., y_m | x_1, x_2, ..., x_m; \theta) = \prod_{i=1}^{m} \frac{e^{y\theta' x}e^{-e^{\theta' x}}}{y!} \tag{10.5}$$

The set of parameters θ that makes this probability as large as possible can be obtained by the method of maximum likelihood. Rewriting the equation (10.5) as a likelihood function in terms of θ, yields,

$$L(\theta|x,y) = \prod_{i=1}^{m} \frac{e^{y\theta' x} e^{-e^{\theta' x}}}{y!} \tag{10.6}$$

It is to be noted that the expression on the right hand side has not actually changed. The log-likelihood may then be written as,

$$lnL(\theta|x,y) = \sum_{i=1}^{m} [y_i \theta' x_i - e^{\theta' x_i} - ln\,(y_i!)] \tag{10.7}$$

It can also be noted that the parameters θ only appear in the first two terms of each term in the summation. Therefore, given the interest in finding the best value for θ, the term ($y_i$!) may be dropped. Then, the log-likelihood is simply,

$$lnL(\theta|x,y) = \sum_{i=1}^{m} [y_i \theta' x_i - e^{\theta' x_i}] \tag{10.8}$$

Applying the standard optimisation techniques solves the equation for the optimal value of θ.

Then, the Poisson regression model can be written as,

$$y = e^{\beta_0} e^{\beta_i x_i} = lny = \beta_0 + \beta_i x_i \tag{10.9}$$

Under Poisson regression model, as the response variable is a count variable and is in log-linear form, the Logit estimation method is applied.

When the variance is equal to the mean, the most common way of testing a count data is by the Poisson regression model. But, when the data is over-dispersed, a negative binomial regression model is commonly used. Over dispersion occurs when the variance of the dependent variable is greater than the mean of the dependent variable.

In the NFHS II data used in this paper, the variance of the number of children, the dependent variable, as reported in the descriptive statistics in Table 10.3 is large. Statistically, the goodness of fit tests of Bayesian information criterion and Akaike information criterion are used to choose to the most suitable model. The AIC is a measure of the relative quality of statistical models for a given set of data. Given a collection of models for the data, the AIC estimates the quality of each model, relative to each of the other models. The models being compared need not be nested, unlike the case when models are being compared using an F-test or a likelihood ratio test. Lower the BIC and AIC values, the model is fit. With the reported AIC and BIC values shown Table 10.2, the decision is to use the Poisson regression model.

**Table 10.2: AIC and BIC Tests of Poisson and Negative Binomial Model Selection**

| *Model* | *AIC* | *BIC* |
|---|---|---|
| Poisson regression | 89751.56 | 89817.26 |
| Negative binomial regression | 89753.56 | 89827.47 |

The estimation empirical model is specified as,

$$ln(Nchild) = \beta_0 + \beta_1 Age + \beta_2 Age^2 + \beta_3 Edu + \beta_4 Work + \beta_5 Conexp + \beta_6 Religion + \beta_7 Residence + u_i \quad (10.10)$$

The Table 10.3 presents the descriptive statistics of the variables used in the empirical analysis of the demand for children. The average number of children a household has is 2. About 66 percent of females are working and about 34 percent of households reside in urban locality. The average years of education completed by the female is 6 years which implies that she has attended primary schooling.

**Table 10.3: Descriptive Statistics of the Variables in the Analysis of Demand for Children**

| *Variable* | *Description* | *Mean* |
|---|---|---|
| Nchild | Number of child in a household | 2.036 (1.531) |
| Age | Age of female (yrs) | 29.863 (6.255) |
| $Age^2$ | Age of female squared (yrs) | 930.902 (374.607) |
| Edu | Education of female (yrs) | 5.932 (4.993) |
| Ln(Conexp) | Logarithm of consumption expenditure (proxy for household income) | 11.532 (0.674) |
| Work | If female is working=1, 0 otherwise | 0.661 (0.474) |
| Religion | If household religion is Muslim=1, 0 otherwise | 0.127 (0.334) |
| Residence | If place of residence is urban=1, 0 otherwise | 0.337 (0.473) |
| N | Sample size | 27275 |

The Table 10.4 presents the estimated results of the Poisson regression along with incidence rate ratios. All the estimated coefficients are statistically significant. As can be observed with an increase in age of female by a year, the preference to have children increases by 1.5 times or by 40.3 percent. The negative coefficient of age square shows that the preference for more children declines with rising age of women. That is, the number of children a household has decreases by 0.99 times or 0.6 percent with further increase in the age of females. The household consumption expenditure has a positive impact on the fertility of households. With increase in household income, the demand for children increases by 22.4 percent or 1.25 times. This observation reflects the Becker's (1960) argument that with an increase in household income, the families tend to increase the quantity of children. The education of women has a negative impact on the fertility decisions showing that for every increase in wife's education, the demand for children decreases by 3.3 percent or 0.97 times. The results are similar to the results obtained by Pandey et al. (1998).

The employment of wife has a positive impact on the number of children reflecting the income effect rather than price effect on the demand for children. With a working wife the family is likely to have 1.12 times or 11.38 percent more children than a household with a non-working spouse. The urban residence of the household has a negative impact on fertility decisions. If a household resides in an urban area, its demand for children is 11.59 percent less compared to a household residing in rural area. Overall, age, employment and income have a positive effect on the demand for children while education and urban residence reduces the number of children a household has in India.

**Table 10.4: Poisson Regression Estimates of the Demand for Children Dependent variable: No. of children in a household**

| *Variable* | *Coefficient* | *Incidence rate ratio* |
|---|---|---|
| Age | 0.403* (0.008) | 1.501* (0.012) |
| $Age^2$ | -0.007* (0.0001) | 0.993* (0.0001) |
| Edu | -0.034* (0.0009) | 0.967* (0.0009) |
| Ln(Conexp) | 0.225* (0.007) | 1.252* (0.008) |
| Work | 0.114* (0.009) | 1.121* (0.011) |
| Religion | 0.240* (0.012) | 1.270* (0.015) |
| Residence | -0.116* (0.009) | 0.891* (0.009) |
| Constant | -7.480* (0.137) | 0.967* (0.0009) |
| Log-likelihood | -44867.781 | |
| LR Chi-square | 5568.22 | |
| Pseudo R-square<br>Prob. > Chi-square | 0.058<br>0.001 | |
| Pearson goodness of fit<br>Prob. > Chi-square | 25466.26<br>1.000 | |
| N | 27,238 | |

**Note:** Standard errors in parentheses. * Significant at 1 percent level.

## 10.5 Conclusion

With economic growth and social development, there has been a rapid decline in the fertility rate of India. The decline or rise in fertility rate is the result of household preference for number of children the family wants to have. Among all decisions made by the household, the fertility decision emphasises the role of females in the household as a spouse. The wife's education and employment forms an integral part of the household preference structure and women empowerment in decision making. The literature on the economics of fertility decisions maps the different factors that influence the fertility decision of couples. Using the India human development survey II (IHDS II) and applying the Poisson regression model, this paper analysed the fertility decision among Indian households. The empirical results of this paper identify that household income, age, educational attainment and employment of wife are the main forces that drive the fertility decisions of a household. The results further show that community (religion) and place of residence (urban) also play significant role in the number of children couples have.

# 11

# Demand for Hospitalisation: Poisson-Logit Hurdle Estimation of Inpatient Care

**Abstract**

*Every individual desires to be in good health and incurs substantial expenditure both on preventive and curative health care. Most individuals seek outpatient healthcare while some illness and ailments require hospitalisation. This paper analyses the demand for inpatient health care and the determinants of expenditure on such hospitalisation using the NSSO 71st round (January-June 2014) morbidity data and applying the Poisson-Logit Hurdle regression model. The number of times an individual hospitalised is taken as the count data and the odds ratio of inpatient care is estimated. The estimated results show that household income, health insurance coverage, hygiene at the household and availability of good drinking water are the important determinants of both the demand for inpatient care and the number of times of hospitalisation. The health expenditure for diseases like cancer and cardio-vascular illness are higher relative to other ailments.*

**Key words:** *Hospitalisation, inpatient care, health expenditure, Poisson-Logit Hurdle regression, odds ratio*

## 11.1 Introduction

Every person in this world desires to be in good health and wants to live a disease free life. In fact, good health is the most basic requirements of an individual to lead a normal life and to be able and productive. In order to maintain a good health, people seek healthcare both as preventive and curative care. Just like individuals, the country also seeks healthy people. For the economy, a good general public health is one of the most important economic goals, since most other goals are conditional on good national health. Health improves efficiency and skills of labour and human capital and such an increase in the productivity of healthy labour force improves the national output. Therefore, health is wealth. In the literature on the economics of health, the demand for healthcare is thus considered as a derived demand. Many issues in health economics such as the demand for healthcare services in the economy, allocation of resources for the development of healthcare facilities, healthcare supply through public and private sector agencies, healthcare utilisation and the gaps that exists between the demand and supply of healthcare services in the economy are some of the critical issues that have been widely recognised as the concerns of an economy.

The healthcare industry in India has been continuously expanding over the years and it contributes annually to around 4 percent to the GDP of India. Though the public healthcare system is wide and vast and highly subsidised, in recent years the private players have been providing significant healthcare services albeit at high costs. Despite such an increase in the quantum of hospital services offered by both private and public hospitals, India still faces severe crisis in providing proper healthcare services to the masses and the issues in the health sector are large. With the fast growth of population with an increasing change in the lifestyle and food habits, the related disease burden is heavy. There is also a constant burden of chronic and communicable diseases added with seasonal and climate related illness and high spread of diseases during natural calamities. As the second most populated country in the world, India shares around 20 percent of the global disease burden. But, India has only 8 percent share of doctors and nursing staff and only about 9 beds per 10000 people. The public expenditure on health is just less than 4 percent of GDP. Also, the infrastructure facilities in public healthcare centres in both the rural and urban areas are inadequate and poorly equipped.

Therefore, there is an increasing reliance on the private sector for healthcare over the last few decades. Consequently, there has been a steady decline in the utilisation of public health services, especially the inpatient care. The Table 11.1 shows that during 1995-2014 the percentage of hospitalised cases in public hospitals has declined, the same for the private hospitals has increased. Further, as the infrastructure rich private hospitals are located in urban areas, the inpatient care has increased dramatically relative to the rural areas where the public hospitals are the only possibility for inpatient care. This disparity in the utilisation of public and private hospitals for inpatient care cannot be overlooked while explaining the demand for inpatient care.

**Table 11.1: Distribution of Hospitalisation by Type of Hospital**

| ***Hospital*** | ***Rural*** | | | ***Urban*** | | |
|---|---|---|---|---|---|---|
| | 1995-96 | 2004 | 2014 | 1995-96 | 2004 | 2014 |
| Public | 43.8 | 41.7 | 41.9 | 43.1 | 38.2 | 32.0 |
| Private | 56.2 | 58.3 | 58.1 | 56.9 | 61.8 | 68.0 |

*Source:* NSSO (2014) Key Indicators of Social Consumption in India, 71st Round.

**Note:** Figures represent percentages.

This paper aims to analyse the demand for inpatient care in India. The main objectives of this paper are to identify and estimate the effects of the individual and household characteristics that determine the demand for inpatient care and to analyse the patterns of expenditure incurred by individuals on account of utilisation of inpatient care. The demand for inpatient care is considered as the number of times inpatient care is sought and the frequency of hospitalisation by an individual. This paper uses the NSSO 71st round (January-June 2014) morbidity data and the health infrastructure data, especially in public hospitals, from the sources of the Ministry of Health and Family Welfare (MOHFW) of Government of India. The Poisson-Logit Hurdle regression model has been used in the empirical analysis of the demand for inpatient care. The Hurdle model or a two-part model estimates two models where the dependent variable is count data and is inflated with zeroes. The first part of the Poisson-Logit Hurdle model is a logistic regression model that analyses the likelihood of an individual seeking inpatient care that includes the zero cases. The second part is a Poisson regression model that analyses only the non-zero counts of the number of times an individual is hospitalised. In the Poisson-Logit Hurdle model dependent variable is assumed to follow the Poisson distribution, and tests for over-dispersion are done to ensure that the mean and the variance of the dependent variable are not statistically different from one another. The Poisson-Logit Hurdle model is estimated by the maximum likelihood estimation method. In addition to analysing the demand for inpatient care, the expenditure incurred on utilising inpatient care is analysed by the linear regression model.

## 11.2 A Brief Review of Recent Studies

Alam and Karim (2006) examine the insecurities faced by the aged in India and Pakistan as a consequence of declines in fertility and mortality. They use Poisson regression to study the causal risk factors of the poor health conditions of the elderly in India analysing the 52nd round NSSO data of India. They model the number of diseases reported by an elderly person as a function of a set of household level socio-economic variables such as consumption expenditure, type of latrines in the household, and source of drinking water and individual demographic characteristics such as age, sex and literacy. The paper concludes that the changing demographic-scenario in India calls for many policy-related actions. The growth in the age category of 25+ would require a matching improvement in work opportunities, and the growth in the number of elderly people would increase demand for healthcare and social security. The authors call for various actions such as the creation of stable savings instruments for the old age income security, increase in insurance coverage for the elderly, increase in efficiency and quality in government hospitals and healthcare facilities, and a general increase in public expenditure on health.

Levesque and Mukherjee (2010) study the changing inequalities in the utilisation of inpatient care in rural India, using the 52nd and 60th rounds of NSSO data and concentration indices to measure inequality of inpatient care utilisation. In most of the major states of India, the utilisation of inpatient care among the poor has shown an increase during 1995-96 to 2004. However, at least in 6 states the utilisation of inpatient care by the rich seems to have declined. But overall, both the rich and the poor seemed to utilise more of inpatient care and therefore there was a reduction in the economic-status related inequality. To measure inequality, Bhandari et al. (2010) measure the impoverishing effect of healthcare expenditure in India by estimating the number of households falling below poverty line as a result of healthcare payments and financial coping mechanisms. The analysis of data on morbidity from the 60th round of NSSO shows a significant healthcare related impoverishment across states with much variation across states.

Kumar et al. (2010) analyse the key health barriers that are responsible for inequities in access to health services in India, focusing on the availability, accessibility and affordability across geographic, social and economic groups and the analysis of NSO as well as NFHS data reveals that there are insufficient investments in the public sector which is a key factor in contributing to the existing inequities.

Yen and Adamowicz (1993) use a multinomial-Poisson hurdle model to analyse the recreation demand in Canada that allows price and quality changes to affect both the choice of recreation sites as well as the frequency of trips. The estimated results show that the decision to participate i.e. to go on at least one trip for recreation does not depend on site attributes, rather income is the significant determinant of the recreation trips.

Lahiri and Xing (2004) analyse the nature of inpatient and outpatient healthcare utilisation, applying a negative binomial hurdle model to the 1992 US National Survey of Veterans. Also a bivariate probit regression model is used to analyse the decision to use Veterans' Administration (VA) or non-Veterans' Administration healthcare facility. Those veterans with lower income, without health insurance coverage or those living near the health facilities are more likely to use the Veterans' Administration health system than the others. Veterans with a service-connected disability or some specific diagnosed health problems use more healthcare services than others. The estimated results show that the family income of the veteran is the most important factor in deciding the veterans' healthcare facility choice. The veteran family income has a negative impact on the inpatient care usage, but a positive effect on the outpatient care usage. Other demographic characteristics such as age, marital status and employment status are not very significant in the healthcare choice of veterans.

Ricker-Gilbert et al. (2011) apply the double hurdle model to investigate how fertilizer subsidies affect farmers' demand for commercial fertilizer. In the first part of the hurdle model, the probability of farmers' participation in the commercial fertilizer market is estimated by a probit regression. In the second part, the demand for commercial fertilizer is estimated by a truncated normal regression model. The estimated results show that the subsidisation of fertilizers has a significant negative impact on farmers' commercial fertilizer purchases. The results from the double hurdle model shows that on average each additional kilogram of subsidized fertilizer reduces farmer purchases of commercial fertilizer by 0.22 kilograms. This means that each additional kilogram of subsidized fertilizer contributes an additional 0.78 kg to total fertilizer use after accounting for the crowding out effect.

Iles (2015), using the National Family Health Survey (NFHS) data from rural north India, estimate the demand for primary healthcare using the mixed multinomial logit model (MMNL) allowing parameter estimates to vary across individuals. The estimated coefficients of variables price and travel distance are negative indicating the declining probability of utilisation of primary healthcare in rural India with rising prices and travel cost. Further, consumer trust is an important determinant of the choice of healthcare provider.

## 11.3 Data and Methodology

In the empirical analysis, this paper uses the 71st round (January-June 2014) of NSSO household survey on morbidity. The NSSO's surveys on social consumption are one of the major sources of basic quantitative information on the health sector such as morbidity, frequency of hospitalisation, pre-natal care and post-natal care by women, treatment expenditure on disease, etc. In the 71st round NSSO questionnaire, the schedule 25.0 (social consumption: health has collected information on the prevalence of different diseases, extent of use of health services provided by the government, hospitalisation or medical care received and expenses incurred as inpatient of medical institutions during the last 365 days, spells of ailment of household members during the last 15 days (including hospitalisation) and expenses incurred during the last 15 days for treatment of members (not as an in-patient of medical institution), pre-natal and post-natal care for women of age 15-49 years during the last 365 days, economic independence and state of health of persons aged 60 years and above as on date of survey, besides household characteristics and demographic particulars of the households.

The 71st round NSSO data covers 65,932 households (36,480 in rural India and 29,452 in urban India) across the Indian states and a total of 3,34,931 individuals living in these households. Out of this, a total of 51,650 individuals had utilised inpatient care in the span of one year (2013-2014). Excluding the cases of childbirth, there are 36,725 individuals had utilised inpatient care for various diseases like cancer, cardio-vascular diseases, genito-urinary diseases, respiratory problems, gastro-intestinal diseases, etc. In the empirical analysis, individuals who had not sought inpatient care in the last one year are also included so as to study the decision behind the seeking of inpatient care. The expenditures towards both inpatient care and outpatient care are analysed for a total of 59,895 individuals who sought outpatient care in the span of 15 days prior to the date of survey, and 36,725 individuals who sought inpatient care in the span of one year prior to the date of survey.

The empirical analysis of the demand for inpatient care in this paper uses a type of count data model, the Poisson-Logit hurdle regression model, to model count variables with excessive zeroes. In the hurdle model, actually a modification of a simple count data model, the underlying assumption is that the statistical process governing individuals with zero counts and individuals with positive counts are actually different. The Poisson-Logit hurdle regression model proceeds in two parts. The first part is a dichotomous model for the counts being zero or positive and the second part is a 'truncated at zero' model for strictly positive outcomes. In this paper, the number of times an individual seeks inpatient care in the span of one year is taken as the dependent variable. The Table 11.2 presents the descriptive statistics of the variables used in the empirical analysis of the demand for inpatient care.

**Table 11.2: Descriptive Statistics of Variables in the Inpatient Care Analysis**

| *Variable* | *Description* | *Mean* |
|---|---|---|
| No. of times of hospitalisation | Number of times an individual seeks inpatient care in the span of one year | 0.17 (0.43) |
| Consumption expenditure | Monthly consumption expenditure (proxy for income) (Rs.) | 9595.67 (7175.09) |
| Age | Age of the individual (years) | 27.96 (19.79) |
| $Age^2$ | Age squared | 1173.68 (1348.91) |
| Disease | If chronic disease=1, 0 otherwise | 0.05 (0.23) |
| Gender | If male=1, 0 otherwise | 0.51 (0.50) |
| Drinking water | If tap/well water=1, 0 otherwise | 0.89 (0.31) |
| Latrine | If flush/septic tank latrine=1, 0 otherwise | 0.47 (0.50) |
| Govt. hospital | If public hospital (including HSC, ANM, ASHA, AWW, PHC, CHC)=1, 0 otherwise | 0.07 (0.26) |
| Health insurance | If any health insurance cover=1, 0 otherwise | 0.15 (0.36) |
| Beds | No. of beds available in public hospitals per 1000 population | 0.31 (0.44) |
| Health expenditure | Per capita health expenditure (Rs.) | 6895.95 (7213.45) |
| N | 3,34,931 | |

The second part of this paper analyses the expenditure incurred for both inpatient care and outpatient services separately using the general linear regression model. Expenditure of an individual's hospital visit has been taken as the dependent variable. Household size and disease types are also used as additional independent variables in the analysis of health expenditure.

The disease groups contain 61 ailments classified into 16 groups of diseases and the mean medical expenditure per hospitalisation for these ailments by hospital type is presented in Table 11.3. The cancer and cardio-vascular diseases are the significant contributors to the average medical expenditure on hospitalisation. Also per individual medical expenditure in private hospitals is significantly higher than that in public hospitals for each disease.

**Table 11.3: Average Medical Expenditure per Hospitalisation for Diseases**

| *Disease group* | *Average expenditure* | *Average expenditure in public hospital* | *Average expenditure in private hospital* |
|---|---|---|---|
| Infection | 8134 | 3007 | 11810 |
| Cancer | 56712 | 24526 | 78050 |
| Blood diseases | 13313 | 4752 | 17067 |
| Endocrine, metabolic and nutrition | 14117 | 4625 | 19206 |
| Psychiatric, neurological | 23984 | 7482 | 34561 |
| Eye | 9307 | 1778 | 13374 |
| Ear | 15285 | 6626 | 19158 |
| Cardio-vascular | 31647 | 11549 | 43262 |
| Respiratory | 12820 | 4811 | 18705 |
| Gastro-intestinal | 17687 | 5281 | 23933 |
| Skin | 10438 | 3142 | 14664 |
| Musculo-skeletal | 21862 | 8165 | 28396 |
| Genito-urinary | 24525 | 9295 | 29608 |
| Obstetric, neonatal | 11707 | 2651 | 21626 |
| Injuries | 23491 | 6729 | 36255 |
| Others | 28003 | 14030 | 35572 |

The Figure 11.1 shows the distribution of the original count variable corresponding to the number of times an individual seeks inpatient care. There are more cases of zeros showing more outpatient care. Out of 3,34,931 observations, 2,83,281 people have not utilised inpatient care in the reference period of one year. In other words, there are 2,87,231 zeroes in the data. The Figure 11.2 presents the frequency distribution for the non-zero counts of hospitalisations. It is observed that the distribution is positively skewed since the probability of being hospitalised a fewer times is significantly higher than the probability of being more frequent hospitalisation. For this reasons, the Hurdle model has been used in this paper to model separately the zero and non-zero values in the first part and model only the non-zero values in the second part of the model.

## Poisson-Logit Hurdle Regression Model

Let $f_1$ and $f_2$ be the probability distribution functions for non-negative integers. If $f_1$ governs the first part of the hurdle model and $f_2$ the second part, then the probability distribution of the hurdle model is given by,

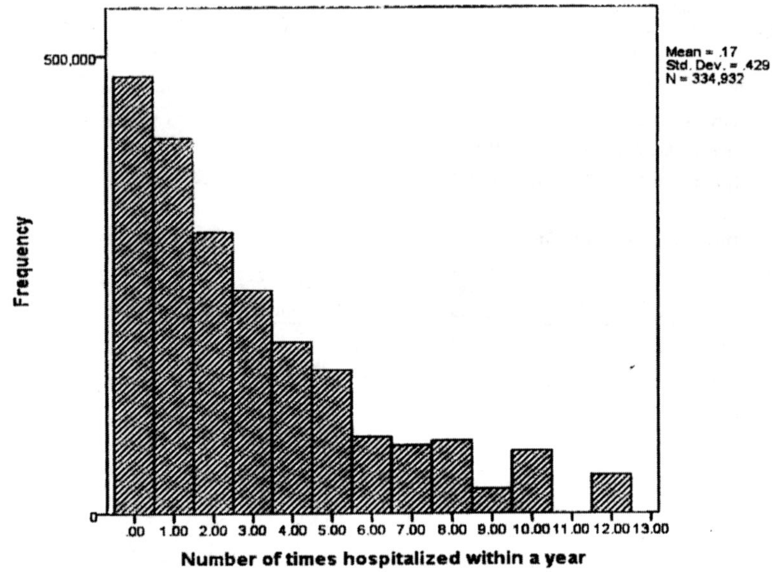


*Figure 11.1: Distribution of Counts of Hospitalisation for Inpatient Care*

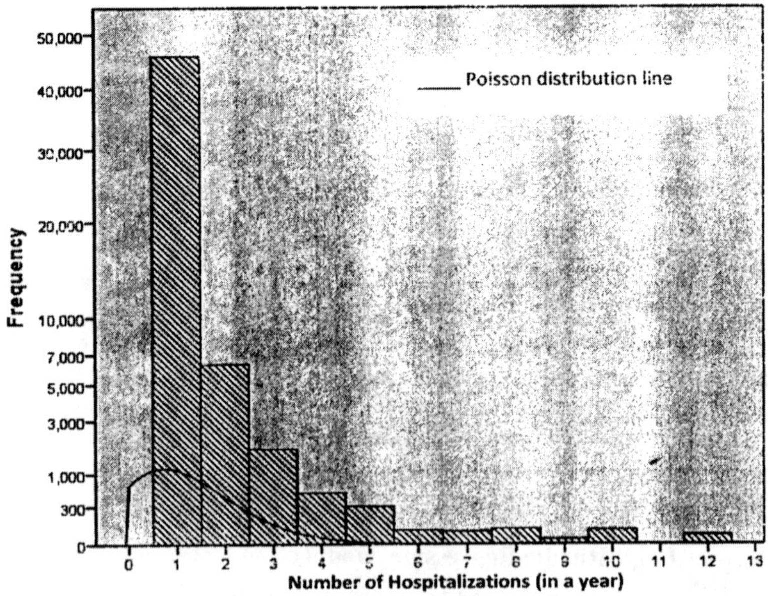


*Figure 11.2: Distribution of Nonzero Counts of Hospitalisation for Inpatient Care*

$$p(y=0)=f_1(0) \tag{11.1}$$

$$p(y=y)=f_2(y)\frac{1-f_1(0)}{1-f_2(0)}=\phi f_2(y) \qquad y=0,1,2,\ldots\ldots \tag{11.2}$$

where 1-$f_1(0)$ is the probability of crossing the hurdle and 1-$f_2(0)$ is the truncation normalisation for $f_2$. The hurdle model specification depends on the probability functions $f_1$ and $f_2$. For the Poisson model, $y_i$ denotes the count data, $x_i$ is the vector of explanatory variables, and $\lambda_i$ is the parameter of the Poisson distribution. Thus,

$$p(y=y_i=0)=\frac{e^{-\lambda_i}\lambda_i^{y_i}}{y_i!}=e^{-\lambda_i} \tag{11.3}$$

The specification for the first part of the model i.e. the logit regression is given as,

$$Logit(p_i)=ln\left[\frac{p_i}{1-p_i}\right]=\beta_0+\beta_k x_k+u_i \tag{11.4}$$

where $p_i$ is the probability of observing the response of an individual $i$ utilising inpatient care expressed in terms of odds ratio. The ß's are the intercepts and the slope coefficients and $u_i$ is the residual term.

The second part of the hurdle model is a truncated Poisson regression model given by,

$$p(y=y_i)=\frac{e^{-\lambda_i}\lambda_i^{y_i}}{y_i!} \qquad y_i=0,1,2,\ldots.. \tag{11.5}$$

where $y_i$ represents the counts, the number of hospitalisations, and $\lambda$ is the mean of the Poisson distribution. The most common specification of the model is the log-linear model given by,

$$\ln(\lambda_i)=\beta x_i \tag{11.6}$$

The expected number of events per period is given by,

$$E[y_i|x_i]=\lambda_i=e^{\beta x_i} \tag{11.7}$$

where $x_i$ is a vector of independent variables and ß is a vector of coefficients to be estimated by the method of maximum likelihood.

The log-linear specification of the Poisson hurdle model is written as,

$$\begin{aligned} ln\lambda_i=\beta_0+\beta_1 Con_{exp}+\beta_2 Age+\beta_3 Age^2+\beta_4 Gender+\beta_5 Water+\\ \beta_6 Latrine+\beta_7 Hospital+\beta_8 Insurance+\beta_9 Beds+u_i \end{aligned} \tag{11.8}$$

## 11.4 Empirical Analysis

The first part of the hurdle model i.e. the Logit model takes into account both zero as well as non-zero values of the variable and analyses the decision to seek inpatient care among individuals. The second part of the hurdle model uses the count variable truncated at zero and analyses the causes of the variation in the demand for inpatient care, conditional on having sought inpatient care in the first place. The estimated Poisson-Logit-Hurdle regression of the demand for inpatient care is presented in Table 11.4.

**Table 11.4: Poisson-Logit-Hurdle Regression Estimates of Inpatient Care Dependent variable: No. of times of hospitalization**

| *Variable* | *Logit model* | *Poisson model* |
|---|---|---|
| Consumption expenditure | 0.0004* | 0.0001* |
| Age | 0.010* | -0.001 |
| $Age^2$ | 0.0002* | 0.0001 |
| Gender-male | -0.090* | -0.002* |
| Drinking water | 0.016 | -0.158* |
| Latrine | 0.302* | -0.010* |
| Govt. hospital | - | -0.181* |
| Health insurance | 0.248* | 0.219* |
| Beds | -0.297* | -0.030 |
| Constant | -3.367* | -1.408* |
| Log-likelihood | -85441.97 | |
| Wald Chi-square | 7081.53 | |

**Note:** * Significant at 1 percent level.

In the logit estimates of the demand for inpatient care all the coefficients with the exception of drinking ware are statistically significant at 1 percent level. For households with higher income (consumption expenditure), the odds of visiting a hospital for inpatient care at least once in the given year are higher. This may be attributed to the fact that the increasing hospitalisation expenditure in India makes inpatient care unaffordable to the poor income households. However, people are more inclined to utilise inpatient care from both public and private hospitals when they have health insurance coverage as shown by the positive coefficient of the health insurance variable. Thus, the odds of an individual seeking hospitalisation are higher if he/she has insurance coverage. The effect of age on the decision to seek inpatient care is significantly positive as the old age related ailments usually require hospitalisation. This is also supported by the positive coefficient of the age squared variable.

The probability of seeking inpatient care is lower for males than for females. Women, especially during the middle age and at times of pregnancy encounter gender-specific illness which require some duration of hospitalisation. The estimated coefficient of flush-type latrine in the household is also significantly positive suggesting that those with good systems of latrine may possess better literacy levels and better awareness of communicable diseases which may help them to report diseases better than an illiterate individuals. Another important factor that determines individual's willingness to be inpatient and hospitalisation is the quality of healthcare related infrastructure in the state. The variable number of beds is an indicator of the infrastructure in the state. Surprisingly, the estimated coefficient of beds is significantly negative showing with more beds per 1000 population, the probability of seeking hospitalisation declines possibly indicating the poor quality of beds in general hospitals.

The Poisson regression model is estimated strictly for positive counts of the number of times an individual seeks inpatient services in a year, conditional on patient seeks inpatient care at least once in the given year. The Poisson regression estimates show that those with higher household incomes tend to utilise the inpatient services in a hospital more frequently. The impact of income is statistically significant at 1 percent level. Males are found to utilise less inpatient services than females. Age has no effect on the number of times an individual is hospitalised. A good drinking water and a good latrine facility significantly reduce the frequency of hospitalisation as they usually contribute to a healthy environment in the family. Individuals with insurance cover use inpatient services more often as the costs of hospitalisation are reimbursable under health insurance. As the hospitalisation costs in India are increasing over the years, the catastrophic payments of the households are increasing and thus health insurance coverage is essential to meet with the hospitalisation expenditures. As in the case of the logit model, the health infrastructure of the state has negative impact on seeking inpatient care, but the coefficient is not statistically significant. Thus, household income, health insurance, household hygiene and good drinking water are the important determinants of both the demand for inpatient care and the number of times of hospitalisation of an individual in India.

In addition to the determinants of the demand for inpatient services, this paper also tries to understand the effect of diseases on the health expenditure of individuals for hospitalisation. An OLS regression has been estimated with the total amount of health expenditure incurred for inpatient treatment as the dependant variable. The estimated coefficients of the determinants of hospitalisation expenditure are presented in Table 11.5.

**Table 11.5: OLS Estimates of Hospitalisation Expenditure**
**Dependent variable: Medical expenditure on inpatient care**

| *Variable* | *Coefficient* |
|---|---|
| Consumption expenditure | 1.10* (2.93) |
| Age | 1.85* (3.19) |
| $Age^2$ | -1.32* (2.99) |
| Household size | -1.02* (2.93) |
| Gender-male | 4.79* (6.43) |

*(Contd...)*

| Drinking water | -2.93* (4.70) |
|---|---|
| Govt. hospital | -1.46* (3.24) |
| Insurance | -1.79 (1.55) |
| Beds | 1.71* (3.09) |
| Chronic disease | 1.53* (2.61) |
| Infection | 1.89* (2.85) |
| Cancer | 8.16* (3.81) |
| Blood diseases | 2.15 (1.50) |
| Endocrine, metabolic and nutrition | 1.25* (2.72) |
| Psychiatric, neurological | 1.84 (1.47) |
| Eye | 0.41 (1.23) |
| Ear | 0.21*** (1.91) |
| Cardio-vascular | 9.15** (2.35) |
| Respiratory | 3.58** (1.96) |
| Gastro-intestinal | 2.74** (2.03) |
| Skin | 1.21*** (1.82) |
| Musculo-skeletal | 1.19 (1.31) |
| Genito-urinary | 2.56** (2.04) |
| Obstetric, neonatal | 4.44* (4.33) |
| Injuries | 0.54** (2.27) |
| Constant | 1.24 (0.96) |
| R-square | 0.32 |
| F-value | 276.29 |

**Note:** Absolute t-values in parentheses. * Significant at 1 percent level ** Significant at 5 percent level *** Significant at 10 percent level.

The expenditure for inpatient care increases with household income as shown by the significant coefficient of consumption expenditure. The age of an individual is a key determinant of the amount of expenditure incurred. As age increases, the expenditure towards inpatient services increases on account of increased utilisation of inpatient services. But the effect of age increases expenditure at a decreasing rate perhaps due to the continuing treatment and medicines for age related illness. Household size has a negative effect on hospitalisation expenditure. Males spend more for inpatient care than females. Chronic ailments increase the expenditure significantly and good drinking water facility reduces the health expenditure. Availability of government hospital services and health insurance cover significantly reduces the hospitalisation expenditure. A better public health infrastructure would mean that individuals would utilise the inpatient services more often as suggested by the significant positive coefficient of the variable beds. Diseases like such as cancer and cardiovascular diseases contribute more towards hospitalisation expenditure than diseases such as infections or any ENT and skin problems.

## 11.5 Conclusion

As health is important for everyone, healthcare and investments in health predominates the behaviour of individuals. People seek healthcare both as outpatient and inpatient in hospitals. The hospitalisation is generally avoided, but for serious diseases and ailments, patients need to be hospitalised at multiple spells. Therefore, this paper analyses the determinants of the health seeking behaviour of individuals with respect to inpatient care in terms of number of times of hospitalisation using the NSSO 71st round (January-June 2014) morbidity data and applying the Poisson-Logit Hurdle regression model for the counts of hospitalisation. The OLS regression model is used to analyse the expenditure on health. The estimated econometric results show that health insurance, availability of drinking water and good latrine and hygienic practices at the household, besides household income, are the important determinants of both the demand for inpatient care and the number of times of hospitalisation of an individual in India. The presence of insurance cover encourages people to utilise inpatient care more frequently. The health expenditure for diseases like cancer and cardio-vascular illness are higher relative to other ailments.

# 12

# The Demand for AYUSH Healthcare: A Multinomial Logistic Regression Estimation of AYUSH Hospital Visits


## Abstract

*Despite the widespread increase in the allopathic system of medicines, the indigenous non-allopathic system of medicine is widely practiced and used in many parts of India. The increasing costs of modern corporate type of hospitals and the less expensiveness of local herbal medicines drives households to use the AYUSH (Ayurveda, Yoga and Naturopathy, Unani, Siddha and Homoeopathy) hospitals for treatments of chronic diseases, acute illness episodes, maternity health care and catastrophic health expenditure. This paper attempts to analyse the use of the AYUSH healthcare system in India using the 68th round (2011-2012) of NSSO data pertaining to the four southern states of India - Andhra Pradesh, Karnataka, Kerala and Tamil Nadu and applying the multinomial logit method to estimate the number of visits to the AYUSH hospitals by household members. Within the AYUSH healthcare system, there are statewise differentials in the use of ayurveda, unani, siddha and homoeopathy systems of medicines. The yoga system is widely practiced. The estimated results show that the relative probability of choosing the AYUSH treatment and the number of visits to AYUSH hospitals is influenced significantly by the cost of medical expenditure, wealth/income/landholding, household size and composition and region. The occupation, household headship and community have no significant effect on the use of AYUSH hospitals in India.*



**Key words:** *Healthcare, medical expenditure, AYUSH hospitals, visits, MNL estimation*

## 12.1 Introduction

India is the second largest populated country with millions of people having health issues and is in need of proper healthcare. Also, India has a vast variety of healthcare systems in itself. These various types of healthcare systems are classified generally into two major healthcare systems. There are allopathic or western system of medicine, generally known as English medicines, and the Indian or traditional or indigenous non-allopathic system of medicines, popularly known as Indian medicines. Generally, it is believed that the modern healthcare system is a curative form, while the indigenous system of healthcare is largely preventive healthcare since the Indian system is said to have a holistic approach. The AYUSH system of medicines consists of Ayurveda, Yoga and Naturopathy, Unani, Siddha and Homoeopathy. The Indian system of medicine is of great antiquity. India has a vast reservoir of natural flora and fauna and also ancient texts and knowledge that have made it an authority in the field of AYUSH. It is the culmination of Indian thought of medicine by great sages or yogis which represents a way of healthy living valued with a long and unique cultural history, It also amalgamates the best of influences that came in from contact with other civilisations be it Greece (resulting in unani medicine) or Germany (homoeopathy) or Indian scriptures/sages which gives the science of ayurveda, siddha, yoga and naturopathy. There are about 6200 indigenous herbal plants in India. India has 6600 medicinal plants found in Himalayan region, around its coastline, desserts and rain forest eco-system. India has unmatched heritage represented by its ancient systems of medicine which are both preventive and curative health care. Like the multifaceted culture of India, traditional medicines have evolved over centuries blessed with a plethora of traditional medicines and practices. The AYUSH system of medicine has certain advantages. Primarily, the AYUSH, unlike the chemical-based allopathic drugs, is safe, no side-effects, non-toxic, cost effective, and do not produce life style disorders. As an indigenous system of medicine with natural forms, it has more of holistic approach to the body for the cure the patient, and attempts to stimulate the self-healing capacity of the body. The yoga is a drugless system and can be applied as an independent modality or as an add-on therapy with other systems. The ultimate goal of this system is to create a balance between man and his environment.

The ayurveda is a classical system of medicine originating from the Vedas, founded around 5000 years ago in India, and currently recognised and practiced in India as well as in of the many subcontinent countries. It is one of the oldest medical systems in the world. The treatment in Ayurveda system is holistic and individualised, mainly uses drugs from medicinal plants (though materials of animal, marine origin, metals and minerals are sometimes are also used) diet and life style systems. The preventive aspect of ayurveda consists of personal hygiene, regular, daily and seasonal regimes, appropriate social behaviour, use of rejuvenate materials/food and drugs. It is believed that ayurvedic medicines are safe and have little or no known adverse side effects.

The yoga and naturopathy refers to traditional physical and mental disciplines originating in India. Yoga is about the union of a person's own consciousness and the universal consciousness. The practice of Yoga has also been found to be useful in the prevention of certain psychosomatic disorders/diseases and improves individual resistance and ability to endure stressful situations. Yoga is a primitive, preventive and curative intervention. Naturopathy is a cost effective drugless, non-invasive therapy involving the use of natural materials in its treatment based on the theories of self healing capacity of the body and the principles of healthy living. Naturopathy, as a system of medicine widely practiced, globally accepted and recognised by the WHO. It has great primitive, preventive, curative as well as restorative potential.

The unani system of medicine originated in Greece is widely used in India, especially among the vast Muslim population, is enriched by imbibing what was best in the contemporary systems of traditional medicines in Egypt, Syria, Iraq, Persia, India, China and other Middle East countries. The unani system of medicine uses naturally occurring, mostly herbal, medicines. The siddha system, said to have been developed by eighteen Siddhars, is one of the oldest systems of medicine in India and is practiced in the Tamil speaking parts of India and abroad. The system has developed a rich and unique treasure house of drug knowledge with the use of metals and minerals. The siddha system is effective in treating chronic cases of liver, skin diseases especially psoriasis, rheumatic problems, anemia, peptic ulcer and many more. The homoeopathy system of medicine has been brought into India around 1810 A.D. by European missionaries and received official recognition. Homoeopathic medicines are prepared mainly from natural substances such as plant products, minerals and from animal sources. Homoeopathic medicines do not have any toxic, poisonous or side effects. Homoeopathic treatment is economical as well and has a very broad public acceptance.

Since the mid 2000s the governments in India have taken innovative initiatives to improve public healthcare in India. For instance, with an objective of raising the public health spending to achieve universal healthcare, the central government has launched the National Rural Health Mission in 2005. Realising the limitations of the state provision of health particularly in rural and remote areas and the growing preference of the consumers for the private health providers, many states have started adopting innovative public-private partnership in health sector for various services (Bhat and Jain, 2006; Baru and Nundy, 2008) with a view of directing the growth of private sector to contribute to public goals. Despite the vast growth and availability of modern allopathic medicines in both public and private healthcare industry, for many in many places in India, the Indian systems of medicines continues to be widely used due to their accessibility and the reason that they offer only the kind of medicine whining the physical and financial reach of the patient. These Indian systems of medicines play an important role even in achieving the national health goal of reducing maternal mortality rate and infant mortality rate, malnutrition and anemia. The AYUSH system of medicine has been preferred by people for various kinds of acute illness and repeating episodes of it, such as cough, cold, fever, gastritis, arthritis, asthma, migraine, injury, heart disease, diabetes and hypertension. Also, women use AYUSH system for maternity healthcare. Different empirical studies have found that a significant proportion of India's population adopt various non-allopathic system of medicine (NSSO, 1992). People who use non-allopathic medicines find it more effective in the long run and they rarely report having any negative reactions or side effects (Chandrasekhara et al., 2002). According to the Ministry of Health and Family Welfare, the AYUSH has also been the strength in managing the non-communicable diseases.

Given the importance of AYUSH system of medicine and its widespread practice in India, a separate Department of Indian Systems of Medicine and Homoeopathy (ISM&H) was set up in 1995 to ensure the optimal development and propagation of AYUSH systems of health care. The Department of ISM&H was renamed as the Department of AYUSH in November 2003 in the Ministry of Health and Family Welfare. The Department of AYUSH has launched the National AYUSH Mission (NAM) during 12th plan. With the objective of promoting AYUSH medical systems through cost effective AYUSH services, strengthening of educational systems, facilitate the enforcement of quality control of ayurveda, siddha, unani and homoeopathy (ASU&H) drugs and sustainable availability of ASU&H raw materials. In 2014, a dedicated Ministry of AYUSH was set up with the aim of providing impetus to these ancient healthcare systems with a targeted thrust.

The AYUSH sector is growing at 20 percent from year to year, and India is the second largest exporter of AYUSH and herbal products. The AYUSH exports has been Rs. 22.7 billion in 2013-14 through raw medicinal herbs, medicaments, and medicinal extracts. The biggest markets for Indian herbal products are Western Europe, Russia, USA, Kazakhstan, UAE, Nepal, Ukraine, Japan, Philippines, and Kenya. As on 2017, the infrastructural facilities with the Ministry of AYUSH consists of 3,943 hospitals, 27,698 dispensaries, 7,73,668 doctors, 55,242 beds, 9,038 drug manufacturing units, 631 educational institutions with 40,151 UG and 5,826 and PG admission capacity. There are more ayurveda hospitals and only few yoga hospitals in India. On an average, AYUSH dispensaries have increased at the rate of 0.8 percent per annum during 1993-2010.

The Figures 12.1 and 12.2 present the growth of AYUSH hospitals in India during the period 1980-2010. It can be observed that when the AYUSH system of healthcare was introduced in 1980s, the number of ayurveda hospitals were greater compared to all other forms of AYUSH hospitals. However, since the 2000s there is appreciable increase especially in the homoeopathy hospitals. As Figure 12.2 shows when the AYUSH system of healthcare was introduced, the number of unani, siddha and homoeopathy hospitals was very less. However, since 1990s, the use of the indigenous system of medicines gradually increased. With the advent of yoga and naturopathy hospitals, the other hospitals such as unani and homoeopathy hospitals saw a decline in its number. However, of late there is an increasing trend in the number of all types of these hospitals.

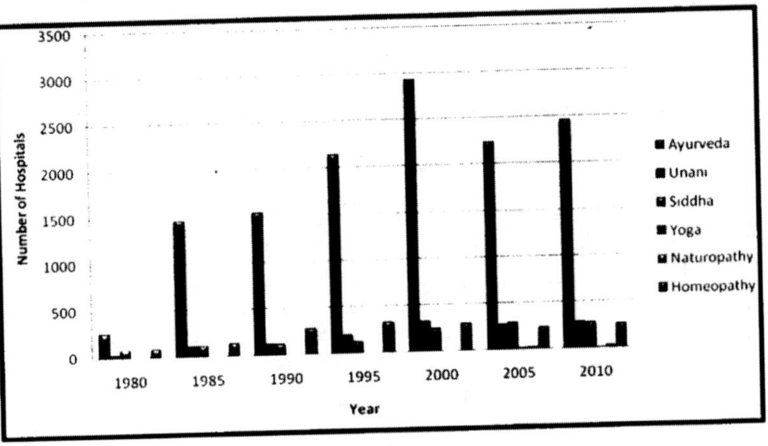


***Figure 12.1: Growth of AYUSH Hospitals in India, 1980-2010***

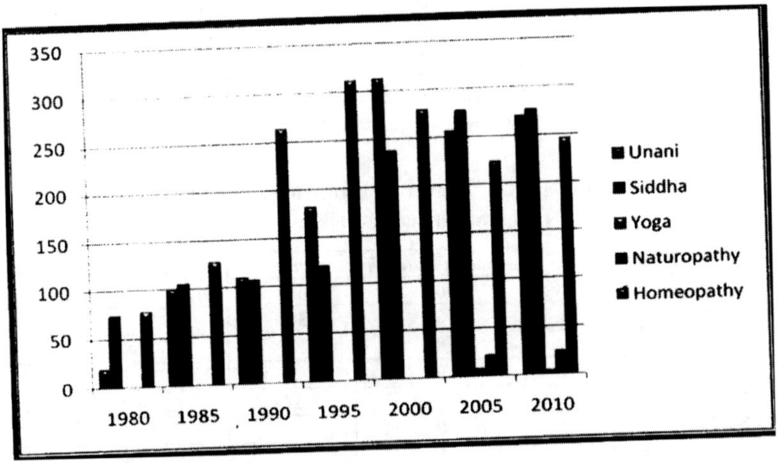


***Figure 12.2: Growth of Unani, Siddha, Yoga, Naturopathy and Homoeopathy Hospitals in India, 1980-2010.***

The Table 12.1 presents the total number of AYUSH hospitals and AYUSH beds across the states and union territories in India. It can be observed that ayurveda is more prevalent in the southern states of Kerala and Karnataka, unani is popular in Andhra Pradesh, Karnataka and Tamil Nadu, homoeopathy is widely practiced in Kerala, Andhra Pradesh and Tamil Nadu, and the siddha system is more acquainted in the southern part of India, especially in Tamil Nadu and the practice of yoga is gaining more acceptance all over India. The Table 12.2 shows that Tamil Nadu has more number of both allopathic and AYUSH, both in both urban and rural areas, government hospitals, followed Kerala and Karnataka. Tamil Nadu is dominated by siddha hospitals due to the historical nature of siddha system of medicine developed by Siddhars in Tamil Nadu.

**Table 12.1: Distribution of AYUSH Hospitals and Beds in India**

| *State/UT* | *AYUSH hospitals* | *AYUSH beds* | *State/UT* | *AYUSH hospitals* | *AYUSH beds* |
|---|---|---|---|---|---|
| Andhra Pradesh | 22 | 1314 | Madhya Pradesh | 57 | 2981 |
| Arunachal Pradesh | 3 | 70 | Maharashtra | 101 | 11388 |
| Assam | 5 | 230 | Manipur | 3 | 75 |
| Bihar | 26 | 2325 | Meghalaya | 8 | 80 |
| Chandigarh | 2 | 145 | Mizoram | 1 | 14 |
| Chhattisgarh | 13 | 605 | Nagaland | 1 | 10 |
| Delhi | 20 | 1094 | Orissa | 14 | 673 |
| Goa | 2 | 65 | Punjab | 21 | 1484 |
| Gujarat | 62 | 2728 | Rajasthan | 114 | 1191 |
| Haryana | 10 | 895 | Sikkim | 1 | 10 |
| Himachal Pradesh | 26 | 455 | Tamil Nadu | 292 | 3225 |
| Jammu & Kashmir | 5 | 355 | Tripura | 2 | 20 |
| Jharkhand | 3 | 242 | Uttar Pradesh | 1988 | 12223 |
| Karnataka | 164 | 9746 | Uttrakhand | 10 | 377 |
| Kerala | 160 | 5327 | West Bengal | 17 | 1099 |

*Source:* Ministry of AYUSH, Government of India: AYUSH in India (2017).

**Table 12.2: Number of Allopathic and AYUSH Hospitals in Southern States of India**

| *Hospitals* | *Andhra Pradesh* | *Karnataka* | *Kerala* | *Tamil Nadu* |
|---|---|---|---|---|
| Allopathy - rural | 308 | 423 | 1091 | 1614 |
| Allopathy - urban | 152 | 342 | 164 | 381 |
| Ayurveda | 8 | 133 | 126 | 8 |
| Yoga and naturopathy | 0 | 9 | 2 | 0 |
| Unani | 6 | 14 | 0 | 1 |
| Siddha | 0 | 0 | 2 | 270 |
| Homoeopathy | 6 | 21 | 32 | 9 |

The Tables 12.1 and 12.2 and Figures 12.1 and 12.2 together shows that people in India need both systems of medicine both for curative and preventive healthcare. Therefore, it is important to understand the factors that determine the use of AYUSH healthcare system in India especially at the household level.

The main objectives of this paper are to understand the trends and patterns of household use of AYUSH healthcare in India and to identify and analyse the determinants of the choice of AYUSH hospital healthcare by households in India. This paper uses the 68th round (2011-2012) of NSSO data on the use of AYUSH hospitals by households for the four southern states of India - Andhra Pradesh, Karnataka, Kerala and Tamil Nadu. Empirically, the multinomial logit method is used to estimate the number of visits to the AYUSH hospitals.

## 12.2 A Brief Review of Recent Studies

Gumber, Dhak and Lalitha (2012) detail the trends in health seeking behaviour of people and the choice between government and private sources, reasons for not accessing healthcare and the cost of treatment by examining three rounds of the NSSO data on healthcare use and morbidity pattern in India. They observe that the public health system play a vital role in meeting healthcare needs in India. They also observe that while majority of both men and women sought treatment for their illness, the percentage of people reporting lack of access to medical facility is more for rural than for urban populations indicating the urban centric position of health providers and the public healthcare needs to fill in this gap. At the same time the percentage of people reporting illness not serious enough requiring treatment has declined over the survey periods, indicating a better health seeking behaviour of people in both rural and urban areas. It also reflects on the increasing level of morbidity in India.

Loera et al. (2001) analyse the characteristics among older Mexican Americans that correlate with the use of herbal medicines using a panel survey that study the health status of community-dwelling elderly persons applying logistic regression method. The empirical results show that, among people aged 75 years and more, 9.8 percent more Mexican American women are likely to use herbal medicine than men in the same age group and younger ones and the usage is based on their financial status. They conclude that herbal medications are relatively common among older Mexican Americans with chronic medical conditions, particularly among those with limited financial resources.

Mukherjee et al. (2012) use a 12 month long panel survey to identify the utilisation pattern of allopathic and non-allopathic providers. The results show that the choice varies with economic status. The households with less landholding having acute episodes of health problem have a slightly higher utilisation rate of non-allopathic provider as compared to households owning more land. The wage labour households have marginally higher utilisation of non-allopathic provider than households belonging to independent cultivators and engaged in occupations. The use of non-allopathic healthcare providers is observed more in rural areas and mostly for chronic diseases across all the age-groups, educational levels and living standards.

Saito et al. (2014), in an attempt to identify which households - richest or poorest - incur out-of-pocket expenditure on the various incidence of ten reported illness by the members of households, use a multivariate Poisson regression approach. They observe that catastrophic health expenditure is mostly met by the out-of-pocket expenditure of the households. The poorest households spend 10.7 percent out-of-pocket on health while the wealthiest households spend only 6.9 percent out-of-pocket on health.

Mukherjee et al. (2013) investigates the incidence, intensity and socio-economic correlates of catastrophic maternal healthcare expenditure using the 60th round (January-June 2004) NSSO data on morbidity and healthcare in India. The logistic regression method is applied to analyse the non-catastrophic expenditure and catastrophic expenditures based on religion, MPCE quintiles, social groups, occupation, educational attainment of the head of the household and age groups. Empirically, the catastrophic head count in rural areas has been 37 percent compared to 35 percent in urban areas. Women of poorer households in both rural and urban areas are burdened by catastrophic expenditure. Also, the Muslim households in urban areas spend less (49 percent) compared to Christian households in rural areas (84 percent). The odds of experiencing a catastrophic expenditure reduce significantly by 99 percent in 5th quintile, 98 percent in 4th quintile, 96 percent in 3rd quintile and 66 percent in 2nd quintile compared to the 1st quintile.

Rahman et al. (2013), noting the high proportion of households incurring catastrophic health expenditure and very limited risk sharing mechanism in Bangladesh, try to identify the determinants of out-of-pocket payments on catastrophic health expenditure. The empirical results of a primary survey show that the relative risk of incurring catastrophic payments significantly increase by 1.12 times and 1.47 times for a single additional average illness in children and adults respectively. The households in the poorest quintile have more than 4 times the risk of catastrophic expenditure than the richest quintile. An increase in the education attainment of the head of the household reduces the relative risk of catastrophic health expenditure increases.

Wang et al. (2015) analyse the determinants of the choice of healthcare type among those reporting at least one chronic non-communicable disease (CNCD) using a population based survey and applying the multinomial logistic regression model. The paper used the healthcare options of no care, informal care and formal care. They find that for the people with higher socio-economic status, a household head, and higher perceived severity significantly increase the probability of using formal care, compared with no care. The proportion of people with CNCDs in a household suffering from 'early detectable CNCDs' and the long duration of illness are negatively associated with formal care utilisation.

## 12.3 Data and Methodology

To study the pattern of the household use of AYUSH system of healthcare, the household consumption expenditure data from 68th round (2011-2012) of NSSO has been used and to examine the use of AYUSH hospitals by households the NSSO data pertaining to the four southern states of India has been used. The four southern India states considered are Andhra Pradesh, Karnataka, Kerala and Tamil Nadu where the AYUSH system of medicines are widely practiced and these states have the large number of AYUSH hospitals and beds. In the NSSO 68th round data, there are 22,095 household observations in total for the four states, out of which 6847 households use AYUSH system of medicine. The NSSO data of the 68th round of household consumption expenditure collected by the category I item group relating to clothing, bedding, footwear, education, medical, and durable goods for the reference period of last 30 days has been used because the usage of AYUSH is taken for the past 30 days and the variables pertaining to the household expenditure on medical expenses are also taken for the same period. The medical expenses include both institutional and non-institutional medical expenses. Empirically the multinomial logistic regression has been used to model the use of AYUSH healthcare by the households as the choice of AYUSH healthcare as well as the number of visits to AYUSH hospitals for treatment is a categorical variable. The number of visits is also unordered because the data pertains to the household level data and the number of visits to AYUSH hospital is reported for the whole household and not for individual household members.

The dependent variable is the choice of number of visits to AYUSH hospital. It is taken as how often do the members of the household visit an AYUSH hospital for treatment in the past 30 days. The data on visits to AYUSH hospital includes nil visits to more than three times. The nil visit data is also included because it has been grouped as household members using AYUSH in the past 30 days. The independent variables included in the paper are medical expenditure, which includes institutional and non-institutional medical expenditure for a period of 30 days. The non-institutional medical expenditure is the expenditure made as outpatient and is taken as an indicator for households with acute illness episodes. The institutional medical expenditure is the expenditure incurred as inpatient and is taken as an indicator of catastrophic health expenditure and maternal health expenditure. The land possessed by the household is taken as an indicator of the income/wealth status of the household as well as the utilisation pattern of AYUSH by households. As observed by Mukherjee et al. (2012), people with less landholdings use more of AYUSH compared to people with more landholdings. Since the indigenous system of medicine is cost effective, household size plays a role in the type of healthcare the household prefers. As household size increases people may tend to use AYUSH healthcare than other forms. However, number of visits to AYUSH hospitals may differ based on the household size. The difference in

AYUSH hospital visits between rural and urban households is captured by the region variable. Studies show that people in urban areas tend to use more of AYUSH healthcare as they have a holistic approach, but rural people also use of AYUSH healthcare because of the easy availability and culture. The other independent variables considered are the type of occupation, household type, gender of household head, age composition of household, social group, and state and religious dummies. The AYUSH is said to be used across different religions holding them to be used by their ancestors and continue the same, for example unani is brought by Muslims and is still is popular system of medicine among Muslim households.

## Multinomial Logistic Regression

Consider a logistic regression model specified as,

$$y_i = \beta_0 + \beta_1 x_i + u_i \tag{12.1}$$

where $y_i$ is the dependent categorical/choice variable and $x_i$ is a set of explanatory variables. When $y_i$ ranges over a limited category, say $j$ choices, the probabilities for the $j$ choices is given by,

$$Pr(y_i = j) = e^{\beta_j x} / (1 + \sum e^{\beta_j x}) \tag{12.2}$$

For multinomial logistic regression model, the linear component is equated to the log of odds of *jth* outcome compared to the Jth outcome. That is, considering the *jth* category to be omitted or baseline category, the logits of the first *J*-1 categories are constructed with the baseline category in the denominator as,

$$log\left[\frac{\pi_{ij}}{\pi_{iJ}}\right] = log\left[\frac{\pi_{ij}}{1+\sum_{j=1}^{J-1}\pi_{ij}}\right] = \sum_{k=0}^{K}\beta_{jk}x_{ik} \quad \text{i=1,...,N; j=1,...,J-1} \tag{12.3}$$

Solving for $\pi_{ij}$ gives,

$$\pi_{ij} = \frac{e^{\sum_{k=0}^{K}\beta_{jk}x_{ik}}}{1+\sum_{j=1}^{J-1}e^{\sum_{k=0}^{K}\beta_{jk}x_{ik}}} \qquad j < J \tag{12.4}$$

$$\pi_{iJ} = \frac{1}{1+\sum_{j=1}^{J-1}e^{\sum_{k=0}^{K}\beta_{jk}x_{ik}}} \tag{12.5}$$

The dependent variables follow a multinomial distribution with J categories. Thus, the joint probability density function is given by,

$$f(y|\beta) = \prod_{i=1}^{N}\left[\frac{n_i!}{\prod_{j=1}^{J}y_{ij}!}\prod_{j=1}^{J}\pi_{ij}^{y_{ij}}\right] \tag{12.6}$$

The likelihood function expresses the unknown values of ß in terms of known fixed constant values for *y*. To maximise equation (12.6) with respect to ß the factorial terms that do not contain any of the $\pi_{ij}$ terms can be treated as constants. The log likelihood function for the multinomial logistic regression model can be written as,

$$L(\beta) = \sum_{i=1}^{N} \sum_{j=1}^{J-1} \left( y_{ij} \sum_{k=1}^{K} \beta_{jk} x_{ik} \right) - n_i log \left( \frac{1}{1+\sum_{j=1}^{J-1} e^{\sum_{k=0}^{K} \beta_{jk} x_{ik}}} \right) \qquad (12.7)$$

Maximising equation (12.7), the estimates of β are obtained.

## 12.4 Empirical Analysis

The Table 12.3 presents the use of AYUSH system of healthcare in the four southern states of India. It can be observed that that out of a total of 22095 observations from all the four southern states, about 6848 households, nearly one-third households (31 percent) have used AYUSH in the last 30 days of the NSSO survey. Out of these observations, the medical expenditure for 1242 households is missing. Thus, omitting the missing observations from the stud, the empirical analysis is based on the 5606 observations, 81.86 percent of households that have used AYUSH for the four southern states. However, 68.16 percent of these households who have used AYUSH system of healthcare have not visited the AYUSH hospitals. Nearly 16.20 households have visited the AYUSH hospital once, 11.33 percent two to three times, and 4.32 percent more than thrice visited the AYUSH hospitals.

**Table 12.3: AYUSH Healthcare Use in Southern India**

| *State* | *AYUSH use* | *No. of visit to AYUSH hospital* | | | | |
|---|---|---|---|---|---|---|
| | | Nil | Once | 2-3 times | >3 times | Total |
| Andhra Pradesh | 2207 (31.99) | 1594 (88.46) | 123 (6.83) | 61 (3.39) | 24 (1.33) | 1802 (81.65) |
| Karnataka | 815 (19.91) | 477 (66.16) | 111 (15.40) | 95 (13.18) | 38 (5.27) | 244 (51.15) |
| Kerala | 1566 (35.12) | 374 (9.79) | 542 (38.71) | 391 (27.93) | 93 (6.64) | 1400 (89.40) |
| Tamil Nadu | 2260 (34.02) | 1376 (81.76) | 132 (7.84) | 88 (5.23) | 87 (5.17) | 307 (22.31) |
| Total | 6848 (30.99) | 3821 (68.16) | 908 (16.20) | 635 (11.33) | 242 (4.32) | 5606 (81.86) |

**Note:** Percentage figures in parentheses.

The pie chart presented in Figure 12.3 shows the percentage share of people in rural and urban regions of the states using the AYUSH. In both the regions the pattern of use of AYUSH healthcare is the same; 68 percent of households use AYUSH, but do not visit the AYUSH hospitals. Only 4 percent of households in both rural and urban areas visited the AYUSH hospitals more than three times. The bar chart presented in Figure 12.4 shows the percentage of households using AYUSH hospitals is relatively higher among

Christians compared to Hindus. Interestingly, households belonging to Jainism, Buddhism, Sikhism and Zoroastrianism have more preference towards the AYUSH system of medicine. As shown in Figure 12.5, among the social groups, about 86.12 percent of schedule tribe households have used the AYUSH hospitals compared to 66.19 percent of other households. While the visits to AYUSH hospitals by schedule tribe households is very low relative to other social groups. Among occupation groups, mostly the regular salaried households have visited the AYUSH hospitals at least once, whereas most of the self-employed households and casual labour households have not visited AYUSH hospitals.

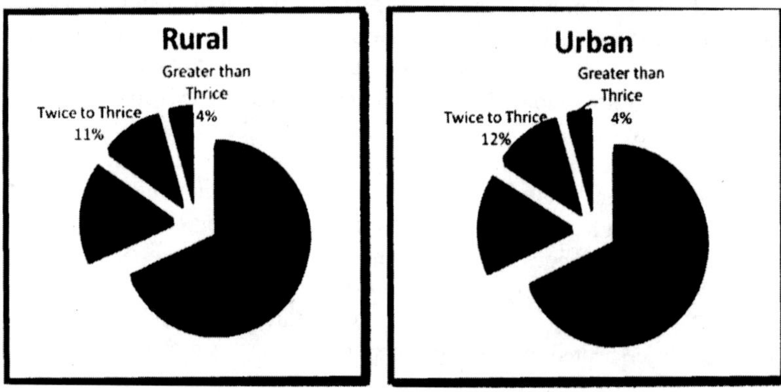


*Figure 12.3: AYUSH Hospital Visits by Region*

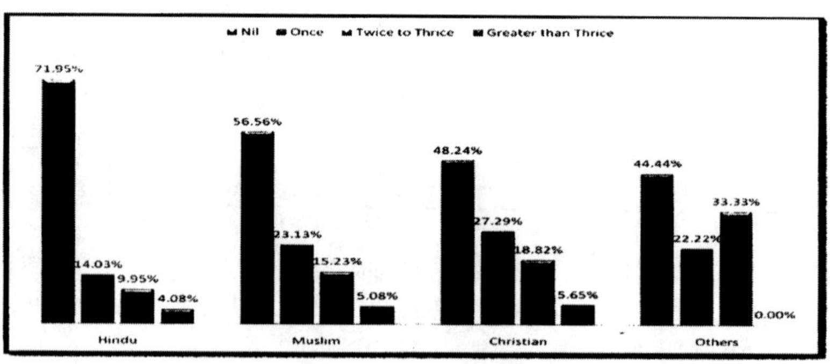


*Figure 12.4: AYUSH Hospital Visits by Religion*

From the Table 12.4 it can be observed that the mean medical expenditure of those households who have used AYUSH healthcare has been Rs. 950 and its log value is 5.864. The households who have used AYUSH, but have not visited the AYUSH hospitals have incurred a mean medical expenditure of Rs.788. The mean medical expenditure of households who visited the AYUSH hospital once has been Rs.1298 and for those who visited more than thrice has been Rs.1459.

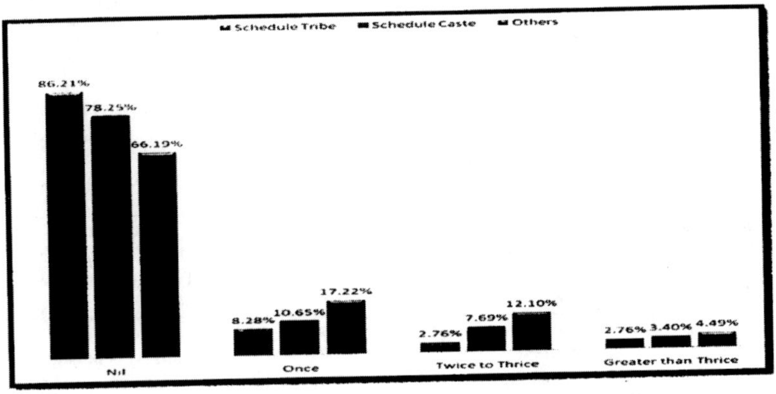


***Figure 12.5: AYUSH Hospital Visits by Social Group***

**Table 12.4: Summary Statistics of AYUSH Medical Expenditure**

| *Variable* | *AYUSH use* | *No. of visit to AYUSH hospital* | | | |
|---|---|---|---|---|---|
| | | *Nil* | *Once* | *2-3 times* | *>3 times* |
| Medical expenditure (Rs.) | 950.22 (4362.81) | 788.31 (4594.25) | 1298.05 (3350.91) | 1233.16 (2258.71) | 1459.12 (6037.90) |
| ln(Medical expenditure) | 5.864 (1.294) | 5.702 (1.239) | 6.208 (1.356) | 6.208 (1.318) | 6.234 (1.332) |
| N | 5606 | 3821 | 908 | 635 | 242 |

**Note:** Standard deviations in parentheses.

**Table 12.5: Description of Variables Used in the AYUSH Healthcare Choice**

| *Variable* | *Definition* | *Measurement* | *Justification* |
|---|---|---|---|
| No. of visit to AYUSH hospital | Number of visits to AYUSH hospital by members of a household | No visit, once, twice or thrice and more than thrice dummies | Dependent variable |
| Ln(Medexp) | Total medical expenditure (institutional and non-institutional) | Log of total medical expenditure (institutional and non-institutional) | A measure for acute illness episodes in the household |
| HHSize | Number of members in the family | Number of persons in the household | As the family size increases, households may prefer to use AYUSH as it is less expensive |
| Land | Land possessed by the household | Land possessed by the household (hectares) | A measure of wealth and income |
| Region | Urban and rural area | Rural = 1, Urban = 0 | Urban and rural difference in visits to AYUSH hospital |

*(Contd...)*

| State | Karnataka, Andhra Pradesh, Kerala and Tamil Nadu | State dummies | Prevalence of AYUSH medication |
|---|---|---|---|
| Religion | Hindu, Islam, Christian and Others | Religion dummies | Religious influence of AYUSH due to tradition |
| Social group | Schedule Tribe, Schedule Castes and Others | Social group dummies | AYUSH medication use varies across social groups. AYUSH is common among ST households |
| Occupation | Self employed, Wage/salaried, Casual labour and Others | Occupation dummies | AYUSH medication Differentials by occupation and affordability |
| Household members in age groups | Child (0-14), Young (15-30), Adult (31-60), Elder (60+ years) | Age group dummies | Effect of demographic factors in choosing the number of visits to AYUSH hospital |
| Male head of household | Head of the household | If household head is male=1, 0 otherwise | Decision on the visit to AYUSH hospital depends on the gender of the head |

In this paper, multinomial logistic regression has been used to model the number of visits to the AYUSH hospital by the households. The number of visits to the AYUSH hospital in the NSSO data has been recorded at the household level as no visit, visited once, visited twice to thrice and visited more than thrice. The data on visits to AYUSH hospital is unordered because the number of visits is the total visits by the household members, and there are no separate data for the visits to the AYUSH hospital by individuals in the household. The estimating multinomial logistic regression includes economic factors, demographic factors and social factors that determine the choice of visits to an AYUSH hospital by the household. The estimated results are the relative risk ratios, since the estimates are eß rather than β.

**Table 12.6: MNL Regression Estimates of Number of Visit to AYUSH Hospitals Dependent variable: No. of visit to AYUSH hospital**

| *Variable* | *Visited once vs No visit* | | *Visited twice or thrice vs No visit* | | *Visited more than thrice vs No visit* | |
|---|---|---|---|---|---|---|
| | *Coefficient* | *z-value* | *Coefficient* | *z-value* | *Coefficient* | *z-value* |
| Ln(Medexp) | 1.142* (0.038) | 4.01 | 1.145* (0.043) | 3.61 | 1.236* (0.067) | 3.91 |
| Land | 0.999 (0.0003) | 0.71 | 0.999** (0.0005) | 1.97 | 0.999** (0.0003) | 2.08 |
| HHSize | 1.035 (0.028) | 1.26 | 1.003 (0.032) | 0.09 | 1.077*** (0.047) | 1.71 |

*(Contd...)*

| | | | | | | |
|---|---|---|---|---|---|---|
| Male head | 1.044 (0.119) | 0.38 | 1.009 (0.128) | 0.07 | 1.106 (0.212) | 0.51 |
| Child | 0.846*** (0.085) | 1.68 | 0.978 (0.113) | 0.19 | 0.850 (0.140) | 0.98 |
| Young | 0.815** (0.078) | 2.11 | 0.808** (0.088) | 1.97 | 0.685** (0.106) | 2.43 |
| Adult | 1.339** (0.201) | 1.98 | 1.212 (0.202) | 1.16 | 1.745** (0.482) | 2.02 |
| Rural | 0.827** (0.074) | 2.11 | 0.739* (0.075) | 2.96 | 0.923 (0.134) | 0.55 |
| Karnataka | 3.001* (0.431) | 7.65 | 5.41* (0.947) | 9.65 | 5.328* (1.435) | 6.21 |
| Kerala | 16.70* (2.075) | 22.65 | 24.70* (3.901) | 20.31 | 13.09* (3.247) | 10.37 |
| Tamil Nadu | 1.166 (0.154) | 1.16 | 1.536** (0.264) | 2.49 | 3.886* (0.915) | 5.76 |
| Self employed | 0.920 (0.146) | 0.52 | 0.923 (0.161) | 0.45 | 0.986 (0.256) | 0.05 |
| Wage/ salaried | 1.072 (0.173) | 0.43 | 0.895 (0.160) | 0.62 | 0.849 (0.227) | 0.61 |
| Casual labour | 0.835 (0.144) | 1.04 | 0.775 (0.147) | 1.34 | 0.849 (0.237) | 0.58 |
| Hindu | 0.854 (0.144) | 1.05 | 0.907 (0.149) | 0.59 | 0.936 (0226) | 0.27 |
| Muslim | 0.828 (0.146) | 1.06 | 0.769 (0.152) | 1.32 | 0.883 (0259) | 0.42 |
| Other religion | 3.082 (2.756) | 1.26 | 6.307** (5.115) | 2.27 | 0.0004 (0.003) | 0.02 |
| ST | 0.613 (0.201) | 1.49 | 0.303** (0.160) | 2.26 | 0.728 (0.383) | 0.60 |
| SC | 0.815 (0.119) | 1.39 | 0.839 (0.141) | 1.03 | 0.785 (0.184) | 1.03 |
| Constant | 0.041* (0.013) | 10.26 | 0.027* (0.009) | 10.22 | 0.003* (0.001) | 10.43 |
| Log likelihood | | | -4375.477 | | | |
| LR Chi-square | | | 1771.23 | | | |
| Prob.>Chi-square | | | 0.000 | | | |
| No. of observations | | | 5606 | | | |

**Note:** Standard deviations in parentheses. Coefficient estimates are relative risk ratios.
* Significant at 1 percent level ** Significant at 5 percent level *** Significant at 10 percent level.

In general, the estimated logistic regression results presented in Table 12.6 show that the cost of medical expenditure, wealth/income/landholding, household size and composition and region are the significant determinants of the household visits to the AYUSH hospitals. The occupation of the household, household head and even community of the household have no significant effect on the use of AYUSH hospitals. The log of medical expenditure, presence of an adult member in the family, and households residing in Karnataka and Kerala have a statistically significant positive effect, while presence of a child and young member in the family and households in rural areas have a significant negative effect on the visit to the AYUSH hospital once compared to no visits. For a 1 percent increase in the log of medical expenditure, the relative probability of visit to AYUSH hospital once is 14 percent higher compared to no visit. The presence of adult persons in the households increases the relative probability of visit to AYUSH hospitals by 33 percent. The relative probability of choosing to visit AYUSH hospital once rather than no visit is 3 times and 16 times higher for households in Karnataka and Kerala respectively compared to households in Andhra Pradesh. The relative probability of visiting AYUSH hospital once is 18 percent lower for rural households compared to urban households and presence of a child and young members in the family reduces the choice of visiting an AYUSH hospital by 16 percent and 19 percent respectively compared to the presence of elderly in the family.

In case of households visiting more than once the AYUSH hospitals, the log of medical expenditure, households in Karnataka, Kerala and Tamil Nadu and households belonging to non-major religions have a positive relative probability ratio, while the presence of a young member in the family, the household in rural sector and household belonging to schedule tribe have a negative probability of visiting AYUSH hospital twice or thrice compared to no visits. The relative probability of choosing to visit AYUSH hospital twice or thrice rather than no visits is 14 percent higher, for a 1 percent increase in medical expenditure, 53 percent higher for household in Tamil Nadu compared to households in Andhra Pradesh. The relative probability of choosing to visit AYUSH hospital twice or thrice rather than no visits is 5 times and 24 times higher for households in Karnataka and Kerala respectively compared to households in Andhra Pradesh. The relative probability of choosing to visit AYUSH hospital twice or thrice rather than no visits is 6 times higher for households belonging to non-major religions compared to Christian households.

The relative probability of choosing to visit AYUSH hospital twice or thrice rather than no visits is lower by 27 percent for rural households compared to urban households, 70 percent for schedule tribe households compared to households belonging to other social groups, and the presence of a young member in the family reduces the choice of visiting an AYUSH hospital by 20 percent compared to the presence of elderly member in the family.

The log of medical expenditure, household size, household from Karnataka, Kerala and Tamil Nadu, male headed family and presence of adult in the family have a positive effect while the presence of a young member in the family and land possessed have a negative effect on visiting AYUSH hospitals more than three visits compared to no visits. The relative probability of choosing to visit AYUSH hospital more than three visits rather than no visits is 23 percent higher for a 1 percent increase in medical expenditure,

7 percent higher for an increase in the household size. The relative probability of choosing to visit AYUSH hospital more than thrice rather than no visits is as high as 5 times, 13 times and 3 times for households in Karnataka, Kerala and Tamil Nadu respectively compared to households in Andhra Pradesh. The male headed households have 10 percent higher probability to visit AYUSH hospitals more than three times compared to a female headed households and the presence of an adult member in the family increases the probability of three times visit to AYUSH hospital by 74 percent compared to the presence of elderly member in the family.

## 12.5 Conclusion

The system of Indian medicine continues to attract patronage from Indian population, even though there has been a tremendous increase in the western healthcare style hospitals and the widespread demand for allopathic care. The indigenous medicine and its practices have been largely described as preventive non-allopathic healthcare and applied for chronic and non-curable illness. This non-allopathic medicinal system is common for acute illness episodes and also for maternity healthcare and catastrophic health expenditure. The increasing medical expenditure through corporate western allopathic health system drives the households to choose the local systems of healthcare which is less expensive and easily available in their locality. Recognising the significance of the traditional healing system, the Government of India has established a dedicated ministry, the Ministry of AYUSH, to promote the ancient healthcare systems of ayurveda, Yoga and Naturopathy, unani, siddha and homoeopathy. Many state governments have also established AYUSH hospitals. The AYUSH system of healthcare is more prevalent in southern India, particularly among religious, regional and traditional households. The AYUSH medicines are largely produced from herbs and minerals by indigenous methods and have fewer side effects. To a significant extent there is a global market for AYUSH products and the Indian exports of AYUSH medicines are steadily expanding.

Given the large scale prevalence and practice of AYUSH healthcare in India, this paper makes an attempt to study the trends and patterns of AYUSH hospitals and the determinants to household demand for AYUSH healthcare. In order to assess the use of the AYUSH healthcare system, this paper analyse the number of visits to the AYUSH hospitals by household members. This paper uses the 68th round (2011-2012) of NSSO data on the use of AYUSH hospitals by households for the four southern states of India - Andhra Pradesh, Karnataka, Kerala and Tamil Nadu. Empirically, the multinomial logit method is used to estimate the number of visits to the AYUSH hospitals. The trends and patterns in AYUSH hospital show that with the advent of the AYUSH hospitals, people gradually increase the usage of AYUSH system of healthcare. Within the AYUSH healthcare system, there are statewise differentials in the use of ayurveda, unani, siddha and homoeopathy systems of medicines. The yoga system is widely practiced.

The empirical analysis shows that the choice of visits to AYUSH hospitals is influenced by the cost of medical expenditure, wealth/income/landholding, household size and composition and region. From the empirical results it is also observed that urban households use more of AYUSH medicines and use AYUSH hospitals more compared to rural households, may be due to the easy access to these hospitals in cities. The relative probability of choosing to visit AYUSH hospitals by schedule tribe households is low. The presence of elderly member in the family has a positive effect on visiting AYUSH hospital compared to the presence of young members in the family, implying that older people prefer AYUSH treatment for their healthcare. The occupation, headship and community of the household have no significant effect on the use of AYUSH hospitals.

# 13

# Sex Discrimination in the Labour Market: Heckit Estimation and Decomposition of Gender Wage Gap


## Abstract

*In the Indian labour market, there exists sizable observed wage gap between males and females for identical job market characteristics. The gender wage gap is one of the many indicators of gender inequality and a manifestation of discrimination against women. The observed wage gap may be due to factors like social and cultural factors, differential preferences and tastes, low attachment of women in the labour market, occupational segregation, and importantly, discrimination. This paper empirically estimates the extent of discrimination in the Indian labour market using the 2011-12 Indian Human Development Survey. The labour force participation decision is estimated by Probit method and separate wage equations are estimated for men and women by OLS. Applying the Oaxaca-Blinder decomposition method, the observed gender wage gap is decomposed into a part that is justified or explained gap by the differentials in the labour market characteristics of men and women, and the other part that is unjustified or unexplained differentials that is mainly attributable to discrimination, among other plausible reasons. The decomposition result shows that there exists 26 percent wage gap against females, attributable sex discrimination in the Indian labour market. There has been very little change in sex discrimination in the labour market since 1981 when 28 percent wage discrimination against women estimated earlier by the present author. Despite the globalisation, labour mobility, women empowerment, and legislative protections, even in the 21st century sex discrimination and unequal pay for equal work persist in the Indian labour market.*



**Key words:** *Gender wage gap, labour force participation decision, probit estimation, wage estimation, Oaxaca-Blinder decomposition, discrimination*

## 13.1 Introduction

The pay or wage or earnings gap by gender is normally defined as the relative difference in the average gross earnings of women and men in the economy. It is one of the many indicators of gender inequality in a country when examining labour market participation in terms of gender. According to the International Labour Organisation, progress in reducing the gender pay gap is very slow in every developed and developing country. In the developed countries, especially in the United States, sizable pay gap is very persistent (ILO, 2018). In the developing countries, specifically in the Latin American countries, the size of the gap as well as the trends towards its growth or reduction vary.

In India, as per 2011 Census of India, women population constitutes almost half of the country's population, accounting for 496 million in absolute number. More than 90 percent of these women in rural areas and about 69 percent women in urban areas have no technical skills. According to the NSSO, in the year 2011-12, the share of regular and salaried wage earners in total employment in India was 12.7 percent for women workers compared to 19.8 percent for their male counterparts. The 2011 Census shows that the work participation rate of females is 25.5 percent and that of males is 53.2 percent. Rural women show a higher work participation rate of 30 percent compared with 53 percent of urban male work participation rate. As per the NSSO, between 2004-05 and 2009-10, increase in overall employment has been 1.1 million, but between 2009-10 and 2011-12 employment grew from 459 million to 472.9 million only. Between 1999-2000 and 2011-2012, male employment grew by 1.9 percent per annum while female employment increased by only 0.3 percent per annum (Verick, 2018). The labour force participation rate for women aged 15 and above in India decline from 37.3 percent in 2004-05 to 27.2 percent in 2011-12. From 2004-05 to 2009-10, the number of women workers dropped by 21.3 million, of which 19.5 million are in rural areas, while the number of men worker has increased by 22.4 million. Urban areas accounted for 57.2 percent of the growth in employment. As per the latest NSSO 68th round 2011-12, in rural areas 55 percent of males and 25 percent of females, and in urban areas 56 percent of males and 16 percent of females participate in the Indian labour market.

Though women are increasingly participating in the labour force, with varying education and skill levels, they are mostly concentrated in private sector as informal and casual workers, and wage/salary earned by women are generally much lesser than their male counterparts. Even then, the annual growth in employment of women in the private sector is only 0.52 percent, just 0.04 percent in the government sector, and 0.27 percent in the entire formal employment (Mohanty et al., 2014). According to Self Employed Women's Association, the wages of women workers were below the minimum wages in some cases and at the same time the average monthly income of women workers was Rs. 1815 compared to Rs. 3842 for male workers (SEWA, 2000). The NSSO 68th round reveals that for 2011-12, the actual wage received by women is Rs. 308 per day compared to Rs. 407 per day by men. The daily wage/salary earnings of a regular rural wage/salaried worker in the active age 15-59 years has been Rs. 298.96, and that of for an urban worker has been Rs. 449.65. By gender, rural males earn Rs. 322.28, rural females Rs. 201.56, urban males Rs. 469.87, and urban females earn Rs. 366.15 per day, showing significant rural-urban as well as male-female wage gap in 2011-12 in the Indian labour market. Thus, the 2011-12 NSSO data reveal that women in India earn approximately 75 percent less than the wages of men, 62 percent less in rural areas and 78 percent less in urban areas.

The Tables 13.1 to 13.4 present the work participation rate in India, relative wage gap between males and females in both rural and urban areas and the relative wage gap with respect to the educational levels in India respectively. From Table 13.1, it is observed that, while the work participation rate of males has increased by 1.6 percent, the female work participation rate has slightly declined by 0.1 percent between 2001 and 2011. However, the gender gap in work participation rate between males and females has increased by 0.9 percent only, suggesting almost stagnant employment.

**Table 13.1: Work Participation Rate and Gender Gap in India, 2001 and 2011**

| *Gender* | *2001(percent)* | *Gender gap* | *2011(percent)* | *Gender gap* | *Percentage change* |
|---|---|---|---|---|---|
| Persons | 39.1 | | 39.8 | | +0.7 |
| Male | 51.7 | 26.1 | 53.3 | 27.8 | +1.6 |
| Female | 25.6 | | 25.5 | | -0.1 |

*Source:* Census of India, 2011.

**Table 13.2: Work Participation Rate in India, 2011-2012**

| *State* | *Rural* | | | *Urban* | | |
|---|---|---|---|---|---|---|
| | *Male* | *Female* | *Total* | *Male* | *Female* | *Total* |
| Andhra Pradesh | 61.2 | 44.8 | 52.8 | 57.6 | 18.0 | 38.0 |
| Assam | 56.4 | 12.9 | 35.9 | 57.3 | 9.7 | 34.8 |
| Bihar | 48.7 | 5.8 | 28.4 | 44.1 | 5.4 | 26.7 |
| Gujarat | 60.2 | 27.9 | 44.8 | 60.7 | 13.5 | 38.7 |
| Haryana | 53.2 | 16.4 | 36.5 | 53.5 | 10.2 | 33.1 |
| Himachal Pradesh | 54.7 | 52.9 | 53.8 | 61.2 | 23.6 | 43.3 |
| Jammu & Kashmir | 55.9 | 26.3 | 41.5 | 56.3 | 14.5 | 36.2 |
| Karnataka | 62.0 | 28.9 | 45.4 | 59.4 | 17.1 | 38.8 |
| Kerala | 58.3 | 25.8 | 41.0 | 56.7 | 22.2 | 38.6 |
| Madhya Pradesh | 56.4 | 23.9 | 40.7 | 53.3 | 11.9 | 33.4 |
| Maharashtra | 58.2 | 38.9 | 49.0 | 56.0 | 17.2 | 37.4 |
| Orissa | 60.6 | 25.1 | 42.7 | 60.3 | 15.8 | 39.5 |
| Punjab | 57.9 | 23.7 | 41.4 | 58.6 | 14.1 | 37.9 |
| Rajasthan | 50.0 | 34.9 | 42.7 | 50.7 | 14.4 | 33.6 |

*(Contd...)*

| | | | | | | |
|---|---|---|---|---|---|---|
| Tamil Nadu | 60.7 | 38.6 | 49.5 | 59.9 | 21.1 | 40.3 |
| Uttar Pradesh | 49.6 | 17.8 | 34.1 | 53.3 | 10.6 | 33.1 |
| West Bengal | 60.2 | 19.4 | 40.0 | 63.0 | 18.6 | 41.9 |
| All India | 55.3 | 25.3 | 40.6 | 56.3 | 15.5 | 36.7 |

*Source:* NSSO 68th Round (July 2011–June 2012).

From Table 13.2 it is observed that female work participation rate is lower than the male work participation rate in all states in India, and the scenario is much worse in urban areas. The women work participation rate in Bihar is much pathetic, whereas Himachal Pradesh seems to be much women friendly labour market.

**Table 13.3: Average Wage/Salary Earnings per day by Regular Employees, 2011-12 (in Rs.)**

| *State* | *Rural* | | | | *Urban* | | | |
|---|---|---|---|---|---|---|---|---|
| | *Male* | *Female* | *Relative wage gap, 2011-12* | *Relative wage gap, 2009-10* | *Male* | *Female* | *Relative wage gap, 2011-12* | *Relative wage gap, 2009-10* |
| Andhra Pradesh | 251.28 | 225.01 | 10.45 | 52.6 | 427.82 | 244.30 | 42.90 | 27.25 |
| Assam | 343.97 | 179.71 | 47.75 | 61.7 | 615.23 | 561.63 | 8.71 | 22.43 |
| Bihar | 450.49 | 188.42 | 58.17 | 7.60 | 417.10 | 369.02 | 11.52 | 4.84 |
| Gujarat | 268.69 | 173.13 | 35.57 | 5.05 | 326.34 | 271.86 | 16.69 | 27.79 |
| Haryana | 396.44 | 357.38 | 3.04 | 32.46 | 810.93 | 635.59 | 21.62 | 44.22 |
| Himachal Pradesh | 434.72 | 250.69 | 42.33 | 37.58 | 426.03 | 306.55 | 28.04 | 10.62 |
| Jammu & Kashmir | 453.56 | 222.37 | 50.97 | 2.2 | 497.61 | 484.71 | 2.59 | 15.22 |
| Karnataka | 237.53 | 151.85 | 36.07 | 78.15 | 518.58 | 391.97 | 24.41 | 24.32 |
| Kerala | 386.44 | 240.45 | 33.12 | 26.6 | 519.84 | 412.47 | 20.65 | 29.30 |
| Madhya Pradesh | 270.94 | 108.56 | 59.93 | 10.32 | 459.66 | 320.58 | 30.26 | 28.86 |
| Maharashtra | 369.14 | 306.76 | 16.90 | 43.99 | 516.55 | 370.30 | 28.31 | 29.16 |
| Orissa | 245.30 | 223.23 | 9.00 | 48.36 | 457.66 | 286.42 | 37.42 | 10.83 |
| Punjab | 302.79 | 157.61 | 47.95 | 48.12 | 352.58 | 399.38 | -13.27 | 33.55 |
| Rajasthan | 328.61 | 177.86 | 45.88 | 56.8 | 417.14 | 412.89 | 1.02 | 8.57 |
| Tamil Nadu | 292.55 | 199.44 | 31.81 | 37.05 | 420.76 | 297.63 | 29.26 | 15.11 |
| Uttar Pradesh | 296.51 | 171.27 | 42.24 | 37.0 | 496.53 | 378.00 | 23.87 | 13.26 |
| West Bengal | 297.35 | 119.76 | 59.72 | 46.05 | 454.61 | 323.56 | 28.83 | 29.73 |
| All India | 322.28 | 201.55 | 37.46 | 37.05 | 469.87 | 366.15 | 22.07 | 18.13 |

*Source:* NSSO 66th Round (July 2009–June 2010) and 68th Round (July 2011–June 2012).

The Table 13.3 presents the average wage received by regular wage and salaried employees in India during 2011-12. The wages for males and females differ substantially in rural and urban areas. Overall, females earn lower wages compared to men in both rural and urban areas. The relative wage gap has been calculated to show the comparable difference in the wages between sexes.

This shows that there is prominent wage gap between male and female workers. In every state there is a significant level of wage difference between male and female workers. Madhya Pradesh has the highest level of wage gap between males and females in rural areas, whereas Andhra Pradesh has the highest difference in gender wages in urban areas. Also, the wage gap is relatively low in urban areas compared to the rural areas. Surprisingly, the relative wage gap is negative 13.27 percent in urban Punjab in 2011-12, dropping from a positive 33.55 percent gender earnings gap in 2009-10, while there is 48 percent relative wage gap in rural Punjab. At the all India level, during 2011-12, women in rural India have been earning more than one-third less and in urban India one-fifth less per day relative to the respective per day earnings of men. While the relative wage gap is almost the same between men and women in rural areas, the urban are gender wage gap has increased between 2009-10 and 2011-12.

The Table 13.4 shows the relative wage gap with respect to the educational levels. The gender gap remains very high among workers without formal education and with lower educational standards, who are mostly working in informal activities. While the gender gap declines with educational attainments in rural areas, except at higher education level, there has been a rise in the wage gap for all educational levels in urban areas, except the case of secondary and higher secondary level. Moreover, relative wage gap has been widened between 2009-10 and 2011-12 in almost all cases, indicating rising income inequality and differential returns to higher education.

**Table 13.4: Relative Gender Wage Gap by Education Level in India (percent)**

| *Education level* | *Rural* | | | | | *Urban* | | | | |
|---|---|---|---|---|---|---|---|---|---|---|
| | *1993-94* | *1999-2000* | *2004-05* | *2009-10* | *2011-12* | *1993-94* | *1999-2000* | *2004-05* | *2009-10* | *2011-12* |
| Not literate | 42.5 | 43.4 | 50.7 | 51.8 | 48.78 | 73.0 | 40.9 | 50.7 | 40.9 | 40.55 |
| Literate upto middle | 47.9 | 45.2 | 51.6 | 49.8 | 48.50 | 76.1 | 38.7 | 41.9 | 37.8 | 44.02 |
| Secondary and higher secondary | 20.3 | 14.9 | 36.6 | 43.3 | 43.66 | 13.3 | 13.3 | 17.6 | 19.0 | 14.38 |
| Graduate and above | 26.1 | 27.6 | 36.0 | 29.0 | 31.33 | 29.5 | 29.5 | 26.6 | 21.3 | 24.03 |

*Source:* NSSO: Employment and Unemployment Situation in India (various rounds).

Gender wage gap mainly occurs when both male and female are in the same industry or in the same occupation, where women are being paid less compared to men. The observed wage gap is generally explained on the basis of occupational differences, educational qualification, industry, religion and community, marital status, etc. Men and women, on an average, work in different industries and occupations and this differential occupation pattern may explain some portion of the wage gap. The hours of work also differ between males and females which may also account for some portion of the gender wage gap in earnings. Generally, women work less hours relative to men. Gender wage gap can go beyond education level, occupation, experience etc. According to Blau and Khan (2017), the wage gap can also be due to some of the factors that can not be observed but are evident.

One such unobserved factor that prompts observed gender wage gap is discrimination. Discrimination takes place when one group (males) are paid higher wage rate than females for the same level of work in the same occupation, with similar education and skills. According to the neoclassical approach to the labour market discrimination, wage differences arise among equally productive workers not based on the objective criteria of productive characteristics, but on the basis of unproductive characteristics like colour, sex of community. Such non-market group specific characteristics are more valued in the market and the values attached to these unproductive characteristics are determined by the preferences of the employer. For Becker (1971), who has pioneered the work on (racial) discrimination, discrimination is practiced because employers have a 'preference' or 'taste' for discrimination. The existence of this 'taste for discrimination' explains the process whereby people who in some sense are equal do not receive the same treatment in economic transactions.

The issue of gender discrimination in labour market in the form of gender wage gap and low labour force participation for women is a well-researched area in labour economics. Gender wage discrimination takes place among the male and female groups based on various factors. Women workers get discriminated more in terms of wage if they also belong to socially and economically backward castes and religious minority. Lakshmanasamy and Madheswaran (1995) observed that there exists caste discrimination even in the in Indian scientific labour market to the extent of 74 percent of earnings disadvantage for the SC personnel compared to the non-SC personnel. Using the 1981 Degree Holders and Technical Personnel survey and the Blinder-Oaxaca decomposition method, Lakshmanasamy and Madheswaran (1996) show that there exists gender discrimination in the Indian labour market to the extent of 28 percent. Subsequent studies also demonstrated the continued existence of gender differences in wages and the persistence of sex discrimination in the labour market of India. Thus, gender wage gap continues to persist in the Indian labour market, despite improvements in women empowerment, labour market regulations and globalisation facilitating much mobility, and the wage gap is partly due to some observable factors and some discriminatory factors. Therefore, it is important and also interesting to see how far discrimination against females operating through gender wage gap has changed/declined since 1981 in the Indian labour market.

Hence, the main objective of this paper is to examine the extent of the gender wage discrimination in the India labour market. The paper analyses the gender wage gap, using the India Human Development Survey (IHDS)

2011-2012 data, applying the Heckman two-step estimation (Heckit) procedure of wage estimation, and the Oaxaca-Blinder decomposition method to quantitatively measure the extent of wage discrimination. In the empirical estimation of male and female wage equations, two econometric techniques are followed: the first step is the ML probit estimation of selection (labour force participation) equation, and the second step is the OLS estimation of the wage equation using the participants only, including the moral hazard (the inverse mills ratio) estimated from the first step as additional regressor. Then, the wage gap between the sexes is decomposed as one part due to the observed labour market characteristic differences and the other part due to unexplained differences between the sexes, normally attributed to discrimination against females.

## 13.2 A Brief Review of Recent Studies

There are only a handful of econometric studies that analyse the gender wage gap in India using nationwide data. The empirical analysis on the extent of discrimination, especially wage gap between the sexes, relies heavily on the Oaxaca-Blinder decomposition method. Navarro (2015) analyse the gender wage gap in Dominican Republic using the 2013 Labour Force National Survey. The key determinants of wages are age, education, type of occupation, marital status and number of children. The empirical results show that there exists gender wage gap in the Dominican Republic and there is discrimination against women. Higher education narrows the degree of the gender wage gap; the hourly wage for college educated women is 8 percent less than hourly wage for college educated men, compared with 24-32 percent less in other levels of education.

Sengupta and Das (2014) analyse gender wage discrimination across social and religious group in India using the 50th and 66th rounds of the NSSO data. Heckman two-step estimation model is used to estimate the gender wage gap. It was observed that the probability of women's participation rate in wage employment was lower as compared to the men's participation. However, the difference has been reduced over time. Hindu women workers were in better position than Muslim women workers, partly due to religious customs and partly due to religious discrimination. The study also shows that female workers were subject to stark discrimination in terms of participation in regular/salaried job market as well as wages. Further, discrimination was more severe for women both from minority religious and tribal groups.

Khanna (2012) examines the gender wage gap using wage data for regular wage workers from the NSSO employment-unemployment data for 2009-2010 and the Oaxaca-Blinder decomposition and the quantile regression methods. The focal point of the analysis was to look at log wage gaps at different points of the distribution, not just at the mean. The main finding is that of a sticky floor effect, that is, the phenomenon of declining gender log wage gaps across the quantiles. The Oaxaca-Blinder decomposition shows the contribution of discrimination to the gender log wage gap at least over 80 percent. The quantile regression technique shows that the factors that contribute to the gender wage gap, however, are not the same at the bottom and the top of the distribution. Further, being married actually has a wage reducing effect for high wage earning women. The decreasing coefficients still mean that the wage dispersion among women falls as the proportion of married women increases, as low wage earners see an increase in while the high wage earners see a reduction in wages.

Sarkhel (2012) estimates the wage gap in the Indian labour market and gender bias, using the 2004-05 IHDS data. The study explains the payment gap by integrating the labour market performance with that of family decision-making practice. The Mincer wage functions estimated incorporate patriarchy as one of the explanatory variables. The Oaxaca-Blinder method is used for decomposing inequality in male-female hourly wage earnings into the contributing factors like observed and unobserved. The results show that women from patriarchal families are earning less than men due to the severe participation constraint.

Deshpande et al. (2018) decompose gender wage gaps not only at the mean, but also along the entire wage distribution applying the quantile regression method, using the 55th (1999-2000) and 66th (2009-10) rounds of NSSO data. The estimated gender wage gap is 55 percent in 1999-2000 and 49 percent in 2009-10. It is shown that though the proportion of educated women among women is higher than that among men, the gender wage gap is almost 38 percent. Further, they observed that between the two periods, the gender wage gap at the median has declined from 76 percent to 53 percent.

In short, most studies indicate that there exists significant gender wage gap between male and female groups in the labour market. This is so despite marked improvements in both education and labour force participation of women relative to men. Given that gender wage gap is common in the labour market, the factors that have been used to analyse the gender wage gap are mainly age, education, community, religion, marital status and occupation. To analyse the gender wage gap and the contribution of discrimination to the male-female wage gap, the most commonly used method is the Oaxaca-Blinder decomposition technique that identifies the discriminatory part of the gender wage gap.

## 13.3 Data and Methodology

The data from the Indian Human Development Survey 2011-12 (IHDS-II) is used to analyse the gender wage gap and the decomposition of the male-female earnings differentials to measure the extent of discrimination in the Indian labour market. The IHDS survey, by the NCAER and the University of Maryland, is a nationally representative survey consisting of 41554 households spread across 1503 villages and 971 urban neighbourhoods. The sample is spread across 33 States and UTs of India, except Andaman and Nicobar Islands and Lakshadweep. The sample size of the data is 204568, out of which 102062 are males and 102506 are females. A detailed discussion on the methodology and survey can in the IHDS technical report (Desai et al. 2010). The data a wealth of information on individual age, income source, employment, wages, occupation, education level, educational expenditure, earnings, number of household members, residence, house ownership, etc. The data contains two categories of income source, the salary employed and self-employed, and wages are reported for the salaried employees. There are 131,365 wage employed individuals and 73,150 self-employed individuals in the data. In the empirical analysis, the income source, which is a dichotomous variable, is taken as the dependent variable for the selection equation that is estimated by the probit regression, and the log of wage is taken as the dependent variable in the wage equations of males and females.

Following Mincer (1974), the wage equation has been estimated separately for men and women. A statistical issue that arises during the estimation of the wage equations is that in the data there are households that do not have wage income. Some households within the sample and some members within a household receive no wage as they select themselves not to work and hence report no wage income. When empirical estimation is carried out ignoring the households with no wage income then the samples become non-random or incidentally truncated and the problem of sample selection bias arise. In order to overcome this selectivity bias in the wage estimation, Heckman (1976, 1979) proposed a two step estimation (Heckit) procedure. First step is to estimate the selection equation, the labour market participation decision model, by the maximum likelihood estimation of a probit equation. Then, in the second step, the wage equations are estimated by the ordinary least squares method incorporation the inverse mills ratio obtained from the first step estimation as an explanatory variable. This way the self-selection bias can be taken care-off. Then, the gender wage gap between the two groups can be decomposed by the Oaxaca-Blinder decomposition method as explained and unexplained parts, and the unexplained part is treated as discrimination against women.

## Heckman Two Step Estimation Method

The wage equation and selection equation included in the model are given by,

$$\text{Wage equation: } \ln wi = x_i\beta + \varepsilon_i \tag{13.1}$$

$$\text{Ln(wage)} = \beta_0 + \beta_1 \text{ Age} + \beta_2 \text{ Age Square} + \beta_3 \text{ Education} + \beta_4 \text{ Religion} + \beta_5 \text{ Community} + \beta_6 \text{ Own house} + \beta_7 \text{ Married} + \beta_8 \text{ Residence} + u_i \tag{13.2}$$

$$\text{Selection equation: } y_i^* = \gamma z_i + u_i \tag{13.3}$$

where $y_i = 1 \text{ if } y_i^* > 0$

$y_i = 0$ otherwise

The selection equation is a latent model, where the *z* vector is not observed, and the latent dependent variable represents the individual evaluation of work choice.

$$\text{Employed} = \beta_0 + \beta_1 \text{ No. Persons} + \beta_2 \text{ Education} + \beta_3 \text{ Religion} + \beta_4 \text{Community} + \beta_5 \text{ Own house} + \beta_6 \text{ Married} + \beta_7 \text{ Residence} + \varepsilon_i \quad (13.4)$$

where Employment status = 1, if salary employed

= 0 if self-employed

In the second step of the model, the estimated inverse mills ratio ($\lambda$) from the selection equation is included in the estimation of the wage equation as an additional regressor to correct for the selectivity bias. The significance level of the estimated inverse mills ratio implies whether there is sample selection bias or not. The inverse mills ratio is the ratio of probability density function to the cumulative density function of a distribution. If *y* is a random variable distributed normally with mean $\mu$ and variance $\sigma^2$, then it is possible to show that,

$$E(y \mid x > \alpha) = \mu + \sigma[\{\phi((\alpha - \mu)/\sigma)\}/\{1 - \Phi((\alpha - \mu)/\sigma)\}] \quad (13.5)$$

where, $\alpha$ is constant, $\phi$ denotes standard normal density function, and $\Phi$ denotes the standard normal cumulative distribution function. The selectivity bias corrected estimating wage equation is then given by,

$$\text{Wage equation: } \ln wi = x_i\beta + \sigma\lambda + \varepsilon_i \quad (13.6)$$

$$\text{where} \quad \lambda = \frac{-\phi(\hat{\beta}'x)}{\Phi(\hat{\beta}'x)} \text{ if } y = 1 \text{ and } \lambda = \frac{\phi(\hat{\beta}'x)}{\{1 - F\Phi(\hat{\beta}'x)\}} \text{ if } y = 0 \quad (13.7)$$

## Oaxaca-Blinder Decomposition Method

The Oaxaca-Blinder decomposition method is used to analyse the wage gap between male and female groups. To estimate the gender wage gap between the two groups, the wage functions of men and women are estimated separately. The estimating wage functions are specified as,

$$\ln w_i^m = x_i^m \beta^m + \varepsilon_i^m \quad (13.8)$$

$$\text{and } \ln w_i^f = w_i^f \beta^f + \varepsilon_i^f \quad (13.9)$$

where the subscript *m* denotes male and f denotes male. The average log wage gap is denoted as,

$$\overline{\ln w_m} - \overline{\ln w_f} = \overline{x_m}\beta_m - \overline{x_f}\beta_f \quad (13.10)$$

The Oaxaca-Blinder decomposition of the wage gap is,

$$\overline{\ln w_m} - \overline{\ln w_f} = (\overline{x_m} - \overline{x_f})\ \beta_m + (\beta_m - \beta_f)\overline{x_f} \tag{13.11}$$

The wage gap is decomposed by imposing the returns (ß) for characteristics of one group to the other group's characteristics. That is, $\overline{x_m}\beta_m - \overline{x_f}\beta_f$ explains the observed wage difference for the differential characteristics of the male and female groups. The unexplained wage difference, $\overline{x_m}\beta_m - \overline{x_f}\beta_m$ obtained by imposing the male returns on the female characteristics is usually attributed to discrimination. This difference shows the unjustified part of the observed wage gap due to some observed factors, primarily discrimination, as well as some personal preferences or similar factors.

## Probit Model Estimation

The probit model is a popular specification for an ordinal or a binary response model. The probit model is a type of regression where the dependent variable is a qualitative and dichotomous variable which can only take two values either the presence or the absence of an attribute, for example working or not working. The purpose of the model is to estimate the probability that an observation with particular characteristics will fall into a specific alternative i.e. one of the categories. Moreover, if the estimated probability greater than ½ is treated as classifying an observation into a predicted category, the probit model is a type of binary classification model. The probit model, which employs a probit link function, is most often estimated using the standard maximum likelihood procedure. The behavior of the dichotomous dependent variable needs a suitable cumulative distribution function, and the probit regression emerges from a normal cumulative distribution function.

The normal cumulative distribution function (CDF) is the function where a variable *y* follows the normal distribution with mean μ and variance $\sigma_2$. Then the probability density function (PDF) for *y* is given by,

$$\phi(y) = \frac{1}{\sqrt{2\sigma^2\pi}} e^{-(y-\mu)^2/2\sigma^2} \tag{13.12}$$

and its cumulative distribution function is,

$$\Phi(y) = \int_{-\alpha}^{Y_0} \frac{1}{\sqrt{2\sigma^2\pi}} e^{-(y-\mu)^2/2\sigma^2} \tag{13.13}$$

where $y_0$ is some specified value of *y*. Consider the following regression model,

$$y_i = \beta_1 + \beta_2 x_i + u_i \tag{13.14}$$

where x is a vector explanatory variables and *y=1* if the individual works in salaried employment and 0 if the individual does not work for salaried employment. Assume that the decision of the ith person to go for salaried employment or not depends upon the unobservable utility index $I_i$ (the latent variable), that is determined by a set of explanatory variables $x_i$ in such a way that the larger the value of the index $I_i$, the greater the probability of going for salaried employment. The index *Ii* is expressed as,

$$I_i^* = \beta_1 + \beta_2 x_i \tag{13.15}$$

Let $y$=1 if salary employed and $y$=0 if not wage employed. It is reasonable to assume that there is critical or threshold level of the index, $I_i$*, such that if $I_i$ exceeds $I_i$*, the person is wage employed, otherwise not wage employed. The threshold $I_i$*, like $I_i$, is not observable, but if we assume that it is normally distributed with the same mean and variance, it is possible to not only estimate the parameters of the index given in the equation $I_i$=β1+ $\beta_2 x_i$ but also to get some information about the unobservable index itself.

Given the assumption of normality, the probability that $I_i$* is less than or equal to $I_i$ can be computed from the standardised normal CDF as,

$$P_i = P(y=1|x) = P(I_i^* \leq I_i) = P(z_i \leq \beta_1 + \beta_2 x_i) = \Phi(\beta_1 + \beta_2 x_i) \tag{13.16}$$

where P($y=1|x$) means the probability that an event occurs given the values of $x$ and $z_i$ is the standard normal variable, i.e. Z. N $(0,\sigma^2)$ Φ is the standard normal CDF which can be written explicitly in the present context as,

$$\Phi(I_i) = \frac{1}{2\pi}\int_{-\alpha}^{I_i} e^{-z^2/2} dz \tag{13.17}$$

$$\Phi(I_i) = \frac{1}{2\pi}\int_{-\alpha}^{\beta_1+\beta_2 X_i} e^{-z^2/2} dz \tag{13.18}$$

where P represents the probability that an event will occur, is measured by the area of standard normal curve from –α to $I_i$. To obtain information on $I_i$, the utility index on $\beta_1$ and $\beta_2$, taking the inverse of the above equation to obtain,

$$I_i = \Phi^{-1}(I_i) = \Phi^{-1}(P_i) = (\beta_1 + \beta_2 x_i) \tag{13.19}$$

where $\Phi^{-1}$ is the inverse of the normal CDF. The estimating probit model would be,

$$y_i = 1 \quad \text{if } I_i^* = x_i\beta + \varepsilon_i > 0 \tag{13.20}$$

$$= 0 \text{ otherwise}$$

## 13.4 Empirical Analysis

The focus of the paper is to estimate the extent of gender wage gap and discrimination between males and females in India. Table 13.5 presents the earnings of the male and female workers in each sector (self-employed and wage-employed) and there is a difference of almost 22413.3 and 40415.4 for self-employed and wage-employed respectively.

**Table 13.5: Gender Wage Gap in India (Rs./annum)**

| *Employment* | *Male earnings* | *Female earnings* | *Earnings gap* |
|---|---|---|---|
| Wage-employed | 76085.9 | 35670.5 | 40415.4 |
| Self-employed | 39687.5 | 17274.2 | 22413.3 |

The Table 13.6 presents the mean wage earnings between males and females for different characteristics. On average earnings, by every characteristic, males have higher earnings compared to females. Therefore, it is evident that there is wage gap between males and females in every respect; the wage gap is almost 20-30 percent between male and female groups. This shows that gender wage gap is prominent in every aspect in the labour market.

**Table 13.6: Average Earnings of Males and Females by Characteristics (Rs./annum)**

| *Characteristics* | *Description* | *Wage earnings* | | *Ln (wage earnings)* | |
|---|---|---|---|---|---|
| | | *Male* | *Female* | *Male* | *Female* |
| Education | Illiterate and primary | 41663.5 | 15718.4 | 9.09 | 9.13 |
| | Secondary and above | 113006.7 | 90918.3 | 11.03 | 11.0 |
| Religion | Hindu | 62838.3 | 25694.3 | 10.40 | 9.31 |
| | Non-Hindu | 66933.1 | 39849.9 | 10.58 | 9.70 |
| Community | General | 91575.1 | 55660.3 | 10.80 | 9.91 |
| | OBC, SC or ST | 54355.5 | 22083.3 | 10.32 | 9.25 |
| Marital status | Married | 68973.7 | 25845.2 | 10.51 | 9.29 |
| | Unmarried | 46722.0 | 32261.0 | 10.21 | 9.54 |
| Residence | Owning house | 60606.0 | 25803.5 | 10.02 | 9.31 |
| | Not owning house | 97895.0 | 53264.1 | 10.99 | 10.02 |
| Region | Urban | 103440.6 | 65485.4 | 11.11 | 11.11 |
| | Rural | 42244.6 | 15950.0 | 10.07 | 9.07 |

The Table 13.7 presents the descriptive statistics of the variables that are used in the empirical analysis. The overall mean earnings is Rs. 52608 per year. The average wage gap between males and females based on their average earnings is 36003. The logarithmic difference in earnings between males and females is 1.08. This wage gap between male and female workers shows that there are chances of discrimination in the market by gender. About 64 percent is the proportion of individuals going for salary employed work to self-employed work. The overall mean value of the education levels indicates that 0.27 is proportion of males have more that primary education, compared to 0.19 proportion of females with secondary education. Similarly, 0.80 and 0.70 are the proportion of Hindu and backward households, and 0.92 is the proportion of households owning house, and 0.48 is the proportion married. Similarly, 0.33 is the proportion of urban households.

**Table 13.7: Descriptive Statistics of Variables in the Gender Wage Gap Analysis**

| *Variable* | *Description* | *Mean (standard deviation)* | | |
|---|---|---|---|---|
| | | *All* | *Males* | *Females* |
| Wage | Wage earnings (Rs./annum) | 52608.2 | 63605 | 27602 |
| Ln(Wage) | Ln (Wages) (Rs./annum) | 10.111<br>(1.313) | 10.44<br>(1.19) | 9.363<br>(1.252) |
| Employment | Wage-employed = 1<br>Self-employed = 0 | 0.642<br>(0.479) | 0.642<br>(0.479) | 0.641<br>(0.479) |
| Age | Age (yrs) | 29.82<br>(20.36) | 29.344<br>(20.33) | 30.29<br>(20.38) |
| Age square | Age squared (yrs) | 1303.9<br>(1525.2) | 1274.5<br>(1509.4) | 1333.3<br>(1540.2) |
| Education | Secondary and above = 1<br>Illiterate and primary = 0 | 0.2291<br>(0.420) | 0.2692<br>(0.4435) | 0.1893<br>(0.39) |
| Religion | Hindu = 1, others = 0 | 0.8010<br>(0.399) | 0.8008<br>(0.3993) | 0.8012<br>(0.3990) |
| Community | Community: OBC, SC or ST = 1, General = 0 | 0.7076<br>(0.454) | 0.7067<br>(0.4552) | 0.7086<br>(0.4543) |
| Own house | Owning house = 1, Not owning house = 0 | 0.9280<br>(0.2584) | 0.9280<br>(0.2584) | 0.9279<br>(0.2585) |
| Marriage | Married =1, Unmarried = 0 | 0.4816<br>(0.499) | 0.4692<br>(0.4990) | 0.4940<br>(0.4999) |
| Residence | Urban =1, Rural = 0 | 0.3394<br>(0.473) | 0.3417<br>(0.4743) | 0.3372<br>(0.4727) |
| N | Sample size | 204568 | 102062 | 102506 |

## Heckman Two Step Estimates

The Table 13.8 presents the probit estimates of the decision to work for wages, along with marginal effects. The estimated coefficients of probit estimation have no direct interpretation, but the marginal effects have direct interpretation as the effect of an independent variable on the dependent variable. The marginal effects show that the number of persons in a household has a negative impact on wage employment decision. Lower the family size, lower the chance for participation in wage employment (salaried work). One extra individual in the household reduces the probability of a male being in a salaried work by 0.62 percentage points and 0.46 percentage points for a female. Similarly, the probability of being in a salaried work by a male or a female with secondary and higher education increases by 0.08 for both. This shows one extra level of education increases male and female working for salary in the labour force by 0.28 percentage points. The probability of an individual who is Hindu going for salaried work is negative, and higher for males than for females. The marginal effect is almost equally negative by 0.63 and 0.65 percentage points for male and female respectively, whereas the probability increases for individuals from other religion to participate in the labour market. Also, the individuals who are from SC, ST and OBC communities have lower probability of salaried work, and the marginal effect of these communities on labour market participation is lower by 12 percent and 16 percent for males and females respectively. Similarly, the probability of wage work of individuals owning house is negative, and it reduces the probability of salaried work by 0.23 percentage points. The probability for an individual who is married to work for wages is also negative, and the marginal effect is lower for women than for men. The urban residence significantly increases the probability of labour force participation, and percentage increase for both males and females is almost 33 percentage points. Overall, from the probit estimates of Table 13.8, both males and females have almost equally probability of labour market participation and being wage earners or salaried employees.

**Table 13.8: Probit Estimates of Selection Equation with Marginal Effects**

| *Variable* | *Employment status (dependent variable)* | | | |
|---|---|---|---|---|
| | *Male* | | *Female* | |
| | *Coefficient* | *Marginal effect* | *Coefficient* | *Marginal effect* |
| No. persons in household | -0.174*<br>(11.46) | -0.0062 | 0.0128*<br>(8.59) | -0.0046 |
| Secondary and above education | 0.0800*<br>(7.80) | 0.0285 | 0.0794*<br>(6.76) | 0.0283 |
| Hindu | -0.1816*<br>(16.21) | -0.0635 | -0.1870*<br>(16.75) | -0.0656 |
| OBC, SC or ST community | -0.0399*<br>(3.46) | -0.0121 | -0.0451*<br>(4.63) | -0.0162 |
| Own house | -0.8367*<br>(6.04) | -0.2375 | -0.8196*<br>(6.09) | -0.2353 |
| Married | -0.0521*<br>(33.64) | 0.0187 | -0.0139*<br>(28.60) | -0.0047<br>(-28.60) |
| Urban | 1.0434*<br>(10.47) | 0.3340* | 1.0277*<br>(18.77) | 0.3301 |
| Constant | 1.1515*<br>(19.08) | - | 1.1129*<br>(18.58) | - |
| LR-chi$^2$ | 16440.46 | | 16024.35 | |
| Prob. > chi$^2$ | 0.0000 | | 0.0000 | |
| Pseudo R-square | 0.1241 | | 0.1202 | |
| Log likelihood | -58022.048 | | -58627.758 | |
| Observations | 101593 | | 102092 | |

**Note:** Absolute t-values in parentheses. * Significant at 1 percent level.

Given the more or less equal labour market participation, the next question to be answered is why there is such a noticeable gender wage gap. To understand this, the wage equations for males and females are estimated separately, which is the second step of the Heckman estimation. The Table 13.9 presents the

OLS estimates of wage equations of males and females with and without selectivity bias correction. The statistical significance of the inverse mills ratio ($\lambda$) shows the presence of sample selection bias in the OLS estimation. The inverse mills ratio is negatively signed suggesting that the error terms in the wage equations and the selection equation are negatively correlated and there is sample selection bias in the estimation. The estimated values have reduced down by 1 to 5 percentage points when selectivity correction term is included compared to the uncorrected wage estimates by the simple regression for both male and female. The wage earnings increase for both males and females with an increase in the age by 8 percent. The negative sign on the age square shows that wage earnings increases at a decreasing rate. Relative to illiterate or primary educated individuals, secondary or higher education increases wage earnings of males by about 6 percent and female earnings by 10 percent. This shows that the returns to education are more for females compared to that of males. An individual of Hindu religion has a negative wage earnings by 14 percent compared to non-Hindus. Similarly belonging to SC, ST or OBC communities has a negative impact on the wage earnings of both male and female workers, the marginal effect being by 0.17 and 0.15 for males and females. Thus, being forward or general community results in positive increase in the wage earnings of both male and female. A married male will have a positive increase in the wage earned by 0.05, whereas for females being married will negatively affect the wage earnings by 0.42 implying women working after marriage have lower labour force attachment. Owning a house has a negative effect on the wage earnings of males and positive effect on female work earnings. Also, being in an urban area positively increases the wage earnings for both male and female respectively by 0.76 and 0.50 as the opportunity for salaried work is higher in urban areas.

**Table 13.9: OLS Estimates of Wage Equations by Gender**
**Dependent variable: Log (wage)**

| *Variable* | *Male* | | *Female* | |
|---|---|---|---|---|
| | *Selectivity bias uncorrected* | *Selectivity bias corrected* | *Selectivity bias uncorrected* | *Selectivity bias corrected* |
| Age | 0.078* (30.31) | 0.077* (30.11) | 0.080* (22.0) | 0.076* (21.25) |
| Age square | -0.0008* (30.09) | -0.0008* (29.99) | -0.0008* (19.86) | -0.0008* (19.39) |
| Secondary and above education | 0.585* (47.84) | 0.572* (41.55) | 1.074* (42.79) | 1.010* (36.99) |
| Hindu | -0.154* (10.98) | -0.149* (10.04) | -0.184* (7.47) | -0.145* (5.68) |
| OBC, SC or ST community | -0.179* (13.84) | -0.178* (13.80) | -0.157* (6.64) | -0.155* (6.59) |

*(Contd...)*

| Own house | -0.137* (6.72) | -0.088* (2.84) | -0.223* (6.52) | 0.026 (0.48) |
|---|---|---|---|---|
| Married | 0.101* (6.15) | 0.055** (2.06) | -0.217* (10.48) | -0.425* (10.29) |
| Urban | 0.828* (69.12) | 0.761* (22.63) | 0.802* (37.31) | 0.501* (8.94) |
| Constant | 8.792* (174.15) | 8.915* (115.80) | 8.039* (102.1) | 8.576* (70.83) |
| Inverse mills ratio (λ) | - | -0.106* (2.13) | - | -0.472* (5.83) |
| Prob. > F | 0.00 | 0.00 | 0.00 | 0.00 |
| R-square | 0.24 | 0.27 | 0.25 | 0.29 |
| Number of observations | 36925 | | 16284 | |

**Note:** Absolute t-values in parentheses. * Significant at 1 percent level.

Thus, from the Heckman two step estimation it is observed that both males and females have equal probability of being wage or salaried workers, but the returns for wage determinants in the labour market are not equal between the sexes. The returns to males are somewhat higher than that of for females. Therefore, here we use Oaxaca-Blinder decomposition method to find the gender wage gap between male and female groups. Oaxaca-Blinder decomposition method analyses how much of the gender wage gap is due to the explained factors and due to the unexplained factors which is the discrimination part.

## Decomposition of Gender Wage Gap

The Blinder-Oaxaca decomposition method decomposes the gender gap in the mean earnings between the two groups into that part that is due to the group differences in the wage determining characteristics of males and females and another part that is due to the differential returns to the same wage determining characteristics. Thus, the total log wage gap of 1.072 between the sexes is decomposed into the explained and the unexplained part, together constituting the gender wage gap in the labour market.

The Table 13.10 explains the decomposition results. The positive results express how much the gender wage gap will be reduced if male and female have equal returns for those attributes, and the negative numbers indicate how much will the gender wage gap fall if females face the same wage functions like males. The unexplained part is in generally attributed to the gender wage discrimination. Almost 74 percent of the mean wage gap between males and females is justified by the differences in male and female wage determining characteristics, the 26 percent of the unexplained part captures gender discrimination and also the plausible unobserved gender differences in productivity and tastes in the labour market. Thus, it is evident that there is sizable gender wage gap and nearly one-quarter of this wage gap can be attributable to the discriminatory rewards against females in the Indian labour market.

**Table 13.10: Decomposition of Gender Wage Gap in India**

| Total log of wage gap: 1.072 | |
|---|---|
| Log of mean wage gap attributable to: | |
| Age | -.077 |
| Age-square | 0.047 |
| Education | 0.046 |
| Religion | 0.00006 |
| Community | 0.023 |
| Own house | -0.0001 |
| Marital status | 0.002 |
| Urban residence | 0.003 |
| Constant | 0.7524 |
| Explained (justified) part (Characteristics difference) | 0.7994 (74%) |
| Unexplained (unjustified) part (Discrimination) | 0.2632 (26%) |

## 13.5 Conclusion

The study analyses the extent of gender wage discrimination in the Indian labour market against females. Taking the log of wage earnings by sex, using the 2011-12 India Human Development Survey, the observed gender wage gap is decomposed into two parts by applying the Oaxaca-Blinder decomposition method. As labour market participation is not likely to be random due to self-selection in labour force participation, the wage equations have been estimated using the Heckman two step estimation method. First, the probability of labour market participation is estimated using the total sample by probit model obtaining the inverse of mills ratio. In the second step wage equations for males and females are estimated separately by OLS method including the inverse mills ratio as an explanatory variable to correct for selection bias.

The study reveals that the probability of women's participation in wage employment is lower than male participation. Women have higher level of education than men, but the wages and the probability of going to work are less compared to men. Women workers with higher level of education are found to have high wage rate than women with lower education level. Women of socially backward community have low wage earnings compared to men. Women workers who are Hindu have significantly lower wages than men. Women who are from SC, ST and OBC communities have also negative impact on their wage earnings. Similarly, married women also earn less but married male earn more, which can also be because the labour force participation of married women are generally low. Women workers in urban area have high probability of going for salaried employment and but are receiving significantly low wages than men. There is high level of wage gap among males and females. Therefore, there is sizable gender wage gap in the Indian labour market.

The Oaxaca-Blinder decomposition of the gender wage gap reveals that there is a significant 26 percent wage gap that is due to unexplained factors. This part is generally attributed to discrimination, besides social and personal factors, and differential tastes and preferences. The 74 percent of the wage gap which is explained by the variables is that part of gender gap that could justified on the basis of differentials in the wage determining characteristics of males and females. Thus, the observed gender wage gap is partly the result of the discrimination that takes place in the Indian labour market. Compared to the estimated 28 percent wage discrimination in 1996, discrimination against females in 2011-12 is estimated to be 26 percent, suggesting only a marginal decline in gender wage gap and labour market discrimination. Thus, the persistence of gender differences in labour force participation, wages, and gender wage gap reveal the continuing phenomenon of sex discrimination in India, even in the 21st century and in the age of globalisation and women empowerment.

# 14

# Economics of Religion: A Censored Regression Estimation of Religious Expenditure


## Abstract

*There are a very few or nobody who have no religious affiliation. In every religious household the expenditure on religion is a part of household expenditure. This paper analyses the socioeconomic determinants and their effects on religious expenditure in India, using the 68th round NSSO data, and applying the censored regression method. The estimated empirical results reveal that in almost every religious household, there is a positive relation between income and religious expenditure. Among the major religious groups in India, Christians spend more on religion relative to the Hindus and Muslims. The study also finds that the size of family and literacy have a negative relation with spending on religion, while the presence of elders in the household increases the religious expenditure. The picture of religious expenditure of households does not vary much even if controlled for religion, social group and education.*



**Key words:** *Religious expenditure, income, socioeconomic background, religion, censored regression*


## 14.1 Introduction

India, the largest democracy and the second most populated country is also a multi-ethnic, multi-cultural, multi-religious and multi-language society. According to the 2011 Census of India, about 80.55 percent of the Indian population is Hindu, followed by 13.4 percent of Muslims, 2.3 percent of Christians and a sizable Sikhs, Jains, Buddhists, and other small religious minorities like Parsis, Zoroastrians. Globally, Hindus constitute 15 percent of world population, compared to Christians 31.5 percent, Muslims 23.2 percent, Buddhists 7.1 percent, Jews 0.2 percent around the globe in 2010 (Iyer, 2016). There also exists enormous diversity within each religious group in India such as sects, castes and sub-castes with vast and distinctive social identities, cultures, customs, norms, values and practices. Many of the major world religions had their origins in India. Apart from the largest dominant, there are a number of mind blowing and interesting facts about major religions of India, such as India has almost as many Muslims as Pakistan, more Christians than the population of Australia, more Buddhists than Tibet, more Sikhs, Jains, and Parsis than any country in the world.

There are a very few or nobody who have no religious affiliation. Any major Indian database or population records by any organisation have religion recorded immediately after gender or age. Though this is the true condition, religion as a factor in either individual behaviour or in economic development has never been explored as other topics like gender, poverty or even marriage do. Almost all religious groups and religious individuals spend substantial amounts on religious festivals and rituals. There are wide differences in religious expenditures among different religious and social groups, ranging from the simple tribal practices to more elaborate and expensive pujas in wealthy households and religious congregations. Though many studies focus on religious beliefs and practices, the relationship between income and religious expenditure is an under-studied topic. Since Indian society is strictly bound to religion and religion pervades every aspect of individual's life, it is interesting to see how people spend on their religious practices.

Therefore, the primary aim of this paper is to identify the socioeconomic and demographic determinants of religious expenditure of different religious groups and to analyse their effects on the religious expenditures in India. The data used in this study is the 68th round NSSO data, which deals with consumer expenditure, including religious expenditure, in India. The nationwide NSSO data base is 101651 observations. The data on religious expenditure consists of extreme expenditure ranging from zero to millions. Some observations of higher religious expenditures are outliers. Therefore, applying OLS to the inconsistent distribution with outliers will produce biased estimates. Hence, the econometric method applied in this paper is the censored regression model.

## 14.2 A Brief Review of Recent Studies

There exists a sizable literature on the determinants of religiosity since Adam Smith. Adam Smith laid the foundation for the economic analysis of religion in a largely ignored chapter of Wealth of Nations. Smith argues that self-interest motivates clergy, and hence market forces constrain churches, just as they do secular firms and producers. Therefore, the benefits of competition, the burdens of monopoly, and the hazards of government regulation are as real for religion as for any other sector of the economy. Almost two decades later, since the 1970s, economists and sociologists have returned to Smith's insights. Viewing religious behaviour as an instance of rational choice, rather than an exception to it, they have analysed the religious behaviour at the individual, group, and market levels. Understanding of religious behaviour is important as it provides information about a neglected area of non-market behaviour, addressing questions about belief, norms, customs, morals, values and culture, and how religion affects economic attitudes and activities of individuals, groups, and societies, and eventually economic development.

The seminal paper by Azzi and Ehrenberg (1975) provides the theoretical foundations of the Economics of Religion, wherein religious behaviour is interpreted from an economic perspective, applying microeconomic theory and techniques. It is shown in a simple model of choice between economic goods and devotional goods across time that church attendance falls with increase in income (Azzi and Ehrenberg, 1975; Iannaccone, 1998). In empirical studies, this choice theoretic microeconomic approach is used to explain patterns of religious behaviour among individuals, groups, and cultures. Lehrer (2004) critically reviews and synthesises research on the role of religion on various aspects of the economic and demographic behaviour of individuals and families in the United States, including the choice of marital partner, union formation and dissolution, fertility, female time allocation, education, wages, and wealth.

Azzi and Ehrenberg (1977), using the US General Social Survey data on self-reported religious beliefs and behaviour and applying Tobit regression model, show that church attendance rises with wealth and falls with income. As wage rates increase, religious participation becomes more money-intensive, with rates of church contributions rising. In addition, a significant positive relationship between income and religious expenditure as well as age and amount of contribution to church are also observed. The results imply that the opportunity cost of time does affect religious behaviour.

Iannaccone (1998) finds that styles of religion do vary with income and education, and belief and religious activity tend not to decline with income, and most rates increase with education. An interesting result is that the college professors are, on average, somewhat less religious than the general public.

Lehrer (2004), analysing the US 1987-88 National Survey of Families and Households data, following the theoretical framework of Gary Becker's (1981) economics of the family, shows that religious affiliation affects family outcomes, because it has an impact on the costs and benefits of many interrelated decisions that people make over the life cycle. In addition, for behaviours that pertains to married couple households, affiliation matters because it is a complementary trait within the context of marriage. It is also observed that, religiosity, another dimension of religion, also affects economic and demographic outcomes, partly because it accentuates differences by religious affiliation, and partly because of the generally beneficial effects that religious involvement has on health and well-being.

Gruber (2004) analyse the impact of charitable subsidies on religious participation and religious giving, using the US General Social Survey and the Consumer Expenditure Survey data and applying OLS and probit regression methods. It is argued that subsidising charitable contributions generates positive externalities of charitable activities, particularly from the religious institutions which are the largest recipients of charitable giving. The religious participation can either be a complement to, or a substitute with, the level of charitable giving. The study shows strong evidence that religious giving and religious attendance are substitutes: larger subsidies to charitable giving lead to more religious giving, but less religious attendance. The results validate economic models of religious participation in that charitable giving and religiosity are substitutes.

Dijkgraaf (2005), using micro data from Netherlands, investigate the relationship between income and religion, measuring religiosity by membership and attendance in church. The single equation estimates show that both the religious measures are inversely related with income. However, simultaneous equation results show insignificant results for both church membership and attendance, rejecting the bicasual relationship between income and religiosity.

Blomberg, DeLeire and Hess (2006) explicitly model the investment aspect of religious expenditure and some storage value of holiness through life time stock of religious contributions. Focusing on expenditures rather than time considerations in religious activity, a dynamic life cycle consumer utility optimisation model is developed with mortality in which intra-temporal utility stems from both ordinary consumption and religious consumption i.e. people decides how to allocate their resources between religious expenditures and other consumption expenditures. Religious expenditure not only includes 'this life consumption value', but also an 'afterlife investment value'. A noteworthy aspect of this approach is that the framework allows for the possibility that the stock of religious contributions can be stored and provide value after death also. The probability of survival or the occurrence of death is also explicitly modeled.

Though the literature on economics of religion is mature and vast in developed countries, countries that are mostly Christianity, very little in known on the relationship between religion and economics in developing countries that are multi-religious, multi-sect, and multi-ethnic societies. In India, the second most populated and the home of Hinduism, virtually no evidence is available on the economic effects of religion. Western religious traditions like Christianity and Islam emphasise exclusivity and organisational affiliation like church membership, claiming that there is one and only correct spiritual path, whereas Eastern religions like Hinduism and Buddhism are non-exclusive and the emphasis is on personal behaviour rather than on organisational affiliation. Most religious practices in developing countries preach the central importance of prayer and meditation as a means for achieving religious goals, even for people who have no specific religious affiliation.

Miller (2000) is an early Asian religious study (indeed Hinduism) which is very rare in this regard. This paper explores the relationship between risk preference and religiosity from a cross-national perspective. Using the World Values Survey data and applying OLS and Logit regressions, the study observes that being irreligious only represents risk taking behaviour in Western societies whereas in Eastern societies' non-participation in the mainstream religion does not necessarily constitute risk taking behaviour.

There are some studies which do not study on economics of religion directly, but taking religion or social identity as an important part of it. These studies analyse the impact of religion and expenditure on it along with other aspects of human life such as philanthropy and donations to a charitable cause. Such philanthropic donation can be to a charity organisation, religious institution or public goods. An altruistic household will choose a rational level of donations along with other consumption expenditure subject to budget and utility maximisation constraints.

Yen (2002), applying a censored system of donation equations by full-information maximum likelihood method on the 1995 US Consumer Expenditure Survey data explores finds a positive effect of income, age and education on all categories of donations. Specifically, the donors of charity are those households with high levels of income, headed by older and educated individuals. Benjamin, Choi and Fisher (2013) apply game theoretic framework study the identity effects of religion on economic behaviour among Cornell University students. Applying OLS and interval regression models, the study finds that religious identity salience causes Protestants to increase and Catholics to decrease contributions to public goods, expect others to contribute less to public goods, and become less risk averse. Jews more strongly reciprocate as an employee in a bilateral labour market gift exchange game. Atheists and agnostics become less risk averse. They also find no evidence of religious identity salience effects on disutility of work effort, discount rates, or generosity in a dictator game.

Khamis, Prakash and Siddique (2010) study social identity and expenditure on status signaling goods in India, focusing on social groups as Indian society is characterised by social stratification based to caste system of Hinduism. Using consumption data from the India Human Development Survey (IHDS-2005) and applying a double log regression model, this study finds that among Hindus the disadvantaged caste groups such as OBCs spend nine percent more on visible consumption than high caste groups, while social groups like Muslims spend eleven percent less. Such social and religious group differences are significant and robust.

Thus, the literature on economics of religion provides more insights to the non-market, philanthropic and social aspects of human behaviour. More specifically, the literature shows how economic models can fruitfully address questions about belief, norms, and values, and exploring how religion (and, by extension, morals and culture) affect economic attitudes and activities of individuals, groups, and societies. Being a behavioural science, economics views religious behaviour as an instance of rational choice, rather than an exception to it, and religious expenditures as investments. The analyses of religious behaviour at the individual, group, and social levels shows that religious behaviour generates some utility for expenditure on religion, and there exists a positive relation between income and religious expenditure.

## 14.3 Data and Methodology

This paper uses the 68th round (July 2011-June 2012) of the NSSO data on household consumer expenditure. The 68th round (Type 2) NSSO data consists of 101651 nationwide observations. In this data set, 9914 households reported positive spending on religious activities. Among the states, in Meghalaya and Kerala, 33 percent and 32 percent households have incurred religious expenditure, followed by Tamil Nadu (22 percent) and Orissa (20 percent). Surprisingly there is one union territory with zero religious expenditure- D&N Haveli. Among the religious groups, 44 percent of Christians, 25 percent of Muslims, and 25 percent of Hindus spend on religion. On an average, a household in India is spending Rs. 93 per month on religious activities. The average religious spending by Christians is Rs.177 per month, whereas Muslims spend only Rs. 67 for the same. The Hindu households spend Rs.80 per month and other religious groups spend Rs. 81 per month on religion.

The dependent variable of this paper, household religious expenditure, is distributed over the range of Rs. 2 to Rs. 7000 per month, with mean expenditure of Rs. 93 and standard deviation of Rs. 288. The distribution of religious expenditure shows a skewed distribution with values highly concentrated on the left side of the mean value. Hence, applying OLS to a skewed distribution may lead to a biased estimation because of the rightward outliers. Moreover, the mean value itself lies away from right extreme end. Hence, to avoid the effect of outliers, the censored regression method is applied for the empirical analysis of religious expenditure. It is observed from the distribution of religious expenditure that about 90 percent of observations fall below or equal to Rs. 165 per month. Therefore, an artificial right censoring of data at the point of Rs. 165 per month is considered taking the mean value plus l/4th of standard deviation (93+72=165). The censoring has left 1022 censored observations out of 9914 total observations. All the higher values are reduced to Rs. 165.

### Censored Regression Model

The censored regression model is essentially a missing data problem, but with some information about missing variables, whether the outcome variable is above or below a known threshold value. In the censored regression model the values of the explanatory variables are observed of all observations, but, the true values of the dependent variable is observed only for a restricted range of observations. Instead, the values of the dependent variable for the certain observations are reported as a single value or clustered around a value, say *c*. Generally, the censored (resembles the Tobit model) is defined as an index function or latent variable model given by,

$$y^* = \beta x + u \tag{14.1}$$

$$y = c \quad if \;\; y^* \geq c \tag{14.2}$$

$$y = y^* \text{ otherwise}$$

where *c* is a constant (threshold value), β is a k x 1 vector of unknown parameters; *x* is a k x 1 set of independent variable, *u* is the residuals that are independently and normally distributed, with mean zero and a common variance s2. Normally, E[*y*|*x*]=0. With censoring, E[y|x] ≠ 0, and OLS estimation is biased. Defining the density function for *u* condition on *y* = *c*,

$$\phi = \phi(u \mid y \leq c) = \phi(u \mid u \leq c - \beta x) = \frac{\phi(u)}{P(u \leq c - \beta x)} \tag{14.3}$$

$$= \frac{\phi(u)}{P\left(\frac{u}{\sigma} \leq \frac{c-\beta x}{\sigma}\right)} = \frac{\phi(u)}{\Phi\left(\frac{c-\beta x}{\sigma}\right)} = \frac{1}{\Phi\left(\frac{c-\beta x}{\sigma}\right)} \frac{1}{\sqrt{2\pi\sigma^2}} e^{-\frac{u^2}{2\sigma^2}} = \frac{\frac{1}{\sigma}\phi\frac{u}{\sigma}}{\Phi\left(\frac{c-\beta x}{\sigma}\right)} \tag{14.4}$$

$$E[y \mid x] = \Phi\left(\frac{\beta x}{\sigma}\right)(\beta x + \sigma\lambda) \tag{14.5}$$

where $\lambda = \phi(\beta x/\sigma)/\Phi(\beta x/\sigma)$, $\phi$ and $\Phi$ denotes density and cumulative distribution functions of *u*. Defining,

$$\Phi(\beta, x, \sigma^2) = \int_{-\infty}^{\beta x} \frac{1}{\sigma\sqrt{2\pi}} \mathrm{e}^{\left(-\frac{(\beta x)^2}{2\sigma^2}\right)} \tag{14.6}$$

$$\phi = \phi(\beta, x, \sigma^2) = \frac{1}{\sigma\sqrt{2\pi}} e^{\left(-\frac{(\beta x)^2}{2\sigma^2}\right)(\beta x)^2} \tag{14.7}$$

$$\Phi = \Phi(\beta, x, \sigma^2) = \int_{-\infty}^{\beta x/\sigma} \frac{1}{\sigma\sqrt{2\pi}} \mathrm{e}^{\left(-\frac{(\beta x)^2}{2\sigma^2}\right)} \mathrm{dt} \tag{14.8}$$

For the observations $y_i$ that are zero,

$$P(y_i) = 0 = P(u < -\beta x_i) = (1 - \Phi_i) \tag{14.9}$$

For the observations $y_i$ that are greater than zero,

$$P(y_i) > 0 = \phi(y_i \mid y_i > 0) = \frac{1}{\sqrt{2\pi\sigma^2}} e^{\left(-\frac{1}{2\sigma^2}\right)(y_i - \beta x)^2} \tag{14.10}$$

Hence, the likelihood contribution of $i^{th}$ observation is given by,

$$L_i = \frac{\frac{1}{\sigma}\phi\frac{(y_i - \beta x_i)}{\sigma}}{\Phi\left(\frac{\beta x_i}{\sigma}\right)} \tag{14.11}$$

Then, the likelihood function is given by,

$$Log\ L(\beta,\sigma) = \sum_{i=1}^{n} L_i = -\frac{n}{2}[log(2\pi) + log\ (\sigma^2)] - \frac{1}{2\sigma^2}\sum_{i=1}^{n} u_i^2 - \sum_{i=1}^{n} log\left[\Phi\left(\frac{\beta x_i}{\sigma}\right)\right] \tag{14.12}$$

That is, $L = \prod_0 (1 - \Phi_i) \prod_1 \frac{1}{\sqrt{2\pi\sigma^2}} e^{\left(-\frac{1}{2\sigma^2}\right)(y_i - \beta x)^2}$ (14.13)

where the first product is over the observations for which $y_i = c$ and the second product is over observations for which $0 < y_i \leq c$.

## 14.4 Empirical Analysis

Viewing religious spending as an instance of consumer expenditure, this paper empirically estimates the determinants of religious expenditure by the censored regression model. The distribution of household religious expenditure presented in Table 14.1 shows that approximately 90 percent of households spend under Rs.165 per month, and only 10 percent of households spend more than that on religion. Most households, around 50 percent, spend less than Rs. 30 per month on religion related activities. The Figure 14.1 reveals that the variable is highly concentrated to the left of the mean, and on the right side the distribution is negligible. This situation may lead to a biased estimation because of the rightward outliers. Moreover, the mean value of the religious expenditure (Rs. 93) itself lies away from the right extreme. Hence, to avoid the effect of outliers, an artificial censoring at the point of Rs. 165 is considered, covering 90 percent of the data, and all the upper values are reduced to Rs.165. More comprehensively, though, the dependent variable, religious expenditure is distributed over a range of Rs. 2 to Rs. 7000 per month, the summary statistics of the data shows the mean value is 93 and standard deviation is 288, which means the values are concentrated to the range of Rs. 90-100 with the maximum value as 7000.The table of frequency distribution for Religious expenditure also shows that 90 percent observations fall to less than or equal to Rs. 165 i.e. mean value plus ¼$^{th}$ of standard deviation (93+72=165). This is the condition where an artificial censoring limit is reformed. So censoring the values greater than or equal to 165 to 165 (censoring limit) provide 1022 censored observations out of 9914 (upper censoring or right censoring case).

**Table 14.1: Distribution of Household by Religious Expenditure (Rs. per month)**

| *Uncensored sample* | | | *Censored sample* | | |
|---|---|---|---|---|---|
| ***Religious expenditure*** | ***No.*** | ***percent*** | ***Religious expenditure*** | ***No.*** | ***percent*** |
| 2 to 9 | 853 | 8.59 | 2 to 9 | 853 | 8.59 |
| 10 to 19 | 2,098 | 21.16 | 10 to 19 | 2,098 | 21.16 |
| 20 to 29 | 1,893 | 19.09 | 20 to 29 | 1,893 | 19.09 |
| 30 to 48 | 1074 | 10.83 | 30 to 48 | 1074 | 10.83 |
| 50 to 99 | 1,812 | 18.27 | 50 to 99 | 1,812 | 18.27 |
| 100 to 175 | 1183 | 11.92 | 100 to 108 | 785 | 7.92 |
| 180 to 306 | 505 | 5.09 | 110 to 160 | 377 | 3.79 |
| 310 to 7000 | 496 | 5.05 | 165 to highest | 1022 | 10.35 |
| Total | 9914 | 100 | Total | 9914 | 100 |

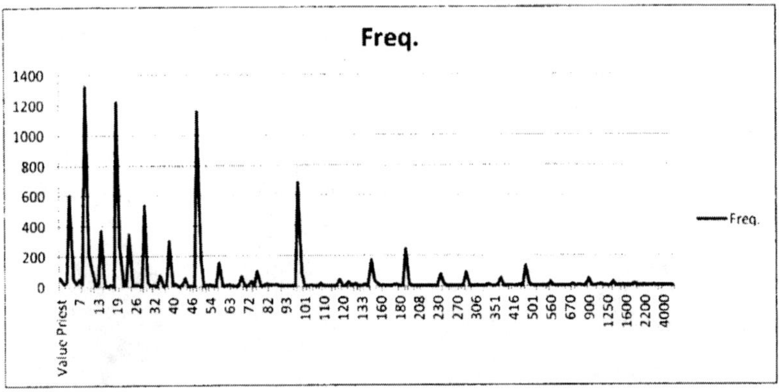


*Figure 14.1: Distribution of Religious Expenditure in India*

The Figures 14.2 and 14.3 present the distribution of households that incur religious expenditure by religion and the average expenditure of households on religious activities by religion. As shown in Table 14.2 and Figures 14.2 and 14.3, among the households that spend on religion, 70 percent are Hindus, 14.55 percent are Christians, and 13.55 percent are Muslims. However, the average religious expenditures by Hindus Rs. 80.78 per month and Rs. 67.40 per month by Muslims are much less than the mean religious expenditure of Rs.177.36 per month by the Christian households. The other religious households spend similar to Hindu religion on religion.

**Table 14.2: Average Religious Expenditure of Households (Rs. per month)**

| *Religion* | *Percent of households* | *Average expenditure* |
|---|---|---|
| Hindus | 70.00 | 80.78 |
| Christians | 14.55 | 177.36 |
| Muslims | 13.55 | 67.40 |
| Others | 2.00 | 81.76 |

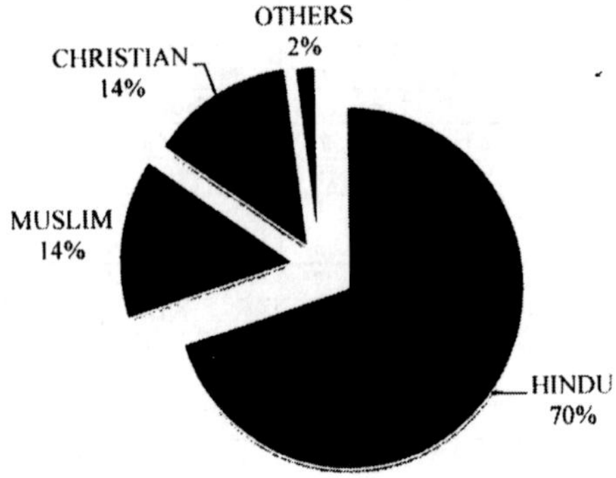


*Figure 14.2: Distribution of Religious Expenditure by Religion in India*

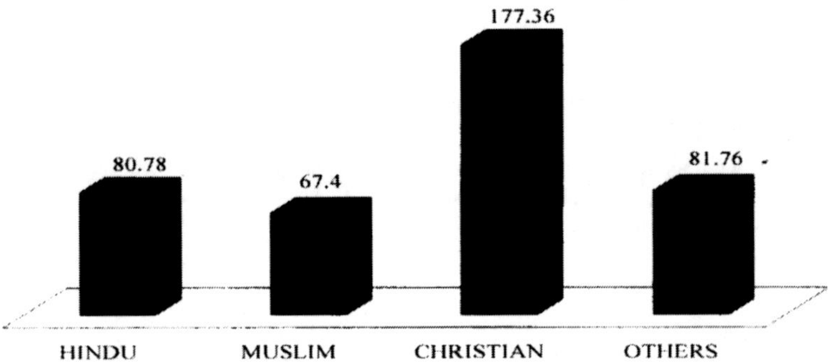


*Figure 14.3: Mean Religious Expenditure by Religion in India*

Much in the same way of differences in religious expenditure pattern across religion, the Table 14.3 shows that more number of urban households report religious expenditure than the rural households. While 36 percent of urban self-employed households spend on religious festivals, about 26 percent of both self-employed agricultural and non-agricultural households in rural areas spend on religion. Among the regular wage/salary earning households, while about 36 percent in urban areas spend on religious activities, only 21 percent in rural areas are spending on religion. A sizable 14 percent of non-agricultural casual labour households report expenditure on religion. It is also to be noted that more non-salary worker households, 68 percent, spend on religion than the 32 percent of regular salary earning households. Approximately 88 percent of households having own shelter are spending on religion compared to the households without own dwelling spending on religion. Overall, urban, salaried, Christians and households with own dwelling spend more on religion than the households with other characteristics.

**Table 14.3: Distribution of Religious Households by Characteristics (percent)**

| *Characteristics* | | | *Percent of households* |
|---|---|---|---|
| Residence | Rural | Self-employed agriculture | 26.94 |
| | | Self-employed non-agriculture | 26.18 |
| | | Agriculture casual labour | 6.45 |
| | | Non-agriculture – casual labour | 13.78 |
| | | Wage/salary worker | 20.83 |
| | | Others | 5.82 |
| | Urban | Self-employed | 36.0 |
| | | Wage/salary worker | 39.0 |
| | | Casual labour | 14.0 |
| | | Others | 11.0 |
| Salaried | | | 31.74 |
| Not salaried | | | 68.26 |
| Own dwelling | | | 87.63 |
| No own dwelling | | | 12.37 |

The definition and descriptive statistics of the variables in the empirical analysis are presented in Table 14.4. The Table 14.4 shows that a household is spending on average Rs. 93 per month on religious practices, with the range of religious expenditure from Rs.2 to Rs. 7000 per month and the standard deviation of Rs. 288 per month. With censoring at Rs. 165 per month, the average monthly religious expenditure is Rs. 50 per month, with a deviation of Rs. 50 per month. In this paper, as the NSSO data does not provide income directly, household expenditure is used as a proxy for household income. A household has an average monthly expenditure of Rs. 10909 per month, excluding religious expenditure. Among the households in the data, 71 percent of them are Hindus, 14 percent are Muslims, 13 percent are Christians and 2 percent belong to other religions such as Buddhism, Jainism, Sikhism, etc. In the same way, mean values of social group dummies show that 42 percent of households belong to OBC category, 34 percent are from other social groups,

**Table 14.4: Descriptive Statistics of Variables in the Religious Expenditure Analysis**

| *Variable* | *Description* | *Mean* | *Std. dev.* |
|---|---|---|---|
| Religious expenditure | Total amount paid in cash and payment made in kind like an item or items of food, pan, tobacco, intoxicants, fuel, clothing, etc. towards religious purpose (Rs.). | 93.062 | 288.08 |
| Religious expenditure1 | Censored religious expenditure (upper censoring at Rs.165) | 51.014 | 50.849 |
| Income | Monthly expenditure of a household excluding expenditure on religion (Rs.) | 10908.62 | 10448.93 |
| Log of income | Natural logarithm of income (expenditure) | 9.082 | 0.638 |

*(Contd...)*

| Household size | Number of persons living in a family | 4.7087 | 2.2480 |
|---|---|---|---|
| Hindu | If Hindu = 1, 0 otherwise | 0.7016 | 0.4577 |
| Muslim | If Muslim = 1, 0 otherwise | 0.1438 | 0.3509 |
| Christian | If Christian = 1, 0 otherwise | 0.1355 | 0.3422 |
| Other religion | If Other religion = 1, 0 otherwise | 0.0192 | 0.1371 |
| ST | If ST = 1, 0 otherwise | 0.1366 | 0.3434 |
| SC | If SC = 1, 0 otherwise | 0.1108 | 0.3138 |
| OBC | If OBC = 1, 0 otherwise | 0.4201 | 0.4936 |
| Other social group | If Other social group = 1, 0 otherwise | 0.3326 | 0.4712 |
| South | If Southern India = 1, 0 otherwise | 0.2349 | 0.4239 |
| West | If Western India = 1, 0 otherwise | 0.2297 | 0.3688 |
| North | If Northern India = 1, 0 otherwise | 0.2687 | 0.4433 |
| East | If Eastern = 1, 0 otherwise | 0.3339 | 0.4716 |
| Own dwelling | If residing in own house = 1, 0 otherwise | 0.8763 | 0.3292 |
| No own dwelling | If no own house = 1, 0 otherwise | 0.1237 | 0.3292 |
| Child | If children <14 years present = 1, 0 otherwise | 0. 5883 | 0.4922 |
| Adult | If adults aged 18-59 years present =1, 0 otherwise | 0. 9708 | 0.1682 |
| Elder | If elders aged > 60 years present = 1, 0 otherwise | 0. 3359 | 0.4724 |
| Uneducated | If head of household illiterate = 1, 0 otherwise | 0. 2344 | 0.4236 |
| Educated | If head of household literate = 1, 0 otherwise | 0.7656 | 0.4236 |
| Male head | If male head of household = 1, 0 otherwise | 0.8815 | 0.3232 |
| Female head | If female head of household = 1, 0 otherwise | 0.1185 | 0.3232 |
| Number of observations | | 9914 | |

13 percent ST category and 11 percent from SC category. Nearly 88 percent of households are headed by males and about 76 of the heads are educated. While 87 households have their own dwellings, the average household size is 4.7. While there are children below 14 years in 59 percent, elders are present in 33 percent of households.

The OLS and censored regression estimates of the socio-economic determinants of the household religious expenditure in India are presented in Table 14.5. The censored regression model estimates show relatively much better fit and more significant coefficient estimates compared to the OLS estimates. The estimated results show that household income and religious spending are positively and significantly related. A one percentage increase in household income will lead to Rs. 41.68 per month increase in religious expenditure. The effect of household size on religious expenditure is significantly negative. An increase in household size will lead to decrease in spending on religion by Rs. 2.65 per month. The religious expenditure of Hindu household is Rs. 3.77 less, whereas the religious expenditure of Christian households is significantly Rs. 24.61 more compared to Muslim households. The other religion households are also spending Rs. 17.74 more on religion than Muslims. However, the effect of Hindu religion on religious expenditure is statistically significant at 10 percent level only. These results show the non-institutionalised religious practice of Hindus, compared to the Christians and Muslims and even other religious groups. The religious expenditure of scheduled tribes Rs. 11.11 more and that of scheduled castes is Rs. 5 less than that of other social groups. The OBC household is also spending Rs. 6 less on religion compared to other social groups. The coefficients of the community dummies are statistically significant. Further, there are also regional disparities in the country in household religious expenditure. Relative to eastern India, south Indian households spend more on religion by Rs. 9.38 per month, while the households in western Indian spending even higher Rs. 15.13 more on religion. However, the north Indian households spend Rs. 2 less on religion compared to east India, but the effect is not significant statistically.

**Table 14.5: OLS and Censored Regression Estimates of Religious Expenditure in India**

| *Variable* | *OLS* | *Censored regression* |
|---|---|---|
| Log income | 141.61 * (27.80) | 41.68* (46.20) |
| Household size | -10.17* (6.72) | -2.65* (10.6) |
| Hindu | 14.35*** (1.68) | -3.77*** (2.54) |
| Christian | 69.53* (5.49) | 24.61 * (11.41) |
| Other religion | 46.29** (2.11) | 17.74* (4.63) |
| ST | 26.44** (2.36) | 11.11* (5.68) |
| SC | 4.94 (0.49) | -4.99* (2.86) |
| OBC | -12.55*** (1.82) | -5.98* (5.00) |
| North | -19.42** (2.28) | -1.95 (1.33) |
| West | 36.03* (3.27) | 15.13* (7.89) |
| South | 2.87 (0.38) | 9.38* (7.10) |
| Educated | -11.13 (1.43) | -2.38*** (1.76) |
| Elder | 8.30 (1.24) | 3.76* (3.23) |
| Adult | -56.77* (3.01) | -17.82* (5.42) |
| Female head | 21.07** (2.38) | 9.56* (6.19) |
| Own dwelling | 19.13** (2.23) | 7.43* (4.99) |
| Constant | -1121.96* (24.31) | -306.35* (37.63) |
| Prob>F / Prob>Chi$^2$ | 0.000 | 0.000 |
| $R^2$ / Log likelihood | 0.0995 | -48205.664 |

**Note:** Absolute t-values in parentheses. * Significant at 1 percent level ** Significant at 5 percent level *** Significant at 10 percent level.

The effect of education on religious expenditure is negative. In the case of education of household head, a literate household head spends Rs. 2.38 less than an illiterate household head, which is significant at 10 percent level. Households with adults spend Rs.17.82 less and households with elders spend Rs. 3.76 more per month relative to households with children less than 14 years. These results are also significant at 1 percent level. This implies elderly spend relatively more on religious activities compared to earning people. The gender of family head plays a crucial role in religious expenditure. A female headed household is spending Rs. 9.56 more on religion compared to a male headed household. It is also significant at 1 percent level. The expenditure on religion will increase by Rs.7.43 if the household has own dwelling compared to household without own dwelling.

As Hinduism is the dominant religion of India and is followed by more 80 percent of population, controlling for religion may reveal more insights.

The Table 14.6 presents the estimated results of the censored regression model by religion. In all the estimates, the coefficient of income is positive and statistically significant. A one percent increase in household income will lead raise religious expenditure by Rs. 39 per month in Hindu households, Rs. 38 in Muslim, Rs. 61.35 in Christian and other religious households. While an increase of household member reduces the religious expenditure, the presence of elders will raise religious expenditure in all religions.

**Table 14.6: Censored Regression Estimates of Religious Expenditure by Religion**

| *Variable* | *Hindu* | *Muslim* | *Christian* | *Other religions* |
|---|---|---|---|---|
| Log income | 38.96* (39.20) | 37.54* (14.93) | 61.35* (17.40) | 60.99* (7.54) |
| Household size | -2.60* (8.83) | -1.86* (3.10) | -5.10* (4.58) | -3.93 (1.50) |
| ST | -1.51 (0.56) | 32.26* (5.52) | -37.29* (3.27) | 29.46** (2.36) |
| SC | -6.18* (3.50) | 25.78 (1.15) | -6.44 (0.47) | 18.93 (1.15) |
| OBC | -6.57* (4.97) | -7.51* (2.63) | -6.18 (1.05) | 26.56 (1.60) |
| North | 6.40* (3.87) | -15.02* (4.89) | -112.95* (3.54) | -61.94* (5.45) |
| West | 19.96* (10.34) | -6.77 (1.01) | -66.71 (1.58) | -10.59 (0.38) |
| South | 12.91* (9.16) | 5.13 (1.20) | -48.05* (4.40) | -61.39*** (1.9) |
| Educated | -4.01 * (2.56) | -3.03 (1.12) | 8.67 (1.37) | 8.49 (0.82) |
| Elder | 4.59* (3.53) | 2.63 (0.94) | 5.68 (1.27) | 12.02 (1.19) |
| Adult | -18.04* (5.11) | -15.65 (1.26) | 0.55 (0.05) | 59.24 (1.06) |
| Female head | 8.86* (5.02) | 8.76** (2.25) | 5.31 (1.07) | 10.47 (0.54) |
| Own Dwelling | 9.67* (6.01) | 0.31 (0.07) | -2.72 (0.49) | 11.33 (0.60) |
| Constant | -288.81* (32.88) | -260.04* (10.96) | -414.51* (12.10) | -537.65* (5.96) |
| Prob>Chi$^2$ | 0.000 | 0.000 | 0.000 | 0.000 |
| Log likelihood | -34141.239 | -6963.7152 | -6024.0853 | -859.81308 |
| N | 6954 | 1425 | 1342 | 189 |

**Note:** Absolute t-values in parentheses. * Significant at 1 percent level ** Significant at 5 percent level *** Significant at 10 percent level.

The estimated results by community and education presented in Tables 14.7 and 14.8 also reveal broadly the same picture. Household income has a significant positive effect on religious expenditure, whereas household size has a significantly negative effect on religious spending. A one percent increase in household income will lead to 65 percent increase in religious expenditure of ST households, 40 percent in SC households and 37.5 percent in OBC households. The presence of elders in the household increases religious expenditure, the dummy for adult has a negative impact on religious spending in both cases. While Christians belonging to ST and ST communities reduce religious expenditure, OBC Christians spend more on religion. However, educated Christians spend less on religion. Both the educated Hindus and Hindus belonging to different communities spend less on religious expenditure. But, female heads belonging to various communities, irrespective of education, incur more religious expenditure. Having own dwelling increases religious expenditure of all communities except STs, whether educated or not.

**Table 14.7: Censored Regression Estimates of Religious Expenditure by Community**

| *Variable* | *ST* | *SC* | *OBC* | *Others* |
|---|---|---|---|---|
| Log income | 65.06* (19.05) | 39.93 * (17.12) | 37.50* (29.13) | 40.01* (25.08) |
| Household size | -3.94* (-4.22) | -3.14* (4.54) | -2.39* (6.32) | -2.72* (5.89) |
| Hindu | -40.80* (4.85) | -31.92 (1.54) | -1.44 (0.70) | -3.93***(1.68) |
| Christian | -16.99** (1.98) | -10.70 (0.48) | 22.50* (6.23) | 22.06* (4.95) |
| Other religion | -0.20 (0.02) | -29.84 (1.31) | 3.30 (0.33) | -0.62 (0.08) |
| North | -37.20* (5.91) | 1.79 (0.51) | 5.13** (2.06) | -0.29 (0.13) |
| West | 4.50 (0.54) | 15.35* (3.03) | 15.51* (5.46) | 21.10* (6.66) |
| South | -12.95*** (1.89) | 8.96* (3.00) | 10.95* (5.65) | 15.42* (5.87) |
| Educated | -2.07 (0.46) | -6.47** (2.26) | -3.06 (1.57) | -0.90 (0.34) |
| Elder | 3.57 (0.85) | 4.55 (1.49) | 3.34** (1.98) | 5.23* (2.63) |
| Adult | -33.83*** (1.95) | -1.94 (0.19) | -17.13* (3.73) | -14.72* (2.78) |
| Female head | -1.39 (0.27) | 5.81 (1.49) | 6.53* (3.00) | 16.64* (5.81) |
| Own dwelling | -16.30* (2.75) | 9.31** (2.81) | 11.67* (5.74) | 5.95** (2.17) |
| Constant | -419.54* (12.57) | -279.99* (9.21) | -282.79* (25.17) | -296.80* (20.8) |
| Prob>Chi$^2$ | 0.000 | 0.000 | 0.000 | 0.000 |
| Log likelihood | -6169.6249 | -5339.64 | -20513.102 | -16065.14 |
| N | 1353 | 1097 | 4164 | 3296 |

**Note:** Absolute t-values in parentheses. * Significant at 1 percent level ** Significant at 5 percent level *** Significant at 10 percent level.

**Table 14.8: Censored Regression Estimates of Religious Expenditure by Education**

| *Variable* | *Literate household* | *Illiterate household* |
|---|---|---|
| Log Income | 41.98* (41.90) | 40.80* (19.32) |
| Household size | -2.58* (8.40) | -2.87* (5.66) |
| Hindu | -4.14** (2.39) | -2.03 (0.71) |
| Christian | 25.32* (10.13) | 10.63** (2.01) |
| Other religion | 21.27* (4.67) | 7.55 (1.12) |
| ST | 12.22* (5.47) | 7.49*** (1.84) |
| SC | -6.06* (2.98) | -1.97 (0.57) |
| OBC | -6.73* (5.05) | -2.41 (0.86) |
| North | -2.44 (1.43) | -1.23 (0.44) |
| West | 16.01* (7.43) | 10.78* (2.60) |
| South | 10.22* (6.89) | 6.69** (2.26) |
| Elder | 4.65* (3.52) | 1.11 (0.47) |
| Adult | -15.79* (4.00) | -22.20* (3.83) |
| Female head | 10.89* (5.77) | 5.77** (2.30) |
| Own dwelling | 7.02* (4.34) | 9.52** (2.40) |
| Constant | -313.69* (32.90) | -294.37* (17.03) |
| Prob>Chi$^2$ | 0.000 | 0.000 |
| Log likelihood | -39687.066 | -8477.0595 |
| N | 8178 | 1732 |

**Note:** Absolute t-values in parentheses. * Significant at 1 percent level ** Significant at 5 percent level *** Significant at 10 percent level.

## 14.5 Conclusion

In almost every religion around the world, the expenditure on religious ceremonies, pilgrimage, festivals, pujas and donations are a part of household expenditure. In fact, religion dominates every aspect of social and economic life of almost every individual. In most religions, like Christianity, expenditure on such religious activities are institutionalised. Hindus, being the dominant religious community as well as population segment of India also spend on religion, but such expenditures are mostly voluntary and not institutionalised. In almost all religious households, there is a positive relation between income and religious expenditure. This paper has also observed the same. Among the major religious groups in India, Christians spend more on religion. The Hindus, as major religion of India, and Muslims, as minor backward community of India, spend approximately 50 percent and 70 percent less expenditure on religion compared to Christians. The study also finds that the size of family and literacy have a negative relation with spending on religion, while the presence of elders in the household increases the religious expenditure. The picture of religious expenditure of households does not vary much even if controlled for religion, social group and education.

# 15

# The Demand for Durable Goods: A Quantile Regression Estimation of Household Expenditure on Durable Goods Consumption

## Abstract

*The objective of this paper is to study is to examine the pattern of household expenditure on durable goods and to analyse the distributional effects of the determinants of durable goods expenditure of households in Tamil Nadu using the 68th round (July 2011- June 2012) of NSSO data. The literate households have high consumption expenditure on durable goods compared to illiterate households. The household consumption expenditure on durable goods is analysed by quantile regression. The study finds a positive relationship between income and durable goods expenditure across all households and such expenditure increases at higher quantiles. The effect of family size is on durable goods expenditure is negative. There also exist significant differences across regions and community. The backward community households spend significantly more on durable goods than the SC/ST households. The households with a regular salary earner and business or self-employment consume more durable goods compared to other households. The households with male head spent more of durable goods compared to female headed households. Households with elders spend more on durable goods. In the quantile regression estimates showing the distributional effects of consumption expenditure on durable goods, most of the variables in the upper quantiles show significantly higher effects on household consumption expenditure on durable goods.*

**Key words:** *Durable goods consumption, expenditure distribution, quantile regression*

## 15.1 Introduction

Generally, household spend on both durable and non-durable goods and services. Durable goods are those goods whose expected life time as well as services from them is expected to be longer. As opposed to many goods that are intended for consumption in short term, consumer durables are intended to endure regular usage for several years or longer before their replacement is required. Durable goods include household appliances like furniture, jewellery, washing machines, air conditioners, automobiles, electrical appliances, etc. Non-durable goods are consumed for short times like food items, medicines and other consumables. Household spending on such durables is much more volatile than spending on non-durable commodities. Durable goods consumption largely depends on. The household purchase of the durables goods are largely influenced by the attitudes, intentions and expectations of consumers as well as by economic position of the household including assets, credit, prices, etc. Household expenditure on durable goods consumption is determined by household occupation, social group and demographic characteristics. They may also reflect household economic and social status, as well as cultural differences, social distinctions and indeed socioeconomic inequalities. Also, there are other characteristics such as that determine the consumption of durable goods by the households.

This paper analyses the characteristics of the household that consume durable goods. The major objectives of this paper are to examine the consumption pattern of durable goods across households, to analyse the influence of household social and demographic characteristics on expenditure on durable goods, and to analyse the differential impact of the determinants of household consumption of durable goods across the distribution of durable goods expenditure of households. This empirical analysis of household expenditure on durable goods consumption is based on 68th round (July 2011-June 2012) of NSS data for Tamil Nadu and the application of quantile regression methodology.

## 15.2 A Brief Review of Recent Studies

Empirical studies on household consumption on durable goods generally examine the household consumption expenditure on the basis of probability of consumption and non-consumption of durable goods. Few studies analyse the durable goods consumption gap of urban and rural households and public and private sector workers. Initial studies used the Probit model and recent studies use the quantile regression methodology.

In an early attempt on the household expenditure on the consumption of durable goods, Wu (1965) analyse the probability of purchase of durable goods as determined by the gap between desired and actual stock, using the 1965 Survey of Consumer Finance data applying the probit model. It is observed that the relative gap between desired and actual stock is important in determining the probability of purchase, while the absolute gap is important in determining the net outlay. There is not much difference with respect to the differential effects of different types of income changes. The empirical evidence also supports the hypothesis that desired stock is a function of expected income.

Fisher (1963) analyses the relationship between liquid assets holding and consumption behaviour using the 1957-1958 Survey of Consumer Finance data applying the Probit model. The study finds that the household purchasing behaviour is related to the types of liquid assets holdings and to the previous and current credit use. The results of this analysis also highlight the relationship between purchasing intentions and subsequent behaviour.

Cragg (1971) study the household total outlay on purchase of durable goods using the 1964 Canadian Survey of Consumer Finances data applying the Probit model. The study finds that lagged income is much insignificant and has different signs in explaining the decision on purchase of durable goods and accounting for the amount spent on such goods. The large effects ascribed to recent marriage and to recently moving into a house are worth noting. These variables are interpreted as being proxies for differences between desired and actual stock of consumer goods.

Ronning and Schulz (2005) use German cross-section micro data (GFK) that contains 9064 households to analyse the relationship between consumption and income using quantile regression. They estimate Engel curve the quantity of beer and wine consumption and find that beer consumption has the largest price elasticity for moderate drinkers compared to light and heavy drinkers. The wine consumption price elasticity is positive for moderate drinkers compared to others. There is also aggregate price sensitivity in beer compared to wine consumption.

Saha, Roy and Kar (2014) analyse the wage and consumption gap between private and public sector employees in India using the 61st round of NSS data for the year 2004-2005 applying quantile regression method. The results of quantile regression show that the expenditure on durable goods is not different between the private and public sector workers, though the private sector workers at upper quantiles of income distribution earn more than the public sector workers.

Caglayan and Aster (2012) investigate the determinants of household consumption expenditure for rural and urban areas in Turkey for 2009 using a sample of 5658 households. The differential effects are analysed using quantile regression methodology. They observe that the consumption expenditure rise as the income increases, where the increase is higher especially at upper quantiles. The consumption expenditure of the urban residents is nearly twice higher than the ones of rural residents at lower quantiles, this decrease at upper quantiles.

Thus, the empirical studies observe that the probability of purchasing durable goods is influenced by household type and household size, and age, household occupation, gender of the household head, income and state region affect the consumption of durable goods. Studies using quantile regression to analyse the distributional effects of consumption of durable goods observe that the consumption pattern are not the same across the distribution of durable goods consumption expenditure.

## 15.3 Data and Methodology

The paper uses the 68th round (July 2011- June 2012) of NSSO data pertaining to Tamil Nadu. The NSSO conducts the nationwide household consumption expenditure surveys at regular intervals as part of its rounds normally of a year's duration. The 68th round is the ninth survey in this series. The 68th household consumer expenditure survey contains information on the level and pattern of consumer expenditure including the household consumption of various goods and services across socioeconomic groups. The sample size for Tamil Nadu is 5442.

## Quantile Regression Method

Quantile regression model, very similar to OLS model in terms of statistical structure, provides a richer characterisation of the data allowing differential impact of covariates on the entire distribution of the dependent variable, not merely its conditional mean as in OLS. The OLS regression analysis estimates the conditional mean or average value of the response variable in terms of the known or fixed variables. A quantile regression models the relationship between explanatory variables and the conditional quantiles of the dependent variable rather than just the conditional mean of dependent variable. A quantile regression gives a more comprehensive picture of the effects of the independent variables on the dependent variable.

The quantile regression is described by the regression equation,

$$y_i = \beta_q x_i + u_i \qquad (15.1)$$

where $\beta_q$ is vector of unknown parameters associated with the $q^{th}$ quantile. While the ordinary least squares minimises the sum of the squares of the errors, $\Sigma u_i^2$, the quantile regression minimises $\Sigma q|u_i|+\Sigma(1-q)|u_i|$ a sum that gives the asymmetric penalties $q|u_i|$ for under prediction and $(1-q)\ |u_u|$ for over prediction. Therefore, the quantile regression is also called median regression or least absolute deviation as it minimises the sum of absolute residuals. The error term is given by,

$$u_i = y_i - \beta x_i \qquad (15.2)$$

On substitution, the $q^{th}$ quantile regression estimator $\beta_q$ minimises over $\beta_q$ the objective function,

$$Q(\beta_q) = \sum_{i:|y_i|\geq x_i\beta}^{n} q|y_i - x_i\beta_q| + \sum_{i:|y_i|\leq x_i\beta}^{n} (1-q)|y_i - x_i\beta_q| \ (0<q<1) \qquad (15.3)$$

where the first term is the actual value of $y_i$ higher than the predictor value and the second term is the actual value of $y_i$ lower than the predictor value. If $L(u) = |u|$, the optimal predictor is the conditional median, $med(y|x)$ and the optimal predictor is that β minimises $\sum|y_i - x_i\ \beta|$. Therefore, the simple minimisation problem yielding the ordinary sample quantiles in the specific location model is the regression quantiles (Koenker and Bassett, 1978). Then, the *qth* sample quantile is defined as any solution to the minimisation problem,

$$min \sum_{i:|y_i| \geq x_i\beta}^{n} q|y_i - x_i\beta_q| + \sum_{i:|y_i|<x_i\beta}^{n}(1-q)|y_i - x_i\beta_q| \quad (0<q<1) \tag{15.4}$$

The case of the median ($q = 1/2$) is the general result. Thus, quantile regression reveals information about the complete conditional distribution of the response variable without any constraints on the error term. Moreover, the estimation is robust with respect to outliers of the response variable.

In contrast to the OLS and the maximum likelihood estimations, the quantile regression uses linear programming methods in computation. In order to convert the regression problem into a linear programming problem, non-negative variables $\varepsilon_i$ and $v_i$ are introduced in the equation,

$$y_i - (\beta_0 + x_i\beta_1) + \varepsilon_i = 0 \qquad i \in (i: y_i \geq \beta_0 + x_i\beta_1) \tag{15.5}$$

$$\varepsilon_i = 0 i \forall (i: y_i \geq \beta_0 + x_i\beta_1) \tag{15.6}$$

$$(\beta_0 + x_i\beta_1) - y_i + v_i = 0 \qquad i \in (i: y_i < \beta_0 + x_i\beta_1) \tag{15.7}$$

$$v_i = 0 i \forall (i: y_i < \beta_0 + x_i\beta_1) \tag{15.8}$$

Since $\varepsilon_i$ and $v_i$ are greater than the complementary sets, equations (15.5) and (15.7) can be rewritten as,

$$y_i = (\beta_0 + x_i\beta_1) + \varepsilon_i - v_i = 0 \qquad \varepsilon_i \geq 0,\ v_i \geq 0,\ \ i \in (1, n) \tag{15.9}$$

Then, the linear regression problem with $\varepsilon_i$ and $v_i$ becomes,

$$min \sum_{y_i \geq \beta_0, x_i\beta_1}^{n} q\varepsilon_i + \sum_{iy_i<\beta_0, x_i\beta_1}^{n} (1-q)v_i \tag{15.10}$$

Note that. $\varepsilon_i v_i = 0\ \forall i \in (1, n)$. Then,

$$\hat{\beta}_1 = \frac{\sum_i^n (x_i - \ddot{x})(y_i - \ddot{y})}{\sum_i^n (x_i - \ddot{x})^2} \tag{15.11}$$

A significant departure of the quantile regression estimator from the linear regression estimator is that in the quantile regression the distance of points from a line is measured using a weighted sum of distances, where the weights is (1-$q$) for points below the fitted line and $q$ for points above the line. The standard conditional quantile is specified as linear,

$$Q_q(y_i|x_i) = x_i\beta_q \tag{15.12}$$

For the $j^{th}$ regressor, the marginal effects is the coefficient for the *qth* quantile,

$$\frac{\partial Q_q(y|x)}{\partial x_i} = \beta_q \tag{15.13}$$

Thus, a quantile regression parameter $\beta_q$ estimates the change at the specified quantile of the response variable $y$ produced by a one unit change in the independent variable $x$.

## 15.4 Empirical Analysis

The Table 15.1 presents the descriptive statistics of the variables used in the empirical analysis of the determinants of household consumer expenditure on durable goods in Tamil Nadu. The mean monthly household income (proxied by the monthly household per capita consumption expenditure) is Rs. 9234 in Tamil Nadu. The natural logarithm of mean monthly per capita consumption expenditure is 11.24. The mean consumer expenditure on durable goods in Tamil Nadu is Rs.7380, showing sizable expenditure on durable goods. The large standard deviation of Rs. 31731 shows sizable differences on durable goods expenditure of households in Tamil Nadu. The natural logarithm of mean durable goods expenditure is 7.24. Of the consumer expenditure on durable goods, the mean expenditure on furniture and fixtures is Rs. 559, on recreation goods is Rs. 1883, on crockery and utensils is Rs. 494, on cooking and other household appliances is Rs. 1878, on therapeutic appliances is Rs. 2920, and the mean expenditure of other personal goods is Rs. 753. The mean expenditure of residential buildings, land and other durables is Rs. 3451 and the mean expenditure of jewellery and ornaments is Rs. 2926.

The mean household size is 3 persons per household. Among the household heads, 80 percent have at least primary education. About 85 percent of households have male headship indicating the patriarchal system of Indian society. Among the social groups, 78 percent of households belong to OBC category, 17 percent from SC category, and 3 percent are from other social groups. Region-wise, 29 percent of households belong to coastal northern region, 18 percent from coastal region, 27 percent from southern region and 24 percent from inland regions. Nearly 49 percent of households have children below the age of 14 years while 31 percent of households have elders above 60 years of age in the family. A household residing in own house is more likely to spend on durable goods consumption while a family with a regular wage/salary earner is less likely to spend on durable. Among the social groups, households belonging to backward community are the highest proportion of households that send on durable goods. A sizable number of households with elderly persons also spend on durable goods.

**Table 15.1: Descriptive Statistics of Variables in the Analysis of Household Expenditure on Durable Goods Consumption**

| *Variable* | *Description* | *Mean* |
|---|---|---|
| HDG Exp | Household expenditure on durable goods | 7380.06 (31731.67) |
| ln(HDG Exp) | Log of household expenditure on durable goods | 7.24 (1.69) |

*(Contd...)*

| MPCE | Total household monthly expenditure (excluding household expenditure on durable goods) (income proxy) | 9234.48 (62660.57) |
|---|---|---|
| ln(MPCE) | Log of household monthly consumption expenditure | 11.24 (0.64) |
| HHSize | No. of persons living in the household | 3.67 (1.64) |
| Literate | Household head at least primary educated=1, 0 otherwise | 0.80 (0.40) |
| Male head | Household head is male=1, 0 otherwise | 0.85 (0.36) |
| Wage Emp | Household head is employed regular wage/salary=1, 0 otherwise | 0.29 (0.45) |
| Self Emp | Household head is self-employed in agriculture/non-agriculture=1, 0 otherwise | 0.34 (0.47) |
| Casulab | Household head is casual labour in agriculture/non-agriculture=1, 0 otherwise | 0.29 (0.26) |
| Oth Emp | Household head is in other work=1, 0 otherwise | 0.09 (0,28) |
| BC | Household belongs to backward community=1, 0 otherwise | 0.78 (0.41) |
| SC/ST | Household belongs to SC/ST community=1, 0 otherwise | 0.19 (0.39) |
| Oth Com | Household belongs to other community=1, 0 otherwise | 0.08 (0.17) |
| North coast | Household lives in northern coastal region=1, 0 otherwise | 0.30 (0.46) |
| Coast | Household lives in other coastal region=1, 0 otherwise | 0.19 (0.39) |
| South | Household lives in southern region=1, 0 otherwise | 0.27 (0.44) |
| Inland | Household lives in inland region=1, 0 otherwise | 0.25 (0.43) |
| Age 14 | Household has children below 14 years age=1, 0 otherwise | 0.49 (0.50) |
| Age 15-60 | Household has adults between ages 15 and 60 years=1, 0 otherwise | 0.95 (0.22) |
| Age 60+ | Household has elders above 60 years age=1, 0 otherwise | 0.31 (0.47) |
| N | No. of observations | 5442 |

**Note:** Standard deviations in parentheses.

The Table 15.2 indicates that approximately 36 percent of households spend Rs. 1000 to 5000 on durable goods while 28 percent of households spend less than Rs. 500 on durable goods. About 10 percent of the households spend Rs. 50001 to Rs. 100000 on durable goods whereas only 0.86 percent of the households spend more than Rs.100000 on durable goods.

**Table 15.2: Distribution of Households by Expenditure on Durable Goods Consumption**

| *Expenditure* | *Percentage of households* | *Expenditure* | *Percentage of households* |
|---|---|---|---|
| Below 500 | 27.84 | Rs. 10001-50000 | 9.67 |
| Rs. 501-1000 | 16.96 | Rs. 50001-100000 | 2.32 |
| Rs. 1001-5000 | 35.78 | Above Rs. 100000 | 0.86 |
| Rs. 5001-10000 | 6.58 | | |

The Figure 15.1 shows the distribution of durable goods consumption across households in Tamil Nadu. Nearly 19 percent of household expenditure is on residential buildings and land, 16 percent on jewellery, 14 percent on furniture, 11 percent for recreation, and 10 percent on cookery. The household expenditure on residential purposes is high compared to the other durable goods expenditure in Tamil Nadu. Among the social groups, about 80 percent of BC community households spend on durable goods and 83 percent of literate households spend on durable goods.

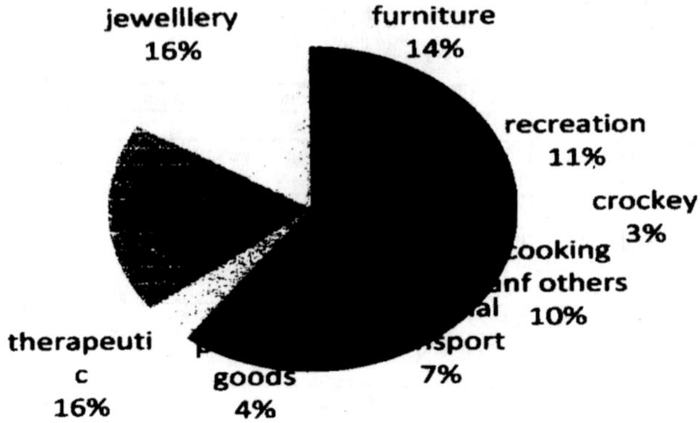


*Figure 15.1: Distribution of Household Expenditure on Durable Goods.*

The causal effects of the determinants of household expenditure on durable goods consumption are usually estimated by the OLS regression analysis. However, the OLS estimates are the same for throughout the distribution of household durable goods expenditure. Therefore, the quantile regression model is applied to identify the differentials effects at the 25th, 50th and 75th quantiles of the distribution of household consumption expenditure on durable goods. The Table 15.3 presents the estimated results for both OLS and quantile regression models. As can be observed the quantile regression model has relatively much better and significant coefficients estimates compared to the OLS model.

**Table 15.3: OLS and QR Estimates of Household Consumption Expenditure on Durable Goods Dependent variable: ln(HDGExp)**

| *Variable* | *OLS* | *25th quantile* | *50th quantile* | *75th quantile* |
|---|---|---|---|---|
| ln(MPCE) | 1.49* (3.36) | 1.25* (3.94) | 1.36* (3.38) | 1.74* (4.46) |
| HHSize | -0.12* (7.50) | -0.10* (4.86) | -0.10* (5.64) | -0.14* (6.59) |
| Literate | 0.09 (1.59) | 0.07 (0.88) | 0.14** (2.27) | 0.20** (2.40) |
| Malehead | 0.03 (0.58) | 0.17*** (1.87) | 0.03 (0.46) | -0.01 (0.12) |
| WageEmp | 0.15** (2.03) | 0.05 (0.63) | -0.05 (0.91) | 0.14*** (1.72) |
| SelfEmp | 0.21* (3.91) | 0.23* (3.29) | 0.19* (3.56) | 0.14*** (1.92) |
| Casulab | 0.008 (0.08) | -0.01 (0.09) | 0.05 (0.91) | 0.16 (1.11) |
| BC | 0.28* (2.59) | 0.25* (2.78) | 0.29* (2.85) | 0.33* (2.91) |
| SC/ST | -0.04 (0.80) | -0.05 (0.67) | -0.07 (1.18) | -0.07 (0.87) |
| Age15-60 | -0.21 (1.55) | -0.15 (0.84) | -0.32** (2.33) | -0.20 (1.07) |
| Age60+ | 0.14* (2.98) | 0.16* (2.60) | 0.10** (1.98) | 0.17** (2.53) |
| Coast | 0.59* (9.76) | 0.37* (4.72) | 0.60* (9.63) | 0.78* (9.27) |
| South | 0.72* (3.39) | 0.62* (4.81) | 0.86* (5.48) | 0.89* (7.72) |
| Inland | 0.51* (9.10) | 0.56* (7.68) | 0.59* (8.35) | 0.68* (7.46) |
| Constant | -9.74* (6.45) | -8.11* (3.60) | -8.36* (7.85) | -11.71* (8.35) |
| $R^2$/Pseudo $R^2$ | 0.25 | 0.14 | 0.15 | 0.15 |

**Note:** Absolute t-values in parentheses * Significant at 1 percent level ** Significant at 5 percent level *** Significant at 10 percent level.

In the OLS estimates, one percent increase in income will significantly increase the household consumption expenditure on durable goods by 1.49 percent. In quantile regression estimates, income is positively associated with the consumption of durable goods. All the coefficients of income are positive and statistically significant at 1 percent level. In the 25th quantile, increase in income increases durable goods consumption expenditure by 1.25 percent, by 1.26 percent in 50th quantile and by 1.75 percent in the 75th quantile. Thus, the income effect on durable goods consumption is not the same across the distribution of household consumption expenditure on durable goods and it increases with the increase in household income. In fact, the income effect increases by 0.50 percent at the upper quantile of expenditure distribution. With regard to employment, the self-employed households like agricultural and business households spend more on the consumption of durable goods. The coefficient estimates are positive and statistically significant both in the OLS and quantile estimates. However, neither wage employed nor casual labour households spend much on durable goods consumption. The coefficient of wage employment at the 50th quantile is in fact negative and insignificant. The other wage employment coefficients are weak and none of the casual labour coefficients are significant.

The negative effect of household size is higher at the upper quantile. The male head of the household has a positive effect on durable goods consumption expenditure at the 25th quantile only. In the quantile regression estimates literacy has positive effect on the consumption of durable goods. The coefficients of literacy are statistically significant at the upper quantiles. Households with elders also spend significant amount on durable goods consumption relative to households with young children. Significantly, the household expenditure on durable goods consumption decreases with more adults in the household. The age group 15-60 has consistently negative effect on durable goods expenditure at all the quantiles. In both OLS and quantile estimates, households belonging to backward community spend more on durable goods compared to other communities. The coefficient estimates are consistently positive and statistically significant. Further, households at the upper quantiles spend more on durable goods relative to households in the lower quantiles. For households belonging to the SC/ST community, the coefficient estimates are negative but statistically insignificant. The backward class community is more status concerned, therefore incur more on durable goods consumption. An increase in household size significantly decreases household consumption expenditure on durable goods. Households in the interior regions of Tamil Nadu incur significant expenditure on durable goods consumption. The positive effect is statistically significant at all quantile of the durable goods expenditure distribution. In 25th quantile, inland household expenditure on durable goods consumption is higher by 0.57, by 0.59 in 50th quantile and by 0.68 units in the upper quantile compared to northern coastal region households. The effect of other regions is also positive and statistically significant and the effect increases with higher quantiles in the distribution.

The southern region household expenditure on durable goods is higher than all other regions both in the OLS and quantile estimates.

The household consumption expenditure on durable goods by literacy and social groups are presented in Tables 15.4 and 15.5 respectively. The estimates OLS and quantile regression show more or less the same effects of the variables as in the general estimates. The effect of income is significantly positive in all estimates and the quantile regression estimates show an increasing effect of income over regression quantiles. In households with literacy, none of the coefficients of wage/salary employment is significant, whereas wage employment has some effects at the bottom quantile of the household durable goods expenditure. While self-employment has a significant effect at the upper end of the expenditure distribution of the illiterate households, the effect is strong and significant at the lower end of the durable goods expenditure. The coefficients of casual labour are positive and significant among the illiterate households, in illiterate households the effect is insignificantly negative. In illiterate households, community background has no significant effect on household expenditure on durable goods, but the literate backward community spends significantly positively on durable goods consumption in Tamil Nadu. Similarly, the presence of elders contributes to increased expenditure on durable goods in literate households, but in illiterate households there is no significant effect of aged persons.

Among the social groups, income has a positive and significant effect on household expenditure on durable goods and the effects are strong in the upper quantiles of the expenditure distribution. The effect of household size is significantly negative in all quantiles among the SC/ST and backward class communities but has no significant effect in other communities. Male headship has some effect in other communities at the lower part of the expenditure distribution while it has no effect in both SC/ST and backward class communities. Similarly, the employment status has no significant effect on durable goods consumption expenditure in SC/ST and other communities, in backward class community households salary/wage employment and self-employment have positive and significant effect in all quantile and OLS estimates. Interestingly, literacy has significant and positive effect on durable goods consumption in the backward class community households while education has no role in the consumption of durable goods either in SC/ST or other community households. The presence of elders significantly positively contributes to durable goods expenditure in only the backward class community households and has no significant effect in other community households.

Irrespective of region of residence, both in the literate and illiterate households and among the social groups, generally all households in Tamil Nadu incur substantial expenditure on durable goods and it increases with the increase in quantiles of the expenditure distribution. Overall, there is some difference between the literate and illiterate households and among the social groups in the expenditure on durable goods.

**Table 15.4: OLS and QR Estimates of Household Consumption Expenditure on Durable Goods by Literacy Dependent variable: ln(HDGExp)**

| *Variable* | *Literate households* | | | |
|---|---|---|---|---|
| | *OLS* | *25th quantile* | *50th quantile* | *75th quantile* |
| ln(MPCE) | 1.50* (3.79) | 1.27* (2.56) | 1.37* (4.14) | 1.83* (6.19) |
| HHSize | -0.13* (7.28) | -0.11* (5.09) | -0.12* (6.72) | -0.17* (6.50) |
| Malehead | 0.07 (0.85) | 0.25** (2.34) | 0.11 (1.25) | -0.17 (1.42) |
| WageEmp | 0.08 (1.18) | 0.03 (0.32) | 0.008 (0.12) | 0.04 (0.45) |
| SelfEmp | 0.19* (3.09) | 0.23** (2.23) | 0.19* (2.93) | 0.07 (0.78) |
| Casulab | -0.08 (0.76) | -0.08 (0.55) | -0.05 (0.49) | -0.13 (0.80) |
| BC | 0.30* (2.47) | 0.33** (2.23) | 0.29** (2.35) | 0.21 (1.27) |
| SC/ST | -0.07 (1.18) | -0.06 (0.81) | -0.06 (0.85) | -0.09 (0.98) |
| Age15-60 | -0.21 (1.25) | -0.20 (0.93) | -0.23 (1.32) | -0.17 (0.70) |
| Age60+ | 0.17* (3.06) | 0.20* (2.87) | 0.15* (2.73) | 0.19** (2.50) |
| Coast | 0.58* (8.74) | 0.38* (4.57) | 0.59* (8.56) | 0.75* (7.88) |
| South | 0.71* (7.34) | 0.61* (8.11) | 0.85* (6.74) | 0.84* (9.90) |
| Inland | 0.53* (8.56) | 0.58* (7.33) | 0.60* (9.20) | 0.60* (6.70) |
| Constant | -9.68* (8.02) | -8.20* (6.05) | -8.39* (5.91) | -12.24* (5.91) |
| $R^2$/Pseudo $R^2$ | 0.23 | 0.13 | 0.13 | 0.15 |
| N | 4498 | | | |

| *Variable* | *Illiterate households* | | | |
|---|---|---|---|---|
| | *OLS* | *25th quantile* | *50th quantile* | *75th quantile* |
| ln(MPCE) | 1.48* (4.49) | 1.21* (7.73) | 1.44* (8.74) | 1.62* (7.65) |
| HHSize | -0.07** (2.28) | -0.06 (1.28) | -0.06*** (1.76) | -0.07 (1.65) |
| Malehead | -0.02 (0.25) | 0.04 (0.26) | 0.06(0.54) | -0.002 (0.02) |
| WageEmp | 0.32* (2.29) | 0.41*** (1.92) | 0.20 (1.37) | 0.16 (0.90) |
| SelfEmp | 0.20*** (1.81) | 0.07 (0.46) | 0.11 (1.03) | 0.23*** (1.73) |
| Casulab | -0.48** (2.07) | 0.23 (0.65) | 0.60** (2.50) | 0.71** (2.40) |
| BC | -0.23 (0.56) | -0.005 (0.01) | -0.36 (0.85) | -0.18 (0.35) |
| SC/ST | 0.09 (0.89) | 0.02 (0.15) | -0.008 (0.09) | 0.04 (0.31) |
| Age15-60 | -0.11 (0.49) | -0.25 (0.71) | -0.28 (1.19) | -0.11 (0.39) |
| Age60+ | 0.07 (0.74) | 0.16 (1.06) | -0.004 (0.04) | 0.08 (0.65) |
| Coast | 0.60* (4.21) | 0.38*** (1.73) | 0.50* (3.41) | 0.63* (3.51) |
| South | 0.83* (6.16) | 0.92* (4.50) | 0.98* (7.15) | 0.91* (5.40) |
| Inland | 0.39* (3.18) | 0.35*** (1.89) | 0.53* (4.31) | 0.53* (3.48) |
| Constant | -7.63* (4.85) | -7.63* (4.85) | -9.27* (8.84) | -10.87* (8.45) |
| $R^2$/Pseudo $R^2$ | 0.30 | 0.14 | 0.19 | 0.22 |
| N | 944 | | | |

**Note:** Absolute t-values in parentheses. * Significant at 1 percent level ** Significant at 5 percent level *** Significant at 10 percent level.

**Table 15.5: OLS and QR Estimates of Household Consumption Expenditure on Durable Goods by Social Groups Dependent variable: ln(HDGExp)**

| *Variable* | *SC/ST households* | | | |
|---|---|---|---|---|
| | *OLS* | *25th quantile* | *50th quantile* | *75th quantile* |
| ln(MPCE) | 1.55* (5.35) | 1.26* (6.23) | 1.55* (4.07) | 1.68* (6.34) |
| HHSize | -0.13* (4.04) | -0.14* (3.75) | -0.15* (4.19) | -0.09*** (1.85) |
| Malehead | 0.05 (0.35) | 0.12 (0.69) | 0.02 (0.09) | -0.09 (0.40) |

*(Contd...)*

| | | | | |
|---|---|---|---|---|
| WageEmp | -0.03 (0.20) | 0.09 (0.69) | 0.16 (1.34) | 0.05 (0.29) |
| SelfEmp | 0.09 (0.76) | 0.22*** (1.67) | -0.02 (0.11) | 0.18 (1.02) |
| Casulab | -0.26 (0.82) | -0.31 (0.89) | -0.25 (0.73) | -0.17 (0.36) |
| Literate | -0.008 (0.07) | 0.01 (0.10) | 0.11 (0.89) | 0.18 (1.06) |
| Age15-60 | -0.31 (0.76) | -0.52 (1.15) | -0.24 (0.54) | -0.75 (1.24) |
| Age60+ | 0.12 (1.08) | 0.13 (1.04) | 0.12 (0.99) | 0.19 (1.14) |
| Coast | 0.43* (3.31) | 0.19 (1.28) | 0.44* (3.11) | 0.61* (3.16) |
| South | 0.73* (5.97) | 0.83* (6.10) | 0.89* (6.73) | 0.91* (5.01) |
| Inland | 0.42* (3.48) | 0.47* (3.50) | 0.63* (4.81) | 0.59* (3.34) |
| Constant | -10.11* (9.40) | -7.63* (6.38) | -10.20* (4.73) | -10.96* (6.93) |
| $R^2$/Pseudo $R^2$ | 0.26 | 0.15 | 0.17 | 0.17 |
| N | 935 | | | |

| ***Variable*** | ***Backward community households*** | | | |
|---|---|---|---|---|
| | ***OLS*** | ***25$^{th}$ quantile*** | ***50$^{th}$ quantile*** | ***75$^{th}$ quantile*** |
| ln(MPCE) | 1.47* (9.35) | 1.22* (8.14) | 1.34* (5.74) | 1.76* (4.97) |
| HHSize | -0.11* (6.35) | -0.09* (3.54) | -0.08* (4.39) | -0.15* (6.04) |
| Malehead | -0.01 (0.17) | 0.14 (1.34) | 0.02 (0.31) | -0.12 (1.06) |
| WageEmp | 0.17** (2.50) | 0.07 (0.80) | 0.12*** (1.76) | 0.17*** (1.86) |
| SelfEmp | 0.25* (4.14) | 0.23* (2.83) | 0.25* (3.93) | 0.15*** (1.76) |
| Casulab | 0.01 (0.11) | -0.01 (0.07) | 0.12 (1.08) | 0.14 (0.89) |
| Literate | 0.13** (1.98) | 0.12 (1.29) | 0.13*** (1.78) | 0.21** (2.11) |
| Age15-60 | -0.13 (0.91) | -0.14 (0.66) | -0.21 (1.35) | -0.13 (0.62) |
| Age60+ | 0.14* (2.62) | 0.17** (2.39) | 0.09*** (1.73) | 0.15** (1.99) |
| Coast | 0.59* (8.66) | 0.37* (3.99) | 0.58* (8.10) | 0.75* (7.71) |
| South | 0.71* (9.49) | 0.55* (6.57) | 0.81* (8.59) | 0.86* (9.87) |
| Inland | 0.50* (7.97) | 0.56* (6.50) | 0.55* (8.32) | 0.54* (6.06) |
| Constant | -9.67* (8.83) | -7.87* (8.25) | -8.21* (7.25) | -11.89* (6.26) |
| $R^2$/Pseudo $R^2$ | 0.25 | 0.12 | 0.15 | 0.16 |
| N | 4323 | | | |

| ***Variable*** | ***Other community households*** | | | |
|---|---|---|---|---|
| | ***OLS*** | ***25$^{th}$ quantile*** | ***50$^{th}$ quantile*** | ***75$^{th}$ quantile*** |
| ln(MPCE) | 1.71* (7.36) | 1.82* (8.05) | 1.52* (4.96) | 1.76* (4.51) |
| HHSize | -0.10 (1.01) | -0.13 (1.39) | -0.009 (0.07) | -0.09 (0.57) |
| Malehead | 1.15* (2.68) | 1.36* (3.25) | 0.46 (0.81) | 0.53 (0.73) |
| WageEmp | 0.29 (0.61) | 0.71 (1.55) | 0.63 (1.01) | 0.53 (0.67) |
| SelfEmp | -0.36 (0.77) | 0.48 (1.07) | 0.72 (1.19) | 0.74 (0.96) |
| Casulab | 0.32 (0.52) | -0.03 (0.06) | -0.15 (0.18) | -0.36 (0.35) |
| Literate | 0.04 (0.07) | -0.30 (0.56) | 0.42 (0.56) | 0.52 (0.58) |
| Age15-60 | -0.91 (1.54) | -1.00*** (1.74) | -0.54 (1.21) | -0.55 (0.55) |
| Age60+ | 0.22 (2.81) | -0.05 (0.23) | -0.05 (0.22) | 0.36 (0.79) |
| Coast | 1.09* (2.81) | 1.47* (3.90) | 0.79 (1.55) | 1.60** (2.46) |
| South | 1.17* (3.72) | 1.44* (4.69) | 1.04* (2.50) | 1.02*** (1.93) |
| Inland | 0.80** (2.54) | 1.01* (3.28) | 0.96** (2.30) | 1.05** (1.99) |
| Constant | -12.85* (4.59) | -14.54* (5.81) | -1029* (3.02) | -12.57* (2.90) |
| $R^2$/Pseudo $R^2$ | 0.31 | 0.24 | 0.19 | 0.20 |
| N | 4323 | | | |

**Note:** Absolute t-values in parentheses. * Significant at 1 percent level ** Significant at 5 percent level *** Significant at 10 percent level.

## 15.5 Conclusion

The objective of this paper is to study is to examine the pattern of household expenditure on durable goods and to analyse the distributional effects of the determinants of durable goods expenditure of households in Tamil Nadu using the 68th round (July 2011 - June 2012) of NSSO data. The literate households have high consumption expenditure on durable goods compared to illiterate households. The household consumption expenditure on durable goods is analysed by quantile regression. The ordinary least square estimation explains the average effects of the explanatory variable, while the quantile regression explains the distribution effects in the different quantiles. The study finds a positive relation between income and durable goods expenditure across all households and such expenditure increases at higher quantiles. The effect of family size is on durable goods expenditure is negative. There also exist significant differences across regions and community. The backward community households spend significantly more on durable goods than the SC/ST households. The consumption expenditure on durable goods of the coastal and southern districts households is more compared to the other regions. The households with a regular salary earner and business or self-employment consume more durable goods compared to the other households. The households with male head spent more of durable goods compared to the female headed households. Households with elders spend more on durable goods. The quantile regression estimates show the distributional effects of consumption expenditure on durable goods – most of the variables in the upper quantile show higher effects on household consumption on durable goods. The effects of variables are increasing from the lower quantile to the upper quantile in case of all major determinants of consumer expenditure on durable goods.

# Section - IV
# Panel Data Econometrics

# 16

# Fiscal Management and Government Expenditure: Panel Estimation of the Relationship between Fiscal Deficit, Interest Payment, Social Expenditure and Capital Outlay


## Abstract

*The Fiscal Responsibility and Budget Management (FRBM) Act, 2003 imposes fiscal discipline on governments by limiting the fiscal deficit to a manageable level of 3 percent of the GDP. With fiscal consolidation, reduction in fiscal deficit reduces interest payment and debt servicing and permits governments to prioritise spending on capital expenditure or on social sector expenditure. By reducing the revenue deficit, falling interest payment further increases the scope of capital outlay. This paper empirically analyses the causal relationship between fiscal deficit, interest payment, social sector expenditure and capital outlay, using panel data on state finances of 17 states of India for 12 years from 2004-2016. The panel data analysis, based on Johansen cointegration test, Granger causality test and error correction mechanism shows that there is long-run relationship between gross fiscal deficit, capital outlay and interest payment. And there is long-run causality running from interest payment to capital outlay. Though there is short-run causality, there is no long-run causality running from aggregate social sector expenditure to gross fiscal deficit. As the empirical results suggest many state governments have increased their capital expenditure with the reduction in gross fiscal deficit and interest payment.*



**Key words:** *Fiscal deficit, interest payment, government expenditure, causality, cointegration, error correction*

## 16.1 Introduction

The Fiscal Responsibility and Budget Management (FRBM) Act was enacted in 2003 by the Parliament of India to institutionalise discipline India's finances, reduce fiscal deficit, improve macroeconomic management, fiscal sustainability, management of public funds, ultimately moving towards a balanced budget. The immediate and the principal aim was to eliminate revenue deficit of the country and bring down the fiscal deficit to a manageable level of 3 percent of the GDP by March 2008. However, due to the 2007 international financial crisis, the deadline for the implementation of the targets in the Act was initially postponed and subsequently suspended in 2009. The FRBM Act provides a legal institutional framework for fiscal consolidation. It is now mandatory for the central government to take measures to reduce fiscal deficit, to eliminate revenue deficit and to generate revenue surplus. The FRBM Act binds the government to hold to the path of fiscal consolidation. The government can move away from the path of fiscal consolidation only in case of natural calamity, national security and other exceptional grounds which the central government may specify.

Subsequently, the state governments have adopted a rule-based framework for fiscal correction and consolidation through progressive enactment of Fiscal Responsibility Legislation (FRL). Karnataka was the first to enact the FRL in September 2002 followed by Kerala and Tamil Nadu in 2003, and Punjab in 2004. Subsequently, twenty-two more states enacted the FRLs. The fiscal position of the state governments broadly followed the pattern witnessed for the central government. There has been a severe fiscal stress in the finances of state governments since the mid-eighties. The fiscal stress emanated from inadequacy of receipts in meeting the expenditure requirements, low and declining buoyancy in tax and non-tax receipts, and constraints on internal resource mobilisation due to losses incurred by state owned public sector undertakings. The deceleration in resource transfer from the centre to states also contributed to the worsening of state finances. The enactment of FRLs has provided impetus to the process of attaining fiscal sustainability as reduction in key deficit indicators viz. revenue deficit (RD) and gross fiscal deficit (GFD). Apart from fiscal sustainability, meeting the targets set in FRLs is crucial not only for maintaining credibility in budgetary operations but also for ensuring prudent debt management and greater transparency.

Following the FRBM and FRL acts, in the process of fiscal corrections, there has been a rise in total expenditure involving both revenue and capital components accompanied by some rise in revenue receipts. Significantly, 13 out of 17 non-special category states have been successful in reducing the proportion of their total expenditure to GSDP after implementation of FRBM. Before the implementation of FRBM, the average total expenditure per GSDP was 17.8 percent and post FRBM the average total expenditure to GSDP was 17.1. Goa, Maharashtra, Haryana, Rajasthan and Jharkhand have experienced an expenditure reduction of two percentage points and above, which is noteworthy since the overall average expenditure GSDP ratio of the 17 states underwent a reduction of about one percentage point between the two points (RBI, 2016). In terms of expenditure composition, 12 states have been able to curtail their revenue expenditure-GSDP ratio in the post FRBM period. While the overall average has reduced by 1 percentage point in the post-FRBM period, four states (Goa, Maharashtra, Haryana, and Gujarat) have been successful in reducing their revenue expenditure-GSDP ratio by 2 percentage points or more. The states, in general, have raised the average capital outlay-GSDP ratio by 0.6 percentage point post-FRBM. Six states (Chhattisgarh, Madhya Pradesh, Uttar Pradesh, Bihar, Karnataka and Tamil Nadu) out-performed the average by improving this ratio by more than 1 percentage point. Overall, 13 states have improved their capital outlay-GSDP ratios. At the overall level, there has been only marginal improvement in the average development expenditure-GSDP ratio. Although no high-income state recorded an improvement in the post-FRBM period, seven states from the low-income group have improved the average development expenditure-GSDP ratio. In contrast, there has been an appreciable decline in the average non-developmental expenditure-GSDP ratio post-FRBM, with majority of states achieving a reduction in the range of 0.4-3.9 points (RBI, 2016). After the implementation of FRBM, there has been an increase in the number of occasions on which various states have recorded revenue balance or surplus.

The Figure 16.1 shows the average gross fiscal deficit (GFD) of the 11 non-special category states over time after the FRBM Act, viz. Andhra Pradesh, Chhattisgarh, Goa, Gujarat, Jharkhand, Karnataka, Madhya Pradesh,

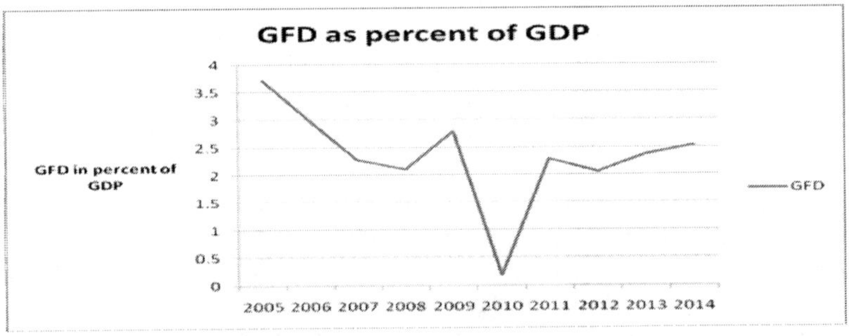


***Figure 16.1: Average GFD of 17 Non-Special Category States in India***

Maharashtra, Orissa, Uttar Pradesh, Rajasthan, Bihar, Haryana, Kerala, Punjab, Tamil Nadu and West Bengal. While the GFD continuously declined since 2005, around 2010 there has been a hike in GFD because of the economic depression and it goes on increasing since then. The Figure 16.2 shows that the average interest payment in these states has been declining, while the capital outlay has been increasing. Thus, after the introduction of FRBM Act, there is

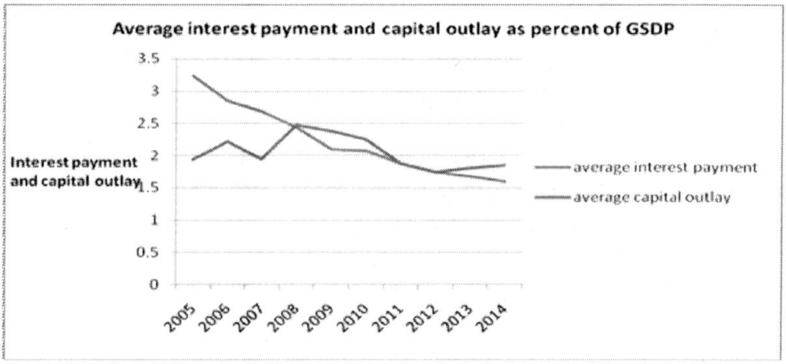


*Figure 16.2: Capital Outlay and Interest Payment in 11 Non-Special Category States*

a significant relationship between the changes in interest payment and capital outlay. Among the 17 non-special category states, 11 states, viz. Andhra Pradesh, Chhattisgarh, Goa, Gujarat, Jharkhand, Karnataka, Madhya Pradesh, Maharashtra, Orissa, Uttar Pradesh and Rajasthan possesses this relationship between the interest payment and capital outlay. The other 6 states, viz. Bihar, Haryana, Kerala, Punjab, Tamil Nadu and West Bengal, has higher interest payment and higher capital outlay.

Thus, reduction in fiscal deficit favours further reduction in future interest payment. Consequently, with a given level of revenue, reduction in interest payment releases funds for other public expenditures. Hence, the falling interest payment may create two immediate effects: (i) increases the scope for social sector expenditure in the revenue account, and (ii) by reducing revenue deficit, increases the scope of capital outlay, for a given amount of borrowing. Thus, after the implementation of FRBM Act, fiscal consolidation at the state level improves not only the quantity, but also the quality of expenditure by the states. For sustainable long-term growth, the revenue account needs to be balanced while borrowed funds should only be used for capital expenditure in order to maintain intergenerational equity. Moreover, lower deficits lead to reduced borrowings which, in turn, would ease interest burden. Thus, there exists causal relationship between fiscal deficit, interest payment and debt servicing, social sector expenditure and capital outlay. However, the direction of causality is not clear as some states show inverse and some positive relation between interest payment and capital outlay. Thus, the main objective of this paper is to empirically analyse the causality between fiscal deficit, interest payment, social sector expenditure and capital outlay, using data on state finances and panel data methodology.

## 16.2 Data and Methodology

The database used in this study is an unbalanced panel data for 17 states of India for 12 years from 2004-2016, collected from 'State Finances: A Study of Budgets' published annually by the RBI with regard to fiscal position of state governments. The 17 states are Andhra Pradesh, Bihar, Chhattisgarh, Goa, Gujarat, Haryana, Jharkhand, Karnataka, Kerala, Madhya Pradesh, Maharashtra, Odisha, Punjab, Rajasthan, Tamil Nadu, Uttar Pradesh, and West Bengal. The data contains not only the statements of GFD, revenue expenditure and capital expenditure of the states, but also it includes data on the policy initiatives of state governments, government of India and the RBI. The consolidated fiscal position of state governments, an assessment of state-wise fiscal performance, outstanding liabilities, market borrowings and contingent liabilities of state governments, fiscal transfers to the state governments and issues and perspectives in the path of fiscal adjustment, expenditure management, fiscal transparency and budget integrity, debt sustainability and infrastructural financing. The variables considered for the causality analysis are gross fiscal deficit, interest payment, capital outlay and aggregate social sector expenditure.

Gross fiscal deficit is calculating by taking the difference between total revenue and total expenditure of the governments. While calculating the total revenue, borrowing is not included. On one hand, interest payment by states, as a borrower, represents the rate charged on lending funds. On the other hand, as an investor, interest payments represents income earned on cash accounts or fixed and variable rate securities. Capital outlay is calculated by adding development expenditure and rural development expenditure. Aggregate social sector expenditure is calculated by adding all the expenditure incurred by the government for development of the social sectors. They include education, sports, art, culture, medical and public health, family welfare, water supply and sanitation, housing, urban development, welfare of scheduled castes scheduled tribes and other backward classes, labour and labour welfare, social security and welfare, nutrition, relief on account of natural calamities, others. The panel unit is state and time variable is year, and natural log of all the variables are used to avoid the surplus value of GFD in some states. As the study focuses on the time series of GFD and its causality between interest payment and debt servicing, capital outlay and aggregate social sector expenditure, panel unit root test, Johansen cointegration test, vector error correction model and granger causality test are used in the empirical analysis.

## Stationarity Test

Stationarity of a time series is an important phenomenon because it can influence its behaviour. Applying OLS to a non-stationery random process (integrated) of variables will only generate a spurious regression. Stationarity is the statistical characteristics of a series such as its mean and variance are constant over time. If both are constant over time, then the series is said to be a stationery process, otherwise, non-stationery process. If a series is stationery without any differencing it is designated as integrated of order 0, I (1). On the other hand, a series that has stationery at first difference is designated I (1). For the stationarity test, the conventional test is the Dicky-Fuller unit root test of the following,

$$y_{it} = \alpha_i + \rho_i y_{it-1} + e_{it} \tag{16.1}$$

The null hypothesis is that each series in the data contains a unit root, i.e. $H_0$: $\rho_i = 0$ for all $i$ and alternative hypothesis is that it does not have a unit root, i.e. $H_1 \neq 0$.

Panel unit root tests are more powerful (less likely to commit a Type II error) than unit root tests applied to individual series because the information in the time series is enhanced by that contained in the cross-section data. In addition, in contrast to individual unit root tests which have complicated limiting distributions, panel unit root tests lead to statistics with a normal distribution in the limit. With the exception of the IPS test (Im, Pesaran and Shin (2003), Levin, Lin and Chu (2002), Breitung (2000) and Hadri (2000) tests assume that there is a common (identical) unit root process across the relevant cross-sections. The LLC and Breitung tests employ a null hypothesis of a unit root using the following Augmented Dickey Fuller (ADF) specification,

$$\Delta y_{it} = \alpha y_{it-1} + \sum \beta_{ij} \Delta y_{it-j} + \delta x_{it} + u_{it} \tag{16.2}$$

where $y_{it}$ refers to the pooled variable, $X_{it}$ represents exogenous variables in the model such as country fixed effects and individual time trends, and uit refers to the error terms which are assumed to be mutually independent disturbances. It is also assumed that $\alpha = \rho - 1$ is identical across the three cross-sections, but the lag order for the difference terms across the 17 states are allowed to vary. By contrast, the less restrictive IPS test (and other widely used tests such as the ADF Fisher Chi-square) estimates a separate ADF regression for each of the 17 cross-sections to allow for individual unit root processes; i.e. $\rho_i$ may vary across cross-sections.

## Cointegration Test

In case of non-stationery data, it is quite possible that there is a linear combination of integrated variables that is stationery; such variables are said to be cointegrated. The cointegration test procedure uses two tests to determine the number of cointegrating vectors: the maximum Eigen value test and Trace test. The maximum Eigen value statistics tests the null hypothesis of $r$ cointegrating relations against the alternative of r+1 cointegrating relations for $r$=0, 1, 2….$n$-1. This test statistics are computed as,

$$LR_{max}(r/n+1) = -T^* \log (1-\hat{\lambda}) \tag{16.3}$$

where $\lambda$ is the Maximum Eigen value and T is the sample size. Trace statistic investigate the null hypothesis of $r$ cointegrating relations against the alternative of n cointegrating relations, here n is the number of variables in the system for $r$=0,1,2,.....,$n$-1. Its equation is computed according to the following formula,

$$LR_{tr}\ (r/n) = -\ T^{*}\sum_{i-r+1}^{n} log\ (1-\hat{\lambda}) \qquad (16.4)$$

In some cases, Trace and Maximum Eigen value statistics may yield different results and then in this case the result of trace test should be preferred. To determine whether a cointegrating relationship exists among the variables, the Pedroni (1999) methodology employs four panel statistics and three group panel statistics to test the null hypothesis of no cointegration against the alternative hypothesis of cointegration. In the case of panel statistics, the first-order autoregressive term is assumed to be the same across all the cross sections, while in the case of group panel statistics the parameter is allowed to vary over the cross sections. If the null is rejected in the panel case, then the variable GFD is cointegrated with all the variables. On the other hand, if the null is rejected in the group panel case, then there is at least one cointegration among the variables.

## Error Correction Model

The Error Correction Model (ECM) is a theoretically driven approach useful for estimating both short-term and long-term effects of a time series on another time series. The term error-correction relates to the fact that last-period's deviation from a long-run equilibrium, the error, influences its short-run dynamics. The ECMs directly estimate the speed at which a dependent variable returns to equilibrium after a change in another variable. If cointegration has been detected between series, then as there exists a long-term equilibrium relationship between them, the ECM is applied in order to evaluate the short-run properties of the grated series. The regression equations for ECM are,

$$\Delta y_t=\alpha_1 + \rho_1 e_1+\sum_{i-0}^{n} \beta_i \Delta y_{t-1} +\sum_{i-0}^{n} \delta_i \Delta x_{t-I} +\sum_{i-0}^{n} \gamma_i z_{t-i} \qquad (16.5)$$

$$\Delta x_t=\alpha_2 + \rho_2 e_{i-1}+\sum_{i-0}^{n} \beta_i\ y_{t-1} +\sum_{i-0}^{n} \delta_i \Delta x_{t-1} +\sum_{i-0}^{n} \gamma_i z_{t-i} \qquad (16.6)$$

In the Vector Error Correction Model (VECM), the cointegration rank shows the number of cointegrating vectors. For instance, a rank of two indicates that two linearly independent combinations of the non-stationary variables will be stationary. A negative and significant coefficient of the ECM indicates that any short-term fluctuations between the independent variables and the dependent variable will give rise to a stable long-rum relationship between the variables.

## Granger Causality Test

A general specification of the Granger-causality test can be expressed as,

$$y_t=\alpha_0+\alpha_1 y_{t-1}+........+ \alpha_i y_{t-I}+\beta_1 x_{t-1}+.........+\beta_i x_{t-I}+ v \qquad (16.7)$$

$$x_t=\alpha_0+\alpha_1 x_{t-1}+........+ \alpha_i x_{t-I} +\beta_1 y_{t-1}+.........+\beta_i y_{t-I}+ v \qquad (16.8)$$

In the model, the subscript denotes time periods and *v* is a white noise error. The constant parameter $\alpha_0$ represents the constant growth rate of the variables and thus the trend in the variables can be interpreted as general movements of cointegration between the variables and *y* that follows the unit root process. We can obtain two tests from the analysis: the first examines the null hypothesis that the *x* does not Granger-cause *y* and the second test examines the null hypothesis that *y* does not Granger-cause *x*. If we fail to reject the former null hypothesis and reject the latter, then we conclude that *x* changes are Granger-cause by a change in *y*. Unidirectional causality will occur between the two variables if either null hypothesis is rejected. Bidirectional causality exists if both null hypotheses are rejected and no causality exists, i.e. neither null hypothesis is rejected.

## 16.3 Empirical Analysis

The Table 16.1 presents the descriptive statistics of the variables used in the study. The dependent variable is gross fiscal deficit (LGFD), and the explanatory variables are total aggregate expenditure (LAGGEXP), total capital outlay (LCO), and the interest payment and debt servicing (LIP), all in natural log forms. It can be noted that the interest payment is almost equal to capital outlay and the gross fiscal deficit. The Table 16.2 presents the correlation matrix of the variables used in the study. The interest payment and gross fiscal deficit are highly correlated. And capital outlay and interest payments are also highly correlated. The least correlation is between interest payment and social sector expenditure.

**Table 16.1: Descriptive Statistics of the Variables in the Fiscal Management and Government Expenditure Analysis**

| *Variable* | *Description (Rs.crore per annum)* | *Mean* | *Std. dev.* |
|---|---|---|---|
| GFD | Gross fiscal deficit (total revenue-total expenditure) | 8648.68 | 7994.86 |
| AGGEXP | Aggregate social sector expenditure(addition of expenditures on education, sports, art, culture, medical and public health, family welfare, water supply and sanitation, housing, urban development, welfare of scheduled caste scheduled tribes and other backward classes, labour and labour welfare, social security and welfare, nutrition, relief on account of natural calamities, others and economic services) | 3979075 | 6076415 |
| CO | Total capital outlay(combined development expenditure and rural development expenditure) | 7610.57 | 7701.50 |
| IP | Interest payment and debt servicing (appropriation for reduction or avoidance of debt and interest payment and debt servicing) | 7600.05 | 6102.66 |
| LGFD | Log of gross fiscal deficit | 8.489598 | 1.411745 |
| LAGGEXP | Log of aggregate social sector expenditure | 15.88242 | 2.559419 |
| LCO | Log of capital outlay | 8.456322 | 1.111498 |
| LIP | Log of interest payment and debt servicing | 8.605580 | 0.931236 |

**Table 16.2: Correlation Matrix of Causal Variables**

| *Variable* | *LAGGEXP* | *LCO* | *LGFD* | *LIP* |
|---|---|---|---|---|
| LAGGEXP | 1.00 | - | - | - |
| LCO | 0.058(0.51) | 1.00 | - | - |
| LGFD | 0.295*(0.00) | 0.328*(0.00) | 1.00 | - |
| LIP | 0.235*(0.002) | 0.555*(0.00) | 0.645*(0.000) | 1.00 |

**Note:** p-values in parentheses. * Significant at 5 percent level (2 tailed).

## Unit Root Test

In order to investigate the stationarity of the variables LAGGEXP, LCO, LIP and LGFD, panel unit root tests (Levin Lin Chu, Breitung, Fisher Phillips Perron, Im, Peseran Shin, Fisher ADF) are applied. The null hypothesis is 'presence of unit root' (i.e. presence of non-stationarity) against the alternative hypothesis 'series is stationery'. It is clear from Table 10.3 that the null hypothesis of no unit root for all the time series are rejected at their first difference at 1 percent level of significance. All the variables have unit root in their level form, but at first difference the variables became stationery and integrated of same order, i.e. I (1).

## Cointegration Test

The cointegrating relationship across the variables is performed by Johansen (1991) cointegration test. The precondition for panel cointegration test is that the variables must be non-stationery at levels, but when all the variables are converted into first difference the variables become stationery. As shown in Table 16.3, all the variables are non-stationery at levels and when taken first difference they become stationery.

**Table 16.3: Unit Root Test for Stationarity**

| *Variable* | *Levin, Lin, Chu test (p values)* | | *ADF-Chi-square (p values)* | | *PP-Fisher Chi-square (p values)* | |
|---|---|---|---|---|---|---|
| | *level* | *1st difference* | *level* | *1st difference* | *level* | *1st difference* |
| LAGGEXP | 0.0416 | 0.0000 | 0.9335 | 0.0000 | 0.9549 | 0.0000 |
| LCO | 0.9367 | 0.0000 | 1.0000 | 0.0000 | 1.0000 | 0.0000 |
| LIP | 1.0000 | 0.0000 | 1.0000 | 0.0000 | 1.0000 | 0.0000 |
| LGFD | 0.9629 | 0.0000 | 1.0000 | 0.0000 | 1.0000 | 0.0000 |

Both the trace statistic and maximum Eigen statistics reject the null hypothesis of no cointegration at 0.05 level in all cases. As shown in Table 16.4, the Johansen methodology shows that there exist at most two cointegrating relationships among LGFD, LCO, LIP, and LAGGEXP. Hence, estimation of VECM model is required in this context. The presence of cointegration between variables suggests a long-run relationship among the variables under consideration. The long run relationship between LAGGEXP, LCO, and LIP for one cointegrating vector for 17 states for the period 2004-2016 is shown in Table 16.5.

**Table 16.4: Johansen-Fisher Panel Cointegration Test**

| *LGFD=f(LAGGEXP,LCO, LIP)* | | | | |
|---|---|---|---|---|
| *No of CEs* | *Trace statistics* | *0.05 critical value* | *Max–Eigen statistics* | *0.05 critical value* |
| None** | 432.1 | 47.85613 | 349.2 | 27.58434 |
| At most 1 | 176.9 | 29.79707 | 137.3 | 21.13162 |
| At most 2 | 109.2 | 15.49471 | 109.2 | 14.26460 |

**Note:** Trace and max Eigen statistics indicates 1 cointegrating equation at 5 percent level. ** Significant at 5 percent level.

**Table 16.5: VECM Estimates of Long Run Coefficients**

| *Independent variable* | *Dependent variable* | | |
|---|---|---|---|
| | *LGFD* | *LIP* | *LCO* |
| LAGGEXP | -0.046 (0.33) | - | - |
| LCO | - 0.431** (0.00) | 0.02** (0.04) | - |
| LIP | - 0.79** (0.00) | - | 0.40** (0.00) |
| R-square | 0.81 | 0.40 | 0.56 |

**Note:** p-values in parentheses. ** Significant at 5 percent level.

The results in Table 16.5 show that there exists long-run relationship between LGFD and LCO and LIP. The estimated long-run coefficients are interpreted in such a way that if the coefficient value is negative and the *p*-value is significant, then there exists long-run relationship among the variables. The coefficient value of LAGGEXP is negative but the p-value is 0.33 i.e. the p-value is insignificant, and hence the null hypothesis that there exists long-run relationship between LGFD and LAGCEXP is rejected. Even though there is budget deficit, the state governments would like to expend on social sectors. The results also show that there exists long-run relationship between capital outlay with interest payment, and there is long-run causality running from interest payment to capital outlay.

## Granger Causality Test - Wald Statistics

Granger causality is used to test the short-run causality among variables. The test statistics for Granger test should follow Chi-square distribution instead of F-distribution. With respect to the short-run causality between LGFD and LCO and LAGGEXP, the *p*-values are significant, as shown in Table 16.6. Therefore, the null hypothesis that there is no short-run causality running from independent variable to dependent variables is rejected, as the chi-square *p*-value for both lags are lower than 0.05. Hence, LCO jointly cause GFD. Likewise, the chi-square *p*-values for the independent variables aggregate social sector expenditure and interest payment are also lower than 0.05, and hence both the lags of these variables jointly cause GFD.

**Table 16.6: Granger Causality Test: Wald Statistics**

| *Variable* | *LGFD* | *LCO* | *LAGGEXP* | *LIP* |
|---|---|---|---|---|
| LGFD | - | 0.2536<br>C(12)=C(13)=0 | 0.0000<br>C(22)=C(23)=0 | 0.0514<br>C(32)=C(33)=0 |
| LCO | 0.0044**<br>C(4)=C(5)=0 | - | 0.0000<br>C(24)=C(25)=0 | 0.0649<br>C(34)=C(35)=0 |
| LAGGEXP | 0.0000*<br>C(6)=C(7)=0 | 0.0004*<br>C(16)=C(17)=0 | - | 0.4069<br>C(36)=C(37)=0 |
| LIP | 0.2006<br>C(8)=C(9)=0 | 0.3492<br>C(18)=C(19)=0 | 0.6090<br>C(28)=C(29)=0 | - |

**Note:** * Significant at 1 percent level ** Significant at 5 percent level.

## Vector Error Correction Model

The error correction mechanism tries to correct the disequilibrium between gross fiscal deficit and interest payment. As shown in Table 16.7, the current log of gross fiscal deficit only depends on the second log of interest payment. And it is not influenced by the one period lag of interest payment. Hence, the error correction of second lag is important than first lag. After error correction, 46 percent of the change in GFD variable is explained by second lag value of the interest payment. In the second error correction, log of capital outlay depends on log of interest payment. Current capital outlay depends on its own first and second lags as well as the first and second lags of the interest payment. After error correction, 55 percent of changes in the capital outlay are explained by change in interest payment. When C1, the error correction term, has negative coefficient and significant then there exists long-run causality from independent variable to dependent variable. In both the cointegrating equations, the C1 coefficient is negative and statistically significant at 1 percent level. This means that there would be a speed of adjustment towards long-run equilibrium.

**Table 16.7: VECM Estimates of Error Correction Model**

| Dependent Variable: Log(GFD) | | | | |
|---|---|---|---|---|
| D(LOG_GFD_) = C(1)*( LOG_GFD_(-1) - 1.05701719659*LOG_INTR_PAYMENT(-1) + 0.555847431289 ) + C(2)*D(LOG_GFD_(-1)) + C(3)*D(LOG_GFD_(-2)) + C(4)*D(LOG_INTR_PAYMENT(-1)) + C(5)*D(LOG_INTR_PAYMENT(-2)) + C(6) | | | | |
| | *Coefficient* | *Std. error* | *t-statistic* | *Probability* |
| (C1) | -0.781860 | 0.148556 | -5.263077 | 0.0000 |
| (C2) | -0.140645 | 0.123666 | -1.137299 | 0.2565 |
| (C3) | 0.011679 | 0.084059 | 0.138934 | 0.8896 |
| (C4) | 1.166086 | 0.909314 | 1.282380 | 0.2009 |
| (C5) | -1.177762 | 0.931022 | -1.265020 | 0.2070 |
| (C6) | 0.137682 | 0.156240 | 0.881216 | 0.3790 |
| (C7) | 0.042976 | 0.013492 | 3.185432 | 0.0016 |
| (C8) | -0.021597 | 0.011351 | -1.902587 | 0.0582 |
| (C9) | -0.001306 | 0.007777 | -0.167905 | 0.8668 |
| (C10) | 0.033366 | 0.083647 | 0.398891 | 0.6903 |

*(Contd...)*

| | | | | |
|---|---|---|---|---|
| (C11) | -0.166504 | 0.086227 | -1.931008 | 0.0546 |
| (C12) | 0.117220 | 0.014570 | 8.045449 | 0.0000 |
| R-square | 0.463259 | | | |
| Adjusted R-squire | 0.441616 | | | |
| S.E of regression | 1.033747 | | | |
| Sum squared residual | 132.5106 | | | |
| Mean dependent variable | 0.129841 | | | |
| S.D dependent variable | 1.383401 | | | |
| Durbin-Watson statistics | 2.106256 | | | |

## Pairwise Granger Causality Test

Pairwise Granger causality test explains which variable Granger causes the other. The Table 16.8 shows that capital outlay Granger cause gross fiscal deficit and gross fiscal deficit does not Granger cause capital outlay. Hence, there exists unidirectional causality between gross fiscal deficit and capital outlay and in the case of interest payment and gross fiscal deficit also there exists unidirectional causality. But, in the case of capital outlay and aggregate social sector expenditure, a bidirectional causality exists. Last causality is bidirectional causality among interest payment and capital outlay.

**Table 16.8: Pairwise Granger Causality Test Results**

| *Null hypothesis* | *Observations* | *F-statistics* | *p-value* |
|---|---|---|---|
| LOG_AGG_ does not Granger Cause LOG_GFD_<br>LOG_GFD_ does not Granger Cause LOG_AGG | 150 | 72.41<br>28.01 | 0.00<br>0.00 |
| LOG_CO_ does not Granger Cause LOG_GFD_<br>LOG_GFD_ does not Granger Cause LOG_CO_ | 150 | 6.72**<br>0.08 | 0.0016<br>0.92 |
| LOG_IP_ does not Granger Cause LOG_GFD_<br>LOG_GFD_ does not Granger Cause LOG_IP_ | 150 | 15.08<br>6.33** | 0.00<br>0.002 |
| LOG_CO_ does not Granger Cause LOG_AGG_<br>LOG_AGG_ does not Granger Cause LOG_CO_ | 170 | 7.69**<br>0.84 | 0.0006<br>0.43 |
| LOG_IP_ does not Granger Cause LOG_AGG_<br>LOG_AGG_ does not Granger Cause LOG_IP_ | 170 | 19.79<br>4.09 | 0.00<br>0.018 |
| LOG_IP_does not Granger Cause LOG_CO_<br>LOG_CO_ does not Granger Cause LOG_IP_ | 170 | 3.33**<br>3.11** | 0.049<br>0.047 |

**Note:** **Significant at 5 percent level.

## 16.4 Conclusion

The Fiscal Responsibility and Budget Management (FRBM) Act, 2003 limits the fiscal deficit of both central and state governments with the objective to impose fiscal discipline. It necessitates that the fiscal management should be conducted in a disciplined manner i.e. government deficits or borrowings should be kept within reasonable limits. Therefore, governments should plan its expenditure in accordance with its revenues so that the borrowing should be within limits. Then it is the discretion of the governments to prioritise spending, whether on capital expenditure or on social sector expenditure. Reduction in fiscal deficit leads to further reduction in future interest payment and debt servicing, an expenditure in the revenue account. Consequently, with a given level of revenue, reduction in interest payment releases funds for other public expenditures. The falling interest payment may create two immediate effects (i) increases the scope for social sector expenditure in the revenue account, and (ii) by reducing revenue deficit, increases the scope of capital outlay, for a given amount of borrowing.

The empirical analysis of this paper shows that the test variables – LGFD, LIP, LCO and LAGGEXP – are non-stationery at levels and they are stationery at their first difference. Hence, the unit root tests are performed, and the cointegration analysis for those variables shows that there are at most two cointegrating equations, implying causality among the variables. With cointegration with each other, there should be some disequilibrium happening between those variables and some causality among the variables. As regards causality, there is no long-run causality running from aggregate social sector expenditure to gross fiscal deficit, but there is short-run causality running from social sector expenditure and gross fiscal deficit. There exists long-run relationship between gross fiscal deficit and capital outlay and interest payment. And the capital outlay and interest payment have long-run relationship with the gross fiscal deficit. And there is long-run causality running from interest payment to capital outlay.

As there is some disequilibrium happening in between those variables, the error correction model is applied for correcting that disequilibrium. For, a reduction in fiscal deficit means low rate of interest payment, and hence, the revenue deficit will reduce or revenue surplus will increase. It will allow the government to spend more for long term expenditure (capital expen diture). Hence, a reduction in interest payment will increase the capital outlay and there will be more spending for meeting long-term capital sector expenditure.

Thus, after the implementation of FRBMA each state government took measures for effective fiscal consolidation which has a positive effect on the reduction in gross fiscal deficit. This means governments have been able to reduce their GFD to certain extent and they could spend more on capital sector development. With the consequent reduced interest payment and debt servicing, the discretion of the state governments to spend either on social sector or on capital sector. As the data suggests many state governments have increased their capital expenditure as the GFD and interest payment and serving of debt reduced. However, in reality, the governments should also have to expend for social sector irrespective of surplus revenue or not, and hence the governments face deficit budget all the time.

**Table 16.A1: VECM Estimates of Error Correction Mechanism**

| *Cointegrating equations* | | | | |
|---|---|---|---|---|
| LOG_GFD_(-1) | 1.000000 | | | |
| LOG_AGG_(-1) | -1.749848<br>(0.05282)<br>[-33.1282] | | | |
| LOG_CO_(-1) | 0.437585<br>(0.08304)<br>[5.26972] | | | |
| LOG_INTR_PAYMENT(_1) | 0.362632<br>(0.09258)<br>[3.91692] | | | |
| Constant | 11.22427 | | | |
| Error correction | D(LOG_GFD_) | D(LOG_AGG_) | D(LOG_CO) | D(LOG_IP) |
| CointEq1 | 0.014175<br>(0.02972)<br>[0.47688] | 1.460886<br>(0.04487)<br>[32.5577] | -0.097282<br>(0.04111)<br>[-2.36645] | -0.003349<br>(0.00495)<br>[-0.67717] |
| D(LOG_GFD_(-1)) | 0.168847<br>(0.07256)<br>[2.32426] | -0.898600<br>(0.10966)<br>[-8.19428] | -0.137086<br>(0.10047)<br>[-1.36447] | 0.023349<br>(0.01209)<br>[1.93182] |
| D(LOG_GFD_(-2)) | -0.104783<br>(0.04560)<br>[-2.29765] | -0.309467<br>(0.06884)<br>[-4.49531] | 0.000307<br>(0.06307)<br>[0.00487] | 0.012019<br>(0.00759)<br>[1.58406] |
| D(LOG_AGG_(-1)) | -0.013200<br>(0.03784)<br>[-0.34885] | 0.594575<br>(0.05712)<br>[10.4096] | -0.172740<br>(0.05233)<br>[-3.30098] | 0.002732<br>(0.00630)<br>[0.43395] |
| D(LOG_AGG_(-2)) | 0.308747<br>(0.02872)<br>[10.7489] | 0.139638<br>(0.04336)<br>[3.22047] | -0.139535<br>(0.03972)<br>[-3.51254] | 0.007555<br>(0.00478)<br>[1.58092] |
| D(LOG_CO_(-1)) | 0171502<br>(0.06201)<br>[2.76561] | -0.892017<br>(0.09361)<br>[-9.52903] | -0.983205<br>(0.08576)<br>[-11.4642] | -0.002264<br>(0.01032)<br>[-0.21939] |
| D(LOG_CO_(-2)) | 0.147940<br>(0.08865)<br>[1.66891] | -0.428857<br>(0.13381)<br>[-3.20487] | -0.427015<br>(0.12260)<br>[-3.48311] | -0.004981<br>(0.01475)<br>[-0.33772] |
| D(LOG_IP_(-1)) | -1.055404<br>(0.53308)<br>[-1.97982] | -1.099800<br>(0.80471)<br>[-1.36670] | -0.470387<br>(0.73725)<br>[-0.63803] | 0.060861<br>(0.08869)<br>[0.68620] |
| D(LOG_IP_(-2)) | -0.317439<br>(0.56930)<br>[-0.55760] | -0.272584<br>(0.85939)<br>[-0.31718] | -0.063181<br>(0.78734)<br>[-0.08025] | -0.095556<br>(0.09472)<br>[-1.00883] |
| Constant | 0.303638<br>(0.09309)<br>[3.26179] | 0.294773<br>(0.14052)<br>[2.09768] | 0.124598<br>(0.12874)<br>[096781] | 0.102132<br>(0.01549)<br>[6.59425] |
| R-square | 0.825557 | 0.960807 | 0.566176 | 0.086797 |
| Adjusted R-square | 0.812473 | 0.957867 | 0.533639 | 0.018307 |
| F-statistics | 63.10024 | 326.8632 | 17.40111 | 1.267298 |
| Log likelihood | -112.6508 | -166.1863 | -154.8039 | 120.5032 |
| Akaike AIC | 1.886936 | 2.710558 | 2.535444 | -1.700049 |
| Schwarz SC | 2.107515 | 2.931138 | 2.756024 | -1.479470 |

**Note:** Standard errors in parentheses and absolute t-values in brackets.

**Table 16.A2: VECM System Equations**

| | |
|---|---|
| Model 1 | D(LOG_GFD_) = C(1)*( LOG_GFD_(-1) + 0.437585003001*LOG_CO_(-1) - 1.74984829559*LOG_AGG_(-1) + 0.362632241814*LOG_INTR_PAYMENT(-1) + 11.2242699371 ) + C(2)*D(LOG_GFD_(-1)) + C(3)*D(LOG_GFD_(-2)) + C(4)*D(LOG_CO_(-1)) + C(5)*D(LOG_CO_(-2)) + C(6)*D(LOG_AGG_(-1)) + C(7)*D(LOG_AGG_(-2)) + C(8)*D(LOG_INTR_PAYMENT(-1)) + C(9)*D(LOG_INTR_PAYMENT(-2)) + C(10) |
| Model 2 | D(LOG_CO_) = C(11)*( LOG_GFD_(-1) + 0.437585003001*LOG_CO_(-1) - 1.74984829559*LOG_AGG_(-1) + 0.362632241814*LOG_INTR_PAYMENT(-1) + 11.2242699371 ) + C(12)*D(LOG_GFD_(-1)) + C(13)*D(LOG_GFD_(-2)) + C(14)*D(LOG_CO_(-1)) + C(15)*D(LOG_CO_(-2)) + C(16)*D(LOG_AGG_(-1)) + C(17)*D(LOG_AGG_(-2)) + C(18)*D(LOG_INTR_PAYMENT(-1)) + C(19)*D(LOG_INTR_PAYMENT(-2)) + C(20) |
| Model 3 | D(LOG_AGG_) = C(21)*( LOG_GFD_(-1) + 0.437585003001*LOG_CO_(-1) - 1.74984829559*LOG_AGG_(-1) + 0.362632241814*LOG_INTR_PAYMENT(-1) + 11.2242699371 ) + C(22)*D(LOG_GFD_(-1)) + C(23)*D(LOG_GFD_(-2)) + C(24)*D(LOG_CO_(-1)) + C(25)*D(LOG_CO_(-2)) + C(26)*D(LOG_AGG_(-1)) + C(27)*D(LOG_AGG_(-2)) + C(28)*D(LOG_INTR_PAYMENT(-1)) + C(29)*D(LOG_INTR_PAYMENT(-2)) + C(30) |
| Model 4 | D(LOG_INTR_PAYMENT) = C(31)*( LOG_GFD_(-1) + 0.437585003001*LOG_CO_(-1) - 1.74984829559*LOG_AGG_(-1) + 0.362632241814*LOG_INTR_PAYMENT(-1) + 11.2242699371 ) + C(32)*D(LOG_GFD_(-1)) + C(33)*D(LOG_GFD_(-2)) + C(34)*D(LOG_CO_(-1)) + C(35)*D(LOG_CO_(-2)) + C(36)*D(LOG_AGG_(-1)) + C(37)*D(LOG_AGG_(-2)) + C(38)*D(LOG_INTR_PAYMENT(-1)) + C(39)*D(LOG_INTR_PAYMENT(-2)) + C(40) |

**Table 16.A3: Overall p-values for Wald Test**

| *Coefficient* | *Estimate* | *Standard error* | *t-statistics* | *p-value* |
|---|---|---|---|---|
| C(1) | 0.014175 | 0.029725 | 0.476884 | 0.6337 |
| C(2) | 0.168847 | 0.072645 | 2.324263 | 0.0205 |
| C(3) | -0.10478 | 0.045604 | -2.29766 | 0.022 |
| C(4) | -0.0132 | 0.037838 | -0.34885 | 0.7274 |
| C(5) | 0.308747 | 0.028724 | 10.74891 | 0 |
| C(6) | 0.171502 | 0.062012 | 2.765611 | 0.0059 |
| C(7) | 0.14794 | 0.088645 | 1.668905 | 0.0958 |
| C(8) | -1.0554 | 0.533081 | -1.97982 | 0.0483 |
| C(9) | -0.31744 | 0.569301 | -0.5576 | 0.5774 |
| C(10) | 0.303638 | 0.09309 | 3.261788 | 0.0012 |
| C(11) | 1.457413 | 0.044689 | 32.61227 | 0 |
| C(12) | -0.87266 | 0.112556 | -7.75313 | 0 |
| C(13) | -0.29194 | 0.070584 | -4.13601 | 0 |
| C(14) | 0.588837 | 0.057136 | 10.30591 | 0 |
| C(15) | 0.145913 | 0.043648 | 3.342928 | 0.0009 |
| C(16) | -0.89108 | 0.09633 | -9.25028 | 0 |
| C(17) | -0.43701 | 0.138053 | -3.16551 | 0.0016 |
| C(18) | -1.70702 | 0.803587 | -2.12425 | 0.0342 |
| C(19) | -0.22973 | 0.877469 | -0.26181 | 0.7936 |
| C(20) | 0.367053 | 0.143209 | 2.563065 | 0.0107 |
| C(21) | -0.09086 | 0.039271 | -2.31377 | 0.0211 |
| C(22) | -0.13612 | 0.098908 | -1.37623 | 0.1694 |
| C(23) | -0.00193 | 0.062025 | -0.03112 | 0.9752 |
| C(24) | -0.16418 | 0.050208 | -3.27007 | 0.0012 |

*(Contd...)*

| | | | | |
|---|---|---|---|---|
| C(25) | -0.13404 | 0.038356 | -3.49451 | 0.0005 |
| C(26) | -0.98558 | 0.08465 | -11.643 | 0 |
| C(27) | -0.42693 | 0.121314 | -3.5192 | 0.0005 |
| C(28) | -0.42859 | 0.706152 | -0.60694 | 0.5442 |
| C(29) | -0.13464 | 0.771076 | -0.17461 | 0.8615 |
| C(30) | 0.123463 | 0.125845 | 0.981076 | 0.327 |
| C(31) | -0.00155 | 0.004776 | -0.32472 | 0.7455 |
| C(32) | 0.022425 | 0.01203 | 1.864069 | 0.0629 |
| C(33) | 0.010755 | 0.007544 | 1.425666 | 0.1546 |
| C(34) | 0.004987 | 0.006107 | 0.816599 | 0.4146 |
| C(35) | 0.008484 | 0.004665 | 1.818482 | 0.0696 |
| C(36) | -0.00309 | 0.010296 | -0.29992 | 0.7644 |
| C(37) | -0.00478 | 0.014755 | -0.32406 | 0.746 |
| C(38) | 0.084485 | 0.085889 | 0.983656 | 0.3258 |
| C(39) | -0.1099 | 0.093785 | -1.17177 | 0.2419 |
| C(40) | 0.099645 | 0.015306 | 6.510053 | 0 |

# 17

# Rainfall and Farmer Suicides in India: Panel Estimation of the Effects of Monsoon Rainfall Deficit


## Abstract

*Farmer suicide in India is the single most manifestation of the distressed and pathetic situation of the agricultural sector and indicates the vulnerability of the rural economy to the vagaries of nature. Frequent failure of monsoon, inadequate rainfall, crop failure, overburden of loan, harassment of moneylenders and lack of accessibility to government support are the prime causes for a farmer ending his life on his own. This paper attempts to estimate the effects of annual rainfall and its shortage, along with gross irrigated area and GSDP, on farmer suicides in India using state-wise panel data for 10 states and for 10 years, 2001-2010. Panel data regression methods of fixed and random effects models are used for analysis. The estimated empirical result shows that with increase in annual rainfall farmer suicides decline. This result is strengthened with the findings that monsoon rainfall is associated with reduced farmer suicides, whereas the shortage in monsoon rainfall increases farmer suicides. Also, female farmer suicides are more responsive to rainfall related factors than the male farmer suicides. Though the Indian growth performance is described as spectacular and even frequently celebrated as a shining example, the life of the Indian farmer still reels under the mercy of nature, and the mere fact that a farmer commits suicide is a dent on face of the surging Indian economy.*



**Key words:** *Monsoon rainfall deficit, farmer suicides, panel data, fixed and random effects estimation*


## 17.1 Introduction

Farmers around the globe have high suicide rates, relative to other professions (Judd et al., 2006). Though farmer suicides may be treated as relatively few and even isolated events compared to all causes of deaths in a large and densely populated India, the sheer phenomenon of suicide by a farmer, who is the backbone for feeding the millions, can not be equated with other forms of suicides and taken so lightly. In fact, it is an indicator of the distressed and ill-fated scenario of development and income distribution. It is an essential facet in a comprehensive assessment of economic development and rural welfare for two reasons. First, the relative frequency of suicides is an objective quantitative measure of the prevalence of extreme individual distress. Second, unlike a transitory shock to household income, a suicide is irreversible. The farmer suicide, that too at a young and prime age, repercussions has not only to the income and debt problems, but also has devastating, pervasive and cascading effects for the entire family, including education and health of children, dependency on others, social neglect, and stigma. Hence, is important to understand the vulnerability of India's rural populations different from the much popular poverty angle and identify whether there is a need for reorienting rural development policies that are necessary to provide protection and mitigation against various sources of risk rather than just aggregate economic or income growth.

In order to understand the magnitude of the issue of farmer suicides, just look at the data on the causes of reported deaths in India available in the national crime records. For example, the actual demographic breakdown by NCRB report shows that out of 134,599 suicides reported in India in 2005, 15,964 belonged to the farming community. Figure 17.1 shows the trends in farmer suicides by gender in Indian states between 2001 and 2010. It can be observed that in Andhra Pradesh and Karnataka farmer suicides are much higher, despite better irrigation facilities and favourable political and government scenario, relative to poor states like Jharkhand and Rajasthan. It can also be noted that almost in every state the male farmer suicide rate is higher than female farmer suicide rate. In Karnataka, male suicide rate is much higher compared to the female farmer suicide rates, showing the glaring dependency on men in rural areas.

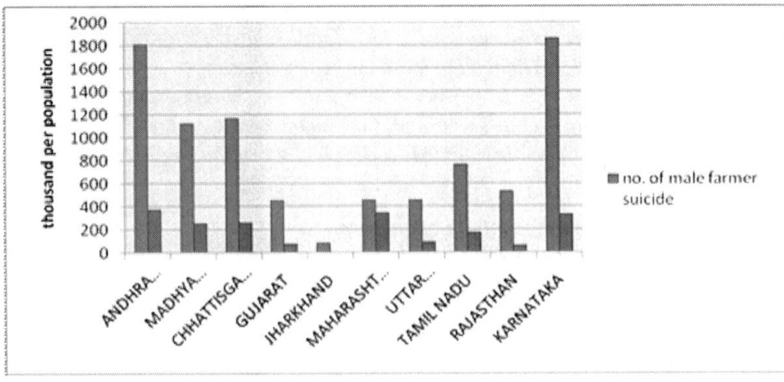


*Source:* NCRB data (2001-2010).

***Figure 17.1: Farmer Suicides in India***

Traditionally, lack of sufficient and timely rainfall and irrigation facilities, frequent crop failure, poor capital investments and credit facilities, high costs of fertilisers and pesticides, inadequate and inappropriate technology, near non-existence of storage and marketing facilities, and total neglect of agricultural sector in the wake of economic reforms have been cited as the main causes for the phenomenon of farmer suicides. The absence of coping any mechanism, land fragmentation, poor organisational structure, high indebtedness, exploitation by local moneylenders, lack of education, large family size, land being the only asset, poor crop diversification, etc. further aggravate the woes of the farmers. The high levels of economic stress due to severe risks in agriculture and the rapid pace of structural change rub the salt to the wound, thus aggravate the pathetic situation faced by the farmers (World Bank, 2007). The rising farmer suicides have often been cited as the manifestation of the destitute situation of poor farmers in the wake of globalisation and crony capitalism. The post reform drive for economic growth emphasising manufacturing and service sector growth and urban development, relative to agricultural sector growth and rural development have been the cause of concern in many developing countries. The plight of farmers and the increasing farmer suicides have been the bone of contention for political controversy and broad media focus around the globe, especially in India. In fact, increasing farmer suicides reflects the distress, destitute and desperate situation of poor farmers in the midst of growing affluence elsewhere. Despite much acclaimed success in rural poverty reduction, increasing education and improving awareness, suicides by farmers in India in rural areas continues to be a sad reflection of poor state of agrarian structure and its performance.

In fact, it is paradox that much of the farmer sucides have happened in an era of increasing income and impressive growth performance in India. Again, most of farmer suicides are in the relatively developed states like Maharashtra and Andhra Pradesh is perturbing. Further, these states are better placed in terms of irrigation, credit, and rural development, compared to other dry land states like Chhattisgarh, Jharkhand or Rajasthan. This poses a paradoxical situation as if the development activities have no impact on farming and on improving farmer income. Thus, the rural scenario still points to the near no hope for farmers and the poor farmers continue to reel under the vagaries of nature expecting good monsoon every season and hoping that rain will tilt their fortunes. Out of the total geographical area of 328.7 million hectares in India, the net sown area is 141 million hectares, out of which the irrigated area is only 48 million hectares and the majority 92.6 million hectares are dependent on natural rainfall (Tyagi, 1984). More than 50 percent of India's agricultural land is dependent on rainfall to see any crop growth (Stein, 2018). This shows that the dry land farming by the Indian farmer is inevitable. The crops that are grown in the dry land farming, jowar, pulses, oilseeds, cotton, etc. often yield poor returns. These crops often depend on timely monsoon rainfall, and the monsoon often fails in India and the feeders of the nation have to stare at crop failure. As the rainfall in India is notoriously unpredictable, Indian agriculture is termed as the gamble of monsoon. Thus, the farmer is forced to turn to their conventional and the only reliable saviours, the moneylenders and other informal sources, in order to cope with nature's onslaught and to survive in the Indian economy.

As so many Indian farmers take out their life so sadly, without even taking the everlasting consequences his suicide will to impose on the rest of the family, the causes that lead him to such a desperate situation need to be probed seriously. Of all the causes for farmer suicides, insufficient rainfall, that too erratic monsoon, and crop failure are the frequently cited primary causes that push the farmers to commit suicide. Hence, this paper investigates the farmer suicides in India by examining the effects of income, irrigated area, and rainfall on farmer suicides using a panel data from 10 major states for 10 years covering the period 2001-2010. To capture the effects of unobservable heterogeneity and individual effects, panel data regression methods of fixed effects and random effects models are used in the empirical analysis.

## 17.2 A Brief Review of Recent Studies

In the literature on suicides, econometric studies on farmer suicide are scanty. In most studies, suicides generally view suicide as an expression of extreme self-perceived misery. Often farmer suicide is considered to the sign of distress and failure of coping mechanism. The literature that examines farmer suicides in India has focused mostly on listing socioeconomic causes and state-level policy recommendations (Parthasarathy, 1998; Revathi, 1998). Among the causes mentioned are inadequate rainfall, low yield, falling commodity price, lack of institutional credit, poor quality of inputs, and increased reliance on informal moneylenders. All of which, incidentally, are also sources of problems in Indian agriculture at large. Of these, moneylenders are widely vilified as being the primary stressor pushing already over-burdened farmers to take their own lives. Contributing to farmer suicides, Bose (2000) highlights that seed quality and lack of pesticides as primary causes.

In a time-series study for the period from 1995-2011, Basu, Das and Mishra (2016) examines the suicide mortality rate (SMR) of farmers and non-farmers in India for 19 major states, that account for more than 97 percent of farmer suicides in India. The study observes that the SMR for male farmers has been consistently and significantly higher than for female farmers. The SMR ratio, i.e. the ratio of farmer SMR and non-farmer SMR, has been less than one, implying that the suicide rate of farmers has been lower than the suicide rate of non-farmers. Further, the SMR ratio for India has increased between 1995 and 2004 and has declined since then.

Hebous et al. (2014) analyses the vulnerability of India's rural populations from the usual consumption or income-based poverty angle. The study, examining district-wise data on suicides in farm households in two major Indian states Karnataka and Maharashtra during 1998-2004, observes marked differences across the two states. In Karnataka, where rainfall and rural poverty varies significantly, suicides among male farmers rise sharply with transitory poverty shocks caused by lack of rainfall. For females, an intriguing opposite effect, though quantitatively smaller, has been observed. In Maharashtra, no such effect has been observed because of the effective rural social protection policies. The results underscore the need for rural development policies that are geared towards protection against various sources of risk rather than just aggregate growth.

Rashmi Bhat (2016) examines the predictive power of monsoon and annual rainfall, which is assessed by a comparison of how agricultural suicide rates differ from non-agricultural suicide rates in the way that they respond to fluctuations in rainfall. Using a panel of suicide data for 25 Indian states, the pathways by which rainfall could affect an individual's decision to commit suicide is analysed. The results show that while both monsoon and annual rainfall are significantly associated with suicides rates, the other factors like real GDSP per capita, real agriculture output per worker and percent of the population employed in agriculture have no impact on farmer suicide.

## 17.3 Data and Methodology

The data used in this paper is a 10 years state-wise panel data covering the period 2001-2010. The states are Andhra Pradesh, Madhya Pradesh, Chhattisgarh, Gujarat, Jharkhand, Maharashtra, Uttar Pradesh, Tamil Nadu, Karnataka and Rajasthan. The panel unit is state and time variable is year. The period or number of years is 10 years starting from 2001 to 2010. The dependent variable of the study is the number of farmer suicides. Independent variables are annual rainfall, GSDP (gross state domestic product), GIA (gross irrigated area). The data on farmer suicides are collected from the Accidental Deaths and Suicides in India (ADSI) database of the National Crime Record Bureau NCRB, annual rainfall data from India Meteorological Department (IMD), gross state domestic product (GSDP) data from Planning Commission,

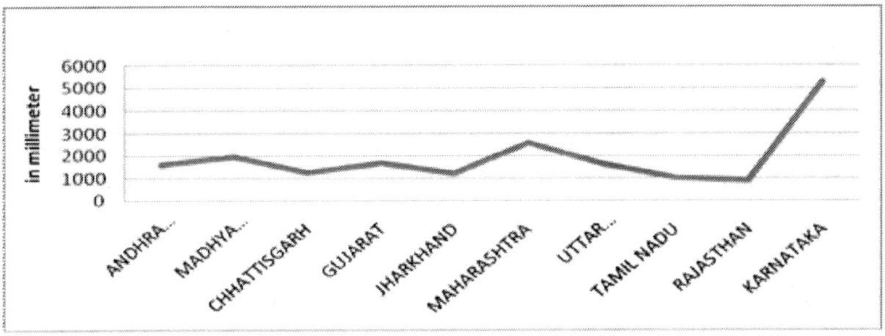


*Source:* Indian Institute for Tropical Meteorology (2001-2010).

***Figure 17.2 Annual Rainfall in India***

Government of India, and gross irrigated area data from CSO (Central Statistical Organization), and the irrigated area data from Ministry of Statistics and Programme Implementation.

The Figure 17.2 presents the pattern of average annual rainfall in India, showing the low level of rainfall in most Indian states. The Figure 17.3 presents

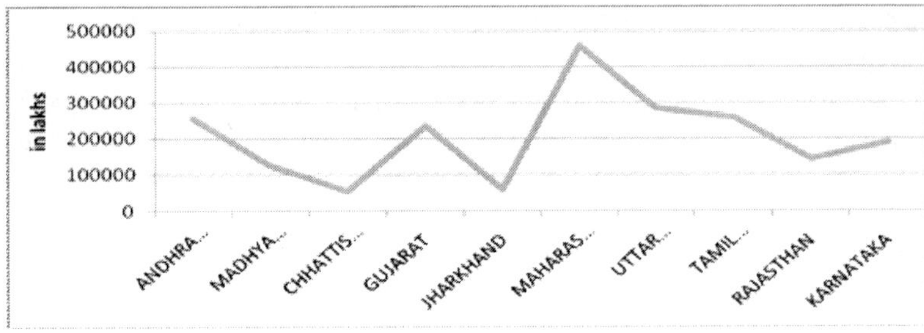


*Source:* Central Statistical Organization (CSO) (2001-2010).

***Figure 17.3 Gross State Domestic Product (GSDP) in India***

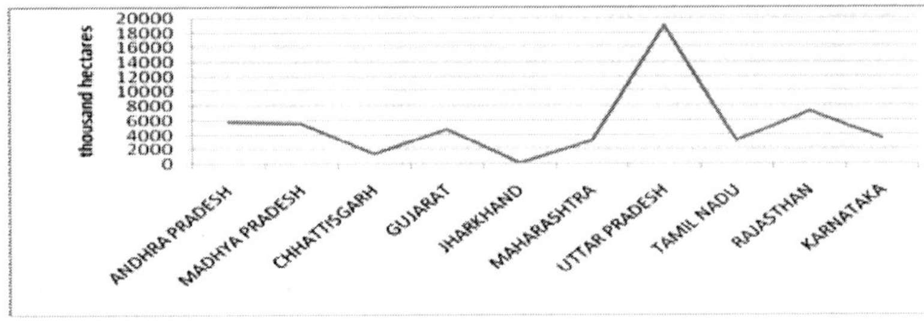


*Source:* Ministry of Statistics and Programme Implementation (2001-2010).

***Figure 17.4 Gross Irrigated Area (GIA) in India***

the average GSDP of the states in India and the Figure 17.4 presents the average gross cropped area in the 10 Indian states together.

## Panel Data Methodology

The fundamental advantage of panel data compared to cross-section data is that it allows greater flexibility in modeling differences in behaviour across states. The panel methods control for both time invariant observed and unobserved individual heterogeneity between the states. The panel model is given by,

$$y_{it} = \beta_i x_{it} + \alpha z_i + \lambda_i + u_{it} \qquad (17.1)$$

$$y_{it} = \beta_i x_{it} + c_i + u_{it} \qquad (17.2)$$

where $y_{it}$ is the number of farmer suicides in state $i$ during time $t$, $x_{it}$ is a set of explanatory variables, $z_i$ is the observed and $\lambda_i$ is the unobserved individual effects, i.e. heterogeneity. As it stands, this model is a classical regression model. If $z_i$ is observed for all individuals, then the entire model can be treated as an ordinary linear model and can be estimated by least squares method. The complications arise when $z_i$ is unobserved, which will be the case in most applications. When $z_i$ is unobserved but correlated with $x_{it}$ then the least squares estimator of $\beta$ is biased and inconsistent as a consequence of the omitted variable bias.

However, if the observed heterogeneity is time invariant i.e. $z_i$ is constant over time, then $z_i$ can be conveniently added with the constant term of the model as,

$$y_{it} = \alpha_i + \beta_i x_{it} + u_{it} \tag{17.3}$$

where $\alpha_i$ specifies an estimable conditional mean. This form of fixed effects estimation approach takes $\alpha_i$ to be a group-specific constant term in the regression model. The fixed effects model allows the unobserved individual effects to be correlated with the included variables. We then modeled the differences between units strictly as parametric shifts of the regression function. If the individual effects are strictly uncorrelated with the regressors, then it might be appropriate to model the individual specific constant terms as randomly distributed across cross-sectional units. The payoff to this form is that it greatly reduces the number of parameters to be estimated. It should be noted that the term 'fixed' as used here signifies the correlation of $c_i$ and $x_{it}$ not that $c_i$ is not-stochastic. If the unobserved individual heterogeneity $\lambda_i$ is, however formulated, assumed to be uncorrelated with $x_{it}$ then the model may be formulated as,

$$y_{it} = \beta_i x_{it} + \varepsilon_{it} \quad (\varepsilon_{it} = \lambda_i + u_{it}) \tag{17.4}$$

That is, a linear regression model with a compound disturbance that may be consistently, albeit inefficiently, estimated by least squares. The random effects estimation approach specifies that $\lambda_i$ is a group specific random element, similar to $u_{it}$. Again, the crucial distinction between fixed and random effects is whether the unobserved individual effect embodies elements that are correlated with the regressors in the model, not whether these effects are stochastic or not.

From the standpoint of causal analysis, a question is which model, fixed effects or random effects, is appropriate for empirical analysis. From a purely practical standpoint, the fixed effects model which uses dummy variables for individual effects has the disadvantage of losing as many degrees of freedom as the number of cross-section units. However, it has an advantage over the random effects; in that there is little justification for treating the individual effects as uncorrelated with the other regressors as is assumed in the random effects model. The random effects modeling suffers from the inconsistency due to this correlation between the explanatory variables and the individual effects. To overcome this specification issue, Hausman's (1978) devised a specification test, using the orthogonality property of the common effects and the regressors, based on the idea that under the hypothesis of no correlation, OLS, fixed effects and random effects estimators are consistent, but OLS is inefficient, whereas under the alternative, fixed effect is consistent, but the random effect is not. Therefore, under the null hypothesis, the two estimates should not differ systematically. Thus, the Hausman specification test is based on the difference in the variances of the two estimators i.e. test the covariance matrix of the difference vector $[b - \beta]$,

$$\mathrm{var}[b - \beta] = \mathrm{var}[b] + \mathrm{var}[\beta] - \mathrm{cov}[b, \beta] - \mathrm{cov}[(\beta, b] \quad (17.5)$$

Note that the covariance of an efficient estimator with its difference from an inefficient estimator is zero, implying that,

$$\mathrm{cov}[(b - \beta), \beta] = \mathrm{cov}[b, \beta] - \mathrm{var}[\beta] = 0 \text{ or } \mathrm{cov}[b - \beta] = \mathrm{var}\,[\beta] \quad (17.6)$$

Then, the covariance matrix is,

$$\mathrm{var}[b\text{-}\beta] = \mathrm{var}[b] - \mathrm{var}[\beta] = \Omega \quad (17.7)$$

on which the Wald chi-squared test can be performed,

$$W = \chi^2[K-1] = [b - \hat{\beta}]'\Omega^{-1}[b - \hat{\beta}] \quad (17.8)$$

The test statistic is,

$$H = [b_{FE} - \hat{\beta}_{FE}]'[V_{FE} - V_{RE}]^{-1}[b_{FE} - \hat{\beta}_{FE}] \quad (17.9)$$

If the computed value of the test statistics is greater than the critical value, the null hypothesis of the random effects is rejected, and the fixed effects model is specified.

## 17.4 Empirical Analysis

The definition and descriptive statistics of the variables used in the empirical analysis are presented in Table 17.1. In 2010 alone, 134599 suicides have been reported, which amounts to a suicide rate of 11.4. According to the NCRB, between 2000 and 2010, the number of suicides has increased by 23.9 percent, compared to the population increase of 18.3 percent during that decade. Out of all the suicides, on average, 1391 farmers per 1 lakh population committed suicide in India during the decade 2000-2010. During this time period, the mean annual rainfall is 1898 millimeters, and the shortfall in monsoon rainfall is 3512 millimeters. The average gross irrigational area is 5369 thousand hectares. The average GSDP at constant prices is Rs. 3891551, and the mean NSDP per capita is Rs. 26652.

**Table 17.1: Descriptive Statistics of the Variables in Farmer Suicides Analysis**

| *Variable* | *Description* | *Mean* | *Std. dev.* |
|---|---|---|---|
| FS | No. of farmer suicides (per 1,00,000 population) | 1391.18 | 1060.643 |
| AR | Annual rainfall (millimeter per annum) | 1898.012 | 1276.057 |
| GSDP | Gross state domestic product (Rs. lakhs in constant price) | 3891551 | 6432563 |
| GIA | Gross irrigated area (thousand hectares) | 5368.6 | 5018.541 |
| MRS | Monsoon rainfall shortage (millimeter) | -3512.593 | 4148.579 |

The empirical specification for panel estimation is,

$$FS_{it} = \beta_0 + \beta_1 AR_{it} + \beta_2 GIA_{it} + \beta_3 GSDP_{it} + \lambda_i + u_{it} \quad (17.10)$$

$$i = 1, 2, \ldots\ldots\ldots\ldots\ldots, 10;\ t = 2001, 2002, \ldots\ldots, 2010$$

The heterogeneity or individual effect term $\lambda_i$ is treated as a random variable with a specified probability distribution in the random effects model, whereas as a set of fixed parameters in fixed effects model. The term $u_{it}$ is the usual stochastic disturbance term that follows normal distribution with mean 0 and variance $\sigma^2$.

The Table 17.2 presents the panel regression results for fixed and random effects models. The variables are taken in the linear form. The coefficient of the main variable annual rainfall is negative and significant at 1 percent level in both models. These results show that for an increase in rainfall, the farmer suicide rate declines. An increase of one unit in rainfall will reduce the number of suicides by 5.6 percent in India. Irrigation is a major factor in farmer suicide. An increase one unit in irrigated area will significantly reduce farmer suicides by 2.0 percent. Better irrigation facilities will improve the agricultural production and hence prevent farmer suicides. Aggregate income GSDP has significant positive effect on farmer suicides, though the effect is only modest. As the fixed effects model also produces close estimates similar to the random effects model, the fit of the appropriate model need to be tested further. For the null hypothesis that there is a random effect, the Hausman specification test accepts the null, as the chi-square value for Hausman test is insignificant. Hence, the fixed effects model is rejected and the random effects model is the better one.

**Table 17.2: Fixed and Random Effects Panel Estimates of Farmer Suicides in India Dependent Variable: No. of farmer suicides**

| *Variable* | *Fixed effects* | *Random effects* |
|---|---|---|
| Annual rainfall | -.0881* (-3.09) | -.0565* (-2.72) |
| Gross irrigated area | -.0102* (-3.27) | -.0205* (-3.62) |
| GSDP | .00002*** (1.70) | .00002*** (1.82) |
| Constant | 155.58* (6.87) | 154.07* (3.85) |

*(Contd...)*

| R-squared (within) | 0.209 | 0.185 |
|---|---|---|
| R-squared (between) | 0.461 | 0.541 |
| R-squared (overall) | 0.337 | 0.406 |
| Rho | 0.9437 | 0.9418 |
| Hausman's specification test<br>Chi-square value | 3.00<br>Prob > chi2 = 0.3920 | |

**Note:** Absolute t-values (fixed effects) and z- values (random effects) in parentheses. * Significant at 1 percent level *** significant at 10 percent level.

The Table 17.3 estimates the effects of monsoon rainfall and the shortage of monsoon rainfall on farmer suicides in India. In specification 1, annual rainfall has a negative impact in farmer suicide and significant at the 1 percent level, showing adequate rainfall improves crop prospects and the tendency for suicide by farmers declines. In specification 2, timely monsoon rainfall also significantly reduces farmer suicides. But, inadequate or a shortage of monsoon rainfall has a statistically significant positive impact on farmer suicides. In all specifications, the effect of gross irrigated area is negative and significant at 10 percent level, showing irrigation facilities reduce farmer suicides. In specification 1, GSDP has a significant positive coefficient, but in other specifications GSDP effect on suicide by farmers is insignificantly negative.

**Table 17.3: Random Effects Panel Estimates of Monsoon Rainfall Shortage on Farmer Suicides in India**
**Dependent Variable: No. of farmer suicides**

| *Variable* | *Specification1* | *Specification 2* | *Specification 3* |
|---|---|---|---|
| Annual rainfall | -.0030* (-3.08) | - | - |
| Monsoon rainfall | - | -.0502* (3.37) | - |
| Shortage in monsoon rainfall | - | - | .0357* (3.08) |
| Gross irrigated area | -.0253** (-1.83) | -.0236** (-1.73) | -.0243*** (-1.73) |
| GSDP | -.0026* (2.81) | -.00009 (-0.27) | -.00009 (-0.26) |
| Constant | 147.707* (4.96) | 146.973* (4.63) | 166.955* (4.68) |
| R-squared (between) | 0.491 | 0.452 | 0.383 |
| R-squared (within) | 0.103 | 0.214 | 0.197 |
| R-squared (overall) | 0.520 | 0.426 | 0.432 |
| Rho | 0.8954 | 0.9019 | 0.9031 |

**Note:** z-values in parentheses. * Significant at 1 percent level *** Significant at 10 percent level.

**Table 17.4: Fixed and Random Effects Panel Estimates of Farmer Suicide by Gender**
**Dependent Variable: No. of farmer suicides**

| *Variable* | *Males* | | *Females* | |
|---|---|---|---|---|
| | *Fixed effects* | *Random effects* | *Fixed effects* | *Random effects* |
| Annual rainfall | -.0301*<br>(3.42) | -.0622*<br>(2.91) | -.0561*<br>(2.93) | -.0819***<br>(-1.70) |
| Gross irrigated area | -.0053***<br>(2.14) | -.0109***<br>(-2.35) | -.0071*<br>(2.71) | -.0119***<br>(-2.28) |

(Contd...)

| | | | | |
|---|---|---|---|---|
| GSDP constant | .0012*** (-1.86) | .0007*** (1.83) | .0012*** (-1.68) | .0015*** (-1.70) |
| Constant | 111.115* (5.38) | 112.903* (3.35) | 297.089* (5.28) | 290.923* (4.66) |
| R-squared (within) | 0.391 | 0.285 | 0.337 | 0.312 |
| R-squared (between) | 0.201 | 0.236 | 0.302 | 0.267 |
| R-squared (overall) | 0.384 | 0.246 | 0.637 | 0.414 |
| Rho | 0.936 | 0.920 | 0.887 | 0.776 |
| Hausman's specification test Chi-square value (with p-value) | 2.07 (0.558) | | 10.15 (0.017) | |

**Note:** Absolute t-values (fixed effects) and z- values (random effects) in parentheses. * Significant at 1 percent level *** significant at 10 percent level.

In the Table 17.4, the estimated results for male and female farmer suicides are presented separately. An increase in annual rainfall reduces both male suicides, as its sign is significantly positive. Female suicide rates are more responsive to rainfall than male farmer suicides. Further, irrigated area also reduces farmer suicides. The GSDP has got less positive effect on farmer suicides. The Hausman specification test shows insignificance for fixed effects and high significance for random effects leading to the acceptance of the null hypothesis that there is random effect.

## 17.5 Conclusion

It is no wonder that the Indian farmer's life and death revolves around the nature. Among all the ill factors that are responsible to a farmer's suicide, rainfall failure that too shortage of monsoon rainfall is the single most effective factor. A crop failure due to monsoon failure causes a farmer to default the crop loan, and his own life. This paper has attempted to estimate the effects of annual rainfall and its shortage, along with gross irrigated area and GSDP, on farmer suicides in India using state-wise panel data for 10 states and for 10 years. Panel data regression methods of fixed and random effects models are used for analysis. The estimated empirical result show that there is a direct relationship between annual rainfall and farmer suicide. With increase in annual rainfall, farmer suicide declines in India. This result is strengthened with the findings that monsoon rainfall is associated with reduced farmer suicides, whereas the insufficient monsoon rainfall increases farmer suicides. It seems that female farmer suicides are more responsive to rainfall related factors than the male farmer suicides. Thus, despite India's enviable growth rates, booming economy, and shinning urban sector, Indian farmers are still at the mercy of the 'rain God' and are 'born in debt, live in debt and die in debt', not because of ageing or natural causes, but by cutting short in his own hands his hopeless life, the sin being carrying out his family's professed occupation of agriculture.

# 18

# The Demand for Credit: Panel Conditional Fixed Effects Logistic Regression Estimation of Sources of Credit


## Abstract

*Financial inclusion drives by RBI and Government aim to give access to financial services for weaker and vulnerable sections of population at affordable costs. Still a majority population has not been brought under formal financial sector services, especially the banking services, and there exists a sizable informal credit sources that charge exorbitantly high interest rates. The formal banking institutions, though lend at lower interest rates, face the constraints of quantity rationing due to high transactions cost of smaller size credit demand, and lending to the poor is restricted due to the inability of poor to provide collateral security and surety. The formal requirements of the banks and the proximity of the borrower with the informal sources, mainly the local moneylenders, influence the household decision to borrow from informal sources even at much higher interest rates. This paper aims to understand the presence of quantity rationing in formal credit by analysing the determinants of the source of credit using the IHDS-I &II (2004-05 and 2011-12) data and applying panel conditional fixed effects logistic regression model. The estimated results of this study show that, even with low interest rates, there is quantity rationing in formal sector lending in India. Further, households borrow from informal sources at much higher interest rates, due proximity with local moneylenders and relatives. It is also observed that, though present, the extent of quantity rationing in the formal credit markets in India is minimal.*



**Key words:** *Financial inclusion, credit sources, quantity rationing, conditional fixed effects logistic regression*

## 18.1 Introduction

The term financial inclusion gained currency in the international policy forms since early 1990s with the success of microfinance approach and the rapid developments in the financial sector both globally and nationally. Though the Reserve Bank of India has initiated some form financial inclusion since the 1960s through schemes like priority sector lending, lead bank scheme, regional rural banks, service area approach, and the like, the importance of the concept financial inclusion has been fully recognised only after a mention about the same in the annual policy statement of the RBI for the year 2005-06 and the self-help group-bank linkage programme initiative. In fact, the National Democratic Alliance Government's flagship programme Pradhan Mantri Jan Dhan Yojana (PMJDY 2014) and Jan Dhan Aadhaar Mobile (JAM) are primarily designed to enhance financial inclusion, especially integrating the vulnerable and weaker sections with the financial services. In fact, the 2016 Economic Survey articulates the PMJDY and JAM trinity and the 2016 demonetisation moves as drivers for financial inclusion and formalisation of banking integration of the public.

The Rangarajan Committee on Financial Inclusion (2008) defines financial inclusion as "the process of ensuring access to financial services and timely and adequate credit where needed by vulnerable groups such as weaker sections and low income groups at an affordable cost" (Government of India, 2008, p. 35). The Raghuram Rajan Committee on Financial Sector Reforms (2009) defines financial inclusion as "universal access to a wide range of financial services at a reasonable cost. These include not only banking products but also other financial services such as insurance and equity products" (Raghuram Rajan, 2009, p. 50). The objective of the PMJDY, which is to ensure that there is universal access to various financial services, is achieved by providing individuals who did not hold an account in the past with bank accounts without any minimum balance requirement, mostly in a public sector bank. As on April 2018, about 31.48 crores accounts have been opened under this scheme. For example, the Punjab National Bank alone has opened 253.9 million accounts as on April 2018, mobilising Rs. 632.8 billion in these PMJDY accounts. The private sector banks have opened 9.9 million PMJDY accounts with Rs. 22.18 billion deposits. Thus, financial inclusion drive provides access to financial sector for the marginalised and formal finance deprived sections of the society.

However, such financial inclusion drives do not mean mere opening of formal bank accounts. The success of the financial inclusion move greatly depends on the availability of credit to weaker sections and low income vulnerable groups at affordable interest rates. The truth seems to be contrary to the objective of financial inclusion. Still a majority of population is not brought under financial inclusion and they depend on the same old modes like moneylenders and borrow at high interest rates. The Table 18.1 reveals that despite financial inclusion drives, still a large number of individuals in the lower income quartiles, as compared to relatively higher income quartiles, borrow at relatively high rates of interest. Despite the RBI's mandate of peer-to-peer lending norm that the maximum rate of interest that can be charged on a loan not to exceed 21 percent per annum, about 67 percent, 50 percent, 45 percent and 35 percent of the individuals belonging to lowest income quartile, second income quartile, third income quartile and the highest income quartile respectively borrow at over and above 24 percent per annum. These facts show that there exist unregulated sources that lend higher rates of interest. This is despite the availability of credit at lower rates from the formal credit institutions such as commercial banks, microfinance institutional and cooperative societies.

**Table 18.1: Interest Rates by Income Quartiles**

| *Income quartile* | *Percentage of persons paying interest (percent per annum)* | | | |
|---|---|---|---|---|
| | *≤12* | *13-24* | *25-36* | *>36* |
| Lowest | 16 | 16.9 | 18.7 | 48.4 |
| Second | 22.8 | 18.8 | 18.7 | 39.7 |
| Third | 29.1 | 26.1 | 18.7 | 26.2 |
| Highest | 40.4 | 24.5 | 11.7 | 23.4 |
| Total | 22.6 | 19.4 | 17.7 | 40.4 |

*Source:* Planning Commission (2009): Invest India Incomes and Savings Survey (IISS).

A further look into the breakup of the sources of credit of individuals belonging to various income quartiles throws greater light on the poor state of affairs in financial inclusion drives in India. The figures presented in Table 18.2 points out that low income groups borrow mostly from informal sources. Nearly 80 percent of individuals in lower income quartiles borrow from friends/relatives and moneylenders. Though about one third in the highest income quartile borrows from friends/relatives, the source of credit from moneylenders is only 15 percent. But, about 80 percent of individuals in the top two income quartiles borrow from formal source, the banks. The role of SHGs and microfinance institutions as source of credit is rather limited even among the low income quartiles. As revealed in Table 18.5, as income increases, the share of total borrowings from moneylenders steadily declines from 39.8 percent to 14.8 percent while that of banks increases from 9.6 percent to 45.8 percent. Thus, from Tables 18.1 and 18.2, it can infer that the low income groups borrow from the informal sources at high interest rates, which goes against the definition of financial inclusion.

The trends in institutional and non-institutional borrowing in rural India since 1951 are presented in Table 18.3 and Figure 18.1. The share of institutional lending has experienced a sharp rise post-1970s i.e. after the nationalisation of banks, while the share of total number of borrowings from

**Table 12.2: Sources of Credit by Income Quartiles**

| Loan Source | Percentage of persons in income quartile taken loan in last two years | | | |
|---|---|---|---|---|
| | Lowest | Second | Third | Highest |
| Relatives/friends | 39.2 | 34.4 | 33.2 | 32.0 |
| Moneylenders | 39.8 | 33.2 | 25.8 | 14.8 |
| Banks | 9.6 | 20.7 | 33.3 | 45.8 |
| Self-help groups | 9.7 | 8.4 | 3.3 | 3.4 |
| Cooperative societies | 5.4 | 4.9 | 6.5 | 7.4 |
| Chit funds | 1.6 | 1.9 | 1.5 | 1.2 |
| Microfinance institutions | 1.1 | 1.4 | 1.2 | 0.9 |
| Others | 1.0 | 0.9 | 0.8 | 1.4 |

*Source:* Planning Commission (2009): Invest India Incomes and Savings Survey (IISS).

the non-institutional sources has declined over the years. However, still about 43 percent of rural credit is from non-institutional sources, and moneylenders constitute nearly 30 percent share in the non-institutional credits. As per the Indian Human Development Survey (2004-05 and 2011-12) about 27.6 percent of the loans have been borrowed from family and friends and the mean lending rate for the same has been 13.8 percent per annum, which is less than that of the moneylenders whose mean lending rate stands at 41 percent per annum. Note that though these sources fall under the informal credit sector, yet they do not charge exorbitantly like the moneylenders.

**Table 18.3: Trends in Institutional and Non-Institutional Rural Credit in India**

| *Source of credit* | *1951* | *1961* | *1971* | *1981* | *1991* | *2002* |
|---|---|---|---|---|---|---|
| Government | 3.3 | 5.3 | 6.7 | 4.0 | 5.7 | 2.3 |
| Co-op. society/bank | 3.1 | 9.1 | 20.1 | 28.6 | 18.6 | 27.3 |
| Commercial bank including RRBs | 0.8 | 0.4 | 2.2 | 28.0 | 29.0 | 24.5 |
| Insurance agencies | - | - | 0.1 | 0.3 | 0.5 | 0.3 |
| Provident fund | - | - | 0.1 | 0.3 | 0.9 | 0.3 |
| Others institutional agencies | - | - | - | - | 9.3 | 2.4 |
| All institutional agencies | 7.2 | 14.8 | 29.2 | 61.2 | 64.0 | 57.1 |
| Landlord | 1.5 | 0.9 | 8.6 | 4.0 | 4.0 | 1.0 |
| Agricultural moneylender | 24.9 | 45.9 | 23.1 | 8.6 | 6.3 | 10.0 |
| Professional moneylender | 44.8 | 14.9 | 13.8 | 8.3 | 9.4 | 19.6 |
| Traders and commission agents | 5.5 | 7.7 | 8.7 | 3.4 | 7.1 | 2.6 |
| Relatives and friends | 14.2 | 6.8 | 13.8 | 9 | 6.7 | 7.1 |
| Others | 1.9 | 8.9 | 2.8 | 4.9 | 2.5 | 2.6 |
| All non-institutional agencies | 92.8 | 85.2 | 70.8 | 38.8 | 36 | 42.9 |
| Total | 100 | 100 | 100 | 100 | 100 | 100 |

*Source:* All India Debt and Investment Survey (AIDIS), 1954-2002 (various rounds).

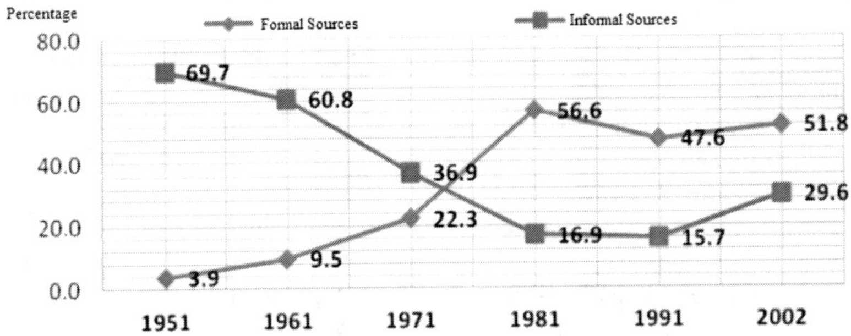


***Figure 18.1: Trends in Sources of Borrowings in India***

The Figure 18.1 depicts the trends in sources of borrowing over the years in India. In the initial phase, between 1950s and 1970s, households were more reliant for borrowings on informal sources like moneylenders, unauthorised lending services, friends, family etc. But after 1970s, with nationalisation of commercial banks and the establishment of cooperative societies, the trend of borrowing has changed. Borrowing from formal sources has increased whereas borrowing from informal sources has gone down. However, the dependence for borrowings on informal sources has been rising since 1990s with the deregulation of financial markets and the corporate orientation of commercial banks since economic reforms.

The existence of a size of informal lending at exorbitantly high rates of interest is not peculiar to India but to the whole of the developing world. To address this issue, the state governments in India have enacted laws that lead to punitive actions against the lenders who charge over the specified rates such as the Kerala Prohibition of Charging Exorbitant Interest Act, 2012 and the Tamil Nadu Money Lenders Act, 1957. The very persistence of the informal credit alongside the credit market points to the fact that mere punitive actions are insufficient to resolve the problem. In order to comprehend the problem of informal lending and the associated high interest rates, it is essential to understand the working of credit market institutions in India.

In the credit market, commercial banks constitute a significant part of the financial system in India. Other formal credit market agencies also cater sizable credit needs of the population. However, commercial banks, as they care about profits, generally provide credit of large sums and the formal agencies satisfy specific purpose credits. Moreover, these formal institutions require collateral security and surety for the credit. The weaker strata of the society cannot provide the type of collateral that commercial banks and formal agencies need to sanction a credit. Moreover, due to high transaction costs involved in handling transactions of smaller size credits, the banks and formal agencies are reluctant to provide credit of smaller amounts and to weaker sections. The information costs associated with screening and monitoring lead to adverse selection and moral hazard in the formal credit market. This problem of small size credits is known as 'quantity rationing' in the literature on credit markets (Stiglitz and Weiss, 1981). Moreover, the economic and investment activities of the poor income groups that borrow from formal agencies, even at lower interest rates, may not earn higher returns on their investment as compared to the investment activities of higher income groups (Conning and Udry, 2007). Hence, the formal credit agencies may not be willing to advance credit to the poor and weaker sections. Therefore, the financial inclusion drive towards the vulnerable groups through, for example, PMJDY may be insufficient in resolving the problem of informal sector lending in India.

To mend the gaps in formal banking sector credits, a number of other forms of formal institutions like non-banking financial institutions, government credit programmes, cooperative societies, self help groups and microfinance schemes have been evolved. However, these institutions also suffer from the same issues associated with the banking credit. Once again the poor are compelled to depend on informal sources, like local moneylenders and relative/ friends, who charge high interest rates. Guirkinger (2008) argues that money lenders have greater access to information about the financial status of the borrower which allows them to substitute screening and monitoring for collateral requirements overcome adverse selection. Though cooperative societies, non-governmental organisations (NGOs) and self help groups (SHGs) do not fall under the informal credit category, their proximity with the borrowers allows them to access as much information as the moneylenders. The lending rates of these institutions are generally lower as compared to that of moneylenders.

Thus, despite availability of relatively cheap credit from formal sources, there exists a huge and sustained demand for informal credits. This is a truly a puzzling phenomenon. The literature shows that the demand for informal credit may be spillover in nature (Bell, Srinivasan and Udry, 1997) or a deliberate choice by the household (Kochar, 1997). The inability to provide collateral security or surety for the loan can also result in quantity rationing in formal credit markets (Stiglitz and Weiss, 1981). Since the source of credit is a result of demand side and supply side interactions in the credit market, the problem is to be approached from both sides. Hence, this paper analyses the determinants of the sources of credit of households, using the India Human Development Survey data (IHDS-I 2004-05 and IHDS-II 2011-12), applying the panel conditional fixed effects logistic model. The main objective of this paper is to identify and estimate the effects of the determinants of source of credit for households in India.

## 18.2 A Brief Review of Recent Studies

In order to study the source of credit of an individual or a household, it is essential to understand the concept of quantity rationing. This is because it is perceived that the demand for informal credit may spill-over in nature due to quantity rationing in formal markets. Rationing refers to not obtaining credit from a particular source despite being able to pay the interest charged by the source. In the context of this study, it refers to not obtaining credit from banks despite being able to pay the interest rates charged by the banks. This concept has been studied, both theoretically and empirically, and most studies carried out are pertaining to credit markets in developing economies. Literature points out that rationing is of three types namely quantity rationing, risk rationing and transaction cost rationing. Of the three, quantity rationing is given greater importance and it refers to formal lenders denying a loan or a borrower voluntarily opting out of the formal credit market due smaller size of the loan. Stiglitz and Weiss (1981) argue theoretically that endogenous quantity rationing may arise because formal lenders have limited local information and thus rely on collateral to overcome moral hazard and adverse selection intrinsic in credit transactions.

Zeller (1994) discusses the quantity rationing in formal and informal credit sectors in Madagascar, Africa. The source of credit depends on the purpose of the loan and its relationship with the repayment rate. Also, the occupation of the borrower has an impact on the source of the loan as it determines both the size of loan and repayment capacity.

Kochar (1997), using a subset of the All-India Debt and Investment Survey 1981-1982 survey data pertaining to Northern Uttar Pradesh, studies quantity rationing constraints in formal rural credit markets in India. The models used in the study are univariate, bivariate and trivariate logistic regressions with three different assumptions. The bivariate probit model has been used to model both access and demand for formal credit. Demand for formal credit is defined as application for credit and access to credit is defined credit sanction by formal credit institutions sanctioning the loan. The study observes that interest rates have a positive effect on both the demand and access to credit by formal credit institutions. The coefficients on interest rate reported are an insignificant 0.0045 for access and significant 0.1224 significant for demand. Further, Kochar argues that the demand for informal credits cannot be perceived as spillover demand as a result of rationing in formal credit markets and that the households may make a deliberate choice of borrowing from informal sources, as they are observed to be cheap compared to the formal credit sources.

Guirkinger (2008) examines the coexistence of formal and informal credit markets, for a primary survey data from Peru of two rounds -1997 and 2003 - for a sample of 499 households, applying random effects logistic regression. As the information on the borrower's source of credit and the type of credit rationing (if any existed) is directly available in the data, the survey permits analysing directly if quantity rationing is a significant problem in the formal credit sector. The coefficient on quantity rationing is 1.64 and statistically significant showing positive impact of credit rationing on the household's credit source being informal source. The results confirm the existence of quantity rationing in the formal credit sector.

Wydick, Hayes and Kempf (2011) study the impact of social capital on access to credit in Rural Guatemala using primary survey data conducted in 2004 and multinomial logit method. The paper argues that social networks facilitate households to secure loans from different sources. In the empirical analysis, church membership of a household is taken as a measure of social capital, specifically social network, for its effect on the household's ability to obtain a loan. The multinomial logit results show that being a church committee member has a significant positive impact of 1.843 on obtaining credit from microfinance institutions.

Campero and Kaiser (2013) study the awareness and use of formal and informal credit institutions in Mexico using Mexican Family Life Survey data for the period 2004-05, employing two-stage multinomial probit method. The estimated results show that average schooling of head and spouse has a significant coefficient of 0.0467for the awareness of existence of banks and a significant 0.0321 coefficient for savings banks. Similarly, the log of annual incomes of the households had a significant positive impact on the awareness of formal credit sources. The estimated coefficients are 0.186 and 0.173 for banks and savings banks respectively, both significant at 1 percent level.

Kumar et al. (2017) study the access to institutional credit and non-institutional credits in India, using the NSSO National Farmers Survey, 2013 data. They report that increasing in farmer education increases the probability of access to institutional credit increases. The estimated coefficients are 0.393, 0.610, 0.870 respectively for primary, higher secondary and graduate levels of education, all significant at 1 percent level. The log of per capita monthly expenditure used as a proxy for income has a positive impact on the access to institutional credit. The reported coefficient is 0.298, significant at 1 percent level.

Thus, the source of credit of a household is influenced by both demand side and supply side factors. The size of the loan, purpose of loan, interest rate, awareness, access, household income and education, repayment capacity and social networks are some of the factors that have a significant effect on the household's demand and/or access to formal credit. The main objective of this paper is to examine whether quantity rationing is a factor in households choice of non-formal institutional credit where the interest rate is higher than the formal credit sources. In addition, the paper also aims to examine whether the proximity of households to the informal sources of credit influence the demand for credit of these households. Further, this paper also tries to identify and estimate the effects of other environmental factors that influence the source of credit of households in India.

## 18.3 Data and Methodology

The source of data for this study is the two rounds of Indian Human Development Survey (IHDS) conducted jointly by University of Maryland and National Council for Applied Economic Research (NCAER). The IHDS is a nationally representative, multi-topic survey spanning across 1503 villages and 971 urban neighbourhoods in India. The first round of the survey was conducted in 2004-05 covering 41,544 households and the second round was conducted in 2011-12 covering 42,152 households. About 83 percent of the households interviewed in 2004-05 were re-interviewed in 2011-12. This allows for the construction of a panel dataset combining the two rounds of data and to perform a panel data analysis. As the objective is to examine the determinants of the source of credit of households in India, all those households that have taken loan in both the time periods have been taken into consideration. The final sample used in the study is 23,008 households that borrowed both in 2004-05 and 2011-12 from any one of the sources, consisting of 82,225 households that borrowed from the formal sources and 14,783 households that borrowed from informal sources.

The Figure 18.2 presents the shares of the sources of credit for households in the sample. Among the sources of household borrowings, commercial banks constitute the single largest share which stands at 30.67 percent of the total number of borrowings in both the years 2004-05 and 2011-12. However, it is only one-third of the total credits by households. Still the share of loans from moneylenders and relatives stands at 27.92 percent and 27.63 percent respectively, together constituting more than one-half of total borrowings of households. Another 8.07 percent share of the total borrowings is from employees and others who also fall under the informal sources category. Thus, the informal sources of credit constitute nearly two-third of the credit sources, a result that also corroborated by the AIDIS data. In total, the informal sources constitute 64.25 percent of the total number of borrowings while the formal sources constitute only 35.75 percent of the same. It is appalling that the cooperatives, NGOs, SHGs and government programmes put together constitute only 5.08 percent of the total share of household borrowings. It has been pointed out in the literature that these institutions are capable of overcoming moral hazard and selection bias pertaining to credit due to their proximity with the borrowers. However, the share of their lending has been abysmally low. Over all, the large share of borrowings from the informal sources shows quantity rationing in the formal sector and inadequacies of the formal sectors in catering to the demand for credit by the households. Therefore, the households demand for credit from informal sources, even though the interest rates are high.

In the empirical analysis, credit source is the dependent variable in the analysis and it is treated as dichotomous variable. Formal credit source is assigned value one, while the informal credit sources are taken as zero. The independent variables are household income, credit size, interest rate,

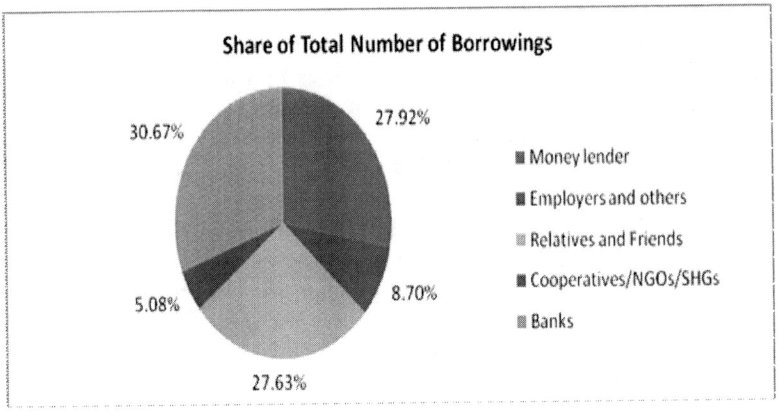


*Source:* IHDS - Round I (2004-05) and Round II (2011-12).

***Figure 18.2: Sources of Credit for Households in India***

education, social network, purpose of the loan, occupation and residence of the borrowers. The size of the loan is use to capture quantity rationing and membership in NGOs, co-operative societies or SHGs is used to capture the impact of social networks. The purpose of loan is classified into four categories as personal, housing, education and business loans, and are used as dummy variables. The occupation of the household is classified into five categories as salaried professional, agriculture and allied activities, organised business, wage labourers and others, and treated as dummy variables.

The Table 18.4 presents the average size of credit and the average interest rates on the loans from the credit sources. Overall, the average credit amount is Rs. 48,590 and the mean interest rate is 19.72 percent. The average size of loan from formal sources is higher than the loan size from informal sources, whereas the interest rate charged is higher for informal credit than for formal credit. The moneylenders charge 42 percent interest rate compared to the bank interest rate of 11 percent. The loan amount from moneylenders is about one-third of the size of credit from commercial banks, showing the presence of credit rationing. However, the interest charged by moneylenders is three times higher than that of formal sources. It seems credit from employers and relatives/ friends is more reliable as the average loan borrowed from these sources is sizable and at the same time the interest charged is moderate, falling between the interest rates of formal sources and moneylenders. Overall, it is observed from the Table 18.4 that the sizable informal credit, though costlier than formal credit, is due to quantity rationing in the formal sources and the proximity of informal sources to households.

**Table 18.4: Average Size of Credit and Interest Rate by Sources of Credit**

| *Source* | *Size of credit (Rs. in 000s)* | *Interest rate (in percentage)* |
|---|---|---|
| Moneylenders | 28.17 | 41.90 |
| Employers and others | 34.87 | 15.50 |
| Relatives and friends | 23.27 | 13.87 |
| Cooperatives/NGOs/SHGs | 44.61 | 11.54 |
| Banks | 94.55 | 11.02 |
| Total | 48.59 | 19.72 |

The Table 18.5 presents the summary statistics of all the variables in the model. The source-wise mean and standard deviations are reported for continuous variables, while the proportion of borrowers of credit from the formal and informal sources is reported for the qualitative variables. It can be noticed from the Table 18.5 that a majority of households, about 65 percent, availed credit from informal sources, whereas only 35 percent of households borrowed from formal sources. The average size of the loans from formal sector is much larger than that of the loans from the informal sector. Similarly, the standard deviations for the two sources differ significantly, and the formal source exhibits much wider deviations from the mean, pointing to the presence of significant quantity rationing. A similar pattern is observed in the case of total household income also. The average and the standard deviation of the total household income for the formal sources are observed to be larger than the mean and the standard deviation of the same for informal sources. Those who borrowed from formal sources have more years of education, 10.25 years, while that of the informal credit source is 8.44.

The average rate of interest charged by the informal sources is more than double (25.85) the interest rate of formal sources (11.08). As noted in Table 18.4, the average lending rate of moneylenders stood at 42 percent per annum. Even though Kochar (1997) finds that some informal sources of credit may be cheaper and thus be a deliberate choice of the borrower, the IHDS data shows that the informal sector credit is costlier than the formal sources. Though 65 percent of the households who are not members in any of the formal or informal networks borrowed from informal credit sources, the observation that about 50 percent of the households who are members of mainly the cooperative societies or SHGs/NGOs borrowed from formal sources suggests that formal membership households exploit social capital in securing credit from formal sources. It can be clearly seen from the Table 12.5 that only 21 percent of the consumption loans are obtained from a formal credit source, whereas 59 percent of the business or agriculture loans, which are investments, are obtained from formal sources. It is also to be observed that still education and land development loans by banks have not penetrated the credit market.

**Table 18.5: Averages and Proportions of Variables in the Sources of Credit Analysis**

| *Variable* | *Informal credit* | *Formal credit* |
|---|---|---|
| Continuous variables - Mean and standard deviation | | |
| Size of the credit (Rs. in 000s) | 26.9 (84.2) | 87.5 (589.5) |
| Total household income (Rs in 000s) | 40.2 (51.4) | 82.2 (159.9) |
| Education (in years) | 8.44 (3.49) | 10.25 (3.67) |
| Interest rate (per annum) | 25.85 (26.33) | 11.08 (5.88) |
| Qualitative variables - Share of total borrowings (percent) | | |
| Membership in co-operative society or NGO or SHG | | |
| Member | 50.85 | 49.15 |
| Not a member | 65.38 | 35.45 |
| Credit purpose | | |
| Education loan | 55.47 | 44.53 |
| Housing/land loan | 58.96 | 41.04 |
| Business /agriculture loan | 40.96 | 59.04 |
| Consumption loan | 78.61 | 21.39 |
| Residence | | |
| Rural | 64.11 | 35.89 |
| Urban | 64.77 | 35.23 |
| Occupation | | |
| Salaried/professional | 54.96 | 45.04 |
| Wage labourer | 76.87 | 23.13 |
| Agriculture and allied worker | 54.81 | 45.19 |
| Organised business | 51.55 | 48.45 |
| Others | 59.42 | 40.58 |
| Number of observations | 14,783 | 8,225 |

Due to greater economic activity in urban areas, awareness about banking and increased concentration of banks, the accessibility and transaction costs for those households applying for a loan is lower than that of rural households. It is to bridge this gap that the RBI has taken efforts such as establishing RRBs and lead banks. Yet, the share of informal borrowings in the urban areas and the share of that in rural areas are similar and sizable 35 percent. It is also to be noted from Table 18.5 that about 40 to 50 percent households belonging to various occupations borrow from formal sources. But, the condition for poor wage earners is pathetic in that only 23 percent of the wage labourers could borrow from the formal sources, and for 77 percent labour households moneylenders and local sources are the only viable and dependable source of credit. This poor state of affairs of wage labourers can be attributed to the absence of collateral security, surety, small credit size and illiteracy. Thus, it is the poor sections of the society that pay the unbearable interest rate to the usurious moneylenders.

## Panel Data Methodology

As the dependent variable the sources of credit is qualitative and binary in nature and the data is for two rounds of IHDS of 2004-05 and 2011-12, this paper uses the panel data approach. A general panel model for logistic regression is given by,

$$y_{it} = \beta' x_{it} + \varepsilon_{it} \qquad i = 1, \ldots, n; \quad t = 1, \ldots, T \tag{18.1}$$

where $y$ is the binary dependent variable and $x$ is the matrix of the independent variables, $e_{it}$ is the stochastic error term, $i$ and $t$ index cross section observations and time periods respectively. As the dependent variable is dichotomous, estimating equation (18.1) directly by maximum likelihood method requires the assumption that the errors in the two time periods $\varepsilon_{i1}$ and $\varepsilon_{i2}$ are uncorrelated. However, in the context of panel data, error terms are correlated within groups and uncorrelated between groups. Hence, it is more appropriate to estimate the panel model by fixed effects or random effects model which takes care of the unobserved heterogeneity and resolve the issue of correlated error terms. Writing $\varepsilon_{it} = \varepsilon_{it} + v_i$ where $\varepsilon_{it}$ is the usual disturbance term and $v_i$ is the unobserved time-invariant individual heterogeneity, the assumption on relationship between $v_i$ and $x_{it}$ is the crucial factor that determines whether the model is to be estimated as fixed effects or random effects model.

## Conditional Fixed Effects Logistic Regression

The fixed effects logistic regression is to be used when the unobserved heterogeneity $v_i$ is correlated with the independent variables $x_{it}$. The fixed effects model takes the form,

$$y_{it} = \alpha_i d_i + \beta' x_{it} + u_{it} \tag{18.2}$$

where $d_i$ is a dummy representing an individual in the sample, and $a_i$ captures the individual time-invariant heterogeneity in the panel model. The log likelihood function for the panel model is constructed by taking the product of the individual probabilities and subsequently taking a natural log of the product.

$$Prob(y_{it} = 1|x_{it}) = \frac{e^{\alpha_i + \beta' x_{it}}}{1+e^{\alpha_i + x'_{it}\beta}} \tag{18.3}$$

$$L = \prod_i \prod_t (P_{it})^{y_{it}} (1 - P)^{1-y_{it}} \tag{18.4}$$

$$lnL = \sum_{i=1}^{n} \sum_{t=1}^{T_i} lnP(y_{it}|\alpha_i + \beta' x_{it}) \tag{18.5}$$

The log-likelihood function (equation 18.5) is maximised by the maximum likelihood method to obtain the parameter estimates of the model. However, in the estimation of fixed effects model, number of parameters to be estimated $(n+k)$, as a constant tern $a_i$ is to be estimated for each individual in the sample, apart from the usual $k$ number of coefficients per variable in the model. As the number of cross-section units in the panel increases with fewer time periods, the number of parameters $a_i$ also increases. Therefore, the data requires more time periods in order to ensure that the estimates for the constant terms are consistent. When the sample size is small, estimates of ß are biased due to the inconsistency in the estimates of $a$, leading to the incidental parameters problem (Hsiao, 2003).

To free the panel model from the incidental parameters problem, Chamberlain (1980) proposes the maximisation of a conditional likelihood function. The conditional likelihood function is given by,

$$L^c = \prod_{i=1}^{n} Prob\left(Y_{i1} = y_{i1}, Y_{i2} = y_{i2}, \ldots, Y_{iT_i} = y_{iT_i} \middle| \sum_{t=1}^{T_i} y_{it}\right) \quad (18.6)$$

$$f(y_{i1}, \ldots y_{iT} | \textstyle\sum_t y_{it}) = \sqrt{T}(2\pi)^{-(T-1)/2}\sigma^{-(T-1)}\exp\{-\frac{1}{2\sigma^2}\sum_t[(y_{it} - \bar{y}_i) - \beta'(x_{it} - \bar{x}_i)]^2\} \quad (18.7)$$

As $i$ term in $L^c$ is just one in any of the alternatives, when taken logs it drops out as it contribute nothing to the conditional likelihood function.

For a balanced panel, Chamberlain (1980) suggests the likelihood function,

$$L_i = \textstyle\sum_i ln\,[exp\,(\beta' \sum_t x_{it} y_{it}) \sum_{b \in B_i} exp\,(\beta' \sum_t x_{it} b_t) \quad (18.8)$$

where $B_i = \{b = (b_1, b_2) | b_t = 0 \; or \; 1 \; and \sum_t b_t = \sum_t y_{it}\}$ (18.9)

Suppose, there is a pair of observations for an individual $i$ for two periods with $y_{i1} = 0$ and $y_{i2} = 1$. Then, the conditional probability is given by,

$$Prob(0,1|sum = 1) = \frac{Prob(0,1 \; and \; sum = 1)}{Prob(sum = 1)} = \frac{Prob(0,1)}{Prob(0,1) + Prob(1,0)} \quad (18.10)$$

which can be expressed as,

$$Prob(0,1|sum = 1) = \frac{\frac{1}{1+e^{\alpha_i+\beta' x_{i1}}}\frac{e^{\alpha_i+\beta' x_{i2}}}{1+e^{\alpha_i+x_{i2}\beta}}}{\frac{1}{1+e^{\alpha_i+\beta' x_{i1}}}\frac{e^{\alpha_i+\beta' x_{i1}}}{1+e^{\alpha_i+\beta' x_{i2}}} + \frac{e^{\alpha_i+\beta' x_{i2}}}{1+e^{\alpha_i+\beta' x_{i1}}}\frac{1}{1+e^{\alpha_i+\beta' x_{i2}}}} \quad (18.11)$$

$$Prob(0,1|sum = 1) = \frac{e^{\beta' x_{i2}}}{e^{\beta' x_{i1}} + e^{\beta' x_{i2}}} \quad (18.12)$$

Thus, the conditional likelihood is maximised to obtain the coefficients vector.

## Random Effects Logistic Regression

The random effects logistic regression is to be used when the unobserved heterogeneity $v_i$ is uncorrelated with (or independent of) the independent variables $x_{it}$. The random effects model takes the form,

$$y_{it} = \beta' x_{it} + (u_{it} + v_i) \tag{18.13}$$

The assumptions on $\varepsilon_{it}$, $u_{it}$, $v_i$ and $x_{it}$ are,

$$\begin{aligned} &E[u_{it}|x] = 0;\ Cov[u_{it}, u_{js}|x] = Var[u_{it}|x] = 1 \quad if\ i = j\ and\ t = s;\ 0\ otherwise \\ &E[v_i|x] = 0;\ Cov[v_i, v_j|x] = Var[v_i|X] = \sigma_v^2 \quad if\ i = j;\ \ 0\ otherwise \\ &Cov[u_{it}, v_j|x] = 0 \quad for\ all\ i, t, j \end{aligned} \tag{18.14}$$

Then,

$$\begin{aligned} &E[\varepsilon_{it}|x] = 0 \\ &Var[\varepsilon_{it}|x] = \sigma_u^2 + \sigma_v^2 = 1 + \sigma_v^2 \end{aligned} \tag{18.15}$$

$$Corr[\varepsilon_{it}, \varepsilon_{is}|x] = \rho = \frac{\sigma_v^2}{1 + \sigma_v^2}$$

where $x$ is the matrix of all the exogenous independent variables in the model for all the observations $i$ across time periods $t$. The new free parameter in the model is $\sigma^2_v = \rho/(1+\rho)$. Conditional on common $v_i$, the $\varepsilon$'s are independent, and hence the likelihood function is maximised to obtain the estimates of the model. The conditional likelihood function is given by,

$$L_i = P[y_{i1}, \dots, y_{iT_i}|X] = \int_{-\infty}^{+\infty} \left[ \prod_{t=1}^{T_i} Prob(Y_{it} = y_{it}|x_{it}'\beta + v_i) f(v_i) dv_i \right] \tag{18.16}$$

Specifying a distribution for equation (18.15) and solving it by Butler and Moffit (1982) method, produces the estimated vector of coefficients as,

$$\hat{\beta} = arg.max \int_{-\infty}^{+\infty} [\prod_{t=1}^{T_i} Prob(Y_{it} = y_{it}|x_{it}'\beta + v_i) f(v_i) dv_i] \tag{18.17}$$

## Hausman Specification Test

The fixed effects approach treats the individual heterogeneity to be correlated with the independent variables in the model, while random effects approach assumes that the individual heterogeneity are uncorrelated with the independent variables. If there is no correlation between the independent variables and the individual heterogeneity both fixed effects and random effects estimators are consistent, while in the presence of correlation, the fixed effects estimator is alone consistent. The specification test due to Hausman (1978) tests for orthogonality i.e. whether the covariance of an efficient estimator with its difference from an inefficient estimator is zero. Therefore, Hausman specification test in essence is to test the covariance matrix of the difference vector $[\hat{\beta}_{CML} - \hat{\beta}_{ML}]$ for statistical significance,

$$Var[\hat{\beta}_{CML} - \hat{\beta}_{ML}] = Var[\hat{\beta}_{CML}] + Var[\hat{\beta}_{ML}] - Cov[\hat{\beta}_{CML}, \hat{\beta}_{ML}] - Cov[\hat{\beta}_{ML} - \hat{\beta}_{CML}] \quad (18.18)$$

$$Cov[(\hat{\beta}_{CML} - \hat{\beta}_{ML}), \hat{\beta}_{ML}] = Cov[\hat{\beta}_{CML} - \hat{\beta}_{ML}] - Var[\hat{\beta}_{ML}] = 0 \quad (18.19)$$

$$Cov[\hat{\beta}_{CML} - \hat{\beta}_{ML}] = Var[\hat{\beta}_{ML}] \quad (18.20)$$

$$Var[\hat{\beta}_{CML} - \hat{\beta}_{ML}] = Var[\hat{\beta}_{CML}] - Var[\hat{\beta}_{ML}] = \Omega \quad (18.21)$$

The chi-squared test is based on the Wald criterion,

$$W = \chi^2[K-1] = [\hat{\beta}_{CML} - \hat{\beta}_{ML}]' \Omega^{-1} [\hat{\beta}_{CML} - \hat{\beta}_{ML}] \quad (18.22)$$

where $\Omega$ is the estimated covariance matrix.

The logistic regression is basically non-linear, and therefore, the logistic estimates do not have the same constant effect throughout the distribution. Hence, the marginal effect i.e. the effect β of $x_{it}$ on $y_{it}$ varies over the distribution as the estimated curve is non-linear. For estimation purpose, the logistic regression curve is linearised by taking the log of odds of the dependent variable, thereby making it difficult to interpret the coefficients straightaway. That is, it is inappropriate to calculate the marginal effect at the mean. Hence, the marginal effect of a variable *j* in the logistic regression is calculated as $\beta_j$ $P_i$ (1-$P_i$) where Pi is the probability that *y*=1. While the evaluation of $P_i$ involves all variables in the model, the rate of change in the probability of obtaining credit from the formal sector for a unit change of a regressor is given by,

$$\text{Marginal effect} = Prob[y = 1|\bar{x}, d = 1] - Prob[y = 1|\bar{x}, d = 0] \quad (18.23)$$

where *x* denote the mean values of the variables in the model.

## 18.4 Empirical Analysis

As the objective of this paper is to identify and estimate the effects of the determinants of source of credit for households, the probability of credit from a source, formal or informal, is taken as a dichotomous variable i.e. *y*=1 or 0 and the dependent variable is measured as logits or the log of odds ratio. The descriptive statistics of the variables in the empirical analysis are presented in Table 18.6. About 36 percent of households have taken loan from formal source, thus, a majority have obtained from informal sources. The average credit size is Rs. 48,590 and the annual interest rate paid by the households is on average Rs. 19.72 on the credit. The standard deviation of both variables is substantial showing wide variations both in loan amount and interest rates across the sources. Note that loan amount is used here as a measure of quantity rationing in the formal sector institutions. About 29 percent of households are members in cooperatives or NGO or SHG. Nearly 28 percent of households borrowed either for business or agriculture purposes, another 15 percent availed loan for housing or land purchase. For about 40 percent of households, agriculture is the primary occupation.

**Table 18.6: Descriptive Statistics of the Variables in the Credit Sources Analysis**

| *Variable* | *Description* | *Mean* | *Std.dev.* |
|---|---|---|---|
| Creditsource | If credit sourced from formal institutions =1, 0 otherwise | 0.36 | 0.48 |
| Irate | Annual rate of interest charged on the credit (in percent) | 19.72 | 21.74 |
| Loanamt | Credit amount measured in 2004-05 constant prices adjusted with GDP deflator (in Rs.000) | 48.59 | 360.07 |
| HHinc | Total of all incomes of all the individuals in a household from various sources measured in 2004-05 constant prices adjusted with GDP deflator (in Rs.000) | 55.22 | 106.05 |
| Edu | Number of years of education by the most literate individual in the household | 9.18 | 3.68 |
| Urban | Urban=1, 0 otherwise (classified on the basis of Census 2001 and Census 2011) | 0.22 | 0.41 |
| Member | Membership in any of three cooperative, NGO or SHG group = 1, 0 otherwise | 0.29 | 0.46 |
| Lnedu | If loan is for education = 1, 0 otherwise | 0.04 | 0.19 |
| Lnbusiness | If loan is for business/agriculture = 1, 0 otherwise | 0.28 | 0.45 |
| Lnhouse | If loan is for housing/land purchase = 1, 0 otherwise | 0.15 | 0.36 |
| Osalary | If occupation is salary employed = 1, 0 otherwise | 0.11 | 0.32 |
| Oagri | If occupation is agriculture = 1, 0 otherwise | 0.40 | 0.49 |
| Obusiness | If occupation is business = 1, 0 otherwise | 0.03 | 0.16 |
| Other | If other occupations = 1, 0 otherwise | 0.04 | 0.20 |
| N | No. of observations | 23,008 | |

Both the panel conditional logistic fixed effects and random effects models are estimated and the results are presented in Table 18.7. The estimating panel logistic regression equation is specified as,

$$\text{Creditsource}_{it} = \beta_1 (\text{Irate}_{it}) + \beta_3 (\text{Loanamt}_{it}) + \beta_4 (\text{HHinc}_{it}) + \beta_5 (\text{Edu}_{it}) + \beta_6 \text{ Urban}_{it}) + \beta_7 (\text{Memberit}) + \beta_8 (\text{Lnedu}_{it}) + \beta_9 (\text{Lnbusinessit}) + \beta_{10} (\text{Lnhouse}_{it}) + \beta_{11} \text{ Osalary}_{it}) + \beta_{12} (\text{Oagri}_{it}) + \beta_{13} (\text{Obusiness}_{it}) + \beta_{14}(\text{Oother}_{it}) + \lambda i + u_{it} \quad (18.24)$$

where $\lambda_i$ indicates the individual effects. The variable loan amount is intended to capture the effects of quantity rationing. Application of the Hausman specification test suggests that the appropriate model is the fixed effects logistic regression model. The Hausman specification test rejects the null hypothesis that the random effects model at 5 percent level of significance. Therefore, the results of the conditional fixed effects logistic regression model only are discussed, and the maximum likelihood results of random effects model are presented only for comparison. Further, as the estimated coefficients indicate the effect of the variables on the probability, the more relevant marginal effects are interpreted.

**Table 18.7: Panel Logistic Regression Estimates of Source of Credit in India Dependent Variable: Source of credit**

| *Variable* | *Conditional fixed effects model* | | *Random effects model* | |
|---|---|---|---|---|
| | *Coefficient* | *Marginal effect* | *Coefficient* | *Marginal effect* |
| Irate | -0.0525* (0.00) | -0.0051* (0.00) | -0.6166* (0.00) | -0.0151* (0.00) |
| Loanamt | 0.0024* (0.00) | 0.0002* (0.00) | 0.0006* (0.00) | 0.0016* (0.00) |
| HHinc | 0.004* (0.00) | 0.0004* (0.00) | 0.0047* (0.00) | 0.0011* (0.00) |
| Edu | 0.1294* (0.00) | 0.0125* (0.00) | 0.0775* (0.00) | 0.0190* (0.00) |
| Urban | 1.129* (0.004) | 0.0879* (0.00) | -0.1484** (0.018) | -0.0362** (0.017) |
| Member | 0.9923* (0.00) | 0.0875* (0.00) | 0.4831* (0.00) | 0.1194* (0.00) |
| Lnhouse | 0.6483* (0.00) | 0.0532* (0.00) | 0.8402* (0.00) | 0.2069* (0.00) |
| Lnedu | 0.9029* (0.00) | 0.0637* (0.00) | 0.8009* (0.00) | 0.1970* (0.00) |
| Lnbusiness | 1.0529* (0.00) | 0.0936* (0.00) | 1.5337* (0.00) | 0.3656* (0.00) |
| Osalary | 0.2138 (0.24) | 0.0195 (0.21) | 0.1876** (0.014) | 0.0464** (0.014) |
| Oagri | 0.0087 (0.94) | 0.0008 (0.95) | 0.2912 (0.00) | 0.7158 (0.00) |
| Obusiness | 0.133 (0.61) | 0.0122 (0.59) | 0.3218 (0.004) | 0.1037 (0.004) |
| Oother | -0.1518 (0.57) | -0.0155 (0.59) | 0.3218 (0.004) | 0.0800 (0.004) |
| Constant | - | | -1.5520* (0.00) | |
| Number of observations | 3350 | | 13333 | |
| Number of groups | 1675 | | 9196 | |
| Log likelihood | -821.43 | | -6878.35 | |
| Prob>Chi$^2$ [Wald chi$^2$] | 0.000 | | 0.000 | |
| Hausman Test – Prob>Chi$^2$ | | | 0.000 | |

**Note:** p-values in parentheses. * Significant at 1 percent level ** Significant at 5 percent level *** significant at 10 percent level.

The estimated results show that credit size has a statistically significant positive effect on borrowing loan from the formal credit source, and the estimated marginal effect is 0.2 percent. This shows that an increase in the demand for credit by Rs.1000, the probability that the household avails loan from a formal source increases only by 0.002. Therefore, it can be inferred that credit size has a very low impact on the formal source of credit for a household, showing the presence of quantity rationing in the formal banking sector. This result is in conformity with the observations in the literature (Guirkinger, 2006). Further, the negligible impact of the demand for credit size on formal sector lending shows the ineffectiveness of financial inclusion through priority sector lending or microfinance taken by the RBI and governments.

The significant presence of quantity rationing in the formal credit sources may induce households to seek credit from informal sources. This finding is also confirmed by the estimated significant negative effect of interest rate on the formal sector credit. An increase in interest rate reduces the probability of credit by 0.5 percent. Note that this result is in line with results in the literature (Kochar, 1997). This implies that though interest rate charged by the formal sources is relatively low, the cost of credit in addition to the transaction costs such as procedural delays acts as a disincentive for the household to apply for formal credit and for the banks to sanction the loan. Even, an increase in household income is not sufficient to provide collateral security to the formal sector credit, as the estimated coefficient on household income shows. Though positive and significant, increase in household income increases the probability that the household borrows loan from a formal source by 0.04 percent only. All these results show the presence of significant presence of quantity rationing in the formal institutional credits. Hence, households borrow from local informal sources such as moneylenders and relatives even at higher interest rates.

On the other hand, the increase in the education of household members increases the probability of credit from formal sources. The coefficient on years of education of highest educated individual in the household is positive and statistically significant. This points out that education promotes financial literacy and awareness of formal credit among households as noted by Campero and Kaiser (2013). Likewise, membership in a cooperative society or NGO or SHG has the greatest effect on borrowing from a formal sector credit institution. The probability that a household borrows from formal credit sources increases by a significant 8 percent when the household is a member of such organisations as compared to non-membership. Since these organisations play a dual role of both offering credit and enhancing the social networking of the households, membership plays a crucial role in a household obtaining formal credit. Thus, social capital has a significant impact on the access to formal credit, as observed by Wydick et al. (2011).

As compared to borrowers in rural areas, there is a greater chance that the borrowers in urban areas have formal credit as their credit source. The estimated results show that the probability that a household borrows from formal sources is greater by 8 percent in urban areas as compared to rural areas. This further indicates the claim that environmental factors and awareness play a greater role in obtaining credit from a formal source. In respect of the purpose of credit, with consumption loans being the reference category, it is found that the housing loans, business loans and education loans cause an increase of 5 percent, 6 percent and 9 percent probability respectively of the credit source being formal institutions. These results are in line with Zeller's (1994) argument that purpose of credit impacts the repaying rate and consequently the source of credit. For occupation categories, though the estimated coefficients are positive, none of the variables are statistically significant. However, the results suggest that, as compared to wage labourers, other categories have a greater probability of borrowing from formal sources. As indicated in the preceding paragraphs, a wage labour cannot afford to provide the required collateral security and surety the formal sector institutions demand for extending a credit. Moreover, the demand for small size of credit by the wage labourer also increases the transactions cost of formal institutions and therefore there is quantity rationing in credit to the sections by the formal institutions. Further, with low education and social networking, the level of awareness and information on the credit availability in formal institutions is poor for a wage labour. The proximity of a wage labour to the informal sources makes it easy the access and repayment conditions, though he has to pay much higher interest rate on the credit.

## 18.5 Conclusion

The financial sector that provides credit to the public in India consists of both formal and informal sources. The formal sector institutions provide credit at low interest rates with adequate collateral security and surety, whereas the informal sources extend credit more on the basis of proximity and high interest rates. The demand for loans by households is constrained by both demand and supply side factors. The small size of credit demand increases the transactions cost of formal sector sources leading to quantity rationing, while the same increases the prospects of informal sector borrowings with less monitoring and enforcement costs for the local moneylenders and relatives/friends. The main objective of this paper is to understand whether there is quantity rationing in credit in formal sector institutions in India. Towards this objective, this paper attempts to identify the determinants of, and their effects on, the source of credit for households, using the IHDS-I and II (2004-05 and 2011-12) data and applying the panel logistic regression models. The estimated results of this study shows that the size of credit, a measure used for the presence of quantity rationing in the formal sector, and interest rate are important determinants of the probability of borrowing from formal institutional sources. These results suggest that, though the interest rates are low, to some extent there is quantity rationing in formal sector lending in India due to the small size of demand for credit and absence of collateral security and surety. And due to this the households borrow from informal sources at much higher interest rates, where the proximity and information flow are the main determinants of lending by local moneylenders and relatives. Further, the size of credit, household income, education, urban residence, membership in NGO/ SHG or co-operatives and purpose of the loan have significant positive effect on obtaining credit from formal sources by the households. Overall, the study shows that extent of quantity rationing in the formal credit markets in India, though present, is minimal.

# 19

# The Technical Efficiency of Commercial Banks: A Multiple Output-Multiple Input Technology Panel Stochastic Ray Frontier Function Estimation


## Abstract

*In recent years, the commercial banking sector in India is in great stress with staggering rates of loan defaults, accumulating non-performing assets, priority lending obligations and high regulation norms. At the same time, as commercial firms, they have to maximise profit in the midst of providing financial services to the public. The banks have to operate to their potential levels and any inefficiency will dent their performance. As potential output levels of banks are not observed directly, this paper uses a frontier function approach to estimate the technical efficiency of commercial banks using the inputs-outputs mix. The multiple output- multiple input stochastic ray frontier function is estimated for a panel of 47 commercial banks in India for the period 2014-17 and the effects of the factors that determine the level of technical efficiency of banks are also estimated. The ML estimates of ray frontier function show that the mean technical efficiency of Indian scheduled commercial banks is on average 33 percent, with a range for individual banks between 23 and 77 percent. The high technical inefficiency of banks is explained by high non-performing assets, priority sector lending and the age of the banks. Improving regulations, technology and management practices are key to improve technical efficiency of scheduled commercial banks in India.*



**Keywords:** *Multiple output-input technology, technical efficiency, stochastic ray frontier function, commercial bank performance, panel ML estimation*


## 19.1 Introduction

Generally, producing units use many inputs and produce one or more outputs. Economic theory usually presents the producers as successful optimisers. They maximise production, minimise cost, and maximise profits.

Typically, the neoclassical theory of firm focuses on the technical relationship between inputs and outputs, assuming that all firms are using the inputs efficiently and producing the maximum outputs given technology. Further, all inputs are assumed to be efficient and inputs are rewarded equal to their marginal product. Moreover, firms are also assumed to employ the inputs to the point of zero marginal product. Hence, in a competitive market, no input will be employed inefficiently and no firms can produce outputs lesser than the maximum outputs. Therefore, all producing units need to be fully efficient for competition in the market. Technical efficiency is the cornerstone of economic profitability as it measures the ability of the firm to produce maximal outputs from a given set of inputs. Hence, it affects the competitive position of a firm directly (Belhassan and Womack, 2000). If there exists any inefficiency either in the inputs or in the outputs, or the firm uses a lesser technology, then the firm cannot sell its outputs at competitive price in the market as other firms and cannot reward the inputs their value of marginal product. Therefore, the firm has to go out of the market due to its inefficiency.

However, in practice, the use of inputs and production of outputs differ markedly among the firms that produce the same type of products. In reality, no two firms will have the same quality inputs and accordingly outputs will not be the same for the two firms. There are a number of factors that operate in the production environment like degree of competitiveness, input and output quality, network characteristics, ownership form, regulation, etc. that is bound to produce different outcomes for each firm. There are also differences in unobserved factors like management skills, motivation, effort, loyalty, or productive efficiency of both the inputs and the producing units. Therefore, firms may be inefficient in realising their full potential, and inefficiency arises when firms produce quantity of outputs that are below the production potential, or technically, their frontiers. Technically stated, production frontier is the locus of the technically efficient input-output combinations wherein each point of the frontier shows how productive a business can be given the fewest inputs, or resources, necessary to do the job. Producing firms that are on or close to this frontier are said to be technically efficient in that they use their inputs efficiently to realise the full potential in the inputs.

Production unit's inefficiency can result from non-optimal allocation of resources into production (allocative inefficiency), technological deficiencies (technical inefficiency) or productive inefficiency (input inefficiency). Both allocative and technical inefficiencies constitute economic (cost) inefficiency and economic efficiency and productive efficiency are very crucial to any firm for its viability. Theoretically, economic efficiency refers to the ability of firms to produce outputs at minimum costs, given input prices. Allocative efficiency occurs when consumers pay a market price that reflects the private marginal cost of production i.e. the firm produces that output where the marginal cost of production just equals the price of that product. Productive efficiency occurs when a firm is combining resources in such a way as to produce a given output at the lowest possible average total cost, that is in effect is the marginal cost. Thus, productive is to be understood in terms of cost minimisation by adjusting the mix of inputs, technical efficiency is output maximisation from a given mix of inputs.

Generally, allocative efficiency of a firm depends on the market conditions, where the prices of the produced outputs are determined, the firm's technical efficiency is determined within the firm, by its own actions like management skills and inputs-outputs decisions. Therefore, measurement of technical efficiency of production units and the identification of sources of their inefficiency are important to improve the performance of any producing unit in order to improve their competitive level.

Technical efficiency relates to how much output can be obtained from a given input, such as a worker or a machine, or a specific combination of inputs. Maximum technical efficiency occurs when output is maximised from a given quantity of inputs. It is the ratio of actual output to potential output. Suppose that a firm has a production plan $(y^0, x^0)$ where the first argument is the set of outputs and the second is the set of inputs. Given the production function $f(.)$, the firm is technically efficient if $y^0$=f($x^0$) and technically inefficient if $y^0$<f($x^0$). Thus, technical efficiency explains their ability to operate close to, or on the boundary of their production set. Hence, the technical efficiency measured by the ratio $0 \leq [y^0/f(x^0)] \leq 1$,) i.e. technical efficiency lies between 0 and 1. Therefore, technical inefficiency is measured as (1-TE).

Measurement of technical efficiency requires estimation of the production frontier, the maximum output from an input mix. The production function $y^m = f(x; \beta)$, shows the potential output ym producible from a given vector of inputs $(x)$, where $\beta$ represents the production function parameters. When the actual output produced $y$ is less than the potential output $y^m$, then there is technical efficiency. Since the potential output is not observed directly like the actual output, a stochastic random variable $u$ is added to the deterministic production frontier and the production frontier can be written as $y^m = f(x; \beta) + v$. Further, as the level of inefficiency is not the same across firms, to capture firm-specific inefficiency, a non-negative random variable $u_i$ is added, and the production frontier can now be specified as $y^m = f(x;\beta) + v - u_i$. There are two families of methods to measure the efficiency frontier, non-parametric methods like Data Envelopment Analysis (DEA) or Free Disposal Hull (FDH) (Farrell, 1957; Aigner and Chu, 1968; Timmer, 1971), and parametric methods like Stochastic Frontier Analysis (SFA), Thick Frontier Approach (TFA) and Distribution Free Approach (DFA) (Aigner, Lovell and Schmidt, 1977; Meeusen and Broeck, 1977).The former methods use linear programming to calculate an efficient deterministic frontier against which firm's efficiency are compared, the latter methods use econometric functions modeling inefficiency as an additional stochastic term. These methods estimate technical efficiency from the input-output mix that is specified for a single output and multiple inputs. A severe limitation of these methods is that they can not measure the technical efficiency when firms produce more than one output, which is in the most production units.

The measurement of technical efficiency in case of multiple output-multiple input mix is feasible if the production function can be specified as a scalar-valued function. That is, an output frontier vector for multiple output mix can be defined as an Euclidean norm of the polar coordinate angles of outputs. The mix of outputs is now specified as a stochastic ray production function *a la* Lothgren (2000). Thus, the multiple output-multiple input production frontier can be specified as, $y^m = \iota\, m(\theta) = \sum_{j=1}^{p} y^j_i = (x;\beta) + v - u_i$ where $i$ is the Euclidean norm of the output vector $y$, $p$ is the number of outputs, and $m(\theta)$ is the output mix angles.

Generally, the production environment considered in technical efficiency measurement is the output producing manufacturing sector where outputs and most inputs are usually in physical units. However, in the service sector, the outputs produced are generally services and are almost in different units of measurement. Therefore, it would be interesting and also important to see the technical efficiency of a service industry. One such important service sector in an economy is the commercial banking sector which does multiple services as well as involves multiple inputs. As commercial units, dealing with deposits and lending along with a host of other services to the public and the financial sector in general, the commercial banks are also profit maximisers, and most importantly, do business in one of most competitive sectors of an economy. Essentially, commercial Banks are multi-product firms and produce a variety of products and services as loans to customers, safekeeping, intermediation and accounting services for deposits (Benston and Smith, 1976). Therefore, this paper attempts to measure the technical efficiency of the commercial banks in India. The banking sector is ideally suited for the technical efficiency analysis of a multiple output-input mix service industry. This paper applies the stochastic ray production function method to 47 scheduled commercial banks in India for the year 2014-17 to measure their technical efficiency, and identifies the factors affecting their inefficiency.

## 19.2 Recent Performance of Indian Commercial Banks

It is important to consider the efficiency of commercial banks per se, for two reasons. First, the commercial banks are the wheel of the industry and commerce in an economy. To cite one such crucial role, bank credit accounted for more than half of the total financial flow (54 percent) to the financial resources of the commercial sector in India during 2013-14, and still constitutes a significant 35 percent, showing the important relevance of commercial banks to economic growth. At the same, in recent years the banking sector is at the receiving end for mismanagement and poor performance. There is widespread concern that most state run commercial banks top the nonperforming assets (NPA) lists and many are bogged down by scams and bad loans. The commercial banks are hard it despite the best efforts by banks to cover it up in restructuring loan strategies, and government's help with recapitalisation. The persistent deterioration in the bank asset quality dented the profitability and consequent deleveraging resulted in historically low credit growth. This poor performance prompted questions on the efficiency of the banking sector and put immense pressure on the regulator of banks in India, the RBI.

Generally, the performance of any firm is judged by the level of profit it makes or the expansion of its business. Being service industry, the performance of commercial banks has to be judged from net profit a bank earns and its growth in credits, the main operation of banks to earn profit. Figure 19.1 presents the net profit of commercial banks in India during 2010-17. It can be seen that there is steady rise in net profit upto 2013, and since 2014 net profit fluctuate with a declining trend. In 2015, RBI came out with a list of over 150 accounts facing problems in servicing debt obligations, which was pruned to 120 later, and asked all the lenders to recognise their exposures to those as non-performing assets or bad loans, reflection of which is clear from the sharp dip in net profits during 2015-16. The RBI has also taken intense efforts to clean up the accumulated NPAs or bad loans of commercial banks and improve the quality of bank assets like introducing the joint lenders forum (JLF) which allows multiple banks that had extended loans to a specific firm to consider a collective mechanism to resolve the problem, the strategic debt restructuring (SDR), a scheme for sustainable structuring of stressed assets.

The position of net profit with respect to capital employed in commercial banks in India in 2016-17 is presented in Figure 19.2. As can be observed the profit levels are generally low despite the varied levels of capital employed. While the HDFC Bank has the highest profit for capital employed, the IDFC Bank is making low profit in relation to the amount of capital employed. Most

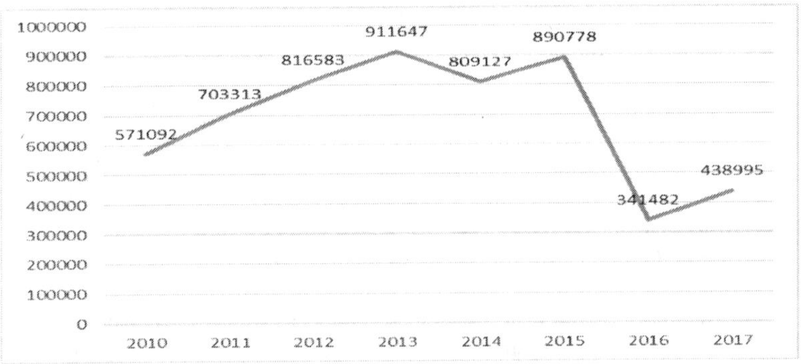


*Source:* RBI (2017): Liabilities and Assets of Scheduled Commercial Banks.

***Figure 19.1 Net Profit of Commercial Banks in India, 2010-17 (Rs. millions).***

of the commercial banks earn low profits. Some banks like IDBI, State Bank of Patiala, and Indian Overseas Bank has incurred losses as well.

The Figure 19.3 shows the growth rate of credit in commercial banks between 2011 and 2017. It is clearly seen that the bank credit growth has declined drastically during this period, from 10.3 percent to 4.5 percent.

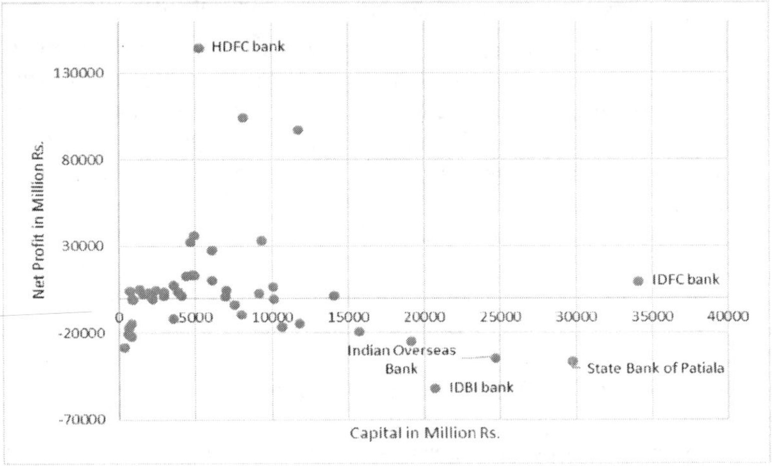


*Source:* RBI: Statistical Tables Relating to Banks in India 2016-17.

***Figure 19.2 Relation of Net Profit to Capital of Commercial Banks in India, 2016-17***

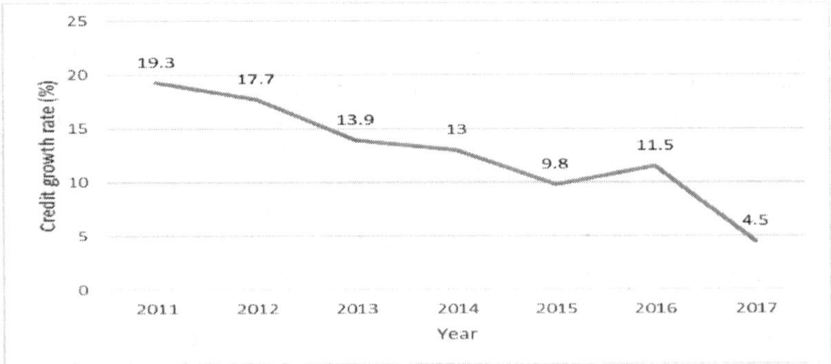


*Source:* RBI: Scheduled Commercial Banks – Business in India.

***Figure 19.3 Growth Rate of Credit in Commercial Banks in India, 2011-17.***

Further, in the financial sector, the efficiency of a firm is usually analysed with efficiency ratios, very important tools used by finance managers in the production planning process. Among those ratios, return on assets ratio is the ratio of operating profits to total assets shows the percentage of profit a company earns in relation to its overall resources. The return on assets ratio is an important ratio because it measures the efficiency with which the firm is managing its investment in assets and using them to generate profit. The return on assets of commercial banks presented in Figure 19.4 shows that there is drastic variation in the efficiency levels of the banks, ranging from -3 percent to 2 percent. The return on assets in commercial banks is bogged down by the NPAs of Rs. 2860 billions, which accounts for 2 percent of the total assets of Rs. 141586.24 billions in 2016-17. The ratio of gross non-performing assets to gross advances, a measure of bad loans, has increased from 2.36 percent in March 2011 to 4.11 percent in March 2014, and still worse, 10.41 percent as of December 2017. However, as presented in Table 19.1, the NPA amount recovered from the various recovery channels like Lok Adalats, Debts Recovery Tribunals (DRTs) and the Securitisation and Reconstruction of Financial Assets and Enforcement of Securities Interest Act (SARFAESI) aggregate merely to about 10 percent of the NPAs.

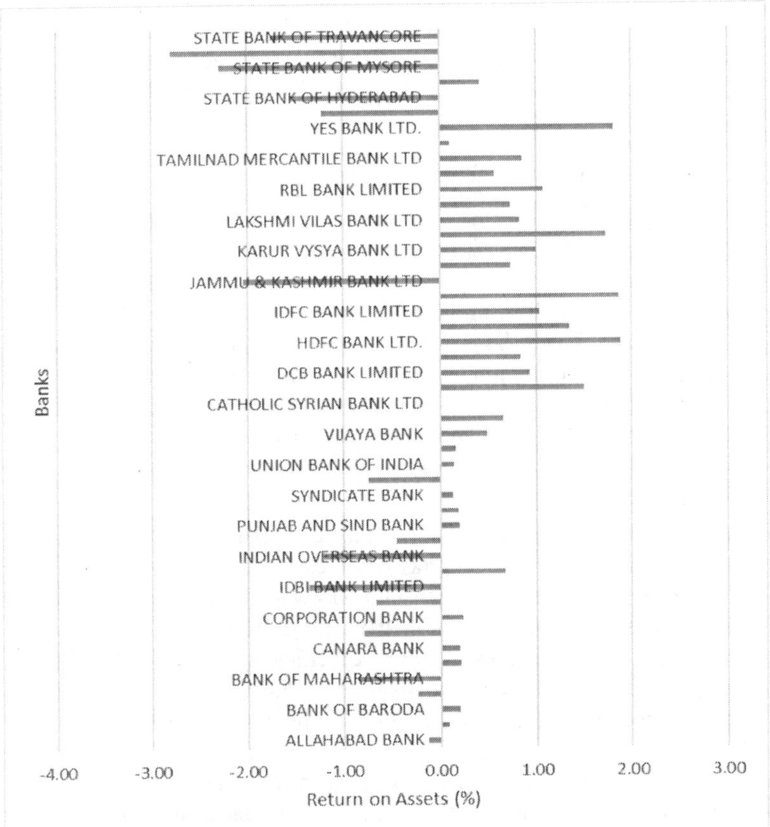


*Source:* RBI: Statistical Tables Relating to Banks in India 2016-17 RBI.

***Figure 19.4 Commercial Banks Return on Assets in India***

**Table 19.1: Non-Performing Assets of Commercial Banks in India, 2016-17(Rs. billion)**

| *NPA* | *Lokadalats* | *DRTs* | *SARFAESI act* | *Total* |
|---|---|---|---|---|
| Total NPA | 1058 | 671 | 1131 | 2860 |
| NPA recovered | 38 | 164 | 78 | 280 |
| Percent NPA recovered to total NPA | 4 | 24 | 7 | 10 |

*Source:* RBI: Statistical Tables Relating to Banks in India 2016-17.

Thus, all these few indicators of bank performance presented show that the commercial banks in India are not operating efficiently and there exists significant levels of inefficiency in bank performance. However, these conventional measures of efficiency do not provide direct measurement of either the bank efficiency or the inefficiency. Therefore, direct measurement of banking efficiency or inefficiency is needed in order to assess the bank performance and to gain insights to the best practice the bank has to follow to be the best performer. The literature on firm efficiency measurement suggests a number of measures of best practices for production units using alternative frontier techniques.

## 19.3 A Brief Review of Recent Studies

Farrell (1957) was the first to estimate the deterministic frontier model (DEA). DEA involves a non-parametric way of plotting input/output ratios of firms in a space of suitable number of dimensions forming the convex closure of the set of points. Following Farrell's initiatives, Aigner and Chu (1968) specified a deterministic homogenous Cobb-Douglas production frontier function. To overcome the limitations of the deterministic approach, Aigner, Lovell and Schmidt (1977) and Meeusen and Broeck (1977) independently developed a stochastic frontier approach (SFA) to measure technical efficiency by adding a firm specific random noise variable along with technical inefficiency term in the production.

Kumar and Gulati (2008) analyse technical efficiency and scale efficiency of Indian public sector banking industry for 1992-2005 using input oriented DEA approach, a method that minimises inputs while keeping output constant. The paper uses logistic regression method to estimate the effect of a set of environment variables on the overall technical efficiency of public sector banks. The output measure is the number of deposits and loan accounts and the input vector included physical capital measured by fixed assets, wages of labour, and loanable funds that include borrowings and deposits. The estimated technical efficiency of public sector banks is above 75 percent, except Bank of India with 63.2 percent, while most of the State Banks show 100 percent technical efficiency.

Dwivedi and Charyulu (2011) seek to determine the impact of various market and regulatory initiatives on efficiency improvements of Indian banks in the post-reform era. The input variables of the study include number of bank branches, total operating expenses and deposits while the output of banks are advances and non-interest income. The DEA-Constant Returns to Scale model estimates show mean technical efficiency of 95.6 percent in 2005 and an improved 97.9 percent in 2010. It is observed that the national banks, new private banks and foreign banks have high efficiency over the period.

Samad (2009) examines inefficiency of Bangladesh banking industry using the stochastic frontier production function model for a cross-sectional data for 2000. The SFA is estimated using loans as output variable and deposits and employees as inputs. The estimated results show that efficiency of Bangladesh commercial banks lies between 12.7 and 94.7 percent.

However, both DEA and SFA consider only a single output, though consider an input bundle, can not provide efficiency measures for multiple output production environment. This severe limitation of the applicability of these methodologies in the case of multiple output technologies, as noted earlier, is solved by the stochastic ray frontier function. Lothgren (2000) was the first to develop and estimate this stochastic ray frontier function approach for specification and estimation of multiple-output production frontiers. He applied the ray function to the healthcare industry of Sweden, using 26 Swedish County Council healthcare data for the years 1984-1994. Using the number of beds as a proxy for capital input in the production of healthcare, Lothgren (2000) specified three different outputs, number of admissions, number of operations and number of physicians. The stochastic ray frontier estimates show that a unit increase in cost of production results in 8.6 percent increase in output and a unit increase in bed results in 92 percent increase in output. The output mix show significant coefficients of -9.62 and - 4.25, indicating that output mix affects the frontier output norm.

Following Lothgren (2000), Lakshmanasamy and Shanmugam (2001; 2003) estimate all the alternative methodologies of frontier techniques to measure the technical efficiency of single as well multi-outputs of 58 commercial banks in India for 1999. The estimated models include non-parametric method DEA, parametric methods SFA, Random Coefficients Approach (RCA) and Stochastic Ray Frontier Function (RAY). Two outputs, interest margin and other non-interest income, and three inputs namely deposits, borrowings and labour employed are considered in the study. The study reveals that the mean technical efficiency estimates by DEA is 65percent, RCA 51.71 percent, SFA range from 52 to 81 percent, and RAY 81.32 percent. The RAY coefficients suggest that the elasticity of Euclidean output with respect to deposits is 89.5 percent, labour 0.5 percent, and borrowing 0.046 percent. The inclusion of non-interest income as a second output of banks adds about 2 percent efficiency in RAY estimates.

Thus, regardless of methodology used, the Indian banking sector seems to have fared well, with mean technical efficiency above the average in pre-2000s and achieving more than 75 percent of technical efficiency in post-2000s. Also, the efficiency levels of most of the units are above 90 percent for the years 2005-10. However, DEA or SFA method used in most of the studies on Indian bank efficiency is either deterministic model which does not consider random noise or single output model. As obvious commercial banks are doing lot of services, banks are multi-output firms. Therefore, the stochastic ray frontier approach is the most suited method to address the efficiency measurement of multiple output-multiple input technology of the commercial banks.

## 19.4 Data and Methodology

The data relating to the input and output variables of 47 scheduled commercial banks from the Statistical Tables Relating to Banks in India, 2016-17 in the Database of Indian Economy (DBIE) of the Reserve Bank of India's data warehouse, have been used in this paper. The scheduled commercial banks are those banks that are included in the second schedule of RBI Act 1934 which carry out the normal business of banking such as accepting deposits, giving loans and other banking services to the public. The RBI's Statistical Tables Relating to Banks in India covers the activities of scheduled commercial banks, rural co-operative banks, non-banking financial companies (NBFCs) and financial institutions (FIs). Information on major items of liabilities and assets, income and expenses, selected financial ratios, number of employees and details of priority sector advances of commercial banks are available in the database. In addition, data on capital adequacy ratios (CRAR), non-performing assets (NPAs), exposure to sensitive sectors, contingent liabilities and unclaimed deposits are also available. The 47 commercial banks operating in India considered in this study consists of state banks, nationalised banks and private banks for the years 2014-17, with total observations of 188. For the purpose of this study, interest margin and non-interest income are the two output variables, and the input variables are borrowings, deposits, fixed assets and expenditure on employees. From assets point of view, deposit services is essentially viewed as inputs which are used to make loans (Sealey and Lindley, 1977). Interest margin is the net of interest income over interest expense. All other income of the banks other than by way of net interest income including fine, fee for their services etc. are accounted in non-interest income. Interest income, interest expense and non-interest income are available in 'Earnings and Expenses of Scheduled Commercial Banks'. The input variables are available in 'Liabilities and Assets of Scheduled Commercial Banks' and 'Bank wise and Category wise Employees of Scheduled Commercial Banks'.

### Stochastic Ray Frontier Function

The Deterministic Frontier Approach (DEA) approach assumes that the actual level of output of a firm lies below the frontier only due to the existence of the technical inefficiency in the production process and applies a linear programming (LP) solution. The stochastic frontier function approach measures technical efficiency as a ratio of actual output to potential output, adding a composite error term that include a random noise variable along with the error (technical inefficiency) term. However, both these approaches apply to a single output-multiple input technology only. To overcome the limitations of both the deterministic and stochastic frontier approaches in this respect, the ray production function for multiple inputs-outputs technology can be specified as a scalar-valued representation of the multiple input-multiple output technology that defines the Euclidean norm of the frontier output vector as a function of the inputs and the output mix, represented by the polar coordinate angles ($\theta$). A stochastic ray frontier model is obtained by introducing a composed error term as in the stochastic frontier model.

To begin with, the multiple output $y \varepsilon R^p_+$ and multiple input $x \varepsilon R^d_+$ technology production is described by the output set $P(x)$ defined as,

$$P(x) = \{y \in R^p_+ : x \text{ can produce y}\} \tag{19.1}$$

The technology is assumed to satisfy a set of axioms as per Shephard (1970),

(i) No free lunch: $(x, y) \in \Gamma$, production set, if $x = 0$ then $y = 0$. This axiom states that inactivity is always possible, i.e., zero output can be produced by any input vector $x \varepsilon R^d_+$, but it is impossible to produce output without any inputs.

(ii) Free disposability: Let $x \varepsilon R^d_+$ and $y \varepsilon R^p_+$, with $x \geq x$ and $y \leq y$, then $(x, y) \varepsilon \psi$. This is the free disposability assumption, named also the 'possibility of destroying goods without costs', on the production set. The weak disposability property allows model congestion and overutilisation of inputs/outputs.

(iii) Compactness: $P(x)$ is bounded $\forall x \varepsilon R^d_+$.The production set $\Gamma$ is closed, $P(x)$ is closed $\forall x \varepsilon R^d_+$, $\forall y \varepsilon R^p_+$.

(iv) Convexity: The convexity of $\Gamma$ can be stated as: If $(x_1, y_1)$, $(x_2, y_2)$ $\varepsilon\Gamma$, then $\forall \alpha \; \varepsilon \; [0, 1]$, $(x, y) = \alpha(x_1, y_1) + (1 - \alpha)(x_2, y_2) \; \varepsilon\Gamma$.

Let the output set be nonempty. The scalar valued representation of the multiple output technology is obtained from the polar coordinate representation of the output vector as,

$$\boldsymbol{y} = \iota\, m(\theta) \tag{19.2}$$

where $\iota = \|\boldsymbol{y}\| = \sum_{i=1}^{p} \sqrt{y_i^2}$ denotes the Euclidean norm of the output vector $y$ with $p$ being the number of outputs and $m(\theta)$ representing the output mix vector. A transformation of the polar coordinate angle vector $\theta \epsilon \left[0, \frac{\pi}{2}\right]^{p-1}$ to the vector $m(\theta) = y/\iota$ can be obtained from the functionm: $m: \left[0, \frac{\pi}{2}\right]^{p-1} \rightarrow [0,1]^p$, defined by $m_i\ (\theta) = \cos\theta_i \prod_{j=0}^{i-1} \sin\theta_j$ where $i = 1, \ldots, p$, $\theta\epsilon\left[0,\frac{\pi}{2}\right]^{p-1}$, $\sin\theta_0 = \cos\theta_p = 1$. The polar coordinate angle θ can be obtained as $\theta = \cos^{-1}\left[\left(\frac{y_i}{\iota}\right)\prod_{j=0}^{i-1}\sin\theta_j\right], i = 1, \ldots, p$, where $p$ is the number of outputs and thus $p$-1 angles are obtained. This is possible by recursive approach i.e. the first angle is given by $\theta_1 = \cos^{-1}\left(\frac{y_1}{\iota}\right)$ and the second angle is given by $\theta_2 = \left\{\cos^{-1}\left(\frac{y_2}{\iota}\right)\sin\theta_1\right\}$ and so on till $p$-1 angles.

This type of polar coordinate representation of the output vector is thus used to define a ray production function,

$$\Psi(\boldsymbol{x},\theta) = max\{\iota\,\epsilon R_+ : \iota\, m(\theta)\epsilon P(\boldsymbol{x})\} \tag{19.3}$$

which is analogous to the single output production function,

$$f(\boldsymbol{x}) = max\{\boldsymbol{y}\epsilon R_+ : \boldsymbol{y}\epsilon P(\boldsymbol{x})\} \tag{19.4}$$

The ray production function equation (19.3) gives the maximum norm of the attainable outputs given inputs and output mix represented by the polar coordinate angles θ. Then, adding the error terms $v$ and $u$, the stochastic ray production function model can be specified as,

$$\iota = \Psi(x,\theta)\exp\,(v-u) \tag{19.5}$$

Taking logarithms, the stochastic ray frontier function can be written as,

$$ln(\iota) = \beta_0 + \beta_i \sum lnx_i + \varepsilon \tag{19.6}$$

The observed ray norm ι is specified as a function of a deterministic ray function $f\ (x,\ \theta)$ and a composed error term $\varepsilon = (v- u)$ where $v$ accounts for random events affecting the production frontier and the truncated random variable $u$, $u$=0, accounts for random events affecting the technical efficiency of the firm. The stochastic frontier norm is given by,

$$\iota^* = \Psi(x,\theta)\exp\,(u) \tag{19.7}$$

Note that the technical efficiency is modeled as affecting the output radial $y$. The observed output is obtained from a radial rescaling of the frontier output level $y^* = \iota^*\ m\ (\theta)$, and equals $y = y^*\ exp\ (-u)$, where the output reduction factor defines the technical efficiency measure, TE = exp (-$u$).

In the empirical analysis of stochastic frontier function, the usual random disturbance term $v$ is assumed to be $v$~NIID(0, $\sigma^2_v$) and the technical inefficiency measure $u$ is assumed to follow half normal distribution $u$~NIID (0, $\sigma^2_u$). The half-normal distribution is a fold at the mean of an ordinary normal distribution giving the exact half of normal distribution. Outputs within the frontier are deemed inefficient, hence, the direction of inefficiency is one sided and therefore follows half normal distribution. The probability density function of $v$ is given by,

$$f(v) = \frac{1}{\sqrt{2\pi\sigma^2}} exp^{\frac{-v^2}{2\sigma_v^2}} \tag{19.8}$$

The probability density function of *u* is given by,

$$f(u) = \sqrt{\frac{2}{\sqrt{\pi\sigma^2}}} exp^{\frac{-u^2}{2\sigma_u^2}} \tag{19.9}$$

The joint distribution of *u* and *v* is given by,

$$f(v,u) = \frac{1}{\pi\sigma_v\sigma_u} exp^{\left(\frac{-u^2}{2\sigma_u^2} - \frac{v^2}{2\sigma_v^2}\right)} \tag{19.10}$$

Denoting ($v_{kt}$-$u_k$) as ε and $v_{kt}$ as *v* for simplicity and rewriting f($u$,$v$) to get,

$$f(u,\varepsilon) = \frac{1}{\pi\sigma_v\sigma_u} exp^{\left(\frac{-u^2}{2\sigma_u^2} - \frac{(u+\varepsilon)^2}{2\sigma_v^2}\right)} \tag{19.11}$$

The composite error ε is thus part of the equation because some white noise is accommodated as the estimation procedures are stochastic, but an additional one-sided error represents any other reason firms would be away from (within) the boundary. Then,

$$f(\varepsilon) = \int_0^\infty f(u,\varepsilon)\,du \int_0^\infty \frac{1}{\pi\sigma_v\sigma_u} exp^{\left(\frac{-u^2}{2\sigma_u^2} - \frac{(u+\varepsilon)^2}{2\sigma_v^2}\right)} = \frac{1}{\pi\sigma_v\sigma_u} exp^{\left(\frac{-u^2}{2\sigma_u^2} - \frac{(u+\varepsilon)^2}{2\sigma_v^2}\right)} \tag{19.12}$$

The observations within the frontier are deemed 'inefficient', and the direction of inefficiency is one sided and therefore follows half normal distribution. However, this distribution is conditional on ε as *u* is derived from the composite error ε. Hence, the conditional distribution that *u* follows is given by,

$$f(u \mid \varepsilon) = f(u, \varepsilon \mid f(\varepsilon) = \frac{\frac{1}{\pi\sigma_u\,\sigma_v} exp^{\left(\frac{-u^2}{2\sigma_u{}^2} - \frac{(u+\varepsilon)^2}{2\sigma_v{}^2}\right)}}{\frac{2}{\sqrt{2\pi}\sigma_\varepsilon} exp^{\left(-\frac{\varepsilon^2}{2\sigma_\varepsilon}\right)\left(1-\phi\left[\frac{\varepsilon\lambda}{\sigma_\varepsilon}\right]\right)}} \tag{19.13}$$

where $\lambda = \sigma_u/\sigma_v$ and ϕ is the density function of ε. Then, the ratio of the observed output of the ith firm to frontier (potential) output determined by the frontier function, given the input vector *x* provides the technical efficiency of the $i^{th}$ firm. Thus, the technical efficiency of $i^{th}$ firm is,

$$TE_i = exp^{-E[u_i|\varepsilon_i]},\quad E[u_i \mid \varepsilon_i] = \int_0^\infty u_i f(u_i \mid \varepsilon_{it})du \tag{19.14}$$

## 19.5 Empirical Analysis

This section presents the empirical estimation of the stochastic ray frontier function to measure the technical efficiency of the 47 commercial banks.

The two outputs of commercial banks considered are the interest margin and non-interest income, and the inputs are borrowings, deposits and wages. The descriptive statistics of the variables used in the frontier function analysis are presented in Table 19.2. The scheduled commercial banks in India are of varying nature in terms of size, scale and operation and the logarithm of the variables have toned down the variability. This variability is shown by the substantial standard deviation of the output and input variables. Maximum output is produced by State Bank of India (ln =13.477) in the year 2017. In the year 2014, the least output was produced by Bharatiya Mahila Bank (ln = 6.045). Also, maximum of each of inputs is also used by State Bank of India and the least by Bharatiya Mahila Bank. The Tables 13.3 and 13.4 present the correlation among the variables. There is high correlation between the inputs, borrowings, deposits and wages, and the Euclidean norm of output.

**Table 19.2: Descriptive Statistics of the Variables in the Panel Stochastic Ray Frontier Function Analysis**

| *Variable* | *Description* | *Mean* | *Std.dev.* |
|---|---|---|---|
| $l$ | Euclidean norm of output | 67147.61 | 101990 |
| BS | Borrowing by banks | 1531121 | 2200302 |
| FA | Fixed assets | 21130.91 | 36902.06 |
| DS | Deposits | 1992129 | 2723125 |
| WS | Wages | 22875.78 | 36420.76 |
| θ | Output mix | 0.395 | 0.126 |
| ln $l$ | Log of Euclidean norm of outputs | 10.384 | 1.309 |
| lnBS | Log of borrowings | 13.490 | 1.460 |
| lnFA | Log of fixed asset | 9.154 | 1.407 |
| lnDS | Log of deposits | 13.787 | 1.428 |
| lnWS | Log of wages | 9.374 | 1.249 |
| ln θ | Log of proportion of outputs | 3.065 | 0.341 |
| N | No. of observations | 188 | |

**Note:** Monetary variables measured in millions of rupees.

**Table 19.3: Correlation between Inputs and Output Norm**

| *Variable* | *ι* | *Borrowings* | *Fixed assets* | *Deposits* | *Wages* |
|---|---|---|---|---|---|
| ι | 1.00 | | | | |
| Borrowings | 0.976(0.00) | 1.00 | | | |
| Fixed assets | 0.769(0.00) | 0.803(0.00) | 1.00 | | |
| Deposits | 0.955(0.00) | 0.993(0.00) | 0.828(0.00) | 1.00 | |
| Wages | 0.951(0.00) | 0.977(0.00) | 0.779(0.00) | 0.970(0.00) | 1.00 |
| θ | 0.200(0.00) | 0.168(0.02) | 0.214(0.00) | 0.162(0.03) | 0.129(0.08) |

**Note:** p-values in parentheses.

**Table 19.4: Correlation between in Logs of Inputs and Output Norm**

| *Variable* | *ln $l$* | *lnBS* | *lnFA* | *lnDS* | *lnWS* |
|---|---|---|---|---|---|
| ln $l$ | 1.00 | | | | |
| lnBS | 0.9761* | 1.00 | | | |
| lnFA | 0.9143* | 0.9253* | 1.00 | | |
| lnDS | 0.9642* | 0.989* | 0.9219* | 1.00 | |
| lnW | 0.9699* | 0.9737* | 0.933* | 0.9778* | 1.00 |
| lnθ | 0.4048* | 0.4255* | 0.4138* | 0.4144* | 0.3898* |

**Note:** p-value significant at 5 percent level.

Following the literature on frontier function analysis, the panel Cobb-Douglas stochastic ray frontier specification (in log form) is specified empirically as,

$$ln(\iota) = \beta_0 + \beta_1 lnDS_{it} + \beta_2 lnBS_{it} + \beta_3 lnFA_{it} + \beta_4 lnWS_{it} + \beta_5 ln\theta_{it} + \delta_i + v_{it} - u_{it} \quad (19.15)$$

where ι is the Euclidean output norm of the vector of outputs, interest margin and non-interest income, θ is the angle between the two outputs that represent the proportion of interest margin to non-interest income, and $\delta_i$ is the individual heterogeneity. Under the assumption that the individual heterogeneity is uncorrelated with the independent variables, equation (19.13) can be estimated by the panel random effects estimation method. As only two outputs are specified, one polar coordinate is obtained in the ray function. The panel random effects GLS regression estimates of frontier function are presented in Table 19.5. The coefficients of all input variables are positive and the coefficients of borrowings and wages are statistically significant. A one percent increase in borrowings increases the bank outputs by results in 49.34 percent. A one percent increase in wages increases the output by 47.29 percent. However, one percent increase in the proportion of outputs in favour of interest margin decreases the outputs by 12.55 percent. The other input variables, deposits and fixed assets, do not significantly impact the outputs. The overall R-square value shows that about 95.83 percent variations in output variables is explained by the variations in the included input variables.

**Table 19.5: Panel Random Effects GLS Regression Estimates of Stochastic Ray Frontier Function Dependent Variable: ln ι**

| *Variable* | *Coefficient* | *Standard error* | *P>\|z\|* |
|---|---|---|---|
| lnB | 0.4934423* | 0.0695486 | 0.000 |
| lnFA | 0.0084673 | 0.0323616 | 0.794 |

*(Contd...)*

| lnW | 0.4728802* | 0.0749925 | 0.000 |
|---|---|---|---|
| ln θ | -0.1255096* | 0.0470459 | 0.008 |
| Constant | -0.9109365* | 0.3177263 | 0.004 |
| Between variation | 0.20510906 | Between R-square | 0.9632 |
| Within variation | 0.1335212 | Within R-square | 0.9312 |
| Wald chi-square | 2928.13 | Overall R-square | 0.9583 |

**Note:** * Significant at 1 percent level.

It is to be noted that the standard GLS random effects regression estimator, as given in Table 19.5, is a generalised method of moments (GMM) estimator that is just a matrix-weighted average of the between and within estimators. The estimate of constant by GLS method is not consistent as it assumes that the composite error term ε follows normal distribution. But this assumption fails in the case of frontier models as the composite error term ε also includes technical inefficiency term *u* which follows half normal distribution. The maximum likelihood estimation takes both *v* and *u* into consideration and gives the variance components of the error terms that compose the composite error term ε and $\lambda(=\sigma_u/\sigma_v)$. The estimation of these parameters is crucial for computing $\int_0^{-\infty} uf(u \mid \varepsilon)du$ as the conditional distribution of *u* depends on them which in turn is used in computing technical efficiency. The Table 19.6 presents the frontier estimation using ML for the multiple output stochastic ray frontier as well as single output stochastic frontier functions.

**Table 19.6: Panel Random Effects ML Estimates of Stochastic Ray Frontier Function**

| *Variable* | *RFA: Dependent variable: ln l* | | *SFA: Dependent variable: ln (Interest margin)* | |
|---|---|---|---|---|
| | *Coefficient* | *p>\|z\|* | *Coefficient* | *p>\|z\|* |
| lnBS | 0.4809* (0.067) | 0.000 | 0.5500* (0.073) | 0.000 |
| lnFA | 0.0116 (0.031) | 0.710 | -0.0505 (0.033) | 0.123 |
| lnDS | 0.0641 (0.082) | 0.434 | 0.0063 (0.089) | 0.944 |
| lnWS | 0.4660* (0.073) | 0.000 | 0.4701* (0.078) | 0.000 |
| ln $\theta_1$ | -0.1367* (0.046) | 0.003 | | |
| Constant | 0.1036 (3.838) | 0.978 | 0.0719 (1.151) | 0.997 |
| $\sigma_\varepsilon$ | 0.0786 (0.015) | | 0.0701 (0.013) | |
| λ | 0.7718 (0.051) | | 0.6798 (0.064) | |
| $\sigma_u$ | 0.0607 (0.015) | | 0.0477 (0.012) | |
| $\sigma_v$ | 0.0179 (0.022) | | 0.0225 (0.003) | |
| Wald chi$^2$ (4) | 2478.18 | | 2391.04 | |

**Note:** Standard errors in parentheses. * Significant at 1 percent level.

In both models, again the coefficients of all input variables are positive and the coefficients of borrowings and wages are statistically significant. In the ray frontier function, the output elasticity with respect to borrowings is 48.09 percent implying one percent increase in borrowings results in 48 percent increase in bank outputs. Also one percent increase in employee expenditure will result in a significant increase of 46.60 percent in outputs. The output elasticity with respect to the polar coordinate angle $\theta_1$ is negative and statistically significant. The estimated coefficient shows the percentage change in the output norm with a percentage change in the output mix is -13.67 percent. Thus, an increase in proportion of interest margin to overall output will result in a negative impact on bank outputs. Further, positive and significant sigma *u* signals the existence of significant technical inefficiency in Indian commercial banks. The input variables deposits and fixed assets have no significant impact on bank outputs. Output elasticity with respect to fixed assets is just 1.16 percent and a percent increase in deposits results in 6.41 percent increase in outputs. The technical terms σ's and λ are positive indicating that the observed outputs significantly differ from frontier outputs. The estimated value of λ is 0.77 implying that about 77 percent of the gap between the actual and potential outputs is primarily due to technically inefficiency of the banks. The statistical significance of Wald chi-square value shows the statistical fit of the model.

The estimated stochastic ray frontier function is,

$$ln(\hat{\iota}) = 0.1036 + 0.4809 \ln BS + 0.0116 \ln FA + 0.0640 \ln DS + 0.4660 \ln WS - 0.1367 \ln\theta \tag{19.16}$$

giving the deterministic frontier that defines the potential output based on which technical efficiency is computed. The estimated stochastic frontier function with only interest margin is,

$$ln(\widehat{IM}) = 0.0719 + 0.5500 \ln BS + 0.0063 \ln DS - 0.0505 \ln FA + 0.4701 \ln WS \tag{19.17}$$

The SFA estimates show a lower technical inefficiency of Indian commercial banks, the sigma *u* being 0.04, compared to 0.06 of RFA. The Wald chi-square test of SFA gives relatively lower value than that of RFA indicating that RFA is a better approach to measure technical efficiency.

The mean technical efficiency of Indian commercial banks as presented in Table 19.7 is only 33 percent by RFA method and 30 percent by SFA method. The bank specific technical efficiency is presented in Table 19.8. Using RFA, the least technically efficient bank is Punjab and Sind Bank (23 percent) while Bharatiya Mahila Bank is the most technically efficient bank at 77.02 percent. Again, Bharatiya Mahila Bank is the most efficient at 70.9 percent by SFA, but Catholic Syrian Bank is the least efficient bank. Nationalised banks (Allahabad Bank and Vijaya Bank) are performing low with a range of 23-32 percent when the exceptional case of Bharatiya Mahila Bank is omitted. With exceptions of Catholic Syrian Bank and Federal Bank, private banks have above 30 percent technical efficiency, but not more than 51 percent (Axis Bank and Yes Bank Ltd). The State Banks are around 30 percent technical efficient. Overall, with an average of 32.90 percent technical efficiency, the banking sector performance in India is very low and poor.

It is interesting to note that Lakshmanasamy and Shanmugam (2001; 2003) estimated mean technical efficiency of commercial banks by ray frontier function as 81.32 percent for 1999, and other estimation methods produced technical efficiency estimates ranging from 52 to 81 percent. For 2005-10, Dwivedi and Charyulu (2011) estimated more than 90 percent technical efficiency of banks by DEA method. However, the mean technical efficiency of commercial banks in India estimated by ray frontier function in this paper for the years 2014-2017 shows a sharp drop to an average of merely 33 percent, and even by the stochastic frontier function estimate the mean technical efficiency is only 30 percent. Thus, the efficiency of the commercial banks has declined drastically in recent years.

**Table 19.7: Mean Technical Efficiency of Commercial Banks in India, 2014-17**

| *Method* | *Mean* | *Std. dev.* | *Min.* | *Max.* |
|---|---|---|---|---|
| RFA | 0.3290 | 0.0953 | 0.2300 | 0.7702 |
| SFA | 0.3004 | 0.0778 | 0.2046 | 0.7090 |

**Table 19.8: Technical Efficiency of Commercial Banks in India, 2014-17**

| *Bank* | *RFA* | *SFA* | *Bank* | *RFA* | *SFA* |
|---|---|---|---|---|---|
| Allahabad Bank | 0.2984 | 0.2902 | DCB Bank Ltd | 0.3416 | 0.3132 |
| Andhra Bank | 0.3043 | 0.2917 | Federal Bank Ltd | 0.2637 | 0.2515 |
| Bank of Baroda | 0.2845 | 0.2838 | HDFC Bank Ltd. | 0.4146 | 0.3919 |
| Bank of India | 0.2551 | 0.2606 | ICICI Bank Ltd | 0.5040 | 0.4335 |
| Bank of Maharashtra | 0.2645 | 0.2677 | IDFC Bank Ltd | 0.4008 | 0.3334 |
| Bharatiya Mahila Bank Ltd | 0.7702 | 0.7090 | IndusInd Bank Ltd | 0.5036 | 0.3879 |
| Canara Bank | 0.2650 | 0.2516 | Jammu & Kashmir Bank Ltd | 0.3149 | 0.3061 |
| Central Bank of India | 0.2429 | 0.2570 | Karnataka Bank Ltd | 0.3507 | 0.3354 |
| Corporation Bank | 0.3068 | 0.2706 | Karur Vysya Bank Ltd | 0.3380 | 0.2950 |
| Dena Bank | 0.2419 | 0.2373 | Kotak Mahindra Bank Ltd | 0.3525 | 0.3199 |
| IDBI Bank Ltd | 0.3291 | 0.2923 | Lakshmi Vilas Bank Ltd | 0.3718 | 0.3206 |
| Indian Bank | 0.2789 | 0.2837 | Nainital Bank Ltd | 0.3224 | 0.2816 |
| Indian Overseas Bank | 0.2574 | 0.2436 | RBL Bank Limited | 0.3646 | 0.3006 |
| Oriental Bank of Commerce | 0.301558 | 0.2854 | South Indian Bank Ltd | 0.3098 | 0.2496 |
| Punjab and Sind Bank | 0.2300 | 0.2407 | Tamilnadu Mercantile Bank Ltd | 0.3241 | 0.2977 |
| Punjab National Bank | 0.3007 | 0.2980 | Dhanalakshmi Bank Ltd | 0.3068 | 0.2849 |
| Syndicate Bank | 0.2483 | 0.2398 | Yes Bank Ltd. | 0.4467 | 0.3406 |
| UCO Bank | 0.3044 | 0.3003 | State Bank of Bikaner and Jaipur | 0.3194 | 0.2935 |
| Union Bank of India | 0.2731 | 0.2621 | State Bank of Hyderabad | 0.3145 | 0.2995 |
| United Bank of India | 0.2898 | 0.2287 | State Bank of India | 0.2954 | 0.2945 |
| Vijaya Bank | 0.2409 | 0.2287 | State Bank of Mysore | 0.2896 | 0.2757 |
| Axis Bank Ltd | 0.507016 | 0.4283 | State Bank of Patiala | 0.2618 | 0.2354 |
| Catholic Syrian Bank Ltd | 0.2371 | 0.2046 | State Bank of Travancore | 0.2833 | 0.2489 |
| City Union Bank Ltd | 0.4386 | 0.3724 | | | |

Apart from the physical inputs, the technical efficiency of banks could be influenced by many global and economy wide changes, and factors like conformity to regulations, quality of assets, technological improvements, improvement in management of operations, etc. Global banking norms are guided by the Basel Norm, the voluntary regulatory framework agreed upon by the members of the Basel Committee on Banking Supervision (including India) in response to the deficiencies in financial regulations revealed by the

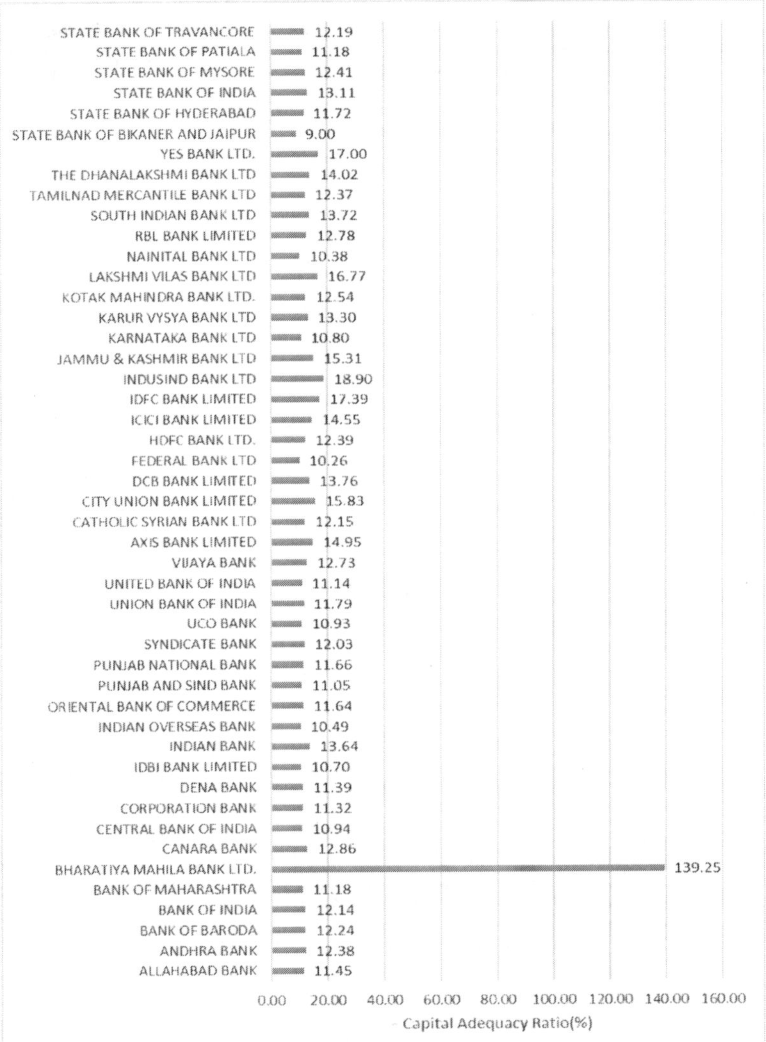


*Source:* RBI: Statistical Tables Relating to Banks in India 2016-17.

***Figure 19.5: Capital Adequacy Ratio of Commercial Banks in India***

financial crisis of 2007-08. The regulatory norms are addressed towards bank capital adequacy, stress testing, and market liquidity risk. The most important aspect of the Basel Norm, the capital adequacy ratio (CAR) measures (Tier 1 capital +Tier 2 capital)/risk weighted assets, where in, tier one capital absorbs losses without a bank being required to cease trading, and tier two capital absorbs losses in the event of a winding-up. Hence, a high CAR of a bank ensures high safety for its depositors.

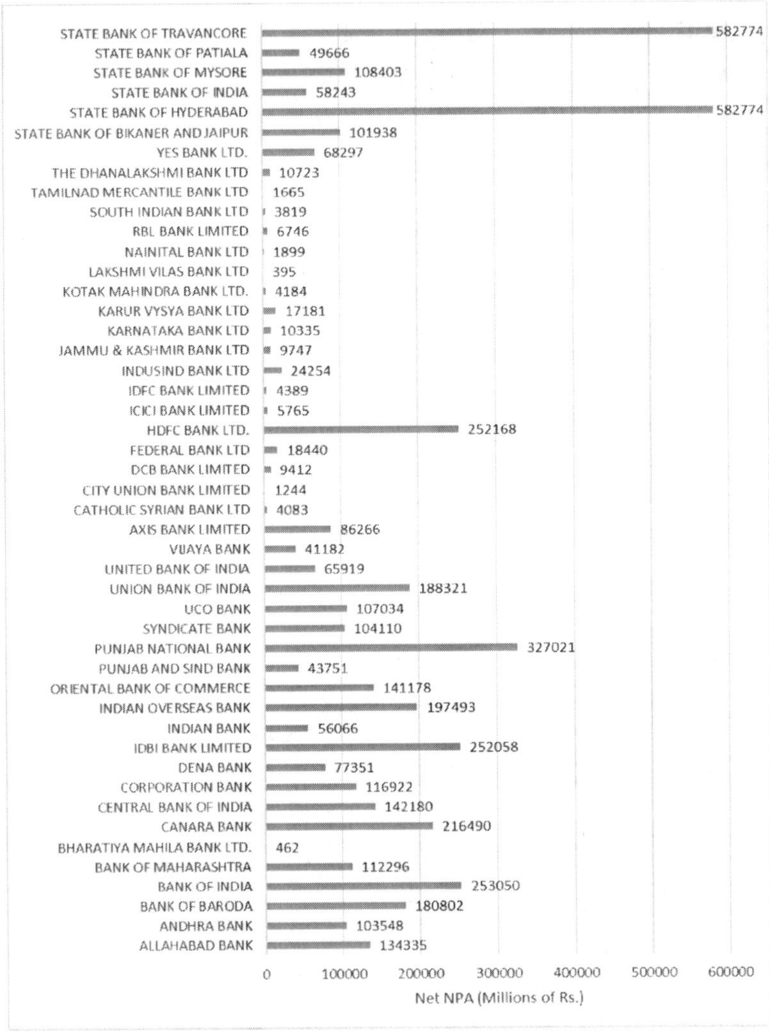


*Source:* RBI: Statistical Tables Relating to Banks in India 2016-17.

***Figure 19.6 Net Non-Performing Assets of Commercial Banks in India***

Domestically, the non-performing assets (NPA) accumulation in banks can be considered as a test of the quality of assets. These NPAs place burdens on bank lending affecting the quantity and quality of banking input-output relationships. The non-payment of interest or principal reduces cash flow for the lenders, disrupting budgets and decreasing earnings. Loan loss provisions, which are set aside to cover potential losses, reduce the capital available to provide subsequent loans. Once the actual losses from defaulted loans are determined, they are written-off against earnings. Hence, a high NPA leads to low performance of a bank and hence poor technical efficiency. From the Figure 19.5, it can be observed that the most technically efficient bank in India, Bharatiya Mahila Bank, has much higher CAR and lower NPA compared to other commercial banks in India.

Further, the commercial banks in India are obligated to lend to priority sectors like agriculture and industrial sectors. To the extent that the priority sectors fail and are sick, the bank lendings to these sectors become irrecoverable, affecting severly the technical efficiency. Within the bank, the efficiency of management is inversely related to the increase in scale of operations, hence, more number of branches for a bank means lesser management efficiency which can lead to technical inefficiency. The number of ATMs of banks can be considered as an indicator for improvement in banking technology and can affect technical efficiency. Years in existence of a bank is a vital factor that affect technical efficiency, as there are several new generation banks competing along with banks that have been established long years ago. The mean age is 80.11 years and standard deviation of 39.06. As shown in Table 19.9, as against the target of 40 percent priority sector loans, on average banks lend 36.76 percent of the total advances to priority sectors. The prioity sector credit of public sector banks as a percentage of gross advances has increased from 31.5 percent in 2013 to 38.1 percent in 2017. For example, the priority sector credit of the Punjab National Bank alone has increased from Rs. 5.04 billion on the eve of bank nationalisation in 1969 to Rs.19889 billion by March 2017. The NPA of the commerical banks forms 5.95 percent of the total bank advances. Capital adequacy ratio is maintained only at 15.36 percent on an average. The average number of bank branches is 2452 and the average number of ATMs is 4406. The public sector banks have nearly 57 percent of

**Table 19.9: Summary Statistics of Factors Affecting Technical Inefficiency of Commercial Banks in India**

| *Variable* | *Description* | *Mean* | *Std. dev.* | *Min.* | *Max.* |
|---|---|---|---|---|---|
| PSL | Ratio of priority sector lending to total advances | 36.76 | 8.37 | 14.48 | 58.32 |
| NPA | Ratio of net NPA to net advances | 5.95 | 4.51 | 0.33 | 16.89 |
| CAR | Capital adequacy ratio | 15.36 | 18.58 | 9 | 139.25 |
| Branch | Number of bank branches | 2452.47 | 2791.47 | 77 | 17167 |
| ATM | No. of automated teller machines | 4406.51 | 7780.24 | 0 | 50188 |
| Age | No. of years in existence | 80.11 | 39.06 | - | - |

their branches in rural and semi-urban areas. Nainital Bank is reported to have no ATM while IDFC bank has the least number of branches. State Bank of India has the maximum number of branches and ATMs.

The Table 19.10 presents the estimated effects of these factors on the RFA estimates of the technical efficiency of commercial banks. An increase in capital adequacy ratio slightly increases banking technical efficiency. Similarly, increasing the number of branches and ATMs also increases the technical efficiency of banks. A unit increase in proportion of priority sector lending decreases the technical efficiency by 0.002 units. Increase in proportion of non-performing assets also decreases technical efficiency by 0.004 units. Similarly, age of the bank impacts technical efficiency negatively.

**Table 19.10: OLS Estimates of the Determinants of Technical Efficiency of Commercial Banks in India**
**Dependent Variable: RFA technical efficiency**

| *Variable* | *Coefficient* | *Std. error* | *p-value* |
|---|---|---|---|
| Age | -0.00014 | 0.00045 | 0.75385 |
| PSA | -0.00248** | 0.00119 | 0.04419 |
| NPA | -0.00540 | 0.00366 | 0.14743 |
| CAR | 0.000001 | 0.00082 | 0.99537 |
| Branch | 0.000001 | 0.00002 | 0.95331 |
| ATM | 0.000001 | 0.00001 | 0.90235 |
| Constant | 0.46858* | 0.06356 | 0.00000 |
| R-square | 0.174 | | |

**Note:** *Significant at 1 percent level ** Significant at 5 percent level.

## 19.6 Conclusion

The commercial banking sector in India is in great stress in recent years due to high rates of defaulted loans, accumulating non-performing assets, priority lending obligations and high regulation norms. At the same time, as commercial banks, they have to maximise profit. But, their outputs are mostly service to the public and their operations are mainly related to receiving deposits paying interest and lending loans for interest, and hence, interest margin and other service income are the measured outputs of the commercial banks. Therefore, understanding the efficiency with which the commercial banks perform is crucial for improving banking operations. Similar to producing units, the commercial banks also use technology and practice management principles, and the inputs are to be used efficiently to realise maximum possible outputs. However, most banks do not realise their full potential outputs and inputs are used with inefficient levels. This paper has estimated the technical efficiency of the scheduled commercial banks in India using panel data of 47 banks for the period 2014-17 and the effects of the factors that determine the level of technical efficiency of banks are also estimated.

Unlike the much used data envelopment analysis and stochastic frontier function methods that use only a single output of firms, the interest margin, this paper considered multiple output and multiple input in measuring technical efficiency. Taking interest margin and non-interest income as multiple output of banks, the stochastic ray frontier function approach is used to specify the input-output mix. The stochastic ray frontier function estimates show that during the years 2014-2017 the technical efficiency of Indian scheduled commercial banks on average is only 32.9 percent. The Bharatiya Mahila Bank is the most technically efficient bank with 77.02 percent and the least technically efficient bank is Punjab and Sind Bank with 23 percent. The results also show that private sector banks generally perform better than public sector banks. The low technical efficiency of banks is explained by high non-performing assets, priority sector lending and the age of the banks. To a low extent, the capital adequacy, number of branches and ATMs increase banking efficiency. Thus, improved regulations, technology and management practices are key to improving technical efficiency of scheduled commercial banks in India.

# References


Abdulai, A. and D. Aubert (2004) "Nonparametric and Parametric Analysis if Calorie Consumption in Tanzania", Food Policy, 29, 2, 113-129.

Adams, H.R. (2008) "The Demographic, Economic, and Financial Determinants of Remittances in Developing Countries", Policy Research Working Paper No. 4583, World Bank.

Adams, H.R. and J. Page (2005) "Do International Migration and Remittances Reduce Poverty in Developing Countries?", World Development, 33, 10, 1645-1669.

Agarwal, R. and A.W. Horowitz (2002) "Are International Remittances Altruism or Insurance? Evidence from Guyana Using Multiple Migrant Households", World Development, 30, 11, 2033-2044.

Agrawal, P. (2005) "Foreign Direct Investment in South Asia: Economic Impact on Economic Growth and Local Investment", in E.M. Graham (ed.): Multinationals and Foreign Investment in Economic Development, London: Palgrave Macmillan, 94-118.

Agrawal, P., S.V. Gokarn, V. Mishra, K.S. Parikh and K. Sen (2000) Policy Regimes and Industrial Competitiveness: A Comparative Study of South Asia & India, UK: Palgrave Macmillan.

Ahmad, M.H., P.Y. Ping, S.R. Yaziz and N.H. Miswan (2015) "Forecasting Malaysian Gold Using a Hybrid of ARIMA and GJR-GARCH Models", Applied Mathematical Sciences, 9, 30, 1491-1501.

Aigner, D.J. and S.F. Chu (1968) "On Estimating the Industry Production Function", American Economic Review, 58, 4, 826-839.

Aigner, D.J., C.A.K. Lovell and P. Schmidt (1977) "Formulation and Estimation of Stochastic Frontier Production Function Models", Journal of Econometrics, 6, 1, 21-37.

Alam, M. and M Karim (2006) "Changing Demographics, Emerging Risks of Economic Demographic Mismatch and Vulnerabilities Faced by the Aged in South Asia: A Review of Situation in India and Pakistan", Pacific Population Journal, 21, 3, 63-92.

Alam, K.J., B.C. Ghosh, M.S. Islam and M.E. Hossain (2014) "Empirical Analysis of Twins' Deficits in Bangladesh", IOSR Journal of Humanities and Social Science, 19, 1, 65-72.

Alkswani, M. A. (2000) "The Twin Deficits Phenomenon in Petroleum Economy: Evidence from Saudi Arabia", Paper presented at the Seventh Annual Conference, Economic Research Forum (ERF), October 26-29, Amman, Jordan.

Amuedo-Dorantes, C. and S. Pozo (2006) "Remittances as Insurance: Evidence from Mexican Immigrants", Journal of Population Economics. 19, 2, 227-254.

Anantha Ramu, M.R. (2017) "Twin Deficits' Hypothesis: An Assessment of Relationship and Transmission Mechanism in India", Foreign Trade Review, 52, 1, 15-29.

Aromolaran, A.B. (2004) "Household Income, Women's Income Share and Food Calorie Intake in South Western Nigeria", Food Policy, 29, 5, 507-530.

Arulampalam, W. and S. Bhalotra (2008) "Persistence in Infant Mortality: Evidence for Indian States", Population Studies, 62, 2, 171-190.

Asher, S., P. Novosad and C. Rafkin (2017) "Intergenerational Educational Mobility in India: Evidence from 1970-Present", Working Paper: The World Bank, Dartmouth College and National Bureau of Economic Research.

Ashik, M.A. and S.K. Kannan (2017) "Forecasting National Stock Price using ARIMA Model", Global and Stochastic Analysis, 4, 1, 77-81.

Aslam, M. and G.G. Kingdon (2008) "Gender and Household Education Expenditure in Pakistan", Applied Economics, 40, 20, 2573-2591.

Ayinde, A., D. Akerele and A.O. Dipeolu (2010) "Socio-Economic Determinants of Calorie Intake Among Members of Farm Households in Ogun State, Nigeria", Journal of Food, Agriculture and Environment, 8, 2, 209-212.

Azam, M. and V. Bhatt (2015) "Like Father, Like Son? Intergenerational Education Mobility in India", Demography, 52, 6, 1929-1959.

Azeez, A. and M. Begum (2009) "Gulf Migration, Remittances, and Economic Impact", Journal of Social Science, 20, 1, 55-60.

Azzi, C. and R.G. Ehrenberg (1975) "Household Allocation of Time and Church Attendance", Journal of Political Economy, 83,1, 27-56.

Babatunde, R.O., A.O. Adejobi and S.B. Fakayode (2010) "Income and Calorie Intake Among Farming Households in Rural Nigeria: Results of Parametric and Nonparametric Analysis", Journal of Agricultural Science, 2, 2, 135-146.

Baharumshah, A.Z., E. Lau and A.M. Khalid (2006) "Testing Twin Deficits Hypothesis for ASEAN-4: Using VARs and Variance Decomposition", Journal of Asia Pacific Economy, 11, 3, 331-354.

Ball, R. and K. Chernova (2008) "Absolute Income, Relative Income, and Happiness", Social Indicators Research, 88, 3, 497-529.

Ballard, R. (2005) "Remittances and Economic Development in India and Pakistan", in S.M. Marimbo and D. Ratha (eds.): Remittances: Development Impacts and Future Prospects, Washington, D.C.: World Bank, 104-118.

Banerjee, B. (1984) "Information Flow, Expectations and Job Search: Rural-to-Urban Migration Process in India", Journal of Development Economics, 15, 1-3, 239-257.

Banerjee, D. (2014) "Forecasting of Indian Stock Market Using Time-Series ARIMA Model", Conference Proceedings Paper, ICBIM-14.

Banga, R. (2008) "Government Policies and FDI Inflows of Asian Developing Countries: Empirical Evidence", in J.M. Fanelli and L. Squire (eds.): Economic Reforms in Developing Countries: Reach, Range, Reason, Cheltenham: Edward Elgar Publishing, 117-146.

Bardhan, P.K. (1974) "On Life and Death Question", Economic and Political Weekly, 9, 32-34, 1293-1304.

Baru, R.V. and M. Nundy (2008) "Blurring of Boundaries: Public-Private Partnerships in Health Services in India", Economic and Political Weekly, Vol. 43, 4, 62-71.

Basole, A. and D. Basu (2014) "What Explains Declining Calorie Consumption in India?", Ideas for India, June 16.

Basu, D., D. Das and K. Mishra (2016) "Farmer Suicides in India Trends across Major States, 1995–2011", Economic and Political Weekly, 51, 21, 61-65.

Basu, K. (2006) "Gender and Say: A Model of Household Behavior with Endogenously Determined Balance of Power", Economic Journal, 116, 511, 558-580.

Basu, S. and D. Datta (2005) "Does Fiscal Deficit Influence Trade Deficit? An Econometric Enquiry", Economic and Political Weekly, 40, 30, 3311-3318.

Battese, E.C. and T.J. Coelli (1992) "Frontier Production Functions, Technical Efficiency and Panel Data: With Applications to Paddy Farmers in India", Journal of Productivity Analysis, 3, 1, 153-169.

Becker, G.S. (1960) "An Economic Analysis of Fertility", in Demographic and Economic Change in Developed Countries, Universities-National Bureau Conference Series No. 11, Princeton: Princeton University Press, 209-231.

Becker, G.S. (1965) "A Theory of Allocation of Time", Economic Journal, 75, 299, 493-517.

Becker, G.S. (1971) The Economics of Discrimination, Chicago: Chicago University Press.

Becker, G.S. (1981) A Treatise on the Family, Cambridge: Harvard University Press.

Becker, G. S. and H.G. Lewis (1974) "On the Interaction between Quantity and Quality of Children", Journal of Political Economy, 81, Part 2, S279-S288.

Becker, G.S. and N. Tomes (1976) "Child Endowments and the Quantity and Quality of Children", Journal of Political Economy, 84, Part 2, S143-S162.

Behrman, J.R. and A B. Deolalikar (1987) "Will Developing Country Nutrition Improve with Income?", Journal of Political Economy, 95, 3, 492-507.

Bell, C., T.N. Srinivasan and C. Udry (1997) "Rationing, Spillover, and Interlinking in Credit Markets: The Case of Rural Punjab", Oxford Economic Papers, New Series, 49, 4, 557-585.

Ben-Belhassen, B. and A.W. Womack (2000) "Measurement and Explanation of Technical Efficiency in Missouri Hog Production", Paper Presented at the Annual Meeting of the American Agricultural Economics Association, July-30-August 2, Tampa, Florida, USA.

Benjamin, D.J., J.J. Choi and G. Fisher (2016) "Religious Identity and Economic Behavior", Review of Economics and Statistics, 98, 4, 617-637.

Benston, G.J. and C.W. Smith (1976) "A Transactions Cost approach to the Theory of Financial Intermediation", Journal of Finance, 31, 2, 215-231.

Bernheim, D.B. (1988) "Budget Deficits and the Balance of Trade", in L.H. Summers (ed.): Tax Policy and the Economy, Volume 2, Cambridge: MIT Press, 1-32.

Bettendorf, L. and E. Dijkgraaf (2011) "The Bicausal Relation between Religion and Income", Applied Economics, 43, 11, 1351-1363.

Bhandari, L., P. Berman and R. Ahuja (2010) "The Impoverishing Effect of Healthcare Payments in India: New Methodology and Findings", Economic and Political Weekly, 45, 16, 65-71.

Bhat, R. (2016) "Agricultural Suicides in India: The Role of Rainfall and Relation to Economic Theory", Econ 199S Senior Thesis, Duke University.

Bhat, R. and N. Jain (2006) "Analysis of Public and Private Healthcare Expenditures", Economic and Political Weekly, Vol. 41, 1, 57-768.

Bicego, G.T. and J.T. Boerma (1993) "Maternal Education and Child Survival: A Comparative Study of Survey Data from 17 Countries", Social Sciences and Medicine, 36, 9, 1207-1227.

Black, S.E. and P.J. Devereux (2011) "Recent Developments in Intergenerational Mobility", in D. Card and O.C. Ashenfelter (eds.): Handbook of Labor Economics, Volume 4B, Amsterdam: North Holland, 1487-1541.

Black, S.E., P.J. Devereux and K.G. Salvances (2005) "Why the Apple Doesn't Fall Far: Understanding the Intergenerational Transmission of Human Capital", American Economic Review, 95, 1, 437-449.

Black, S.E., P.J. Devereux and K.G. Salvances (2009) "Like Father, Like Son? A Note on the Intergenerational Transmission of IQ Scores", Economic Letters, 105, 1, 138-140.

Blake, J. (1968) "Are Babies Consumer Durables? A Critique of Economic Theory of Reproductive Motivation", Population Studies, 22, 1, 5-25.

Blanden, J. and L. Macmillan (2014), "Education and Intergenerational Mobility: Help or Hinderance?", CASE Paper 179, LSE, London, UK.

Blau, F. and L. Kahn (2017) "The Gender Wage Gap: Extent, Trends, and Sources, Journal of Economic Literature, 55, 3, 789-865.

Blinder, A.S. (1973) "Wage Discrimination: Reduced Form and Structural Estimates", Journal of Human Resources, 8, 4, 436-455.

Blomberg, S.B., T. DeLeire and G.D. Hess (2006) "The (After) Life-Cycle Theory of Religious Contributions", CESifo Working Paper No. 1854, Munich.

Blomstrom, M. and H. Persson (1983) "Foreign Investment and Spillover Efficiency in an Underdeveloped Economy: Evidence from the Mexican Manufacturing Industry", World Development, 11, 6, 493-501.

Boes, S. and Winkelmann, R. (2006) "Ordered Response Models", Allgemeines Statistisches Archiv, 90, 1, 167-181.

Bollerslev, T. (1986) "Generalised Autoregressive Conditional Heteroskedasticity", Journal of Econometrics, 31, 3, 307-327.

Bongaarts, J. and R.G. Potter (1983) Fertility, Biology and Behavior: An Analysis of the Proximate Determinants, New York: Academic Press.

Borensztein, E., J. De Gregorio and J.-W. Lee (1998) "How Does Foreign Direct Investment Affect Economic Growth", Journal of International Economics, 45, 1, 115-135.

Borkotoky, K., S. Unisa and A.K. Gupta (2015) "Intergenerational Transmission of Education in India: Evidence from Nationwide Survey", International Journal of Population Research, Article ID 251953, 1-11.

Borooah, V.K. (2006) "What Makes People Happy? Some Evidence from Northern Ireland", Journal of Happiness Studies, 7, 4, 427-465.

Bose, A. (2000) "From Population to Pests in Punjab: American Boll Worm and Suicides in Cotton Belt", Economic and Political Weekly, 35, 38, 3375-3378.

Bose, N., M. E. Haque and D.R. Osborn (2007) "Public Expenditure and Economic Growth: A Disaggregated Analysis for Developing Countries", The Manchester School, 75, 5, 533-556.

Bouis, H.E. and L.J. Haddad (1992) "Are Estimates of Calorie-Income Elasticities too High? A Recalibration of the Plausible Range", Journal of Development Economics, 39, 2, 333-364.

Bourguignon, F. and P.A. Chiappori (1992) "Collective Models of Household Behavior: An Introduction", European Economic Review, 36, 2-3, 355-365.

Bourguignon, F., M. Browning, P.A. Chiappori and V. Lechene (1993) "Intra-household Allocation of Consumption: A Model and Some Evidence from French data", Annales d'Economie et de Statistique, 29, 1, 137-156.

Box, G.E.P. and G.M. Jenkins (1976) Time Series Analysis: Forecasting and Control, San Francisco: Holden Day.

Boyce, C.J., G.D.A. Brown and S.C. Moore (2010) "Money and Happiness: Rank of Income, Not Income, Affects Life Satisfaction", Psychological Sciences, 21, 4, 471-475.

Breitung, J. (2000) "The Local Power of Some Unit Root Tests for Panel Data", in B.H. Baltagi (ed.): Advances in Econometrics, Volume 15: Nonstationary Panels, Panel Cointegration, and Dynamic Panels, Amsterdam: JAI Press, 161-178.

Brooks, C. (2008) Introductory Econometrics for Finance, New York: Cambridge University Press.

Brown, G.D.A., J. Gardner, A.J. Oswald and J. Qian (2008) "Does Wage Rank Affect Employees' Well-being?", Industrial Relations: A Journal of Economy and Society, 47, 3, 355-389.

Browning, M. and P.A. Chiappori (1998) "Efficient Intra-Household Allocations: A General Characterisation and Empirical Tests", Econometrica, 66, 6, 1241-1278.

Budijanto, S.S., S. Hadi and S. Susilo (2016) "International Migration, Remittances and Impact on the Locality of Origin", Research on Humanities and Social Science, 6, 10, 52-62.

Buthe, T. (2010) "Politics and Institutions in the Regulation of Global Capital: A Review Article", Review of International Organizations, 3, 2, 207-220.

Butler, J. and R. Moffitt (1982) "A Computationally Efficient Quadrature Procedure for the One Factor Multinomial Probit Model", Econometrica, 50, 3, 761-764.

Caglayan, E. and M. Aster (2012) "A Microeconometric Analysis of Household Consumption Expenditure: Determinants for both Rural and Urban Areas in Turkey", American International Journal of Contemporary Research, 2, 2, 27-34.

Cain, M.T. (1983) "Fertility as an Adjustment to Risk", Population and Development Review, 9, 688-702.

Calwell, J.C. (1979) "Education as a Factor in Mortality Decline: An Examination of Nigerian Data", Population Studies, 33, 3, 395-413.

Campero, A. and K. Kaiser (2013) "Access to Credit: Awareness and Use of Formal and Informal Credit Institutions", Working Paper, Banco de Mexico.

Cantril, H. (1965) 'The Pattern of Human Concerns, New Burnswick, NJ: Rutgers University Press.

Chamberlain, G. (1980) "Analysis of Covariance with Qualitative Data", Review of Economic Studies, 47, 1, 225-238.

Chami, R., A. Barajas, T. Cosimano, C. Fullenkamp, M. Gapen and P. Montiel (2008) "Macroeconomic Consequences of Remittances", IMF Occasional Papers 259, IMF.

Chami, R., C. Fullenkamp and S. Jahjah (2003) "Are Immigrant Remittance Flows a Source of Capital for Development?", IMF Working Paper No. WP/03/189, IMF.

Chandrasekhara, S., T. Anilkumar and S. Jamuna (2002) "Complementary and Alternative Drug Therapy in Arthritis", Journal of the Association of Physicians of India, 50, 2, 225-227.

Chaudhuri, K. and S. Roy (2006) "Do Parents Spread Educational Expenditure Evenly across the Two Genders? Evidence from Two North Indian States", Economic and Political Weekly, 41, 51, 5276-5282.

Chernichovsky, D. (1982) "Fertility Behaviour in Developing Economies: An Investment Approach", in J.L. Simon and P. Lindert (eds.): Research in Population Economics, Volume 4, Greenwich: JAI Press, 235-285.

Chimhown, A., J. Piesse and C. Pinder (2005) "Socio-Economic Impact of Remittances on Poverty Reduction", in S.M. Marimbo and D. Ratha (eds.): Remittances: Development Impacts and Future Prospects, Washington, D.C.: World Bank, 84-102.

Chinn, M.D. and H. Ito (2006) "What Matters for Financial Development? Capital Controls, Institutions and Interactions", Journal of Development Economics, 81, 1, 163-192.

Chinn, M.D. and H. Ito (2008) "A New Measure of Financial Openness", Journal of Comparative Policy Analysis, 10, 3, 309-322.

Clark, A., D. Masclet and M-E. Villeval (2010) "Effort and Comparison Income", Industrial and Labor Relations Review, 63, 3, 407-426.

Clark, A., N. Kristensen and N. Westergaard-Nielsen (2009) "Economic Satisfaction and Income Rank in Small Neighbourhoods", Journal of the European Economic Association, 7, 2-3, 519-527.

Clark, A.E., P. Frijters and M.A. Shields (2008) "Relative Income, Happiness and Utility: An Explanation of Easterlin Paradox and Other Puzzles", Journal of Economic Literature, 46, 1, 95-144.

Clarke, K. and S. Drinkwater (2001) "An Investigation of Household Remittance Behaviour", Manchester School of Economic Studies Discussion Paper Series.

Cleland, J.G and J.K van Ginneken (1988) "Maternal Education and Child Survival in Developing Countries: The Search for Pathways of Influence", Social Sciences and Medicine, 27, 12, 1357-1368.

Cleland, J.G. and Z.A. Sathar (1984) "The Effect of Birth Spacing on Childhood Mortality in Pakistan", Population Studies, 38, 3, 401-418.

Cleveland, W.S. (1979) "Robust Locally Weighted Regression and Smoothing Scatter Plots", Journal of the American Statistical Association, 74, 368, 829-836.

Conning, J and C. Udry (2007) "Rural Financial Markets in Developing Countries", in R. Evenson and P. Pingali (eds.): Handbook of Agricultural Economics, Volume 3, 2857-2908.

Corak, M. (2013) "Income Inequality, Equality of Opportunity, and Intergenerational Mobility", Journal of Economic Perspectives, 27, 3, 79-102.

Cragg, J.G. (1971) "Some Statistical Models for Limited Dependent Variables with Application to the Demand for Durable Goods", Econometrica, 39, 5, 829-844.

Das, A. (2000) "Efficiency of Public Sector Banks: An Application of Data Envelopment Analysis Model", Prajnan, 28, 1, 119-131.

Das Gupta, M. (1987) "Selective Discrimination Against Female Children in Rural Punjab, India", Population and Development Review, 13, 1, 77-100.

DaVanzo, J. and J.P. Habicht (1986) "Infant Mortality Decline in Malaysia, 1946-1975: The Roles of Changes in Variables and Changes in the Structure of Relationship", Demography, 23, 2, 143-160.

De Haan, A. (1999) "Livelihoods and Poverty: The Role of Migration – A Critical Review of the Migration Literature", Journal of Development Studies, 36, 2, 1-47.

De La Cruz, B.E. (1995) "The Socioeconomic Dimensions of Remittances: Case Studies of Five Mexican Families", The Berkeley McNair Journal, 3, 1-10.

Deardon, L., S. Machin and H. Reed (1997) "Intergenerational Mobility in Britain", Economic Journal, 107, 440, 47-66.

Deaton, A. (1989) "Looking for Boy-Girl Discrimination in Household Discrimination Data", World Bank Economic Review, 3, 1, 1-15.

Deaton, A. (1997) The Analysis of Household Surveys: A Microeconometric Approach to Development Policy, Baltimore: Johns Hopkins University Press for the World Bank.

Deaton, A. (2008) "Income, Health and Well-being around the World: Evidence from the Gallup World Poll", Journal of Economic Perspective, 22, 2, 53-72.

Deaton, A. and J. Dreze (2009) "Food and Nutrition in India: Facts and Interpretations", Economic and Political Weekly, 44, 7, 42-65.

Delgado, M.A. and P.M. Robinson (1992) "Nonparametric and Semiparametric Methods of Economic Research", Journal of Economic Surveys, 5, 3, 201-249.

Deltoro, L.S. (2015) "Twin Deficits Hypothesis for European Countries", Masters Thesis, James I University, Spain.

Desai, S. and R. Vanneman (2011-12) India Human Development Survey-II (IHDS-II), 2011-12. Ann Arbor, MI: Inter-University Consortium for Political and Social Research.

Desai, S., A. Dubey, B.L. Joshi, M. Sen, A. Shariff and R. Vanneman (2009) India Human Development Survey: Design and Data Quality, IHDS Technical Paper 1.

Deshpande, A. (2018) "Bad Karma or Discrimination: Male-Female Wage Gaps among Salaried Workers in India", World Development, 102, 331-344.

Deshpande, R.S. and K. Shah (2007) "Agrarian Distress and Agricultural Labour", Indian Journal of Labour Economics, 50, 2, 257-272.

Dickey, D.A. and W.A. Fuller (1979) "Distribution of the Estimators for Autoregressive Time Series with a Unit Root", Journal of the American Statistical Association, 74, 366, 427-431.

Diener, Ed., E.M. Suh, R.E. Lucas and H.M. Smith (1999) "Subjective Well-being: Three Decades of Progress", Psychological Bulletin, 125, 2, 276-302.

Doepke, M. and F. Kindermann (2017) "Intrahousehold Decision Making and Fertility", in M. Cervellati and U. Sunde (eds.): Demographic Change and Long-Run Development, Cambridge: MIT Press.

Dolan, P., T. Peasgood and M. White (2008) "Do We Really Know What Makes Us Happy? A Review of the Economic Literature on the Factors Associated with Subjective Well-being", Journal of Economic Psychology, 29, 1, 94-122.

Doss, C. (2013) "Intrahousehold Bargaining and Resource Allocation in Developing Countries", World Bank Research Observer, 28, 1, 52-78.

Dritsaki, C. (2015) "Forecasting Real GDP Rate through Econometric Models: An Empirical Study from Greece", Journal of International Business and Economics, 3, 1, 13-19.

Dwivedi, A.K. and D.K. Charyulu (2011) "Efficiency of Indian Banking Industry in the Post-Reform Era", Working Paper No. 2011-03-01, Ahmedabad: Indian Institute of Management.

Easterlin, R.A. (1974) "Does Economic Growth Improve the Human Lot? Some Empirical Evidence", in P.A. David and M.W. Reder (eds.): Nations and Households in Economic Growth, New York: Academic Press, 89-125.

Easterlin, R.A. (1975) "An Economic Framework for Fertility Analysis", Studies in Family Planning, 6, 1, 54-63.

Easterlin, R.A. (1995) "Will Raising the Incomes of All Increase the Happiness of All?", Journal of Economic Behavior and Organization, 27, 1, 35-47.

Easterlin, R.A. (2003) "Explaining Happiness", Proceedings of the National Academy of Sciences, 100, 19, 11176-11183.

Easterlin, R.A. (2017) "Paradox Lost?", Review of Behavioral Economics, 4, 4, 311-339.

Easterlin, R.A. and L. Angelescu (2010) "Happiness and Growth the World Over: Time Series Evidence on the Happiness–Income Paradox", in H. Hinte and K.F. Zimmermann (eds.): Happiness, Growth, and the Life Cycle, Oxford and New York: Oxford University Press, 56-81.

Easterlin, R.A. and E.M. Crimmins (1985) The Fertility Revolution: A Supply-Demand Analysis, Chicago: University of Chicago Press.

Easterlin, R.A. and O. Sawangfa (2010) "Happiness and Growth: Does the Cross Section Predict Time Trends? Evidence from Developing Countries", in Ed Diener., J. Helliwell and D. Kahneman (eds.): International Differences in Well-being, New York: Oxford University Press, 162-212.

Easterlin, R.A., L.A. McVey, M. Switek, O. Sawangfa, and J.S. Zweig (2010) "The Happiness-Income Paradox Revisited", Proceedings of the National Academy of Sciences, 107, 52, 22463-22468.

Engle, R. and C. Granger (1987) "Co-integrationand Error Correction: Representation, Estimation, and Testing", Econometrica, 35, 2, 251-276.

Engle, R.F. (1982) "Autoregressive Conditional heteroskedasticity with Estimates of the Variance of UK Inflation", Econometrica, 50, 4, 987-1007.

Epaphra, M. (2017) "Modeling Exchange Rate Volatility: Application of the GARCH and EGARCH Models", Journal of Mathematical Finance, 7, 121-143.

Faini, R. (2005) "Migration, Remittances and Growth", in G.J. Borjas and J. Crisp (eds.): Poverty, International Migration and Asylum: Studies in Development Economics and Policy, London: Palgrave Macmillan, 171-187.

FAO (2008) The State of Food Insecurity in the World, 2008, Rome: Food and Agriculture Organization.

FAO (2015) The State of Food Insecurity in the World, 2015, Rome: Food and Agriculture Organization.

Farrell, M.J. (1957) "The Measurement of Productive Efficiency", Journal of the Royal Statistical Society, Series A, 120, 3, 253-281.

Fisher, J.A. (1963) "Consumer Durable Goods Expenditure, with Major Emphasis on the Roleof Assets, Credit and Intentions", Journal of American Statistical Association, 58, 303, 648-657.

Frey, B.S. and A. Stutzer (2001) "Happiness, Economy and Institutions", Economic Journal, 110, 466, 918-938.

Frey, B.S. and A. Stutzer (2002) "What Can Economists Learn from Happiness Research?", Journal of Economic Literature, 40, 2, 402-435.

Fry, M.J. (1993) "Foreign Direct Investment in a Macroeconomic Framework", Policy Research Working Paper No.1141, International Economics Department, World Bank.

Fuchs, R., E. Pamuk and W. Lutz (2010) "Education or Wealth: Which Matters more for Reducing Child Mortality in Developing Countries?", Vienna Yearbook of Population Research, 8, 175-199.

Funkhouser, E. (1995) "Remittances from International Migration: A Comparison of El Salvador and Nicaragua", Review of Economics and Statistics, 77, 1, 137-146.

Gibson, J. and S. Rozelle (2002) "How Elastic is Calorie Demand? Parametric, Nonparametric and Semiparametric Results for Urban Papua New Guinea", Journal of Development Studies, 38, 6, 23-46.

Glaeser, E.L., J.D. Gottlieb and O. Ziv (2014) "Unhappy Cities", NBER Working Paper No. 20291.

Glosten, L.R., R. Jagannathan and D.E. Runkle (1993) "On the Relation between the Expected Value and the Volatility of the Nominal Excess Return on Stocks", Journal of Finance, 48, 5, 1779-1801.

Gopalan, C., B.V. Rama Sastry and S.C. Balasubramanian (2012) Nutritive Values of Indian Foods, National Institute of Nutrition, Indian Council of Medical Research, Hyderabad.

Government of India (2008) Report of the Government of India Committee on Financial Inclusion, New Delhi: Government of India.

Govindasamy, P. and B.M. Ramesh (1997) "Maternal Education and the Utilization of Maternal and Child Health Services in India", National Family Health Survey Subject Reports, No. 5.

Greene, W.H. (2005) "Reconsidering Heterogeneity in Panel Data estimators of the Stochastic Frontier Model", Journal of Econometrics, 126, 2, 269-303.

Grosse, R. and L.J. Trevino (2005) "New Institutional Economics and FDI Location in Central and Eastern Europe", Management International Review, 45, 2, 123-145.

Gruber, J. (2004) "Pay or Pray? The Impact of Charitable Subsidies on Religious Attendance", Journal of Public Economics, 88, 12, 2635-2655.

Gruere, G., P. Mehta-Bhatt and D. Sengupta (2007) "Bt Cotton and Farmer Suicides in India: An Evidence-based Assessment", Journal of Development Studies, 47, 2, 316-337.

Guerin, S.S. (2011) "Law and Foreign Direct Investment", IES Working Paper No. 4/2011, Institute of European Studies, Belgium.

Guha, B. and G. Bandhopadhyaya (2016) "Gold Price Forecasting Using ARIMA Model", Journal of Advanced Management Science, 4, 2, 117-121.

Guirkinger, C. (2007) "Understanding the Coexistence of Formal and Informal Credit Markets in Piura, Peru", World Development, 36, 8, 1436-1452.

Gumber, A., B. Dhak and N. Lalitha (2012) "Declining Free Healthcare and Rising Treatment Costs in India: An Analysis of National Sample Surveys 1986 and 2004", Journal of Health Management, 14, 2, 97-116.

Haddad, L. and T. Reardon (1993) "Gender Bias in the Allocation of Resources within Households in Burkina Faso: A Disaggregated Outlay Equivalent Analysis", Journal of Development Studies, 29, 2, 260-276.

Hadri, K. (2000) "Testing for Stationarity in Heterogeneous Panel Data", Econometrics Journal, 3, 2, 148-161.

Hagerty, M.R. (2000) "Social Comparisons of Income in One's Community: Evidence from National Surveys of Income and Happiness", Journal of Personality and Social Psychology, 78, 4, 746-771.

Hagerty, M.R. and R. Veenhoven (2003) "Wealth and Happiness Revisited: Growing Wealth of Nations Does Go with Greater Happiness", Social Indicators Research, 64, 1, 1-27.

Hajdu, T. and G. Hajdu (2014) "Income and Subjective Well Being: How Important is the Methodology", Hungarian Statistical Review, Special Number 18, 110-127.

Hallward-Driemeier, M. (2003) "Do Bilateral Investment Treaties Attract Foreign Direct Investment? Only a Bit ... and They Could Bite", WPS 3121, World Bank.

Hausman, J. (1978) "Specification Tests in Econometrics", Econometrica, 46, 6, 403-426.

Haveman, R. and B. Wolfe (1995) "The Determinants of Children's Attainments: A Review of Methods and Findings", Journal of Economic Literature, 33, 4, 1829-1878.

Heaton, T.M., R. Forste, J.P. Hoffmann and D. Flake (2005) "Cross National Variation in Family Influences on Child Health", Social Science and Medicine, 60, 1, 97-108.

Heckman, J.J. (1976) "The Common Structure of Statistical Models of Truncation, Sample Selection and Limited Dependent Variables and a Simple Estimator for such Models", Annals of Economic and Social Measurement, 5, 4, 475-492.

Heckman, J.J. (1979) "Sample Selection as a Specification Error", Econometrica, 47, 1, 153-161.

Hertz, T., T. Jayasundera, P. Piraino, S. Selcuk, N. Smith, and A. Verashchagina (2008) "The Inheritance of Educational Inequalities: International Comparisons and Fifty-Year Trends", The B.E. Journal of Economic Analysis and Policy, 7, 2, 1-48.

Hnatkovska, V., A. Lahiri and S.B. Paul (2013) "Breaking the Caste Barrier: Intergenerational Mobility in India", Journal of Human Resources, 48, 2, 435-473.

Hobcraft, J.N. (1993) "Women's Education, Child Welfare and Child Survival: A Review of Evidence", Health Transition Review, 3, 2, 159-173.

Holmlund, H., M. Lindahl, and E. Plug (2011) "The Causal Effect of Parents' Schooling onChildren's Schooling: A Comparison of Estimation Methods," Journal of Economic Literature, 49, 3, 615-651.

Holst, E., A. Schafer and M. Schrooten (2012) "Gender and Remittances: Evidence from Germany", Feminist Economics, 18, 2, 201-229.

Hsiao, C. (2003) Analysis of Panel Data, 2nd edition, New York: Cambridge University Press.

Husain, Z. (2011) "Gender Disparities in completing School Education in India: Explaining Geographical Variations", Journal of Population Research, 28, 4, 325-352.

Iannaccone, L.R. (1998) "Introduction to the Economics of Religion", Journal of Economic Literature, 36, 3, 1465-1496.

Iles, R. (2015) "Demand for Qualified and Unqualified Primary Healthcare in Rural North India", mimeo, Griffith University, Australia.

Im, K.S., M.H. Pesaran and Y. Shin (2003) "Testing for Unit Roots in Heterogeneous Panels", Journal of Econometrics, 115, 1, 53-74.

IMF (2005) "India: Selected Issues", IMF Country Report No. 05/87.

Inglehart, R., R. Foa, C. Peterson and C. Welzel (2008) "Development, Freedom and Rising Happiness: A Global Perspective", Perspectives on Psychological Science, 3, 264-285.

International Labour Organisation (2018) World Employment and Social Outlook: Trends for Women, Geneva: ILO.

International Monetary Fund (2005) World Economic Outlook, Washington, D.C.: IMF.

Irving, J., S. Mohapatra and D. Ratha (2010) "Migrant Remittance Flows: Findings from a Global Survey of Central Banks", Working Paper No. 194, World Bank.

Iversen, V., A. Krishna and K. Sen (2017) "Rags to Riches? Intergenerational Occupational Mobility in India", Economic and Political Weekly, 52, 44, 107-114.

Iyer, S. (2016) "The New Economics of Religion", Journal of Economic Literature, 54, 2, 395-441.

Iyer, S. (2018) "The Economics of Religion in India", Cambridge: Harvard University Press.

Jalan, J. and M. Ravallion (2003) "Does Piped Water Reduce Diarrhoea for Children in Rural India?", Journal of Econometrics, 112, 1, 153-173.

Jalan, J. and R. Murgai (2007) "Intergenerational Mobility in Education in India", Working Paper, World Bank.

Javeed, S. and A. Manuhaar (2013) "Women and Wage Discrimination in India: A Critical Analysis", International Journal of Humanities and Social Science Invention, 2, 4, 6-12.

Jha, R. (2013) "The Determinants of Household Level Fertility in India", ASARC Working Paper Series, 2013/13.

Johansen, S. (1991) "Estimation and Hypothesis Testing of Cointegration Vectors in Gaussian Vector Autoregressive Models", Econometrica, 59, 6, 1551-1580.

Jones, L.E., A. Schoonbroodt and M. Tertilt (2010) "Fertility Theories: Can they explain the Negative Fertility-Income Relationship?", in J. Shoven (ed.): Demography and the Economy, Chicago: University of Chicago Press, 43-100.

Juarez, F.W.C. (2015) "Intergenerational Transmission of Education: The Relative Importance of Transmission Channels", Latin American Economic Review, 24, 1, 1-44.

Judd, F., H. Jackson, C. Fraser, G. Murray, G. Robins and A. Komiti (2006) "Understanding Suicide in Australian Farmers", Social Psychiatry and Psychiatric Epidemiology, 41, 1-10.

Kaicker, N. and R. Gaiha (2013) "Calorie Threshold and Undernutrition in India", Journal of Policy Modeling, 35, 2, 271-288.

Kannan, K.P. and K.S. Hari (2002) "Kerala's Gulf Connection: Emigration, Remittances and Their Macroeconomic Impact, 1972-2000", Working Paper No. 328, Centre for Development Studies, Trivandrum.

Kapsos, S. (2008) "The Gender Wage Gap in Bangladesh", Bangkok: ILO Asia-Pacific Working Paper Series.

Khamis, M., N. Prakash and Z. Siddique (2012) "Consumption and Social Identity: Evidence from India", Journal of Economic Behavior & Organization, 2012, 83, 3, 353-371.

Khanna, S. (2012) "Gender Wage Discrimination in India: Glass Ceiling or Sticky Floor?", Working Paper No.214, Delhi School of Economics.

Kim, S. and N. Roubini (2008) "Twin Deficits or Twin Divergence? Fiscal Policy, Current Account, and Real Exchange Rate in the US", Journal of International Economics, 74, 2, 362-383.

Kingdon, G.G. (2005) "Where Has All the Bias Gone? Detecting Gender Bias in the Intra-Household Allocation of Educational Expenditure", Economic Development and Cultural Change, 53, 2, 409-451.

Kishan, P.K.P. (2018) "Is the Past Still Holding Us Back? A Study on Intergenerational Education Mobility in India", Working Paper No. 2018-01-03, Indian Institute of Management, Ahmedabad, India.

Kochar, A. (1997) "An Empirical Investigation of Rationing Constraints in Rural Credit Markets in India", Journal of Development Economics, 53,2, 339-371.

Koenker, R.W. and G. Bassett (1978) "Regression Quantiles", Econometrica, 46, 1, 33-50.

Kumar, S.S. (2013) "Total Factor Productivity of Indian Banking Sector – Impact of Information Technology", RBI Occasional Papers, 34, 1&2, 66-86.

Kumar, A., A.K. Mishra, S. Saroj and P.K. Joshi (2017) "Institutional versus Non-institutional Credit to Agricultural Households in India: Evidence on Impact from a National Farmers' Survey", Discussion Paper No. 01614, International Food Policy Research Institute.

Kumar, N. (2001) "Host Country Policies, WTO Regimes and the Global Patterns of FDI Inflows: Recent Quantitative Studies India's Strategic Response", Economic and Political Weekly, 36, 1, 39-50.

Kumar, N. (2009) "FDI and Economic Development: Indian Experience in Global Comparative Perspective", in S.R. Hashim et al. (eds.): Indian Industrial Development and Globalization, New Delhi: ISID and Academic Foundation: 409-428.

Kumar, S. and K.S. Hari (2011) "International Migration, Remittances and Its Macroeconomic Impact on Indian Economy", Working Paper No. 2011-01-06, Indian Institute of Management, Ahmedabad.

Kumar, S.S. and R. Gulati (2008) "An Examination of Technical, Pure Technical and Scale Efficiency in Indian Public Sector Banks using Data Envelopment Analysis", Eurasian Journal of Business and Economics, 1, 2, 33-69.

Kumar, A.K., A. Acharya, K. Nagaraj, R. Baru and S. Acharya (2010) "Inequities in Access to Health Services in India: Caste, Class and Region", Economic and Political Weekly, 45, 38, 49-58.

Lahiri, K. and G. Xing (2004) "An Econometric Analysis of Veterans' Health Care Utilization Using Two-Part Models", Empirical Economics, 29, 2, 431-449.

Lakshmanasamy, T. (1988) "Economic Utility and the Demand for Children: A Theoretical and Empirical Analysis", Artha Vijnana, 30, 4, 421-453.

Lakshmanasamy, T. (1989a) "Economic Contribution of Rural Children and the Family Fertility Behaviour: A Rationale for High Fertility in India", Asian Economic Review, 31, 1, 51-78.

Lakshmanasamy, T. (1989b) "Old Age, Risk, Security and Children: An Empirical Evidence from Rural India", Indian Journal of Economics, 70, 276, 51-68.

Lakshmanasamy, T. (1990) "Family Survival Strategy and Migration: An Analysis of Returns to Migration", Indian Journal of Social Work, 51, 3, 473-485.

Lakshmanasamy, T. (1991a) "Income Smoothing, Risk and the Family: Household Relationships as Risk Diversification Strategy", Journal of Social and Economic Studies, 63-79.

Lakshmanasamy, T. (1991b) "Hours of Work of Rural Children: Its Determinants and Effect on Fertility", Indian Journal of Labour Economics, 34, 1, 54-59.

Lakshmanasamy, T. (1991c) "Demand for Children in Rural Families: Children as Consumption Utility", Journal of Family Welfare, 37, 4, 3-12.

Lakshmanasamy, T. (1991d) "Intergenerational Transfers and Wealth Accumulation: Motivations for Savings and the Effects of Annuities", Indian Journal of Economics, 71, 283, 465-487.

Lakshmanasamy, T. (1991e) "Risk, Consumption Smoothing and the Family: Portfolio Management of Children and Assets in Rural Families", Artha Vijnana, 33, 4, 24-40.

Lakshmanasamy, T. (1991f) "The Demand for Children: A Survey", Asian Economic Review, 33, 1, 49-102.

Lakshmanasamy, T. (1991g) "The Family, Risk and Self-Insurance: An Application of Portfolio Selection Model", Indian Journal of Social Science, 4, 4, 567-589.

Lakshmanasamy, T. (1991h) "Agricultural Modernisation, Risk, and Migration: Family Strategy for Innovation", in J. Mahender Reddy and S. Kisan Rao (eds.): Agricultural Development and Rural-Urban Disparities, New Delhi: Sterling Publishers, 153-165.

Lakshmanasamy, T. (1992) "Income Smoothing, Risk and the Family: Inter-and Intra-Family Relationships as Risk Diversification Strategy", Indian Economic Journal, 39, 4, 30-43.

Lakshmanasamy, T. (1993a) "Intrafamily Relations, Migration and Remittances", Artha Vijnana, 35, 1, 86-94.

Lakshmanasamy, T. (1993b) "Hours of work of Rural Children: Its Determinants and Effects on Fertility", in B.P. Singh and S. Mahanty (eds.): Children at Work: Problems and Policy Issues, New Delhi: B.R. Publishing House, 153-163.

Lakshmanasamy, T. (1993c) "Economic Valuation of Pristine Quality: Some Issues", in Anil Agarwal (ed.): The Challenge of the Balance: Environmental Economics in India, New Delhi: Centre for Science and Environment, 42-45.

Lakshmanasamy, T. (1997a) "Educational Infrastructure and Economic Benefits in Tamil Nadu", IEA 1st Amrit Jubilee (80th) Conference Volume, 803-810.

Lakshmanasamy, T. (1997b) Economics of Human Behaviour: Essays in Honour of A.M. Nalla Gounden, New Delhi: Allied Publishers.

Lakshmanasamy, T. (2000a) "The Household Costs and Willingness to Pay for Higher Education", Journal of Educational Planning and Administration, 14, 2, 187-196.

Lakshmanasamy, T. (2000b) "The Economics of Corruption and Development", IEA Conference (83rd) Volume of the Millennium, 2000, 681-688.

Lakshmanasamy, T. (2000c) "Education and Economic Growth in a Knowledge Based Economy", in K.B. Powar (ed.): Higher Education for Human Development, New Delhi: Association of Indian Universities, 166-181.

Lakshmanasamy, T. (2001a) "Education, Search, Matching and Age at Marriage of Females", Asian-African Journal of Economics and Econometrics, 1, 1, 63-77.

Lakshmanasamy, T. (2001b) "Microeconometrics of Selective Samples and Discrete Choice: Contributions of Heckman and McFadden for the Analysis of Microdata", in Department of Economics, Annamalai University (ed.): Papers on James J. Heckman and Daniel L. McFadden: Nobel Laureates in Economics - 2000, Annamalai University, 1-25.

Lakshmanasamy, T. (2001c) "The Economics of Corruption and Development", in D. Narasimha Reddy (ed.): Crime, Corruption and Development, New Delhi: Deep & Deep Publishers, 24-34.

Lakshmanasamy, T. (2002a) "Nash Bargained Household Decisions: Testing the Economic Models of Family in India", Indian Economic Journal, 50, 3-4, 99-115.

Lakshmanasamy, T. (2002b) "Imperfect Information, Knowledge and Development", IEA 85th Conference Volume, 135-147.

Lakshmanasamy, T. (2002c) "A Test for the Economic Empowerment of Women", in A. Ranga Reddy (ed.): Empowerment of Women and Ecological Development, New Delhi: Serials Publications, 353-373.

Lakshmanasamy, T. (2002d) "Human Capital: An Infrastructure for Economic Growth", in S. Murty (ed.): Infrastructure and Social Sector Development for Economic Growth, Jaipur: RBSA Publishers, 91-109.

Lakshmanasamy, T. (2003a) "New Information, New Institutions and Economic Development", Asian Economic Review, 45, 3, 425-439.

Lakshmanasamy, T. (2003b) "Testing the Unitary and Nash Bargaining Household Models in India", Indian Journal of Social and Economic Development, 5, 2, 197-217.

Lakshmanasamy, T. (2003c) "The Microeconometrics of Selective Samples and Discrete Choice", India Development Review, 1, 1, 47-63.

Lakshmanasamy, T. (2003d) "Nash Bargained Household Decisions: Testing the Economic Models of Family in India", Indian Economic Journal, 50, 3&4, 99-115.

Lakshmanasamy, T. (2003e) "Household Costs and Willingness to Pay for Higher Education", in J.B.G. Tilak (ed.): Financing Education in India, Delhi: Ravi Books, 255-266.

Lakshmanasamy, T. (2003f) "Economic Empowerment of Women: Implications for Household Decision Making Process", in G. Vidya Rani, H. Grija Rani and V. Bhagyalaxmi (eds.): Status of Women: Post Independence Era, Warangal: A.S.M. College of Women, 133-148.

Lakshmanasamy, T. (2004a) "Some Critical Issues in Financing of Higher Education", Perspectives in Education, 29, 1, 5-22.

Lakshmanasamy, T. (2004b) "Willingness to Pay for Higher Education: An Econometric Analysis using Contingent Valuation Method", Indian Educational Review, 40, 2, 3-23.

Lakshmanasamy, T. (2004c) "New Institutions and Economic Development: The Significance of Governance and Social Capital for Economic Growth", Indian Journal of Economics, 75, 336, 65-94.

Lakshmanasamy, T. (2004d) "Intergenerational Mobility of Income and Education in India", Quantonomics, 1, 1, 9-19.

Lakshmanasamy, T. (2004e) "Social Capital, Institutions and Development", in G. Gopal Reddy and T.L.N. Swamy (eds.): Institutional Policy Options for Sustainable Agricultural Development, Hyderabad: Department of Economics, Osmania University, 88-99.

Lakshmanasamy, T. (2005a) "The Economic Theory of Bribery and Corruption", in A. Ranga Reddy (ed.): Dimensions of Crime and Corruption in India, New Delhi: Serials Publications, 128-144.

Lakshmanasamy, T. (2005b) "Modernisation and Development: Institutional Reforms under Globalisation", in S. Narsimhan and D.Y. Kim (eds.): Korea and India: A Forging Relationship, New Delhi: Manak Publications, 2005, 45-77.

Lakshmanasamy, T. (2006a) "Women's Education, Dowry, Bargaining and Gains to Marriage", Journal of Educational Planning and Administration, 20, 1, 27-51.

Lakshmanasamy, T. (2006b) "Demand for Higher Education and Willingness to Pay: An Econometric Analysis using Contingent Valuation Method", Manpower Journal, 41, 1, 97-120.

Lakshmanasamy, T. (2006c) "Imperfect Information, Institutions and Development", in D.M. Nachane and B. Chatterjee (eds.): Economics of Asymmetric Information, New Delhi: Deep & Deep Publishers, 46-63.

Lakshmanasamy, T. (2007a) "Social Capital, Economic Reforms and Economic Development", in A. Banerjee and R. Arunachalam (eds.): Indian Economic Reforms and Response of States, New Delhi: Kanishka Publishers, 260-280.

Lakshmanasamy, T. (2007b) "Women's Education, Dowry, Bargaining and Gains to Marriage", in J.B.G. Tilak (ed.): Women's Education and Development, Delhi: Gyan Publishers, 249-281.

Lakshmanasamy, T. (2008a) "Agglomeration Economies, New Economic Geography and Industry Clusters", Indian Geographical Journal, 83, 2, 105-120.

Lakshmanasamy, T. (2008b) "Social Exclusion and Inclusion: Meaning, Identification and Strategy", Journal of Development and Social Change, 5, 1-2, 193-212.

Lakshmanasamy, T. (2008c) "Understanding Social Exclusion and Empowering for Inclusion", in R.G. Dandge (ed.): Social Exclusion and Inclusive Policies in South Asia, Kolhapur: Shivaji University, 1-9.

Lakshmanasamy, T. (2009a) "Unequal Chances: The Intergenerational Transmission of Economic Advantage under Marital Sorting" in B. Dutta, T. Ray and E. Somanathan (eds.): New and Enduring Themes in Development Economics, New York: World Scientific Publishing, 41-56.

Lakshmanasamy, T. (2009b) "Equality among the Unequal: Choice vs Luck under Individual Heterogeneity and Non-Subordination in Economic Distribution", International Research Journal of Social Sciences, 2, 2, 253-271.

Lakshmanasamy, T. (2009c) "Women in Business: Human Capital versus Family Background", Annamalai Economic Papers, 20-29.

Lakshmanasamy, T. (2009d) "Financing the Poor and Marginalised: Financial Institutions vs Microfinance", Journal of Development and Social Change, 6, 3&4, 59-69.

Lakshmanasamy, T. (2009e) "Social Justice and Welfare State: Including the Excluded", in G. Bhadru Naik and V. Rajasekhar (eds.): Reservations in the Era of Globalization and Privatization – Emerging Trends and Issues, Hyderabad: Sree Bhagavan Publications, 2009, 31-47.

Lakshmanasamy, T. (2009f) "Equality and Social Justice: Opportunity vs Choice under Disadvantage", in G. Bhadru Naik and V. Rajasekhar (eds.): Dr.B.R. Ambedkar's

Philosophy of Social Justice and Its Relevance, Hyderabad: Sree Bhagavan Publications, 76-91.

Lakshmanasamy, T. (2010a) "Are You Satisfied with Your Income? The Economics of Happiness in India", Journal of Quantitative Economics, 8, 2, 115-141.

Lakshmanasamy, T. (2010b) "Global ICT Revolution and the Indian Service Sector Growth", Journal of Development and Social Change, 7, 1&2, 14-33.

Lakshmanasamy, T. (2010c) "Corruption, Inequality and Poverty: Cracking the Guardian Knot through a Smart Card", in S. Sarkar (ed.): Tackling Poverty Challenges: Key Approaches and Policy Implications, Germany: Lambert Academic Publishing.

Lakshmanasamy, T. (2010d) "Positional Aspirations, Relative Income and Happiness: Money and Well-Being under Status Comparison" in G.B. Naik and V. Rajasekhar (eds.): Buddhism: World Harmony and Peace, Hyderabad: Sree Bhagavan Publications, 262-284.

Lakshmanasamy, T. (2010e) "Agglomeration Economies and Industry Clusters", in E.M. Thomas and C.J. Unny (eds.): Industrial Growth Through Clusters, Department of Economics, Christ College, Irinjalakuda, Thrissur, Kerala, 7-25.

Lakshmanasamy, T. (2010f) "Expanding Opportunity, Widening Inequality and Worsening Income Distribution under Economic (Market) Globalization", in A.K. Thakur and P. Singh (eds.): Globalisation – Inclusive Growth and Indian Economy: Issues and Policies, New Delhi: Regal Publications, 1-29.

Lakshmanasamy, T. (2010g) Population Dynamics and Human Development: Opportunities and Challenges, Delhi: Bookwell Publishers.

Lakshmanasamy, T. (2011) "Expanding Opportunity, Widening Inequality and Worsening Income Distribution under Economic (Market) Globalisation", in P. Arunachalam (ed.) Mahatma Gandhi National Rural Employment Guarantee Programme and Poverty in India, New Delhi: Serials Publications, 214-242.

Lakshmanasamy, T. (2012a) "Ageing and Security: Savings and Transfers Behaviour of Indian Households", Indian Journal of Gerontology, 26, 4, 484-501.

Lakshmanasamy, T. (2012b) "Are Indian Households Impurely Altruistic? Testing for Bequest Motives and Intergenerational Transfers in India", Indian Economic Journal, 60, 1, 39-66.

Lakshmanasamy, T. (2012c) "Neuroeconomics: The Science of the Art of Decision Making", Asian Economic Review, 54, 1, 49-98.

Lakshmanasamy, T. (2012d) "Economic Development and Transition of Youths: Differential Perceptions of Changing Lifestyles and Behaviour of Youths in India", Indian Journal of Youth Affairs, 16, 2, 114-129.

Lakshmanasamy, T. (2012e) "Connecting the Poor to Economic Prosperity", in N. Mani (eds.): Paradox of Poverty and Economic Prosperity, New Delhi: Serials Publications, 16-35.

Lakshmanasamy, T. (2012f) "Digital Governance: Potential Uses of NPR and UID as Smart Card for Economic Efficiency", International Journal of Management Research and Technology, 6, 1, 101-113.

Lakshmanasamy, T. (2013a) "Team Capital and Productivity: A Panel Analysis of the Effect of Unit Specific Nursing Care on Patient Outcome", Artha Vijnana, 55, 3, 252-271.

Lakshmanasamy, T. (2013b) “How Deep Are Caste Discrimination and Social Exclusion? Methodologies for Measuring Economic Deprivation of Dalits”, Indian Journal of Dalit and Tribal Studies and Action, 1, 1, 18-34.

Lakshmanasamy, T. (2013c) “So Near Yet So Far! The Elusive Quest for the Engines of Economic Growth”, Shanlax International Journal of Economics, 1, 2, 82-90.

Lakshmanasamy, T. (2013d) “Health Capital and the Rights to Health Care”, Shanlax International Journal of Economics, Special Issue on Health Economics, 98-109.

Lakshmanasamy, T. (2014a) Economics of Household Non-Market Behaviour: Analysis of Household Relations and Decisions, Delhi: Bookwell Publishers.

Lakshmanasamy, T. (2014b) “From Wealth of Nations to Wealth of Relations: The Power of Social Networks and the Small World of Economics”, Indian Journal of Economics. 95, 376, 93-177.

Lakshmanasamy, T. (2014c) “Is Economics in Genes? The Genoeconomics of Economic Behaviour and Economic Development”, Indian Economic Journal, 61, 4, 593-625.

Lakshmanasamy, T. (2015a) Economics of Growth, Inequality, Institutions and Development: Reforms, Social Capital, Inclusion and Distribution, Delhi: Bookwell Publishers.

Lakshmanasamy, T. (2015b) Applied Microeconometrics of Human Decisions, Delhi: Bookwell Publishers.

Lakshmanasamy, T. (2015c) “Economic Challenges of Greying Population: Problem or Predicament?”, Ageing and Society: The Indian Journal of Gerontology, 25, 1-2, 1-26.

Lakshmanasamy, T. (2015d) “Economics of Business Networks: Theory and Empirics of the Structure and Properties of the Network among Trading Firms”, Artha Vijnana, 57, 1, 49-79.

Lakshmanasamy, T. (2015e) “Why the Apple Doesn’t Fall for the Poor? The Elusive Invisible Veil between the Poor and the Economic Prosperity”, mimeo, Department of Econometrics, University of Madras.

Lakshmanasamy, T. (2016) “Does Conditional Aid Promote Performance? A Regression Discontinuity Analysis of the Impact of GAVI Alliance on Immunisation in Developing Countries”, Artha Vijnana, 58, 1, 19-55.

Lakshmanasamy, T. (2017a) “Demand for Private Tuition: A Quantile Regression Analysis of Household Expenditure on Private Coaching in India”, Journal of Educational Planning and Administration, 31, 2, 115-139.

Lakshmanasamy, T. (2017b) “Empirics of Dynamic Network in Actor-Oriented Model: Panel Estimation of the Parameters of Co-evolution of Network and Behavior Effects in Business Relations”, South Asian Journal of Management, 24, 2, 136-168.

Lakshmanasamy, T. (2018a) New and Evolving Economics: Biological and Behavioural Perspectives on Economic Behaviour, Delhi: Trinity Press.

Lakshmanasamy, T. (2018b) “Sex Discrimination in India: A Two Step Estimation and Decomposition of Gender Wage Gap in the Labour Market”, Labour and Development, 25, 1, 35-58.

Lakshmanasamy, T. (2018c) "Are Commercial Banks in India Technically Efficient? A Multiple Output - Multiple Input Technology Panel Stochastic Ray Frontier Function Estimation", WEALTH - International Journal of Money, Banking and Finance, 7, 3, 4-16.

Lakshmanasamy, T. (2018d) "Women's Education, Dowry, Bargaining and Gains to Marriage", in R.M. Sudarshan and J.B.G. Tilak (eds.): Gender in Contemporary Education Research, New Delhi: Gyan Publishing House, 225-250.

Lakshmanasamy, T. (2019a) Econometrics of Networks and Efficiency: Social Network Analysis of Business Relations and Economic Performance, Delhi: Bookwell Publishers.

Lakshmanasamy, T. (2019b) "Is There Educational Mobility in India? A 2SLS-IV Estimation of Intergenerational Effects of Parental Education on Child Education" Journal of Indian Education.

Lakshmanasamy, T. and C. Anil (2012) "Link Loyalty in Social Networks: An Econometric Analysis of Marketing Channel Networks in India", International Journal of Economics and Business Research, 4, 5, 501-513.

Lakshmanasamy, T. and C. Anil (2015a) "Product Seasonality and Benefits of Linking with Marketing Networks: A Discriminant Analysis of Dealer Relations in Business", Journal of Marketing Vistas, 5, 2, 49-58.

Lakshmanasamy, T. and C. Anil (2015b) "The Effect of Attributes of Distribution Channel Member on Supply Chain Management: An Empirical Analysis of Social Networks in Business", International Journal of Logistics Systems and Management, 21, 2, 160-180.

Lakshmanasamy, T. and C. Anil (2015c) "Social Network Analysis of Marketing Intermediaries – An Empirical Analysis", International Journal of Management and Network Economics, 3, 3, 181-198.

Lakshmanasamy, T. and C. Anil (2015d) "Relative Rankings and Risks in Marketing Management: An Empirical Analysis of Dealer Perceptions and Trade Factors in Dealer Networks", Journal of Management Research, 15, 4, 197-210.

Lakshmanasamy, T. and C. Anil (2016) "Economic Utility on Social Networks: Utility of Linking and Delinking in Dealership Networks", Journal of Economic Policy and Research, 11, 1, 70-83.

Lakshmanasamy, T. and R. Arunachalam (2005) "Economic Reforms and Development: Reflections on Economic Paradigms and Public-Private Partnership", in P. Jegadish Gandhi and M.J. Joseph (eds.): Public–Private Partnership in Nation Building, New Delhi: Deep and Deep Publications, 22-61.

Lakshmanasamy, T. and R. Arunachalam (2006) "Public–Private Partnership in Development: Some Theoretical and Empirical Reflections", in S.N. Misra and B.K. Sahu (eds.): Globalisation, Economic Growth and Human Development, New Delhi: Anmol Publications, 60-80.

Lakshmanasamy, T. and R. Arunachalam (2008) "Vulnerability of Landholdings to Income Shocks", in A. Vinayak Reddy and M. Yadagira Charyulu (eds.): Indian Agriculture: Challenges of Globalisation, New Delhi: New Century Publications, 303-322.

Lakshmanasamy, T. and S. Madheswaran (1993) "Determinants of Earnings in Scientific Labour Market", Journal of Educational Planning and Administration, 7, 2, 181-196.

Lakshmanasamy, T. and S. Madheswaran (1994) "Education and Earnings among Science Graduates in West Bengal", Indian Journal of Regional Science, 26, 2, 63-75.

Lakshmanasamy, T. and S. Madheswaran (1995) "Discrimination by Community: Evidence from Indian Scientific and Technical Labour Market", Indian Journal of Social Science, 8, 1, 59-77.

Lakshmanasamy, T. and S. Madheswaran (1995a) "Discrimination by Community: Evidence from Indian Scientific and Technical Labour Market", Indian Journal of Social Science, 8, 1, 59-77.

Lakshmanasamy, T. and S. Madheswaran (1995b) "Dual Selection Criteria for Simultaneous Decisions: Migration and Sector Choice of Scientific and Technical Females in India", Indian Journal of Applied Economics, 4, 3, 89-104.

Lakshmanasamy, T. and S. Madheswaran (1996) "Occupational Segregation and Earnings Discrimination by Sex: Evidence from India", Artha Vijnana, 38, 4, 372-386.

Lakshmanasamy, T. and S. Madheswaran (1996a) "Employment Decision and Earnings: Issues of Self-Selection and Selectivity Bias", Indian Economic Journal, 43, 4, 56-72.

Lakshmanasamy, T. and S. Madheswaran (1996b) "Occupational Segregation and Earnings Discrimination by Sex: Evidence from India", Artha Vijnana, 38, 4, 372-386.

Lakshmanasamy, T. and S. Madheswaran (2001a) "Household Characteristics, Financial Aid and Financing Higher Education", Perspectives in Education, Special Issue, 17, 65-76.

Lakshmanasamy, T. and S. Madheswaran (2001b) "Stochastic Frontier Function and the Measurement of Sex Discrimination", in S. Elumalai (ed.): Optimization Techniques in Industrial Mathematics, Chennai: Ramanujan Institute for Advanced Study in Mathematics, University of Madras, 124-135.

Lakshmanasamy, T. and S. Madheswaran (2002) "Asymmetric Information or Ignorance in the Labour Market: A Two-Tiered Earnings Frontier Estimation", Indian Social Science Review, 4, 2, 223-237.

Lakshmanasamy, T. and S. Madheswaran (2004) "Determinants of Earnings in Scientific Labour Market", in D. Thakur and D.N. Thakur (eds.): Vocational and Technical Education, New Delhi: Deep and Deep Publishers, 565-586.

Lakshmanasamy, T. and K.S. Mandal (1989) "Rural Poverty during 1970s and 1980s", Yojana, 33, 23, 8-10.

Lakshmanasamy, T. and K. Maya (2017) "Money and Happiness in India: Are the Poor Unhappy and Rich Happy?", Indian Economic Journal, Special Issue, 64, 571-588.

Lakshmanasamy, T. and A.M. Nalla Gounden (1992) "The Sources of Academic Achievement and School Effectiveness", New Frontiers in Education, 22, 1, 89-103.

Lakshmanasamy, T. and C. Ramanurthy (2005) "Corruption in Development Perspectives", in A. Ranga Reddy (ed.): Dimensions of Crime and Corruption in India, New Delhi: Serials Publications, 509-533.

Lakshmanasamy, T. and S. Ramasamy (1999) "An Econometric Analysis of the Worker Choice between Public and Private Sector", Indian Journal of Labour Economics, 42, 1, 71-83.

Lakshmanasamy, T. and K.C. Roy (2007) "Does Human Capital and Dowry Raise Women's Bargaining in Household Decisions?" in K.C. Roy and C.B. Prasad (eds.): Governance and Development in Developing Countries, New York, USA: Nova Science, 141-159.

Lakshmanasamy, T. and K.C. Roy (2012) "Institutional Reforms and Governance Restructuring for Distribution of Gains under Globalisation", in J.A. Mancini (ed.): Globalisation: Partnerships, Modernisation and Future Perspectives, New York, USA: Nova Science Publishers, 207-220.

Lakshmanasamy, T. and U. Sankar (1993) Methodology of Applied Economic Research, New Delhi: Sterling Publishers.

Lakshmanasamy, T. and K.R. Shanmugam (2000) "Labour Use Efficiency of Banking Sector in India", Indian Journal of Labour Economics, 43, 4, 989-999.

Lakshmanasamy, T. and K.R. Shanmugam (2001) "Production Frontiers and Efficiency Measures: An Analysis of the Banking Sector in India", Asian-African Journal of Economics and Econometrics, 1, 2, 211-228.

Lakshmanasamy, T. and K.R. Shanmugam (2001) "Production Frontiers and Efficiency Measures: An Analysis of the Banking Sector in India", Asian and African Journal of Economics and Econometrics, 1, 2, 211-228.

Lakshmanasamy, T. and K.R. Shanmugam (2003) "Technical Efficiency Measures for Single and Multiple Output Technologies", in P. Thangavel (ed.): Algorithms and Artificial Systems, Chennai: Allied Publishers, 277-295.

Lakshmanasamy, T. and K. Shanthi (1999) "Family Background, Choice and Participation of Women in Higher Education in Tamil Nadu", in Association of Indian Universities (ed.): Women Participation in Higher Education, New Delhi: Association of Indian Universities, 15-26.

Lakshmanasamy, T. and K. Shanthi (2010) "Will the Emerging Asian Giants China and India Overshadow Japan?" in G. Balachandirane (ed.): Japan in a Resurgent Asia, New Delhi: Manak Publications Pvt. Ltd, 94-108.

Lancaster, G., P. Maitra and R. Ray (2008) "Household Expenditure Patterns and Gender Bias: Evidence from Selected Indian States", Oxford Development Studies, 36, 2, 133-157.

Lau, E. and A.Z. Baharumshah (2006) "Twin Deficits Hypothesis in SEACEN Countries: A Panel Data Analysis of Relationships between Public Budget and Current Account Deficits", Applied Econometrics and International Development, 6, 2, 213-226.

Layard, R. (2005) Happiness: Lessons from a New Science, London: Penguin.

Lehrer, E.L. (2004) "Religion as a Determinant of Economic and Demographic Behavior in the United States", Population and Development Review, 30, 4, 707-726.

Levesque, J.F. and S. Mukerjee (2010) "Changing Inequalities in Utilisation of Inpatient Care in rural India: Evidence from the NSS", Economic and Political Weekly, 45, 46, 84-91.

Levin, A., C.-F. Lin and C.-S.J. Chu (2002) "Unit Root Tests in Panel Data: Asymptotic and Finite-Sample Properties", Journal of Econometrics, 108, 1, 1-24.

Linssen, R. (2009) "Happiness Among the Rural Poor in India: Effects of Absolute, Relative and Status Consumption", Master's Thesis, Radboud University, Nijmegen.

Litchfeld, J., B. Reilly and M. Veneziani (2012) "An Analysis if Life Satisfaction in Albania: An Heteroscedastic Ordered Probit Approach", Journal of Economic Behaviour and Organisation, 81, 3, 731-741.

Loera, J.A., S.A. Black, K.S. Markides, D.V. Espino and J.S. Goodwin (2001) "The Use of Herbal Medicine by Older Mexican Americans" Journal of Gerontology: Medical Sciences, 56A, 11, M7l4-M718.

Lothgren, M. (2000) "Specification and Estimation of Stochastic Multiple-Output Production and Technical Inefficiency", Applied Economics, 32, 12, 1533-1540.

Lumbila, K.N. (2005) "What Makes FDI Work? A Panel Analysis of the Growth Effect of FDI in Africa", Africa Region Working Paper Series No. 80, World Bank.

Maitra, P. and A. Sharma (2009) "Parents and Children's Education Across Generations in India", Working Paper, Department of Economics, Monash University, Australia.

Maity, B. And B. Chatterjee (2012) "Forecasting GDP Growth Rates of India: An Empirical Study", International Journal of Economics and Management Sciences, 1, 9, 52-58.

Majumdar, C. and G. Gupta (2015) "Don't Worry, Be Happy: A Survey of the Economics of Happiness", Economic and Political Weekly, 50, 40, 50-62.

Majumder, R. (2010) "Intergenerational Mobility in Educational and Occupational Attainment: A Comparative Study of Social Classes in India", Journal of Applied Economic Research, 4, 4, 463-494.

Makepeace, G. and S. Pal (2006) "Effects of Birth Interval on Child Mortality: Evidence from a Sequential Analysis", World Health and Population, January, 1-14.

Makepeace, G. and S. Pal (2008) "Understanding the Effects of Siblings on Child Mortality: Evidence from India", Journal of Population Economics, 21, 4, 877-902.

Mare, R.D. and V. Maralani (2006) "The Intergenerational Effects of Changes in Women's Educational Attainments", American Sociological Review, 71, 4, 542-564.

Markova, E. and B. Reilly (2007) "Bulgarian Migrant Remittances and Legal Status: Some Micro-Level Evidence from Madrid", South-Eastern Europe Journal of Economics, 5, 1, 55-69.

Matuschke, I., R.R. Mishra and M. Qaim (2007) "Adoption and Impact of Hybrid Wheat in India", World Development, 35, 8, 1422-1435.

McGillivray, M. (2007) Human Well-Being: Concept and Measurement, New York: Palgrave Macmillan.

Meeusen, W. and J. van den Broeck (1977) "Efficiency Estimation from Cobb Douglas Production Function with Composed Error", International Economic Review, 18, 2, 435-444.

Merriott, D. (2015) "Factors Associated with the Farmer Suicide", Journal of Epidemiology and Global Health, 6, 217-227.

Merza, E., M. Alawin and A. Bashayreh (2012) "The Relationship between Current Account and Government Budget Balance: The Case of Kuwait", International Journal of Humanities and Social Science, 2, 7, 168-177.

Miankhel, A.K., S.M. Thangavelu and K. Kalirajan (2009) "Foreign Direct Investment, Exports, and Economic Growth in South Asia and Selected Emerging Countries: A Multivariate VAR Analysis", Crawford School of Public Policy, Australian National University, Australia.

Miller, A.S. (2000) "Going to Hell in Asia: The Relationship between Risk and Religion in a Cross Cultural Setting", Review of Religious Research, 42, 1, 5-18.

Mincer, J. (1974) Schooling, Experience and Earnings, New York: Columbia University Press.

Ministry of AYUSH, Government of India (2017) AYUSH in India 2017 Annual Report.

Mishra, S. (2014) "Farmers' Suicides in India, 1995-2012: Measurement and Interpretation",

Mitra, P. and G.S. Khan (2014) "Twin Deficits Hypothesis: An Empirical Analysis in the Context of India", International Journal of Commerce and Business Studies, 2, 2, 10-23.

Mohanty, R.K. (2012) "Fiscal Deficit – Economic Growth Nexus in India: A Cointegration Analysis", Working Paper, CESP, JNU, New Delhi.

Mohanty, S.S., M. Bisht and P. Mohapatra (2014) "Gender Wage Gap among Salaried Workers in India: Results of a Principal Component Analysis of State Level Statistics", Economic Affairs, 59, 2, 175-190.

Motiram, S. and A. Singh (2012) "How Close Does the Apple Fall to the Tree? Some Evidence on Intergenerational Occupational Mobility from India", Economic and Political Weekly, 47, 40.

Mulligan, C.B. (1999) "Galton vs The Human Capital Approach to Inheritance", Journal of Political Economy, 107, S61, S184-S224.

Mukherjee, S., S. Haddad and D. Narayana (2012) "Patient's Choice for Non-Allopathic Providers for Acute Illness: Evidence from a Rural Setting in Kerala", Indian Journal of Human Development, 6, 2, 225-244.

Mukherjee, S., A. Singh and R. Chandra (2013) "Maternity or Catastrophe: A Study of Household Expenditure on Maternal Health Care in India", Health, 5, 1, 109-118.

Mukhtar, T., M. Zakaria and E. Ahmad (2007) "An Empirical Investigation for the Twin Deficits Hypothesis in Pakistan", Journal of Economic Cooperation, 24, 4, 63-80.

Munshi, K. and J. Myaux (2006) "Social Norms and the Fertility Transition", Journal of Development Economics, 80, 1, 1-38.

Myrskyla, M., J.R. Goldstein and Y.A. Cheng (2013) "New Cohort Fertility Forecasts for the Developed World: Rises, Falls, and Reversals", Population and Development Review, 39, 1, 31-56.

Navarro, A.G. (2015) "Gender Wage Gap and Education: Case in Dominican Republic", All Graduate Plan B and other Reports Paper 485, Utah State University.

Nelson, D.B. and C. Cao (1992) "Inequality Constraints in the Univariate GARCH Model", Journal of Business and Economic Statistics, 10, 2, 229-235.

Ngwenya, E. (2008) "Determinants of Calorie Intake in Widowhood in Vietnam", Discussion Paper 2008-02, School of Economics and Finance, University of Tasmania, Australia.

Nordhaus, W.D. and J.Tobin (1973) "Is Growth Obsolete?", in M. Moses (ed.): The Measurement of Economic and Social Performance, Cambridge: National Bureau of Economic Research, 509-564.

Normandin, M. (1999) "Budget Deficit Persistence and the Twin Deficits Hypothesis", Journal of International Economics, 49, 1, 171-193 .

NSSO (1992) Morbidity and Utilisation of Medical Services, 42nd Round NSS (1986-87), National Sample Survey Organisation, Department of Statistics, Ministry of Planning, Government of India.

NSSO (2008) Education in India: 2007-08, Participation and Expenditure, NSS 64th Round (July 2007-June2008), National Sample Survey Office, National Statistical Organisation Ministry of Statistics and Programmed Implementation, Government of India.

NSSO (2012) Consumer Expenditure Survey, 68th Round, 2011-2012, National Sample Survey Organisation, Department of Statistics, Ministry of Planning, Government of India.

NSSO (2013) Key Indicators of Employment and Unemployment in India: 2011-12, National Sample Survey Organisation, Department of Statistics, Ministry of Planning, Government of India.

NSSO (2014) Key Indicators of Debt and Investment in India, NSS 70th Round, 2013, National Sample Survey Organisation, Department of Statistics, Ministry of Planning, Government of India.

Nugent, J.B. (1985) "The Old Age Security Motive for Fertility", Population and Development Review, 11, 1, 75-97.

Nugent, J.B., K. Kan and R.J. Walther (1983) The Effects of Old Age Pensions on Household Structure, Marriage, Fertility and Resource Allocation in Rural Areas of Developing Countries, Report to AID.

Oaxaca, R.L. (1973) "Male-Female Wage Differentials in Urban labor Markets", International Economic Review, 14, 3, 693-709.

Ohri-Vachaspati, P., B.L. Rogers, E. Kennedy and J.P. Goldberg (1998) "The Effects of Data Collection Methods on Calorie-Expenditure Elasticity Estimates: A Study from the Dominican Republic", Food Policy, 23, 3-4, 295-304.

Oliveria, R.A., C.W. O'Connor and G.W. Smith (1979) "Short-Run Forecasting Models of Beef Prices", Western Journal of Agricultural Economics, 4, 1, 45-55.

Onafowora, O.A. and O. Owoye (2006) "An Empirical Investigation of Budget and Trade Deficits: The Case of Nigeria", Journal of Developing Areas, 39, 2 153-174.

Oreopoulos, P., M.E. Page and A.H. Stevens (2006) "The Intergenerational Effects of Compulsory Schooling", Journal of Labor Economics, 24, 4, 729-760.

Orewa, S.I. and C.O. Iyanbe (2010) "Determinants of Daily Food Calorie Intake among Rural and Low-Income Urban Households in Nigeria", Academic Journal of Plant Sciences, 3, 4, 147-155.

Orozco, M., B.L. Lowell and J. Schneider (2006) "Gender Specific Determinants of Remittances: Difference in Structure and Motivation", Report to the World Bank Gender and Development Group.

Ozcan, Y.Z., S. Ucdogruk and K.M. Ozcan (2003) "Wage Differences by Gender, Wage and Self-employment in Urban Turkey", Journal of Economic Cooperation, 24, 1, 1-24.

Pal, S. (1999) "An Analysis of Childhood Malnutrition in Rural India: Role of Gender, Income and Other Household Characteristics", World Development, 27, 7, 1151-1171.

Pandey, A., M.K. Choe, N.Y. Luther, D. Sahu, and J. Chand (1998) "Infant and Child Mortality in India", National Family Health Survey Reports 11, International Institute for Population Sciences, Mumbai and East-West Center, Honolulu, U.S.A.

Parthasarathy, G. and Shameem (1998) "Suicides of Cotton Farmers in Andhra Pradesh: An Exploratory Study", Economic and Political Weekly, 33, 13, 720-726.

Pebley, A.R. and J. DaVanzo (1993) "Maternal Depletion and Child Survival in Gautemala and Malaysia", RAND Labor and Population Working Paper No. 93-18.

Pebley, A.R., N. Goldman and G. Rodrigruez (1996) "Prenatal and Delivery Care and Childhood Immunization in Guatemala: Do Family and Community Matter?", Demography, 33, 2, 231-247.

Pedroni, P. (1999) "Critical Values for Cointegration Tests in Heterogeneous Panels with Multiple Regressors", Oxford Bulletin of Economics and Statistics, Special Issue, 61, 653-670.

Pena, R., J. Liljestrand, E.Zelaya and L.A. Persson (1999) "Fertility and Infant Mortality Trends in Nicaragua 1964-1993: The Role of Women's Education", Journal of Epidemiology & Community Health, 53, 3, 132-137.

Philips, P.C. and P. Perron (1988) "Testing for Unit Root in the Time Series Regression", Biometrika, 75, 2, 335-346.

Pitt, M.M. and M.R. Rosenzweig (1985) "Health and Nutrient Consumption Across and Within Farm Households", Review of Economics and Statistics, 67, 2, 212-223.

Preston, S.H. (1978) The Effects of Infant and Child Mortality on Fertility, New York: Academic Press.

Raghupathy, S. (1996) "Education and Use of Maternal Care in Thailand", Social Science and Medicine, 43, 4, 459-471.

Rahman, M.M., S. Gilmour, E. Saito, P. Sultana, and K. Shibuya (2013) "Health-Related Financial Catastrophe, Inequality and Chronic Illness in Bangladesh", PLOS ONE, 8, 2, 1-9.

Rajan, Raghuram G. (2009) A Hundred Small Steps: A Report on the Committee on Financial Sector Reforms, Planning Commission, Government of India.

Ram, R. and K.H. Zhang (2002) "Foreign Direct Investment and Economic Growth: Evidence from Cross-Country Data for 1990s", Economic Development and Cultural Change, 51, 1, 205-215.

Rangarajan, C. and D.K. Srivastava (2005) "Fiscal Deficit and Government Debt in India Implications for Growth and Stabilization", Working Paper, NIPFP, New Delhi.

Rangarajan, C. and D. Subba Rao (2007) "Importance of Being Earnest about Fiscal Responsibility", Monograph 3/2007, Madras School of Economics, Chennai.

Ravallion, M. (1990) "Rural Welfare Effects of Food Price Changes with Induced Wage Responses: Theory and Evidence for Bangladesh", Oxford Economic Papers, 42, 3, 574-585.

Ravinthirakumaran, N., S. Premaratne and M. Kesavarajah (2013) "Twin Deficits in Sri Lanka: An Econometric Analysis", Sri Lanka Economic Journal, 12, 1-2, 31-63.

Rawlings, J.S., V.B. Rawlings and J.A. Read (1995) "Prevalence of Low Birth Weight and Preterm Delivery in Relation to the Interval between Pregnancies among White and Black Women", New England Journal of Medicine, 332, January 12, 69-74.

Ray, R. (2000) "Analysis of Child Labour in Peru and Pakistan: A Comparative Study", Journal of Population Economics, 13, 1, 3-19.

Reddy, D.V. and B. Mohanty (2007) "Impact of Foreign Direct Investment on the Gross Domestic Product, Exports and Imports of Four Asian Countries", Delhi Business Review, 8, 1, 1-20.

Reserve Bank of India (2005) Annual Policy Statement for the Year 2005-06, Mumbai: Reserve Bank of India.

Reserve Bank of India (2009) Handbook of Statistics on the Indian Economy, Mumbai: Reserve Bank of India.

Reserve Bank of India (2016) State Finances: A Study of Budgets, 2015-16, Mumbai: RBI.

Ricker-Gilbert, J., T.S. Jayne and E. Chirwa (2011) "Subsidies and Crowding Out: A Double-Hurdle Model of Fertilizer Demand in Malawi", American Journal of Agricultural Economics, 93, 1, 26-42.

Ronning, G. and N. Schulz (2005) "A Microeconometric Characterization of Household Consumption using Quantile Regression", IAW Discussion Paper 05, IWA.

Rosenzweig, M.R. (1977) "The Demand for Children in Farm Households", Journal of Political Economy, 85, 1, 123-146.

Rosenzweig, M.R. (1986) "Birth Spacing and Sibling Inequality: Asymmetric Information within the Family", International Economic Review, 27, 1, 55-76.

Rosenzweig, M.R. and R.E. Evenson (1977) "Fertility, Schooling and the Economic Contribution of Children in Rural India", Econometrica, 45, 5, 1065-1079.

Rosenzweig, M.R. and T.P. Schultz (1983) "Consumer Demand and Household Production: The Relationship between Fertility and Child Mortality", American Economic Review, 73, 2, 38-42.

Sacks, D.W. and B. Stevenson (2012) "The New Stylised Facts About Income and Subjective Well-Being", Emotion, 12, 6, 1181-1187.

Sadashiv, K.R. (2015) "Farmers Suicide in India - Causes and Remedies: 2006-2010", Journal of Economics and Sustainable Development, 6, 1, 147-153.

Saeed, S. and A. Khan (2012) "Twin Deficit Hypothesis: The Case of Pakistan 1972-2008", Natural and Applied Sciences, 3, 2, 155-162.

Saha, S., P. Roy and S. Kar (2014) "Public and Private Sector Jobs, Unreported Income and Consumption Gap in India: Evidence from Micro-Data", North American Journal of Economics and Finance, 29, 1, 285-300.

Saito, E., S. Gilmour, M.M. Rahman, G.S. Gautam, P.K. Shreshta and K. Shibuya (2014) "Incidence of and Illnesses Associated with Catastrophic Household Expenditure on Health in Nepal: A Cross-Sectional Survey", Bulletin of the World Health Organisation, 92, 760-767.

Samad, A. (2009) "Measurement of Inefficiencies in Bangladesh Banking Industry using Stochastic Frontier Production Function", Global Journal of Business Research, 3, 1, 41-48.

Sangeethamani, S. and M.L. Louis (2017) "Maximization of Technical Efficiency of a Normal-Half Normal Stochastic Production Frontier Model", Global Journal of Pure and Applied Mathematics, 13, 10, 7353-7364.

Sarkhel, S. (2012) "Wage Gap in Labour Market, Gender Bias and Socio-cultural Influences: A Decomposition Analysis for India", Working Paper, St. Xavier's College, Kolkata.

Sathye, M. (2003) "Efficiency of Banks in a Developing Economy: The Case of India", European Journal of Operational Research, 148, 3, 662-671.

Schultz, T.P. (2008) "Population Policies, Fertility, Women's Human Capital, and Child Quality", in T.P. Schultz and J. Strauss (eds.): Handbook of Development economics, Volume 4, Amsterdam: Elsevier, 3249-3303.

Sealey, C.W. and J.T. Lindley (1977) "Inputs, Outputs, and a Theory of Production and Cost at Depository Financial Institutions", Journal of Finance, 32, 4, 1251-1266.

Self-Employed Women's Association (2000) Labouring Brick by Brick: A Study of Construction Workers, Ahmedabad: SEWA.

Semyonov, M. and A. Gorodzeisky (2005) "Labour Migration, Remittances and Household Income: A Comparison between Filipino and Filipina Overseas Workers", International Migration Review, 39, 1, 46-68.

Sengupta, A. and P. Das (2014) "Gender Wage Discrimination across Social and Religious Groups in India", Economic and Political Weekly, 49, 21, 71-76.

Shephard, R.W. (1970) Theory of Cost and Production Functions, Princeton: Princeton University Press.

Singh, P., R.J. Yadav and A. Pandey (2005) "Utilization of Indigenous System of Medicine and Homeopathy in India", Indian Journal of Medical Research, 122, 2, 137-142.

Sinha, K. (2005) "Household Characteristics and Calorie Intake in Rural India: A Quantile Regression Approach", ASARC Working Paper 2005-2, Department for International Development, UK.

Sinha, R. (2018) "Closer, But Not Cigar: Intergenerational mobility Across Caste Groups in India", Working Paper No. 8401, World Bank.

Skoufias, E. (2003) "Is the Calorie-Income Elasticity Sensitive to Price Changes? Evidence from Indonesia", World Development, 31, 7, 1291-1307.

Smith, R.H., E. Diener and D.H. Wedell (1989) "Intrapersonal and Social Comparison Determinants of Happiness: A Range-Frequency Analysis", Journal of Personality and Social Psychology, 56, 3, 317-325.

Solon, G. (1999) "Intergenerational Mobility in the Labor Market", in O.C. Ashenfelter and D. Card (eds.): Handbook of Labor Economics, Volume 3A, Amsterdam: North Holland, 1761-1800.

Srivastava, D.K. (2006) "FRBM Act and Eleventh Plan Approach Paper", Economic and Political Weekly, 41, 43/44, 4553-4559.

Srivastava, D.K. (2008) "Fiscal Responsibility Rules in India Impact And Reassessment", Paper presented at the V.K.R.V. Rao Centenary Conference on National Income and Other Macroeconomic Aggregates in a Growing Economy, April 28-30l, 2008, Delhi School of Economics and Institute of Economic Growth, Delhi.

Stahl, C. (1982) "Labor Emigration and Economic Development", International Migration Review, 16, 4, 869-899.

Stark, O. (1991) "Migration in LDCs: Risk Remittances and the Family", Finance and Development, 28, 39-41.

Stark, O. and R.E. Lucas (1988) "Migration, Remittances, and the Family", Economic Development and Cultural Change, 36, 3, 465-481.

Stark, O. and R.E.B. Lucas (1988) "Migration, Remittances, and the Family", Economic Development and Cultural Change, 36, 3, 465-481.

Stein, D. (2018) "Dynamics of Demand for Rainfall Index Insurance: Evidence from a Commercial Product in India", World Bank Economic Review, 32, 3, 692-708.

Stephansson, O., P.W. Dickman and S. Cnattingius (2003) "The Influence of Interpregnancy Interval on the Subsequent Risk of Stillbirth and Early Neonatal Death", Obstetrics and Gynecology, 102, 1, 101-108.

Stevenson, B. and J. Wolfers (2008) "Economic Growth and Happiness: Reassessing the Easterlin Paradox", Brookings Papers on Economic Activity, 1, 1-84.

Stiglitz, J.E. and A. Weiss (1981) "Credit Rationing in Markets with Imperfect Information", American Economic Review, 71, 3, 393-410.

Su, C. (2010) "Application of EGARCH Model to Estimate Financial Volatility of Daily Returns: The Empirical Case of China", Master Degree Project No.2010:142, Graduate School Master of Science in Finance, School of Business, Economics and Law, University of Gothenburg.

Subramanian, S. (1995) "Gender Discrimination in Intra-Household Allocation in India", mimeo, Department of Economics, Cornell University.

Subramaniam, S. and A. Deaton (1991) "Gender Effects in Indian Consumption Patterns", Sarvekshana, 14, 4, 1-12.

Subramanian, S and A. Deaton (1996) "The Demand for Food and Calories", Journal of Political Economy, 104, 1, 133-162.

Suresh, K.G. and V. Gautam (2015) "Relevance of Twin Deficit Hypothesis: An Econometric Analysis with Reference to India", Theoretical Economics Letters, 5, 2, 304-311.

Tan, E.C. (2006) "Fiscal Deficits Inflation and Economic Growth in a Successful Open Developing Economy", Review of Applied Economics, 2, 1, 29-139.

Taniguchi, K. and A. Tuwo (2014) "New Evidence on Gender Wage Gap in Indonesia", Economics Working Paper Series No.404, Asian Development Bank.

Tansel, A. (2015) "Intergenerational Educational Mobility in Turkey", IZA Discussion Paper No. 9590.

Taylor, J.E. (1992) "Remittances and Inequality Reconsidered: Direct, Indirect, and Intertemporal Effects", Journal of Policy Modeling, 14, 2, 187-208.

Thaler, R.H. (1987) "Anomalies: The January Effect", Economic Perspectives, 1, 1, 197-201.

Thangavelu, S.M. and G. Rajaguru (2004) "Is There an Export or Import Led Productivity Growth in Rapidly Developing Asian Countries? A Multivariate VAR Analysis", Applied Economics, 36, 10, 1083-1093.

Timmer, C.P. (1971) "Using a Probabilistic Frontier Production Function to Measure Technical Efficiency", Journal of Political Economy, 79, 4, 776-794.

Tiwari, A.K. and A.P. Tiwari (2011) "Fiscal Deficit and Inflation: An Empirical Analysis for India", Romanian Economic Journal, 14, 42, 131-158.

Tiwari, A.K., K.G. Suresh and M. Mihai (2015) "A Structural VAR analysis of Fiscal Shocks on Current Accounts in Greece", Theoretical and Applied Economics, 22, 3, 5-20.

Toor, I.A. and M.S. Butt (2005) "Determinants of Health Care Expenditure in Pakistan", Pakistan Economic and Social Review, 43, 1, 133-150.

Topalova, P., S. Cole, X. Gine, J. Tobacman, R. Townsend and J. Vickery (2013) "Barriers to Household Risk Management: Evidence from India" American Economic Journal: Applied Economics, 5, 1, 104-135.

Townsend, R.M. (1994) "Risk and Insurance in Village India", Econometrica, 62, 3, 539-591.

Tyagi, B.P. (1984) Agricultural Economics and Rural Development, Meerut: J.P.Nath & Co.

Vardharajan, S. (2003) "The Pitfalls of Proxies of Power in Intra-Household Analysis", mimeo, Cornell University.

Variyam, J.N., J. Blaylock and D. Smallwood (1996) "A Probit Latent Variable Model of Nutrition and Dietary Fiber Intake", American Journal of Agricultural Economics, 78, 3, 628-639.

Veenhoven, R. (2004) "Happy Life Years: A Measure of Happiness", in U. Karma and G. Karma (eds.): Gross National Happiness and Development: Proceedings of the First International Seminar on Operationalisation of Gross National Happiness, Center of Bhutan Studies, Thimphu, Bhutan, 287-318.

Veenhoven, R. (since 1984) World Database of Happiness: Happiness in Nations, https://worlddatabaseofhappiness.eur.nl.

Verick, S.S. (2018) "The Puzzles and contradictions of the Indian Labour Market: What will the Future of Work Look Like?", IZA Discussion Paper No. 11376.

Wang, W. and F. Famoye (1997) "Modeling Household Fertility Decisions with Generalized Poisson Regression", Journal of Population Economics, 10, 3, 273-283.

Wang, Q., S. Brenner, G. Leppert, T.H. Banda, O. Kalmus and M. De Allegri (2015) "Health Seeking Behaviour and the Related Household Out-of-Pocket Expenditure for Chronic non-Communicable Diseases in Rural Malawi", Health Policy Planning, 30, 2, 242-252.

Wilson, W. (1967) "Correlates of Avowed Happiness", Psychological Bulletin, 67, 4, 294-306.

World Bank (1981) World Development Report 1981, Washington, D.C.: World Bank.

World Bank (2001) Engendering Development, Washington, D.C.: World Bank.

World Bank (2007) World Development Report, 2007, Washington D.C.: World Bank.

World Bank (2010) Migration and Remittances Data, Washington, D.C.: World Bank.

Wu, De-Min. (1965) "An Empirical Analysis of Household Durable Goods Expenditure", Econometrica, 33, 4, 761-780.

Wydick, B., H.K. Kayes and S.H. Kempf (2011) "Social Networks, Neighborhood Effects and Credit Access: Evidence from Rural Guatemala", World Development, 39, 6,974-982.

Yang, D. (2011) "Migrant Remittances", Journal of Economic Perspectives, 25, 3, 129-151.

Yaziz, S.R., N.A. Azizan, R. Zakaria and M.H. Ahmad (2013) "The Performance of Hybrid ARIMA-GARCH Modeling in Forecasting Gold Price", Paper presented at the 20th International Congress on Modeling and Simulation, 1-6 December 2013, Adelaide, Australia.

Yen, S.T. (2002) "An Econometric Analysis of Household Donations in the USA", Applied Economics Letters, 9, 13, 837-841.

Yen, T. and W.L. Adamowicz (1993) "Participation, Trip Frequency and Site Choice: A Multinomial-Poisson Hurdle Model of Recreation Demand", Canadian Journal of Agricultural Economics, 42, 1, 65-76.

Yushkina, Y. (2010) "The Determinants of Happiness and Its Changes: An Empirical Analysis Based on Panel Data from Russia", Master's Thesis, Amherst College.

Zachariah K.C. and S. Irudaya Rajan (2000) "Socioeconomic and Demographic Consequences of Migration in Kerala: Working Paper No. 303", Centre for Development Studies, Trivandrum.

Zeller, M. (1994) "Determinants of Credit Rationing: A Study of Informal Lenders and Formal Credit Groups in Madagascar", FCND Discussion Paper No. 2, International Food Policy Research Institute.

# Index

## P



## Q



## R

## S



## T